DUQUESNE STUDIES

Philosophical Series

16

METAPHYSICS

A Systematic Survey

Library of Congress Catalog Card Number: 63-8144

DUQUESNE STUDIES

Philosophical Series

16

METAPHYSICS

A Systematic Survey

by

JOHN A. PETERS, PH.D.

DUQUESNE UNIVERSITY PRESS, Pittsburgh, Pa.

EDITIONS E. NAUWELAERTS, LOUVAIN

1963

DUQUESNE STUDIES
Philosophical Series

Andrew G. van Melsen, D.Sc., D.Ed., and Henry J. Koren, C.S.Sp., S.T.D., editors.

Volume One—*Andrew G. van Melsen*, From Atomos to Atom. Pp. XII and 240. Price: paper $3.50, cloth $4.25. Published also in Dutch, German, Spanish, and Italian.

Volume Two—*Andrew G. van Melsen*, The Philosophy of Nature. Pp. XII and 265. Third edition, fourth impression. Price: paper $3.75, cloth $4.50. Published also in Italian and Dutch. Polish edition in preparation.

Volume Three—*P. Henry van Laer*, Philosophico-Scientific Problems. Out of print.

Volume Four—*Cajetan's*, The Analogy of Names and the Concept of Being. Pp. X and 93. Second edition. Price: $2.25, cloth.

Volume Five—*Louis de Raeymaeker and others*, Truth and Freedom. Pp. VII and 132. Second impression. Price: $3.00, cloth. Published also in French.

Volume Six—*P. Henry van Laer*, The Philosophy of Science. Part One: Science in General. Pp. XVII and 164. Price: cloth $3.75. Second impression.

Volume Seven—*Stephan Strasser*, The Soul in Metaphysical and Empirical Psychology. Pp. X and 275. Second impression. Price: cloth $6.00. Published also in German, Dutch, and French.

Volume Eight—*Albert Dondeyne*, Contemporary European Thought and Christian Faith. Pp. XI and 211. Price: paper $5.00, cloth $5.75. Published also in French. Second impression.

This book has been translated from *Metaphysica. Een systematisch overzicht*, published by Het Spectrum N. V., Utrecht. Copyright 1957.

Volume Nine—*Maxwell J. Charlesworth*, PHILOSOPHY AND LINGUISTIC ANALYSIS. Pp. XIII and 234. Second impression. Price: paper $4.75, cloth $5.50.

Volume Ten—*Remy C. Kwant*, PHILOSOPHY OF LABOR. Pp. XI and 163. Price: paper $4.50, cloth $5.25.

Volume Eleven—*Remy C. Kwant*, ENCOUNTER. Pp. VIII and 85. Price: cloth $3.25. Published also in Dutch.

Volume Twelve—*William A. Luijpen*. EXISTENTIAL PHENOMENOLOGY. Pp. XIII and 355. Second impression. Price: paper $6.00, cloth $6.75. Published also in Dutch.

Volume Thirteen—*Andrew G. van Melsen*, SCIENCE AND TECHNOLOGY. Pp. X and 373. Price: paper $6.20, cloth $6.95. Published also in Dutch.

Volume Fourteen—*P. Henry van Laer*, THE PHILOSOPHY OF SCIENCE. PART TWO: A STUDY OF THE DIVISION AND NATURE OF VARIOUS GROUPS OF SCIENCES. Pp. XIV and 342. Price: paper $5.75, cloth $6.50.

Volume Fifteen—*Remy C. Kwant*, THE PHENOMENOLOGICAL PHILOSOPHY OF MERLEAU-PONTY. Pp. ix and 257. Price: paper $4.50, cloth $5.25.

Volume Sixteen—*John A. Peters*, METAPHYSICS. A Systematic Survey. Pp. XVIII and 529. Price: paper $9.00, cloth $9.75.

In preparation:

M. G. Plattel, SOCIAL PHILOSOPHY.

Joseph A. Kockelmans, PHENOMENOLOGY AND PHYSICAL SCIENCE.

Nihil Obstat

Rev. Donald W. Kraus, Ph.D.
censor librorum

Pittsburgh, November 26, 1962

Imprimatur

Rt. Rev. Msgr. Vincent M.
Leonard, Vicar General

Aristotle:

"The question which was raised of old and is raised now and always and is forever embarrassing us is, viz.: What being is, is just the question, What is beingness?" *Metaphysica,* bk. VI, ch. 1, 1028 b 3.

Thomas Aquinas:

Illud quod est maxime formale omnium, est ipsum esse.
That which is most formal of all is "to be."

Summa theol., p.I, q.7, a.1

Ipsum esse est actualitas omnium rerum.
"To be" is the actuality of all things.

Summa theol., p.I, q.4, a.1, *ad* 3

Ipsum esse est perfectissimum omnium.
"To be" is the most perfect of all.

Ibid.

Esse est illud quod est magis intimum cuilibet.
"To be" is what is most intimate to every being.

Summa theol., p.I, q.8, a.1

Ipsum esse, absolute consideratum, infinitum est.
"To be," considered absolutely, is infinite.

Contra gentes, bk.I, ch.43

Gradus in ipso esse inveniuntur.
Grades are to be found in "to be" itself.

Summa theol., p.I, q.48, a.2

Illud quod per se est appetibile, est esse.
That which is desirable in itself is "to be."

Summa theol., p.I, q.5, a.2, *ad* 3

TABLE OF CONTENTS

PREFACE

"It has long since been commonplace to assert that philosophers agree on practically nothing and that the history of philosophy is perhaps the strongest evidence against the truth value of philosophical opinions." Thus writes Louis de Raeymaeker in an article about Thomism as a living philosophy.[1] In replying to the question whether or not there is really no agreement among philosophers, de Raeymaeker seeks a mean: each philosopher considers the same whole, but in his own personal way. Lavelle, likewise, held as one of his fundamental convictions that there is only one philosophy. What he meant may be rendered in this way: as soon as skepticism, relativism, and absolute empiricism are passed, there reveals itself to each philosopher a perspective on one and the same unique absolute, but each of them will approach this unique absolute in a different way. The greatest possible diversity of opinion among philosophers does not exclude but precisely includes a basis of unanimity, although this unanimity remains concealed under their explicit diversity. For the divergence does not arise from what we ultimately have before us as the *matter intended,* but from the names we give to it and from the concepts, judgments, and reasoning processes in which we explicitate it. Thus Maydieu[2] was able to show that even in the most radical differences of views—those concerning being itself—the fundamental agreement continued to exist.

Aristotle called the matter intended "being" and "beingness."[3] These terms "being" and "to be" also and even especially fall under the discussion. Nevertheless, we have chosen these most comprehensive terms to indicate the matter intended by the philosophers. But, according to Aristotle, what being is, always remains a question and even an embarrassing question.[4] Gabriel Marcel adds that precisely because of the all-embracing character of this question the philosopher himself is primarily involved in it. Here, then, lies the source of the divergence characterizing the philosophical systems. Like life itself, they remain essentially unfinished, they are sketches and in-

---

[1] "Thomisme als levende filosofie," *Tijdschrift v. philosophie,* vol. 18 (1956), p. 12.
[2] A. J. Maydieu, *Le désaccord,* Paris, 1952.
[3] *Metaphysica,* bk. VI, ch. 1, 1028 b 3.
[4] *Ibid.*

troductions which from different viewpoints forever try to name again the ineffable and to explain the inexhaustible again and again in new explicitations. Not all of these philosophies are equally true, some even err, but none of them has the monopoly of the truth.

How can one offer a systematic survey of the fundamental questions of philosophy under the title *metaphysics* without losing sight of the problematic and unfinished character of philosophy? First of all, one could offer an introduction to philosophy by raising questions in an orderly way and leaving it to the listener or the reader to supply the answers. This was the method of Socrates. On the other hand, an introduction may be given by proposing orderly replies to orderly questions and letting these replies give rise to new questions. This system was followed by Aristotle and Thomas Aquinas. They propose a succinct whole of theses which, on the one hand, did not lose sight of the problematic character of philosophy while, on the other, it offered a synoptic view as a first demarcation of the unsurveyable realm. This method offers the advantage of a greater order and tranquillity. Of course, the judgments they pronounced may not be handled as arguments from authority, but should merely be proposed for consideration to the intellect of the reader.

The systematic survey of metaphysics offered in the subsequent pages attempts to explain in a Thomistic perspective the *matter intended* by all philosophers, which we call the "to be" of beings. According to Etienne Gilson,[6] the characteristic feature of Thomas Aquinas consists in having always considered "to be" as the center of philosophical reflection. He thinks that only rarely St. Thomas's adherents have followed in his footsteps and that the fruitfulness of this starting point is far from exhausted. In agreement with many recent interpreters, our metaphysical survey attempts to show Thomism as a metaphysics of the *being* of beings.

The disadvantage of a systematic survey is that the careful progress of phenomenal analyses has to give way to summaries which in their conciseness are sometimes not sufficiently refined. However, the very order in which the problems are raised may serve to clarify what is meant by thought processes that are only summarily expressed. Moreover, toward the end of the survey some of the questions raised in the beginning will be taken up again in a more extensive way.

---

[6] *L'être et l'essence,* Paris, 1948, pp. 321-22.

Because this work is meant as a survey, the text has been sub-divided into many sections and subsections. These sections are numbered continuously and all references to them are made by means of the marginal numbers.

The Index of Names and the Index of Subject Matter were made by Dr. Herman Berger, to whom I owe a debt of gratitude for his advice and assistance in the preparation of this volume.

The University of Nijmegen JOHN A. PETERS, Ph.D.

The American edition differs only slightly from the Dutch text. Subtitles have been added for greater readability and a few minor modifications have been made, as suggested or approved by the author. References to Dutch sources have been retained, except in the general bibliography, because all too often no similar works are available in English. A word of thanks is due to the Reverend John R. Kanda, C.S.Sp., Ph.D., for reading the translation and suggesting a few improvements.

In the translation of this work several linguistic difficulties had to be solved. One of these concerns the rendering of the Dutch term "zijn" (German *sein*), "to be," which plays a crucial role in the author's thought. Unlike Dutch, English usage demands "being" after a preposition and not "to be." However, in this way we would get the same term for being in the sense of "that which is" (*ens*) and "to be" (*esse*). Following the example of several recent metaphysical studies, I have not hesitated to retain "to be," despite its grammatical awkwardness, for the sake of clarity, wherever there would be danger of confusing "to be" with "that which is" (*ens*).[7] Where this danger did not exist, I have used *being* in italics to indicate that the term stands for "to be" and not for "that which is." As a rule, however, no italics have been used where being occurs in compounds, such as being-together.

Dr. Peters had planned to come to Duquesne University as a visiting professor for the Spring semester of 1962, but his sudden death, a few months before his scheduled departure, prevented him

---

[7]The suggested substitutions of "existence," "act of being," and *"esse"* had to be discarded. "Existence" often has a special sense in contemporary thought, the meaning of "act of being" is too differentiated as a translation of the author's term "zijn," and *"esse"* was explicitly rejected by him as a tacit admission that the implied metatphysical idea cannot be expressed in English.

from becoming personally acquainted with philosophical life in the
United States and sharing the fruit of his penetrating thought with
American students. The volume which is here presented to the
English-speaking world may serve as a fitting memorial to the
maturity of his search for wisdom.

Henry J. Koren C.S.Sp.

Duquesne University
September 6, 1962

CHAPTER ONE

INTRODUCTION

1. *First Approach to Metaphysics*

Divergent Descriptions. The term "metaphysics" does not always evoke the same idea in different minds. In some people it gives rise to a feeling of aversion because for them it means vague speculations, uncontrollable assertions and a trespassing of the boundaries of reason which is more akin to poetry than to thinking. Others see just the opposite in metaphysics—namely, an extraordinarily obstinate effort to think clearly and cogently. Some will speak of philosophy and metaphysics as soon as there is question of the more general principles which constitute the foundation of art and science in any realm of human endeavor. Others reserve the term for a connected whole of statements that claims to point the way toward a final and definitive explanation of the whole world of experience. In this case the emphasis may be laid either on the mode of knowing or on the object known. In the first way one arrives at such descriptions as absolute knowledge, integral knowledge, reflective knowledge, intuitive knowledge as opposed to abstracted knowledge, knowledge by reason as contrasted with knowledge through the senses. If, on the other hand, the object is emphasized, metaphysics is described as knowledge of the absolute, of the totality, the immutable and eternal as opposed to the mutable and temporal, knowledge of ideas as source of the facts, knowledge of first causes or ultimate foundations, knowledge of beings in their essence and not merely in their appearance, knowledge of what is not accessible to the senses, and knowledge of beings as beings.

Undoubtedly, these descriptions are very divergent. Moreover, the terms which express them have already a definite meaning flowing from the philosophical views of their users. Thus they give very little information to anyone who approaches the subject from without. Apparently the term "metaphysics" does not indicate an object of research which all determine alike or a mental attitude that is common to all its students. For this reason the term has received the most divergent meanings in the course of its history. A measure of clarification, however, can be obtained by returning to its historical origin.

1

Aristotle. Among Aristotle's works there are a few short treatises concerned with what he calls "first philosophy" or sometimes "theology." These treatises were united into a work of ten (later fourteen) books which, as is supposed, Andronicus of Rhodes (60 B.C.) in his edition of Aristotle's works called *"ta meta ta physica"* because of their location after the physical treatises.

Both the sequence and the name originated from the idea that we must proceed from what is best known to us to what is less known to us although "in itself" the latter may be best known. For by *physis* or nature Aristotle meant everything that is mobile and mutable, has a definite place in space and a definite duration in time— briefly put, "the material." The living and the psychical, including man, fall also under the science of *physis* or nature. Hence we may say that physics considers everything which can be directly reached by human experience. However, there remain some questions which aim at the ultimate reason for the unity in the experienced plurality of beings, and this reason is not directly open to experience.

Aristotle does not always indicate in the same way the object of this inquiry regarding the realm beyond experience. Sometimes he speaks of "being as being," sometimes also of *"ousia"* or beingness. Properly speaking, *ousia* has an abstract meaning and indicates that by which a being is constituted a being (for Aristotle this usually is the immanent *"eidos"* or form). Sometimes, however, *ousia* is used concretely for what is eminently and primarily being. By this he seems to mean sometimes substantial or subsistent being and sometimes the causes of the beings composed of matter and form which we experience. These causes he endeavors to find in supra-material pure forms as the immutable and immovable causes of the mutable and the mobile, and finally in the first absolutely immovable Mover.

Provisional Description. On the etymological basis of the term we may provisionally describe the still unnamed examination of that which is "after the physics" as *the science of what transcends experience.* Despite its negative character, this approach gives rise to many questions and even implies a certain viewpoint regarding this branch of human knowledge. What is science? Can this investigation be called a science in the same sense as the research which aims at particular objects of experiece? What is meant by transcending, and what is the relation between physical and metaphysical knowledge, between the physical and the metaphysical object? And especially, what is experience? Is it concerned only with what is offered through the senses or also with the life of the spirit? We may even ask: Is it not possible to experience the all-embracing and the absolute itself?

As a first effort to render the description more precise we may say that experience aims at the factual and that insight aims at the necessary.[1] Thus experimental knowledge is concerned not only with the physical (in the modern more restricted sense) and the chemical, but also with the biological, the psychological and sociological, and with all spheres of human activity. Relying on experience, reason is capable of arriving in these realms at insights into the connection of experienced facts; it can discover order, regularity and relationships of interdependence, and it is capable of formulating hypothetic necessities in general propositions. One cannot say that knowledge based on experience is entirely devoid of essential insights.

The question, however, is whether or not reason can rise above facts and above the hypothetically necessary essential relationships implied in these facts so as to arrive at insights into the absolutely necessary, into that which cannot not-be in any hypothesis—not even in the hypothesis that the facts would not be or would be different from what they are.

This question really includes two problems. First, is anything absolutely necessary or does the totality of all that appears to us as de facto real have no reason for being as it is? Is pure chance the ultimate "why" of everything? Is the contingent the absolute? Secondly, assuming that something is absolutely necessary, is this something perhaps the totality itself of the beings which de facto are, so that they cannot be other than they are and have within themselves the ultimate foundation of their *being*? Or do the events and beings of our experience, each separately and all jointly, point to a transcendent basis of the facts which in themselves are not absolutely necessary? Do they point to a cause which is not conditioned by anything else but is itself the condition of everything else? Is it possible for us to have any knowledge of this absolute? And if so, is this act of knowing, knowledge by means of an insight of our intellect?

2. *Attitudes Toward Metaphysics*

The history of philosophy teaches us that the most divergent views have been held regarding the questions whether or not there

---

[1]Cf. no. 21.

there can be a science of the unconditionally necessary or absolute
and how such a science is related to experiential knowledge. A few
of these opinions may be indicated here in a very brief way.

Materialism. According to this view, there is nothing which is not
in principle accessible to sense experience. Not only is everything
that is, extended in space and time, but vegatative and sense life and
even the mind are nothing but higher and more complex organization
patterns of one and the same substratum. They can be explained, for
instance, by means of dialectic evolution, in accordance with the general methodical rule that every instance of the so-called higher has to
be understood in terms of the so-called lower.

Empiricist Views. Empiricism considers experience not only as
the starting point but as the one and only source of our knowledge.
It limits the role of reason to bringing order in the data of experience.
According to *nominalism,* we do not have any general and necessary
insights. What passes for a universal proposition is nothing but a
provisional synthetic view of a manifold of convergent individual
experiences. *Positivism* limits the data of experience to sense-perceptible facts. For the *neo-positivists* propositions are meaningful only if
they are intersubjectively verifiable by reduction to the data of sense
experience. Statements have to be expressed in a symbolic language
which may be chosen arbitrarily, provided one remains faithful to his
choice. Logic has to be observed, but this logic, albeit independent of
experience, does not offer any new knowledge. It is merely a syntac-
tical aid in the systematization of the experiential data. It is the task
of philosophy, conceived as the logical analysis of language, to eliminate as meaningless statements all propositions that are concerned
neither with the data of experience nor with the way in which we
express these data in a logical language.

Agnosticism. This view does not reject the possibility that there
could exist something which is above the reach of man's experience.
However, it considers that the human mind, at least speculative reason, is unable to reach certainty regarding the existence, and *a fortiori*
the essence, of any absolute reality which transcends experience, even
if the contrary claim is modestly based on indirect and analogous
knowledge.

Nicolai Hartmann. This German philosopher has a very broad
notion of experience and extends it also to aspects of reality that are

not perceptible by the senses. Everything that we can experience, Hartmann argues, possesses a common trait, which since antiquity has been considered an object of science. This common characteristic consists in this that everything *is* in many different modes. Thus being as being can be studied in a "formal ontology," which is based on experience and culminates in a theory of the modes of *being* and of the categories. However, such an "ontology" is not a doctrine about an Absolute that would be beyond experience; it is not metaphysics. Metaphysics is nothing but a collection of as yet unsolved and partially insoluble problems which remain as an irrational residue at the limits of our knowledge.

Inductive Metaphysics. Some, such as G. Heymans, advocate an inductive metaphysics. On the basis of experience it is possible to formulate, as the ultimate offshoots of more specialized scientific theories, more or less probable and always provisional hypotheses about an absolute basis of unity. Through these hypotheses man tries to conceive the totality of phenomena as necessary in their mutual interdependence.

Immediate Experience of the Absolute. Diametrically opposed to these views which reject metaphysics or at least assume a very critical attitude toward it are other trends of thought. They do not limit human experience to sense knowledge or to intellectual knowledge built on sense perception, but extend it to everything which man can attain in any way whatsoever. René Le Senne, for instance, defines philosophy as the description of integral experience. According to views of this kind, integral experience comprises also the absolute itself. True, proponents of such positions realize that a preparation is needed before the mind can rise to the metaphysical standpoint, but once this standpoint is reached, the mind has immediate contact with the absolute. Their views, however, about the nature of the metaphysical act differ considerably, as appears from the names they give to it, such as, remembrance, contemplation, intuition, absolute thought, *Einfühlung,* sympathy, love, and surrender. In the same way the character of the attained absolute receives divergent descriptions. The Platonists call it the subsistent Idea, the Neo-Platonists the One and the Good, Spinoza Substance, the ontologists God as the fountain-head of ideas, Hegel Absolute Thought, Bergson Pure Duration, the phenomenologists of the first generation Essence, Heidegger *Being.*

Mediate Knowledge of the Absolute. Others think that man can approach the absolute, but not by means of direct experience. Our knowledge of the absolute is mediate. It is given to us in the concept itself which we have of an infinitely perfect being, for "that than which a greater cannot be thought" includes "to be" itself in its very concept. This view of metaphysics is implied in the so-called "ontological proof" for God's existence. With variations, this proof is proposed, for instance, by St. Anselm, Descartes, and Leibniz.

Others, again, emphasize the limitation of our world of immediate experience. They do not simply accept the "ontological proof," but claim that the beings of experience, as finite and mutable beings, by the very fact of their reality point beyond themselves to the absolutely necessary as their cause. They admit that by means of reasoning about metaphysical causality we are capable of discovering the existence, but not the inner essence, of the absolute. For Aristotle this absolute is the Immovable Mover, the Pure Act, the Thinking of Thinking, Scotus calls it Infinite Being, Thomas Aquinas Subsistent "To Be."

3. *Critique of Knowledge*

These differences of opinion show that many doubt whether metaphysics is possible and even whether metaphysical problems are meaningful. They show also that the proponents of metaphysics are far from being unanimous regarding the nature and method of metaphysics.

Metaphysics Lacks an Immediately Determinable Object. Apparently metaphysics is characteristically diverse from the specialized sciences. These possess an immediately determinable object of inquiry that is not subject to reasonable doubt within the particular science in question; for instance, the earth, the stars, colors and sounds, measurements and numbers, plants, animals and men, perception, imagination, language, social intercourse, group formation, law, labor, art, and history. No such clearly determinable object can be assigned to metaphysics. Or should one have to say that metaphysics, too, considers each of these realms—namely, from the viewpoint of the interconnection each one has with the others? In this case the question must be raised whether it would not be sufficient and adequate to limit ourselves to a summary of the results obtained by the special sciences. Or would it be possible to say something about the whole before one has finished with the study of the parts?

The answer would have to be in the negative if there is question of a whole that is constructed of parts and therefore presupposes these parts, for in such a case the study of the whole appears to be dependent on the study of the parts. But even if we assume that we are concerned here with a whole that is prior to the parts and gives rise to them, the question arises whether such a whole, as the source of the parts, is *given to us* prior to these parts. Shouldn't we say that only the parts are given to us immediately? It does not seem possible to assign to metaphysics an immediately given object that can serve as an indubitable starting point.

The Problem of the Object of Metaphysics. If metaphysics cannot start from a clearly determinable and indubitable object that is given to us immediately, it will have to begin by formulating the problem of its object. Thus it is only in the process itself of metaphysical thought that it can become clear whether or not there is a metaphysical object and whether metaphysical knowledge is possible. This, however, raises the question whether man could not refuse to engage in metaphysical thought because, prior to metaphysical reflection, there is no datum of experience given to him which would force him to go beyond the study of the experiential datum offered to him in one or the other of the special sciences.

The object of metaphysics remains uncertain before one pursues metaphysics. Therefore, what has to be shown is not so much that man *must* pursue metaphysics, but rather that willy nilly he always is already implicitly doing metaphysical thinking and that he cannot avoid doing it. However, this demonstration can be given only by showing that even the attitude of doubt or denial of metaphysics implies a metaphysical attiude. For this reason we must examine the grounds which give rise to doubt about the claims of metaphysics.

Is Man Capable of Metaphysics? From the foregoing it follows that one can share Kant's view that the first point to be investigated is whether or not man is capable of doing metaphysics.

Undoubtedly, no matter how one conceives metaphysics, it claims to be *knowledge* of the absolute if knowledge is understood in the broadest sense as the activity by which we have access to beings in order to discover whether, how and why they are. This assertion does not exclude that also other acts, such as feeling, willing and doing, if they are distinguished from knowing, may play an essential role in metaphysics.

Knowledge, however, is not completed by perceiving that something is. It is directed also to discovering *what* and *how* this something is, why it is and why it is as it is. Knowledge seeks essence, foundation and reason. As *"logos,"* it wants to gather everything into an interconnected whole. It reaches its completion in insight, understanding, and comprehension. Knowledge essentially includes intellect (*intellectus*) and reason (*ratio*).

Accordingly, we may render Kant's question more precise in this way: Are man's intellect and reason of such a nature that they can transcend experience and arrive at genuine knowledge and true judgments about the absolute? Thus a critique of man's cognitive faculty is a necessary condition if metaphysics is ever to be justified in its claim of being genuine knowledge.

Epistemology. Critique, in general, is the act of *"krinein,"* of discerning and judging value or lack of value according to certain norms. In a special sense, we call critique the determination of the value or lack of value of an achievement by looking back over the road travelled from the starting point to see if any deviation or error has crept in anywhere. In this sense critique is reflection or self-analysis.

Critique of knowledge or epistemology is the self-analysis of the knower who reflects on the limits which his capacity to reach the truth may have. Any such limits would be present in the very exercise of the cognitive power and consequently would have to be discovered by means of reflection.

Epistemology belongs to every science insofar as every science has an aspect that could be called its self-analysis. However, the epistemology which investigates the possibility of metaphysical knowledge must be a radical and most critical critique, for it is concerned with the highest claim of human knowledge—namely, that of bringing man into contact with the absolute and thereby to some extent of embracing and comprehending everything. For this reason metaphysical epistemology should subject the totality of human knowledge to a reflective analysis and not leave any proclaimed certainty unexamined.

4. *Critique of Knowledge and Metaphysics*

Two Ways of Viewing Man's Cognitive Power. If man's cognitive capacity is considered in itself, the study of knowledge is an aspect of the study of man's integral activity, and this study, in its turn, is but an aspect of the study of the particular being called "man."[2] But the problem of man's nature, studied in philosophical anthropology, is not a question which lies at the foundation of metaphysics but is itself a special problem within the realm of metaphysics.

Man's cognitive power, however, can and must be considered also in a different way—namely, as avenue to the realm of being. Whoever inquires about the nature of the things that are, and especially one who searches for their absolutely necessary foundation, must have access to them and even to their all-embracing and unconditioned foundation. But, as we have said, knowledge in its broadest sense is the general instrument by which we can approach beings in their *being*. Thus it is on the value and range of this instrument that depends the possibility of metaphysics. If the cognitive power is considered in its relation to what can be known through it, its investigation does not constitute a special study, but is the general foundation of critically justified science and especially of critically justified metaphysics.

Relation of Epistemology to Metaphysics. Accordingly, epistemology is the critical or reflective aspect of metaphysics itself. It raises the question whether it is possible for us not only to know the de facto given real world as it is in itself, but also, beyond the totality of the beings that de facto are and their interconnections, to have access to that which does not just happen to be, but is of itself and independently of all conditions absolutely necessary.

Conceived in this way, epistemology is not related to metaphysics as a special science to the general science. On the contrary, the critique of knowledge and metaphysics reveal themselves as the retrogressive and progressive aspects of one and the same fundamental attitude. We have to revert to every metaphysical assertion in a critical way to check its epistemological value by investigating how it was reached. Reversely, this critique may not *a priori* close itself and be antimetaphysical, but must be willing to surrender to whatever reveals itself to the mind as evident.

Accordingly, in the construction of philosophy both viewpoints have to compenetrate each other. Thus the general critical question itself is already a metaphysical problem. It is impossible to raise

---

[2] Concerning the difference between knowing as a particular object and as a general instrument for attaining every object, see M.-D. Roland-Gosselin, *Essai d'une étude critique de la connaissance*, Paris, 1932, pp. 9-19.

this question outside or previously to metaphysics. For only when we actually endeavor to pursue metaphysics, i.e., when we actually attempt to approach that which transcends experience, will it become clear whether or not a successful attempt is within our capacities.

There is no objection against placing special emphasis on the critical question at the beginning of metaphysics, so long as one realizes that this question itself is metaphysical. We may go even further and say that the inquiry about the possibility of metaphysics remains a central problem which cannot be solved for once and for all but returns constantly on a higher and higher level in the development of metaphysics. For with every forward step we become more and more conscious of the fact that we did not yet have a complete insight into what we previously had called acquired results. Thus these prior acquisitions are taken up again in a subsequent stage of our inquiry and are subjected to a new search in the light of a more profound setting. In this way critique and metaphysics remain united by an unbreakable bond.

CHAPTER TWO

PROVISIONAL DESCRIPTION OF HUMAN

KNOWLEDGE

5. *Introduction*

The critique of knowledge judges the value or lack of value of man's cognitive capacity. We have to subject man's knowledge to an inquiry because knowledge has become a problem for us. This, however, presupposes that we have already been concerned with knowledge and to some extent know what it is to know, so that we are at least able to distinguish it from other operations such as to desire and to move. As a matter of fact, we always have a spontaneous, pre-critical knowledge of knowing. This knowledge is implied in the very exercise of our cognitive ability, both in our everyday way of dealing with our fellow men and in the more systematic way of knowing called "science."

We will now examine what is implied in this spontaneous knowledge of knowing. Its first description does not yet claim to be philosophical. It proceeds from the standpoint of everyday life and presupposes the cultural pattern of our civilization. The intention of this description is merely to discover what the purpose is of man's cognitive activity. It will be the task of a further radical critique to investigate knowledge and to determine to what extent and under which conditions this purpose can be reached.

6. *Subject and Object*

Subject. Knowing always presents itself in our everyday life as knowing something or somebody. We speak of a subject which knows and of an object that is known, regardless of whether this object known is I myself or something or someone else. Through my cognitive activity I know about this object. It has revealed itself to me and somehow, in a way difficult to describe, it is present to me. However, this mutual presence does not change me, with respect to my own nature, into the object known, nor does it change the object with respect to its own nature, into me. As is often said, in

11

human knowledge there is an "intentional" relationship between the knower and the event, thing or person known, between "subject" and "object."

Object. Among the objects which we think we know more or less, each finds first of all himself, for we constantly use the term "I" as the subject term of our statements and speech. Next, there are "you" and "we," "he," "she" and "they," for we think that we know our fellow men with whom we converse and have dealings. We know also beings below man: animals, plants, and minerals, which we encounter and which we utilize on the basis of our knowledge of them. Sometimes we put together all the objects encountered by man before he acts on them under the collective title "nature." As the opposite of nature we consider the objects originating from man's active interference in natural conditions, i.e., the results of his activity. Among these objects, which we sometimes collectively indicate as "products of culture," we may enumerate utensils, instruments, machines, objects of art, such as statues and paintings, but also musical compositions, stories, poems, argumentations, sciences, customs, laws, legal institutions, etc. All these objects we think we know insofar as we understand their meaning and value with respect to human life.

7. *Perception and Thought*

External and Internal Perception. Perception is the basis of our knowledge of objects. It is the openness to, and the reception of a real being which shows itself to us in its own individual appearance.

External perception by means of the so-called "senses," such as touch, hearing, and sight, is primarily directed toward an individual object which is supposed to be present outside our bodily organs. We perceive such an object as it appears to us in a definite perspectice, at a definite place and at a definite time. We know that what we perceive of the object depends on the condition of our sense organs. We know also that the object has other aspects which at present we cannot perceive, e.g., we cannot see its other side, and that it is not certain whether the object will be in the same condition a little later. Moreover, the object delineates itself against a background that is not sharply perceived; this background itself, however, may become foreground. Accordingly, perception is never complete, but always relative and capable of being perfected.

The inner perception of our own acts of perceiving, thinking, feeling, hoping, fearing, deciding, acting, etc. seems to be even less complete than external perception, for the attention proper to "reflection" modifies the spontaneous acts that constitute the stream of our "lived" events. While the stable spatial aspect characterizes external perception, the volatile temporal aspect is fundamental in inner perception.

Memory and Imagination. In our acts of perception we have the impression that the object makes itself present to us. But by means of memory and remembrance we are capable of making interiorly present to ourselves an object which in time and space is no longer present. In such acts of knowing, images (representations) occur which are for us a means of arriving at the knowledge of something that is no longer present in itself. Memory, however, hardly ever establishes complete contact with what has been formerly perceived. The reason is not only that we forget, but also that, apart from memory, we possess a so-called "creative" imagination which produces new forms from elements borrowed from the data of perception. This imagination plays a very important role in our spontaneous knowledge. It is a powerful aid in our efforts to learn more about the objects of the real world, but at the same time it harbors also the danger of misrepresentation and error.

Concepts. Perception, memory, and imagination all refer to real or possible events and beings in their individuality, their concrete appearance in a definite place and at a definite time. But we have also higher cognitive powers by which we are able to analyze perceptive acts and their objects, interconnect them, and discover similarities and differences. From the concrete whole appearing to us we single out a certain feature which we can find also elsewhere, a "general" characteristic, i.e., one which can be realized in many individual events and beings. Such characteristics are expressed in concepts. Accordingly, a concept has as its content a mode of *being,* an "essential feature," in the broadest sense of the term, which precisely because it has been "detached from" ("abstracted out of") the individual also disregards ("abstracts from") the individual and in principle can be found in an unlimited number of spatio-temporally determined individuals (c.f. no. 51). Concepts can be compared and classified according to the group to which they belong and according as they are more or less general. We are able to resolve more complex concepts into more elementary ones and, reversely, use more elementary concepts to build more complex types.

Judgments. The concept is an element of the judgment. In the concept the intellect represents to itself a certain thought content without pronouncing itself regarding the presence of this content in real or possible beings. But in the judgment the intellect reverts to experience and either affirms or denies that certain thought contents are "in" certain beings or groups of beings. Accordingly, in the judgment the intellect makes a statement by saying whether and how beings are or are not. There are different types of judgments; e.g., hypothetical and categorical, affirmative and negative, general, particular and individual judgments.

Reasoning. Some judgments, such as certain individual judgments, originate in immediate experience. Others, and in particular certain general judgments, stem from an immediate insight into an essential relationship. Many judgments, however, are deduced from other judgments; they result from thinking, i.e., from the reasoning process of human thought. A reasoning process seems to be the act by which the human mind concludes from two or more admitted statements to a new statement which flows logically from the others. It may be inductive and lead from the singular to the general, or deductive and go from the general to the particular.

8. *Conditions of the Knowing Mind*

Both perception and concept are completed in the judgment. The judgment is concerned with a proposed reply to the question whether this or that is this way or that way.

With respect to the proposed situation submitted to its judgment the human mind may find itself in different conditions. First of all, there is the state of ignorance—namely, when there is no cognitive connection at all with the object of the question. Secondly, the mind may be in the conditions of certitude and doubt, of suspicion and opinion.[1]

Certitude. Certitude is a condition of firmness of judgment regarding the proposed situation. When the question is asked whether a thing is so or not so, the mind limits itself to one part of this contradictory opposition by its yes or no, its affirmation or negation. It assents to one of these contradictories in such a way that fear of the

---

[1]Cf. Geny, *Critica,* Rome, 1927, pp. 59-64; C. Schoonbrood "Analyse van het begrip waarschijnlijkheid," *Algemeen Nederlands Tijdschrift voor Wijsbegeerte en Psychologie,* vol. 48 (1956), pp. 138-153.

opposite is excluded; the very thought that the opposite could be true is absolutely rejected.

Certitude can be spontaneous or reflex; it may be purely putative or well-founded. Well-founded certainty has a cognitive basis which guarantees that the situation is really as the mind in its firm judgment considers it to be. This foundation lies in the self-revelation of the object. Such a self-revelation is called "evidence," and the self-revealing object is said to be "evident."

However, the firm foundation of certainty may lie also outside the object to be known—namely, in the trustworthiness of a person who testifies about the object. If the conditions of trustworthiness are fully satisfied with respect to the testimony of a person, knowledge obtained through faith likewise is capable of offering certitude.[2]

Doubt. Doubt, which is etymologically connected with the Latin *duo,* two, is the state of a mind which abstains from judging when it is faced with two contradictory opposites. This suspension of judgment may flow from the lack of reasons for either one or the other opposite, and in this case we speak of a *negative* doubt. Such a doubt is not far removed from ignorance. It occurs especially at the start of an investigation.

Doubt may originate also from the fact that there are grounds for both opposites which counterbalance one another in such a way that the scale of judgment does not incline to either side. In such a case we speak of a *positive* doubt. It occurs when we are in the midst of an investigation and sometimes persists until its very end.

Just as certitude, doubt may be spontaneous and reflex. If reflex doubt is used in a systematic process of research in which the grounds for certitude only gradually become the object of our consideration, it is called *methodic* doubt. It starts as a negative doubt and sometimes persists later as a positive doubt. Such a methodic doubt lets the natural spontaneous certitudes be what they are on their own level, but abstains from using them in its progressive chain of thoughts until they have been subjected to a critical reflection.

Suspicion. This is a slight inclination of the mind in favor of one side of contradictory opposites without, however, eliminating doubt.

Opinion. Opinion refers to the state of a mind which adheres to one part of a contradictory opposition, but retains the fear that the

---

[2]Cf. no. 132.

other part may be true. There remains a measure of reason for doubt, because the motive in favor of the opinion is not wholly apodictic and does not fully warrant the judgment. For instance, there is a certain amount of darkness or vagueness in perception, memory, insight, or argumentation. The object in question does not reveal itself fully but only with imperfect evidence, i.e., with probability. Such a situation will arise especially when the object in question is not open to direct inspection but presents itself as probable merely because of certain data. The probability is not a property of the object taken in itself, but belongs to it only insofar as it is approached by our imperfect knowledge.[3]

It may happen that the same proposed situation is probable for some reasons and improbable for others. In such a case we can come to an opinion only if the reasons in favor of one or two contradictory statements present themselves as considerably more probable than those for the second; otherwise we cannot go beyond doubt or suspicion.

9. *Truth and Falsity*

Truth. The judgment is a statement of the mind by which it says whether and how something is or is not. According as the mind adheres with greater certainty to a proposed statement, it thinks more firmly that its judgment is true. The mind claims to reach truth in its judgment. What, however, is truth?

In the first place, we speak of truth with respect to a cognitive act, that of judging, insofar as the judgment "says of what is that it is, and of what is not that it is not."[4]

A concept also may be called true—namely, when it is not conceived as expressing merely a thought content but also "something that *is*"; for example, my "concept of the French Revolution." In such a case the concept implicitly contains one or more judgments.

It cannot be denied that the judgment always pronounces itself about the *being* or the mode of *being* of someone or something. The affirmation of *being* is the most general form as well as the most general content of all possible judgments.[5] Moreover, a judgment

---

[3]Cf. Schoonbrood, *art. cit.*
[4]Cf. Aristotle, *Metaphysica,* bk. IV, ch. 7 (1011b 26) : "To say of what is that it is not, or of what is not that it is, is false, while to say of what is that it is, and of what is not that it is not, is true."
[5]Cf. no. 36.

that is posited with certitude claims to pronounce itself as to whether something truthfully is, or truthfully is this or that way.   For this reason the truth of a judgment is often defined as the *adequatio intellectus et rei,* i.e., the (known) agreement between, on the one hand, the thought the knower has of a being and, on the other, the being that is thought.   The knowledge of this agreement itself does not necessarily have to become explicitly the object of the judgment, as happens in the reflex judgment: "I know that this is so."   Nevertheless, the claim of having knowledge of this agreement is implicitly contained in the taking of a position, the act of pronouncing and determining itself, which distinguishes the judgment from a solitary concept merely expressing a thought content.   For this reason the judgment always claims to be a mode of self-knowledge, even when it aims at other beings than the knower and his acts, for it is always concerned with the cognitive relationship of the subject itself to its objects.

Thus truth, as the agreement of knowing and *being,* appears to be the *purpose* of the cognitive act as it reveals itself to us in spontaneous life.   Accordingly, the critical question will be: Is it possible to reach this purpose?   Can the claim of cognition that through it we always, or sometimes, reach, or at least will at some time reach, the truth be justified?

Falsity.   A judgment is false insofar as it does not agree with "that which is as it is."   This disagreement should not be understood as only a partial agreement—for that would be the incomplete truth which seems to characterize all human knowledge—, but as a positive deviation insofar as "what is not, is said to be, and what is, is said not to be."[6]   As for truth, so for falsity there must be question of known disagreement.   How it is possible to know the disagreement, although the false judgment is posited with the claim of being true, i.e., whether and how error is possible, is just as much an epistemological problem as the question whether and how truth is possible.[7]

Justification of Logical Truth.   The truth (and falsity) spoken of above is usually called *logical* truth (and falsity).   We do not like this expression too much, for we attribute a more restricted sense to the term "logical."[8]   For this reason we would prefer to speak of

---

[6]Cf. Aristotle, *loc. cit.*
[7]Cf. no. 29.
[8]Cf. no. 166.

the truth (and falsity) of presumed knowledge. Whether and on what conditions this truth can be reached is a question pertaining to the critique of knowledge. One can conceive, as it were, three ways to arrive at a cognitive agreement:

1. There is a pre-established harmony of knowing and *being*. This view is held, e.g., by the theory of illumination.

2. Knowing, in the sense of thinking, establishes the very "to be" of beings. This is so-called idealism.[9]

3. The "to be" of beings reveals itself to the cognitive act. This is called realism, although the name is not quite correct.[10]

In all these views one could speak of an *ontological* truth, i.e., the *being*-true of beings themselves. In the first view, this ontological truth is the *being* of that which is, as in pre-established harmony with knowing; in the second it is the *being* of that which is, *as* caused by thinking; in the third, it is the *being* of that which is, *as* the cause of true judgments because that which is unveils itself as it is to the cognitive act.[11]

However, the question of what ontological truth means does not yet concern us here, for first an answer has to be given to the question whether "logical" truth can be reached. Must we not first subject all possible judgments to doubt and see whether there exists a judgment which is capable of surviving every critical investigation and whose certitude is beyond any doubt? Should we not start with the attitude of universal doubt?

---

[9]Cf. no. 24.
[10]Cf. no. 34.
[11]The Greek *aletheia*, truth, is sometimes said to mean literally the state of being unveiled, revealed. Cf. Heidegger, *Platons Lehre von der Wahrheit* (Bern, 1947) and *Vom Wesen der Wahrheit* (Frankfurt, 1943).

CHAPTER THREE

THE INITIAL METAPHYSICAL ATTITUDE

10. *The Spontaneous Certitudes of Life*

Universal Doubt. Serious objections are raised against universal doubt as the correct initial metaphysical attitude. The main objection is that the critique of knowledge is of a reflective nature while that which is the object of a reflection, obviously, is prior to this reflection itself. This prior object consists in the life of the mind as it spontaneously runs its course in perception and thought. Should we, then, not decide to withdraw the spontaneous certitudes of life from doubt and even make them the undoubted starting point of philosophy, for otherwise we would undermine the very foundation on which we stand?

Uncertainty of Spontaneous Certitudes. The question arises as to what exactly are these spontaneous "lived" certitudes of "sound thinking" or "common sense." Even a superficial examination reveals that in different cultural surroundings there is very little agreement on the way of looking at life. Not only the structures of thought often differ, but even perception itself reveals a divergent structure—the world is "viewed" in a different way. The so-called "natural" world in which we live appears to be highly conditioned by man's historical development.[1]

Moreover, in more recent times the mathematical and physical sciences, followed by psychology, sociology and the historical branches of learning, have subjected the accepted world view of ordinary perception and spontaneous thought to a sharp critique.

Phenomenological Description. If it is said that one may start from his own concrete existence and that of his fellow men in a common spatio-temporal world, one should first reply to the question: On what grounds can one decide what belongs to the structure of this world and what not? A "phenomenological" description may not be satisfied with the analysis of experiences and convictions that apply

---

[1]Cf. Andrew G. van Melsen, *Science and Technology*, Pittsburgh, 1961, ch. XIII. Tr.

to us Westerners of the twentieth century, but will be adequate only when it indicates what pertains to man as man. Such a description, however, would demand an essential insight into the meaning of being-human as such, into the value which perceiving, judging, and thinking possess for man as man. But such an insight implies that one already has critically and reflectively left behind the spontaneous everyday world.

Aim of Critical Attitude. Nevertheless, this critical consideration does not at all imply that we set aside the spontaneous certainties of our life in a negative judgment. On the contrary, we reverently let life continue on its way, including our own life during the time of our investigation. The reflective attitude must not choke what is spontaneous, but only render it more refined. For this reason we inquire about its validity and search for the root from which it stems. Precisely because of our respect for truth, we want to declare ourselves convinced only when we encounter this truth, as it were, bodily in immediate and inescapable presence, so that we can do nothing else than affirm it. What the critical attitude aims at is the absolutely undeniable that manages to maintain itself in every supposed situation, even the most foolish one, because it affirms itself in everything.

11. *Dogmatism*

Should not the methodic doubt of all certitudes stop short of a few certainties, above all doubt, which are necessarily implied not only in every judgment but also in every inquiry and every doubt? We mean:[2]

1. The first and indubitable fact: I am.

2. The first and indubitable principle: nothing can be and not-be in the same respect.

3. The first and indubitable condition of all knowledge: I have the power to reach the truth.

Critique. These three so-called primordial truths certainly are not to be denied. But how can we know they are absolutely indubitable? Because we are convinced that they can resist all doubt. But

---

[2]Cf. J. Balmès, S. Tongiorgi, D. Palmieri, e.a. See G. Van Riet, *L'épistémologie thomiste*, pp. 3-133.

how can we know this? Because we have tried to doubt them. If they really are well-founded, they will pass a critical examination. But it is only by means of a critical analysis that their undeniable character will be absolutely established.

For this reason the initial attitude is not simply a question of accepting these three certainties, but extends its reflection also to these certainties and accepts them only after making an effort to doubt them.

12. *Relativism*[3]

Serious objections, however, remain against the very possibility of such a universal doubt as the initial metaphysical attitude. Everyone's mind is influenced by his previous history and surroundings. It would be naïve to pretend that one could eliminate all his previous knowledge and start philosophizing afresh, *ab ovo*. Everyone's judgment proceeds from his own pre-existing situation and therefore can indicate only how beings appear to *him*. Only relativism, the attitude which respects this actual situation, is a sincere starting point of philosophy.

Relativism teaches that, just as perception, so also thinking depends on the situation of the subject: "As it appears to me, so it is for me, and as it appears to you, so it is for you." In other words, "to be" is "to be so for me" (Protagoras).[4]

Critique. Extreme universal relativism cannot be maintained. For the relativistic attitude itself either is included or not in its own relativism. If it does not fall under it, the truth that all our knowledge is relative will be absolute and consequently not all our knowing is relative. If, on the other hand, it falls under it, the relativistic attitude, by virtue of its self-posited relativism, will be valid only for the positing subject and not for knowledge as it is in itself. In this case the relativist admits that he is just as unable to make a statement regarding

---

[3]Cf. J. Peters, "Défense de la métaphysique," in *Mélanges Philosophiques*, 10ème Congrès international de philosophie, Amsterdam, 1948, pp. 132-145.

[4]Protagoras: "Of all things the measure is man, of the things that are, that they are, and of the things that are not, that they are not." "What appears to each one and seems so to him, that is for him, what does not appear to him and seems not so to him, that is not for him." Diehls, *Fragmente der Vorsokratiker*, 8th ed., vol. 2, Berlin, 1956, p. 263. Probably these statements are to be understood primarily with respect to individual human beings who can differ in their perceptions in an infinite variety of ways. Cf. Plato, *Theaetetus*, 166 d.

knowledge as it is in itself as he is with respect to everything else that is, and thus he has become a skeptic.

This critique of universal relativism leads to the following insight. Whoever identifies "to be" with "to be for me" implies a reference to a "to be in itself" which is excluded and therefore, *as* excluded, is again admitted.[5] "To be so for me" can never be the first meaning of "to be," because "to be so for me" would have to mean that "it is in itself in such a way" that it "appears so to me." Even what appears so to me, the phenomenal, *is,* for it *is* "appearing to me." "To be" (= "to be in itself") is included in "to be for me," for "to be for me" is a mode of *"being"* (= "to be in itself").

However, this denial of universal relativism as the initial philosophical attitude does not mean the denial of all subjective conditions of knowledge. What one can know depends to a large extent on the situation in which he lives. We may even say that the highest knowledge will also be the most precarious and impose the highest conditions on the knowing subject. Not everything is equally accessible to all. The only thing we want to say here is that "to know" with respect to the content known cannot be the purely subjective impression of the individual subject. The relativist either contradicts himself or is really a skeptic.

13. *Skepticism*

Should universal skepticism be considered the correct initial metaphysical attitude? Let us try to analyze the skeptical attitude. The skeptic thinks that we do not know whether there is even a single judgment expressing "what is, as it is" and therefore wants to abstain from all judgments. In favor of his skepticism he puts forward *inter alia* the following reasons:[6]

1. Men hold different opinions about everything that can be perceived or thought. Apparently, therefore, not a single statement is self-evident.

---

[5]The expression "to be in itself" can be understood in two ways. It may be taken, as is done here, in opposition to "to be for me," but it may also be opposed to "to be in something else" as subsistent being or substance is opposed to accident. Whenever the expression is to be understood in this second sense, we will italicize *in.* Tr.

[6]The "diallelos tropos" or the vicious circle is one of the five ways to give a foundation to skepticism against the dogmatists which Sextus Empiricus (2nd cent. A.D.) quotes from Agrippa in his *Pyrrhoneioi Hypotyposeis.* These five ways are reducible to two: the argument to infinity and the vicious circle.

2. It is likewise impossible to make any statement evident in the light of something else as a norm or criterion. For such a criterion needs to be established as the true criterion by means of another criterion, and so on to infinity.

3. Even if in any way whatsoever reasoning would make us understand a certain assertion, the very process of reasoning would have to use the power itself whose value we want to establish and therefore presupposes its validity (the *argumentum dialleli* or vicious circle).

4. The idealistic skeptic has an additional reason to believe that being itself always escapes us. For the agreement of intellect and being, in which for the non-idealist truth consists, can be known as such only when we compare our concept of being with being itself; but this comparison has to be made by means of a concept, and so on to infinity.

Critique. Absolute or universal skepticism cannot be maintained. One who really wants to suspend *all* judgments is in the following position:

1. He cannot posit the general proposition: "Man cannot know anything with certitude."

2. He is unable to restrict his assertion to: "I cannot know anything with certitude."

3. He cannot limit it to: "I do not know anything with certainty," even if this proposition would be stated only as a probable thesis.

4. He is unable to doubt deliberately whether he knows anything with certainty, for such a doubt presupposes that he knows his own existence as well as the difference between knowing and not knowing, and between certitude and doubt.

5. He cannot even take his doubt as a practical attitude of life, for otherwise he would give his doubt a purpose to be intended—namely, to live wisely by abstaining from judging—and thereby pronounce himself in favor of something.

6. He is unable simply not-to-will, for this would be to will not-to-will because he would have to face the problem of willing or not-willing.

7. Finally, he cannot even simply live or exist unconsciously, for this, too, implies the rejection of non-*being* and therefore contains an affirmation. Only non-*being* is wholly without any affirmation.

The Arguments of the Skeptic. Thus it appears that the skeptic may not offer any reasons for his skepticism. If he does it anyhow, his arguments can be refuted in the following way.

It is not true that the difference of opinions extends to everything that can be perceived or thought. There are primordial and fundamental insights which everyone who has to make use of his reason cannot escape from admitting at least implicitly because they reveal themselves at once. A critical reflection on this point will follow later.[7]

As soon as one considers something as an error—and skeptics commonly albeit inconsistently do this—there is already a recognition of truth, for to deny that something is true is to affirm as true that it is false.

It is not necessary to go on to infinity in seeking a criterion of truth if there is a self-revealing truth which affirms itself even when we try to deny it.

Epistemological reflection does not consist in proving one "thing" through another—obviously, not everything can be proved—but in a reflex analysis of one and the same being by itself.

The intellect can know its agreement with being when in its judgment it reflects on the nature itself of the concept as essentially referring to being, as representing a mode of *being,* although not always in a perfect way. In and through the concept, being itself, in accordance with its mode of *being,* becomes manifest to the mind.

14. *Raising the Most Universal Question*

Absolute skepticism is impossible as a radical and successful attitude of abstaining from judgment. The universal skeptic does not exist. Universal skepticism can exist only in a provisional way as an *attempt* to see whether it is possible. The authentic initial attitude of metaphysics consists precisely in raising the most universal question without touching the point whether this question can maintain itself as a question or perhaps implies already an affirmation.

Accordingly, we must raise this universal question—the question about "all," and therefore about truth as truth—not as a positive

---

[7]Cf. nos. 26, 36-44.

doubt but only as a methodic-negative initial doubt. It does not yet affirm itself as a really admitted or asserted doubt, but only asks whether it is possible to doubt everything. For this reason it would be better to avoid the term "doubt" altogether and to speak only of asking a question. For, as was indicated above, we leave our spontaneous certitudes for what they are and merely avoid using them as an established starting point in our investigation.[8]

---

[8]We may quote here an appropriate commentary of Thomas Aquinas on Aristotle's *Metaphysics:*

Aristotle was accustomed, in nearly all his works, to set forth the problems which emerge before investigating and establishing what is true. But while in other works Aristotle sets down the problems one at a time in order to establish the truth about each one, in this work he sets forth all the problems at once, and afterwards in the proper order establishes the things that are true. The reason for this is that other sciences consider the truth in a particular way, and therefore it belongs to them to raise problems of a particular kind about individual truths. But just as it belongs to this science to make a universal study of truth, so also does it belong to it to discuss all the problems which pertain to the truth. Therefore it does not discuss its problems one at a time but all at once. *Commentary on the Metaphysics of Aristotle,* translated by John P. Rowan, vol. One, bk. III, lect. 1, no. 343, Regnery, Chicago, 1961, p. 143.

CHAPTER FOUR

THE QUESTION OF BEING AND THE
AFFIRMATION OF BEING

15. *The Primordial Question*

The Nature of Judgment. Every particular act of knowledge reveals a characteristic duality when it is explicitated in a judgment. Knowledge always refers to something or someone and makes an assertion about this something or someone in either an affirmative or a negative way. From this explicitation of knowledge in the judgment it appears that to know something or someone always means for us to know it or him as being this way or that way or not this way or that way.

The judgment is not merely a predicative synthesis, i.e., a "proposed" connection or separation of a subject and a predicate. Such a synthesis is merely a proposition. The judgment intends to make a statement about this proposed state of affairs with respect to that to which the proposal refers—namely, the being itself that is in question. The judgment claims to make a truth-positing synthesis, i.e., to reach truth as the known agreement between what is thought of someone or something in a proposition and this same someone or something as he or it *is.*[1]

The Primordial Judgment. Every particular judgment may be considered as a reply to the question: Is the being in question as it is asserted to be in the proposition? This question, however, is raised on the basis of a series of previously accepted suppositions. If, for instance, the question refers to the "what" or "how" of a person or thing, it presupposes that they *are.* If it is concerned with the actual occurrence of a particular event, it assumes a framework of successive events. If it aims at essential relationships, e.g., between certain numbers, it takes for granted that a world of numbers is possible or at least can be thought of as a whole of relationships.

All such presuppositions themselves may be put into the form of questions and thus allow constantly more profound assumptions to reveal themselves. Ultimately, it appears that they all point to

---

[1]Concerning the judgment as a predicative synthesis and as a truth-positing synthesis, cf. J. B. Lotz, *Sein und Wert,* Paderborn, 1938, pp. 53-63.

one and the same most fundamental presupposition. No other assertion is prior to this first supposition and all other assertions are further determinations of it. It is expressed by the statement: *something* (no matter what) *is* (no matter how).

The Primordial Question. If this primordial assumption is expressed in the form of a question, one arrives at the most radical and most universal question, i.e., a question to which no other is prior and which all others presuppose to have been answered, the question: *Is* there (no matter how) *anything* (no matter what)?[2]

Usually this most radical of all questions, which should be answered first of all, is omitted because the reply to it seems evident. Attention is turned at once to more special problems, and the fundamental question is omitted and neglected. However, as soon as universal wonder is struck not only by what is sensational and clamorous, but pays attention also to the hidden and silent, the unobtrusive, and the so-called "obvious," as being most important, reflection sheds full light on the peculiar and unique nature of the most universal question.

Inadequate Formulation. This question cannot be formulated in an adequate way. What it asks cannot be expressed in words. The term "anything" is used, but should not be taken here in opposition to "anybody," for in its universality it refers to persons as well as things and includes also qualities, activities, events, relations, imaginations, thoughts, etc. The question uses the third person singular, but does not convey as yet any opposition between first, second, and third person, singular or plural. It is formulated in the present indicative, but does not yet make a distinction between present, past, and future, between indicative, optative, and imperative, or between possibility, reality, and necessity. All modes of *being* are indiscriminately included in this question, which may be called only the question of *being*.

Radical Epoche. This question puts everything into question, it is all-embracing. More particular questions presuppose a ques-

---

[2]Regarding the question of *being,* cf. M. Heidegger, *Sein und Zeit,* Tübingen, 6th ed., 1949, pp. 1-15, *Einführung in die Metaphysik,* Tübingen, 1953, pp. 1-7; K. Rahner, *Geist in Welt,* pp. 35-36, *Hörer des Wortes,* München, 1941, pp. 42-50. However, *we* conceive the question of *being* first of all as the question: Is there anything? It is only after this question that the others arise: "What is 'to be'?" and "Why is there something?" The authors cited above do not mention the first question, but conceive the question of *being* as referring to the meaning of *being.*

tioner from whom the query proceeds as something distinct from him, as well as one to whom the question is addressed, one who is asked something. In the question of *being,* however, both the "to be" of the questioner and that of the one who is questioned are also object of the question. Even the "to be" of the question itself is put into question, for the inquiry is precisely whether there is anything, no matter what.

The *epoche* or attempt to abstain from judging must, therefore, be made in such a radical way that nothing remains except only this question, which subjects everything to itself, puts itself also into question, and does not even affirm its own "to be": Is there anything or is there nothing? Is it so self-evident that "something is"? Would not "there is nothing" be even so much easier?

Impossibility of Absolute Denial and Absolute Abstention. The question is not raised by a questioner who is distinct from it, but raises itself. It is not addressed to someone distinct from it, but addresses itself. If the question can ever find an answer, it will have to find it in itself.

It is wholly impossible to reply to it in a negative way, for the negating assertion "nothing is" is something. Thus an absolute denial contains a contradiction between what is stated and the act itself of stating it. It annihilates itself. Consequently, the viewpoint of absolute nihilism can never be adhered to in a self-consistent way.

Likewise, the question cannot remain a pure question which does not supply an answer, but stays between *being* and non-*being,* as absolute skepticism attempts to do. As soon as the question understands itself as the all-embracing question, it knows that it has already answered itself, for the very question "Is there anything?" is something. It satisfies what is asked and therefore, as soon as the question is put, there is something "no matter what it is."

Accordingly, the impossibility of absolute denial and absolute abstention from judgment is rooted in the necessity of the affirmation that is present to and in the question itself of *being.* Therefore, the question can never be a pure question, one whose answer is expected from without. It always contains already within its bosom the certainty that something is and by reflecting on its all-embracing nature as a question, it becomes conscious that it itself has the character of a reply and that certainly something is.

Thus we may say that the irreducible and primordial starting point of all further questions and all further replies lies in the self-presence and self affirmation of the "not-nothing" contained in the question of *being*. This question is a being which, asking about its being, says that it is and therefore excludes that nothing is.

16. *The First Affirmation*

Inadequate Expression. The *"Urdoxa"* or fundamental conviction which is the basis of all further research is expressed by the statement: "something (no matter what) *is* (no matter how)." However, just as the question of *being* cannot be stated adequately, so also the affirmation of *being* that is contained in the question defies expression. It precedes all further distinctions, even that between the something which is and the "to be" of this something. It posits neither identity nor distinction between being and "to be" in any explicit fashion. For this reason the affirmation of *being* is not a judgment which distinguishes and connects a subject and a predicate, but a kind of pre-predicative knowing that precedes all concepts and judgments, even though it is true that it somehow finds expression in the judgment.[3]

The Affirmation of Being *is Immediate.* It is important to emphasize that the affirmation of *being* is present in, and coincides with the question of *being*. For this reason this question is not a pure question, i.e., it does not originate in not-yet-knowing and does not face affirmation and negation as two possibilities of equal value. Thus the affirmation of *being* is indubitable. For, if asking a question is a way of thinking, this thinking can be a pure doubt only when it faces two possibilities without being able to determine which of the two has to be admitted. But such a case arises only when the point is whether or not a subject should be connected with a predicate. This connection constitutes a problem only when there is a certain distance between the questioning thought and the object to be known, so that the cognitive object is not in the knowing subject with its own immediate illuminative presence. But as long as the *Urdoxa* retains its character of undifferentiated knowing of *being*, there is not yet question of any twofoldness and opposition, or of any intermediary. It is an immediate knowledge and for this reason wholly above doubt, so that it necessarily includes its own truth in itself.

---

[3]Concerning the pre-predicative knowing of the *Urdoxa*, cf. E. Husserl, *Erfahrung und Urteil*, Hamburg, 1948, pp. 13, 21, 34, 60 and *passim*.

The Immediacy of Being *Cannot be Doubted.* This unity of thinking and *being* in the pre-predicative knowledge of *being* is manifested by the failure of any attempt to doubt its immediacy.

1. One could assume that the affirmation of *being* is merely a subjective necessity of our thinking, based on the *a priori* structure of the mind, so that it would not include the "to be" of what is thought. However, such a subjective necessity of thinking itself would *be* and thus would verify what it claims—namely, that something is.

2. One could claim that knowledge of *being* is mediated by a subjective medium of thought, a concept or a judgment, which intentionally refers to the *being* itself of something. But this concept or judgment of *being* itself would *be;* consequently, of itself and not merely by referring to something else, it would verify what it asserts—namely, that something is.

3. One could suppose that the knowledge of *being* refers only to a mere appearance without there being anything corresponding to this appearance. But then this appearance itself would *be* and would manifest itself as such. Purely apparent "to be" therefore, is excluded as the terminus of the fundamental affirmation of *being.*

4. One could assume that the knowledge of *being* has as its intermediary an image or phenomenon which is distinct from *being* and points to it. This very phenomenon, however, through which "to be" would reveal itself would *be* and therefore would manifest itself directly. Consequently, there would necessarily be something that reveals itself as it is, without the intermediary of a distinct phenomenon. Accordingly, "to be" is immediately present to thinking in the affirmation of *being.*

Intuition of Being. The immediate self-presence of *being* in the questioning thought is the highest form of evidence. The affirmation of *being* is the central point in which there is no longer any distance or otherness of the affirmer, the act of affirming, and the affirmed. The affirmation of *being,* which coincides with the question of *being,* always truthfully affirms that something is, for it itself is.

For this reason the act of affirming *being* may be called an act of vision or intuition. But then this term must be divested of its original connotation of sensitive seeing, which always implies an opposition of subject and object. Intuition should be understood here as the supreme immediacy of self-revelation. For the *being* of questioning is self-illuminatingly present in the questioning thought, so that here to-open-itself-to is tantamount to to-be-open-to.

Nevertheless, the knowledge of *being* which precedes the explicit formation of all concepts and judgments is not at all a perfect intuition. Although the affirmation that there is not nothing is indubitable, this affirmation is only the affirmation already present in the question of *being* itself and does not strip this quesion of its interrogative nature. In its indifferentiation it is the foundation of all further unfolding of the ontological question. All subsequent questions about it remain open—questions about the essence: What, then, is? In what ways is it? Questions about ground: What is "to be"? and: Why is whatever is and why is there not rather nothing? The more the affirmation of *being* unfolds itself into more particular queries, the more new questions does it raise. Thus it is far from being an explicit intuition of everything-that-is in its essence and grounds. Nevertheless, to some extent, it contains all further replies, albeit only in the form of questions. It would not go on searching if it had not to some extent already found what it was looking for.

A Middle Position Between Dogmatism and Skepticism. Thus the development of thought does not originate in an isolated, unsolved, and wholly insoluble question, but in a question that possesses a nucleus of absolute certainty. Neither does it originate in an isolated problemless assertion, but in an affirmation which constantly gives rise to new questions. The initial attitude of philosophy is neither a doubt containing no certitude nor a certitude containing no doubt. Philosophy has to preserve the mean between skepticism and dogmatism.

All Judgments Aim at Being. The only thing which shows itself with all clarity in this imperfect intuition of *being* is that all acts of judging are directed to *being*. For the most general question of thinking receives its most general answer through the certainty that whatever there may be—this point is still left open—there is not nothing. But if thinking thus appears to come to rest in the certitude of *being,* then the first condition which something must fulfill to be affirmed in a judgment is that it *be.* If it were not at all and in no way whatsoever, then, and only then, could it never play the role of a cognitive object. In any case knowing refers to *being* and not to non-*being,* even though we must provisionally leave undecided how this reference should be conceived—viz., as total identity, or as the relationship of knowing to *being* so that a thing is known because it is, or as the relationship of *being* to knowing, so that a thing is because it is known.[4]

"To Be" is Irreducible. What does "to be" mean? What is meant by to-be-red can de determined by indicating its agreement with, and distinction from other modes of being-colored, such as to-be-blue or to-be-green. In a similar way "to be" can only be placed alongside and opposite "not-to-be." However, if "to be" and "not-to-be" are claimed to be contrasted as each other's opposites within the realm of a higher unity, "not-to-be" would have to be before it would be capable of being an opposite. Because, however, "not-to-be" is not, "to be" has no opposite which it excludes from itself; therefore, it includes "everything" and applies to "everything".[5]

What "to be" means, therefore, cannot be understood by reducing it to something other or higher than "to be." It can be understood only in and of itself. But, because in its affirmation "to be" does not yet reveal itself explicitly in a perfect intuition, its full richness can be understood only from subsequent particularizations which flow from it and are intelligible through it. Accordingly, in the affirmation of *being* a primordial knowing of *being* reveals itself, but this knowing remains implicit, and all subsequent explicit and more particular knowledge is an explicitation of it.[6]

---

[4]Cf. nos. 9, 23-26, 42.
[5]See, however, what will be said about the *concept* of non-being in nos. 167 and 179.
[6]Cf. no. 172.

CHAPTER FIVE

EXPERIENCE AND INSIGHT AS APPROACHES TO EVIDENCE

17. *The Affirmation of My Own Being*

Self-Consciousness and Self-Love. Although the pre-predicative knowledge that something (no matter what) is, which is implicit in the question of *being,* is an absolute and intuitive certainty, nevertheless it is a very imperfect intuition, for it leaves all further questions unanswered. Especially this question is urgent: What, then, *is,* and how is it?

A first reply to this question, however, is immediately given in the undifferentiated affirmation of *being.* For there is not-nothing, because at least the question of *being* itself is. As soon as the question whether anything is interrogates itself, it knows that it itself is and that, by being, it includes its own answer in itself. It affirms itself as *being.* Therefore, the undifferentiated affirmation of *being* implies at least that the affirmation itself is, i.e., it is a self-affirmation. But "to know that one is" is the self-present identity of the knower and the known, it is to be conscious of oneself, to be in *self-consciousness.*

Moreover, the question of *being* is not indifferent to its answer, for it itself falls under the question. Therefore, the answer concerns it, for its own "to be" or "not to be" is at stake. "To be" is of interest to the question. It desires not only to know but above all *to be* knowing. And if it knows that it is, "to be" is the fulfillment of this desire. The question exists not only as knowing—to-be-known, but also as loving—to-be-loved, to be *self-love.*

I Am. That which is conscious of itself and contains its own *being* as knowing—to-be-known and loving—to-be-loved calls itself "I." For the term "I" expresses precisely the identity of the one who knows and the one who is known, the knower and the known, the lover and the loved.[1]

---

[1]When someone says: "I am" (or "I see," "I feel," etc.), he wants to express that the one who is said to be is the same as the one who says it and knows it. Saying, knowing and being pertain to the same. This is evidently the meaning of the term "I."

Of course, this "I," which now is inevitable, had to be avoided hitherto in order to emphasize as strongly as possible the undifferentiation and universality of the affirmation of *being*. For this reason we spoke of something that is. But we added that the expression was deficient, for it was not our intention to give preference to the third person neuter. We merely wanted to maintain as long as possible an attitude of undecidedness and to remain above the distinction of persons and that of the conscious and the unconscious.

However, the self-reflection of the question of *being* shows that it implies at least the first person: *I am.* All other persons presuppose the first person, and the use of the neuter is preconditioned by the personal or conscious. Thus the *epoche* has to give way for the first person.

Inadequacy of "I." Prudence, however, remains necessary. Just as the affirmation "something is" leaves other questions open, so also does the affirmation "I am." Just as the expression "something" has another meaning here than the one accepted by the differentiated usage of speech, so also has the term "I," as used here. Again, we are concerned with something that defies adequate expression—namely, a pre-predicative knowing of being self-conscious which is not further differentiated. In everyday usage "I" is opposed to you, he, she, we, it, and they, and excludes these others. But here there is not yet question of others and therefore neither of opposition to such other personal or impersonal beings. No attention is yet paid to the question whether there are any opposites. The only thing which has become clear is that the neutral indications of the question and of the affirmation of *being* were provisional indications of what at least is: I, who am. *Who* I am is still wholly contained in the *epoche*. Perhaps I am "to be" itself unqualifiedly. Perhaps I am everything that is or everything that is is I, without any qualification. But in any case this much is certain: if ever any distinction will reveal itself, it will never be possible to speak of the other without there being in this other a reference to the non-other, to what is identical with itself, to the self I am for myself.

18. *The Finiteness of My* Being

Nevertheless, self-affirmation as the first concrete form of the *Urdoxa* contains already the beginning of an answer to the question which the questioner necessarily asks himself: Who am I? I am the one who in his questioning desire for *being* "feels" in a pre-predicative immanent grasp that he himself is. I am present to myself in a kind of immediate self-illumination and self-inclination.

The Becoming "I." However, this reply is not sufficient. Just as the intuition of *being* is an imperfect intuition which seeks further, so also my self-presence in *being,* knowing, and loving is an imperfect self-intuition which continues its search. For it is only as a questioning, desiring being that I am. But can perfect knowing have the nature of a question, and perfect love the character of a desire? I question only because I do not yet know fully, I desire only because I do not yet fully possess. The question of *being* which I myself am reveals itself to me as a thinking and searching knowing, as a desiring and striving love. Mine is a becoming and growing consciousness, directed to something that transcends what I know of myself in my initial self-affirmation.

Pure "to be" on the other hand, just as pure knowing and pure loving, is all-embracing, because it is opposed only by pure "not to be" and therefore has no opposite. Even if we leave undecided whether "to be" necessarily includes coming-to-be, whether knowing implies thinking, and loving contains desiring,[2] it is certain that there is not yet full identity of what-comes-to-be with pure *being,* of what-thinks with pure knowing, of what-desires with pure loving.

If we call pure "to be," all-embracing as it is, *unqualified "to be,"* I, as a coming-to-be-conscious, cannot fully coincide with this unqualified *being.* For, while questioning and desiring, I am directed toward what is not yet perfectly present but can become present; and unqualified "to be" embraces both my imperfect consciousness and that to which my questioning and desiring are directed. I, as coming-to-be, questioning, and desiring, am necessarily in a certain sense distinct from unqualified *being.*

Particularized "To Be." This distinction between me and unqualified "to be" reveals itself in the form of the judgment in which my pre-predicative self-grasp has to express itself. The composite statement "I am" is the connection of elements which of themselves do not fully coincide—namely, "I" and "to be." Thus the judgment reveals that "to be" is not that which fully coincides with me, i.e., is not "what" I am, although "to be" is that "through which" I am. I encounter "to be" only as particularized in my *being.*

---

[2] Cf. no. 179.

I am not unqualified "to be," but I am be-ing. This participle indicates that I share in "to be," participate in it. Unqualified "to be" appears to transcend me, yet it somehow is immanent in me, for it makes me share in itself. It is in me particularized to my *being*.

I am Finite. That unqualified "to be" is particularized to my *being* means that my "to be" is *finite*. While unqualified "to be" is opposed only by "not to be" and therefore has no opposite, my "to be," as a particularization, necessarily expresses a relationship of opposition to other possible modes of *being* which I do not necessarily include.

For this reason the judgment "I am" is essentially incomplete, for it leaves open precisely the question about the particular mode of *being* which is mine and through which I am distinct from unqualified *being*. In the undetermined self-affirmation I appear not yet to have grasped myself adequately. Although there is nothing in me that does not fall under my *being,* not enough light has yet been shed on the question of how my "to be" is further determined.

19. *My Self-Affirmation is Not Based on an Essential Insight*

If I am distinct from unqualified *being,* the question arises of why I cannot doubt my *being,* why I am certain that I am.

Only Unqualified "To Be" and its Implications are Absolutely Undeniable. Absolutely undeniable is only that which cannot be denied in any hypothesis, only that for which it is absolutely impossible not to be, only that which is of necessity. For, if one says of that which absolutely cannot not-be that it is not, there would be a contradiction in the content itself of the assertion and thus the assertion would destroy itself.

That for which it is absolutely impossible not to be is that which is perfectly opposed to "not to be." But only unqualified "to be" and what is necessarily included in it are opposed in this way to "not to be."[3]

Thus it follows that my "to be" is wholly undeniable only if it either coincides entirely with unqualified *being* or is necessarily included in it, e.g., as a part in a whole, a property in an essence, or a conclusion in the premises.

---

[3]Cf. no. 176.

My "To be" is Not Absolutely Undeniable. My complete identity with unqualified *being* has already been excluded in the preceding pages. On the other hand, I have no perfect intuition of unqualified *being;* until now it manifests itself to me only in the particular form of my *being,* and therefore I cannot yet decide whether or not my "to be" is necessarily implied in unqualified *being.*[4] Thus I will have to leave undecided whether or not it is absolutely necessary that I am.

The ground, then, for my self-knowing can lie neither in the complete identity of me and *being*—such an identity does not exist— nor in the necessary implication of my *being* in unqualified *being*— for such an implication is not known to me.

Accordingly, the hypothesis that I would not be is not evidently absurd. It is not from the understanding that unqualified "to be" is absolutely necessary that I can deduce the necessity of the judgment "I am." The undeniable impossibility of self-negation does not find its ground in an insight that "I" and "not to be" evidently contradict each other—at least, this contradiction is not known to me. The negation of my *being* does not necessarily imply the absolute negation of *being,* for the other-than-me is possible.

"I am" is Not an Essential Insight. Because I do not know whether "I," taken in myself, with absolute necessity imply "to be," the judgment "I am" cannot be grounded on itself, i.e., purely on an essential insight into the relationship of "I" and *being,* as implying each other with absolute necessity.

20. *My Self-Affirmation is Based on Experience*

Alongside essential insight there is another approach to evidence or self-revelation—namely, experience.

I cannot deny that I am. However, the reason is not that the denial would imply a contradiction in the contents of my judgment, as happens in evidence which is an insight. I cannot deny that I am, because *I* cannot exercise an act whose content would be the denial of the exercising act: *I* cannot deny that I am, because in the very act of denying I already *am.*

For this reason the pre-predicative knowing of my *being* that is expressed in the judgment "I am" must be based on a pre-given (but imperfect) unity of "I" and *being* which precedes my knowing,

---

[4]Cf. nos. 172, 181.

not as a necessity—at least, not as a known necessity—but as *de facto* present. My *de facto being* has a certain priority over my consciousness. My consciousness is not a pure self-illumination that does not need any other explanation than itself, but it is a becoming acquainted with "me-as-already-being," it is a self-experience.

To experience is to meet, to encounter, to find that something is, to undergo it.[5] Whoever experiences, observes and, as long as the observed presents itself to his attention, it is impossible for him to deny it, he has to admit it.

21. *The Difference Between Insight and Experience*

Insight.[6] Insight is concerned with necessity and is fully present only in absolutely apodictic evidence, i.e., such evidence that the contradictory opposite is wholly unthinkable because it is absolutely impossible. To deny such an absolutely apodictic evidence is the denial of *being* itself, for it is to assert that "to be" and "not to be" are identical.

Experience. Experience is concerned with facts, in the broadest sense of the term. It tends to another form of evidence—namely, experiential evidence. As such, it can never reach apodictic evidence, for it does not know whether or not its opposite is wholly unthinkable because of its absolute impossibility. Nevertheless, in its own way experience can reach indubitableness—namely, if it is affirmed in its very negation. We do not mean that the content of the act denying such an experience implies the affirmation but that the very exercice of this act implies it.

Experiences which in this way are inevitable and undeniable, because they are present as soon as I am there experiencing and observing, may nonetheless be said to be apodictic to a certain extent. They may be called primordial experiences. Their apodicticity, however, is based only on my experience of my *being* and of whatever is given together with my *being* as I experience it. To deny such experiences is not the same as to negate unqualified "to be," but it is to negate the "to be" of the negating "I."

---

[5]Cf. the German words *Erfahrung, Vernehmen,* and the Latin *percipere.*

[6]Concerning the difference between absolutely apodictic evidences and primordial existential experiences or perfect evidences of experience, see the theory proposed by Stephan Strasser in his study of Husserl, "Beschouwingen over het vraagstuk van de apodicticiteit en de critische verantwoording van de phenomenologie," *Tijdschrift voor Philosophie,* vol. 8 (1946), pp. 226-270.

CHAPTER SIX

HOW METAPHYSICS IS POSSIBLE

22. *Introduction*

We could now try to describe more in detail the primordial experiential evidences of the "I who am." For instance, I could say: "I am a temporal being which, while it remains itself, is constantly in different states according as it unfolds itself." Or, "I am a social being which is subsistent *in* itself and, at the same time, in its experiential encounters is concerned with other beings with whom it is together."

Such a description of my existence and of the undeniable world of experience "to" which I "ec-sist" cannot be avoided in the process of our investigation. However, in itself such a description is not yet metaphysics, it is not yet a science of the absolute which transcends experience. It remains a fundamental question whether it is possible to rise from such a description of what I experience to knowledge which is not only concerned with what de facto is but also with what absolutely cannot not-be.[1]

The Two Crucial Questions. For this reason I want to postpone such a further description as long as possible and hold fast to the first experiential evidence of my *being* as not yet differentiated but most certain. I want to ask myself two questions. First of all, Do I have access to absolutely apodictic evidences, i.e., can I arrive at an insight into truths that do not depend on what de facto is but are true in every hypothesis or absolutely? And secondly, What is the relation between such evidence of insight and the evidence of experience?

These two questions are decisive with respect to the possibility of metaphysical knowledge and its relationship to experiential knowledge.

---

[1]Concerning the relationship between phenomenology and metaphysics, see, for instance, Albert Dondeyne, "Belang voor de metaphysica van een accurate bestaansbeschrijving van de mens als kennend wezen," *Kennen en metaphysiek* (*Verslag der 12e Alg. Verg. v.d. Ver. voor Thom. Wijsbegeerte*), Nymegen, 1947, pp. 37-51; Stephan Strasser, *The Soul in Metaphysical and Empirical Psychology*, Pittsburgh, 2nd impr., 1961, pp. 1-6; Etienne Gilson, *L'être et l'essence*, Paris, 1948, pp. 19-20, 327-328.

If I call knowledge that is based on the experience of facts *a posteriori knowledge* (for it is posterior to experience), and knowledge that does not depend on experience *a priori knowledge* (for it is prior to experience), the second question may be formulated also in this way: If there are any insights into the absolutely necessary, can they be *a posteriori* or only *a priori?* And if they are *a priori,* how should I conceive their independence of experience? What is the basis for the certainty of *a priori* knowledge and how is it possible that the validity of this knowledge extends beyond a mere arranging of experiential data in orderly fashion?

23. *The Impossibility of Radical Empiricism*[2]

A Fact Implies a Hypothetical Necessity. On the basis of experience I have to affirm categorically that I am, although I do not yet know why I am or whether my *being* is absolutely necessary, so that it would be absolutely impossible for me not to be. However, now that I am and as long as I am, it is impossible for me to deny truthfully that I am. Not only can this fact not be denied by me, but it is also undeniable in itself. The categorical affirmation of a fact, therefore, contains a hypothetical judgment—namely, the affirmation of a hypothetical necessity: "If and insofar as something is, it cannot be denied."

Thus I come a step closer to the absolute. For now it becomes clear that *to affirm* a fact as a fact goes already beyond the purely factual and implies the discovery of a certain necessity. Wherever "to be" reveals itself, even if it be merely in the experience of the *de facto being* of something, there it reveals to some extent also a necessity, albeit only a hypothetical necessity.

The Hypothetical Necessity Itself is Absolutely Necessary. I can make further progress by considering this hypothetical necessity in itself. The hypothetical proposition itself, insofar as its intended content is concerned, is absolutely true, independently of the question whether the hypothesis is fulfilled. For even in the supposition that the being in question *de facto* is not, it remains true that "if it is, it is of necessity." Therefore, the hypothetical proposition itself is true in every hypothesis, it is absolutely true. Hence what the hypothetical proposition wants to express is no longer merely a fact, as was the

---

[2]Cf. Thomas Aquinas, *Summa theologica,* I, q 2 a. 3 (tertia via); *Contra Gentes,* bk. I, ch. 15.

case in the two categorical propositions hitherto considered: "Something is," and "I am." What is meant by the hypothetical proposition is absolutely undeniable, it is unqualifiedly or absolutely true.

My Possibility is Absolutely Necessary. Another step has to be taken. Now that *de facto* I am, I know that my *being* is not absolutely impossible. I am at least possible. From "it *is* de facto" follows clearly "it *is* possible" with respect to the *de facto* being in question. Therefore, the categorical affirmation of a fact implies still another judgment—namely, the affirmation of its necessary possibility.

Is this possibility hypothetically necessary, i.e., does it depend on the fact that I am? I know, of course, that I am possible, because through experience I know that *de facto* I am. But it is evident that I am not possible because *de facto* I am. On the contrary, my possibility is a condition of my actuality. Although the fact that I am is for me the *cognitive* ground of my possibility, the possibility itself is the *ontological* ground of the fact in question, even if perhaps it is not its adequate ground.

Accordingly, we may conclude: once I have experienced that a being *de facto* is and thus know that this being is possible, I know also that it is of necessity possible and that this possibility is not merely hypothetically necessary, i.e., dependent on the fact that the being in question *is,* but absolutely necessary. At the same time, I know also the absolute necessity of whatever may be necessary to make the being in question possible.

It is Absolutely Impossible that There be Nothing. This knowledge contains an insight of the greatest importance—namely, not only is it impossible for me to say that there is nothing, but also *it is in itself absolutely impossible that there be nothing.* For, if "ever" there was absolutely nothing, there would not even have been the possibility that I could be because this possibility is not nothing. But the possibility that I am *is* at all events; in every hypothesis, whether *de facto* I am or not, this possibility is. Therefore, even if what I experience myself to be would "ever" not be, there would not be nothing, for there would be the possibility of what I experience and of whatever may be necessary to make this experience possible.

Radical Empiricism is Impossible. The preceding reflex analysis of experience shows that my experiential evidences include insights of absolute apodicity. Therefore, the first of our two questions has been given a provisional answer, which subsequent considerations can render more profound.

Radical empiricism, however, denies that experienced facts reveals us anything of the absolutely necessary. It teaches that knowledge offers us nothing else than the data of experience and that at most we can analyze and synthetize them without ever getting beyond the hypothetical necessity of the fact as long as it is a fact. We cannot arrive at insights possessing validity independently of the experienced facts.

Radical empiricism, however, contradicts itself. It may mean one of two things. Either it says that it is *impossible* for me to rise above experience, and then it asserts an absolute necessity. Or it does not want to speak about the impossibility of metaphysical knowledge but only to observe the fact that in my knowledge I do not transcend experience. But then it asserts that this fact is undeniable and therefore necessarily to be affirmed, and it affirms especially that with absolute necessity a being, such as I, is possible which does not know anything else than the facts of experience.

24. *The Impossibility of Radical Idealism*

The extreme opposite of radical empiricism is radical idealism. Radical empiricism conceives knowledge as a perception of what presents itself as being *de facto,* so that the knower remains purely passive with respect to what is known. Such knowledge can never arrive at knowing whether what *de facto* is cannot be other than it presents itself or cannot not-be, i.e., whether of necessity it is, and is as it is.

Radical Idealism. Radical idealism, on the other hand, conceives knowledge only as thinking, as the constructing or constituting of being by the act of knowing, so that the knower is fully active with respect to that which is known. Such knowledge would possess an insight into the necessity of *being,* for in that case "to be" is of necessity constituted by thought itself.

Accordingly, in radical idealism "to be" has as its condition that it be thought: "to be" means "to be thought." Thus thinking is the absolutely necessary, but not so "to be," taken in itself. Since experience presupposes a priority of *being* over knowing, in radical idealism there cannot be any question of experience in the strict sense of the term.

The Self-Contradiction of Radical Idealism. Radical idealism contradicts itself. On the one hand, it conceives "to be" as "to be thought" and thus makes it wholly dependent on the thought that constitutes it. On the other, it cannot conceive thought itself otherwise than as a mode—and even the fundamental mode—of *being,* for who could deny that to-be-thinking is to be? Accordingly, it cannot logically maintain the priority of thinking over *being,* but at most can take refuge in their identity in a perfectly self-illuminating consciousness.

However, as we have seen, I, who asking about *being* know that I am, do not coincide with unqualified *being.* To explain my finiteness, radical idealism has to admit that the identity of thinking and *being* necessarily includes a thinking that is finite and has to experience itself, as one of the forms in which this identity appears. Thus the finite "I" would of necessity belong to the self-construction of thought which thinks that it is. But, as we have seen, I do not know anything about the necessary inclusion of my *being* in unqualified *being.* If I did know about it, I would not need experience to know that I am.

A Less Radical Form of Idealism. Descartes' rationalism of "clear and distinct ideas" is a less radical form of idealism. In this theory there is no longer question of absolute identity but only of a perfect harmony between the "idea" present in my thought and the "real," distinct from this idea. Rationalism posits a parallelism between my thinking which is independent of experience, and my *being* which is independent of my thinking. In this conception the main problem is to explain how I have gotten this "idea" (e.g., as innate) and for what reason this idea harmonizes with the *being* that is distinct from it.

When this rationalism maintains experience alongside the idea and says, for instance, that what we have first experienced we can next deduce from the idea (Christian Wolff's "empirical" and "rational" method), it is still less radical. Its problem would be to explain how the world of experience harmonizes with the world of thought.

Accordingly, we can only conclude that my knowing is not pure thinking, but first of all experiencing. Because I know about *being* only through my own *being,* and because I know about my own *being* only through experience, we must say that metaphysical knowledge, if it is attainable, presupposes experience.

25. *The Impossibility of Radical Phenomenalism*

Kant's Criticism. Kant endeavors[3] to assume a middle position
between empiricism and idealism insofar as he accepts the evidence of
both experience and insight. According to his criticism, we receive
certain impressions; hence his system accepts *a posteriori* knowledge.
However, these impressions do not contain any kind of necessity, but
are "empirical and therefore contingent." Nevertheless, we appear
capable of arriving at knowledge of the necessary, for in science we
are able to form universal and necessary judgments. Since this necessity cannot stem from experience, it is *a priori*. According to Kant,
this *a priori* element of our knowledge, which cannot arise from
experience, must be explained through subjective mind forms. These
forms, the so-called "categories," are subjectively necessary modes in
which we "think" that which was given to us in experience.

Thus the object of knowledge is constructed by the intellect, inasmuch as the intellect adds an *a priori* element, which is subjectively
present independently of experience, to the *a posteriori* data, which
are deprived of any kind of necessity. Knowledge which is not a
synthesis of experience and concept is not "objective." Therefore, a
metaphysics of what lies beyond experience cannot be a knowledge
of "transcendent" objects but only a knowledge of the "transcendental" analysis of our cognitive power—"transcendental" being taken
here as the subjective *a priori* conditions of objective knowledge.
Metaphysics consists in the unveiling of the subjective structure implied by "I think," and this structure alone is the foundation of the
necessity revealing itself in our knowledge. For I know only that
beings must of necessity *appear* in this or that form *to me* since I
think in these forms, but I do not know whether beings must of
necessity also *be* so *in themselves,* for I do not have any knowledge
of things in themselves.

Radical Criticism is Untenable as a Middle Position. Considered
as an attempt to establish a middle position between empiricism and
idealism, radical criticism is untenable.

First of all, it asserts that any necessity which reveals itself in
the judgment is an addition made by the intellect. But if this is so,
would it not be logical to maintain doubt about the "objective" value
of this necessity and to limit oneself in a radically empiricist way to

---

[3]Cf. Kant, *Kritik der reinen Vernunft,* 2nd ed., 1787, *Einleitung.* Concerning the different meanings of "phenomenon," see Heidegger, *Sein und Zeit,*
pp. 28-31.

the mere description of beings as experienced in their individuality and contingency, without wanting to make any universal and necessary judgments (Hume)? Kant is not satisfied with this empiricism, because he accepts the objective value of science before reflecting critically on it. Yet the value of science also must be subjected to the *epoche*. Empiricism can be overcome only by showing that necessity reveals itself not only in the universal and necessary judgments of science but also in the judgments expressing individual experiences of individual facts.

Secondly, although criticism considers any necessity that reveals itself in the judgment as an element added by the intellect, it accepts that "the things in themselves" exercise influence on me in my sense experience. This position leaves two alternatives. Either the way in which these things influence me, i.e., their causality, is based on these "things in themselves," and then the necessity in question lies in the data of experience. Or, if one insists that all necessity arises only from the intellect, then the causal influence of "things in themselves" has to be scrapped, so that one arrives at radical idealism (Fichte in his earlier works.)

Criticism as Radical Phenomenalism. Criticism can be appreciated as an attempt to make experience and insight, senses and intellect, the *a posteriori* and the *a priori* collaborate in the production of man's finite and always imperfect knowledge. But it contradicts itself when it remains a radical phenomenalism, i.e., when it maintains that we cannot at all know beings as they are "in themselves," but only as they are "conceived" by our thinking on the basis of our sense data. Let us see in what this contradiction consists.

The term "phenomenon" may be used in different senses. It may mean:

1. What is merely "apparently" this way or that way; it merely seems to be this way or that way, but it is not as it appears to be.

2. The "appearance" of something that directly shows itself as it is, but is understood only as a manifestation of, and a pointer to *something else* which does not show itself; e.g., the symptoms of a disease.

3. The "phenomenon" in the Kantian sense of the term, i.e., as the object of sense experience insofar as this object is connected with, and is *something of* being "as it is in itself" (the noumenon).

4. "Self-revealing," in the sense of the modern phenomenologists (Husserl and Heidegger), as something which shows itself "as it is in itself." This "self-revealing" may be something which manifests itself already in everyday life. Often, however, the phenomenologists speak of "phenomenon" with respect to the more profound ground of what manifests itself in everyday life, a ground which is still hidden and perhaps even misunderstood, so that it has to be brought to light by the phenomenological method.

If the object of human knowledge is seen purely as the phenomenon in the Kantian sense, one cannot deny that this phenomenon itself in its own way *is,* even though it be nothing but the subjectively necessary mode in which that which does not reveal itself "as it is in itself" appears to our thought, so that the phenomenon in question arises from subjective influence. The phenomenon *is,* for this appearing-to-us is a way of *being*—namely, *being*-a-phenomenon. Thus we would know at least the phenomenon itself "as it is in itself" and in this way the phenomenon would belong to "self-revealing" in the sense of phenomenology. Accordingly, our knowledge appears to be directed to being as such, and this being is what, properly speaking, "reveals itself," no matter how imperfectly.

The opposition of being and phenomenon is untenable especially with respect to Kant's critique of the cognitive faculties and the knowing subject. He determines what sensitivity, intellect, experiencing, and thinking *are* and investigates their value. But, is there question here merely of these faculties as they necessarily appear to us or as they are in themselves? And regarding the knowing subject, Kant seeks the root of our knowledge in "I think" or transcendental apperception, the consciousness which synthetizes all cognitive objects. But if this synthesis is an empty, contentless form, can I really say that "I am"? Leaving aside the exact determination of how I am because my limited way of knowing myself would play a role in this determination, is it not rather true that the "to be in itself" of my *being* imposes itself on me with undeniable experiential evidence?

26. *The Possibility of Metaphysics as Ontology*

The preceding pages excluded skepticism, relativism, and dogmatism as initial attitudes of philosophy. Next, we showed that one cannot maintain the various epistemological systems that are more or less related to these initial attitudes—namely, the radical forms of empiricism, idealism, and phenomenalism, although it was not excluded that they could be maintained in a mitigated form. We must now present the positive results of our investigation in a summary fashion.

Positive Results. I have undeniable primordial experiences, especially that there is not nothing, and that I, asking about being, am. In these experiential evidences I know at least *something* as it is in itself, even though this knowledge may be very imperfect. I cannot absolutely oppose being as it presents itself to me to being as it is in itself, for to present itself or to appear is a mode of *being* belonging to being in itself. Especially, the phenomenon, in the Kantian sense of the term, itself is something.

The experience that something *de facto* is teaches me at least something about the possible, for in any case what *de facto* is real, is possible.

It teaches me also something about the necessary. For what *de facto* is real, as long as and insofar as it really is, i.e., at least hypothetically, is of necessity real. And the possible is of necessity possible, regardless of whether it is *de facto* or not, and therefore it is possible by absolute necessity.

Accordingly, I have a certain insight into the necessity that there is something. I know that it is absolutely impossible that there be nothing. But I do not know this independently of all experience of what *de facto* is real, I do not know it by means of an adequate and perfect intuition as to what unqualified "to be" means and what it necessarily includes. My immediate intuition of *being,* as pre-predicative knowledge, is very imperfect. It unfolds itself only by means of experience, insofar as I discover a certain necessity in what I experience as soon as I affirm that the experienced is being: insofar as it is, it is of necessity.

The Possibility of Metaphysics. The way in which metaphysics is possible discloses itself through opposition to the excluded viewpoints.

In opposition to radical empiricism, I cannot *a priori* doom to failure the attempt to express the necessity which is the foundation on which what I experience *de facto* is.

In opposition to radical phenomenalism, I cannot admit that this necessity is purely a necessity of my thinking to arrange what I

experience in subjective *a priori* categories. For the discovered
necessity belongs not merely to what is experienced insofar as I
grasp it, but pertains to what is experienced as it is in itself because,
as something that is, it participates in unqualified *being*.

In opposition to radical idealism, I must admit that this necessity
of being is not constructed by my thinking. For I have an imperfect
insight into this necessity which finds its source in unqualified *being*.
Only by means of a reflex analysis of what is experienced as being,
i.e., only through the discovery that it participates in *being*, do I
arrive at the explicit knowledge of the *being* in which it participates.

Metaphysics as Ontology. What was provisionally indicated as
"metaphysics" may now be appropriately called "ontology." By this
term one should understand primarily the study of being as being as
a way to come closer to the essence and the meaning of the unqualified
being which reveals itself as the all-embracing ground of being. Constant care will have to be taken not to let metaphysical thought lapse
into any conception which identifies "to be" itself which one or the
other of its general or special modes.[4] "To be" is what first reveals
itself with absolute necessity in my thinking, and therefore it cannot
be understood by means of something prior to it.

For this reason it is not correct to stipulate as the condition for
the *being* of a being that it present itself as *de facto* real to passive
experience. Yet this is done by empiricism in its positivistic form.

It is also contrary to the priority of *being* as *being* to stipulate as
a condition that it depend on the activity of thinking itself. Yet
this is maintained by radical idealism.

Finally, because the absoluteness of *being* reveals itself in the
experience of beings, it implies a contradiction to conceive the "to be"
attributed to the experiential data by the judgment as a purely subjective synthesis of phenomena and, on the other hand, to accept that
there is something that, transcending the phenomena, "is in itself."
Yet this is done by phenomenalism in its agnostic form.

Ontology necessarily has to conceive "to be" as "to be in itself."
To-be-experienced-by, to-be-conceived-by, to-be-understood-by are

---

[4]Concerning this danger, see Gilson, *L'être et l'essence, passim,* e.g., p.
311: "Aristotle . . . a dénoncé l'erreur la plus grave qui n'allait pas cesser
de mettre la philosophie première en peril: substituer à l'être en tant qu'être,
comme objet de la métaphysique, l'une quelconque des formes de l'être . . .
Elle [la raison] identifie à l'être même ce qui n'est que l'un de ses modes,
et érige en méthode de la philosophie première celle de la science particulière
qu'elle vient de fonder."

not conditions of *being* but derivative meanings of it which presuppose and include its first meaning.[5]

A Fundamental Difficulty. If ontology is an attempt to express the absoluteness of *being* revealing itself in the experience of being, i.e., an attempt to say something about *being,* its very possibility becomes at once problematical. Ontology, so the objection goes, can express itself about *being* only in judgments, but a judgment asserts that something is and how it is; it speaks about a bearer of *being* as a subject, whose way of *being* it determines in a predicate. Thus the great difficulty of ontology lies in this: Is the judgment capable of saying anything about *being* itself? Is it possible to separate from the judgment itself that which reveals itself *within* the judgment in the verbal copula "to be" as that by which whatever is, is and to set it apart in a formal-abstract concept as the subject of a judgment? Such a judgment would have to state that "to be" *is,* but by what new "to be" would "to be" be? Is it really possible to seize "to be" truthfully in a concept, since every concept contains either as a formal-concrete concept *something* that is in one way or another or as a formal-abstract concept the *way* in which something is?[6]

The reply is that in principle it is not impossible to speak about *being* itself in true judgments if one keeps in mind that in such metaphysical judgments the way of signifying and understanding is not adequate to that which is signified and understood. For "to be" reveals itself to us primarily in its "exercise" by a being. But through reflex analysis of being as being we can aim at "to be" itself. Even though we know that "to be" is ineffable in explicit judgmental knowledge, nevertheless we are capable of expressing the ineffable at least to some extent in reflex judgments. Such judgments are not untrue, as long as we are aware of their inadequacy and constantly correct their mode of expression. We have to add all the time: I do not want to say that what I conceive as if it were something is itself something to which "to be" belongs, but I am concerned with the principle and ground through which whatever is, *is*—the "to be-ness" of being. While we deny the metaphysical propositions insofar as their mode of expression is concerned, we affirm the identity with

---

[5] The term "ontology" was used as a title by J. B. Du Hamel in 1681, by J. Clauberg in 1691, and by Christian Wolff in 1730. Note, however, that ontology does not necessarily have to be imbued with the rationalism which Wolff introduced into the concept, for ontology is based on Aristotle's conception that being as being (*to on*) is the object of the first philosophy.

[6] Cf. no. 51.

itself of that which they express and intend. Thus we indicate that the whole of the conceptual and judgmental world of expression used in ontology should debouch in a silent openness to that which is most knowable in itself and the source from which whatever we know explicity derives its knowability.

27. *The Starting Point of Metaphysics*

The experience of what *de facto* is real constitutes *for me* the cognitive ground of the absolutely necessary, which presents itself as the foundation or the "why" of the facts, as the condition of their possibility, their *de facto* reality, and their hypothetical necessity.

However, the *de facto* reality which I experience is not *in itself* the ontological ground of the absolutely necessary, for I understand that the necessary is necessary even in the hypothesis that the facts are not. Only the insight that the necessary is independent of the facts is a metaphysical insight, for it arrives at truths which are true of necessity, even if the world of experience would not exist or would be entirely different. Metaphysics as ontology is concerned with *being* insofar as it cannot not-be.

A Twofold Starting Point. Thus we may speak in a twofold way of the starting point of metaphysics :[7]

For me and insofar as the *pursuit* of metaphysics is concerned, the starting point lies in the undeniable but necessary affirmation of the *being* of the experienced real being I am and that of the other real beings, if there are any, with whom I find myself together. This necessity is only hypothetical, for it is based on experience. It consists in the undeniability of whatever is implied in the *act* by which I experience that I am.

In itself and insofar as the *content* of metaphysics is concerned, the starting point lies in the absolute, essential necessity of *being* as *being* which reveals itself to some extent, but only imperfectly and inadequately, in the *de facto* reality of my *being*. This necessity consists in the undeniable absolute identity of *being* with *being*.

---

[7]Concerning the starting point of metaphysics, cf. L. de Raeymaeker, *Philosophy of Being,* St. Louis, 1953, pp. 11-32.

CHAPTER SEVEN

REALITY, POSSIBILITY, AND NECESSITY AS GENERAL MODES OF *BEING*

28. *Introduction*

Ontology as Theory of the Real. Metaphysics as ontology is often conceived as the theory of reality. Being as being, it is said, is the real, and thus realism is opposed to idealism.

Insofar as this view identifies "to be" with reality, it runs the risk of forgetting that "to be" is all-embracing. It is in danger of making the same mistake as empiricism, phenomenalism, and idealism— namely, that of considering a mode of *being* as more fundamental than "to be" itself.

Moreover, it is not always clear what they mean by reality. One gets the impression that the real is opposed to something else. But in that case we must ask: Is no "to be" at all attributed to this other, the unreal, or *is* it nevertheless in some way or other? If the real is identified with the actual, then what is to be said about the potential? If the real is conceived as the present, what about the past and the future? Or if real is whatever *de facto* ever is at any time, what must be said about the possible as possible? And if the real is taken to be that which is or can be the object of knowledge, what about the subject of knowledge as subject? Again, if the real is supposed to be whatever *is* independently of thought, what are we to say about that which *is* in dependence on thought?

It should be clear that "to be" extends also to the non-real. There- fore, ontology is not entirely the same as theory of reality, no matter in what sense the term "reality" be understood. Ontology has to determine also the mode of *being* proper to what is potential, temporal, possible, subjective, merely thought, imagined, apparent, supposed, etc. The first task of ontology as the theory of *being* is to rise to the all-embracing unqualified *being* which reveals itself in these modes of *being* as their explanatory ground.

Special Modes of Being. In different ways there can be question of modes of *being*. First of all, there are particular modes which do not necessarily include one another, sometimes even exclude one

51

another, and never coincide completely. If finite beings are admitted, they are distinguished from one another by the particular mode in which they share in unqualified *being*. These modes constitute their individual, specific, or generic essence and their accidental determinations. The most fundamental particular modes of *being* are classified in the supreme genera or categories.[1] If the categorical determinations refer to beings that come to be, these beings have either the mode of being-in-act or that of being-in-potency.[2] If they are concerned with temporal beings, these beings can have the mode of being-present or that of being-past or being-future.[3]

General Modes of Being. The general modes of *being* concern every being as being. They are not only distinct, but also compenetrate one another, and to some extent coincide with one another. They have to be treated at the beginning of ontology, because they raise the metaphysical problem of the essence and meaning of the *being* of beings as sharply as possible. Such general modes are, first of all, the modes of reality, possibility, and necessity, which were discovered in the reflection on the experience of what *de facto* is. Next, there are the ontological properties which flow of necessity from being as being, in which "to be " unfolds itself as in its "aspects," and which are formulated in the first ontological judgments or principles.

29. *Reality*

Realism is undeniably right when together with empiricism it claims that I understand by "that which is" first of all that which presents itself to me in my actual experience. This present being encountered by me is called "the fact," insofar as it is considered to have arisen from some kind of operation—"fact" being derived from *facio,* I do or I make. It is called "the actual," insofar as in its turn it reveals itself by its action or operation.[4] It is known as "the

---

[1] Cf. no. 69.

[2] Cf. no. 74.

[3] Cf. no. 75. Let us suppose, moreover, that there exists an imperfect knower who thinks of beings in a way that does not fully agree with the mode proper to them as they are in themselves. In that case we have to accept that such a knower will have to use thoughts in which what itself is not a being is thought of in the manner of a being.. In this way there arises the pure *being of reason* as the mode of *being* proper to relationships which have their foundation in being but are created by thought. Such relationships can exist between real or possible beings or also between the contents of thought as contents of thought (cf. no. 165).

[4] We use the term "actual" here as an approximation of the untranslatable "werkelijke," which is derived from the verb *werken,* to work. Tr.

real," insofar as it presents itself as a *res,* an existing thing, or at least something belonging to an existing thing—the term "thing" being used here in its broadest sense, so that it does not yet imply an opposition to living being or person.

Past and Future. If I accept—it has not yet been explicitly established—that my experience is variable and changing, and therefore temporal, I have to admit the past and the future alongside the present. The modes of *being* proper to the past and the future are connected with the present, for the past has been the present, and the future will be the present. Moreover, despite the fact that they relatively are-not, past and future beings are to some extent implied in the present, in a way that is still to be determined, for they *are* receding or approaching.

Being, in the sense of the real, therefore extends not only to what is real at the moment of my actual experience, but also to what really has been or really will be. It extends to everything that "ever" is real.

Central Meaning of Being. This "to be real" is *for me* the *central* or unmodified meaning of *being,* the starting point from which I discover its other meanings and with which I connect them. When I speak without any further determination of being and "to be," I mean real being and real "to be." The contradictory opposite of this "to be real" is "not to be real."[5]

30. *Necessity*

Insofar as I know reality through experience, I know it as *de facto* being. Insofar as I know it only as *de facto* being, I can merely say that it cannot not-be as long as and insofar as it *de facto* is. But I ask myself the question whether the real, taken "in itself," is merely *de facto* and therefore could also not-be, or is such that "in itself" it cannot not-be. In this way I oppose, on the one hand, what is not necessary but contingent being, what merely happens to be and is merely real and, on the other, what is real in every hypothesis or with an absolute necessity.

I use a categorical affirmation for what I experience to be real. I affirm apodictically only what I see to be of necessity as something that is real in every hypothesis.[6]

---

[5] Cf. no. 38.
[6] Cf. no. 21.

The necessary is farther removed from non-*being* than is the merely real or contingent. The necessary is even as far distant as is possible from non-*being*, for it positively excludes this possibility which is implied in contingent real *being*.

Accordingly, to-be-necessary is the strongest and strictest sense and in itself the most proper and even the most narrow sense of *being*. The contradictory opposite of the necessary, of not being able not-to-be, is the not-necessary or being able not-to-be.

The Necessary and the Real. At the beginning of metaphysics I am not yet able to give a reply, at least a positive reply, to the above-mentioned question whether the *de facto* reality I experience is merely contingently real or perhaps "in itself" necessarily real. I do not know whether the real and the necessary coincide completely, for I do not yet know what is of necessity implied in unqualified *being*. I can say only that provisionally there seems to be room for the not-absolutely-necessary but merely-real or contingent, because I experience real beings first of all in their *de facto being*. Although the hypothetical necessity of what *de facto* is demands to be given a further foundation in the absolute necessity of *being*, I do not yet know how this foundation has to be conceived.

31. *Possibility*

The Possible and the Real. In any case the real is possible. The real is not possible because it is real, but because it is possible it *can* be real. In this sense possibility is the condition of reality.

The possible *is* not only when it is realized, but, even as a possible not-absolutely-nothing. It *is* a being in a new meaning of the term. It is not subject to doubt that to-be-possible is also a mode of *being*, even though this mode is difficult to grasp. There is, therefore, a certain opposition between what is for me the first meaning of *being*— namely, "to be real" and the broader sense which pertains to something even insofar as it not impossible. "That which is" must extend to whatever is absolutely possible. Only what is absolute impossible is in no way whatsoever, it is "that which is not at all."

Accordingly, the broadest sense of *being* is "to be possible." The contradictory opposite of "to be possible" (to be able to be) is "to be impossible" (to be unable to be). But the impossible has no longer any reference to *being* and therefore "to be possible," in the all-embracing sense of *being*, has no opposite. If, however, one conceives the possible as implying a negation of its realization, then the possible is limited to the purely possible and thus it does not convey the broadest sense of *being*. In that case it has a contrary opposite—namely, that which is not purely possible but is a realized possible, a real being.[7]

Possibility as the Foundation of Reality. Although possibility is the necessary foundation of reality, one may ask: Is it the sufficient foundation? In other words, does the possibility of something include also the necessity of its realization? Or is there room for the purely possible? This question also cannot be answered definitely at the beginning of metaphysics. For I do not yet know whether the necessity of *being* includes the realization of everything possible and therefore I do not know whether the possible and the real (understood as whatever is "ever" real) coincide completely. I can only say that provisionally there seems to be room for the merely possible because there seems to be room for the merely real. For, if all that is possible is necessarily realized, then there is no room for the purely possible; on the other hand, there is room for it if not everything possible is necessarily realized.[8]

32. *Summary*

The general modes of *being* and non-*being* may be presented schematically as indicated below. In this schema, "to be" in the sense which is fundamental and central for me, i.e., unmodifiedly to-be-real, is placed between quotation marks. If to-be-possible and to-be-real are considered merely according to the characteristics indicated above the heavy line, then they apply also to the subsequent modes of *being*—namely, to-be-real and to-be-necessary. If, on the other hand, the characteristics below the heavy line are added, then to-be-possible and to-be-real positively exclude the subsequent modes

---

[7] Cf. no. 38.

[8] In the elaborate second part of his ontology *Möglichkeit und Wirklichkeit*, Berlin, 1938, Nicolai Hartmann takes up again the thought of the old School of Megara that nothing is fully possible unless it be real. For something is "really possible" (*realmöglich*) if all conditions required for its possibility are fulfilled. But when the chain of conditions is complete, that which is conditioned by them follows of necessity. Therefore, "really possible" is at the same time "really necessary" (*realnotwendig*) and therefore also "really existent" (*realwirklich*). In this way the modes of being coincide. Aristotle defends a difference by means of his distinction between *dynamis* and *energeia*. Cf. *Metaphysica*, bk, IX, ch. 3 (1046b 29 - 1047b 2) and St. Thomas' *Commentary*, nos. 1795-1806. Since we are here only at the start of metaphysical thought, we can only indicate the foundations but not the solution of the problem. Cf. nos. 174-176.

and thus are conceived as merely to-be-possible (not-to-be-real) and merely to-be-real (to-be-not-necessary or to-be-contingent).

We must emphasize that the negative modes of *being*, "not-to-be" and "cannot be" and the combination of these two, "to-be-impossible" are merely *thought of* as modes of *being*, although we know that they *are* not modes of *being*.[9] "Cannot 'not-be'," however, is the negative way in which the most positive mode of *being* has to be *thought of*, although we know that it is not a negative mode of *being*. Accordingly, all modes of *being* may be thought of by means of the terms "to be," "not," and "can." These three appear to be irreducible.

to be impossible	to be possible	to be real	to be necessary
cannot "be"	can "be"	can "be"	can "be"
"to be" (is) not	"to be" (is) not	"to be" (is)	"to be" (is)
can "not-be"	can "not-be"	can "not-be"	cannot "not-be"
to be impossible	to be unreal	to be not-necessary	to be necessary

33. *The Modes of* Being *as Including One Another*

Possible. If whatever is in any way whatsoever is in any case possible, then to-be-possible applies also to the real and the necessary. In this way to-be-possible, unlike to-be-purely-possible, is no longer a definite state of *being* which positively excludes the other two. It is now the all-embracing mode of *being* which belongs to all that is and excludes only what is absolutely not because absolute non-*being* is not only not-real but cannot even be: it is absolutely impossible. Insofar as to-be-possible is opposed to absolute not-to-be and therefore has no opposite, it is, as all-embracing, no longer a mere mode of *being*, but expresses the absoluteness of *being* which transcends all modalities, the relation of *being* itself to absolute non-*being* or rather its relation to nothing at all, the non-relativity or all-embracingness of *being*.

Possible, therefore, applies not only to the purely possible but, conceived in an absolute way, it extends to pure possibility, mere reality, and necessity as its modes. For the real and the necessary also belong to the domain which is contradictorily opposed to absolute non-being, or rather the domain that has no opposite but is the domain of that which belongs in any case to every being *as* being, whether it is purely

---

[9]Cf. no. 167.

possible, merely real, or necessary—namely, to have a reference to all-embracing unqualified *being*.

Necessary. To-be-able-not-to-be, which in the merely possible accompanies to-be-able-to-be, does not arise from the being-able-to-be of the possible as possible. For otherwise whatever is possible would be positively not-necessary and thus would positively exclude necessity, so that the necessary could not be possible. But the necessary is possible; hence the possible, considered precisely *as* possible and, therefore, as to some extent already being, does not include to-be-able-not-to-be. But what does not include to-be-able-not-to-be, i.e., what does not include the contingent, is considered precisely as such, not positively contingent. Now what is not positively contingent, taken as such, is non-contingent or necessary—the term "necessary" being understood here in a broader sense, which includes whatever is not positively contingent. The possible, therefore, is necessary not with respect to its being real or not-real, but with respect to its being possible itself, i.e., insofar as it *is* possible, it is necessary. It is not only *de facto* possible, but it cannot not-be possible.

Likewise, to-be-able-not-to-be which in the merely real accompanies its being-real does not arise from the being-real of the real as real. For otherwise everything real would be positively non-necessary and thus would positively exclude necessity, so that the necessary could not be real. But the necessary is real. Therefore, the real, taken precisely *as* real, does not include to-be-able-not-to-be. But what does not include to-be-able-not-to-be, to-be-contingent, is, considered precisely as such, not positively contingent and thus in the broader sense necessary. The real, therefore, is necessary not with respect to its being-able or not-being-able to-be-real, but with respect to its being-*de-facto*-real itself. It is, at least hypothetically, necessarily real.

Necessary, therefore, is not only the absolutely necessary, but to some extent necessity permeates also reality and possibility and contains them as its modalities. Taken in this sense, necessity is no longer a mode of *being* alongside the other modes, but expresses the absoluteness which accompanies "to be" wherever it reveals itself. Even the purely possible and the merely real, insofar as they are, belong to the domain of the necessity of *being*: by virtue of their own mode by which they refer to unqualified *being*, they cannot not-be.

Real. Not-to-be-real which in the purely possible accompanies its being-able-to-be does not arise from the being-able-to-be of the possible as possible. For otherwise everything possible would positively not be real, it would positively exclude reality, and therefore the real could not be possible. But the real is possible. Therefore, the possible, considered precisely as possible and insofar as it already *is* to some extent, does not include not-to-be-real. But what does not include not-to-be-real is, considered precisely as such, not positively non-real. Now what is not positively non-real, taken as such, is real in a broader sense of reality which extends to everything that is not positively non-real. Therefore, the possible is real with respect to its very being-possible, i.e., insofar as it *is* possible. It is of necessity really possible, it participates in reality in the mode proper to possibility.

Real, therefore, applies not only to being "ever" present (in time), in the sense which is for me the first and central sense. To some extent, reality contains also the other modes as its modalities. It is a property of *being* itself wherever "to be" reveals itself: not only the supra-temporal and absolutely necessary is real in an eminent sense, but even the extra-temporal possible is real in a degraded sense insofar as even the possible in its own way refers to unqualified *being* and therefore to reality.

34. *The Meaning of Realism*

To-Be-Real and To-Be-Objective. To-be-real often evokes the idea of being-objective, i.e., of belonging to the structure of an object facing a subject, regardless of whether, with empiricism and realism, one conceives the subject as more or less dependent on the object or, with idealism and phenomenalism, one takes the object to be more or less dependent on the subject.

However, the subject as subject also is real, no matter whether it be thought of as passive or active. To-be-real transcends the opposition of subject and object, or knower and known. It is against the all-embracing nature of *being* to make it a condition of *being* that it be an object of at least possible knowledge. "To know" does not constitute all-embracing "to be," as idealism asserts with respect to thought, for "to know" is itself a mode of *being*. At most, one could say, although it has not yet been explicity established, that to be known or at least to be knowable is essentially implied by *being*.[10]

---

[10]Cf. no. 42.

To-Be-Real and To-Be-Merely-Thought. Sometimes to-be-real is opposed to purely-being-thought. This happens when one accepts a certain opposition between knowing and thinking. To know, they say, is correlative to the real, but to think can be concerned also with the non-real, so that the non-real is purely thought.

First of all, we must remark that thought, as a product of the act of thinking, is something real; hence what is opposed here to the real is a certain *content* of thought, a represented object to which nothing real corresponds and which *is* only as being-thought.

Secondly, the opposite of such a purely-thought-being is not only the real but also the possible. For the "to be" of the possible is not circumscribed by being represented in thought because the possible is really possible.[11]

Ontology and Pure Being of Thought. Even pure beings-of-thought fall under all-embracing *being,* for they are contents of thought which are represented "in the mode" of something, real or necessary. Because of this relationship to beings in the proper sense, which they presuppose and "imitate," they have a kind of shadowy *being* in thought. Such a "to be" is not absolutely "not-to-be," but has to be called "to be" in a broader and analogous sense of the term.

Consequently, even pure beings-of-thought, and especially logical relations,[12] belong to the domain of ontology. Ontology has to investigate what their particular mode of *being* is, how they arise, and how they are related to all-embracing *being* in its possibility, reality, and necessity.

---

[11]Pure being of thought may be understood in more than one sense.

1. Sometimes it refers to something which in the eyes of the thinker expresses a true situation of possible, real, or necessary being, although it contains merely what he *thinks* to be the situation. In this case he errs and his thought content is a pure being-thought, even though all its elements are borrowed from possible and real beings (cf. no. 129).

2. Sometimes the thinker knows that his representations are pure beings-of-thought—namely, when he *imaginatively* constructs quasi-real beings in a world of fancy. Here, too, the elements of his representations are taken from real and possible beings (cf. no. 124).

3. Finally, there are thought contents which the thinker knows to be mere beings-of-thoughts, but which he can express in true judgments with reference to possible and real beings. These are pure beings-of-thought, *entia rationis,* in the strict sense of the term; for instance, the contents of negative and privative concepts, the logical relationships between concepts, judgments, and processes of reasoning. Such beings are indispensable aids for an imperfect knower who needs negation and reasoning, who thinks of and expresses beings in a way that does not fully correspond with the way in which beings are "in themselves" (cf. no. 165).

[12]Cf. no. 166.

Metaphysics and Realism. Accordingly, "to be," as considered in metaphysics, is not opposed to merely-being-thought, but extends also to this secondary, derivative, and analogous mode of *being*. Nevertheless, metaphysics is primarily concerned not with pure being-of-thought but with real being. For this reason we are justified in calling the theory presented here *realism*.

This assertion should be understood in such a way that for the metaphysician the starting point lies in the real, i.e., in what presents itself in experience. But from this starting point he endeavors to discover what is in-itself-necessary and especially the necessary possibility of the real. Hence possibility also falls under *being* in the metaphysical sense, and "not to be" in the metaphysical sense means to-be-impossible.

The "to be," therefore, which metaphysics attempts to approach is primarily that through which everything real is real, but it is also the possibility of the possible and the necessity of the necessary. It is the undifferentiated absolute which contains inseparately the modes of the possible, the real, and the necessary and, as has still to be shown, lets them come forth separately as soon as it manifests itself in finite and contingent beings which it makes participate in itself in a particular way.

CHAPTER EIGHT

BEING AS BEING. THE FIRST PRINCIPLES

35. *The Universal Interconnection. The Problem of Monism*

Being-with-Me. In the experiential evidence of my *being* there reveals itself a certain apodictic evidence of insight into unqualified *being* and its modes. Therefore, I know already something about "all that is," for I can indicate a condition which all that is has to fulfill in order to be. This condition is that, no matter what else there would be, it cannot be opposed to me in such a way that its *being* would imply my non-being or vice versa. All that *is*, regardless of its degree of opposition to me, is at least *together-with-me* and constitutes together with me a certain unity, for it communicates together with me in *"being."* Therefore, the pre-predicative experience of my *being* contains, but only in a very implicit way, the presence of "all that is, insofar as it is," i.e., being *as* being.

Apodictic First Principles. If "all that is, insofar as it is" is to some extent together with me and in the broadest sense of the term present with me—no matter how absent from me it may be in other respects—, then I am able to say at least something of "all that is" in absolutely general judgments.

Sometimes it is assumed that these first judgments are hypothetical judgments which indicate *how* every "something," if it is, *is* necessary. Although it is true that the mode of expressing these judgments is somewhat hypothetical, nevertheless their intention is not at all of a hypothetical nature. For in the form of general assertions about every being as being, i.e., about every being insofar as it participates in *being,* they want to show what *being* implies wherever it reveals itself. But the fact *that being* reveals itself is not a hypothesis but something real. Even in my experience which in a very implicit way extends somewhat to "all that is" *being* always reveals itself as the non-hypothetical but unconditioned and necessary.

Therefore, the first principles intend to express evidences that are absolutely apodictic and transcend experience and are concerned

with the "essence" itself of *being,* at least if the term "essence" is
still appropriate in this context.[1]

It is possible, therefore to speak with apodictic evidence in the
mode of necessity about being as being, because the three modes
are not yet being considered insofar as they are distinct from one
another, but precisely insofar as they are mutually inclusive. The
possible is not yet considered as the merely possible or the purely
realizable, and the real not yet as the merely real or the purely
contingent, as long as the question has not yet been explicitly raised
whether whatever is possible has been realized. This question has
not been asked because we did not yet raise the question whether
whatever is real is necessary. Thus the possible and the real are
not yet opposed to the necessary, but are viewed insofar as they
include some necessity in their very being the way they are. In
this way there arise propositions which are valid for being as being,
regardless of any presupposition one might make, including that of
radical monism.

Radical Monism. Accordingly, the force of the first principles
lies precisely in this that they do not explicitly determine the *mode
in which everything is one,* the universal interconnection. They
speak about being as being without deciding whether being is wholly
identical with "to be" or whether there are many finite and imperfect things which participate in *being.* Radical monism seeks
to base itself precisely on the first principles. It says that being as
being can have only identity but not a distinction between one and
the other, plurality and finiteness. As long as one does not speak
of finite being as such but only of being as being, without attaching
any value to the grammatical form of this participle, absolute
monism cannot yet be excluded. On the other hand, it cannot be
affirmed either, for such an affirmation would require that first the
possibility of finiteness be positively excluded.

Strictly speaking, however, radical monism is already excluded by
reason of the finiteness of my *being,* the distinction between my *being*
and unqualified *being.* Nevertheless, it is very important to ask once
more whether in metaphysics it is possible to place oneself on the
"absolute standpoint" and to view all previously made distinctions as
"provisional" or merely "apparent" distinctions which disappear in
the distinctionless One. It is precisely through such an attempt that

---

[1]Cf. no. 58.

the problem of radical monism may perhaps be placed in a clearer light. True, the principles of *being* do not explicitly determine the mode in which everything is one. Nevertheless, it is not excluded that they presuppose a way of thinking which, *starting from* the finite and multiple, attempts to grasp something of infinity and unity, so that even the apodictic insights would be merely finite and inadequate ways of knowing the infinite.

36. *The Principle of Identity*

This Principle is Implied in All Judgments. In the affirmative judgment I say that something is and that it is as it is, i.e., according to the mode and the measure in which it is.[2] It is itself. I affirm the necessary identity of that which I affirm with itself. Because this identity is valid for the affirmed precisely insofar as it *is,* I know at once that it is valid for everything of which I will ever be able to affirm that it is. Therefore, the particular judgment "this is," e.g., "I am," contains a general judgment which embraces all judgments—*whatever, is,* insofar as it is, *is and is what it is.*

This absolutely general primordial judgment finds expression, but only in a limited way, in all particular judgments. Therefore, it is not just another judgment alongside particular judgments, but in the form of a judgment it expresses the essence of every judgment. Thus it may be called the "judgment of judgments," i.e., that by which all judgments are judgments, and in this sense it is the first or most excellent,[3] the most general *form* of affirmative categorical assertion.[4]

This Principle is Not a Tautology. Nevertheless, the principle of identity is not merely an empty, subjectively necessary form of my thinking,[5] but includes also all my judgments insofar as their *content* is concerned. It makes present to me what is the very foundation of all that, thinking, I can know: the *being* itself of that which is.

---

[2] The true nature of the first principles and their mutual relationship are treated with great clarity in Clement Schoonbrood's analyses, "Is metafysiek als wetenschap mogelijk?" *Studia Catholica,* vol. 18 (1942), pp. 68-85; "Het beginsel van identiteit als wet van het zijn," *op. cit.,* vol. 22 (1947), pp. 105-122 and 163-176; "Over vorm en betekenis van het beginsel van de uitgesloten derde by Aristoteles," *Tijdschrift voor Philosophie,* vol. 4 (1942), pp. 489-522; "Onbepaaldheid en ontkenning," *op. cit.,* vol. 10 (1948), pp. 595-606; "Propositie en oordeel," *op. cit.,* vol. 12 (1950), pp. 431-452; "Tertium non datur, de norm van de disjunctie," *op. cit.,* vol. 13 (1951), pp. 418-465.
[3] Whence the Greek expression *axioma* and the Latin *dignitas.*
[4] Cf. no. 169.
[5] Cf. no. 25.

For this reason the principle of identity is not a pure tautology, i.e., it is not concerned with such an obvious repetition as A=A. For the predicate adds to the subject the mode of necessity which stems from the *being* of being. True, "to be" does not allow itself to be expressed adequately in the form of a judgment, because to judge is to state something about something and therefore implies a certain duplicity.[6] Nevertheless, the judgment about being as being reveals that "to be" is precisely "to be," self-sufficient, self-explanatory, and not referring to something else or dependent on anything else (for it does not exclude anything), and therefore unconditioned and necessary.

What it Expresses. The principle of identity expresses precisely the connection of what by *being* is with the *being* by which it is. Therefore, it predicates of being that it is-itself that it is "in" itself, that it is unconditionally and necessarily. For all this belongs to a being precisely as being, by virtue of the *being* by which it is.

Because the principle of identity does not determine whether the connection of what by *being* is with the *being* by which it is consists in a perfect identity or merely in an identity by means of participation,[7] the principle is valid in every supposition, including that of radical monism.

37. *The Principle of Non-Contradiction*

Judgment and Non-Contradiction. To affirm is to connect. Therefore, the affirmative judgment is a reply to a question regarding a proposed situation, a proposition. But a question allows two possible replies—namely, to connect or to separate, yes or no. The point here is whether the judgment which affirms the connection includes a negation of the separation.

The reply is affirmative. Connection and separation of one and the same thing in the same respect, i.e., the same mode of *being,* cannot go together, because *only* one of the two is true. Or also, because *at least* one of the two, if not both, are not-true, false. This logical principle is based on the general ontological insight that *whatever is,* insofar as it is, *is-not not,* i.e., cannot not-be, *and is not what it is not.*

This principle is founded on the all-embracing nature of *being.* Outside *being* there is only and of necessity only non-being, but non-

---

[6]Cf. no. 26.
[7]Cf. no. 170.

being cannot be. Therefore, "to be" extends to everything, and it is impossible to predicate not-to-be, in the absolute sense, of any being *as* being. Accordingly, the all-embracing affirmation implies the impossibility of the all-embracing negation: it is absolutely impossible that there would be nothing.[8]

The Principle of Non-Contradiction is Not a Negation. The *general* principle of non-contradiction is not a negation in the proper sense of the term. When I say "whatever is is-not not," I do not yet deny anything. Although in the judgment absolute non-being assumes the form of a predicate, it is precisely its being-a-predicate that I deny. Therefore, insofar as the principle denies the possibility of the all-embracing negation it is not distinct from the principle of identity.[9]

In a genuine negation the subject is never the total unity of "whatever is," but always a particular being. What is denied is never the *being* of the subject in the absolute sense but always a particular mode of *being*. I first affirm being as being and then judge that certain modes of *being* are not, at least not necessarily, included and perhaps even positively excluded. In this way there arises the distinction between the *one* and the *other*.

Principle of Identity and Principle of Non-Contradiction. Accordingly, the principle of non-contradiction is a special principle only for a way of thinking which needs the genuine negation because its thinking is first of all concerned with particular beings and particular modes of *being*. In radical monism the principle of non-contradiction fully coincides with the principle of identity. Accordingly, the fact that for my way of thinking the principle of non-contradiction has a new content shows that my thought, *starting from* thinking about the many and the finite, reaches *toward* unity and all-embracingness.

For this reason human thought, in which negation always accompanies affirmation, will be inclined to consider the principle of non-contradiction even as its *central* principle. Man's way of thinking in the process of his investigations always need both affirmation and negation *together,* and in this sense the principle is even more important than the principle of identity, considered in itself.[10] However, one

---

[8]Cf. no. 23.

[9]Cf. no. 167.

[10]Aristotle explicitly studies the principle of non-contradiction as the first principle, and next the principle of excluded middle. Cf. *Metaphysica,* bk. IV, chs. 3-8 and bk. XI chs. 4-6.

should not forget that, just as negation and finiteness presuppose affirmation and all-embracingness, so also the principle of non-contradiction presupposes the principle of identity as prior "in itself."

38. *The Principle of Excluded Middle*

Excluded Middle. The principle of non-contradiction excludes the identity of a being with its contradictory opposite, for *being* cannot be non-being. To express it logically, a "proposal" or proposition cannot be both affirmed and denied at the same time. Either the affirmation or (Latin *vel*[11]) the negation, at least one of the two, is not true. To affirm implies not-to-deny, and to deny includes not-to-affirm.

However, is it not possible that a "proposal" has to be neither affirmed nor denied? Does not-to-affirm include also to deny, and not-to-deny also to affirm? Or is a middle ground, distinct from both, possible between *being* and non-*being?*

This third possibility is excluded by a new principle: every "proposal" is either true or (*vel*) not true (or both). Without determining which position, that of affirming or that of denying, agrees with "that which is," it is certain that at least one of the two is in agreement with it.

Identity and Excluded Middle. The principle of excluded middle is based on the impossibility of a middle ground between *being* and non-*being*, distinct from both, for it there were such a medium it would have to *be*. It is, however, impossible to formulate the principle meaningfully as a distinct ontological principle. If one states: "Being as being is or (*vel*) is not" or "Being as being is-not neither being nor non-being," the statement is clear by virtue of the principle of identity which has already decided in favor of one of the two possibilities. Accordingly, the principle is distinct from that of identity only when no decision has yet been taken with respect to the *being* or non-*being* of something, for in that case it refers merely to a "proposal" and therefore is formulated in a logical way.

The fact that, just as the principle of excluded contradiction, the principle of excluded middle has a new content for our thought means that our thinking is primarily directed toward the finite and therefore leaves open the possibility of non-being, thought only in a relative sense. It implies even that our thinking is a kind of "pro-

---

[11]The Latin *vel* is indifferent to which of two or more suppositions is chosen. Tr.

posing," for it asserts of this "proposing" that it always and of necessity refers to *being*: every proposed situation, even a self-contradictory thought, has a relationship of agreement or (*vel*) non-agreement with "what is," and this principle is certain even before it is decided which of the two possibilities, if not both, is *de facto* present.

Excluded Middle and Non-Contradiction. Together with the principle of non-contradiction, the principle of excluded middle is sometimes formulated in this way: everything is or is not (*quodlibet est "aut" non est*). In this formula *everything* should be understood as a proposed way of thinking, and *is* as a special mode of *being*. Sometimes also the formula is: every proposed situation is 1) not both true and not true (principle of non-contradiction), and 2) not neither true nor not-true (principle of excluded middle).

It should be clear that these two principles do not have the same content. If *p* stands for the affirmation of a proposition, and -*p* for its negation, then the principle of non-contradiction says:

> if *p* is true, then -*p* is false, and
> if -*p* is true, then *p* is false.

But the principle of excluded middle says:

> if *p* is false, then -*p* is true, and
> if -*p* is false, then *p* is true.[12]

----

[12]Concerning oppositions see Aristotle, *Metaphysica,* bk. V, ch. 20, bk. X, chs. 4-5, and St. Thomas' *Commentary,* nos. 922-935, 2023-2074.

Types of Opposition. The principle of non-contradiction states that combination and separation, affirmation and negation of one and the same thing in the same respect cannot go together. The principle of excluded middle asserts that affirmation and negation do not allow a third possibility. Both indicate the properties of *contradictory* opposition between propositions as well as concepts or thought contents.

The contradictory opposition between a positive thought content and its pure negation should be distinguished from other forms of opposition, which imply a certain negation and consequently a certain exclusion and impossibility of union, but only in a qualified way.

1. *Privative* opposition, i.e., between having and lacking, is the opposition between a thought content which is enunciated relative to a being that can or ought to have it and the negation of this same content in reference to the same being. In such a case the mode of *being* is not only not-present but "lacking": the being in question is deprived of it. Between seeing and blind, which are privative opposites, there is not-seeing as the purely negative opposite: not-seeing can be predicated of a being that is not supposed to see (cf. no. 167).

2. *Contrary* opposition or contrast between two extremes, is the opposition between two positive thought contents which within a more general class are at a distance from each other and cannot in their pure form belong to

39. *The Principle of Unity*

Being is One. Being as being is itself and not not-itself. But that which does not include its opposite, the not-itself, but excludes it and puts it in contrast to itself we call "one."

One, undivided in itself and divided from what is not-itself, is that which does not contain in itself any "not-itself" because it contains only itself in itself, it is wholly itself, wholly identical, and therefore not in part its opposite.

But being as being has no other opposite than non-being, and this opposite is wholly excluded from being as being, for it is impossible that non-being is.

Therefore, in being as being there is no opposition whatsoever. It is wholly one and undivided in itself, divided only from non-being, and therefore not divided from anything.

The foundation for the unity of being as being lies in the impossibility that "to be" and "not to be" be together. For "not to be" does not stand alongside "to be" as the "other" to which "to be" would be related and with which therefore it would have to be combined at least in a certain opposition. Accordingly, "to be" is not opposed to anything, but identifies everything with itself in unity.

No Absolute Plurality and Opposition. Consequently, *if* there exist distinction, plurality, and opposition, they do not pertain to being precisely *as* being. If one particularized thing is not the other particularized thing, their distinction cannot be concerned with their *being* as such, but in *being* they are always somehow the same and one.

Accordingly, absolute plurality and opposition, i.e., of such a nature that there would be nothing but distinction without any connection, is impossible. Opposition also, insofar as it *is,* is a form of

---

one and the same thing in the same respect, although they do not eliminate each other entirely. Middle terms or forms of transition are not always excluded, so that the two extremes can go together in a tempered way. For instance, between red and yellow there is orange, and between white and black there is grey (cf. no. 79).

3. *Relative* opposition is the opposition between a relationship or order of one being to another and the reciprocal relationship of this other to the first. These relations cannot go together in one and the same being in the same respect. Nothing, for instance, is greater and smaller with respect to the same, no one is father and son with respect to one and the same person. However, these relations eliminate only the identity of the related beings in question, but the two relatively opposed beings themselves are presupposed by, and included in the relationship. To be related is the mode of being-together of opposites (cf. no. 163).

identity, a diminished, degraded, and participated identity. Likewise, plurality, insofar as it *is,* is a form of unity, a diminished, degraded, and participated unity.

40. *The Principle of Infinity or Perfectness*

Infinity is grammatically the negation of finiteness. Finiteness is not yet understood here in a purely spatial or purely temporal sense as here and not there or now and not then, but in the general ontological sense of limitation to a particular mode of *being.*

Being is Infinite. Nothing is foreign to being, so that being is not opposed to anything.[14] Limitation, however, presupposes an opposite which as "other" is excluded or at least not included. But what is absolutely not, cannot be a limit. Therefore, whatever is, insofar as it is and to the extent that it *is,* is not limited and therefore unlimited and infinite. If being to the extent that it is were limited, "to be" to the extent that it is would be not-to-be, and this would mean that "to be" would be identical with not-to-be.

Accordingly, the infinity of being as being is founded on the absolute infinity of "to be," which of itself says nothing but perfection and all-perfectness. Infinity is negative only with respect to our way of understanding and expressing it, but in itself it is a pure affirmation.

No Absolute Finiteness. Consequently, *if* there exists finiteness, it does not pertain to being as being. If a being does not include an "other" way of *being,* the reason for it is that it participates only in a limited way in the infinity of *being.*

Consequently, absolute finiteness, i.e., finiteness which would be nothing but finiteness, pure particularity without connection with other particular things and with the universal, is impossible. Insofar as the finite *is,* it refers to the infinite, although only in a deficient way. Thus to some extent it is infinite, albeit only in an analogous and limited way.[15]

41. *The Principle of Determinateness*

The Two Meanings of "Determined." The finite or limited is sometimes also called "the determined." It is restricted, bounded, and limited through opposition to the "other" which is not included in it and perhaps even excluded from it.

---

[14]Cf. St. Thomas, *Contra Gentes,* bk. I, ch. 43: "Considered absolutely, 'to be' is infinite, for there are infinite and infinite modes in which it can be participated."

[15]Cf. no. 63.

However, "the determined" sometimes has an almost opposite meaning—namely, when determination is opposed to indetermination and the latter is not understood as positive all-embracingness, i.e., as infinity and perfectness, but precisely as a lack of positive content, as not yet having the perfectness of *being* which should pertain to a being.[16]

In this sense that which is still without content but ordered to content is the undetermined-but-determinable; the positive content which "fills" the determinable is the determination; and the full or the perfect is the determined because its fullness of *being* does not lack anything, except non-being, from which it is distinct.

It is in this positive sense that we speak here of enriching determination and all-embracing determinateness. The term's etymological connotation of restriction with respect to positive otherness should be eliminated from its meaning.

Being is Determined. Being as being is what it is, it is already itself. Thus it has the perfectness of *being* which it should have. Therefore whatever is, insofar as and to the extent that it *is,* is not still-undetermined-but-determinable, but is already determined and individual. If being, to the extent that it is, were undetermined, it would to the extent of its *being* not yet be, so that "to be" and "not to be" would be identical.

Accordingly, the determinateness of being, as being, is founded on the absolute infinity of *being,* which of itself is identical with itself, includes all-perfectness, and therefore excludes all possibility of any further positively enriching determination, all further determinability.

No Absolute Indeterminateness. Thus it follows that *if* there is indetermination, it does not pertain to being *as* being. If a being is further determinable, i.e., if it has not yet reached the fullness of its mode of *being,* the reason is that it is only in an imperfect way "what it is," because it has not yet arrived at full identity with itself.

---

[16]Concerning the two meanings of determinateness see Chr. Barendse, "Over de graden in het zijn," *Tijdschrift voor Philosophie,* vol. 11 (1949), pp. 155-202. Fernand Van Steenberghen, *Ontologie,* p. 59, formulates the principle of determinateness as follows: "Every being, insofar as it is, is absolutely opposed only to non-being. This is an extrinsic relation of opposition which gives rise to the first attribute: every being is *distinct* or *determined* insofar as it is." According to him, the logical principles of identity, non-contradiction, and excluded middle are based on this ontological principle of distinction (pp. 61-64).

Accordingly, absolute indeterminateness cannot be. Insofar as the undetermined *is,* it is no longer fully undetermined, but has already received some determination of being.[17]

42. *Being as Being is True. The Principle of Ground*

Knowledge strives for logical truth. This truth is to some extent within my reach, not only in certain undeniable experiences, but also in a few fundamental insights. There is in me not only an openness to the beings which I "experience" to be (the proportionate object of knowing insofar as it is *my* knowing), but even a measure of openness to all that is in its universal interconnection (the universal object of knowing as *knowing*). We must now investigate how the agreement of knowing and *being* comes about, i.e., how logical and ontological truth are related.[18]

Being and Knowing. Because my knowing is open to all that is, being as being is knowable in the absolute sense. The question, however, is whether it *is* because it is known, or known because it *is.*

1. The thory of harmony[19] evades the question, for it fails to understand that knowing comes to rest only in the clarity of the known itself and consequently only in an immediate reciprocal openness or immanence.

2. Radical empiricism[20] limits the question unduly, for it places the ground of knowability (as perceptibility) only in what is de facto, and is unable to ascribe truth to apodictic evidences.

---

[17]What the pre-predicative certainty of my *being* contains about unqualified *being* has to some extent shown itself in the preceding axioms about being as being—namely, necessity, identity, unity, infinity, determinateness. These judgments explicitly speak about the being itself to which evidently I am always in reference.

Being as being, therefore, is present in my knowing and loving. I can reflect on this presence. This reflection will show that being as being is *knowable* and *lovable,* that truth is the foundation of knowability, and goodness that of lovability. As Thomas Aquinas expresses it: "In the logical structure of thought (*ratione*) that which is first understood by the intellect is prior. But the intellect first apprehends being itself, next it apprehends that it understands being, and thirdly that it tends to being. Whence being is first understood, truth in the second place, and goodness in the third place." *Summa Theologica,* p. I, q. 16, a. 4, *ad* 2.

[18]Cf. no. 9.

[19]Cf. no. 9.

[20]Cf. no. 23.

3. Radical idealism[21] puts the foundation of *being* in being-known, but it can conceive this foundation at most as an identity of being-knowing with being-known in the sense of radical monism.

4. Realism, understood here as ontology,[22] rejects not only the absolutely posited priority of knowing (as activity) over *being,* but also the absolutely posited priority of *being* over knowing (as passivity). It does not absolutely reject the identity of being-knowing and being-known, but strips it of its monistic character by accepting a participation in both being-knowing and being-known in particular modes. This point will be explained later.

Being as True. In the hypothesis of a monistically conceived self-consciousness as well as in the doctrine of participation, care must be taken to safeguard the principle that whatever is, is open to knowledge because it *is,* and that therefore the ground of the knowability of being lies in the "to be" itself of being, regardless of whether this "to be" coincides with knowing or not. "To be" is the clear manifestation or truth, the unconcealedness, itself of the true.

If being as being is knowable because it is true, it is not only perceptible in its de facto existence, but also intelligible in its necessity. For knowing is not only perceiving, as empiricism claims,[23] but also understanding. To understand, in the broadest sense of the term, means to discover the explanatory ground, the reason "why" being is as it is. Accordingly, if being as being is intelligible, *whatever is, insofar as it is, has a ground on which it is as it is.* This is the principle of ground or sufficient reason.

Because being has a ground precisely insofar as it is, the groundless ground of the intelligibility of all that is must be found in *being* itself, for of itself *being* says identity, unity, infinity, and determinateness.

The intelligibility of all that is leads to the following conclusions. What is absolutely unintelligible, because it makes thought contradict itself, i.e., implies the affirmation and negation of one and the same in the same respect, absolutely cannot *be*. The absurd is not only unthinkable but also "un-be-able," impossible.

The all-embracing character of the intellect and the impossibility of a "transintelligible" world reveal themselves in the intelligibility of all that is.

---

[21]Cf. no. 24.
[22]Cf. no. 34.
[23]Cf. no. 23.

No Absolute Mystery. Accordingly, there exists "no absolute mystery," i.e., something which would contain *nothing else* than concealedness for the mind. But does this mean also that there is "absolutely no mystery"?

Radical monism is compelled to answer in the affirmative. However, it shows itself untenable here, for in every reply new questions present themselves to me the questioner. I do not yet know the particular mode in which I am and how I am connected with the unity of all that is. I do not yet know the meaning of my *being*. Especially, I do not yet fully know what is included essentially in unqualified *being,* for even my apodictic evidences are inadequate approaches to unqualified truth.

As a finite knowing, my thinking is only a stretching forward from and through the beings of experience *to* the transcending horizon of *being*. This ultimate explanatory ground, which itself does not need any other ground, contains me (I experience that I am), but I do not contain it, for I am not unqualified "to be."

"For me" there is much that cannot yet be rationally explained, but nevertheless I know already that "in itself" nothing is totally irrational. It is precisely here that lies the reason for my everlastingly continued thinking, the dynamism of my searching mind, which cannot give up in the face of "seeming" contradiction and has to surmount it, because *being* is identically also intelligibility and truth. My knowing, therefore, is a wondering and questioning, i.e., a finite openness to the all-embracing infinite.

The Meaning of My Knowing. Thus unqualified "to be" transcends my finite knowledge. For this reason even my apodictic insights are a grasping from afar which is ruled by being as being. *My* knowing is not an absolute identity of logical and ontological truth, but a reconstruction in the form of judgments of that which has revealed itself somewhat to me in pre-predicative certitude. It is a participation of the logical truth of judgment in the ontological truth.

Provided one lets the "real" extend to all modes of *being,* the more profound meaning of the realism of *my* knowing lies in this that *for me* a being is knowable because it is.[24]

---

[24]Cf. no. 34.

43. *Being as Being is Good. The Principle of Directedness*

The question of my *being* concerns me.[25] I have an inclination to my *being,* and my *being* attracts me: there is a reciprocal order of one to the other. However, I do not strive for my being-limited as such, for otherwise the more I am limited, the more I would be myself, but I strive for the fullness of *being* that is possible for me. Therefore, from *my* desire for *being* I know something about all that is—namely, that it is in communion with me in directedness to *being*. And insofar as it is, this directedness is fulfilled. By calling that which fills or perfects "good," we may say that being as being is inclined to *being* as its good.

Being and Good. The question, however, is whether the good is good because it is valued and loved, or is valued and loved because it is good.

1. According to the formalism of Kantian ethics, happiness or self-perfection does not determine the (moral) tendency, but is an *a priori* moral law. For Kant, this means that it is purely formal, without any empirical content, and autonomous. For this reason the critical axiology of Windelband accepts that everything is good which has to be done unconditionally and precisely because it has to be done.

2. Other axiologist, such as Max Scheler and Nicolai Hartmann, admit "objective" values which serve as norms for our value judgments.

3. Radical monism is forced to maintain the identity of to-be-loving and to-be-loved.

4. Realism, understood here as ontology,[26] rejects both the absolutely posited priority of love (as activity) over *being* and the absolutely posited priority of *being* over loving (as passivity). It does not wholly reject their identity, but strips it of its monistic character by accepting a participation in both the inclination and the good in particular modes. This point will have to be explained later.

In the hypothesis of monistic self-love as well as in the doctrine of participation care has to be taken to safeguard that whatever is, is the terminus of the tendency because it *is*. The ground of the lov-

---

[25]Cf. no. 17.
[26]Cf. no. 34.

ability of a being, therefore, lies in its *being* itself, regardless of whether this *being* coincides with love or not. "To be" as all-perfectness is what perfects or is the goodness itself of the good.

No Absolute Evil. If being as being is good "no absolute evil" is possible. What is, insofar as it is, is something positive and therefore in a way already perfect. For it is what it is and "fully" so. However, does it follow therefore that there is "absolutely no evil"?

Radical monism accepts no evil, not even the lack of any good. Here, again, it shows itself definitely untenable, because for me, who desires, every satisfaction gives rise to new desires, since there is so much good that I do not yet have. Of itself, such imperfect goodness is not yet evil, for evil is a being which lacks a good it *should* have. But finiteness, as such, entails the possibility of falling short of the required goodness and thus the possibility of evil.

Accordingly, if there are finite beings, there are beings which in an inadequate way tend to unqualified goodness. As a finite inclination, my desire is a stretching forward *from* and *through* satisfaction in finite being *to* the transcending horizon of absolute perfectness and goodness. This absolute perfectness contains me, for I am already made-good to some extent by *being,* but I do not contain it, for I am not unqualified goodness.

Accordingly, for a finite being, the primary sense of good is the *ontological good,* that which perfects through fullness of *being.* Appreciation or tendency, e.g., the will as good or virtue, is called good in a derivative sense by analogy of attribution, insofar as it lets itself be influenced and directed by the attraction of the ontological good.

Directedness of Being. If being as being tends to its good, and this good is found in the fullest possible participation in *being,* then being as being is not without meaning or directedness. The directedness of a thing is that to which it tends of itself and in reference to which therefore it has to be considered if it is to be understood in the interconnection of all that is. If something were directed to non-*being,* it would have given up its connection with all that is, so that it would be wholly without any direction. But if all that is, insofar as it is, is directed to *being* and thus in its direction is connected with everything, nothing can be wholly deprived of direction. The undirected cannot be. To be, to the extent of their possibilities, is the meaning or directedness of all beings.[27]

---

[27]Consequently, even evil, considered as an evil tendency, cannot be wholly without directedness, although we do not fully understand its meaning.

44. *Being as Being is Beautiful*

Delight in Truth. Knowledge strives for logical truth. Thus this truth is the good of the knower as knower. When he reaches this good through true knowledge, he is pleased. The logical truth of knowing, however, is nothing else than the ontological truth of being revealing itself to the knower. Therefore, being itself, insofar as it manifests itself in its unconcealedness with full clarity, is the ultimate good of the knower as knower. He is pleased not only with the subjective fullness of his knowledge, but in it also with the illuminating presence of the being known.

This delight in the truth of being is the more eager according as a being reveals itself more immediately with a certain splendor in its full evidence and clarity and holds the attention of the knower in such a way that he does not have to make any effort to find this being through intermediaries. The more a being presents itself in all its richness in an act of contemplation or intuition, the more it moves the knower in an "aesthetic" or feelingly-contemplating way.

Being is Beautiful. Being as being is accessible to knowing as knowing: there is a reciprocal openness of *being* and knowing. And since being as being is one, perfect, and determined, it has integrity, is in harmony with itself, full of splendor and attractiveness. **Thus it** satisfies the contemplating knower precisely insofar as it is known intuitively.

If we call beautiful that whose contemplation pleases, then being as being, because of its truth, is beautiful.

Being and Beauty. Is being as being beautiful because it pleases when contemplated, or does it please when contemplated because it is beautiful? Since beauty is nothing else than the goodness of truth, the views concerning the *being* of beauty parallel those about the *being* of truth and goodness. We may name two of them:

1. Aesthetic subjectivism (Kant) claims that beauty belongs to the content of an act of knowledge by virtue of the reference of the content not to the object but to the subject. The pleasure of the knower make a being beautiful.

2. Aesthetic objectivism holds that beauty is an objective property of being, a "value," which is the norm of taste.

Against both these views it must be pointed out that the aesthetic is precisely the moment of equilibrium and harmony between subject and object, the immediate identification of the knower with the known, through which the subjective delight loses itself in objective clarity. Their mutual identity may not be simply rejected, although the particular knower's delight in beauty is only a participation in this identity.

Nothing is Absolutely Ugly. The fact that being as being is beautiful implies that nothing can be absolutely ugly in itself. However, this does not mean that something cannot be relatively ugly with respect to a finite knower who can approach the resplendent truth of being only in an inadequate way. Since my knowledge is only very imperfectly intuitive,[28] I can discover beauty only under certain definite conditions. In this respect one has to admit that the aesthetic is dependent on the situation of the knowing subject.[29]

---

[28]Cf. no. 16.

[29]An object is fully proportionate to man's cognitive powers only when it manifests itself in sense-perceptible splendor, harmony, and integrity, for the purely spiritual is not open to our immediate intuition. Thus for man the aesthetic feeling is not merely the harmony of subject and object but also that of the sensitive and the intellectual. This means that what is immediately present in a pleasing way to the higher senses (sight and hearing) must be grasped as a *symbol* in which the infinity and all-embracingness of the intellectual order of *being* receives a living form and concrete embodiment.

So far as man's aesthetic sensitivity is concerned there is, therefore, an essential contrast between the ugly and the beautiful, just as there is between the true and the false, the good and evil. And there are all kinds of degrees and shades of beauty in a general sense: neat, pretty, elegant, charming, lovable, idyllic, beautiful, splendid, admirable, grandiose, delightful, overwhelming, sublime, etc.

Because of the identity of delight and clarity, which remains present to some extent even in the man's aesthetic feeling, this feeling is not merely a passive acceptance of an impression, but also a certain active production of the beautiful form, a participation in *being* as the active source of beauty. It is, as it were, a re-creation of the beautiful form from its universal "idea." For this reason aesthetic feeling and artistic creation are clearly related. Cf. no. 148.

CHAPTER NINE

MULTIPLE, FINITE, AND IMPERFECT BEINGS

45. *Between Radical Pluralism and Radical Monism*

Radical Pluralism. It would be radical pluralism if one were to assert that there is a plurality of beings, each of which stands wholly isolated and is what it is without forming any unity together with the others. Such a view contradicts itself, for each one of these many would *be* and agree with the others in *being,* so that they would *be* together.

Absolute opposition, plurality, finiteness and isolation, therefore, are impossible. Even opposition, plurality, finiteness, and isolation are degraded modes of identity, unity, infinity, and all-embracingness.

Radical Monism. Unlike radical pluralism, radical monism is not *in itself* absolutely impossible. However, as we have already seen and will see again, it contradicts undeniable *experience.*

1. First of all, it is against the content of experience. From experience I can say provisionally at least this much: a) I experience myself as questioning, desiring, and therefore as being in a finite way, i.e., I do not fulfill all possible modes of *being;* b) I do not know whether I am of necessity, i.e., whether unqualified *being* includes my real *being* of necessity.[1]

2. Radical monism is against the very possibility of experience. In absolute identity there is no room for imperfect knowledge. But experiential knowledge is imperfect, because it can reach apodictic insights into the absolutely necessary only in the following ways.

a. By thinking in an investigating and "proposing" way—whence the proper function of the principle of excluded middle, which prior to the decision states that every "proposal" is related by agreement or non-agreement with "that which is."

b. By affirmation as well as by negation—whence the proper function of the principle of non-contradiction, which is the foundation

---

[1]Cf. no. 30.

of negative judgments regarding the particular modes of *being* of particular beings.

c. By starting from the merely hypothetical necessity which reveals itself in the perceived facts of experience—whence the inadequacy of the principle of identity, which speaks explicitly only about being as being without committing itself regarding the mode in which a being is.[2]

But a way of thinking which can arrive at the truth only by means of investigating and proposing, negating and starting from facts is a finite mode of knowing and therefore does not fulfill all possible modes of knowing.[3]

Therefore, finiteness, and consequently also the possibility of manifoldness, is more than pure appearance. Besides, even this appearance would be. Hence finiteness and multiplicity are undeniable.

46. *Moderate Monism*

Moderate monism accepts a single bearer of *being,* one thing, which fully coincides with *being* itself, as well as with knowing and loving. But this one thing, in order to be itself, needs finite, and therefore many, opposite aspects, modes, forms of manifestation, emanations, etc., which in their mutual interconnection constitute the All-One.[4]

Thus there is not a plurality of beings as bearers of *being,* to which it pertains to be *in* themselves and therefore to be subsistent. But in the self-identity of *being* there is necessarily an infinite plurality of aspects of *being*. This plurality is explained in different ways:

1. Spirit, Soul and Matter emanate in a certain plurality from the One—Plotinus.

2. The One Substance has an infinite plurality of attributes, each of which has an infinity of finite modes—individual man being a coupling of the modes of thought and extension—Spinoza.

3. The Ego has to arrive at self-realization through its opposition to the non-ego that has arisen from the Ego—Fichte.

4. The absolute Idea comes to the synthesis of itself (Spirit) only through thesis (Logos) and antithesis (Nature)—Hegel.

---

[2]Cf. no. 169.
[3]Cf. no. 128.
[4]Cf. no. 179.

Finiteness and Plurality Remain Unexplained. From the monistic viewpoint, finiteness and multiplicity remain inexplicable. For if the All-One, to be itself, needs to multiply itself under different aspects, it is itself only through this plurality. But each of these aspects is opposed to the others and therefore finite. Granted even that there were an endless series of finite aspects, as long as the One Being is conceived as coinciding with the totality of its finite aspects, it is constituted by these aspects, without which it cannot be. Therefore, it is a whole which depends on its necessary parts, so that the parts are prior to the whole,[5] not absolutely but at least relatively. But that which depends on the finite, even on an infinite series of finites, itself is finite. It is "something" that is, but it does not coincide with "to be" itself in absolute identity.[6]

Since the infinite, as infinite, includes no non-identity with itself, no limited or finite otherness, but is absolutely one and indivisible, there would be a contradiction if the infinite and the finite were to coincide absolutely. As soon as the finite is accepted, it is to some extent *distinct* from the infinite as well as from other finites. This distinction is not based on the *being* in which the finite shares, but in the limited way in which it participates in the fullness of *being,* in the mode of its *being.*[7]

However, if the finite does not fully coincide with the infinite, and if the finite is not a constituent part of the infinite and therefore is distinct from it, the question arises as to how it is possible that there *be* finite beings.

47. *A Plurality of Finite Beings is Possible*

Moderate monism is unable to assign a place to finite beings as be-ings in the strict sense, i.e., bearers of *being* to which it pertains to be *in* themselves. It can consider them only as aspects, as parts of a whole which alone is the bearer of *being.* The untenability of moderate monism, therefore, means that certainly not all finite beings can be considered merely as parts of a single whole which alone is. In other words, they cannot be considered as non-subsistent beings.

Thus, for instance, I experience myself as a subsistent being. I find that, in a certain measure of active identity with myself, I

---

[5] Cf. no. 178.
[6] Cf. no. 179.
[7] Cf. no. 181.

make "to be" *my* "to be," so that it is I who is, and so that I am not merely a part of an all-embracing whole which alone *is* in the strict sense.

The fact, however, that I am a finite subsistent being means that I am a *particular* being and thus implies that alongside me other particular beings are possible.

Non-Subsistent Beings. It cannot yet be established in detail which beings have to be called subsistent. On the other hand, we can determine that the following are not subsistent beings:

1. The accidental, which is only an aspect of a being that itself is; for instance, my knowing will at once appear to be something-of-me, to which it pertains to be only insofar as it pertains to me.

2. The universal, which I conceive as a mode of *being* that can pertain to many beings as a predicate; e.g., the universal concept "man." The universal exists only a) in a general way in the one who forms the concept in himself, and b) in an individual way as something pertaining to an individually subsistent being.

3. What is purely "proposed" by thought, which perhaps is even unable to be in the first sense of *being;* e.g., a square circle.

On the other hand, to some extent the non-subsistent may be called a being by analogy of attribution insofar as everything *is* which somehow is connected with *being.* However, the primary sense of being does not refer to the non-subsistent, as something pertaining to something, but to the subsistent as something that itself is.

The same conclusion follows from an analysis of the judgment. Although it is true that the subject of judgments can be everything which in any way whatsoever is connected with being, nevertheless there is a privileged judgmental subject—namely, the ultimate bearer of *being* which itself cannot at all be predicated of anything else. This bearer is the *real, individual, subsistent being,* Aristotle's *"tode ti,"* which is *in* itself and appropriates "to be" as its own in the central sense of being-real.

"This" and "That" Being. Accordingly, the judgments about being as being or the first principles are inadequate knowledge. A proper judgment of being as being cannot be made, for it is not possible to predicate of it a special mode of *being* but only a general

reference to *being*. Being as being implies only opposition to absolute non-*being* and therefore is not opposed to anything else. But
as soon as I accept a *plurality* of beings, *this* being is not only
opposed to non-*being* but also, as this, to *that*. Although it is
true, therefore, that the first principles refer primarily to individual,
real, subsistent beings and next to all aspects of *being* pertaining
to these beings, to general predicates, and all possible conceivable
beings and aspects of *being*, nevertheless, with respect to the first
principles, these beings are not yet considered in their individuality
and particular modes of *being* but only in the light of their interconnection with other beings, in other words, *as* beings.

Thus we still have to investigate the *modes* of identity, unity, infinity and all-embracingness of *being* in each of the many finite beings
given to me in experience. These modes cannot be deduced from the
first principles, although all particular modes are contained in them,
but have to come to light through a closer description of further experience.

48. *Experience of Real Subsistent Beings*

My knowledge is imperfect. It is a degraded form of possession
of truth and a presence of *being* which includes absence. Although I
know something of "all that is," insofar as it is, nevertheless, much
of "that which is" is unknown to me. Even my own mode of *being* is
not yet given to me in immediate experience in the undetermined
self-affirmation. Nevertheless, knowing about my lack of knowledge,
I am in my "learned ignorance" on the road to more perfect knowledge. In other words, as a knower, I am in the process of *becoming*.

A Plurality of Acts. This character of becoming means that my
knowing unfolds itself in a plurality of activities or acts which do not
coincide with one another or with me from whom they came forth.
Remaining myself, I glide successively through a plurality of distinct
stages which push one another aside with respect to being-present:
They are first future, then present, and then past. This successive
character of my acts stems from the *temporality* of my *being* as a
degraded form of self-presence. But I do not aim at the temporal
dispersion of my knowing, for temporality is being-limited, but endeavor to reach more perfect knowledge, although I have to use the
temporal succession of distinct acts of knowing.

Other Real Beings. The question, however, is how this otherness
of cognitive acts can originate within the unity, imperfect as it is,

of my *being*. My acts of knowing can be distinct from one another only because they endeavor in different ways to overcome the distance existing between my finite *being* and "all that is" in its universal interconnection, i.e., the universal object of knowing as knowing.[8] Every cognitive act is an effort, in an ever finite and different way, to integrate into my knowledge the riches of everything that through "to be" is being.

And since both the necessary and the possible can be known by me only through and from the real, which "for me" is the central sense of *being,* I am in my self-unfolding directed to *always-other real beings* which I can encounter in experience.

Although the other finite beings are always already somewhat present to me "as beings,"[9] they are at the same time still absent from me as long as I do not explicitly know the many particular modes of their *being*.

Moreover, it is only by means of the encounter with these other beings which are together with me that I arrive at *determinate* knowledge of my own mode of *being*. Without knowing them, I have only a very undetermined knowledge of my own individuality as a knower and, therefore, also of my own individuality as a being.

Accordingly, no matter how much we have stressed that in the development of our metaphysics the statement "I am" is the primordial evidence because of the undeniable character of this experiential evidence, nevertheless now we must equally emphasize that all *explicitation* of self-consciousness takes place through knowledge of other beings. Spontaneous knowing is directed toward the real fellow beings present-to-me, but aiming at the knower himself is a "reflex" attitude.[10]

Thus my self-presence becomes actual only through my presence to other beings, and this presence is dependent not only on the direction of my attention but also and even more on the fact that the other beings make themselves present and reveal themselves in time only in a successive way.

Such a cognitive presence with others, which presupposes as its foundation their ontological presence, is a perceiving act of knowing, a receiving of what is truly other.[11] The *perception of fellow beings,*

---

[8]Cf. no. 42.
[9]Cf. no. 35.
[10]Cf. no. 122.
[11]Cf. no. 20.

therefore, is the foundation on which human knowing can be further explicitated. Without it, no knowledge of determined beings in their determined mode of *being* would be possible. More precise self-knowledge likewise is knowledge of the knower in his changing inter-relationships with the others in a "situation."

Moderate Pluralism. Later when the more determined modes of *being* will be explicitly considered, we shall have to describe how perception arises only from our being affectively tuned by the others in the intercourse of life, and how being influenced in this way, as pertaining to sensitivity, presupposes that both the knower and his immediate object are bodily in a "world" which is not only temporal but also spatial.

For the present, however, it is sufficient to have shown with in-dubitable certainty, from undeniable perception as the basis of more precise knowledge, that there are, alongside and together with me, *real finite subsistent beings* to which in my judgment I attribute "to be" and whose mode of *being* I endeavor to determine more accurately.

Moderate pluralism accepts a plurality of real subsistent bearers of *being* which, however, are not wholly self-contained and isolated from others, because at least they all share in *being* and therefore are together in a unity of order.

The problem, then, that on the basis of the first principles arises is as follows. How is it possible that there are many finite subsistent beings? How can they be distinct, since they are by *being* which of itself is pure identity? How can they be finite, since they are by *being* which of itself is infinite? How can they be imperfect, since they are by *being* which of itself is pure perfectness? How can they be undetermined and yet determinable—for they become—since they are by *being* which of itself is pure determinateness? The antinomy is constantly the same: the ground of distinction, plurality, finiteness, imperfection, and indetermination cannot lie in *being* as such nor in non-*being* as such, for non-*being* is not the ground of anything. Yet there is no middle ground between *being* and non-*being*. Thus we face once again the old dilemma of Parmenides and monism.

CHAPTER TEN

THE IDEA OF BEING IS ANALOGOUSLY
PREDICATED OF MULTIPLE BEINGS

49. *Introduction*

Because of the indubitable, inseparable, and immediate self-presence of being *as* being to my knowing *as* knowing in a pre-predicative certainty which precedes the formation of all explicit concepts and judgments, we may call the knowledge of *being* an act of intuition. But this intuition is so imperfect that it leaves all further questions still open and can be developed only through experience. It does not yet say anything explicit about identity or participation, unity or plurality, etc. In other words, it does not yet say anything about the mode of *being* of that which is and still less about any definite beings. Even the insight into what "to be" itself means finds expression only in inadequate general judgments about "being as being," so-called first principles, which are based on the experience of certain beings, i.e., the experience contained in "I am."

Because of this imperfection of our intuition we are forced to express the knowledge of *being* by means of a *judgment* and consequently first of all through a *concept*—that of being.

Now that the problem facing us is no longer that of being as being, but the possibility of many, finite, imperfect beings, we will have to investigate more accurately the nature of the predicate which is common to all and ask ourselves how a predicate that does not express any plurality, finiteness, imperfection, or indetermination can be predicated of distinct, manifold, finite, imperfect, and determinable subjects. This investigation will have to show how the most universal concept to some extent expresses everything at the same time, but simultaneously falls short because of its inadequacy.[1]

50. *The Idea of Being is the Absolutely General Concept*

Taken in an absolute sense, the predicate "be-ing" or "to be" pertains to everything: the necessary, the real, and even the possible, the

---

[1]Because of the infinity and all-embracingness proper to the concept of being, we shall most of the time prefer to use the term "idea" instead of "concept," so as to distinguish it from concepts that are more restricted in content and less universal in extension.

object known and the knowing subject, the concept and that which is
conceived, what is perceived and what is purely "proposed" in imagination or thought, and even the purely apparent.[2] For "to be" is
all-embracing and excludes only absolute not-to-be.   Therefore,
"being" or "something to which it pertains to be" is the absolutely
all-embracing concept.

A Collective Idea?   Should being be conceived as a collective concept, one that pertains only to many-taken-together as, e.g., people or
army?[3] But if being merely expressed the added bond by which
members are joined to a whole, to what could this bond be added?
The members as distinct members would not be. Moreover, against
monism we accepted a plurality of subsistent beings, each of which
appropriates "to be" in its own way. Not only the whole *is* but also
each of the members. Hence it is impossible that only the *being-*
together, isolated from the proper *being* of the members, would have
to be considered as *being*.

On the other hand, it is equally impossible to consider as *being*
only the proper *being* of the members and not their *being*-together.
Hence, by *being,* the many beings are, each, itself and also are-
together with all the others. Thus the idea of being has something
collective, for everything that is necessarily constitutes a certain unity,
an interconnection.

The Most General Concept. Being, therefore, is a general concept.
By "general" is meant one which refers to many. Thus it means here
that "being" is predicated of each of many beings distributively as
multiplied in these many.

Being is even the absolutely general concept, because it has to be
predicated not merely of a group of beings but of absolutely all.

Being is Not Definable. If being is the absolutely general concept,
it cannot be defined properly, at least when "definition" is understood
in the sense of indicating its limits—*finis* means limit—in reference to
other concepts.[4]

The reason is that a definition places the concept defined under a
more general thought content or genus and indicates how it differs
from other concepts falling under the same genus by means of a more

[2]Cf. no. 34.
[3]How being has something of the abstract, the intuitive, and the collective,
see in Louis de Raeymaeker, *The Philosophy of Being,* St. Louis, 1954, pp.
33 ff.
[4]Cf. no. 41.

special characteristic or specific difference. Hence the combination of the genus and the specific difference, the species, is less known than the genus and is reduced to it as to something higher.[5]

But the idea of being does not fall under a higher, more general concept and therefore is not a species. It is the first known in which everything else that is known, thought or proposed is already present and presupposed.

Description of Being. The idea of being allows a description only if we recognize a certain structure in it. Like all our concepts, it is not perfectly simple, but shows a certain dichotomy of bearer and form. Being is that which is, that which has "to be," that which has a reference to "to be" and through "to be" *is.*

If being is considered as a predicate, it is a participle and emphasizes the participation in "to be." If, on the other hand, it is used as a subject, it is a noun and stresses that which participates in "to be," the bearer or the subject of "to be."

51. *The Idea of Being is Not Abstract*

Is the idea of being not all-embracing at the expense of its content? Is the absolutely universal extension not in inverse ratio to the comprehension? What is predicated of a smaller number of beings expresses more about them than what is predicated of a larger number of beings. What possible importance, then, can be attached to the fact that I can say of *everything* that it *is*? Does it still have *any* meaning? Is it not the greatest possible commonplace, the most self-evident statement? Knowledge becomes important only when I know how the various beings are distinct. But I cannot arrive at this distinction from the concept of being. Accordingly, is being not the most abstract concept?[6]

Abstraction. Abstraction is the operation by which the mind leaves aside, abstracts *from* certain aspects of a being to place one characteristic that is considered to be of central importance in the focus of attention. When the intellect lifts this feature out of the complex whole of a being, abstracts it *out of* the whole, it does so

---

[5] Cf. nos. 83 and 116.
[6] Hegel begins his *Wissenschaft der Logik* with pure, empty being, the undetermined, immediate and wholly undifferentiated, which therefore has to be identified with pure nothing. However, it should be mentioned that, according to Hegel, being and nothing are not the same and therefore distinct, and that their change into each other is motion. Hence even Hegel's starting point of philosophy is not as *abstract* as it may appear at first sight.

because it discovers that other beings also exhibit this same feature. The more the content of a thought or its comprehension is abstract and leaves aside more particular contents, the more does its extension become general, universal and predicable of a larger number.

The opposite of abstraction is contraction. It is a process by which the mind adds again to the central characteristic of a being the aspects which were left behind through abstraction. Since this central feature was universal precisely because of the abstraction, contraction will limit a concept from the more universal to the more particular. Accordingly, an increase in comprehension is accompanied by a decrease in extension.[7]

Proper Abstraction. The abstraction referred to above is so-called *proper* abstraction. The differences between the beings in question are not "actually" contained in the abstracted characteristic. However, they are sometimes contained in it "potentially"—namely, when the differences, despite their distinction from the central feature, are connected with it in such a way that they give a further determination to it. In such a case the differences refer to the central characteristic as something to which they are essentially ordered as determinations. Thus, e.g., black, brown and white do not essentially refer to the persons who can be divided in this way, but refer to them as colored beings divided by their species of "color." Round and square do not primarily refer to tables but to surfaces. Sentient refers to vegetative life, and rational to sentient life. In this way the specific difference is "potentially" included in the genus.[8]

Total Abstraction. The abstraction in question is generalizing abstraction, so-called *"total"* abstraction, a logical process in which one and the same concrete whole, e.g., John, is considered under an increasingly more general aspect, for instance, as man, sentient being, living being, corporeal being.

---

[7]For example, compare the comprehension and extension of the following concepts: surface, quadrangle, trapezoid, parallelogram, rhombus, square.

It is possible that what is considered as a central or essential feature from one viewpoint may be held to be accidental from another. A series of colored surfaces, for instance, may be arranged by color (green, red, blue) but also by shape (round, square, oval). In the first case one abstracts from the shape, in the second from the color. Likewise, a group of persons can be classified by height, age, sex, profession, nationality, etc.

[8]With respect to the idea of being, sometimes use is made of the term "improper" abstraction and contraction to indicate that this idea also is imperfect. Cf. no. 53.

Total abstraction, therefore, means that the being from which the concept is abstracted is not expressed as to one of its parts only but as a whole, albeit in a general way or under a general aspect and not under more particular aspects: the totality is expressed but not totally. For this reason the concept obtained through total abstraction can be predicated of more particular concepts and of the individual being, e.g., John is a man, or man is a sentient being.

Total and Formal Abstraction. 1. It is very important to distinguish this generalizing or total abstraction from so-called "formal" abstraction,[9] which is an entirely different logical process. Formal abstraction detaches from a being an ontological constituent principle by means of which this being is what it is, and the detached constituent principle isolated in this way, which in a very broad sense is called "form," is considered by the mind as a quasi-being, a quasi-subsistent "essence," capable of acting as the subject of judgmental statements. For instance:

> animality is that through which an animal is an animal;
> color is that through which a surface is colored;
> number is that through which a being can be counted;
> goodness is that through which the good is good;
> reality is that through which a being is real;
> subsistence is that through which a being is subsistent;
> activity or action is that through which a being acts;
> power is that through which a being can act;
> habitus is that through which a being can act easily or well;
> motion is that through which a being moves;
> "to be" is that through which a being is a being.

2. The formal-abstract concept is opposed to the formal-concrete concept, which is the concept obtained through the above-mentioned process of total abstraction. This concrete concept in general indicates the bearer or subject of the "form," the one to which it pertains to be in accordance with this characteristic that was isolated in the formal-abstract concept. Both the formal-abstract and the concrete

---

[9] The expressions "total" and "formal" abstraction were probably used for the first time by Cajetan in the *prooemium* of his *In de ente et essentia*. However, see Thomas Aquinas, *In Boethium de Trinitate*, q. 5, a. 3, and *Summa Theol.*, p. I, q. 40, a. 3. Cf. G. Van Riet, "La théorie thomiste de l'abstraction," *Revue philosophique de Louvain*, vol. 50 (1952), pp. 353-393.

concept may be more or less general and therefore more or less abstract in the sense of total abstraction.

The concept obtained through formal abstraction cannot be predicated of the concrete whole from which it is abstracted. For instance, this dog is an animal but it is not animality.

3. Language often uses suffixes to indicate abstracts nouns; e.g., (ous)ia, (substant)ia, (mensur)a, (ver)itas, (dulc)edo, (bon)té, (van)ity, (companion)ship, (good)ness, (warm)th, (activ)ity, (Christen)dom.

4. If abstract nouns, *as* abstract, are used in the plural, they do not indicate individuals, but species which fall under the same general characteristic; e.g., colors, numbers, virtues.

5. The formal-abstract term is sometimes used to express the *de facto* realization of an essence in a being, i.e., that this being *is* indeed such, e.g., the well-known generosity of John, the proved innocence of the accused, the justice of his punishment.

6. In the evolution of a language the formal-abstract term often acquires a concrete meaning—a situation which philosophically may lead to confusion. As early as Aristotle, for instance, *ousia* or beingness did express the concrete being. With respect to substance, people hardly think of its original abstract meaning. The same is true for "reality," which originally meant the totality of everything real.

Being is Not Abstract. If we suppose that the idea of being is the most abstract in the sense of total abstraction, it would be the poorest in content of all concrete concepts. It would retain only that in which the many beings agree, but leave aside that in which they differ. The differences would be expressed in differentiating concepts that would stand independently alongside the concept of being. They would have to be added to it through contraction as positive enrichments of its content if one wanted to arrive at knowledge of the various beings.

Thus there would be a plurality of concepts. Nevertheless, these many thought contents would have to constitute a certain unity, no matter how imperfect and how much subject to further precision, for plurality itself is a degraded mode of unity. Hence the idea of being and the differentiating concepts would have to show a certain similarity with one another. But then this similarity itself through a process of abstraction could be isolated in a higher and more general concept and so on to infinity, without ever allowing us to reach the absolutely supreme and first concept.

However, because of the unity of thinking as well as that of the thinkable, there has to be a supreme and all-embracing concept; hence the most general concept cannot be obtained through abstraction which leaves aside the differences. Therefore, this concept is of another nature than abstract concepts. It has to include also the differentiating concepts, not merely potentially as in concepts that are obtained through total abstraction, but *actually*.

Thus it is not possible to perform a perfect conceptual separation of that in which beings are similar and that in which they differ. Otherwise, since they are similar in this that they all *are,* their dissimilarity would have to lie in something that is beyond *being,* i.e., in non-being. But non-*being* cannot be the foundation of a difference, for to differ is *to be* different, to be in a different way. Therefore, the various beings differ in *being* itself—everyone's "to be" is different.

Accordingly, the differentiating concepts which express the distinct modes of *being* of the various beings, such as subsistent, accidental, material, or spiritual, do not contain absolutely nothing. But in that case they are not additions, in the proper sense of the term, to the idea of being. Consequently, they must lie within the content itself of being as *its immanent precisions.*

Thus it follows that the idea of being is not abstract in the proper sense of the term "total abstraction." It does not indicate a separate characteristic that is distinct from more special characteristics.

52. *The Idea of Being is Transcendental*

In a certain sense there is only one concept—the idea "being," for it extends to all beings not only insofar as they are similar but also insofar as they are dissimilar, and contains them in all respects.

For this reason we call the idea of being transcendental. It is not only the absolutely general concept, transcending all other concepts in extension, but it is at the same time absolutely all-embracing with respect to its comprehension, inasmuch as it somehow includes all other possible thought contents.

Being transcends every genus and all differences: it contains in an eminent way the highest abstract concepts or genera, but also the differentiating concepts and therefore also the concepts of species. Everything in every concepts is permeated with the idea of being, which thus is their unity.

The Meaning of Transcendental. 1. The term "transcendental" is opposed to "categorical." A concept is called "categorical" insofar as it falls under one of the categories or predicaments. The categories are fundamental concepts which are positively distinct and thus opposed to one another and do not agree in a higher general concept obtained through proper abstraction.[10] It is to these categories that univocal concepts of genus and species are reduced. In a wider sense there is sometimes question of categories as distinct fundamental concepts of a certain realm or of certain sciences.

2. As opposed to categorical, the predicate "transcendental" belongs first of all to "being." But also whatever pertains to being as being by its very concept embraces the highest abstract concepts and pervades everything in all concepts. For this reason we give the name "transcendental properties of being" to the properties which, according to our way of thinking, flow from being as being. Such characteristics, flowing from the identity of being with itself, are the following: unity, infinity, perfectness, determinateness, truth, goodness, beauty;[11] also presence,[12] individuality,[13] active potency and activity.[14] In a somewhat *broader* sense one may consider as transcendental properties those which pertain not to all beings but to beings having a higher mode of *being,* inasmuch as they do not include any imperfection in themselves; e.g., to live,[15] to love,[16] and liberty.[17]

3. "Transcendental," however, has still many other meanings in philosophy. In the Kantian sense, for instance, it is opposed to "empirical" and applies to *knowledge* insofar as this knowledge is not concerned with objects but with the subjective[18] *a priori* possibility of knowing objects.

4. "Transcendental" should be distinguished from "transcendent," i.e., what transcends a given order of *being* and is independent of it. With reference to the cognitive object, "transcendent" means that which is above the cognitive immanence of the object; with respect to the world of experience, it indicates what lies beyond the world of

---

[10]Cf. no. 69.
[11]Cf. nos. 39-44.
[12]Cf. no. 75.
[13]Cf. no. 90.
[14]Cf. nos. 93-95.
[15]Cf. no. 117.
[16]Cf. no. 139.
[17]Cf. no. 144.
[18]Cf. no. 25.

experience; and with regard to the finite, it applies to what transcends everything finite.

5. The verb "to transcend" allows several usages. Special attention should be paid to distinguish: a) to transcend something, i.e., to be transcendent with respect to something, to be absolutely or relatively independent of it, to contain it as the ground contains what is grounded on it; b) to transcend "toward" something, i.e., to rise above oneself, to go out of oneself in the direction of something outside or above oneself—in which case that "to" which one transcends oneself may sometimes be called the "transcendent."

Accordingly, the difference between the transcendental idea of being and abstract-general concepts lies in this: "to be" belongs to a being not only because of its similarity but also because of its dissimilarity with the other beings. To be a triangle, on the other hand, pertains to a triangle only insofar as it has three angles, regardless of its being equilateral, rectangular, etc. The unity of the abstract-general concept results from its abstraction. The source, however, of the unity proper to the transcendental idea of being has still to be investigated.

53. *The Idea of Being is Imperfect*

Our knowledge of *being* is somewhat intuitive. But because of its imperfectness, this knowledge needs the intermediary of the idea of being and also of the judgment. True, the idea of being actually contains anything whatsoever that in any way has a reference to "to be" and includes even the differences through which the various beings are in their own way. But, on the other hand, as a concept or intermediary representation of our thinking, it is unable to give us adequate knowledge of the universal interconnection uniting "everything that is."

Being Implicitly Contains the Modes of Being. This imperfectness cannot consist in this that new independent concepts have to be added to the idea of being, but consists in the fact that, although this idea contains the different modes of *being* actually, it contains them only implicitly and confusedly. Despite their being contained in this idea, they are not yet known explicitly and distinctly. For this reason sometimes the term "improper" abstraction is used with respect to the idea of being, for it does not leave anything behind but, on the other hand, it does not yet say everything explicitly.

Thus there is need for other concepts. However, these concepts are not wholly and entirely different, but only more explicit renderings of what is already contained in the idea of being. For this reason occasionally the term " 'improper' contraction" is used with respect to the transcendental idea of being, to express that the idea of being can be added-to only in the sense that more precise concepts are more explicit expressions of the same thought content.[19]

Immanent Explicitation of Being. Accordingly, the development of thought consists in an immanent explicitation of the idea of being, so that in an increasingly more adequate way everything which through *being* is possible and all its realizations are brought to explicit knowledge in more determined concepts. It is only in this way that the full richness of the idea "being" reveals itself.

On the other hand, for us the transition from the confused idea to the explicit grasp of "that which is" depends on experience and the insight contained in it. It is only through experience that we are placed in the presence of the various modes of *being,* which we cannot immediately deduce from the general idea of being itself.

54. *The Idea of Being is Analogous*

If being is the absolutely general concept, it belongs to everything. But if at the same time it is transcendental and thus contains not merely potentially but actually the differentiating concepts, how can it be predicated of the various beings and aspects of *being* in the same undifferentiated sense?[20]

Being is Not Univocal. A general concept which is said of many in exactly the same sense is called *univocal.* Univocity is possible only because of proper abstraction. The concept expresses only that in which the inferiors, the beings of which it is predicated, agree

---

[19]As Thomas Aquinas expresses it: "That which the intellect conceives first as most evident and to which it reduces all concepts is being. . . . Therefore, all other concepts of the intellect must be obtained through additions to being . . ., for every thought content (*natura*) essentially is a being. . . . But some thought contents may be said to add to being inasmuch as they express a mode of *being* which is not expressed by the term "being" itself. . . . This expressed mode may be a special mode of *being* . . . according to the different grades of *being* [leading to the categories] or a general mode that is common to and consequent upon every being [leading to the transcendental properties of being]." *De veritate,* q. 1., a. 1.

[20]The term "sense" indicates here the meaning, the thought content conveyed by the concept. Thus the question is whether being has always the same content, i.e., whether the same is always understood or meant by it.

and leaves their differences entirely out of consideration. It is possible that different beings exhibit one and the same characteristic from an abstract point of view, and then their difference lies, logically speaking, outside this characteristic.[21]

The idea of being, however, is not abstract, it does not unqualifiedly leave the differences behind and, therefore, it is not univocal. Although one may and, methodically speaking, even should *attempt* to form a concept of being that is univocal and minimal in content, the effort is doomed to failure. The effort has similar results as the universal methodic doubt: such a concept bears its own negation in its bosom, for it has to consider all the differences between the various beings as non-being.

Thus it follows that every being, precisely also as a being, is distinct from the other beings; hence the idea of being cannot be predicated of different beings in absolutely the same sense.

Being is Not Equivocal. Must we say, therefore, that being is predicated of all its inferiors in an ever absolutely different sense? Such a sense would constitute an absolutely different concept, for a concept is a unit of meaning and refers wholly to what is meant by it. For this reason one has to exclude entirely that there could be perfect ambiguity or equivocity in the realm of concepts.[22]

Accordingly, the idea of being is predicated of many in a sense that is neither absolutely the same nor entirely different. It has a unity of meaning because its sense reveals not an absolute but a *relative similarity* in the judgments we make about different beings. Such a concept is called analogous or, as it is sometimes inaccurately said, "partially similar."[23]

---

[21]Ontologically, however, this difference will exercise influence. The characteristic will be realized in dissimilar ways when one considers it in the various beings not in an abstract way but in their concrete reality. For instance, the being-sentient of man differs from that of an animal. In Cajetan's language, there exists an "analogy of inequality" even in the logically univocal. Cf. no. 116.

[22]Accidental equivocity is possible only on the level of the expression of concepts by means of gestures and words. According to the context, a single symbol may be used at different times with different meanings. For instance, the same word may have different meanings in different languages, e.g., "jumper" in English (one who jumps) and in Dutch (a garment), "was" in English (past tense of "to be") and in Dutch (laundry); or also one and the same term in the same language, e.g., blade, pen, blue.

[23]Concerning the analogy of being, cf. Cajetan, *De nominum alalogia;* English edition, *The Analogy of Names,* translated by Edward A. Bushinski, Pittsburgh, 2nd ed., 1959; A. van Leeuwen, "L'analogie de l'être," *Revue néoscol. de Louvain,* vol. 38 (1936), pp. 293-320 and 469-496; Angelinus, "De eenheid van het analoge zijnsbegrip," *Verslag der Achtste Alg. Verg.*

55. *The Idea of Being is Not Improperly Analogous*

In what way should the relative similarity, expressed in the idea of being as predicated of different beings, be understood? If we do not every time mean the same when we say of something that it *is,* but convey constantly a varied meaning according to the nature or mode of *being* proper to the being in question, what can be the general content of the term "being"?

Should we perhaps explain the agreement between the various senses of being in such a way that being is intrinsically predicated in its proper and primary meaning only of one among the many beings and that the others are called beings not by virtue of their own internal nature, but because of a relationship to the primary being which relationship is added to their own nature?

Analogy of Attribution. The analogy in question is known as analogy of extrinsic attribution or external relationship. The thought content is intrinsically present in one being, but the others are called by the same name because of a certain dynamic relationship to the first being.[24] This being may be the purpose to which the others are directed, the cause which makes them real, the object of which they are a sign or, reversely, they are the cause, occasion, or condition of it. Thus, for instance, "healthy" is an intrinsic determinant only of an animal organism, but complexion may manifest health, and food, medicine and climate may promote it, and therefore they also may be called healthy.

Strictly speaking, however, this analogy does not deviate from univocity, for the concept in question remains one and the same in meaning. All that happens is this—for brevity's sake language uses the term "healthy" to summarize a complex of meanings that includes among others health-revealing, health-promoting, and purposive of health. It is possible, however, to disentangle the many meanings and to indicate exactly what relation each separate meaning has to the primary intrinsic sense of the term which belongs to a single being— namely, healthy as the state of an animal organism.[25]

---

der *Ver. voor Thom. Wijsbegeerte,* 1942, pp. 5-30; P. Kreling, "De Betekenis van de analogie in de kennis van God, *ibid.,* pp. 31-54; A. de Witte, *Analogie (Wijsgerige Grondbegrippen),* Roermond, n. d.; G. Muskens, *De vocis analogiae significatione ac usu apud Aristotelem,* Groningen, 1943; "Aristoteles en het probleem der analogia entis," *Studia Catholica,* vol. 21 (1946), pp. 72-86.

[24] Cf. no. 163.

[25] The analogy of extrinsic attribution occurs especially in adjectives; e.g., *military* hospital, *medical* instruments. The dynamic relationship is considered in itself without regard to its foundation, and the related object is given a

Being is Not Merely Analogous by Attribution. If the idea of being were analogous in this way, the question would arise as to what would have to be asserted about the proper nature of the many things which would be beings in a secondary sense. What would they be if we leave aside this added relationship to the one being in the primary sense to which alone "to be" supposedly belongs in an intrinsic way?

The answer to this question does not allow any doubt. *Absolutely the first* thing that has to be said of everything is that it *is*. But if this is true, then the idea of being must primarily indicate something that pertains intrinsically to each of the many beings to which it belongs. It cannot *merely* mean their reference to something else without saying anything about what is the bearer and the foundation of this reference, for reference always means a connection of something with something. Accordingly, if the analogous idea of being indicates also the connection of a thing with the other beings in *being*,[26] it has to express a reference which accompanies and is included in the very *being* of every being—the "to be" itself and the to-be-related to the other beings may be distinguished, but they cannot be separated. Thus the idea of being does not primarily express merely an added relationship of the many to the first, but says something intrinsic or essential about every being. However,

---

name solely in reference to the term of the relation. Closer analysis shows that the added relationship has an intrinsic foundation and that cause and object-caused, purpose and directed-to-the-purpose, sign and object-signified always show a certain *intrinsic* similarity. Thus, for instance, medicine possesses chemical qualities through which it promotes certain processes in the organism by which it is absorbed, and these processes facilitate other processes, such as the circulation of the blood or digestion; finally, a complex of conditions and causes gives rise to the equilibrium called "health." Medicine, therefore, does not directly cause health as such, but whatever exactly its consumption causes has to be present in it.

The intrinsic similarity of cause and effect is sometimes univocal (cf. no. 107). However, it may also be analogous insofar as the proper cause *is* by its very essence what the effect *has* by participation. In such a case there is analogy in the strict sense, i.e., analogy based on an ontological relationship, for it implies a relationship arising from the very nature itself, and therefore is an intrinsic attribution. Analogy in the improper sense of the term or analogy of extrinsic attribution, on the other hand, is based on a summarizing use of language arising from a brief and uncritical observation. As soon as beings "have something to do with one another" and become associated in our thinking, we are able to denominate one after the other. A quasi-effect, e.g., healthy color, is called after its quasi-cause; a quasi-cause, e.g., healthy exercise, after its quasi-effect; a sign, e.g., the American Flag, after what it signifies; the symbolized, e.g., Uncle Sam, after its symbol.

[26]Cf. no. 50.

this intrinsic element is such that it implies a reference to the other beings which flows from its very essence or is essential.

Being is Not Analogous by Metaphor.   Because the idea of being belongs intrinsically to each and every being, it must be excluded that the many would be called beings only in a metaphorical sense as accidentally resembling the one which is being in the primary and non-metaphorical sense.

Metaphor is based on the analogy of improper proportionality, i.e., the thought content belongs intrinsically only to one of the inferiors, but the others are indicated by the same name, not in virtue of their inner nature, but only because of an added static relationship of proportional similarity or resemblance to the first.[27] For instance, only man can laugh in the proper sense of the term, only his face can be smiling, yet a blooming meadow may be said metaphorically to be smiling, because it reminds us of man by reason of the proportional similarity between the flourishing sight of the meadow in bloom and the radiant countenance of a human face wreathed in smiles.   Likewise, the relation of the lion to the other animals may be called that of a king; Christ calls himself the vine and the shepherd, and his disciples branches and sheep. However, in metaphors it is always possible to isolate the proportional similarity and distinguish it from the difference between the beings in question.   For this reason, just as the analogy of the added dynamic relationship, metaphor can be conceptually reduced to strict univocity.[28]

56. *The Proper Nature of the Analogy of Being*

The idea of being pertains intrinsically to all beings and therefore these beings must show a certain similarity with one another.   At the

---

[27]Cf. no. 163.

[28]Like analogy of extrinsic attribution, so also metaphor is extensively used as a human way of expression. Everywhere we see proportional similarities. We do not merely express them in comparison, but speak about one being in terms and concepts borrowed from the other and even simply refer to one by the name of the other. Metaphor constitutes the proper strength of poetic language. It is not at all excluded, however, that for the poet there is question here of analogy in the strict sense, i.e., that the conceptual content is experienced as intrinsically present in all the inferiors of the concept, for everything is internally connected with everything else and therefore present everywhere. When for example, Guido Gezelle writes: "I am a flower, blooming in Thy sight, O Giant Sun," this sentence means much more for him than, and expresses something entirely different from "I am *like* a flower." The very term "flower" is endowed with a more extensive as well as a richer or more profound meaning and thus is given a properly analogous sense.

same time, the idea of being indicates each being in its distinction from all the others. Nevertheless, there are no two meanings. As was mentioned above, with respect to the idea of being as a transcendental concept, it is not possible to make a strict conceptual separation between resemblance and dissimilarity, because the idea of being is not subject to proper abstraction and contraction. For this reason there is here an analogy that is not at all reducible to univocity—namely, analogy in the *proper* sense or metaphysical analogy.

A suitable name cannot be given to the analogy of the idea "being." Any qualifier would create the impression that there is question here only of a special kind of analogy which would univocally fall under a general idea of analogy as just another species alongside those of extrinsic attribution and metaphor. Strictly speaking, these two are not analogy in the full sense of the term, i.e., one that is not reducible to univocity. The primordial analogy of the idea of being can be described only by investigating the unity in which this most primordial concept contains its inferiors.

Being and Modes of Being. The ground of the unity proper to beings lies in "to be," the ground of their multiplicity lies in the modes of *being*. If these modes could be left out of the idea of being, so that there would remain only "something that *is* in any way whatsoever," then there would be univocity. But any attempt to leave the modes out is doomed to failure, because they cannot be conceived as absolutely independent of *being*—the modes are not absolutely nothing, they are permeated with *being* and thus have to be included in the idea of being. Hence the different modes are not added to the idea of being from without, as if everyone would first be allotted one and the same "to be" and then receive as an additional positive perfection his own mode of *being*. "To be" is not a property alongside which others can be added, for every property is a property of *being*. It is only through their particularization or finiteness that the characteristics of a being are distinct from unqualified "to be" and become this or that mode of *being*.

Although the idea of being is the most primordial of all concepts, nevertheless it exhibits in itself an essential proportion or composition —namely, the reference of the being to "to be" in accord with its own mode. This inner or essential reference differs from being to being, because each being is in a different way. But because "to be" and the mode of *being* cannot be conceptualized in fully separate ideas as if all beings agree in "to be" and differ in their modes, the mode is contained in the idea of being. Thus the meaning is different in every case when the idea of being is predicated of distinct beings. And nevertheless being means the same for every being, for all agree in this that they are intrinsically related to "to be" in their own way.

A Twofold Analogy. How should this difference and resemblance of proportion be conceived? Is every being related in a different way to one and the same "to be"? Or is the proportion the same, but both the mode and the "to be" different? Both suggestions are inadequate, for "to be" as "to be" is one and all-embracing, but in every being it is modified and particularized by the mode of this being and therefore proportioned to this mode.

The analogy of being, therefore, should be conceived in two supplementary ways:

1. The idea of being expresses the ever different essential relationship of every being to unqualified "to be."

2. The idea of being expresses the similarity of every being with every other being, and this similarity consists in this that in every being the proper mode and the proper "to be" are proportioned to each other.

From the first standpoint one may speak of analogy of dissimilar *intrinsic relationship,* from the second of analogy of *proportional similarity* or *proper proportionality.*

Analogy of Proper Proportionality. The analogy of proper proportionality is a mode of predication in which the thought content is intrinsically present in each of the inferiors, but in such a way that the intrinsic relationship expressed by the thought content—the relation between mode and "to be"—in each inferior is both essentially the same and essentially different. There is an identity of proportion or a proportional identity, but it implies essentially also a proportional otherness.

Thus it appears that the term "proportionality" does not accurately express this analogy. The analogy in question does not consist in the equality or exact agreement of two or more proportions. In pure proportionality, such as occurs in mathematics, it is possible to separate conceptually the proportion as such from the terms proportioned by it. For instance, in the proportions 1:2, 2:4, 3:6, 4:8, etc. one can

leave aside the variant terms and abstract the univocally general concept of "one-half" as something that is realized in exactly the same way in each of the proportions.

In the analogy of being, however, the proportion between the two terms—mode and "to be"—is always both similar and dissimilar to that in the other cases, for, because of its *being*-other than the other beings, a being is related in a somewhat different way to its own "to be" which it modifies. Thus the abstractly conceived pure proportionality is inadequate to express the relationship of the idea of being to its inferiors. Hence the description of the analogy of being as "analogy of proper proportionality" does not perfectly fit the case. It is meant only to draw attention to the aspect of the similarity of proportion, although even this aspect cannot be conceptually separated from that of the dissimilarity of proportion.

No Proper Similarity and Dissimilarity. "To be" therefore is predicated of each being in a sense that is neither entirely the same nor entirely different. Nevertheless, the meaning is always both essentially the same and essentially different. The distinct meanings immediately and of themselves constitute a unity because they do not partially agree and partially differ. There is no question of a difference added to an agreement. There are no "differences" and differentiating concepts in the proper sense of the terms, but there is an immanent diversity of one and the same. The hitherto used expression "in what beings agree with one another therein they also differ" was meant to express that there cannot be question here of similarity and difference in the proper sense of the terms. Rather than speak of different beings which are supposed to differ in something, we prefer to speak of distinct beings—distinct from one another and determined by their very mode of *being,* by the measure in which they are distinct from non-*being.*

Order of Modes. The identity and non-identity of every being with every other being are inseparably united in the idea of being. Thus there are many distinct meanings of *being* and nevertheless they constitute an immediate unity because all beings communicate with one another in their intrinsic relationship to unqualified "to be."

Accordingly, the analogous idea of being expresses actually, albeit only confusedly, all beings in all possible modes of *being.* Nevertheless, there is an order among the distinct explicit meanings of being, for their unity is essentially heterogeneous.

There is order and connection between the analogous meanings of *being* in a twofold way: the order in which the distinct meanings are discovered by progressive acts of *knowledge,* and the order in which the distinct senses are *in themselves* dependent on one another.

Order of Knowledge. One who apprehends a particular being as being explicitly knows a definite mode of *being,* but implicitly also all possible meanings of *being* because of the relationship of proportional similarity which the other meanings must have to the one that is first known.

We must now try to explicitate the other meanings of *being.* It is not possible for us, however, to discover in a purely deductive way all other modes of *being* from a single one, for we do not have a perfect intuition of unqualified *being* and of whatever is of necessity included in it.[29] Two ways are open to us if we want to arrive at explicit knowledge of the other meanings of *being*:

1. Starting from what is explicitly known, to widen our experience, but upon the basis of the all-embracing idea of being, by means of which we know already *something* about everything.

2. To discover through thinking the conditions which make possible the finite and particular beings that are given to us in experience, in order to acquire by means of their relationship of dependence an analogous knowledge of the sense of *being* which in itself is first and absolute.

Cognitive and Ontological Order. The analogy of the idea "being" makes our observation and thought progress from what is better known to us to what is less known to us and known only in dependence on what is first known. We proceed from what for us are primary modes of *being* to what for us are derivative modes.

However, this order of cognitive dependence does not necessarily correspond to the order of ontological dependence which beings have. Nevertheless, in this case we can readily see that the meanings which *for us* are secondary are *in themselves* primary. Since "to be" does not pertain to all beings in a like manner, we are able to discover a grading, a hierarchical order of priority and posteriority, of more

---

[29]Cf. no. 30.

or less, in accordance with the *intrinsic relationship* which all meanings that *in themselves* are secondary or derivative have to the meaning of being that *in itself* is first and absolutely perfect.[30]

---

[30]Not only the idea of being is analogous in the proper sense but also all concepts in which this idea explicitates itself in our thought, such as the transcendental properties of being, one, true, good, beautiful, etc. Likewise, the activities of knowing and loving which are directed toward the transcendental are analogous. As we will see later, even more particular concepts may participate in the analogy of being (cf. no. 130).

If the analogy is valid for individual beings as beings according to their unequal participation in *being*, it is all the more valid for the primary general divisions of being. These two, are analogously enclosed by the idea of being and clearly so by virtue of the intrinsic relationship of the derivative or dependent meanings on the first or independent sense: the secondary, relative and modified sense participates in a particular way in the fullness proper to the primary, absolute and unmodified meaning to which it refers. However, in these divisions of being it becomes clear that in certain cases the derivative sense is first for us according as we encounter beings in experience and that we have to ascend from what is first for us to what is first in itself. To give a few examples—

contingent—**necessary**	imperfect—perfect
real—**possible**	determinable—determined
purely thought—**possible or real**	accidental—substantial
opposite or distinct—**identical**	in-potency—in-act
many—one	past or future—present
composed—simple	temporal—eternal
finite—infinite	effect—cause
part—whole	means—purpose

CHAPTER ELEVEN

FINITE BEINGS PARTICIPATE IN *BEING* IN THE MEASURE OF THEIR ESSENCE

57. *Participation*

How Beings Can be Distinct. A being could be "other" than another being for the following reasons:

1. It possesses a characteristic, thought content or quality, in the broadest sense of the term, which is lacking in the other.

2. It possesses the same characteristic in another or higher way. If the other or higher mode is conceptually separable from a fundamental quality possessed by both, then this case is reducible to the first—namely, the presence or absence of the other or higher characteristic. Both of these analyses lead to the orderly arrangement of univocal concepts.

However, with respect to the *being*-other of beings as beings, the fundamental characteristic—"to be"—cannot be conceptually separated from the presence or absence of other qualities, for there are no "other" or "higher" qualities. Therefore, the presence itself of "to be" has to be "other" in each being.

Such a distinction in the presence of one and the same characteristic can arise only because unqualified "to be" is not fully present in each of the beings but only to a certain extent. This kind of presence is called the participation of beings in *being*.

Meaning of Participation. "To participate"[1] means to take part (*partem capere*) and thus to have a part. It can be understood in more than one sense. Quantitatively taken, it means to divide a whole among several. Qualitatively, it expresses that a whole as a whole is present in several through knowing, feeling, or willing; e.g., to

---

[1]Concerning participation cf. L. B. Geiger, *La participation dans la philosophie de S. Thomas,* Paris, 1942 (see especially pp. 27-31 about the two forms called "participation by composition" and "participation by similarity" or "formal hierarchy"); C. Fabro, *La nozione metafisica di partecipazione secondo S. Tommasso d'Aquino,* Torino, 1950; *De Thomistische Participatieleer* (Verslag der 10e alg. verg. v.d. Ver. voor Thomist, Wijsb.), Nijmegen, 1944.

share in one's knowledge, joy or sorrow. In the present context, however, it should be understood in a strictly philosophical sense as to contain in oneself a characteristic or quality, not in the whole fullness and richness of its content, not universally, but only in a special, limited, and finite or particular way. This should not be taken to mean that only a part or an aspect of the perfection is present, for in that case this part could be considered separately as a common fundamental characteristic to which differences could be added. The sense is that the whole indivisible perfection is present in its self-identity, not however fully but in a diminished or defective way which gives rise to the distinction or non-identity of the many finite participants.[2]

Accordingly, the otherness of beings can be conceived only as an unequal presence of the universality of *being* which gives rise to distinct beings in particular modes of *being*. For this reason there has to be a *gradation* of beings in their participation in *being*.

Inadequacy of the Idea of a Hierarchy. Just as the idea of proportionality is inadequate in the logical order, so that of gradation or hierarchy inadequately expresses the particular distinctness of beings. A mathematically conceived gradation, which puts all on one line at a greater or lesser distance from the limit, fails to take into consideration the possible complexity of the modes of *being*. There is no question here of quantitatively "more or less" by means of addition or multiplication of the same unit, nor of a qualitative gradation or intensification, but the point is here that the fullness of *being* is spread and multiplied *ontologically* in such a way that it retains for each being heterogeneity and originality in its interconnection with the other beings. We have to keep in mind that

---

[2]A different philosophical conception of participation uses the term with respect to a being which *is* not of itself or by identity, but is what-it-is because it has received this (from another). This participation, therefore, expresses first of all a composition of subject and a "form," distinct from the subject, which has been received. Supposing that the recipient receives in its own way and therefore limits, it follows that such a form will have been received only in a limited way. Hence the composition results in a limitation. However, this participation *presupposes a receiving subject* for the perfection that is to be received. With Geiger, we think that according to Thomas Aquinas the view of participation which we have explained above—in which limitation results in composition and not vice versa—should be considered as most fundamental insofar as participation in *being* is concerned. Otherwise one would have to oppose a plurality of receiving potencies as subjects to the *being* that is received, although even the possibility of *being*-a-subject has to be explained through all-embracing *being*. Thus the doctrine of composition, which later we will call the theory of potency and act, ultimately has to find its foundation in the theory of participation (cf. no. 97).

the ontological hierarchy of beings is known to us to some extent only and merely from our experience of real beings. Thus we may not schematize *a priori,* for we do not know the limitless possibilities of finite modes of *being* because we are unable to have a perfect intuition of unqualified *being* and all that is of necessity contained in it.

58. *Essence*

Before considering the grades of *being* more in detail, we must first raise this general ontological question: If every finite being participates in a particular way in *being,* what are we to think of the self-*identity* of this being in *being,* for this self-identity is the fundamental law of being as being? But if the self-identity of the finite is a participated identity, it includes also a certain non-identity of the finite with itself. How are we to reconcile identity and non-identity? Should there not be an opposition in the finite, as a finite mode of unity? In other words, what is the structure of the finite as finite?

We distinguish the many finite beings as *this* and *that,* though not yet in a spatial sense but as an ontological distinction. Although I have answered the question: "Is this?" with "This is"—a reply to which nothing can be added—nevertheless, I do not yet know *this* precisely in its *being*-this. Whence the further question, which is not exactly new but merely an explicitation of the first: *"What is this?"* The new reply, likewise, cannot be exactly new but nonetheless is an explicitation of the affirmation of *being.*

Thus the question of *being* unfolds itself in the question of what-it-is, whatness, or quiddity—that through which this is *what* it is.[3]

---

31. We usually reply with a general substantive noun to the question: "What is this being?" But these substantive nouns, e.g., man, animal, body, are to be explained through adjectival additions to being, such as rational, sentient, living, extended. Thus we know the *whatness* of a thing by means of its *howness.*

In our present problem we are not concerned with the formal-concrete "what," e.g,. "man," but with that through which something is what it is. In other words, we inquire about the formal-abstract whatness. We will use the term "essence" for whatness. Whatness is primarily individual.

2. The term "essence" has the following uses:

a. The formal-abstract essence is the beingness of a being.

b. The formal-abstract essence is the whatness (*ousia* or *essentia*) of a being. This is the sense in which the term will be used here.

c. The formal-concrete essence is the being itself, in a general sense, as, e.g., in the proposition: man is a rational being.

Every individual finite being has its own essence through which it is *what* it is, or through which it is itself and distinct from every other being. There are no words to express this individual whatness, although occasionally we speak of the "Peterness" of Peter. We should conceive this essence as the *mode of being* of *this* being which lies contained in the reply to the question of how this being is, i.e., in what way it participates in *being*.[4]

59. *Relationship of Essence and "To Be"*

"To Be" is Not a Mere Substratum. Does perhaps the important point lie not in "to be," conceived as the "to-be-there" of de facto real being, but precisely in its whatness or essence? Thus "to-be-there" would merely mean the common and trivial fact of "being encountered in experience," but a being would get its value from the content and richness of *what* is-there?

The reply has to be in the negative. "To be" cannot be conceived as a mere substratum on which the modes of *being* are raised as perfections. Logically speaking, "to be" is not a potential substratum for added determinations.[5] From the ontological viewpoint, likewise, "to be" is not perfectible in any way or determinable by added "forms" or essences.[6]

For, where would these essences that complete "to be" find their origin? The assumption that they presuppose a common substratum does not explain their distinction, richness, and hierarchy.

Therefore, "to be" is not determinable through enriching determinations, but the determinations must be considered as "limitations," as limited modes of *being*.[7]

Essence is Not a Presupposed Substratum. Should we then conceive first an order of possible essences and then ascribe to some of them existence as real "to be"?

The answer again is in the negative. With Suarez, one could identify the "existing" individual essence, which first was merely conceived,

---

[4]From a phenomenological standpoint essence is considered by J. Hering, "Bemerkungen über das Wesen, die Wesenheit und die Idee," *Jahrbuch f. Phil. und Phänomenologie,* vol. 4 (1921), pp. 595-643.

[5]Cf. no. 51.

[6]Cf. no. 41.

[7]Perhaps Aristotle sought *ousia,* beingness, too much in the essence, conceived by him as eidē or intelligible principles, whose multiplicity he observed empirically, and neglected to investigate their necessary origin in "to be" (*einai*) itself as pure perfection. If this is true, then the Arabian philosophers and especially Thomism are an improvement over Aristotle.

with its "existence." But, if this essence and this "to be" are fully
identical, how could one maintain that this finite being participates,
imperfectly of course, in the identity of unqualified *being?*

On the other hand, one could conceive "existence" as an added
perfection of the individual essence—not in the sense that something
is added to the conceived content of this essence, but in the sense that
the essence is placed outside its causes. In this way a distinct order of
"existence" is admitted which presupposes and leaves untouched the
order of essence. "Existence" is predicated in a quasi-accidental way
of the conceived essence. However, in this case the order of "existence"
is understood as a pure to-be-there, a "to-be-encountered in experience," which would merely give "existence" to a presupposed content.
But *the content itself* is unthinkable save through its connection with
being. The all-embracing nature of *being* means that it constitutes also
all contents, all essences. An essence is an essence only as a *mode of
being.* It has value only because it contains more or less of *being;*
because it indicates the measure in which a being participates in *being,*
which as "to be" does not include any imperfection.

Accordingly, it is false to conceive the distinction of essence and
"to be" as if the essence were a ready-made receptacle for *being,* a substratum that is supposed to be prior to *being.* Such a view of the composition of essence and "to be" exaggerates the opposition of essence
and "to be." It fails to realize that in a being essence and "to be" are
also somewhat identical in the "to be in this way" which makes this
being this being. The essence, therefore, should not be understood as
a positive perfection that is conceivable in separation from *being.* It
owes all its perfection to the measure in which the being participates
in unqualified *being.*

60. *The Distinction Between Essence and "To Be"*

The Necessity of a Modifying Principle. How should one conceive
the opposition and distinction between essence and "to be"?[8] The two
assertions *that* this is and *what* this is are not distinct merely because
of my imperfect knowledge which first seizes the aspect "to be" and
then that of essence, for there are here no abstract aspects which supplement each other. Both assertions are concerned precisely with the

---

[8]Concerning the history of the real distinction between essence and "to be"
cf. M. D. Roland-Gosselin, *Le "De ente et essentia" de S. Thomas d'Aquin,*
Paris, 1948, pp. 135-205.

same *concrete* thing and include each other without, however, coinciding completely.

Therefore, the finite being itself has to give rise to the imperfect way in which the two assertions coincide. In other words, essence and "to be" are not fully identical in the being itself.

On the other hand, to some extent the finite being has to be identical with "to be," for "to be" is immanent in this being because this being *is*. This identity, however, cannot be perfect because alongside *this* being other beings also are possible and real. "To be," insofar as it is immanent in this being through a certain identity, therefore, is not unqualified "to be," for unqualified "to be" transcends *this* being. The immanent "to be" in question is a modified, finite, and limited "to be," the *proper "to be"* of this being. But how did this modification arise? "To be," taken precisely as "to be," is not a limiting and modifying principle. Thus we have to admit a modifying principle which in a way is opposed to "to be" as "to be."

Opposition of Essence and "To Be." How should the opposition of "to be" and a distinct limiting principle be conceived within the immanence of the single being? Not in such a way that the limiting principle would be *absolutely* opposed to "to be," i.e., be non-*being*, for non-*being* cannot modify anything. Hence essence and "to be" are not in contradiction. Likewise, not in such a way that the modifying principle would all by itself be a being and share in "to be," for a being is not composed of beings.

Of itself the limiting principle is neither "to be" nor being; nevertheless, it constitutes *this* being as this *being* and expresses a modification, imminent to this being, of unqualified "to be" into a limited "to be this" and nothing else. Whatever it has, therefore, it derives from the *relative* opposition to "to be," to which as a modifying principle it refers by its whole nature and from which it has also its modifying capacity. Evidently, "to be" lets itself be modified or limited, and according to this limitation the finite being participates in unqualified "to be."

Distinction of Essence and "To Be." Within a being, then, there is a distinction, not between beings, but between:

1. The immanent principle which makes the being *be*, and this principle is the *proper "to be"* of the being, the limited mode of unqualified *being*.

2. The immanent principle which makes the being be only in *this way*, and this is the essence or limiting principle which modifies the "to be" into the proper "to be" of the being.

The reason for this distinction and duality of principles lies in the transcendency of unqualified *being* over the modified proper "to be" of the being in question.

A Twofold Distinction. Thus there is a double distinction. First of all, unqualified "to be," which transcends all modes, does not fully coincide with the *proper "to be"* of each being which is only in a limited way. This distinction arises from the fact that the finite being is through *participation* in unqualified *being*.

Secondly, to explain this participation, we must admit that within the finite being there is a distinction between its *proper "to be"* and the principle through which "to be" becomes its own limited "to be"— namely, its modifying and limiting essence. This distinction of essence and "to be" is the composition found in the finite being.

Like the first, however, this second distinction is not an absolute opposition. For in this being essence and "to be" are somewhat identified insofar as this being is precisely in its own way. But "to be" is not of itself the proper and limited "to be" of this being, and for this reason there is a distinction of two principles which together constitute the unity of the being in question.

Essence and Judgment. Just as it is impossible to make "to be" adequately the subject of a judgment,[9] so also the essence cannot be such a subject. Neither one nor the other is a being, but they are that through which a being *is* and that through which the being is *what* it is, and their mutual relationship constitutes the being. Nevertheless, we are forced to speak about the essence in the form of judgments; hence it is important to keep in mind that this mode or expression is deficient. This deficiency is lost sight of by anyone who first conceives "to be" and then the determinations or, reversely, first the essence and then the "to be."

Priority of "to Be" Over Essence. The relativity of essence and "to be" *cannot be fully reciprocal.* While the essence is fully relative to "to be," "to be" as "to be" transcends all modes of *being* and therefore all modifications through an essence. In the finite being,

---

[9]Cf. no. 26.

however, "to be" has let itself be modified and has become a correlated principle "through which" the being is in this determined way.

In a sense, therefore, the essence is prior to "to be," for the mode modifies "to be" into "to be this." But this priority cannot be absolute, for the mode also arises from the "to be" which includes in itself the possibility of being-finite. *Absolutely speaking,* therefore, *"to be" is prior to essence,* for "to be" makes the mode a mode of *being.*

However, we know "to be" only as "to-be-of-beings," as modified, limited, and multiplied. Whether unqualified "to be," which we encounter only *in* finite beings as the proper "to be" of every being, is the ultimate ground of all beings we cannot determine before we have studied these finite beings themselves in more detail. Perhaps unqualified "to be" will point to a ground above itself which is transcendent not only relatively to finite beings but absolutely.

CHAPTER TWELVE

THE FINITE BEING IS NECESSARILY DYNAMIC

61. *Finiteness and Infinity*

The problem with which we were concerned was this: since experience shows that there really are finite beings, how can their possibility be understood, for of itself "to be" is infiniteness?[1] As we know, however, infiniteness is not a condition of *being*—for "to be" is unconditioned and absolute—but is a consequence of it. True, it follows, therefore, that all that is, *insofar* as it is, is infinite, but it can be infinite in a finite way insofar as the infiniteness of *being* does not attain to fullness in *this* particular being.

There seems to be a contradiction in this finite infinity. In a provisional reply we have solved the antinomy by accepting, aside from the contradictory opposition of *being* and non-*being,* which strictly speaking is no longer opposition, the relative opposition and relative identity of this "to be" and this essence which together constitute this being. The "to be" which of itself is infinite can be present in a finite way, as the proper "to be" of this being, insofar as it accepts a condition—namely, the essence as the measure of *being*.

On the other hand, an absolutely finite being is impossible.[2] It would be totally encompassed by its limits and absolutely deny the other beings, have nothing to do with them. But in that case to-be-with-others would be impossible.[3] An absolutely finite being would be a being in which *"to be"* and *limit* coincide, a being that would be more, the more it were limited. This, however, would mean the identity of *being* and non-*being*. For this reason every being is a being not according to the measure of its finiteness but according to the measure of its infinity.

---

[1] Cf. no. 48.
[2] Cf. no. 40.
[3] Cf. no. 35.

62. *The Limitless Multiplicity of Possible Finite Beings*[4]

Every finite being stands in contrast not only to non-*being* but also to all other finite beings, because it has only a particular mode of *being* and therefore does not include the other modes. Experience reveals that alongside me other beings are real, but my very finiteness itself implies already the possibility of other finite beings. Together we constitute a plurality, not in the sense of the mathematical number, but in the sense of the ontological distinctness (multitude), the otherness of content of every individual being.[5]

But the whole of all possible modes of *being* can never be constituted by the combination of a particular mode which through opposition refers to all other possible modes and a *limited plurality* of other modes. No matter how differentiated we make this limited plurality of essences, the total will never equal all possible modes of being-real.

The reason is that "to be" as "to be" is infinite and transcends not only each mode in particular but also all modes together, as long as these modes constitute a limited plurality. Alongside them, other particular modes of being-real are always possible "to infinity," i.e., without out end or limitlessly.

Therefore, no limit can be assigned to the multiplication of finite beings in ever distinct ways. No matter which limited whole of finite beings be taken, it will never equal the limitless plurality of finite beings that could possibly participate in *being*.

For the present we will leave undecided whether all possible finite beings are already realized and, therefore whether all reality is necessary.[6] On the other hand, it is certain that, if all possibilities had to have been realized, this reality would constitute a limitless plurality. It seems doubtful, however, whether one could still speak of *finite*

---

[4]According to Thomas Aquinas, a sharp distinction should be made between limitlessness and true infinity. Matter is limitless in its potency and is determined through form. This determination, however, is a perfection, while limitlessness is an imperfection. Form as act is infinite, but determined through potency. This determination, however, is not a perfection but a restriction, a limitation, while the infinity is pure perfection. When Greek philosophy calls the circumscribed and finite perfect, it opposes the determined to the limitlessness of what is further determinable. On the other hand, when later philosophers call the unlimited perfect, they are concerned with the infinity of all-embracing absolute *being*, which is also the perfectly determined.

[5]Because of their analogy and unequal participation in *being* the many beings are not numerable in the most proper or mathematical sense of the term. Cf. no. 78.

[6]Cf. no. 30.

real beings if there were no unrealized possibility, for the finite is perfectible "to infinity."[7]

63. *The Dynamic Infinity of Every Finite Being*[8]

Every being *as* being is *what* it is, is itself in the measure of its essence (the principle of identity).[9] Nevertheless, since the finite is constituted by two principles connected in a certain opposition, it is not fully identical with its essence, just as it is not wholly identical with its "to be." The finite being *is* not its essence.

Essence is Not Merely a Principle of Limitation. The essence should not be conceived merely as the principle of limitation in opposition to "to be." For it is essence only by virtue of its reference to "to be."[10] Hence the essence is "more" essence not according as it is more a limiting principle and excludes the other modes of being, not "more" according as it is more finite, but "more" according as it includes in itself the other modes of *being* and thus identifies itself more with the fullness of unqualified *being*.

The same thought may be expressed in a different way. The essence is that through which a being is *determined* to what it is. If we conceive the essence in opposition to "to be," it is a principle of determination in the sense of limitation.[11] However, we should conceive the essence also as not opposed to "to be," but as originating in "to be" as a mode of *being* which is contained in "to be." Taken in this way, the essence is a principle of determination in a sense that is opposed to indeterminateness, imperfectness, and finiteness. It is the expression of the perfect determination, which is proper to *being,* as distinct from non-*being*. Thus essential determination does not mean that a being is more limited in its mode of *being* and excludes more modes, but means just the opposite— namely, that the being contains more modes of *being* in a higher

---

[7]Cf. no. 178.

[8]Concerning the connection between finiteness and dynamism, cf. J. de Finance, *Etre et agir*, Paris, 1945, p. 160: ". . . l'inadéquation du fini à l'égard des virtualités de l'*esse*. A ce qui, dans l'Acte pur, est richesse, possession par identité, coincidence parfaite avec soi, répond, dans l'acte mixte, la tendance, qui dit précisément multiplicité, séparation du sujet et du terme. Fils de Poros et de Penia, le désir nait de cette opposition même de l'acte et de la limite. Et c'est pourquoi toute forme créee s'accompagne d'une inclination, qui est l'*appetit naturel*".

[9]Cf. no. 36.

[10]Cf. no. 59.

[11]Cf. no. 41.

unity and therefore through its closer approach to the fullness of unqualified *being* is more strongly opposed to absolute non-*being*.

The Finite Being is Further Determinable and Perfectible. From these considerations it follows that the finite being, which *is* not its essence, is always imperfectly determined.   But what is not fully determined is further *determinable,* for as participating in *being* it is directed to determinateness.   Therefore, although the finite is not fully identical with its essence, it has within itself a directedness to identification with this essence, a possibility to become more "itself" by approaching more closely its full essential determination.

As further determinable, the finite being is *perfectible* in such a way that no restricting limit can be assigned to its perfectibility.   Because of its directedness to unqualified *being,* it is subject to further perfection "to infinity," i.e., without end or limitlessly.

Thus it is impossible that there be a finite being which is "fully closed" because it has reached absolute perfection.   A finite being is never fully "itself," never fully identical with its essence.[12]

The finite being is perfectible, because its mode of *being* is not the absolute denial of the other modes, but is-together with them and thus includes them to some extent.   This ever-present radical *being-together* of the modes of *being* can be perfected through reciprocal communication, by means of which the finite being enriches itself in the direction of the infinite and approaches its essence more closely.

Dynamic Infinity. The measure of infinity hitherto expressed as "whatever is, insofar as it is, is infinite" may now be described as a *being-directed-to-the-infinite.* Keeping in mind that the perfectibility in question is not purely passive, not a mere possibility of being perfected from without, but an active *directing-itself-to* further perfection, we may speak here of a dynamic infinity. For *dynamis,* as power, expresses a "being-able" which through an inner impulse aims at reaching a higher degree of *being*-itself and of realizing all the possibilities that lie in the essence.[13]

---

[12]For this reason the finite "optimum" in the absolute sense, the best possible world, as well as its opposite, the finite "pessimum," the worst possible world, cannot exist.

[13]Cf. no. 72.

64. *The Nature of the Finite Being as Principle of Tendency*

Essence and Nature. The finite being is already to some extent *what* it is according to the measure of its essence. But it is also always directing-itself-to *being* more what it is, to a fuller realization of its essence.

Thus the essence of the finite is both terminus and starting point of a directedness. As terminus, it is an "ideal" of perfection to be realized; as starting point, it is the origin of the "power" to realize this ideal. To indicate the essence insofar as it is the power for further determination and perfection we use by preference the term "nature."[14]

Tendency and the Good. The primordial exercise of the capacity for self-realization which originates in nature is called in a very general sense *"inclination."* If the absence of the terminus in the starting point is emphasized, it goes by the name of *desire,* but if the active directedness to the terminus is stressed, it is known as *tendency.*

The perfection to which a being strives as to the fuller participation in *being* that is possible for its essence is "the good,"[15] and more specifically the "natural" good insofar as it is in agreement with this determined being. It should be emphasized that the natural good is nothing else than the ontological good itself viewed as the good of this determined being.

Because a being cannot cease to direct itself in accordance with its essence to a fuller participation in *being* unless it cease to be altogether, the natural inclination is (hypothetically) necessary for the finite being. It is the same necessity which pertains already to the

---

[14]Concerning the concept of nature, see i.a. Aristotle, *Metaphysica,* bk. V, ch. 4 (1014 b10 -1015 a19) and St. Thomas' *Commentary,* nos. 808-826. The primary sense of "nature" appears to be the *ousia* or essence of beings which have within themselves the principle of their motion, taken as such.

Nature, which is derived from *nasci,* to be born, or *physis* has several meanings:
1. The origin itself, especially with respect to living beings.
2. The proper character or essence arising from this origin.
3. The proper character, as the principle from which other perfections originate. This is the sense in which the term is used here.
4. Collectively taken, the whole of originating and self-unfolding beings (cf. no. 146).
5. Sometimes also, normatively taken, the laws governing self-development.

[15]Cf. no. 43.

being because of its participation in *being,* but here this necessity reveals itself more explicitly.

Not only the inclination but also that to which nature is inclined, the good, is necessary, although in a different way. For the good *is* still only as an "ideal" in the intention or directedness of the inclination. The necessity of the good, which consists in this that the good must "necessarily" be tended-to, is strictly speaking the necessity of *being* itself. "To be" of necessity has to perfect and therefore to attract *if and as soon as* there are real finite beings. (The extent to which finite beings are necessary will provisionally be left undecided.)[16]

The good, as necessary, is *natural law* for the finite and especially for the tendencies through which the finite is directed to the natural good. This means that the natural good implies which tendencies are necessary. It means also that the natural good is the norm[17] which determines the goodness of a finite tendency and of the finite being itself. The tendency itself also is called good by analogy of intrinsic attribution or proportion. And the finite being is called good insofar as it is made good or perfected by the natural good.

Foundation of the Tendency. That the finite being has to desire and tend arises from the fact that there is a certain non-identity or opposition between the starting point and terminus of its self-unfolding. The good is not yet fully present but in many respects still absent. This opposition is precisely what the tendency has to overcome.

Moreover, we should keep in mind that self-realization consists in the growth of the essence through communication with beings that have different modes of *being.* Precisely because of their otherness, these beings are at first experienced as obstacles and impediments. Hence the tendency aims at absorbing their otherness in the immanence of the essence, so that this essence becomes more-embracing and more closely approaches the fullness of *being.*

---

[16]Cf. no. 30.
[17]Cf. no. 150.

CHAPTER THIRTEEN

THE FINITE BEING IS THE SUBSISTENT BEARER
OF ACCIDENTS

65. *The First Meaning of Substance: Subsistence*

The Primary Sense of Being. Being as being is, and is what it is. This principle of identity[1] applies in the primary and most proper sense to that which is "*in* itself," makes "to be" its own, and identifies it with itself. "That which is" in the primary sense, therefore, is *real, individual, subsistent being,* as we know it from experience. The reasons are as follows:

1. Possible *being* refers to real *being* as the central sense of *being.*

2. Universal *being,* i.e., that which can be predicated of many, which is proper to being only as it appears in our concept as a thought content, refers to the *being*-individual of reality, which is the ultimate subject of predication.

3. Non-subsistent *being,* i.e., the *being* proper to aspects and determinations of *being,* refers to the *being*-subsistent of the being to which these aspects and determinations belong.[2]

Imperfect Subsistence. The subsistence, however, of the finite is imperfect. For participation, which is only a sharing in *being,* implies that the identity of a being with "to be" is imperfect and even that its immanent proper "to be" does not coincide with it but is only a principle through which this being is.[3] Hence there can be no question of perfect appropriation of "to be," for otherwise being, essence, and "to be" would have to be fully identical.

Now if the subsistence of a being is imperfect, then this being *is* not its subsistence, but participates imperfectly in *being*-subsistent— namely, insofar as it can make "to be" its own in accordance with its essence. Therefore, there is a distinction between the finite subsistent being and its subsistence "through which" it is subsistent.

---

[1]Cf. no. 36.
[2]Cf. no. 47.
[3]Cf. no. 60.

118

"Subsistence" is the term by which we indicate the primary meaning of *being*-a-substance—namely, appropriating "to be" as one's own without sharing it with others. The being which does this is said to be "subsistent" or also to be a "supposit" or "hypostasis" insofar as it is that which appropriates the *modes* of *being* and therefore is *that which* by virtue of its own "to be" is, e.g., man or also acting in this or that way.

Nature of Subsistence. In what does this subsistence consist? Some, as Capreolus, reply: in the "proper to be" of what is *in* itself; others, as Cajetan,[4] place it in the essence insofar as the essence is terminated through an ultimate mode, as a point terminates a line, so that it can no longer share the same "to be" with another being but has to receive its "own to be." With Absil,[5] however, we think that subsistence does not consist in a mode but in the active modification which the essence produces in the "to be" and through which it makes "to be" the proper "to be" of the being in question. Thus the appropriation of "to be" is explained in the sense that it makes the being itself be, makes it subsistent.

66. *"Ex-sistence"*

Taken in the generality of its many meanings, "to be" is not the same as "to exist." The reasons for this assertion are the following:

1. First of all, "to exist" refers only to real being.

2. "To exist" indicates only the reality of the finite as this real being, insofar as the proper "to be" of this limited being is a participation in unqualified *being* and therefore *comes forth* (*ex-sistit*) from the one source of the multiple, finite and imperfect which we have not yet investigated. Thus "to exist" as "ex-sisting" points to a certain connection of effect and cause.

3. "To ex-sist" also indicates a "directedness to the external," a being directed to other beings as to that which the finite "ex-sisting" being, because of its dynamic infinity, needs to become more "itself."[6]

---

[4]Cf. G. van Rijsbergen, *Doctrina Cajetani de personalitate cum doctrina D. Thomae Aquinatis comparata, Roermond,* 1940.

[5]Cf. Th. Absil's important articles about this neglected subject "Gedanken über die Weise," *Studia Catholica,* Nijmegen, vol. 7 (1930-31), pp. 41-71, 73-101; vol. 8 (1931-32), pp. 39-47.

The finite "ex-sistent" tends to more perfect subsistence through more intimate appropriation of *being*. It reaches such a more perfect subsistence by progressively realizing the possibilities of its essence in its communication with beings that are in different ways. The question, however, is: How must this self-realization which originates in the nature of the finite subsistent being be explained? This query leads us to the second meaning of substance.

67. *The Second Meaning of Substance: Support*

The finite subsistent being is perfectible "to infinity" and tends to perfection. Hence it is a self-unfolding, "ex-sistent" being which by merely *being* has not yet reached the fullness of its "to be." A distinction has to be made at least between a more initial and a more final state, a state of determinability and a state of determination.

This self-development can be explained only if the subsistent being is determinable in different ways while it remains the same being. Thus there is an identity of one and the same with itself as well as a non-identity of more or less distinct states in which this being is found.

This identity and non-identity can be understood only if there is a distinction between the subsistent being insofar as through its essence it is already somewhat itself and the further determinations through which it becomes more and more "itself."

Accordingly, the finite being is not only because of its limited subsistence the subject of its essence and "to be" without being fully identical with them, but is also the subject of possible further accidental determinations of *being* because of its growing subsistence and its "ex-sistence" as standing "open" to others.

---

[6] "To ex-sist" may mean:

  1. To come forth from a ground or to be outside the causes.
  2. To be "open" to the world of persons and things.
  3. The dispersion of *being* in the temporal moments of past, present, and future.
  4. The openness to unqualified *being*.
  5. The directedness to the absolutely transcendent—God.

In any case due importance should be attached to the *ex*, and "to exist" should not be confused with all-embracing "to be," which extends also to the possible as well as to the purely thought, or even with "to be real," taken as such.

This condition of being-subject as such, i.e., the real receptivity to further determinations which more and more remove the indeterminateness of the finite being by making it share more intimately in "to be," we call the supporting function or substantiality (from *substo,* I stand under, I support) of the finite subsistent being.[7]

68. *To Be in-Another or Accident*

Distinction of Essence and Further Determinations. The finite subsistent being is perfectible through further determinations. These determinations are, on the one hand, explicitations of possibilities present in the essence and find their origin in the essence as nature, so that there is a certain identity of essence and determinations. On the other hand, they are in a certain way opposed to the essence because the essence, considered in itself, does not yet necessarily include their realization.

The opposition to the essence and the distinction between essence and further determinations is greatest when there is question of conditions which may be successively present and absent, while the subsistent being remains identical.

Modification of "To Be." The accidental determinations presuppose the subsistent being as making "to be" its own through its essence. Thus they modify "to be," but not in the same way in which the essence modifies it and makes it the proper "to be" of a subsistent being. Hence they should not be conceived as if they were, together with the "to be" which they determine, the constituent principles of a subsistent being. The accidental being constituted by the accidental determination is not something which is *in* itself. The

---

71. The term "substance" most literally expresses this "standing-under accidents." It expresses the property of being the subject of accidental determinations. But it was also often used to indicate the being-*in*-itself or autonomy, which we have called "subsistence" and which is proper to the first category (*ousia*) of Aristotle, as taken in itself and not in reference to the other categories.

2. Gradually, as had already happened with the term *ousia,* the formal-abstract meaning of the state of beingness, subsistence and supporting changed into the concrete meaning, so that *substantia,* substance, came to mean *substans,* i.e., the subsistent being. Thus there is a certain lack of clarity in the terminology.

3. It should be kept in mind that the distinction between subsistence and support is especially important because "to subsist" is the primary sense of *being* and does not include any imperfection, while "to support" is applicable only to the finite subsistent being insofar as it is not yet fully "itself" but receptive of accidental determinations.

determinations modify a "to be" which through the essence has already become the proper "to be" of a definite subsistent being. Thus they modify the proper "to be" of a subsistent being in an additional or secondary way. Accordingly, the accidental is something which "pertains to something else"—namely, something pertaining to the subsistent being. However, since the accidental is not nothing, it is a "being" in an analogous sense. This sense is not only intrinsic to the accidental, for it is in a certain way, *but* also always expresses a relation to "being" in the primary sense, the subsistent being which is the support or subject of the *being* of the accidental. Hence the analogy in question is one of intrinsic attribution or proportion. The accidental is not an ultimate subject of *being* but merely its relative subject and, as such, refers intrinsically to the ultimate subject.

From these considerations it follows that the accident may be described in relation to its supporting subject as "that to which it pertain to be in something else."

Essence of Accident. The essence of the accident is, therefore, an essence only in a secondary or analogous sense. It is the further determination of an essential determinateness which is not yet fully determined in itself. Therefore, it presupposes the essence in the primary sense, i.e., that through which the subsistent being is what it is. The essence of the accident is not the quiddity of a being but rather a further state or quality, in the broad sense of the term, of a being which already possesses a quiddity.

Essence and "To Be" of Accident. The essence of the accident does not coincide with either the accident itself or the subsistent being. The finite subsistent being *is* not fully identical with the accidental perfection, but participates in it to the measure of its growing subsistence or its growth in becoming more itself. For this reason the subsistent, as support, is really distinct from the accidental.

Likewise, the "to be" of the accident does not fully coincide with the proper "to be" of the subsistent being. One could think that "to be in this or that accidental way" would be an addition to "to be in the subsistent way," e.g., "to be running" would be added to *being*-man. The objection, however, against such a view is that "to be" as "to be" cannot receive any positive enrichment, it is not further determinable or perfectible in any way.[8]

8Cf. no. 41.

For this reason the enrichment in *being* implied by the accidental determination of a subsistent being should be understood in this way. The proper "to be" of a finite being is only a limited participation in unqualified *being*. Therefore, the finite can more intimately participate in the fullness of *being* through enriching determinations which take away its indeterminateness and derive their determining capacity from *being*, which of itself says perfect determinateness. This growth of participation in *being* is the fuller unfolding and result of the *virtus essendi,* the inner power of *being*, which was already implied in the "proper to be" of the subsistent being and therefore is not an addition of "to be" to "to be."

69. *The Categories in General*

Necessity of Categories. Metaphysics does not only analyze the general modes of *being*, but examines also how these modes are analogously particularized.[9] For in the primordial experience of the one who raises the metaphysical question, a multiplicity of real finite beings comes to light and this multiplicity demands an explanation in the light of *being*. Such an explanation should pay attention not only to the universal interconnection but also to the fundamental distinction of the beings if it is to clarify the ground from which their possibility, reality, and necessity arises. Hence the fundamental structure of the world given in experience has to be critically analyzed before a decision can be taken with respect to the absolute ground of this world. True, the detailed study of perceived beings belongs to the positive sciences of experience. Nevertheless, if metaphysics is to raise its problems in a satisfactory way, it will need both the general critique of perception and the hierarchical classification of perceived beings according to their "regions" or general modes of *being*.

Thus one cannot simply stop with the assertion that every subsistent being has an individual essence and that this essence, as nature, is the foundation of its self-explicitation in accidental determinations. An attempt has to be made to assign an order to the essences, to give a general classification of subsistent beings according to their generic and specific nature.

As soon, however, as one asks *what* each being is, we depend on the manifestation of this whatness in "howness," of the essence in attributes and especially in accidental determinations.[10] By way of

[9]Cf. no. 28.
[10]Cf. no. 58.

observing the accidents we are able to construct "regions" of subsistent beings. It is important, therefore, to fix the most fundamental
accidental modes of *being* in concepts and to propose a hierarchy of
accidental categories.

Meaning of Category. By categories or predicaments we mean
fundamental concepts which are positively distinct from one another
without being mutually opposed in the strict sense and irreconcilable,
but merely juxtaposed, and under which we can classify finite beings
in their particular modes of *being*. As fundamental concepts, the
categories are as general as possible. However, they are not absolutely
general or transcendental,[11] for they are distinct fundamental modes
of *being* which may be found in the finite being and therefore have
above themselves the idea of being as applicable to finite beings. They
are analogous realizations of this idea and the most general diversifi-
cations of everything which experience shows us to be possible, real,
or necessary.[12]

Substance and Accident. When one attributes to a subsistent
finite being a mode of *being,* this mode may express, first of all, the
whatness or essence of the being in question, that which makes it
what it is. In that case this mode of *being* is the mode of *"being in*
itself," proper to the subsistent being, and falls under the category
"substance."

It may happen, however, that the mode of *being* does not express
the whatness but, presupposing it, further determines what the condition is of that which is already this or that. Such a mode of *being*
does not constitute the being *"in* itself," but is something *belonging to*
this determined being, something *of* that which is already constituted
this or that being. Such an accidental mode of being is called
"accident." The accident or the "being-something-of-something"
does not form a single category but is divided into a plurality of
predicaments.[13]

---

[11]Cf. no. 52.

[12]What is imagined or thought to be falls indirectly into the corresponding
category of the real; what is purely a being of thought is a logical relationship
with a foundation in reality and indirectly pertains to the category of relation
(cf. nos. 34 and 165).

[13]In a very general sense, *how* (*poion, quale*) may be placed alongside *what*
(*ti, quid*), and the accidental essence, as distinct from the quiddity, may be
called *"howness"* or quality. However, if this is done, quality in its broad
and analogous sense as applicable to all accidental determinations should be
carefully distinguished from quality in the strict and proper sense as a
special category.

Logical and Ontological Accident. The term "accident" used for the non-subsistent modes of *being* according to which the subsistent being unfolds itself may give rise to the impression that we have to do here with accidents lying wholly outside the essence, incidental forms of appearance which could just as well have been different or even entirely absent. This impression arises because the term "accident" is transferred from the logical to the ontological order.

In the logical order of predication *any thought content whatsoever* can be made the subject of a judgment about which one may ask which predicates belong to it "esentially" and which accidentally or by chance. The logical acicdent is a mode of predication[14] in which a thought content receives a determination that is neither its "essence," in an analogously broadened sense, nor flowing from its "essence" of necessity. Every science seeks to separate what pertains *per se* to its object from what belongs to it only "by accident," e.g., what is essential to a triangle or other figure, to a phlegmatic or choleric temperament, from what is irrelevant to it. This purification is performed by means of the phenomenological method of variation. In a rudimentary form this method was already practiced by Socrates and Plato when they attempted to determine the essence of courage, justice, etc.

Ontology, on the other hand, starts with the ultimate subjects of *being,* concrete subsistent reality as being in the primary sense. It asks itself in which fundamental modes this being can be. Thus it places alongside the mode indicating *what* the being is the modes that express how, how much, and in relation to what it is. These modes presuppose that the being is already determined in its essence and express what "accedes" to the subsistent being without being this subsistent being itself—in other words, they express something pertaining to the subsistent being.

These non-constituent but "inherent" modes of *being* are rooted in the essence and refer to it. For:

1. There are accidents which of necessity flow from the essence, so that the essence cannot exist without them. They are called properties.[15]

---

[14]Cf. no. 83.
[15]Cf. no. 83.

2. All accidents are actuations of a capacity given with the essence and flow from this capacity even if they arise under certain external conditions or influences.[16] Activities show this very clearly.

3. All accidents modify the subsistent being itself which through them becomes different.

4. The *meaning* of the accidents lies in the dynamic infinity through which the finite being is directed to becoming more and more "itself"; hence the *value* of the accidents lies in the enrichment and broadening which they give to the subsistent being. The measure in which a being attains its purpose or natural good is found in its "accidental" perfection.

70. *The Categories According to Aristotle*[17]

The following summary is meant only for orientation purposes and not as a derivation of the categories. It is only in the process of developing metaphysics that it can become clear which are the most fundamental distinct modes of *being,* how their distinction and number are discovered how they are to be arranged in orderly fashion, and what scope should be assigned to each category.[18]

1. Aristotle calls the first category *ousia,* which literally means beingness. Sometimes this term has the formal-abstract meaning of the essence of the subsistent being, sometimes the formal-concrete meaning of being in the primary sense or subsistent being.

Next, he distinguishes:

2. Being as dispersed in parts outside parts through *quantity.*

3. Being as determined in itself through *qualities.*

4. Being as referring to other things in *relations.*

5. Being as actuating its reference to others through transient *action.*

---

[16]Cf. no. 100.

[17]Concerning the categories in Aristotle, cf. L. de Rijk, *The Categories of Being in Aristotle's Philosophy,* Assen, 1952; I. van den Berg, *Logica,* vol. I, Nijmegen, 1946, pp. 150-179.

[18]Undoubtedly, the system of ontological categories or supreme modes of *being* shows a certain connection with logic and especially with grammar, which distinguishes nouns, adverbs, numbers, prepositions, verbs, etc. Nevertheless, it should be clear that ontology has to rise above the distinctions existing between various languages and investigate the essential structure which in different languages finds different ways of expression.

6. Being as undergoing the action of others in being acted upon, or *"passion."*

7. Being as finding itself somewhere in the order of *place*.

8. Being as "located" in the order of *time*.[19]

Value of the Categories. Not all these logical categories or predicaments have the same ontological value, for the mode of predication does not always simply coincide with the mode of *being*. However, this coincidence usually does occur when a subsistent being is denominated by a concept expressing the essence of this being or a determination which belongs to it intrinsically; in other words, in the categories of substance, quantity, and quality. It is disputed whether the relation of one being to another being adds a new mode of *being* to the ontological foundation of the relations.[20]

Regarding the Aristotelian categories of action, passion, where, and when, they denominate a being according to a concept that does not express a positive mode of *being* pertaining to it intrinsically. The denomination in question is extrinsic and based on the relationship of cause and effect, or of the spatial or temporal order one being has to another.[21] These four determinations also Aristotle classifies as categories, because they can be correctly predicated of beings and because they find their ontological foundation in the modes of *being* expressed by the first four categories. In themselves, however, they

---

[19]To these he adds in two texts:

9. The *posture* (*situs*) as the reciprocal situation of the parts of a being within its place, e.g., seated, lying down.

10. The immediate surroundings or garments (*habitus*) as the reference of a being to what is has "with" or "on" itself, e.g., vested, shod, armed.

[20]Cf. no. 164.

[21]That the Aristotelian categories of action, passion, where, and when should be conceived as extrinsic denominations is explicitly asserted by Thomas Aquinas in his *Comment. in Physica,* bk. III, nos. 321-323. After explaining that the modes of *being* reveal themselves in the modes of predication, he continues: the third manner is "when something extrinsic is predicated of something by way of denomination," i.e., something is denominated according to something else that is non-intrinsic to it. This something else is either the cause or the measure. Cf. *De potentia,* q. 7, a. 10, *ad* 8: That according to which a thing is denominated does not always have to be a real intrinsic form, but it is sufficient that it be *grammatically* expressed in the way of a form. A man, for instance, is called "working" according to the operation which he executes in others, or "clothed" according to the clothes he wears. Cf. also *Summa Theol.,* p. I, q. 37, a. 2. Thus it appears that Thomism wants to be a very critical realism which does not lightheartedly recognize all predicates as indications of real modes of *being*.

do not add any new intrinsic denominations to the beings of which they are predicated.

Consequently, the fundamental categories are substance, quantity, quality, and relation. But quantity presupposes the corporeity or materiality of the beings which we experience. It is less fundamental for finite being as such than are substance, quality and relation.

71. *Activity as the Guiding Principle in the Ordering of the Categories*[22]

The accidental categories have to be derived from experience, especially with respect to the division of their particular manifestations. When we ask ourselves in which accidental determinations the dynamic infinity of the finite being manifests itself first to us, we should keep in mind that self-explicitation as enlargement of the subsistent being comes about through the actuation of the being-together with beings of different modes which is radically present in the finite being.[23]

Thus to become more what one is means to be more related to other beings. The more intimate the relation is, the more also the others are to some extent present *in* this being, and the more also this being is to some extent present *in* them. It is by participating in the others and making them participate in itself that a being overcomes its non-identity with them and that their mutual opposition is replaced by communication.

Two Aspects of Activity. The actuation of the relationship to the others originates, on the one hand, in the finite subsistent being itself, for the nature of this being gives rise to a tendency. On the other hand, it depends on the others which communicate their own perfection to the being in question. With respect to the first point, we speak of action, doing, or activity, in the broadest sense of the term; with respect to the second, of being acted upon, passion, or passivity. Both condition the origin of accidental perfections.

Thus activity has to be understood in two ways—1) as the self-actuation of a being, albeit under the influence of a communication

---

[22]Louis de Raeymaeker expresses that activity is the guiding principle in the ordering of the categories in this thesis: "Finite being, insofar as it is active, is composed of substance and accidents as really distinct from one another." Cf. *Metaphysica generalis,* Louvain, 1935, p. 162.

[23]Cf. no. 63.

from the others; 2) as actuation of the others insofar as this being communicates itself to them.

Activity and the Categories. If activity and passivity are conceived in this broad sense—which is wider than the Aristotelian categories of action and passion, for these indicate only the mutually transient interaction of bodies—they can act as a guiding principle in the derivation of the categories. For we know beings from their activities and behavior, we argue from these activities to their permanent dispositions or active potencies, and we deduce from these their innermost nature. Thus the following distinctions appear to be most important:

1. The essence of the subsistent being.

2. Its powers, dispositions, and abilities.

3. Its activities.

4. Its relations.

Now that the problem of the categories has been raised, the various forms in which beings unfold themselves and influence one another, the forms of activity and passivity, have to be discovered through a more elaborate description of experience.

The foundation for this task was laid in a preceding chapter when perception was described.[24] Perception is an activity of attention, of the "I who am," but presupposes that the perceived places itself in my presence and influences me. Thus it reveals also the passivity of the perceiver and the activity of the perceived being. Through a continued analysis of perception the fundamental accidental modes of *being* will manifest themselves and in this way prepare an orderly derivation of the grades of *being* proper to subsistent being.

---

[24]Cf. no. 48.

CHAPTER FOURTEEN

PERCEPTION AS A TEMPORAL ACTIVITY

72. *The Perceiver as the Principle of His Perception—Active Potency*

Knowledge unfolds itself in a plurality of perceiving activities which do not fully coincide.[1] The basis for this distinction between the acts of perception lies in this that the perceived beings do not present themselves all at once and fully to the knower but only gradually and that the perceiver in his activity depends on the presence of what he perceives, for to perceive is to accept cognitively.

Provisionally leaving aside this *passivity* of the perceiver with respect to the changing presence of perceived beings, we will concentrate here on the undeniable experience that the perceiver unfolds himself in a plurality of perceiving *activities*.

Self-Identity in Perception. The act of perceiving is an act of a perceiver. I perceive, i.e., I direct my attention to the perceived, and I am actively with the perceived. In a certain sense, I am even identical with this act, for I *am* perceiving, and to perceive is my mode of *being*.

However, the acts of perceiving are many. They are distinct and succeed one another. On the other hand, they also fuse into one another, for perception is constantly developing since the cognitive situation which cannot remain static is constantly altered. Every perception is an event, something that takes place. As such, it has not only a distinct beginning and end, but is also divisible "to infinity" into parts that are always different, for not a single part perdures in the same condition. Perception is a continuous process.

Nevertheless, this "infinitely" divisible plurality of activities is not wholly without identity. The acts are connected not only because one presupposes the other, but also because each one of them is identical with the same "I."

It is I who perceive first *this* and then *that*. The I is the same and not another. I know that I am the same who knew *a*, knows *b*, and eventually will know *c*, and I know this because I, who perceive

---

[1]Cf. no. 48.

130

what is actually present, remember that I perceived what is no longer actually present, and expect that I will perceive what is not yet actually present.

But if I am one and the same and, nonetheless, identical with a plurality of acts that do not coincide but exclude one another, then there must be a certain distinction between me *as* perceiving *this* and me *as* perceiving *that*. I do not remain entirely the same. Within my identity with myself there has to be an opposition between me and my successive distinct acts. In one respect I have to remain the same, and in another I have to be constantly different.

I am the same as to my subsistent being, as this determined being with this individual essence. I am constantly different in my activities, which are further accidental determinations according to which my participation in *being* unfolds itself.

My activities are distinct from me within the unity of my *being*. As non-subsistent determinations, they are to be attributed to me as the subsistent being. I am the subject which supports these acts.

However, this is not all. The expression "I perceive" has also a more profound meaning. Perception is not only something *in* me and *of* me, but also something *from* me. It originates from my essence, considered as nature; it finds in me the source from which it emanates. I *do* the act of perceiving.

Active Potency. The fact that I successively make *many* acts originate from me reveals that I, as their permanent origin, dispose of them to a certain extent, I have a certain superiority over them.

For it should be clear that, when I do a certain particular act, I have the power and am able to do this act. Since, however, all acts have to originate from one and the same self-consistent nature, I am by virtue of this nature permanently enabled to do acts, even though certain conditions have to be fulfilled if certain acts are to be done.

This permanent ability to perceive (to hear, see, etc.), as such, is a perfection and not an imperfection. It is rooted in my *being* as a subsistent being with a certain essence.

Accordingly, the necessary—though perhaps not yet sufficient—ground of my being-active lies in my being-subsistent. And if we call the activities "acts" in the more original sense of the term, we may call being-subsistent in a certain essence an "act" in a derivative way through analogy of intrinsic attribution, for this being-subsistent is the ground of being-active.

If this terminology is used, the *activity* will be called perfect or "second" act, while the term "initial" or "first" act is reserved to indicate the *essence* of the subsistent being. In this sense we may say that a being is active in the measure in which it is in act.

Nature and Active Potency. My essence or nature and my capacity for perceptive acts do not fully coincide. For my essence is actuated by my "to be" as being-subsistent. But my being-active is a "to be" in an accidental sense, in a plurality of successive acts, and therefore a continuous modification of my being-subsistent, which remains identical. Hence the immediate principle of being-subsistent, my essence, is distinct from the capacity, which is the immediate principle of my being-active.

Consequently, we must admit, that the capacity of perceiving (hearing, seeing, etc.), as the immediate subject and principle of activity, which flows of necessity from my essence or nature, is distinct from this nature, although it corresponds with it.

Such a capacity is a perfection in the order of accidents, but a perfection which results from the nature and cannot be separated from it. Although the capacity is not the essence, it is an essential property through which the subsistent being can exercise its activity as by means of an instrument.[2]

Such a capacity is called a faculty, operative power, or *active potency.*

With Aristotle, we may distinguish between:

1. *Energeia* or activity, which is act in the original sense.

2. *Dynamis* or faculty, which is potency in the original sense.

Active Potency and Possibility. This *dynamis* or power is not a static property, although it is of a permanent nature. It is "dynamically" directed to activity and does not rest until its being-able is changed into action. It is a being-able in the sense of having the power to do the action. As the principle from which the action proceeds, it does not indicate a want but a richness, for it flows from the substantial essence which is the "first" act of real being.

Accordingly, the active potency itself is something real and should not be confused with pure possibility, i.e., "being able to be" without being-real, which is opposed to being-real.[3]

---

[2] Ontologically speaking, the capacity is an accident, but logically it is a property and not an accident. Cf. no. 83.
[3] Cf. no. 31.

73. *The Problem of Becoming and Change*

Twofold Relationship of Subsistent Being and Action. Provisionally we may leave undecided whether or not active potency and activity are essentially distinct. Nevertheless, the experience that acts of perception succeed one another and are mutually exclusive makes me conclude with certainty to their distinction not only from my being-subsistent but also from my capacity to act.

On the other hand, the acts are not perfectly distinct from the active potency, for they are not in an autonomous way but are variable, present or absent, non-subsisting determinations within the identity of my *being*. Thus, although they originate from the subsistent being and its power, they remain contained in this being and its power as further perfections of it.

The question arises of how it is possible that the subsistent being with its power is at the same time the source of the activities and their bearer or subject. As their source, the being is superior to its acts and gives them their perfection and "to be," as their subject, however, it is inferior to them and receives from them a further perfection, a more determinable mode of *being*. On the one hand, then, the power is the necessary ground of *being* for the activities emanating from it, but, on the other, it is of itself still imperfect and for its perfection needs the activities that are distinct from it.

This twofold relationship can be explained only by the fact that of itself the power is not the sufficient ground of the activities, although it is a necessary ground. Of itself it is not fully able to realize the actions. These actions require also an explanation on the basis of other origins on which the power is dependent—namely, both the beings that are to be perceived, which have to present themselves to the power, and a higher power which is already active and which makes the perceptive faculty go into action.[4]

Successive Non-Identity of the Identical. Without as yet inquiring more in detail about the passivity of the active power of perception, we may consider the activities precisely insofar as they are accidental, present or absent, determinations of the power which is determinable through them. The question to be asked here is: How is it possible for one and the same subsistent being and its permanent power to be determined in ever different ways by a multitude of successive activities?

---

[4]Cf. no. 95.

In this way we arrive at the more general problem of becoming and change. Under what conditions can the *permanent unity of the subsistent* be reconciled with the changing plurality of the accidental? Or in more general terms, how is the successive non-identity of the identical possible?

Heraclitus and Parmenides. Should we perhaps make a choice here between becoming and *being?* Does not *becoming* express constant otherness, while *being* says permanent identity? Is there not a clear contradiction between non-identity and identity, so that one of the two has to be considered mere appearance: either the apparently indubitable experience of ever-changing becoming or the apparently equally indubitable insight into the permanence of *being?*

In an indubitable primordial experience we perceive that becoming is a fact: being changes all the time. Hence Heraclitus identified the real with pure becoming and admitted nothing else than the continuous transition of events into their opposites, a pure process, in which the only thing permanent is the law of change itself.

In an indubitable primordial insight *being* reveals itself to us: being is, and being as being is itself, one and undivided in itself, it excludes all otherness from itself. For this reason Parmenides identified *being* with pure permanence. If *being* is *being,* and non-*being* is non-*being,* then what-is can never not-be, and what-is-not can never be. Hence a transition from non-*being* to *being* or from *being* to non-*being* is unthinkable and therefore impossible. And, as others added later to his theory, even if we accept a plurality of distinct beings, every being is *what* it is, and as being-this it cannot be now or ever other than it is. Thus it is fully determined and not further determinable and consequently it is immutable.

Temporality. Being and becoming, however, are not contradictorily opposed, for to become is not not-to-be but a mode of *being*—namely, coming to be.

On the other hand, *being* may not be identified with permanence, for to perdure is not a condition of *being* but only a mode of *being*—namely, to be lasting.

To become and to perdure are two modes of *being* which are opposed to each other. But, apart from *being,* they have another feature in common—namely, both are modes of being-successive, i.e., of temporality.

For temporal is whatever can change. Hence "to be temporal" can have two modes: that of being-changing and that of being-non-changing. To perdure is the being-non-changing of the mutable, and to become is the being-changing of the mutable. Thus to become and to perdure are opposed as two modes of temporality.

Motion. We cannot yet raise the problem of becoming in its full scope. Especially the question whether a subsistent being can begin to be or cease to be cannot yet be considered.[5] The experience of changing perception, whose conditions of possibility we are now investigating, allows us to speak only about the coming and ceasing to be of non-subsistent activities. This improper coming and ceasing to be is a continuous and gradual transition of one and the same subsistent being—the perceiver—from one accidental determination to another. The perceiver changes constantly: he is becoming different now, he became different, and he will become different, but he does not lose his substantial identity in the process. Such a continuous transition from one state to another without stability is sometimes called *motion,* in the broader sense of the term.[6]

Change or motion does not exist *in* itself as a subsistent being. It is motion *of something* that changes—namely, concrete being. It is that "through which"—in a formal sense—the changing being changes. The concept of change or motion is a formal-abstract concept.

The concrete being which changes, the subject of the change is what is permanent. For it is the same being which first is in this and then in that condition. Only that which remains can become different without becoming something different.

Here another question arises. Does it not imply a contradiction to say that the permanent changes, i.e., that the changing is the permanent, for to change means not to be remain, and to remain is not to change? Thus change would seem to be impossible.

74. *The Changing Being is Composed of Passive Potency and Act*

That what changes is permanent can be a contradiction only if it would become different and remain the same in one and the same respect. If change is to be possible, a distinction has to be made in that which changes between one respect in which it remains what it

---

[5]Cf. no. 88.

[6]In its narrowest sense motion means locomotion or movement from one place to another. Cf. no. 79.

is and another respect in which it does not remain what it is but becomes what it is not.

Thus the ground on which change is possible lies in this that the changing being is not fully identical with itself but contains an opposition.

To express the opposition which must be present in the changing being if change is to be explained, Aristotle[7] gave a second meaning to the concepts of act and potency. This meaning, however, is still connected with their most original sense of activity and active potency or power.

As we have seen, even the substantial essence of a being, as the basis of activity, may be called act in a derivative sense, for from the nature of a being's activity we obtain knowledge about its essential perfection. We may, therefore, in a very general sense call "act" anything through which a being in some way or other is perfect.[8]

Whatever is, to some extent is perfect[9] and therefore "in act." The changing being also is at every moment *what* it is at that moment and in that respect "in act." However, it is not yet what it *will be* through the change. Nevertheless, could one maintain that it is in no way whatsoever what it will be in the future? Is it totally unrelated to the perfection which will give it a further determination?

Receptivity of Active Potency. When I reflect on my perception, I must say that the power or active potency has already a certain relationship to possible future acts of perception,[10] not only insofar as these acts can emanate from the power, but also insofar as the power can be determined, completed, and perfected through these acts. While in the first respect the power is in active potency and superior to its acts, it is inferior to them in the second respect, for it is "in capacity" to be actuated by these acts at the proper time and under the proper conditions. If we do not take the term "to receive" as "to receive from another" but merely as being-open-to the influence of the act as a determinating and perfecting principle, we have to say that the power is receptive to the acts to which it is in capacity and

---

[7]The difficulties of Aristotle's doctrine of act and potency are analyzed in detail by S. Smeets, *Act en potentie in de metaphysica van Aristoteles,* Louvain, 1952.

[8]In many texts Aristotle uses the term *entelecheia* instead of *energeia,* which in its original sense indicates activity. *Entelecheia* means having the terminal status of completion and perfection or also this perfection itself with respect to its content.

[9]Cf. no. 40.

[10]Cf. no. 171.

to which it is oriented. Therefore, the unfolding active potency is related also in a receptive way to its acts, with respect to its being-the-subject of the acts it is also in *passive potency.*

Thus we arrive at a new meaning of the term "able." Between "able" as the pure possibility that something will be and "able" as having the power to *do* there is another "able"—namely, a possibility pertaining to the real itself insofar as the real is directed in an initial way to being-in-act as something which it is really capable of *becoming.*

However, the power, which is constantly developing in distinct and successive acts, is not merely in a permanent passive potency to its acts. It is always already actuated to some extent, although it is in transition from one act to a further act. This transition or change itself is not yet explained by speaking about being-in-potency.

The Essence of Motion. What is the "essence" of continuous change or motion in the broader sense of the term? It is "already" a certain actuation of the initial receptivity. It is already an act, but not yet the crowning, perfecting act in the strict sense through which a being *is* what it first was in capacity. For what is changing or *becoming* is still on the way to this final act and thus it is still in potency.

Continuous change, then, actuates the capacity of a being in such a way that this being, precisely because of this actuation, stands open to further perfection. At everyone of its moments, which can be multiplied "to infinity," such a change is the act of a being in potency precisely insofar as through this act it is still in potency.[11]

Thus change is an act of a being in such a way that the being in question in and through its being-in-act is at the same time in-potency. For it is on the basis of an incipient actuation that the perspective of further actuation arises. The potency of the mutable is a complex potency which initially is directed to the successive phases of change and only through them to the properly intended final act.

Change, therefore, can be understood by means of a modification of the concepts "power" and "actuality" into "passive potency" and "act." The question now is how these two are related, i.e., whether or not they are distinct from each other.

If a changing being by the very fact of *being* in a certain act is in potency to further actuation, change means that potency and act

---

[11]See Aristotle's definition in *Physica,* bk. III, chs. 1-3; *Metaphysica,* bk. XI, ch. 9. The various views about this definition are explained by A. Kockelmans, "Aristoteles' definitie van de verandering en de Scholastiek," *Tijdschrift v. Philosophie,* vol. 17 (1955), pp. 663-689.

coincide. They are change itself, but change is not in one and the same respect both potency and act. Change is an act in comparison with the preceding stage of imperfection, but a potency when compared with the succeeding stage of further perfection. Change or motion in the broad sense, as such, i.e., as the transitional stage between initial imperfection and final perfection, is an imperfect perfection.

No Complete Identity of Being, Potency, and Act. When through change a being passes from being-in-potency to being-in-act, one can no longer say that it is "in-potency," i.e., in a state of being merely in capacity without being actuated.

Has, then, the changing being become fully identical with the act to which it was in potency? Not at all. Despite the change, it has remained itself, and "of itself" it is not in-act, for otherwise it would always have had to be "in-act." Hence we must say that the changing being "of itself," i.e., insofar as it remains identical, does not include the act without, however, positively excluding the act. Although it is not always "in a potential state" with respect to the act but sometimes "in an actual state," nevertheless even in the actual state *it is not of itself* or according to its essence *the act* which actuates it. This act is an accidental perfection "through which" the being in question is now "in-act."

Accordingly, a being which of itself is only in potency to an act is never fully identical with the act. When a being passes into *being* "in-act," there is a distinction in it between that through which "of itself" it is only in potency to the act and that through which it has become "in-act." Thus its structure contains two principles—the *potency* to the act and the *act* itself. Although these two are to some extent identified in the one actualized potency, they do not fully coincide. The potency is the permanent fundamental principle which must be conceived as the immediate *substratum* or bearer of the realized accidental act which "forms" the being and therefore is also called *form*.[12]

---

[12]Accordingly, we should distinguish the following:
1. To be in-potency, as a state, i.e., not yet to be in act.
2. To be in-act, as a state, i.e., no longer to be in potency.
3. The potency itself, as the permanent principle or substratum.
4. The act itself, as acceding principle or form.

It is better not to speak of a "transition from potency to act." The correct expression is "transition from being-in-potency to being-in-act.

We may ask whether the principle of excluded middle, between "to be" and "not-to-be" there is no middle ground, applies to change-able being, because concerning this being, insofar as it *remains itself,* one can neither affirm act—for then it would always be in-act—nor deny act—for then it would never be in-act.

The reply is: act must be denied of it, provided the negation be understood not as positively excluding act but merely as of itself not including act. Nevertheless, the potential being is not indifferent to its act, and therefore it not meaningless to affirm act of it provided, however, one be willing to have recourse to analogy of attribution and extend the use of the term "act" also to any orientation to act.

75. *Changing Being as Temporal*

A Broader Sense of Perception. The distinct acts or states in which the changing being is are individually together with the permanent subject, but they are not together with one another. They exclude one another in a continuous transition from not-being-actual to being-actual, and vice versa. The changing being is actually only in one state. Thus the question arises how it is possible to *perceive* that one state is distinct from the other if they are not actual at the same time, for only the actually present is perceptible.

This distinction can be perceived only if perception is given a broader meaning and no longer restricted to the actually present. Only a being which retains cognitively present in itself states that are no longer actually present is capable of seeing together distinct states, as states which are not together, of one and the same permanent being.

I am capable of such knowledge because of the knowledge I have of my perceptive acts:[13] my perception of the actually present is internally connected with the memory of having perceived what is no longer actually present and with the expectation of what is not yet actually present. By means of these three acts joined together in unity, which we may call *"perception in a broad sense,"* I know that I "remain" in the modification of my acts, I know their distinction as well as their connection. If we call the powers of memory and imagination "internal senses" because they make what is really absent present to me to some extent in my knowledge,[14] we may say that the internal senses effect a being-together

[13]Cf. no. 72.
[14]Cf. no. 124.

of what in the real course of events is never together but only successively.

Time. The experience of time occurs when in perception, in the broad sense, the successive stages of the changing being are not considered precisely according to their internal determinations, but only according to their *order of succession with respect to "before" and "after."* The experience of time is a perception in the broad sense in which a being, knowing that it remains itself in its mutually exclusive yet merging states of perception, arranges these distinct phases in orderly fashion and "counts" them.

This perceived time, therefore, is neither the changing being itself nor its change or motion, viewed as to its content, but it is the being-in-transition or motion precisely insofar as this *is* a being-dispersed in a plurality of "infinitely" divisible mutually exclusive phases. Accordingly, time is motion insofar as it is numerable with respect to priority and posteriority, or the numerability of motion according to "before" and "after."[15]

In the perception, broadly, conceived, of time, the continuous parts of time are always separated by an indivisible "break," the "now" of actual perception. This division gives rise to the past and the future, both of which are divisible "to infinity." The now-moment, however, cannot have any parts, for any such parts would be either past or future. On the other hand, unlike past and future, the now-moment has actuality.

Temporality of the Changing Being. If only the present moment has actuality, time, as the being-dispersed, and therefore numerable, of the changing being, does not have any actuality except insofar as it is present somewhat in this moment. This presence, however, is only *potential.* Hence the basis for the temporality of a being lies in the incapacity of its potency or power to pass all at once and fully into act. Precisely because the changing being is always *in transition* from being-in-potency to being-in-act by means of intermediary, imperfect, "infinitely" divisible acts, it cannot realize the actuality of its *being* all at once and fully, but only in a series of mutually exclusive, yet merging nows. The perfections to which this being can be further determined are always possessed by it merely on a kind of "touch and go" basis and according to a constantly changing

---

[15]Concerning the definition of time, see Aristotle, *Physica,* bk. IV, ch. 11, 219 b2, and St. Thomas' *Commentary,* no. 580.

pattern. It actuates the plurality of its possibilities only in such a way that they are not actually together with one another.

Actuality of Time and Change. Both change and time, therefore, have their complete *being,* the unity of their parts, only *potentially* or dynamically *in* the momentaneous actual state of the changing being insofar as the states through which this being has already passed are still somewhat present to it in their after-effects and the states through which it has not yet gone are already somewhat present to it by making their influence felt.

The *complete being* of change and time is fully *actual* only in the perceiver who in the actuality of his knowledge through memory and expectation makes the no-longer-actual and the not-yet-actual phases of change and the passage of time be together with the real actual state at this moment. This, it would seem, is what Aristotle and St. Augustine meant when they said that time would not "be" without the "soul."[16] The dispersed and mutually neutralizing temporal phases of past and future, which in themselves would rather indicate modes of non-being, are modes of *being* when the "internal senses" relate them to the present and thus to each other, so that they are to some extent identified with each other and with the changing being.

Nevertheless, the remark must be made that, when the temporality of a being is explained in the sense that distinct determinations or states of *being* are not *actually* together, this should not be conceived as if these states are *not at all* together. For in a certain degraded sense all successive and mutually exclusive states are together as states of one and the same subsistent being. Even dispersion in time is a kind of being-together, albeit a deficient kind. We express this togetherness by saying that the past is virtually present and the future potentially present in the actual *now* of the being, independently of their actual perception.[17]

As we will see, there are grades of lesser or greater dispersion in time corresponding to the grades of *being* proper to material, living, and knowing beings.[18] In the higher grades of *being* the plurality

---

[16]Concerning the relation of soul and time, see Aristotle, *Physica,* bk. IV, ch. 14, 233 a21-29 with St. Thomas' important *Commentary* no. 629; Plotinus, *Enneads,* bk. III, ch. 7 (about eternity and time) ; St. Augustine, *Confessions,* bk. XI, no. 33. Cf. J. Moreau, "Le temps selon Aristote," *Revue Philosophique de Louvain,* vol. 46 (1948), pp. 57-84 and 245-274; M. de Tollenaere, *Een philosophie van de tijd,* Louvain, 1952.
[17]Cf. no. 87.
[18]Cf. no. 87.

is more synthesized in unity than in the lower grades, but even the temporally most dispersed beings still reveal a certain connection or unity of their moments of time, a remote form of history.

The same applies to the dispersion of temporally separated beings and events. We not only live together with our contemporaries, but there is also a certain togetherness of all present beings with all past and future beings, because all communicate not only in *being,* but also in the actual and final interconnection which unites everything that happens in time through a common bond.

For this reason a changing being which *knows* about its own temporality and therefore has its past and future not merely potentially present, but through memory and expectation also more or less actually present has overcome the dispersion of time in a higher way than a changing being which is not aware of its temporality. For in the actual *now* of consciousness even the receding past and the approaching future states are to some extent actually present as known, they are joined together and no longer wholly opposed to each other. And to the extent that this mutual integration takes place, the participation in *being* is less fragmentary and more integral.

Being and Time. No mode of non-being, no indetermination, pertains to being *as* being, for a being, to the extent that it is, is determined. Hence to-be-not-yet and to-be-no-longer do not belong to being as being. Being, as such is, is neither past nor future, but determined, i.e., actual and present. To the measure in which it is, the perfection of a being is "present" to it. Presence is a transcendental property of *being.*

From this it follows that the measure of temporal dispersion is inversely proportioned to the participation in *being.* Participation in *being* is a participation in self-presence, i.e., in a-temporality or eternity.[19]

---

[19]Thomas Aquinas sees time as a participation in "duration." Duration, according to him, is a transcendental property of *being* whose absolute realization is called *"eternity,"* and whose degraded modes are *"aevum"* and *"time."* Cf. *Scriptum super Sententiis,* p. I, d. 19, q, 2, a. 1.

CHAPTER FIFTEEN

PERCEIVED CORPOREAL BEINGS. THE GENERAL CONDITIONS OF SENSE-PERCEPTIBLE BEING

76. *Introduction*

Dependence of Sense Perception on Objects. My imperfect knowing has the mode of becoming, i.e., it develops in time. It unfolds itself in a plurality of successive acts which both originate in the cognitive power and are received in it as further perfections of this power.

The reason for this temporality of the knower lies in this that he is not pure self-consciousness, but arrives at self-knowledge only through being perceptively open to the many other real beings which reveal themselves only in a gradual way.[1]

Thus the undeniable experience of my temporality reveals to me that the change of my perceptive acts is based on the changing presence of the perceptible *objects*. Even the very act of directing my attention to these acts implies a reflex attitude which includes in its essence a spontaneous directedness toward the objects as a condition and starting point.

Accordingly, no matter how much perception, as activity, originates in the subject and its power, this very origin is conditioned by the objects as presenting themselves to the perceiving subject. Perception is based on experience and therefore depends on the perceived.

It should be clearer now why the perceptive power is not merely an active power but also, in a sense, a receptive or passive potency. Of itself, the power is still incomplete. It is completed and perfected through the active collaboration of the self-revealing beings which make an impression on the power.

Sense Experience Does Not Reach the Essence. Although the beings that are to be perceived, *as* beings, are always to some extent present to the knower, this implicit pre-knowledge does not extend to the explicit apprehension of their individual mode of *being*.

Even when they present themselves to experience in the course of the cognitive process, the ignorance of their individual essence does not cease entirely. Even then, as will become increasingly clear,

---

[1] Cf. no. 48.

143

we do not have an *intellectual* intuition of *what* each of them is in its own original way and as distinct from the other individual beings.

The reason is that these beings present themselves to us only in a *lower* order of experience (which remains to be described in detail). Although this experience is concerned with the individual, it is not yet knowledge of their essence, but is based on the impression the beings in question produce in a particular situation in accordance with their *external* character. This order of experience is called "sense experience."

The Three Moments in the Integral Act of Perception. Nevertheless, intellectual knowledge of *being* penetrates the experience of the senses. It raises this experience to the level of understanding, even though it remains true that it does not go further than the essential characteristics which this individual shares with others.

Thus one may distinguish three partial acts in the integral act of perception:

1. The *more* passive moment of being affected by the individual "external appearance."

2. The *more* active moment of abstractly forming general concepts.[2]

3. The *more* synthetic moment of connecting the general with the individual or of referring the idea to experience—the judgment.[3]

77. *Sense Experience*

To experience something sensitively or to sense is founded on a certain immediate presence with the other, but this other is not yet opposed to the subject *as* other, *as* object. Thus, although to sense is not to know intellectually, it possesses "something" of an indubitable intuition. However, this intuitive element is very restricted. It is concerned only with the immediately present, insofar as this is accepted in pure receptivity and is not yet brought to bear on the non-present or conceived *as* being this way or that way. Every active elaboration, on the other hand, of what is immediately present, made by the inner senses and the intellect, is subject to critical revision.

Nevertheless, it is only *in* the active elaboration of the experienced that we become aware of our sensitivity. Whence it is only

---

[2] Cf. no. 83.
[3] Cf. no. 85.

on the basis of the more integral cognitive acts of perceiving and thinking that we can speak about sensitive receptivity or sense experience as the source from which perception and thought arise.

The Role of Touch. Sense experience is a contact with our surroundings, a being "formed through" and "present with" the other, even before the subject becomes aware of the other as an opposite. The unity of the other and the subject is present in the most simple and most fundamental fashion in the sense of touch, provided touch be understood not as a tactile reconnoitering but more as a being "struck" by a touching object exercising some "pressure" on the subject.

The other senses are based on this receptive contact as more differentiated and complex modes of being "in touch" with the surroundings. Contact is fundamental not only in the sensing of hardness or softness, heat or cold, etc., but also in the sensation of odor and flavor.[4] True, especially in the "higher" senses of hearing and sight there is a more developed awareness of otherness and opposition because these senses encounter the surroundings from a certain distance, but nevertheless, even in them, contact is not lacking, although it is mediated by something intermediary.

Thus, it is the sense of touch which will reveal to us in the most simple way the *general conditions of the sensible,* the characteristics proper to all that is sense-perceptible, the so-called "common sensibles."[5]

78. *The Corporeal as Extended. Space*

Extension. Contact means to touch. But this touching occurs in time, for the coincidence of the one who experiences with his surroundings undergoes modifications: a whole becomes present one part *after* another. Nevertheless, these parts are characterized by

---

[4]Concerning the fundamental importance of the sense of touch, cf. Aristotle, *De anima,* bk. II, ch. 2, 413b 4; ch. 3, 414b 7 (touch is the sense of food); ch. 9, 421a 20 (man excels all other animals in his sense of touch and therefore his discrimination is more exact), cf. St. Thomas' *Commentary* nos. 484 and 485 about the proportion of the sensitive disposition to affective life and intellect; bk. III, ch. 12, 434b 12 (every body is tangible); ch. 13, 435b 2-25, cf. St. Thomas *Scriptum super Sententiis,* p. II, d. 1, q. 2, a. 5, *De anima,* q. 8, *Summa Theol.,* p. I, q. 76, a. 5; q. 91, a. 3, ad 1.

[5]Aristotle, *De anima,* bk. II, ch. 6, 418a 17, names as common sensibles motion, rest, number, figure, and size. The fact that, alongside spatial extension, he does not mention explicitly temporal extension but merely implies it in motion and rest probably has to be explained by this that he was thinking here primarily of the external senses and not of the internal ones.

their being-together in time, for around the area of actual contact there extend areas of past or future contacts, experienced as at a certain *distance,* which even now still remain or even now already await touch.

This dispersion in "parts alongside parts" which are together in time, yet lie "outside" one another, is called "extension" or "dimensive quantity." Extension constitutes a fundamental condition of perceptibility.[6]

Potential Parts. If the parts of the extended whole lie merely alongside one another, their extremities would only touch without fusing and thus they would be contiguous. However, we must admit that the extended whole manifests itself at first to us as a certain unity, in which one may observe distinction without separation. Hence the "parts" of the extended whole are continuous, i.e., there are no divided and actually present parts, but the whole is divisible into parts "to infinity." Consequently, the parts are only "potentially" parts, and each of them in its turn consists of potential parts. It is only by means of this potential multiplicity that Zeno's old antinomy of extension can be solved.[7]

Number. If the extended whole is actually divided, there arises a plurality of actual parts that are contiguous. This plurality is homogenous, for each part is extended and itself divisible in the same way as the whole. Counting the plurality takes place by means of the number (discrete quantity) which indicates how many actual parts there are.[8]

---

[6]Just as dispersion in succession or temporality, dispersion in simultaneity or extension cannot be defined without an appeal to experience. When extension is said to imply "parts outside parts," the mode of *being* proper to the extended is described by means of the concept "outside." This concept points to a sense intuition and should be distinguished from ontological non-identity or otherness. In other words, there is question here of "empirical" concepts—namely, those which conceive the conditions of experience as general modes of *being* of the experienced object (cf. no. 84).

[7]Cf. no. 87.

[8]The plurality in question arises through the *repetition of the same.* Therefore, it consists of homogeneous units which can be counted in the proper sense by adding them to one another. However, this counting requires that abstraction be made of the differences of the parts, such as their places and qualities. Accordingly, the term "the same" applies univocally to each of the many.

In a previous chapter we spoke about the plurality of beings *as* beings. This plurality arises from *participation in the same in constantly different and particularized ways.* Because each being differs from the others precisely in that in which it is similar to them—namely, "to be"—no abstraction can be made of these differences. Hence the term "the same" pertains to the many in a constantly different, analogous and merely particularized way. For this reason

Corporeal Beings. The being which we experience in our sensation as possessing distant "parts outside parts" at the same time
and which extends in the three dimensions of height, width, and
length is called "corporeal being" in the broadest sense of the term.
Thus, we may say that the senses are directed to the corporeal according to the various *qualities* presenting themselves to us on its
extension and especially on its *surface* or outer side. For this reason
we call the senses which aim directly at present corporeal beings
"external senses" in opposition to memory and expectation.[9]

Sensing Implies Being-Corporeal. If sensitivity presupposes contact, the dispersed parts of the corporeal that is being experienced
must touch the experiencing subject, as is most simply and most
clearly the case in the sense of touch. But if this is true, then the
sensitively experiencing subject, as such, must also be corporeal, for
the boundaries of the experienced object are together with its own
limits.

Accordingly, a sensitive knower is a corporeal being which in
certain corporeal parts (sense organs) is influenced by its surroundings and reacts to this influence through sensitive knowing. Therefore, the "I am" of a sensitively knowing being is not merely a vague
knowledge that he is, but the consciousness that he is a certain body
in certain surroundings.

Experience of One's Own Body and Surroundings. Nevertheless,
the experience of one's own body differs from that of the surroundings. In the reflection which begins in the inner senses and reaches
its term in the judgment "I am" of our intellectual knowledge, the
parts of the body are experienced as organs of the same being which
knows that it is. On the other hand, it is very difficult to answer
the question whether the surrounding beings, or at least some of them,
present themselves to us directly as self-knowing beings. In any case,

---

beings cannot be counted in the proper sense, and their plurality is a participated and therefore deficient mode of unity (cf. nos. 39 and 62). In opposition
to this "transcendental" plurality we call the other plurality "predicamental." It
belongs to the category of quantity and is the special form in which transcendental plurality manifests itself in corporeal beings.

[9]Cf. no. 123. Through mathematical abstraction the dimensions of length,
width, and height may be considered purely in themselves, separately from the
sense-perceptible qualitative "natural" body whose dimensions they are. In this
way our imagination and thought give rise to a product representing a so-called
"mathematical body."

In addition, the term "body" is often used in a narrow sense to indicate the
natural, living body of animal and man (cf. no. 115).

we have to maintain that they reveal themselves to us always also in a certain "exteriority," in a being-extended according to perceptible qualities.[10]

The experiencer appears to himself as a central whole composed of organs "out of which" his senses aim at what touches, is nearby, or more distant. Thus the extended is experienced from a perspective that is determined by the perceiving body. It reveals itself, as we may now say, in an "exterior appearance" in which it *itself* is present but only in a limited respect.

It is to be noted that the standpoint of the perceiver is in motion and that the perceived object does not always turn the same side to the perceiver. In other words, the perspective undergoes modifications. However, these various perspectives are given a first interconnection by the internal senses, and then intellectual knowledge gives rise to the unity of "the same object" which presents itself successively to the subject in different perspectives.

Place. Extended beings are situated with respect to one another; they are located. Place or *locus* is the innermost boundary, conceived as motionless, of the container and the content.[11] Hence place is essentially relative. To be *somewhere,* the extended being has to be touched by another extended being. This contact may be direct, and then there is question of place in the strict or immediate sense, or indirect, and then we have to do with place in the broader sense, as determined by means of other located beings, e.g., John is in this room, this house, this city, or this country.[12]

Space. By space is meant the distance intervening between extended beings in which there is room for other beings.[13] If reciprocally-situated beings are said to form a space in this way, the space is just as real as the extended beings themselves are. If, however, we represent space to ourselves as still empty extension in which corporeal beings can be located and which we can conceive to stretch "to infinity," then this space is not something real but merely an imaginary representation. For extension does not precede the totality

---

[10]Cf. nos. 115 and 131.

[11]Cf. Aristotle, *Physica,* bk. IV, ch. 4, 212a 20.

[12]Two extended beings, therefore, which would not be in contact either directly or indirectly would not have any mutual relationship of place.

The whole of all extended beings, which is not imaginable, does not have a place. It is neither here nor there; it is not "anywhere." Hence it does not have a boundary.

[13]Cf. Aristotle, *Physica,* bk. IV, ch. 4, 211b 7.

of corporeal beings, but is consequent on them as their property insofar as these beings are one only in a deficient way and lie dispersed
in "parts outside parts."[14]

79. *The Corporeal as in Motion. Time*

Local Motion is a Common Sensible. When we determined the
conditions—namely, potency and act—which make change possible,
we limited ourselves to the continuous change in our perceptive acts
themselves.[15] We may now remove this restriction, for it has become
clear that perception changes under the influence of the object which
reveals itself constantly in different ways. The cognitive changes *refer*
to changes in the surrounding bodies as well as to the central sensitively experiencing body as presuppositions required by their
occurrence.

Just as extension or quantity is the foundation of the various perceptible qualities, so also change in the local relationships is the
foundation of the variable experience of qualities. For the sensitive
influence of the perceived on the perceiver is based on the occurrence
of contact, and such contact takes place because of a change in the
situation or local relationship.

Consequently, change of place is a common sensible, a general
condition of sensitive perceptibility.

Continuous Character of Motion. Change of place is usually called
"motion," in the sense that a body is on the way from "here" to
"there." It is motion in the narrowest sense of the term.[16] Locomotion,
just as place itself, is relative—namely, in reference to something that
is thought of as immovable.

Because locomotion, e.g., approaching or going away, is based on
continuous extension, it is continuous change *par excellence.* All
places between the starting point and the terminus have to be passed
successively. But between each point and the next there is a plurality
of intermediary points "to infinity." Hence the problem of the con-
tinuum returns here in a pressing way. Again, however, its solution
demands an appeal to a "potential" plurality of points that are already
passed or still to be passed. Locomotion is the act of a transient being

---

[14]Cf. no. 87.
[15]Cf. no. 74.
[16]Cf. no. 73.

as transient, an act which, as a transition, implies potency in its very essence.[17]

Continuity of Augmentation and Qualitative Change. The extension of a body can increase or decrease with respect to the extension of the surrounding bodies which is conceived as constant. Augmentation or diminution is continuous because of the local motion implied by it.

The sensible qualities proper to each of the sense are subject to modifications. In opposition to motion in the narrow sense, which refers only to local motion, the change of these qualities is change *par excellence* and in the narrow sense of the term. For "motion" modifies only the local relationship of beings, while change means that these beings become other with respect to their "content."

Change in quality may be continuous—namely, insofar as it is based on quantity.[18]

Time. Time has been considered hitherto as the numerability of the changes occurring in the perceptive acts.[19] Meanwhile it should have become clear that the perceptible, the corporeally mutable also is temporal.

Even what is in motion in the strict sense of the term, the continuously extended as such, is more dispersed in temporal parts that do not coincide than the perceiver who, despite everything, is

---

[17]Cf. no. 74.

[18] 1. Continuous changes always have an intermediary, as can be seen most clearly in local motion. Every state is in contrary opposition to a subsequent state; e.g., between hot and cold there is lukewarm, between red and blue lies yellow. However, such transitions may be considered also as transitions from, say, not-here to here, not-cold to cold, not-blue to blue. Taken in this way, the opposites are contradictories and have no intermediary. The transition from one to another is discontinuous, and the changes are not successive but instantaneous. The moment of becoming coincides with that of being.

2. Perhaps there are also positive accidental qualities whose transition into one another is immediate, so that their change is instantaneous. In any case, the change by which something becomes not merely "other" but "something else," i.e., essential change, is instantaneous. In a broader sense such a change is still called "change" and even "motion," for here, too, there is transition from the state of being-in-potency to that of being-in-act (cf. no. 88).

3. In the broadest possible sense, the metaphysician speaks of "being in motion" even when there is no longer question of a temporal transition from being-in-potency to *being*-in-act—namely, when a being, even if it did not originate in time, does not possess its act by virtue of its very essence. For even such a case still implies that a potency is perfected through its act. Thus, for instance, every finite being, even if it be supra-temporal, is not its "to be" through its essence but participates in it, and in this sense is "moved" to its *being* (cf. no. 101).

[19]Cf. no. 75.

conscious of his unity in time. Continuity, taken precisely in the sense of divisibility "to infinity" into non-coinciding parts, is proper to the reality of the extended. Through the extended reality, this continuity belongs to locomotion, and through locomotion it pertains to the most "extriorized" and most homogeneous time, which is the numerability, in the strictest sense,[20] of locomotion according to priority and posteriority of potential parts.[21]

Perception of Time and Motion. Time, therefore, together with locomotion, is a general condition of sense-perceptibility.

Motion and time, however, cannot be experienced except by means of the internal senses.[22] Sense acts, then, are never pure acts of the external senses alone, for what is sensitively experienced is always already somewhat synthetized through memory and expectation. How, indeed, would it be possible to arrive at any awareness of spatial distance if one were not aware of the possibility to traverse this distance? Accordingly, motion and time are required for the awareness of spatial distance. A purely instantaneous impression of the actually present, which would not imply an awareness of transition and therefore of time, would not be experience, i.e., knowledge, but could be called only an infra-sensitive biological connection.

True, one may ascribe an intuitive moment to sense experience because and insofar as the subject is passive and coincides with the self-impressing object. However, here it should be recalled that this intuitive moment alone, because of the non-intellectual character of its presence in "exteriority," is insufficient to qualify as "knowledge," but needs to be completed through the synthetizing activity of the subject and consequently through an opposition of subject and object.

80. *The Corporeal as Moving and Moved. Transient Action*

In sensitive contact corporeal beings impress the organs of the perceiver through their qualities in constantly different ways. This ever-changing mode of impressing the perceiver finds its origin

---

[20]Cf. no. 78.

[21]Thus there are grades of dispersion in time. The corporeal as such, insofar as it implies extension and locomotion, is most dispersed of all. Time is already more "interiorized" in living bodies, and still more so in knowing beings which are more or less conscious of their own *being* and self-identity in time.

[22]Cf. no. 75.

in the modifications of the local relationships between the organs and their surroundings, inasmuch as both the perceiver and the perceived are constantly changing their place. However, the perceived beings change also with respect to one another both in place and extension as well as in qualities.

Do Changes Influence One Another? We have considered all these motions and changes as transitions from being-in-potency to being-in-act. But is the transition itself sufficiently explained by means of the dynamic "nature" proper to each of these changing bodies? Even if we assume that the perceived has the power to transfer itself from one place or state to the next, this active potency would still reveal passivity insofar as it would be the support of the new states and relationships which perfect it. Thus the question arises whether such a self-actuation is not connected with the condition of the bodies present to it in mutual contact. In other words, is it not conditioned by these other bodies? Is it not true that we experience an *order* which interconnects movable and changeable spatio-temporal beings? Do we not experience a mutual dependence?

Let us make the question more precise. Previously, we have learned to see perception in a broader sense, in such a way that it implies, alongside instantaneous external contact, also retention and expectation by means of the internal senses. But perception has to be conceived still more broadly, because knowledge of *being* always penetrates even the moment of sensitive experience. In the light of of the intellect we always see what appears to us as something that already is, no matter in what way; we ask about the mode of *being* or the essence of what appears, about the reason why it appears and why it appears in this or that way.

It is not subject to doubt for the perceiver that what appears either is itself something that is, or belongs to something that is. The corporeal world manifests itself as a world of beings which are subsistent to some extent, however much degraded this subsistence may be. But to investigate which beings of this world are subsistent is an entirely different matter, which immediate perception does not at all clarify. Nevertheless, in our intercourse with the world we arrange the spatial whole in orderly fashion into parts behaving with a certain unity. We consider such parts as separate objects, without committing ourselves as to whether they are agglomerates, subsistent units, or merely distinct parts.

Thus the question regarding the order of the events occurring in these parts of the spatial whole may be formulated as follows: Do we perceive that the change in certain parts has a relationship of dependence to the change occurring in other parts? Do we perceive that the one influences the other?

Immediate Evidence of Mutual Influence. Perception does not merely, as Hume's empiricism claims, refer to spatially dispersed and temporally successive parts. At least in certain cases it offers us immediate evidence that the condition of one part changes not merely *while* but *because* another, contactually present part, is in a certain condition. We perceive that corporeal objects influence one another in their becoming-different.

This assertion applies first of all to locomotion, even though such motion is always merely relative. Corporeal objects are not only "in motion," but also move actively something else, and in turn are "moved" by them. They exercise pressure not only on the perceiving body but also on other perceived bodies. They move one another. Even if we admit that certain objects, e.g., living beings,[23] move themselves by virtue of their own nature, we observe and "see" at least that there are also some objects which begin to move because another object has a certain motion; e.g., a moving billiard ball through collision sets a ball "at rest" in motion.

Thus in our perception every being-in-motion presents itself as a being-moved passively and consequently refers to an active motion. To move and to be moved may coincide to some extent in self-movement, but they do not always coincide. Sometimes we perceive immediately the active motion of one part and the passively being-moved of another.

The same applies to some qualitative changes. We perceive that certain objects become different as a result of the spatio-temporal position of other objects. Hence the change in the former is dependent on the influence of the latter. We speak, for instance, of illuminating and heating, and ascribe the origin of noises and sounds to the friction or collision of objects.

Causal Interaction is a General Condition of the Sense-Perceptible. Just as sense experience, taken in itself and in the strict sense, does not explicitly manifest the subsistent nature of objects appearing in this experience, so also it fails to reveal explicitly their causal inter-

---

[23]Cf. no. 111.

relationship. Nevertheless, at least certain privileged perceptions evidently imply a causal connection in their spatio-temporal inter-dependence.[24] In such a case it is the intellect which collaborates, in continuity with the external and internal senses, in integral perception, thus brings to light the concrete causal connection, and obtains an *insight* into the influence on the basis of experience.

Concrete causal interaction also, therefore, belongs to the general conditions of the sense-perceptible, even though it cannot be immediately experienced in the same way as extension and temporality are experienced. Subsistence, which likewise is not immediately perceptible, and causality are something *pertaining* to the sensitively experienced and are discovered by reason in the object experienced. Though they are not directly or *per se* sensible, they are sensible indirectly or *per accidens* and as such they fall under integral perception.

Transient Action. We perceive changes in objects, transitions from being-in-potency to being-in-act, which find their ground not merely in the nature of the object in question, but occur also because other objects act on it in a spatio-temporal order of contact.

The change of the changed object must be considered as a "passion," i.e., as a being acted upon, insofar as the object is changed passively, and as an action insofar as another object actively changes the first.

In reality there is nothing else than the change or motion itself as something *pertaining to* the changed or moved object. But this change is perceived by us as a transition and is considered in a double relationship. First of all, it is considered as supported by, and received in a passive subject—namely, that which is changed or moved by something. As such, change constitutes the category of passion or being-acted-upon. And we denominate the changed being after the agent from which it receives the change. Secondly, it is considered as effected by, and dependent upon an active source—namely, that which changes or moves something. As such, it constitutes the category of action, and we denominate the agent after the changed being which receives the change from the agent.

---

[24] A. Michotte has shown, from the viewpoint of empirical psychology, that we can have in our perception immediate "impressions" of relationships and especially of causal relations. Cf. his works "La causalité physique est-elle une donnée phénoménale?" in *Tijdschrift v. Philosophie*, vol. 3 (1941), pp. 290-328; *La perception de la causalité*, Louvain, 1946.

Accordingly, the imperfect act which change is, is an act of both the changed and the changer. It is *in* the recipient, the one that is acted upon, but *from* the agent.

Transient Action and Perception. The transient action of one thing on another is a form of activity, but in a wholly different way from perception. Perception is a perfection of the perceiver; it not only originates in the power of the perceiver, but is also received in it as a final act, by virtue of which the perceiver cognitively possesses the perceived. It is called an "immanent action."[25]

Transient action, on the other hand, taken in itself, is not a perfection of the agent. A being which influences another must already possess the perfection or act that is to be communicated. Its action is the perfection of the other, the recipient, which receives and supports the action. For this reason such action is *in* the recipient, although it comes *from* the agent.[26]

---

[25]Cf. no. 93.

[26]Cf. Aristotle, *Physica*, bk. III, ch. 3 and St. Thomas' *Commentary*, nos. 297-325; A.D. Sertillanges, *La philosophie de St. Thomas d'Aquin*, Paris, 2nd ed., 1940, vol. I, pp. 104-113.

In this chapter we have investigated the conditions common to everything perceived by the senses—namely, extension, temporality, active and passive locomotion, and qualitative change.

The discovery of these conditions, as conditions, does not take place in experience itself but through intellectual reflection. Nevertheless, they are concretely experienced in the individual externally appearing events which show order and interconnection in place, time, and interaction. The fact that this concrete order and connection are experienced means that the inner senses are always involved in external experience. However, the explicit recognition of the causal order of action and reception takes place in the concepts and judgments of analytic reason (cf. no. 105).

Hitherto the content itself of the many data of experience, the various perceptible *qualities,* have not yet been spoken of. It will have to be done now. Their order also is prepared by the inner senses and brought to completion in the intellect, which wants to know the perceived as being and conceptually attempts to grasp its essence or nature. It is in the experiential judgment that the perceiver pronounces himself as to *what* the individually experienced beings are in themselves. Thus it is here that the perceptive activity finds its ultimate completion.

CHAPTER SIXTEEN

PERCEIVED CORPOREAL BEINGS. KNOWLEDGE OF ESSENCE

81. *The Sensitive "Average" or Phantasm*

Of themselves, the external senses would offer nothing else than a pure plurality of disconnected and always different individual experiences, for the individual cannot be repeated. However, the plurality in question is always framed in a kind of unity by the inner senses, which arrange the experiences in orderly fashion not only according to time and place but also according to their *qualitative* similarities and dissimilarities. Similar contents of experience are brought together, and dissimilar ones are kept separate. From a complex of temporally successive similar experiences the inner senses construct an average or schema which can serve as a first criterion for subsequent experiences.[1]

Nevertheless, the average picture or phantasm, which is the product resulting from the assimilation of a complex of experiences by the inner senses, remains a representation of something *individual* located somewhere in time and place, no matter how vague, how flexible and adaptable such a representation may be. The phantasm, therefore, can never be recognized unqualifiedly as "exactly the same" in a new datum of experience.[2]

82. *The Sensitively Experienced as Being*

Knowledge of *being* pervades sense experience from its very beginning. For this reason we know that the experiential plurality constitutes an internal unity, because whatever is already experienced and whatever is still to be experienced somehow *is* (even appearing is

---

[1]Cf. no. 124.

[2]Concerning the permanent role of the phantasm in human knowledge, cf. Thomas Aquinas, *Summa Theol.*, p. I, q 84, a. 7 and the penetrating commentary of K. Rahner, *Geist und Welt*, Innsbruck, 1939, pp. 1-34. See also St. Thomas, *in Boethium de Trinitate*, p 6, a. 2, ad 5: "The phantasm is the principle of our knowledge as that from which the operation of the intellect begins, not as something passing, but enduring as a kind of foundation of intellectual activity." Heidegger considers the problem on the occasion of the transcendental schematism and the imagination in Kant. Cf. *Kant and the Problem of Metaphysics*, Bloomington, 1962.

a mode of *being*). And we know that through the immediately experienced we enter into contact with the ultimate individual subsistent bearers of *being,* for the non-subsistent, as "accident," refers to
the subsistent. Even the "external appearance" is "something pertaining to" a subsistent being which to some extent manifests itself
in the appearance.

In the experiential judgment the subject refers to the individual
experienced here and now, and the predicate attributes *being* to it.
However, the judgment remains confused and imperfect as long as
the proper mode of *being* of this individual is not made more precise.[3]

We do not have this individual mode of *being* present in an immediate intellectual intuition,[4] but conceive it as a particularization here
and now of an intelligible mode of *being* which, in principle, can pertain also to other beings in different places and at different times.
When in the experiential judgment we affirm that "this here and
now" is "in this way," we mean, of course, that this mode of *being*
makes this being be *what* it is, but this being and the whatness
attributed to it do not cover each other so completely that the essence
expressed by the predicate cannot pertain also to other beings. In
other words, we seize the individual datum of experience in a *universal
concept,* i.e., a concept that in principle can be affirmed of many.
Although we possess knowledge of the essence, this knowledge is very
imperfect, because we do not know the individual as individual but
only in general characteristics.

83. *The Universal Concept.*

Nominalism. Nominalism recognizes general names but claims
that these names do not express one and the same thought content
present in many. Names represent only a collection of singular
representations which the experience of *this* individual recalls to our
mind. For this reason nominalism considers the "universal" judgment as a collection of singular experiences of the past which justify
only a probable expectation of the future. Knowledge of a universal
essence is excluded because there is no universal essence to be found
in many: everything in the individual is singular.

However, nominalism contradicts itself when, on the one hand, it
admits that the one individual reminds us of other related and similar
individuals, thereby constituting classes or groups, and on the other

---

[3]Cf. no. 53.
[4]Cf. no. 76.

hand, it denies universal concepts. Whoever knows similarity distinguishes it from differences. This is precisely what happens in the formation of a universal concept by means of abstraction.[5]

Moreover, nominalism is unable to assign meaning to the experiential judgment. We attribute the same predicate to this being and to that one, e.g., this is red and that is red. But if the term "red" has one meaning, it should be clear that this meaning is not entirely different in the two cases, for otherwise there would be pure equivocity.[6] But by using the same term, we want to express that just as *this* is red so also *that* is red, in exactly the same sense. Hence the term expresses one and the same thought content. This whole content is realized in each of the subjects with a certain identity: this *is* a "something that is red." But, then, the universal term does not express a collection, for a collection cannot be predicated of each of many with identity. The thought content is not singular, for the singular is itself and not something else and pertains only to one individual. Therefore, there is an opposition between what is experienced and the concept, and this opposition is that of the singular to the universal.

Radical Realism of Ideas.[7] This system considers universal concepts as exact representations of real beings existing "in themselves." By way of analogy to sense experience with its intuitive character, it sees concepts as passively related to intelligible reality. Usually its proponents appeal to Plato's distinction between essences which contain nothing but themselves in pure identity and the beings of the extended, changing, and temporal world, which through participation are merely imperfect imitations of these essences.

Such a view cannot be simply rejected when there is question of real particularizations or limited realizations of a thought content which in itself is unlimited.[8] But it is powerless to explain the origin of concepts which are predicated of many through a certain identifi-

---

[5] Cf. no. 51.
[6] Cf. no. 54.
[7] Radical realism was the most controversial solution offered for the problem of universals, which began to draw attention even before the eleventh century (Odo of Tournai) on the occasion of Boethius' commentary of Porphyry's *Isagoge*. It seems to have been defended for some time by William of Champeaux (*ca.* 1070-1121). Peter Abelard (1097-1142) prepared the way for the correct solution, later formulated by Thomas Aquinas. Cf. F. Sassen, *Geschiedenis der patristische en middeleeuwse wijsbegeerte*, Nymegen, 4th ed., 1950, pp. 95-99; M. de Wulf, *History of Medieval Philosophy*, London, 1952, pp. 140-146, 170-172, 194-205.
[8] Cf. no. 57.

cation in exactly the *same* sense and, therefore, with *equal* perfection. Such univocal concepts are not more perfect than the beings of experience, for they originate through a process of abstraction. They are the products resulting from our active elaboration of sense experience and make sense only as predicates of experiential judgments, but not outside these judgments.[9]

Conceptualism reacts against the realism of concepts and seeks the origin of universal ideas in the knower. Thus these ideas do not represent modes of *being* pertaining to beings as they are in themselves. We may distinguish two kinds: empirical and idealistic conceptualism.

Empirical Conceptualism. This viewpoint, which was defended by the old nominalists, such as William of Ockham, sees the universal concept as a (natural) symbol, a term,[10] which sums up the beings of experience and may be used in logical supposition for each one of them, but does not contain anything of *what* these beings are. Concepts are pure aids in classification; they have a certain extension but no comprehension.

This viewpoint correctly emphasizes the gulf separating the richness proper to the stream of experience and the penury rewarding our efforts to express this experience in concepts. Knowledge by means of universal concepts is, in a way, an impoverishment. Moreover, we do not even have any adequate intuitive knowledge of the universal essence of beings.

Nevertheless, concepts are more than mere symbols. To some extent they contain, albeit only in an "intentional" way, what they signify. If to understand means to know how beings are, there must be a certain identity of the concept, taken as to its thought content, and the being that is understood through the concept.[11]

Idealistic Conceptualism. This Kantian form of conceptualism seeks the origin of the universal validity proper to the concept in the subjective structure of the knower, who organizes the sheer plurality of the "raw material," supplied by sense impressions, according to *a priori* forms and thus constructs the unity of the object known.

---

[9]Sometimes authors speak here of a "logical participation" of the individual in the species or of the species in the genus. However, this is an improper terminology, unless one leaves the realm of univocity and enters that of analogy to view the individual as a limited realization of the fuller idea expressing the species. Cf. no. 90.

[10]Whence it is also called terminism.

[11]Cf. no. 128.

Hence concepts do not express beings as they are in themselves, but only as they have to appear to our limited capacity of knowledge.[12]

This viewpoint justly affirms the validity of universal and necessary judgments. However, it considers the senses and the intellect too much as independent sources of knowledge. It leaves unanswered the question why certain data of experience and not others are placed in certain categories. An appeal to a preparatory synthesis made by the inner senses does not suffice, for then the question simply returns on another level. For this reason it is more correct to admit that the datum of experience is never a sheer plurality, but contains the potentiality of being understood by the intellect in certain ways because it is a plurality of "beings," no matter in what way these beings are. In other words, *the actual percept of the senses is potentially intelligible.* But then the activity of the intellect consists in discovering the mode of *being* proper to the being which manifests itself to some extent "as it is" in sense experience, for even to appear *is,* and is something of what appears in the appearance.

Mitigated Conceptual Realism. This is the same as moderate conceptualism. It admits, on the one hand, that the universal concept is opposed to the individual being but, on the other hand, it maintains the identity of the two. The identity is found in what is understood by the concept, its content; and the opposition concerns the way in which this content is understood in the concept and realized in the being.

The content of our original concepts is a mode of *being,* a characteristic or "essence," in the broadest sense of the term, and applies to the whatness not only of subsistent being but also to that of non-subsistent being and of everything which is in any way whatsoever.

The characteristic which constitutes the content of the concept is present in self-identity in both the intellect and the experienced being, but there is a difference in the *modes* of its presence:

1. In the judgment the characteristic is identified with the being in question: "this *is* that." However, the identification is not perfect. The characteristic does not express the being in its full concreteness but only in a certain respect. Together with others, this characteristic is concreted in this individual and therefore present in it in a singular way.

---

[12]Cf. no. 25.

2. The intellect discovers that there is a gulf separating the characteristic as it is, on the one hand, realized in a singular way in the individual, and as it can be considered, on the other, in itself from the viewpoint of its content alone. "In itself" the characteristic is neither singular nor universal.

3. Because the characteristic, considered in itself, abstracts from the other characteristics which have individualized it in this being, it possesses the possibility of being present also in other individuals "to infinity," i.e., the characteristic, *as* "de-individualized" through total abstraction in the intellect, is universal.[13]

4. If the intellect reflects on the way in which the concept is present in the intellect, on the concept's ability to be present in many, and connects the concept with these many as possible subjects of predication, then *formal* universality arises as the product of thought. In this reflection the intellect is no longer directly concerned with the characteristic as the content of its concept (so-called "first intention"), but with the concept itself as a means, produced by the intellect in its own way, to understand beings according to their characteristics (so-called "second intention").[14]

Modes of Predication. When the intellect reflects on the characteristic precisely insofar as it applies to many, it sees that the characteristic can be said of a being in one of the five following ways:

1. As its universal essence which is logically not yet fully determined but further determinable—the genus.

2. As the further logical determination of the universal essence—specific difference.

3. As the further determined universal essence—species.

4. As a characteristic which flows with logical necessity from the universal essence—logical property.

---

[13]Cf. no. 51.

[14]As it is in the individual, the characteristic is not universal, although some call it a "material universal" because it is the foundation of the general characteristic. Taken as the content of the concept, the characteristic has universality as its property and is sometimes called a "direct universal." Universality itself, as the purely thought relationship of the concept to the many of which it may be predicated, is the object of logic and often called a "reflex universal." However, the terminology of the various authors is not constant. Cf. no. 166.

5. As a characteristic that is logically fortuitous with respect to the universal essence—logical accident.[15]

84. *The Insufficiency of Univocal Universal Concepts*

Sometimes authors convey the impression that, despite the fact that we have no intellectual intuition of the individual, we are able to arrive at a full understanding of the universal essence, the specific whatness of the subsistent as well as of the accidental, by means of an abstracting simple apprehension. Is this view correct or should we lean somewhat in the direction of conceptualism by expressing ourselves more prudently?[16]

Empirical Concepts. We are not concerned here with the concepts formed through reflection on our own activities and passivities, but with those which arise from "external perception," and which through abstraction reveal the intelligible aspect that is potentially present in the sensitively experienced object. In other words, we are concerned with empirical concepts.

The seed of such a concept is already present when I judge that "this here and now" *is* "as I experience it," thereby referring to my actual impression. However, indubitable as such a judgment may be, its intelligible content, the mode of *being* proper to "this here and now" is still undetermined. To arrive at a determined concept, I have to see this content of experience in connection with the whole of what can be experienced and assign it its proper place in this whole. The connection in question is prepared by the schematic representations or phantasms. However, it reaches its perfection only when a limitless plurality of possible experiences is unified in a single unvaried concept. In such a concept we conceive, under reference to exemplary experiences, a "mode of *being*" which always and everywhere "to infinity" could be found again in new instances.[17]

---

[15]These five fundamental modes in which a predicate expresses something about a subject are called "predicables." They are derived from Porphyry's *Isagoge.* As divisions of the logical "reflex universal," they should carefully be distinguished from the *predicaments* or categories of the ontological "direct universal." Especially the predicable accident should not be confused with the predicamental accident. Properties which flow with logical necessity from the universal essence are ontologically accidents (cf. no. 69).

[16]Concerning the insufficiency of our concepts, see P. Rousselot, *L'intellectualisme de S. Thomas d'Aquin,* Paris, 3rd ed., 1936, pp. 90-171, especially the note on pp. 106-107.

[17]Without wanting to suggest that such concepts are the most fundamental univocal concepts—for sense experience is broader and richer than what is often understood by the term "the objects of the senses" (cf. nos. 110 and

Content of Univocal Concepts. What is the content of such univocal concepts? Do they merely summarize our experiences, our impressions, so that at most, through reasoning, we are able to form concepts about surrounding beings as causes of our impressions? Or do they directly refer to the surroundings "as they are in themselves" independently of our experiences?

We may ask whether it is legitimate to make such a contrast. Because of the receptive character which experience undoubtedly possesses, it must be admitted that univocal concepts express a thought content or characteristic which pertains to the surrounding beings, but only insofar as they act upon our organism. This influence is conditioned by both the organic state of the experiencer and the state of the extended being which is experienced. The influence is in that which is influenced—action is in the recipient[18]—and consequently depends on the mode in which it is received.

However, this mutual compenetration of the active object and the receptive subject in "causal unity" is *something real,* a real determination of both at the same time. For this reason their contact can be understood in the judgment as "something that is," as an object of true knowledge. Starting from the state he shares with the perceived, the perceiver reverts to himself, opposes the active element to himself as something which influences him, and ascribes the qualities, experienced as modes in which corporeal beings can influence sensitive beings, to these "objects" as their modes of *being.*[19]

The *active qualities,* as they are correctly called, therefore, would not exist, except potentially, if these sense organs did not exist. Nevertheless, they are *real* characteristics of the experienced beings, because the modes in which these beings reveal themselves to us and which depend on us to whom they reveal themselves, are modes in

---

131)—we may name the following as examples of empirical concepts: the various forms, colors, flavors and their properties; also concepts of affection such as agreeable and disagreeable, pleasant and unpleasant, easy and difficult, useful and harmful; likewise, concepts based on perceptions of space, motion, and time, e.g., far away, close by, slow, quick, earlier, later.

[18]Cf. no. 80.

[19]Even the general conditions of sense-perceptibility are modes of *being* of the corporeal, but only *as* they are experienced by a being, which itself is extended, moving, temporal, and endowed with such and such external and internal senses. This assertion applies to extension, but even more to motion, and most of all to temporality.

which these beings are—namely, modes in which they *are* revealing themselves.

Moreover, the active qualities are important for us not only insofar as we receive them in our experience, but especially insofar as this reception is the foundation of our self-unfolding activity with respect to our surroundings.[20] This importance is sensed through the estimative power,[21] but it also finds expression in the formation of our concepts, for we understand and name beings according to their value for our activity.[22]

Even in everyday life, but more deliberately in science efforts are made to understand corporeal beings indirectly through characteristics possessed also independently of the conditions existing in our perceiving organs. The convergence and divergence of the various senses play an important role in these efforts. Nevertheless, this process of objectivation shows fully how difficult it is to separate what is objective from the subjective element in our perception.

Indirect Knowledge of Substantial Essence. Both in spontaneous observation and in critical reflection on this observation all characteristics attributed to corporeal beings remain in the sphere of activity and passivity and, consequently, of accidental determinations and perfections. A direct knowledge of the *substantial* whatness or *essence* of perceived beings is beyond our reach.

Indirect knowledge, however, is possible. We know that what surrounds us must be one or more subsistent beings with a substantial essence. From the aggregation of regularly combined accidental qualities we may derive a certain concept of what the principle of unity can be which gives rise to this multiplicity. In this way through a laborious process of analysis and synthesis of our experiences there gradually arise *generic and specific concepts* of substantial beings, e.g., of the various kinds of animals.

Accordingly, we know the substantial through the description of its accidentals, the essence and powers through the study of activities.[23] But even for our knowledge of the determinations of

---

20Cf. no. 100.

21Cf. no. 124.

22Cf. no. 130.

23Cf. Thomas Aquinas, *De spiritualibus creaturis,* a. 2, *ad* 2: "Substantial forms are not known in themselves, but become known to us through their proper accidents."

accidental genera and species we usually have to rely on a description of experience without knowing the specific "essence" of the accidents, e.g., of the various colors and sounds. It is on the level of mathematical abstraction that the relations between more universal and more particular concepts seems to be known best of all.

Univocal Concepts are a Posteriori *Concepts.* There is no realm in which we can simply derive specific concepts from generic concepts. The very necessity of having recourse to definitions demonstrates this point. We clarify a specific concept by reducing it to a more generic one, but have to add to it from without a new concept— namely, the specific difference—to arrive at the concept of the species. We know that the specific concept is potentially contained in the genus, but we are unable to make this concept arise from the genus as one of its possible particularizations.

Still less is it possible for us to deduce from the specific concept which individual realizations of it are possible. We do not understand the individuals from the specific concept, but form this concept from our experience of the individuals. For instance, starting from the idea of man, we are unable to understand all possible and real men in their distinct individual modes of being-man.

All this indicates that our univocally general concept is nothing but an *a posteriori* summarization of the many in a certain unity devised by our thought. Experience supplies us with similarities between existing things and we proceed to arrange these things according to genera and species. We predicate the same characteristic or essence of many. Although we know that there must be a real foundation, a *"cause of species,"* on which this similarity of many in one essence can be understood,[24] we do not understand the many on the basis of this real general cause which lets the many participate in its fullness in always limited ways.[25]

85. *The Judgment as Synthesis of Concept and Experience*

Abstract Nature of Empirical Concepts. Our empirical concepts are neither an intuition of individual beings nor even of their general substantial essence. As compared with sense experience, such concepts are, on the one hand, an enrichment, insofar as they disclose

---

[24]St. Thomas calls the real general origin of the species the "cause of the species." See, e.g., *Contra Gentes*, bk. III, ch. 65. This cause cannot be univocal, but must be analogous.

[25]Cf. no. 90.

unity and connection in plurality but, on the other, they are an impoverishment, insofar as this unity is obtained through abstraction from the individuals' differentiation and is not the real unity which makes the plurality in question come forth from itself.

For this reason our univocally general concepts, considered in themselves separately from any judgment of which they would be a part, do not yet have any cognitive value. They do not yet express any definite relation to *being* as it is "exercised" by concrete real beings, except insofar as they represent modes of *being* thought to be possible for possible beings. However, even this being-possible is merely thought and not yet explicitly attributed to the modes of *being*.

Formal abstract concepts[26] detach the mode of *being,* or the characteristic constituting their content, from every being which would be characterized by this mode. What is a constituent principle through which a being could be what it is, is as a kind of "form" detached from this being and conceived by thought as if it were a being, a quasi-subsistent "beingness." Nevertheless, the formal abstract concept shows a tendency to concretization, an implicit pointing to being in the first sense of the term, which is not that through which something is, but that which itself is, the subsistent.

Formal concrete concepts connect the characteristic constituting their content or essence, in the broad sense of substantial or accidental determination, with a being to which it pertains to be in accord with this determination. The concept "man," for instance, expresses a being to which it belongs to be in the mode of being-man, a being that is man. The bearer or subject, however, of the characteristic is indicated only in a general way in the concrete concept and not determined to this or that individual thing. Nevertheless, the concrete concept contains a tendency to individualize, to indicate the subsistent bearer who *is* in the mode determined by the conceptual content. The concept remains incomplete as long as it is not identified with the real or possible individual beings which by means of this characteristic are what they are.

Concretization of the Concept in the Judgment. The individualization of the concrete universal concept takes place in the experiential judgment in which the concept is "returned" to its origin in experience. In its most basic form the experiential judgment is a singular affirmative categorical judgment in which the subject, taken in itself,

---

[26]Cf. no. 51.

does not have any conceptual content but is merely an indication of the sensibly experienced individual, and the predicate is a more or less universal concrete concept; for instance, this is a man, that is red, this runs.

The experiential judgment does not have the foundation of its truth in itself, it is not based on the insight that the predicate-concept is of itself by absolute necessity implied in the subject, it does not rely on apodictic evidence.[27] It is a synthetic *a posteriori* judgment, which is true insofar as the concept truthfully is the intellectual assimilation of the *de facto* being presenting itself in experience and consequently the expression of this being in its general characteristics. The total abstraction through which the concept originated is thus reduced to the concrete and individual experiential starting point by means of a reflection on the phantasm. Accordingly, abstraction and contraction or concretization are the two sides of our perceptive knowledge.

Thus, our perceptive knowledge comes about through this that 1) the beings which pre-predicatively are always already somewhat present and whose modes of *being* are known only confusedly and implicitly in the idea of being,[28] present themselves to us in time and space, so that they become our guides in the formation of our concepts; 2) reflecting on the origin of our concepts, we revert to these beings to explicitate their distinct modes of *being* in a predicative way.

Reflection of Judgment on the Concept. The judgment contains a twofold reflection on the concept. First of all, the concept is understood as originating, with respect to its *form,* from the activity of the intellect. For thought images, which represent intelligible modes of *being,* arise from thinking. In forming these thought content, the intellect is governed only by the laws of identity, exclusion of contradiction and excluded middle, for whatever is non-contradictory can be thought.

However, the construction, analysis, and synthesis of separate concepts is not yet an understanding *knowing*: we do not first understand concepts—except, of course, in reflection—but *in* and through concepts we understand being. Accordingly, the concept arrives at its perfection only when it is considered as the concept of or about

[27] Cf. no. 21.
[28] Cf. no. 53.

something. It has to be attributed to a being as an intelligible mode of *being.*

Consequently, the judgment includes a second reflection on the concept. The concept is understood as owing its origin, with respect to its *content,* to sensitive passivity or receptivity. For it is only when the concept is understood not merely as an arbitrary thought construct, but as the actuation of an intelligible content which exists potentially in the sensitively experienced being, that it can be correctly understood at the representation of this being and predicated of it.

Accordingly, the concept, as it is used in the judgment, is the product of our activity of thinking. But the judgment asserts that this activity has been guided by the potential intelligibility of the being perceived in experience.

What the True Judgment Reveals. Thus it follows that the true judgment is at the same time:

1. A revelation of the *being* proper to the object known, insofar as it has been seized in the concept, which raises the sensitively experienced to the level of consciousness by actuating its potential intelligibility.

2. A revelation of the *being* of the knower, insofar as the knower in the concept understands the *being* of the object by making it participate in his own actual intelligibility.[29]

In this way we see that the judgment connects the proper *being* of the knower (the thought image he has formed) with the proper *being* of the object that is (the mode of *being* in which it participates) as related to each other as perfection and capacity. The judgment says: "As I conceive this being in the synthesis of subject and predicate, so this being is truthfully in itself."

Imperfection of the Judgment. Perfect coincidence of knower and known, of predicate and subject of the judgment, can never be reached by the judgment. On the one hand, the judgment elevates the sensitively experienced in the light of *being* but, on the other, the richness of experience is impoverished. For, as a synthesis, the judgment is a reply to a twofold question:

1. Is *this* so? Does the being indicated in the subject of the judgment fall under the extension of the predicate?

---

[29]Cf. no. 125.

2. Is this *so*? Does the predicate fall under the content of the modes of *being* pertaining to the being indicated in the subject of the judgment?

Consequently, it follows that 1) the predicate exceeds the subject and has a greater extension; 2) the subject exceeds the predicate and has a richer content.

Thus the judgment has these implications:

1. Other beings are possible "to infinity" which possess this general characteristic; the poorer the content of the predicate, the wider its extension.

2. There are other general characteristics "to infinity" possessed by this being. For no general characteristic, even if it occurs in a particularized way in a judgment, expresses the individual mode of *being* proper to this being, nor can the individual be reached by adding characteristics to characteristics, for the complex of these characteristics remains general.

It is only when reference is made to "here and now" that the universality ceases, for every place and every time of every individual is distinct from others as this and that. However, "here" and "there," "now" and "then" are not intelligible contents, but data of experience obtained by the external and internal senses.[30]

The general characteristic is predicated of the individual being only as it is experienced "here and now" ("this is here and now so"), so that there is no absolute identity between the being in question and its characteristic. Therefore, one may not exclude that this being has never been not so or that it will never not-be as it is now. Consequently, this being is mutable.

---

[30]Cf. H. Reynders "De verstandelijke kennis van het materieel-singuliere in de philosophie van St. Thomas," *Tijdschrift voor Philosophie,* vol. 12 (1950), pp. 281-316.

CHAPTER SEVENTEEN

CORPOREAL BEING AS COMPOSED OF MATTER AND FORM

86. *Proof from the Structure of Judgment*

The Dual Nature of the Judgment Has an Ontological Basis. In the experiental judgment a characteristic which of itself is general becomes identified with an individual subject. This is true for both accidental and substantial characteristics and, therefore, applies also to the substantial determination of a being called "species." The species is predicable of many individual subsistent beings. The question which we want to ask now is whether or not this dual phase of our perceptive knowledge, these abstracting and concretizing moments, indicate that the object known *itself* has a structural composition of matter and form.[1]

Such a transition from the cognitive to the real order cannot be made immediately. For the structure of the judgment arises certainly also from our defective knowledge of the individual material being. It cannot be maintained that an intellectual intuition of the corporeal individual is *in itself* impossible, for every being *as* a being must be intelligible. Therefore, the corporeal individual as *this* individual must have its own mode of *being,* although it remains true that the intelligibility of this mode escapes us.

Nevertheless, the structure of the judgment does not arise solely from our defective mode of knowing. For, with respect to cognition which is at the same time sensitive and intellectual, perceptible corporeal beings are the most appropriate or "proportionate" object. If, then, cognition is directed to beings as they are in themselves, there must be a proportion between the cognitive act and its proportionate object. Hence, if the cognitive act whereby the proportionate object is known shows a necessary structure, this structure must contain an *indication* of a necessary structure in the proportionate object. In the being itself there must, therefore, be a *ground* why it presents itself to us as a subject which of itself is conceptually empty and to which a general conceptual content is attributed. The being in question itself can possess only a degraded measure of intelligibility.

[1]Concerning the hylomorphic proof from the species-individual structure, see Andrew G. van Melsen, *The Philosophy of Nature,* Pittsburgh, 4th impr., 1961, pp. 107-153; Louis de Raeymaeker, *The Philosophy of Being,* St. Louis, 1954, pp. 155-169.

Subject-Predicate Structure and Ontological Structure. It does not follow, however, that the duality of subject and predicate immediately portrays two structural elements in the being under consideration. For subject and predicate are identified and, therefore, express the same concrete being, although one does it in an individual and sensitive way and the other in a general and intellectual way: this is "something that is man." The reason is that the predicate is a formal-concrete concept obtained through total abstraction and not through formal abstraction.[2]

On the other hand, subject and predicate must *indicate* a certain lack of identity in corporeal being with respect to its mode of *being* or essence. The individual essence cannot be simple, it cannot mean a *totally self-contained and exclusive degree* of participation in *being*. The being in question must really possess the same essential perfection as the other individual of which the same specific characteristic is predicated in an univocal sense. Accordingly, in addition to the principle of specific determination, there must be present in it a principle of individuation, and this principle, of itself, does not express a certain mode of *being* but a limitation of the same specific content to the "here-now" of this individual.

The Matter-Form Structure of Material Being. Because the specifying and individuating principles do not coincide of themselves, the individual essence of the corporeal being reveals a structural unity composed of two principles:

1. A principle which, although of itself it is not individually limited, is present in the being as an individual principle. It is called form (*morphē* or *eidos*).

2. A principle which, although of itself it is not specifically determined, is present in the being as a specified principle. It is called matter (*hylē*).

Thus it follows that:

1. The form, taken in itself, can be individually limited in manifold other ways also. And *this* (sensibly indicated) matter is one of the limitless many possible limitations of the form to a "here-now."

2. The matter, taken in itself, can be determined in many other ways also. And *this* (conceptually expressed) form is one of the

---

[2]Cf. no. 51.

limitless many possible specifications of matter to "such" or "such" a kind of being.

Accordingly, the matter-form unity expressed in the judgment means that *this* being is indeed *such*. But the imperfection of this unity (the composition of matter and form) means that this being, as *this,* does not necessarily have to be *such* nor that, as *such,* it is necessarily *this.*

With respect to its *specific essence,* therefore, the material being is diffused over a possible plurality of contentless limitations—it is multiplied. The individuals of the species can be numbered.[3] On the other hand, with respect to its *individuality,* the corporeal being is not once and for all determined by these specific qualities—it is mutable. In individuals the species can vary.[4]

87. *Proof from Extension and Temporality*

Extension and temporality are general conditions of sense perceptibility. Although they do not constitute the essence itself of the corporeal, they flow from this essence as its properties. This assertion should be understood in the sense that, because a corporeal being changes and moves. its actual place and actual time are constantly modified. Actual place and motion, therefore, are accidents in both the predicable and the predicamental (where and when[5]) sense. However, the fact that a corporeal being must necessarily be "somewhere" and "at some time" is a property flowing of necessity from its essence.

The question we want to raise here is whether it is possible to approach the essence of subsistent corporeal being through the analysis of the "essence" (in the broad sense) of extension and temporality.[6]

Proof from Extension.[7] The subsistent corporeal being, as a being, is one and not divided in itself. But as corporeal it is extended, i.e.,

---

[3]Cf. no. 78.
[4]Cf. no. 85.
[5]Cf. no. 70.
[6]Concerning the proof from extension and temporality, cf. Fernand Renoirte, *Cosmology,* New York, 1950, pp. 233-239; J. Peters, "De plaats van het hylemorphisme in de metaphysiek," *Verslag v. d. 18e Alg. Verg. der Vereniging v. Thom. Wijsb.,* Utrecht-Brussel, 1953, pp. 18-39; also "Matter and Form in Metaphysics," *The New Scholasticism,* 1957, pp. 447-483; M. de Munnynck, "La notion du temps," *Philosophia perennis* (Geyser), Regensburg, 1930, vol. II, pp. 857-868.
[7]Cf. no. 78.

it has parts which negate one another as "here" and "there" insofar as one part is not the other. If, however, this being were actually divided into these parts, it would not be one. But it is not actually divided, although it has parts—"to infinity" even, for each part itself is extended. Accordingly, it has potential parts, i.e., it can be divided "to infinity." It is actually one but potentially many.

However, it is not one *insofar* as it is spatially divisible, nor is it spatially divisible *insofar* as it is one. Hence the foundation or principle of potential divisibility does not coincide with the foundation or principle of actual unity.

The corporeal is one insofar as it has one individual essence. However, this one essence must imply a principle of divisibility, for it is not absolutely one but only relatively, i.e., its unity is a unity of a plurality, a union. Because of this principle of divisibility, the being is constantly forced to *become one* again. Although this principle is not a perfection, it is not purely nothing. It is a *capacity* for unity and, at the same time, the reason why the unity is never perfect and always threatened by dissolution.

Note. In a similar way an argument may be built on the opposition between passivity and activity in corporeal being, or between inertia and energy.[8] The same could be done by starting from the opposition between quantitative and qualitative aspects. In such arguments form is seen not only as the principle of unity but also as a dynamic principle in the sense of active potency.[9]

Temporality. The subsistent corporeal being, as a real being, is actually "now" and present. But, as corporeal, it is temporal, i.e., its "to be" is dispersed in parts of time which negate one another as "then" and "then." These temporal parts, which are past and future, are divisible "to infinity." If, however, this plurality were absolute, and "now" were nothing but the dividing point separating parts of time, then the temporal being would not "be," for the past is no longer and the future is not yet. "Now" unites also the past and the future insofar as "now" implies them at least in the unity of becoming—the being passes from what it was to what it will be, so that being-future passes into being-past. "Now" is the bond uniting the parts of time, so that these parts are not absolutely divided against each other but also always to some extent together in "now."

---

[8]Cf. no. 80.
[9]Cf. no. 72.

However, the temporal is not one precisely *insofar* as it is temporally divided, nor is it temporally divided *insofar* as it is one. The ground or principle of the actuality or presence of its *being* does not coincide with the foundation that divides its *being* in time. Accordingly, in the very essence of the temporal being there is not only a measure of its actual participation in *being* but also a ground of limitation with respect to this participation, a ground of relative non-*being,* i.e., being-past or being-future. Hence the individual essence itself of a being that comes to be, unites two principles which in themselves are opposite. On the one hand, there is a principle of plurality which forces it to be unstable and non-permanent in dispersed moments, on the other, there is a principle through which it is capable of participating, by constant becoming, in *being* with a certain mode of unity of temporal parts, so that it perdures and maintains itself while passing all the time into other situations.

Dynamic Character of Hylomorphic Being. The argument from temporality provides an immediate insight into the dynamic nature of a being which in its individual essence is composed of matter and form. For coming-to-be in time is a tendency toward more being-one-self,[10] toward making plurality or matter serve unity or form. This tendency is realized insofar as through the present the past is retained in the future. Accordingly, even in the purely corporeal, temporality should not be considered as a continuous transition of purely homogeneous moments but, as the numerability of *motion,* it must be connected with motion and therefore with the transition from potency to act. The being that becomes does not tend to unchanged permanence in time, but through change it tends to a greater participation in the modes of *being* of other beings and in this way to have "accidentally" a greater participation in *being.* The more intense the mode of *being* possessed by a form, the more it unifies the heterogeneity of temporal flux and, consequently the plurality implied by matter. Hence the relationship of matter and form is not the same in all corporeal beings—in beings which in and through change are more self-actuating, form will more intensely "inform" the dispersion of matter.

88. *Essential Change*

Both Aristotle and Thomas Aquinas, followed by most neo-Thomists, proved the hylomorphic composition of corporeal beings

---

[10]Cf. no. 64.

from so-called substantial change.[11]   They admitted not only that subsistent material being, remaining itself, becomes "other" in its accidents through so-called accidental change—the kind of change thus far considered—but also that it can become "another."   In such a change the subsistent being does not remain *what* it essentially is, but becomes another subsistent being with a different essence.   This coming-to-be is not the total ceasing-to-be of one accompanied by the *totally* new origin of the other but a *transition* of the one into the other.   Therefore, here, just as in accidental change, there has to be something common which connects the two successive beings, for here too it is true that only the permanent changes.[12]   The difficulty, however, is that it is impossible for this common substratum to be a being which, as endowed with subsistence and its own essential determination, can be conceived as a support and can function as the subject of predicates.[13]   The substratum has to be conceptually empty, for the primary determination of being itself, the substantial essence is included in the change.

Because in substantial change something of the essence has to remain, but not the essence insofar as it has a conceptual content, the essence of the essentially mutable being must be composed of 1) a principle which of itself is without any content-determination, and 2) a first principle determining the content.   Essential change, then, means that contentless "matter," which is in potency to all possible essential determinations or "forms" is successively actuated by distinct forms of essence.

Starting Point of this Proof.   The Ancients saw the starting point of this logically coherent argument in the (supposed) transition of the four elements—earth, water, air, and fire—into one another. More recent proponents appealed to chemical compositions.   However, it is doubtful whether we are able to indicate which beings are really subsistent in the realm of the non-living.[14]

Sometimes the argument starts from the transition of non-living into living matter and vice versa.   But in that case this process of as-similation itself needs first to be analyzed accurately.   Moreover, it is

---

[11]Concerning substantial change, cf. E. Lowijck, *Substantiele verandering en hylemorphisme,* Louvain, 1948; A. Kuiper "Substantiele verandering en hylemorphisme" *Verslag der 18e alg. verg. der Ver. v. Thom. Wysbegeerte,* Utrecht-Brussels, 1953, pp. 2-18.

[12]Cf. no. 73.

[13]Cf. no. 67.

[14]Cf. no. 80.

only by means of analogy that one can extend this hylomorphism to *everything* corporeal *as* corporeal, although it is precisely the corporeal as such that should be reached by hylomorphism.

Essential change in the Light of Hylomorphism. Once the hylomorphic composition has been established, we understand that essential change is possible. Because corporeal being is composed in its individual essence, it can "lose" its own form and be changed into another, essentially different, corporeal being, by virtue of the "remaining" contentless matter. We can even understand that the hylomorphic being may be forced to change essentially. First of all, its spatial unity is only a kind of unification, and this unification is never perfect but constantly threatened. Secondly, its *being* is essentially a mode of coming-to-be in time, for all ontological determinations of the corporeal are temporal, successive determinations—including the determination which expresses *what* this being is in its substantial essence. The essential composition of matter and form is the last ground of the temporality of its *being* and therefore of its corruptibility. The temporal being *is* only in a constant tension between coming-to-be and ceasing-to-be, even when it perdures for some time. Accidental changes may promote its duration, but they can also threaten it.[15]

89. *Matter and Form as Distinct Principles of the Individual Essence*

First Meaning of Form and Matter. The term "form" indicates first of all the external sense-perceptible or geometric shape or figure, an accidental qualitative determination of extended being. For this reason some other qualities, such as certain structural wholes, are called "forms."

---

[15]A corporeal being is more subsistent according as it brings temporally and spatially dispersed plurality more together in the unity of the form. The important element here is not the quantity as such but the intensity of the concentration. There may be non-living corporeal things that perdure longer than living or knowing beings, but their duration shows less unity because past and future are less present in their "now." Living and knowing beings, on the other hand, are more themselves because of the greater unity of their temporal parts. But their duration, *as* corporeal beings, is also more subject to threat. True, no corporeal being can absolutely prevent its essential change. But inorganic beings are less dependent on the assimilation of their surroundings for their persistence, while living beings, precisely because of their greater dynamism and self-enfolding, need favorable surroundings. It is for this reason that their duration is more precarious, although it is of a higher order, than that of the non-living. Likewise, their transition into something else is more striking because it usually means the disintegration of something that was built up with great effort. Only the essential change of living beings is called birth and death (cf. no. 113).

The first meaning of matter is the material from which man makes something, usually by modifying its external form. Hence the term "matter," in the broad sense, is used for everything from which something is made or composed and for everything that still needs to be formed or structured.

Contrasting matter and form is a procedure which has spread to all kinds of sciences and techniques.[16]

Primary Form and Prime Matter. The primary or substantial form is the constituent principle determining the essence of a being and by virtue of the form this being participates in "to be" according to a definite degree of perfection.

Prime or pure matter is the other constituent principle of the essence of a being; of itself it is wholly undetermined with respect to content and it is the reason why the degree of perfection proper to this being is limited to a "here and now."

Because the essence of a corporeal being does not wholly coincide with its form but includes also prime matter, such a being is said to be material.[17]

Universal Essence, Form and Matter. Form is not the same as universal essence. The *universal essence* is the content of a universal concept.[18] It includes not only the form, but also a generalized substratum, a "common matter," of that form. Moreover, it should be kept in mind that the formal-concrete universal concept of subsistent being indicates also in a general way the bearer which is "such"—e.g., "man"—through the essence. It is to this bearer, which is called the supposit, that are attributed both the substantial and the accidental determinations as determinations of its own *being*.[19]

Form, on the other hand, is an ontological principle in the individual being. Through its form this real being participates in a certain grade of *being*. But the form is always this individual form because it "informs" this matter.

Matter also is an ontological principle in the individual being. Through its matter this real being participates in the grade of *being*

---

[16]Cf. no. 146.

[17]The term "matter" is often applied to the totality of all corporeal beings. This use of the term is justified only if matter is taken as a collective concept embracing the many individual material beings not only with respect to their matter but also as regards their forms.

[18]Cf. no. 83.

[19]Cf. no. 65.

merely in a mode limited to a "here and now." But matter is always such or such specific matter because it materializes such or such a form.

The primary form in a corporeal being is the principle through which this being participates in "to be" according to a determined degree; consequently, it constitutes together with prime matter the whatness or essence of the subsistent being. For this reason the corporeal being has only one substantial form. All further determinations possessed by the corporeal being pertain to it only by virtue of secondary or accidental forms.[20]

Matter's Potentiality for All Forms. Matter should be conceived as potential with respect to all forms which have to be individuated through a contentless substratum, i.e., all forms that are not yet individuated of themselves.

"Informed" matter—and matter *is* only as "informed" matter—retains its potential openness to all forms. Of itself, it is and remains pure potency. Nevertheless, "informed" matter is not equally open to all forms. Not everything becomes everything else without any transitory stages, although in principle everything must be capable of becoming everything else. The reason why there is no equal openness to all forms is that, because of its actual information by such or such a form, matter has certain dispositions, and these dispositions make it more immediately appropriate to some forms and more remotely open to others.[21]

90. *The Corporeal as Individual*

In the preceding paragraphs we contrasted form and matter as specifying and individualizing principles. A further consideration of individuality will show in what sense this opposition should be understood.

---

[20]The primary form, however, may have a virtual structure insofar as it is the fountainhead from which different distinct powers flow. Thus, the living body has not only the actions of all that is corporeal but also higher operations of its own. The same is true for the being endowed with knowledge. However, this plurality emanates from the one and only essential form of the living or knowing subsistent being. Cf. no. 94.

[21]Accordingly, the assertion that matter, which of itself is contentless, has dispositions means only that, being actuated here and now by this kind of a form, it constitutes this kind of being, and that this kind of being, as experience shows, can immediately change into that other kind but not arbitrarily into any kind.

Transcendental Character of Individuality. "Everything has individuality in the same respect in which it has 'to be'."[22] For to be an individual, i.e., to be undivided in the self and divided from the nonself, means nothing else than to be one-self or to have self-identity; consequently, it means the being-one and being-determined that pertain to a being *as* a being by virtue of "to be" which is fully distinct from "not-to-be." Accordingly, individually is a transcendental property of *being.*[23]

Finite Individuality. The real finite being, however, is imperfectly itself, imperfectly one and determined, and therefore also imperfectly individual. Together with other finite beings, it participates in *being* in distinct ways. Hence it is individual only in accordance with the limited mode of its participation in *being,* i.e., according to its *essence,* which is what distinguishes it from the other finite beings.

This distinction, however, is not absolute but includes also a being-together with the others. The finite being, therefore, refers to the others in its individuality. It is not yet wholly itself, it is dynamic and further determinable—in an accidental way—in its mode of *being* or essence by means of communication with the modes of *being* of the other finite beings. Consequently, the individuality of the finite being is not perfectly self-contained, but is a being-on-the-road-to self-perfection through interaction with others in the community of finite realities.

Corporeal Individuality. Real corporeal being is not even itself and distinct from the others through the determined grade of *being* pertaining to it by its essence, for it shares with other beings in the

---

[22]Thomas Aquinas, *De anima,* a. 1, *ad* 2. Cf. *Super libr. de causis, prop.* 9 (Saffrey ed., 1954, pp. 65f.), where individuality is clearly attributed to the infinite as such.

[23]Note that individuality is closely connected with determinateness (cf. no. 41). A proposed thought content may still be undetermined in itself and need to be complemented in this or that way by mutually exclusive determinations, before it fully expresses the mode in which a being is. As long as this is the case, this thought content—which arises through abstraction from the differences—is still univocally universal; it can be predicated of many in the same way and therefore is not yet individual. For whatever *is,* insofar as it *is,* is determined.

On the other hand, even the universal, insofar as it *is,* is individual. In real beings the thought content is always particularized and individuated. In the conceptual order, on the other hand, the universal thought content, taken as such, is what it is, i.e., it is distinct from other contents of thought, and therefore is individual in the order of concepts. Even when the content is formally referred to the many modes in which it can be, as happens in reflex universality, this logical relationship is what it is and therefore is individual on the level of logical relationships (cf. no. 83).

same specific perfection. It is individual only insofar as the specific perfection is limited to a "here and now." In other words, its individual essence does not coincide with its form, but has become this individual essence by virtue of the limitation of the form through *matter,* which makes the being in question distinct from the other corporeal beings.

Nevertheless, even here the distinction is not absolute, but implies a togetherness in the order of time and space. Therefore, even the corporeal being in its individuality is related to the other corporeal beings. It is much less fully itself than the finite being (taken as such), but is constantly further determinable through the mutual interaction of bodies in the processes of change. Not even essential change is excluded. For this reason the being-individual of the corporeal is not only never complete but also essentially subservient to the welfare of the species and the whole realm of corporeal beings. It is an individuality which comes to be and passes away.[25]

Summarizing we may say this: to be an individual belongs to every being on the ground of its *being.* That the finite being is individual only in a limited way (and in togetherness with other finite beings) arises from the limitation of "to be" through its *essence*— "to be" individuates the finite being only as a *"to be" such or such.* That the corporeal being is individual only in a limited way (and in togetherness with other spatio-temporal beings), even with respect to its essence, has its reason in the limitation of form through *matter*— "to be" individuates the corporeal being only as a *"to be" here and now such or such.*

Matter as Principle of Repeatability. Matter, therefore, is not the foundation of individuality in the sense that it gives to the material being its being-itself, its being-one and its being-determined. These pertain to the individual by virtue of its "to be," albeit only according to the limited mode of *form,* as the principle of the individual essence. It is only because the material individual cannot realize the full content of its specific determination that the limited mode in which it still can be individual within the species reaches the here-and-now through the limitation of the form, i.e., through prime *matter.*

Matter is a principle of determinability, and itself without any determination of content. It is a pure capacity for all material forms.

---

[25]Concerning fluid continuity within the species, cf. A.D. Sertillanges, *La philosophie de S. Thomas d'Aquin,* vol. 2, pp. 18-27.

No predicate can be assigned to it, certainly not that of numerical unity or of numerical plurality. Matter is a principle of divisibility "to infinity" and, consequently, the substantial root of the extension that belongs to the material as material. Precisely insofar as matter is the foundation of extension in space (and, we should add, in time,[26]) it is the passive principle of individuation, i.e., it is the fundamental reason why specifically the same beings are numerically repeatable "to infinity."[27]

Material Beings Are Not Mere Repetitions of the Same Specific Content. Are material beings nothing but mere repetitions, distinct only in place and time, of exactly the same specific content? True, the univocal judgment with its subject and predicate structure conceives them in that way. We have even used this structure to deduce the hylomorphic composition of material beings from it. However, here we should not forget that, despite its truth, the experiential judgment remains inadequate. The ineffable character of the material individual arises not only from its degraded intelligibility but also from the defective nature of our knowledge.

Moreover, the univocal character of our conceptual knowledge is to some extent transcended in our analogous knowledge of *being*. As soon as the individuals which we conceptually grasp as instances of a species are considered as beings, we know that each of them necessarily participates in its own distinct way in *being*. Therefore, their individual essences cannot be mere repetitions of a species, but each of them must have a content that is somewhat different, although they are similar in specific perfection.

Individual Differences. Accordingly, there are individual differences which, despite their origin in matter, are differences in the individual *forms themselves* because they are unequal participations in *being*. But then it follows that the species is not equally present in all, as we thought when we considered our universal judgments. On closer inspection, there must be a participation of the individuals in the fullness of the species, so that each of them merely approaches the species more or less closely.[28] But in that case the "species"

---

[26]Most authors use here the formula *materia signata quantitate,* i.e., matter marked by quantity.

[27]Accordingly, "matter" should not be conceived as "matter in general," i.e., as a kind of formal-abstract universal concept. It is a principle which in itself is not repeatable; yet it is the foundation of numberless possibilities for determinations to "here-and-now," all of which are rooted in the divisibility stemming from matter.

[28]Cf. no. 83.

is no longer a universal concept obtained through abstraction from the individual differences but, as the real universal origin,[29] it is an all-embracing "idea" containing the individual forms as its possible particular realizations.

Non-living beings spend themselves in acting on others and, as a result, their individual differences are to a greater extent reducible to conditions of time and place. Living beings, on the other hand, display activities that are more directed toward their own self-development. For this reason the originality of every living individual is more striking and their individual forms are more distinct.[30]

Our Knowledge of the Corporeal Individual. It must be pointed out that we do not have any direct intellectual knowledge of either the "species idea" or the individual participations. Just as the univocally universal essence has to be approached by means of sense-perceptible accidents,[31] so also knowledge of the individual beings, in which the fullness of the "species idea" reveals itself, has to be obtained through sensitive contact and experience of life, through the observation of characteristic diversities in the activity and passivity or behavior of the individuals.

91. *Corporeal Beings as Mutually Active and Passive*

At the end of our study of the most general structure proper to corporeal bengs we return to the starting point—sense experience. The hylomorphic composition found in the essence of corporeal being, which is the most degraded mode of *being,* renders intelligible why we observe bodies precisely in their external action on one another and on our organic body. In other words, it becomes understandable why the material always appears as continuously moving and moved according to active qualities, as an *ens mobile,* a mobile being.

The Corporeal is a Being in Transition. The materiality of the corporeal implies that the essential determination, the intelligible

---

[29]Cf. no. 84.

[30]As a corporeal being, man is individuated by matter. However, as we shall see, man is spiritual also and, therefore, his form (the spiritual soul) is a principle having its own *being*. Accordingly, man is, as it were, the transition from individuation through *form,* proper to non-corporeal beings, and individuation through *matter.* In man the originality of the individual manifests itself more clearly than in subhuman beings: on the one hand, each man is an individual of the human species but, on the other hand, he is an unrepeatable realization of being-human having an original content. Cf. no. 153.

[31]Cf. no. 84.

characteristic or form, is not in unity "all by itself," but is divided, multiplied, and dispersed through a principle of limitation to "here-and-now"—through content-less prime matter.   The material individual *is* not unqualifiedly *what* it is.   It participates in being such or such together with any others in a spatio-temporal order.   It is only here-and-now such; it is already potentially "other" and even "something else."   It is in immediate or remote transition from one substantial or accidental determination to another.

However, this transition, in which determinable matter is successively determined through different forms, depends on the presence of beings that are already actually determined by these forms.

Transcient Action.   Consequently, the activity through which material things unfold themselves to become "more themselves" does not consist in an immanent perfection emanating from their nature. For their perfection they are dependent on the influence of their contacting surroundings and, with respect to these surroundings, they are passive.   Their collaboration consists merely in allowing themselves to be influenced by virtue of the dispositions which they actually possess.   The only activity emanating from themselves is not an act that perfects them, but an influence they exercise on other nearby beings according to the form which they themselves have received.   Their activity is an exteriorization of the self in their surroundings by means of contact.[32]

Even this transient action is not at their disposal.   It has more the character of an anonymous event of nature which runs its course through their nature.   It takes place of necessity as soon as the required conditions are present, such as the possession of a received moving power or active quality, the presence of the object to be moved or changed with its passive potency to the act of change, and the spatio-temporal presence of this object to the agent.

Reciprocity of Transcient Action.   This presence or contact, however, is mutual.   Both its being-somewhere and its qualities are of such a nature that the agent is superior only in a certain respect, while the object on which the agent acts is superior in another respect. For this reason the object which in contact becomes open to influence, in its turn exercises influence also.   This unity of action and reaction manifests itself most clearly in locomotion (resistance).   But it is present also in the qualities; for instance, one object heats the

---

[32]Cf. no. 80.

other, but the latter cools the former. Material beings, therefore, are always at the same time reciprocally active and passive. Their exercising-influence is a being-influenced also. The parts of the materially extended world refer to one another and are interconnected.

Purpose of Transient Activity. To reach its perfection, the material object needs the *other* and in this other, through its transient action, it reaches its highest *being*—outside itself. Moreover, through its very activity itself, it is engaged in losing the perfections it possessed, for it is at the same time influenced by the other. For this reason the purpose of the activity does not lie in the material thing considered in itself, but in a certain orderly disposition of the various parts pertaining to the spatio-temporal whole. To this whole the material thing is subservient and for this whole it operates.

Degraded Subsistence of Material Beings. Just as the material, because of its hylomorphic composition, does not fully coincide with its *being* or with its essential content, so also is it not fully identical with its activity. It effects neither the *being* nor the *being-such* of what it changes, but merely that this changed reality is here-and-now in a spatio-temporal order such. And even this it does only as long as its influence perdures through contact. In a subsequent situation, the changed reality is subject to new influences, and the material agent itself has changed in such a way that its influence also is modified. In its activity the material being does not merely refer to its surroundings, but is truly dependent on them.[33]

Accordingly, the material being is *subsistent* in the most *degraded* way both in its *being* and its activity. In the end, it even loses its own subsistence while acting, for the local and qualitative changes which it undergoes in acting are dispositions preparing its essential change into something else.

The material being, therefore, should be conceived as a member of a whole in which the parts are mutually dependent. However, this does not mean that the whole or cosmos is more subsistent than the parts. The cosmos is a whole whose parts are to a greater or lesser extent *on the road* to becoming subsistent and therefore, they are already subsistent in an incipient way. What we want to reject here is the idea that corporeal beings constitute a mosaic of self-contained beings which are all equally and fully self-sufficient.[34]

---

[33]Cf. no. 107.
[34]Cf. nos. 116, 153.

CHAPTER EIGHTEEN

RETROSPECTIVE VIEW: POTENCY AND ACT IN THE PROPER SENSE

92. *Introduction*

The original meaning of the Greek term *energeia or* act is activity, and that of *dynamis* or potency is active power or faculty.[1] It is proper, indeed, to any finite being to be dynamic, i.e., to direct itself to self-realization by means of activity.[2] Moreover, activity is what I experience first explicitly both in myself and in other perceived beings and through which I learn to some extent to know beings in their power and their nature or essence.[3]

However, the term "potency" is used not only for the power to act or operate, but also in a proper, albeit derivative, sense for the capacity to undergo action or to receive, i.e., the potency which is actuated in change. In a corresponding way "act" no longer signifies only activity but also every perfection which determines the potency of a being.

It will be useful to summarize here the results reached in the preceding chapters, before we investigate whether it is possible to amplify the meaning of act and potency in such a way that their application is not limited to solving the problem of how a being unfolds itself temporally in activity and passivity while retaining its self-identity.

93. *Activity*

Its Meaning. Like being and "to be," activity in its most general sense cannot be strictly defined. However, it can be clarified by saying that the meaning of activity is to make the finite, essentially limited being participate more and more in "to be" through communication with the modes of *being* of other beings. As such, activity is the *being-more* or *most perfect actuality* of the finite. This *being-more* is the manifestation of the dynamic infinity which pertains to the finite as a being.

---

[1] Cf. no. 72.
[2] Cf. no. 63.
[3] Cf. no. 71.

Because the finite is essentially limited, it can participate only in an accessory way in the modes of *being* of the other beings. Its essence is distinct from its "to be," and therefore in the finite being to-be-subsistent and to-be-active have to be distinct.

Accordingly, to-be-subsistent is the presupposition and essential foundation of being-active. For this reason being-active is sometimes describe as "second" actuality in opposition to the "first" actuality of being-subsistent.

Its Limitation. The activity through which the finite participates in the modes of *being* of other beings is never a perfect identification with these beings. It always remains a *definite* activity, i.e., a *limited* approximation of the other being. For this reason these other beings, precisely from the viewpoint under which they are the object of an activity, are said to distinguish this activity from other activities. As it is traditionally expressed, the action is specified by its formal object.[4]

Immanent and Transient Activity. In its most general sense, activity is an analogous concept or idea and applies to very different modes of being-active. The classical division distinguishes immanent and transient activities.[5]

1. In an *immanent* act the activity itself is the terminus intended, it perfects the agent by making him enter into an immanent union with beings. Examples of immanent are external perception and reflective self-consciousness.[6] As we shall see later, understanding and loving are the immanent acts of man in the most proper sense.

2. In *transient* action the activity itself is not the terminus intended by the agent. As a perfection of the other, material being, it is *of* the agent—whence it is called action—but *in* the recipient—whence it is called reception ("passion"). It coincides with change which is the act of the changing being.[7]

---

[4]It is customary to distinguish the material and formal object. The material object is the being which is object of an activity; the formal object is the aspect under which the being in question is object of an activity. One and the same object, e.g., an apple, may be touched with respect to its shape, seen through its color, tasted by means of its flavor, etc.

[5]The distinction of transient and immanent activity stems from Aristotle, *Metaphysica*, bk. IX, ch. 8, 1050a 21 -b -2 (Cf. St. Thomas, *Comment.* nos. 1861-1865), *Ethica*, bk. I, ch. 1 (*Comment.* nos. 12-18) and bk. VII, ch. 4, 1140a 1 (*Comment.* nos. 1150-1152). However, for Aristotle, it was more a question of dividing human activities than a general metaphysical distinction.

[6]Cf. nos. 72 and 17.

[7]Cf. no. 80.

Transient action, in the strict sense, is a natural event of the material world and thus implies a large measure of passivity.[8] An immanent act, in the strict sense, is a conscious and free self-determination of a spiritual being and therefore implies a large measure of activity, of control or dominion over the act.

Between these two there exist other intermediary forms of activity which share to some extent in both. For instance, the biological functions, sense cognition and sense affections. Moreover, both biological functions and sensitive as well as intellectual acts exercise influence on other beings, especially material things. These actions are something in the agent—namely, his immanent self-unfolding—but they are called *virtually transient* action because they exercise a causal influence. With respect to these actions, it is not fully true that the action is only in the changing object.[9]

94. *Active Potency*

The activities emanate from the subsistent being. Insofar as this being is the source of these activities, it must contain the germ of the perfection which unfolds itself in the activities. If, then activity is the complete actuality of a being, the essence through which this being participates in *being* will also have to be qualified as being "in act" in a proper, albeit derivative, sense of act. This sense is expressed by the term "initial" or "first" act.

Distinction of Potency and Nature. Because of its being-in-act, the subsistent being is capable of activity. Nevertheless, essence and capacity or active potency do not wholly coincide. For the essence is actuated through "to-be-subsistent', and the potency through successive actualities which are distinct by reason of their object. Because these actualities are accidental determinations, their immediate and proportionate principle must lie in the accidental order, even though

---

[8]Cf. no. 91.

[9]It is a linguistic problem how to include all these activities in a single formal-abstract term and how to express their difference. Perhaps the vague term "activity" can be used here. In Latin sometimes, but not always, a distinction is made between *actio* and *operatio*. In English perhaps the most general meaning could be reserved for "action" and "to act." However, we prefer to use the term "action" for transient activities and "act" or "deed" for immanent activities, especially when the latter are considered as free acts. On the other hand, it remains true that it is difficult to call all immanent activities "deeds." Not all of them have the character of an event taking place in time, as the term "deed" seems to suggest. In contrast with perceiving, thinking, desiring, and deciding, the terms "knowing" and "loving" refer to permanent attitudes rather than to deeds occurring here and now at this moment. The more perfect an activity is, the more it approaches the permanence which characterizes subsistent being.

it remains true that the potency is an essential property emanating of necessity from the essence as nature.[10]

Plurality of Potencies. The active potency is the intermediary between the subsistent being that remains identical with itself and the plurality and diversity of successive activities. It is adapted to the specifically different activities which can have their source in one and the same nature. For every subsistent being is *one* according to its essential form, but may virtually contain different grades of *being*.[11] This virtuality of the essence expresses itself in an ordered plurality of potencies for specifically different activities, directed to distinct formal objects. Nevertheless, the many potencies constitute an inner unity, they emanate hierarchically from one another and, therefore, in their proper nature are attuned and ordered to one another; hence the integral activity of a subsistence being find its source in the confluence of these powers.[12]

Potency as "in Immediate First Act." If the potency is to be the immediate and proportionate principle of activity, if it is to be a power or faculty in the full sense of the term, ready for action, then it must be complete as first act. It has to be "in immediate first act."

Such a readiness, however, presupposes several conditions in the finite and especially the temporal being. For the activities of the finite and temporal being do not simply emanate from the potency,[13] but, as communications with other beings, presuppose also that these other beings present themselves as being "at their disposal" in a certain way.

As regards transient action, which coincides with the change of the recipient object, the material being itself is ready for action as soon as it possesses the power of locomotion or active qualities. However, it cannot exercise its influence unless the subject of the

---

[10]Cf. no. 69.

[11]Cf. no. 89.

[12]Purely corporeal non-living beings have only potencies for transient actions. These potencies are usually called powers or energies. Such beings do not always possess these powers in a permanent way. For instance, the power to move surroundings actively is the being-in-motion itself of the corporeal being, and its power to change actively is identical with its active qualities themselves.

Vegetative beings have special powers for vital functions. They consist in a higher organization of physico-chemical forces.

Sentient beings have, in addition, external and internal sensitive and appetitive powers.

In intellectual beings intellect and will are joined to these active powers.

[13]Cf. no. 43.

change with its passive potency is present to it in a spatio-temporal contact.[14]

95. *The Relation of Active Potency and Activity*

The Actuation of Active Potency. In itself, active potency is not an imperfection but a perfection. Abstractly considered, therefore, there would not have to be an opposition and distinction between active potency and activities. "To be able to act" would coincide with the infinite act if the essence were identical with infinite "to be" and thus would include all possible modes of *being* in its active communication. In this case there could be no transition from active potency to actuality.

However, the finite being is not identical with "to be," but participates in it in a particular mode determined by its essence. For this reason it is also not identical with "to act," but participates in it in a particular mode determined by its power. Just as the participation in *being* reveals itself in the distinction of essence and "to be,"

---

[14]Cf. no. 80.

"Passive" Powers. The immanent acts of knowing and loving presuppose the knowability and lovability of their objects. The active potency, therefore, is not ready as long as these objects have not influenced it. (With respect to knowing, this influence is exercised through formal causality, and with regard to loving, it is exercised through final causality.) The objects have to become united with the potency in a certain intentional way. Only this unity of subject and object is the completed "first act" or "ready" potency from which activity can originate.

For this reason the potencies for immanent acts are sometimes said to be "passive" powers. Nevertheless, they are, and even *par excellence,* operative or active powers, although they have to prepare their action by being in a certain state of receptivity with respect to their object.

Habitus. Human powers may be disposed to certain activities in a more or less permanent way, so that these activities are easily and spontaneously performed. Such a disposition, which becomes a kind of second nature, is called a *habitus,* which may be approximately translated by ability, skill, talent, proficiency, "know-how" and also habit.

Certain *habitus* are naturally present in every human being. Thus, for instance, the intellect spontaneously has certain insights into the first principles of being as being, which are called the *habitus* of principles pertaining to the theoretical intellect. The practical intellect, likewise, has a spontaneous insight into the first principles or supreme norms governing deeds and behavior. With respect to moral acts this habitus is called "synderesis."

Experience shows that there are also abilities which vary from person to person. This variation may result from a native disposition or be the effect of practice, i.e., the repeated performance of actions. In the latter case the dispositions are called acquired abilities. Examples are the following:

for the theoretical intellect, science and wisdom;
for the practical intellect, prudence in acting, art in making things;
for effective and volitional life, moral virtues.

so the participation in acting manifests itself in the distinction of power and activity. The power, even the "fully ready" power, has to become active. This activity, which finally makes the power fully actual, is a new and ultimate actuality, distinct from the power. This actuality is "to do," "to operate," or "to work."

Is the Active Potency the Complete Explanation of its Activity? Thus, we may ask this question: Is the potency alone *fully* able to explain the emanation of its act and, consequently, the *being-more* arising from the transition to the act? We mean, even when, through the existing influence of objects and its own abilities, the potency is fully disposed to let activity emanate from itself and to act by virtue of the dynamism of nature.

The analogy that exists between, on the one hand, the relation of power to act in the accidental order and, on the other hand, the relationship of essence and "to be" in the substantial order may throw some light on this difficult problem.

Activities are expressed by verbs, i.e., terms expressing action. Grammatically even "to be" is a verb,[16] because "to be" is known to us through "acting." In itself, however, "to be" is not a form of action, but "to act" is the perfected form of "to be" proper to subsistent being.

In the substantial order the essence has a certain priority over "to be"—namely, insofar as the formal principle of a being determines the mode of its participation in "to be." However, absolutely speaking, "to be" is prior as that through which the subsistent being *is* according to the measure of its essence.[17]

In a similar way, in the accidental order the potency has a certain priority over activity—namely, insofar as it is the "first act" and therefore determines the mode of participation in activity. But absolutely speaking, activity is prior as that through which the active being *is* active according to the measure of its potency.

Thus, although the ready potency is the source from which the activity emanates, it does not *completely* explain this emanation. For the transition from active potency to activity implies for this potency a becoming-changed, an acquiring of the ultimate, hitherto absent actuality. This becoming-changed or transition is undoubtedly a self-

---

[16]Concerning the relationship of *being* and acting see J. de Finance, *Etre et Agir;* Y. Simon, *Introduction à l'ontologie du connaître,* Paris, 1934, pp. 57-123; J. M. Henri-Rousseau, "L'être et l'agir," *Revue Thomiste,* vol. 53 (1953), pp. 488-531; vol. 54 (1954), pp. 267-297; vol. 55 (1955), pp. 85-118.
[17]Cf. no. 60.

change, a making-oneself-be-more, for it is the potency, or more accurately the subsistent being through its potency, which exercises the act. However, as a pure *self-actuation* this change would be a contradiction in terms, for then the potency would have to be both active and passive in the same respect. We must say, therefore, that the potency is passive in exercising the act, not with respect to itself but in relation to a prior and higher activity in which it is made to participate. The potency *is actuated to actuate itself*.

This situation may be expressed also by saying that the potency is *moved* to its activity, provided to move and to be moved are not understood as a kind of locomotion but in the broad sense of change.[18]

The Actuation of the Active Potency. Consequently, there must be a prior or higher power which is already in activity and which communicates its activity to the "ready" active potency. However, this prior power does not necessarily have to be a different power. If a potency is already actually directed to its formal object in its totality, it can move itself to partial activities with respect to partial objects and proceed to the explicitation of what is implicitly present in the totality.[19]

However, it is possible also that in one and the same subsistent being various powers constitute a unity of order in which one potency that is already in activity moves another.[20]

On certain conditions one subsistent being that is already in activity may move another to activity. In this case the one is the cause of the activity of the other.[21] Thus there appears to exist a network of activity and passivity between hierarchically ordered beings. Experience alone can provide more detailed information about this network.

Nevertheless, the ultimate origin of the activity pertaining to finite beings, *as* finite beings, does not seem to be sufficiently explained through this hierarchical order. For the ultimate foundation of the possibility that a finite being will pass from active potency to activity would have to lie in an activity which does not proceed from

---

[18]Cf. no. 77.

[19]For instance, the intellectual power proceeds from the actual knowledge of the premises to actual knowledge of the conclusion; the will moves from the actual willing of the purpose to free self-determination with respect to the means.

[20]The appetitive potencies move both the cognitive powers and the bodily forces to the execution of their activities.

[21]Cf. no. 80.

an active potency but which, as pure activity, is identical with active potency.[22]

Thus the participation in *being* repeats itself much more explicitly and urgently in the problem of the participation in activity. What is, we must ask, to "participate in unqualified activity" in a merely particular way, which characterizes every finite activity and certainly every temporal and every material activity?

96. *Passive Potency and its Act*

Even in the continuous transition from active potency to successive multiplicity of activities we encounter the problem of becoming and change and, therefore, of passive potency.

Immanent Acts and Passive Potency. Immanent acts originate from the power, but are also received by it. Therefore, this power has two aspects under which it is in passive potency: 1) because it is only through the influence of the objects that the power is "in complete first act";[23] 2) because it passes from first act to the exercise of activity or second act under the influence of prior activities.

Transient Actions and Passive Potency. Transient action likewise presupposes that the agent is already in possession of a perfection or form, a motive power or quality, which we may call an act, a "first act," in a derivative but sitll proper sense.[24]

However, the transient action itself is not the perfection of the agent but of the recipient. The object that undergoes the action receives, as a result of the action, a similiar perfection to that which the agent possesses as the action's source. Accordingly, the recipient also is "in act" because of the action.

Of itself, however, the recipient is not "in act" but only in potency with respect to the perfection. This potency is passive, although it may still be called a potency in a derivative but proper sense.[25]

The active potency of the agent causing the change both resembles and differs from the passive potency of the recipient which undergoes the change. There is resemblance insofar as both refer to a perfection or act of the same specific content. On the other hand, there is a difference insofar as the active potency is the power to

---

[22]Cf. no. 185.
[23]Cf. no. 43.
[24]Cf. nos. 74 and 84.
[25]Cf. no. 74

cause this act in the recipient through action, and the passive potency is the capacity to receive this act through undergoing the action of the agent.

Potency-Act Structure. While active potency itself is an act, although it is distinct from its activity, passive potency is related to its act as capacity is to fulfillment. Passive potency and its act, therefore, are really distinct, not merely as the distinct and successive states of being-in-potency and being-actuated, but as complementary principles pertaining to the structure of the being that becomes and changes. *Of itself,* the changing being remains merely in potency to this act, even when through change it is in-act. It possesses the act only in a passing way, only now and then, but not forever or by virtue of its own nature.

Accordingly, the potency-act structure does not refer primarily to active potency and activity, but to passive potency and act, whether this act is activity or act in the more general sense of perfection.

We have arrived at this structure through an analysis of change. It serves to explain the change or mutability found in a being which remains identical with itself insofar as further determinations of content (forms or acts) are concerned. The potency is the determinable and permanent constituent principle, and the act is the determining but variable constituent principle. The identity of the non-identical or the change of the permanent is explained by means of two contrasting distinct principles within the unity of the mobile being. Such a being possesses perfections or acts with which it is not fully identical.

CHAPTER NINETEEN

RETROSPECTIVE VIEW: POTENCY AND ACT IN A BROADENED ANALOGOUS SENSE

97. *Introduction*

Composition or Participation? Some authors consider Thomism as a philosophical system whose characteristic feature lies in the radical way in which it carries through the opposition of act and potency discovered by Aristotle. They view potency primarily as a passive capacity, and act as the fulfillment or perfection of this capacity. According to them, potency and act can be found in a multitude of ways as distinct structural elements or principles of the beings which they constitute through their mutual relationship. Accordingly, this composition does not serve only to explain change, as Aristotle thought, but also all limitation and plurality, wherever they may be found. The absolutely Immutable, the Infinite and the One, on the other hand, are conceived as Pure Act. The key thesis of the system is seen to lie in the principle that act is limited and multiplied only through the potency in which it is received.[1]

Others object to the conception which considers potency and act as the primordial all-embracing metaphysical principles. They ask themselves whether such a doctrine of composition does not become irretrievably entangled in a fundamental dualism of, on the one hand, pure act and, on the other, pure potency (of prime matter). Does the doctrine sufficiently explain the origin of the receptive potency which it opposes to the act?

---

[1] At least since Liberatore, the division of being into act and potency follows as a rule immediately after the analysis of the concept of being in the textbooks of ontology. See, e.g., Zigliara, Remer, de Mandato, Hugon, Farge-Barbedette, Gredt, Jolivet, Maquart, Thonnard, and Angelinus.

In his work *L'enseignement de la métaphysique,* Louvain, 1950, p. 98, J. Pirlot raises the following question about this procedure: Does one have to make these notions the key that opens metaphysics or use them only as a convenient way to synthetize the results achieved?

Among those who understand Thomistic metaphysics as the theory of potency and act special mention must be made of G. Manser, *Das Wesen des Thomismus,* Fribourg, 3rd ed., 1949. Cf. also P. Grenet, *Le Thomisme.*

These authors do not want to view Thomism primarily as a philosophy of composition but rather as a philosophy of *participation*.[2] True, St. Thomas combats the Platonic or quasi-Plantonic hypostatization of univocally universal concepts on the basis of Aristotle's critical realism. Nevertheless, he retains one central point pertaining to the very core of Plato's theory—namely, that all beings, all modes and structures of *being* are seen in relation to all-embracing "to be" and its transcendental properties.

In this conception of Thomism the distinction of act and potency remains important. Act and potency are even very generally applied in all ontological problems. However, this application does not take place until the meaning of these concepts, as derived from the problem of change, has been broadened and thus rendered suitable for expressing certain aspects of the participation structures which have already been discovered through reflection on the *being* of beings, such as those of essence and "to be," matter and form, substance and accidents.

In this treatise we have proceeded in accordance with the second view and avoided beginning our philosophical train of thought with axioms concerning act and potency in a broadened sense. On the contrary, we have started with the "to be" of beings, then raised the problem of the multiplicity and finiteness of beings, continued with that of time and mutability, and ended with that of space and materiality. Thus we are now in a position where we may revert to our starting point and ask ourselves whether act and potency are useful only in the more particular problem of becoming and remaining, i.e., change, or play a role also in the more universal problem of *being*.

98. *General Metaphysical Theses About Act and Potency*

Limitation of Perfection. Potency and act, in a broadened sense, are used to explain, first of all, how it is possible for a determined content or perfection to be present in a being in a limited way.

Limitation, so it is said, is imperfection and therefore cannot pertain to a perfection as such. Accordingly, if a perfection is found in a being in a limited way, there must be in this being a principle of limitation, alongside and opposed to the principle of perfection. This distinct principle of limitation is a receptivity or capacity for the perfection in question. The being which possesses a principle of capacity for perfection, even when this capacity is filled with the perfection,

---

[2]Cf. no. 57.

itself is not the perfection in full identity, but merely participates in it in the limited measure of its receptivity.

Multiplication of Perfection. Secondly, potency and act, in the broad sense, are used to explain how it is possible for one and the same determined content or perfection to be present in many beings.

Taken in itself, so it is said, this determined content or perfection is what it is, it is itself and one. If, then, it, nonetheless, is found to be multiplied, this multiplication is possible only because the perfection exists as realized in distinct subjects. Because these subjects differ from one another, they cannot be fully identical with the perfection which they possess. And because whatever is received, is received according to the mode of the receiver, the distinction of the subjects means that the perfection in question is present in always-different ways. For this reason the perfection is present also only in a limited way in each of these subjects.

Broadening of Meaning. The concepts of act and potency used in this view are broadened to such an extent that the term "act" indicates every determination, regardless of its nature. It applies to every categorical qualification in the broadest sense, whether substantial or accidental, every determination of time and place as well as of content or relationship, every super-categorical or transcendental qualification, such as unity, truth, and goodness, and even the qualification "to be" itself. The term "potency" is used in a corresponding way for every capacity for such determinations.

Principles of Act and Potency. Concerning potency and act in this broadened sense, the following assertions are generally made:

1. Act and potency divide being and every category or genus of being.

2. It is impossible for one and the same reality to be in both potency and act in the same respect.

3. Act and potency are really distinct.[3]

4. Act as act is unlimited, but potency as potency is limited.

5. With respect to its proper content, an act can be limited only because it is in potency to an act of a higher order.

---

[3] If, however, the terms are used in the logical order, e.g., for the determinable genus and the determining specific difference (cf. no. 83), then there will be question only of a logical distinction.

6. An act can realize its own perfection in a limited way only if it is received in a potency.

7. Act as act is unique, but potency as potency is manifold.

8. An act can be multipled only because it is received in a potency.

9. In one and the same subject potency may be prior to act, but absolutely and in itself act is prior to potency.

10. A being can pass from being-in-potency to being-in-act only under the influence of a being-in-act.

11. What is two beings in-act, cannot constitute a single subsistent being.

A Problem. In the problem of change the concepts of potency and act have a clearly defined meaning. The question, however, which from our viewpoint has to be raised is whether these concepts can be broadened in such a way that, abstraction made of change, they can be used wherever there is question of limitation and multiplication.

We may begin this investigation by pointing out that our viewpoint also has lead to the acceptance of ontological distinctions and structures:

1. The plurality and finiteness of beings and the analogy of the idea "being" led to the participation in "to be," which is expressed in the distinction of being, essence, and "to be."[4]

2. The dynamic character of finite beings, which flows from the distinction of essence and "to be," induced us to admit the structure of substance and accidents within the unity of the subsistent being.[5]

3. The multiplicity and limitation of beings that are specifically the same and the univocity of the specific concept led us to the structure of matter and form within the essential unity of such a being.[6]

The question, therefore, is whether or not these structures may be considered relationships of act and potency in an analogously broadened sense.[7]

---

[4]Cf. nos. 57-60.
[5]Cf. nos. 65-71.
[6]Cf. nos. 86-91.
[7]J. D. Robert ("Le principe 'actus non limitatur nisi per potentiam subjectivam realiter distinctam,'" *Revue philosophique de Louvain,* vol. 47, 1949, pp. 44-70) agrees with C. Fabro ("Un itinéraire de S. Thomas," *Revue de philosophie,* vol. 39, 1939, p. 307) when the latter asserts that St. Thomas

99. *Matter and Form*[8]

Potency and Act in Essential Change. It was the accidental change of the same subsistent being which led us to accept that the changed being is composed of potency and act as determinability and determination.[9] If, however, one admits also the occurrence of essential change, then prime matter and primary form may be conceived as potency and act. Nevertheless, these concepts apply only in an analogous sense to matter and form, because there are essential differences in the relationship of accidental act and potency, on the one hand, and essential act and potency, on the other. These differences are the following:

1. The accidental potency is something pertaining to a subsistent being—namely, insofar as this being is capable of being-in-potency with respect to certain accidental acts; hence the potency can be present even when it is deprived of its act. Prime matter, however, is not an accidental capacity of a subsistent being, but the capacity for the first form itself of the subsistent being. Thus it is not founded in an act, but pure potency. And because whatever is, insofar as it is, is determined, pure determinability can be only as *actuated,* i.e., as "informed," as the constituent principle of a subsistent being. Accordingly, matter and form are immediately component principles, while potency and act, of themselves, refer first to states of *being* and only then are conceived as component parts.

2. The accidental potency can be a capacity for different acts which complement and perfect one another, as e.g., in the increase of size, heat or knowledge. Only in some cases, for instance, in certain active qualities such as colors, does the fulfillment of the potency by one act impede its fulfillment by other acts. For matter, on the other hand, the capacity is essentially directed to mutually exclusive

arrived at the composition of essence and "to be" only through the theory of participation and that only subsequently he expressed this composition in terms of potency and act. But Robert thinks that Aristotelian metaphysics may begin with the theory of limitation of act through receptive potency. Fernand Van Steenberghen expresses himself more circumspectly in the second edition of his *Ontologie* (Louvain, 1952, pp. 261-263) than in the first (*Louvain,* 1946, pp. 91-92), but maintains his view that potency and act should not be introduced before the problem of change. Subsequently, however, once the existence of a transcendent Origin has been demonstrated, it is permissible, he says, to make a synthesis and to oppose God as Pure Act to finite beings as compared of potency and act. In our view it is not necessary to defer this synthetizing retrospective view till the end of the metaphysical train of thought.

[8]Cf. nos. 86-91.
[9]Cf. no. 74.

acts, because matter is pure potency with respect to *all* of the many distinct material forms. Accordingly, matter has a potential indetermination. This indetermination is called also infinity, but in a radically different sense from the infinity of being which is perfect determination.[10] This infinity of matter cannot be wholly filled by an act, for every material form implies a limited mode of *being* which excludes other forms from the being in question. For this reason matter is the principle of essential change, a change which is always both generation and corruption.

3. The accidental potency remains something pertaining to the same subsistent being, even when it is actuated by other acts. Prime matter, on the other hand, remains a constituent principle of *this* subsistent being only as long as it is actuated by *this* first form. In an essential change the subsistent being loses its "being-itself," its identity, and becomes "something else," so that matter becomes a constituent principle of another being. Prime matter is what prevents a being from remaining perfectly itself but, on the other hand, it also links this being with the other being into which it is changed and, therefore, makes a being remain to some extent itself.

Species-Individual Structure and Potency-Act. When the logical distinction of species and individual serves as the starting point of hylomorphism, a twofold role is assigned to matter.

1. It serves to explain the *multiplication* of one and the same specific characteristic. If matter and form are considered here as potency and act, these two terms are evidently used in a broadened sense, for change does not play a primary role. There is no objection to this extension of these concepts, provided one accepts the possibility of change or the transition of a being from one species to another as a consequence flowing from the non-identity of the specifying and individuating principles.

2. Matter serves also to explain the *limitation* of the specific character. In this respect too, one may speak of act and potency as long as one does not forget that concretely act is not realized equally in the individuals, despite the fact that in the judgment the concept of species, because of its abstract nature, is predicated univocally of these individuals. If each individual form is different, the individuals participate in a limited and unequal way in the specific idea, so that

---

[10]Cf. no. 63.

one has to conceive act as transcending as well as embracing its
limited realizations.

The Proofs from Extension and Temporality and Potency-Act.
In the argument based on extension there is question of actual unity
and potential division or divisibility. In the proof from temporality
we spoke about the limitation of the participation in *being* through
the plurality of dispersed "nows." Thus it is easy to see how potency
and act apply here in a broad sense. Moreover, divisibility explains
how one subsistent being can be dissolved into many, which is kind
of substantial change. Temporality, on the other hand, demonstrates
the successive and transitory character as pertaining even to the very
essence itself of the subsistent being. In addition, these arguments
show that the relationship of potency and act is not the same in all
subsistent beings, but that in higher beings divisibility is conquered
to a greater extent by act as the principle of unity.

100. *Substance and Accidents*[11]

Use of Potency and Act with Respect to Substance and Accidents.
Insofar as potency and act correspond fully to each other and potency
is essentially a capacity of act, an accidental act is the immediate
fulfillment of an accidental potency, just as first form, as substantial
act, is the fulfillment of prime matter, as substantial potency.[12]

On the other hand, we have admitted accidental determinations
of the finite subsistent being precisely because of the participation in
being through which this being is dynamically infinite and directed
to activity as its perfection. Thus the finite subsistent being is not
yet fully determined by its essence but, as substance, remains further
determinable. Accordingly, it is permissible to consider the substance
as the potential principle and the accident as the actual principle.
Nevertheless, potency and act are given here a still broader and still
more analogous sense than when they are used for matter and form.

Analogous Nature of the Usage. Although substance is the
determinable and receptive principle with respect to accidents, nevertheless the accidental being constituted by substance and accidents is

---

[11]Cf. nos. 65-71.

[12]Thus, for example, actually being-white is the fulfillment of the capacity
of being-white found in a colored body. Being-colored is a property belonging
to the extended with respect to its surface. In general, the active qualities
of the corporeal being are borne primarily by continuous extension. Activities
also are the fulfillment of powers as capacities.

something that is attributed to the individual subsistent being itself, the supposit, as *its* perfection. Through these accidental acts this supposit *itself* is in this or that way; it is a subject in a much higher sense than the potency, for it is that which through the accidents is in this or that way. These accidents, then, have an "essence" only in a derivative sense—namely, by an analogous relationship insofar as they modify the essence of the subsistent being in a secondary way and therefore always refer to the "essence" in the first sense, i.e., the whatness of that which itself is.

For this reason the *being* of the accidental is not a "to be itself" or "*in* itself", but accidents "are" only insofar as they are *in* the subsistent. Not the accidental is, but the subsistent is according to the accident. Thus the roles of potency and act are almost reversed, for the subsistent gives *being* (as in-*being*) to the accidental and, as being already actual in its subsistence, extends this actuality to the accidents.

Accordingly, the subsistent is not only the subject but also the *origin* of the accidents, which to a greater or lesser extent all flow from its essence. We say "to a greater or lesser extent." For properties of a being, such as its powers, flow from the essence immediately and of necessity;[13] activities flow from it by means of the powers through participation in prior or higher activities;[14] spatial and temporal determinations through the intermediary of the situation;[15] and some qualities through the influence of the active qualities of the surroundings.[16] However, the subsistent, according to its essential form, is always the dynamic origin of its determinations. Hence it is not merely in passive potency but also and primarily in a kind of active and "emanative" potency.

Finally, the subsistent being is the *purpose* also of the accidents, which are for the sake of perfecting the dynamic subsistent being. This assertion applies even to the highest accidental perfections, viz., activities. When it is said that "to be" is for the sake of "to act" and essence for action, the meaning is not that action, taken as it were in isolation, is the purpose and that the subsistent is directed to this action as a means. The purpose is the active subsistent being, i.e., the subsistent in its highest self-sufficiency, in its drawing the action

---

[13]Cf. no. 94.
[14]Cf. no. 95.
[15]Cf. nos. 78-79.
[16]Cf. no. 80.

from itself, especially when the subsistent being has full dominion over its acts through free self-determination.

From all this it follows that it is an oversimplification of their mutual relationships to call subsistent being and its accidents "potency and act" in exactly the same sense as these terms apply to the potency-act structures which reveal themselves in accidental or substantial change. It is only in a certain sense and with the necessary restrictions that these terms can be used here.

101. *Essence and "To Be"*

The distinction of essence and "to be" hardly played a role in Aristotle, but it is clearly present in Arabian philosophy (Avicenna). Thomas Aquinas, especially in his later works, characteristically explained all perfection through "to be," which he describes as the act of all acts, the form of all forms, and the perfection of all perfections.[17] These expressions do not mean that "to be" is a form or even an act in the proper sense of the terms, but that it is the *actuality* of all acts, that through which the real is real, the possible is possible, and the necessary is necessary.[18] If Plato's philosophy is said to be characterized by the primacy of the Idea, Aristotle's by that of substance, (*eidos* as *ousia*), Hegel's by Logos, Bergson's by Life, etc., one may speak also of the primacy of "to be" in the philosophy of St. Thomas.

The fact that finite beings merely participate in unqualified *being* implies that there is in them a certain non-identity of essence and "to be." However, this non-identity does not mean absolute opposition, for ultimately the essence derives its modifying capacity from "to be," which transcends and encompasses all possible modes of *being*.

The question we have to consider here is whether this opposition may be considered as a relationship of potency and act.

---

[17]Cf. St. Thomas, *De potentia,* q. 3, a. 7; q. 7., a. 2, *ad 9*; *Summa* theol. p. 1, q. 3, a 4, a. 1, *ad* 3; q. 4, a. 2; q. 7, a. 1; q. 8, a.1; q. 105, a. 5. See also Louis de Raeymaeker, "De zin van het woord *esse* by de H. Thomas van Aquino," *Tijdschrift* v. *Philosophie,* vol. 8 (1946), pp. 407-434; "De lange tocht naar een uitgesproken philosophie van het zijn," *Miscellanea de Meyer,* 1946, pp. 106-116; J. van Boxtel, "Existentie en waarde in de eerste werken van de H. Thomas van Aquino," *Tijdschrift* v. *Philosophie,* vol. 10 (1948), pp. 211-288; "Existentie en Waarde in de latere werken van de H. Thomas van Aquino," *Tijdschrift* v. *Philosophie,* vol. 11 (1949), pp. 59-133; "Metaphysiek van het wezen of metaphysiek het zijn?" *Verslag der 16e Alg. Verg. voor Thomist. Wijsb.* (*Annalen van het Thijmgenootschap,* vol. 39 (1951), pp. 129-144; *Waarde-ethiek en Zijnsleer,* Nijmegen, 1948. [18]Cf. nos. 28-34.

Essence—"To Be" and Potency—Act. Such a final broadening of act and potency to include "to be" and essence is permissible, provided one defines exactly in which analogous sense potency and act are used here. The reasons are as follows.

1. Potency is the principle of determinability and mutability. But the essence is not determinable to *many* acts of a distinct content but only to the act of *being*. And this determination through the act of *being* constitutes also the essence itself which, without "to be," is not and therefore also is not essence. For this reason the aspect of mutability is wholly absent from the essence as essence, unless one says that a being which is not wholly identical with its "to be" is "moved" to "to be" in the broadest sense of being-moved.[19]

2. Act is the principle of determinateness. But the act of *being* undoubtedly is the principle *par excellence* of determinateness, insofar as whatever is, insofar as it is, is determinate. On the other hand, however, the finite being owes the determinateness of its content to the essence, for the essence is the principle of determinateness insofar as it indicates *what* a being is. Nevertheless, an analogous similarity with potency in the broad sense may be discovered when one considers that 1) every determination of content of a finite being is a *limitation* with respect to the infiniteness of *being;* 2) because of this limitation there can be a *plurality* of essentially distinct beings.

3. Potency and act, in the proper sense, are opposed as two principles; and a being is not in-potency through the same entity which makes it pass to being-in-act. Nevertheless, essence and "to be," as the recipient and the received, cannot be reduced to a *twofold* origin because otherwise the recipient or essence, would remain unexplained. For how could the essence be recipient and how could there be distinct recipients which receive in always-different ways, save through "to be"? Even to-be-recipient is a mode of *being* and therefore finds its ultimate origin in *being*.[20]

---

[19]Cf. no. 79.
[20]Cf. no. 57.

CHAPTER TWENTY

FINITE BEING AS CAUSE AND EFFECT

102. *Perception of Causality*

Empiricism and Phenomenalism. According to *empiricism* (Hume),[1] which is at the same time also nominalism,[2] we observe only successive facts without ever being capable of knowing necessary connections. However, when definite phenomena are regularly followed by definite other phenomena and we suspect that this state of affairs will continue, we refer to the first phenomena as "cause."

Phenomenalism (Kant),[3] which is at the same time also idealistic conceptualism,[4] does not admit that casuality is experienced. We think, its adherents say, that phenomena which follow one another in time are of necessity connected according to the categories of cause and effect. These categories, however, are *a priori* in the Kantian sense of the term and therefore subjective. Therefore, the laws of physical science apply to objects as they appear to us.

Empiricism contradicts itself when it endeavors to indicate the subjective cause of the necessary illusion of causality. Phenomenalism does the same thing when it speaks about "things in themselves" as causing the data of experience and about categories of thought as the cause why we of necessity require a connection between these data.[5]

Perception of Causality. Leaving aside these contradictions, we have indubitable perceptions of causality based on experience. First of all, there are our own conscious activities. They are attributed to the individual subsistent being not only because they are *in* this being as their ultimate subject, but also and especially because they emanate *from* the subsistent being as their ultimate origin. This *emanation* is a kind of "making real," and in this respect we must be

---

[1]Cf. nos 23 and 80.
[2]Cf. no.83
[3]Cf. no. 25.
[4]Cf. no. 83.
[5]Moreover, these trends of thought conceive cause and effect in a much too one-sided fashion as the interaction of material beings. Causality does not always mean temporal succession, for effect, as effect, is always simultaneous with cause, as cause. Likewise, causality does not always mean regularity, for the more the cause is cause, the more it has control over the production of the effect and the more the effect will be new, unique, and unforeseeable.

called the cause of the activities which we exercise, even though it remains true that we are never their total cause.[6]

Secondly, in some cases we perceive *transient* actions of corporeal beings in our surroundings, which influence us sensitively[7] or act upon one another.[8] This transient action is a "making real" of a perfection in an object that is acted upon; hence there is a distinction between the active being and the being acted upon as cause and effect. However, here again the respect under which these two are cause and effect is very limited and, in addition, there is always a certain reciprocal action.[9]

Finally, our *immanent* acts of knowing and tending can move the motor functions hierarchically subjected to them to exercise their activities and thus can produce mediately something real in other corporeal beings. The actions of a craftsman exemplify this point. No matter how obscure may be the connection between immanent act and external result, we cannot deny the experience provided by our own active dealings with beings.[10]

Insight into Causality. These considerations sufficiently show that the perception of causality is an indubitable perception implied in our own *being* and activity. Cause and effect may present themselves in a threefold way to our perception:

1. Sometimes it is from the standpoint of the cause that we experience the resultance of an effect—namely, in our experience of our immanent acts and our deeds.

2. Sometimes, we experience a cause and an effect in their dynamic "bi-unity"—namely, in the external perception of certain movements and changes.

3. Finally, we sometimes perceive events or beings which we recognize as effects of a cause that is not yet known in itself.

---

[6]Cf. nos. 93-95.
[7]Cf. no. 84.
[8]Cf. no. 89.
[9]Cf. no. 91.
[10]The most proper form of human causality is the moral influence exercised on fellow human beings *as* persons. This influence is a free act which is freely also accepted by the others. Although this influence is the purest form of causality experienced by us, we cannot yet discuss it here. Cf. no. 154.

Still less is it possible for us to show at the present stage that the absolutely highest form of knowing and loving must be *capable* of exercising external influence in an immediate way, i.e., without the intermediary of executive powers, and that this pure causality must be the *total* cause of its effect, i.e., does not presuppose that the effect influences it in any way (cf. no. 181).

This third case shows that on the basis of our experience of causality we possess a certain *insight*[11] into the essential relationship of cause and effect and that we know of certain beings that they must necessarily be brought into a causal relationship with other beings, whatever may be the nature of these other beings. This insight has to be clarified in philosophical reflection. Which beings refer of necessity to other beings as their causes and why? Before we consider this question, however, it will be useful to describe first somewhat more accurately what is meant by the terms cause and effect.

103. *Cause and Effect*

General Relationship. The statement that every effect has a cause expresses the relation which the effect must necessarily have to the cause. In this sense the statement may be called a first clarification of cause and effect. However, it says nothing about the ground or reason why a definite being in a definite respect must be considered as an effect and, consequently, as of necessity dependent in its *being* on something else.

The statement that every cause has an effect is still less illuminating, for we do not usually conclude from cause to effect but from effect to cause.[12]

Description of Effect and Cause. An effect is a being which is real, and is as it is, only insofar as it proceeds from something other than itself. To-be-an-effect, therefore, is a relationship of dependence which pertains of necessity to certain beings in certain respects. It is a property flowing from their mode of *being*.

A cause is a being which makes something else proceed from itself as dependent on it in its being-real. In other words, it is a principle which exercises influence on the being-real of a certain being in a certain respect.[13]

---

[11]Cf. no. 21.

[12]Moreover, as will become clear later, there is no absolute correlativity of cause as cause and effect as effect. The cause does not necessarily have a real relation to its effect; it does not even of necessity have an effect.

[13]A principle, in the broadest sense, is anything from which something else follows or proceeds in any way whatsoever. Thus in the order of space a point is the principle of a line, in the order of time the earlier is the principle of the later, in the order of being-known the premises are the principles of the conclusion. In the last-named example there is a certain cognitive influence and therefore the principles in question are said to be the cognitive ground or reason. However, the term "reason" may indicate also a ground of *being*. If this ground of *being* is identical with that which is grounded by it, then the distinction between the two arises only from our way of thinking. If, on the other hand, the ground of *being* is really distinct from what is grounded by it, then we call such a principle a cause.

Internal Causes. Cause and effect are distinct. If this distinction does not refer to two subsistent beings but lies within a single being, it can refer only to the constituent principles which are fully identical neither with each other nor with the being itself, insofar as these principles exercise a certain influence on the way a being really is. In this sense these principles are called *material* and *formal* causes. The terms are used in a broader sense than prime matter and primary form, for they apply also to potency and act in a narrow sense—including not only passive potency and act but also active potency and activity—and even the relationship of substance and accidents.[14]

External Causes. When the distinction of cause and effect refers to two subsistent beings, the terms are used in a stricter sense. In this case it is customary to speak of external causes. We will follow this terminology, which indicates only that cause and effect are ontologically not identical but distinct beings, and does not have the connotation of the spatial exteriority implied by such terms as "external perception" and "external senses."

Causes in this sense are:

1. The operative or *efficient* cause, which in the order of execution influences the "to be" of a being.

2. The *final* cause, which in the order of intention is that for the sake of which something is made real.

3. In addition, there is question sometimes of an *exemplary* cause, i.e., the original idea according to which something is made real, e.g., the idea which governs an activity guided by the intellect.

Analogy of Cause and Effect. The terms cause and effect are predicated analogously of the various types of causality. Internal causes are causes only in a secondary sense, but to external causes the term applies in the primary sense. For us, the first meaning of cause is efficient cause, even though it is true that the final cause has to be called the cause of the efficient cause. Moreover, causal influence may assume all kinds of differentiated forms for which it is difficult to find a place in the classical schema of four causes. As an example we may refer to the causal influence exercised in personal "moral" relationships.[15]

---

[14]In the relationship of the subsistent being to its accidents and especially to its powers and activities there is an "emanative" causality which has something of the efficient cause (cf. no. 100).

[15]For the schema of the four causes, cf. Aristotle, *Physica,* bk. II, chs. 3 ff. and St. Thomas' *Comment.,* nos. 176 ff.; also *Metaphysica,* bk. V, ch. 2 and St. Thomas' *Comment.,* nos. 763-794.

104. *The Inadequacy of the Internal Causes*

The Principle of Intelligibility. The principle guiding the reply to the question of why a certain being under a certain aspect must necessarily be conceived as the effect of another being is the principle of intelligibility or sufficient reason:[16] Whatever is, insofar as it is, has a ground or reason why it is as it is.

Because being is intelligible precisely insofar as it is, the ultimate or groundless ground of intelligibility lies in *being* itself. In other words, insofar as a being *is* and, consequently, is identical with itself, it finds its explanation in this *identity:* it is its own "why." To some extent, therefore, every being has within itself the reason for its *being*—namely, insofar as, as being, it cannot not-be.

Identity and Causality. However, the identity of a being with itself may be relative only. It may imply non-identity and, consequently, opposition,[17] division,[18] imperfection,[19] and indeterminateness.[20] If, nevertheless, such a being *is,* and therefore is, though only relatively, one, perfect, and determinate, the ground of this unity, perfection and determinateness cannot be found in the identity of its essence with itself, because its essence does not coincide with this ground. If such a finite and particular being is to be intelligible in its *being,* it has to include a reference to something else, with which it is not identical, as the ground and reason why it is as it is. This reference to the other as the ontological ground of a being is the relationship of effect to cause.

Causality of Matter and Form. Several times already we have encountered the non-identity of a being with itself as its composition of constituent principles which coincide neither with each other nor with the being itself. These principles are related to each other in a certain opposition, although through their union the being is *what* it is.

This assertion applies in particular to the corporeal being, which in its individual essence is composed of prime matter and primary form. As constituent principles, matter and form are in a certain sense prior to the being which they constitute. We may even say that they *are* only insofar as they constitute the *essence* of the being and that, as such, they exercise influence on the "to be" of the being in

---

[16]Cf. no. 42.
[17]Cf. no. 36.
[18]Cf. no. 39.
[19]Cf. no. 40.
[20]Cf. no. 41.

question. For this reason the material cause is said to be that through which the being is constituted according to its individuation as "here and now" and the formal cause is that through which the being is constituted according to the determination of its content. The causality of matter consists in *bearing* and *limiting* form, while that of form is the *actuating* and *determining* of matter. Through this mutual influence and composition, the individual essence arises as the principle from which to some extent "to be" flows.[21]

An analogous relationship may be discovered on the accidental level in the structures of passive potency and accidental act,[22] active potency and activity,[23] and even substance and accidents.[24] For this reason the matter-form causality, in a broader sense, is found also in accidental acts and forms, although always in essentially different ways.[25]

The Insufficiency of Internal Causes. The internal causes, however, can never offer the ultimate explanation of why a being is according to perfections, determinations, forms, and acts which, albeit its own, are not identical with it. For the constituent principles of such a being are not wholly identical with each other. Although matter, or more generally potency, is a capacity for form or act, *of itself* it is not form or act. The act, therefore, has to proceed or come forth, as it is said, from the capacity, the capacity has to be actuated. But the potency is not the complete foundation or reason why an act, distinct from it, would come forth. This assertion applies even to the active potency, so that this potency includes a certain passivity.[26]

If the material being is to have a ground or reason for its *being,* the coming forth of the form or act from matter or potency and the union of these two opposite constituent principles in a certain identity requires, therefore, a ground in another subsistent being which communicates its actuality to the potential being. For this reason the subsistent being, as "other" in the strict sense, effects, in the narrow sense of the term, the realization of the being in question and, therefore, is called its **efficient cause.**

---

[21]Cf. no. 89.

[22]Cf. no. 96.

[23]Cf. no. 95.

[24]Cf. no. 100.

[25]Even in the association of distinct subsistent beings in all kinds of units of order and quasi-subsistent beings, such as active organizations, one may find the constituent causality of matter and form. In such cases the form lies in the mutual relationships.

[26]Cf. no. 95.

105. *Whatever Changes in Time is Caused*

The clearest *sign* by which we recognize something as an effect is
that it originates in time. Such a thing necessarily refers to something else in which it was virtually present or pre-existed as in cause.

Locomotion. The local motion of bodily beings relative to one
another implies a being-moved and consequently an active moving.[27]
If the mover is another being, the mechanically communicated motion
refers to a series of moved movers. If, on the other hand, a being
begins to move itself, the motion arises from a concentration of motive
power or energy, which refers to preceding qualitative processes.
Moreover, the transition from energy to actual motion has to be
explained either by means of a change in the surrounding conditions
or, in the case of the living, through the influence of a higher vital
power which was already active, for even the self-motion of the living
body is not perfect. Accordingly, in any case, *whatever is in motion,
ultimately is moved by something else.*

Because of the resistance of the moved body, the whole process
of motion takes place not only in space but also in time. Local motion
is a complex of interrelationships of corporeal beings which escapes
our comprehension to such an extent that we can speak about motion
and rest only in reference to an arbitrary, supposedly immobile standpoint in the spatio-temporal whole. It depends on this standpoint
whether we conceive one being as in motion with respect to the
other or vice versa.

Pure locomotion is not a change, in the strict sense, of the corporeal being itself. Except from the viewpoint of the living being
which comes closer to the objects of its desires, locomotion is so little
something new that there is barely question of a genuine distinction
between cause and effect and of a genuine dependence of one on the
other. Everything is reciprocal here, and this proves that the moving
world of bodies must be conceived as a single whole governed by
laws.[28]

Qualitative Changes. Qualitative changes are changes, in the
strict sense, of beings. For their origin, these changes refer not only
to the nature of the changing being that is capable of being qualified
but also to the actuation of this capacity by another being which
actually possesses the quality in question.[29]

---

[27] Cf. no. 80.
[28] Cf. no. 91.
[29] Cf. no. 96.

Because with respect to corporeal qualities the capacity is always in a certain state of actuation, the qualitative influence has to modify the dispositions of the capacity in a gradual way. Thus, here also there is resistance and a process of assimilation that runs its course in time. Moreover, the being which undergoes the change, because of its opposite condition, exercises influence also on the being which causes the change; hence there is always a reciprocal action and the cause is influenced by the effect. Here also, therefore, there is an interconnection and no complete independence of the one from the other.

Essential Change. Essential change[30] lies in the perspective of qualitative changes. The qualities emanate from the subsistent being and, when they are changed, it may happen that the being gradually loses more and more the dispositions required for the persistence of its essential form. For this reason the subsistent being, which exercises its influence *according* to its essential form *by means of* active qualities as its instruments, is capable of communicating its essential form to something else by gradually changing the dispositions of matter, and in this way it can cause an instantaneous essential change.

However, the subsistent being itself which acts through its active qualities undergoes a change in its own qualities because it is passive also; hence the dispositions required for its own essential form are modified also, so that its own essential change is being prepared.

In this way the qualitative change in both beings is connected with the relationship between their matter and form. Their gradual reciprocal influence in the realm of qualities prepares them both for essential change. Through matter both of them are in potency not only to the essential form of each other, but also to a median essential form which may originate from their mutual assimilation and give rise to a more complex being. Thus, there is in the realm of beings which influence one another a constant tension between integration and disintegration, even with respect to their own individual essence.

However, even the essential forms of the more complex beings which may arise from the mutual interaction of corporeal beings hardly reveal any newness and originality. They can be explained by means of the mutual compenetration of activity and passivity in accord with the predetermined laws contained in the capacity of matter.

---

[30]Cf. no. 88.

Vital Actions. It is only when life breaks through the interaction proper to the parts of the material cosmos and reveals a certain immanence of activities that new and more original states of *being* manifest themselves through the action of the living on the purely corporeal. Here the opposition of cause and effect, of activity and passivity assumes a clearer meaning, because there is less reciprocity of influence. It is here also that causality manifests itself more strikingly as a superiority of the living over its surroundings, although at the same time it becomes less predictable in its effects.[31]

Cultural Products. Finally, new forms arise in the material world which point to the organizing action of a knowing being. True, products of culture rise from the potentiality of material substances by means of locomotion, insofar as "nature" is in potency to these products. Nevertheless their organized form indicates that they have been given a meaning from the standpoint of a human purpose and a human "idea." They can be explained only by an intelligent cause which knows the nature of the various beings and realizes in them, in a deliberate way, original forms of order. Here there is still less reciprocity, and the superiority of cause as well as the dependence of effect reveal themselves most strikingly.[32]

Cause and Condition. In all these changes the action of the causes requires certain real conditions. The most important of these conditions are: 1) bodily contact of the extended beings, and 2) the simultaneity of the influencing being with the being that is influenced.[33]

A condition is conceptually distinct from a cause insofar as it does not directly influence the effect, but makes it possible for the cause to exercise influence. If, however, the condition consists in the removal of obstacles, it exercises in this respect a certain causality. More generally, we must even say that, with the exception of the conditions of time and place, all other conditions, i.e., the qualitative states of the immediate and more remote surroundings, can be understood only as a less direct influence and therefore as causality. The whole of the concurrent circumstances which contribute to the exercise of the influence by one being on another plays an active role in the origin of this influence. Often it depends merely on the particular

---

[31]Cf. no. 113.
[32]Cf. no. 145.
[33]Cf. no. 94.

viewpoint with respect to a certain change whether we will call this a cause and that a condition or vice versa. It is especially our limited knowledge of the proper and immediate causes of certain events which makes it impossible for us to separate causes from conditions, although we are certain that all kinds of factors have contributed to the origin of the result and have exercised a direct or indirect influence, in the broad sense of the term. For this reason we may also give the name of cause in a broader sense, i.e., as including condition, to everything without which a certain being would not be exactly as it is. And if we keep in mind that, concretely speaking, every being has relationships with every other being, then everything in the world of bodies exercises influence on everything.[34]

106. *Whatever is Capable of Change but Remains Unchanged in Time is Caused*

All the influences hitherto considered presuppose the being which is influenced as a being and as in-capacity to certain acts, as expressed by the pairs matter-form, potency-act, substance-accidents. The causes make the being-in-potency go into act, so that we may summarize the preceding considerations in the statement: *whatever passes in time from being-in-potency to being-in-act does so under the influence of a being that is already in act* with respect to the perfection in question.

When a being which does not coincide with its act, but *of itself* is only in potency to the act and, consequently, changeable with respect to this act, *remains in-act* after the transition, there must be an actual cause which maintains this actuation of the potency. It is in this connection especially that there is question of necessary favorable conditions and of keeping away incompatible obstacles. But it is here also that it becomes manifest why these conditions must exercise continuous influence to make the being remain what it has become.

If we add the consideration that the temporal being is constantly developing and changing at least in some respects and, therefore, continually in danger of losing the dispositions required by its form or act, the necessity of a favorable environment to maintain the existing condition becomes even more evident. We will therefore *enlarge* the concepts of effect and cause in such a way that we consider the unchanged but changeable being causally dependent on a series of

---

[34]Cf. no. 91.

causes, even though it is true that we know still less of these causal influences than of those which give rise to a change occurring in time.

Accordingly, we may draw the following conclusion about any being which possesses a perfection (form, act, or activity), but is not identical with this perfection because of itself it is only in potency to this perfection. At every moment at which it possesses the perfection actually, it is caused by an external cause which effects or maintains the union of the internal causes (matter and form in the broad sense). In other words, *every being which is not identical with the form or act determining its content is caused with respect to its being-actual according to this form or act.*

107. *The Univocal Cause as Inadequate Cause*

Causality and Concrete Causes. To understand that the coming or ceasing to be and the change or permanence of a being require an external cause does not mean to be able to indicate what the cause in question is. The principle of causality, of which in the preceding pages we gave two provisional formulations, sometimes makes us affirm that something is caused, although this cause itself is not given to us in our immediate perception. In such cases there are two ways to discover the possible cause. We may reason by way of analogy from privileged internal experiences and external perceptions in which the immediate connection of cause and effect is given[35] to cases in which the cause-effect relationship is not directly evident. Or, if the same phenomenon occurs repeatedly in different situations, we may investigate which factors are essential and which accidental with respect to the phenomenon in question. However, even if in this way we arrive at certainty regarding the necessary and sufficient ground of certain facts, we do not always obtain an insight into the causal relationship itself, we do not always know *why* these grounds give rise to these facts or *how* the causality in question operates.

Univocal Cause. Leaving aside the influence exercised by living and knowing beings on their surroundings,[36] and limiting ourselves to the interaction or "natural events"[37] common to everything corporeal, we may say that it is possible to indicate a condition which must be fulfilled if the being is to act as the cause of motions and changes. This condition is that this being must possess either actu-

---

[35] Cf. no. 102.
[36] Cf. no. 145.
[37] Cf. no. 91.

ally or virtually the determination which it communicates to the object in immediate contact with it. For instance, what is in motion, actively moves, what is hot makes warm. The effect *resembles* the cause in which the determination in question pre-exists.

This determination, form, or act is present in the cause in the same sense as it is in the effect. Just as the effect is an individual which of itself is merely in potency to the act, so the cause possesses this act only as the fulfillment of a capacity and does not wholly coincide with it. Both cause and effect participate in one and the same univocal general determination, which they both can lose again and which the cause has only as received through the influence of another cause. Such a cause, which is situated on the same level as the effect, is called a *univocal* cause.[38]

Analogous Cause. The univocal cause is a link in a series of dependent entities. It explains only why a certain being with which it is in contact becomes here and now such a being, provided the chain of conditions required for its influence is present. The univocal cause is not the cause of the specific determination, form, or act, e.g., being-warm, as such wherever this determination occurs. For, it itself participates only here and now in the determination and therefore is caused with respect to it. The priority of the cause over the effect, then, lies only in the difference of their individual situation within the surrounding spatio-temporal whole. Both refer to a higher cause which makes them, although in a certain order of dependence, participate in the determination, form or act as such. This higher, still unknown, cause of being-"such" unqualifiedly, which above[39] we have called the real general cause, lies outside the series of reciprocal causes and effects. It is the basis of their order, and possesses the perfection or action in which the individuals participate, not in an univocal way but eminently. We may call such a cause an *analogous cause.*[40]

Presuppositions of the Univocal Cause. The univocal cause presupposes that the being on which it exercises influence possesses a

[38]Cf. no. 54.
[39]Cf. no. 84.
[40]Concerning univocal and analogous causes, causes of becoming and causes of *being,* see St. Thomas, *De potentia,* q. 5, a. 1 (causes which "in the order of things are on the same level as" the effects dispose matter and "educe the form from the potency of matter") ; *Summa theol.,* p. 1, q. 45, a. 5, *ad* 1. Cf. J. Legrand, *L'univers et l'homme dans la philosophie de S. Thomas d'Aquin,* Bruxelles, 1946, vol. 1, pp. 128-197.

capacity for the determination that is to be received by it. This capacity arises from the fundamental capacity for determinations, the *prime matter* of a being. As to the question whether the material being is self-explanatory from the viewpoint of prime matter, the answer has to be in the negative. For, if prime matter were the sufficient ground of beings, it would be identical with the *being* of the beings. But, of itself, prime matter is merely privatively infinite, i.e., without any actual determinateness, while "to be" of itself is positively infinite and fully determinate.

The univocal cause presupposes also that the object of its influence is *real*. The question whether the being-real of material beings is self-explanatory, likewise receives a negative reply. The "to be" of a material being is identical neither with matter or form nor with the essence; hence the internal causes do not appear to offer the sufficient ground for its being-real. Thus the question arises whether the material cosmos does not refer to a ground of *being* transcending matter.

A Broader Inquiry into the Ground of Being. This question leads us to a renewed inquiry into the ground of *being* on a broader basis which embraces not only the material world but everything finite. Hitherto we have explained finiteness through participation in unqualified *being* but the precise meaning of this assertion was left undecided. Now that we have learned to see all non-identity, plurality, indeterminateness, as dependence on an explanatory cause, we must ask whether perhaps the principle of causality is valid for everything finite and has to be formulated as: *Whatever participates in unqualified* being *is the effect of a cause.*

This cause would have to contain eminently not only the particular modes of *being* but also the unqualified "to be," which functions as an internal principle of all possible and real beings. It would have to be conceived as fully independent of all caused beings, as self-subsistent "To Be."

However, we do not yet want to raise this last metaphysical question, which constitutes the transition from formal to causal participation. First we must continue our analysis of experience with respect to the higher grades of *being* called "living" and "knowing" beings. In this way we will arrive at a clearer insight into the immanent order of finite beings to the "world" in which we human beings find ourselves first in our passivity and our active self-enfolding.[41]

108. *The Purpose as Cause*

The produced effect is dependent on the producing cause. It is the *end* of the production just as the cause is its *beginning*. Effect and cause, therefore, are relatively opposed.

The Principle of Finality.[42] Why is it that the causal action terminates in the *being* of *this* definite effect and no other? The answer usually given is that the causal action was predetermined to this definite effect by its cause as the beginning or principle in which this end was pre-contained. To this it is usually added that this principle was directed to this end, and the effect, as present in the direction of the cause is called the "intended end" of the causal action. This expression is used to convey the idea that the end, as the "why" of the activity, is the cause of the causal action—every agent acts for an end.

Is this view correct and does it hold also when the activity does not seem to be guided by any knowledge, i.e., in the purely material influence occurring in a natural event?

---

[41]Now that we have seen the inadequacy of the univocal cause which has always to be together with its effects, we can understand better how the cause in the strict sense, is a higher and analagous cause, which does not depend on its effect. Just as the effect, as effect, is necessarily dependent on the cause, so the cause, as cause, is necessarily independent of the effect.

The reason is as follows: A being which of necessity requires that another being be dependent on it cannot be without this other being. But then it depends in a certain sense on this other being, for it needs the other to be itself, i.e., to be a cause. Now a cause which somehow depends on its effect is no longer a pure cause; it is dependent not precisely insofar as it is a cause. The cause, therefore, must be considered as something which, being what it is, is *capable* of making something else arise from itself as dependent on itself.

When we speak here of being capable or capacity, we mean the full power to dispose of its own causality and, ultimately, the full *freedom* of the cause with respect to its effect. Accordingly, causality does not find its origin, motive, or reason in the effect, but only in the liberality of the cause. In other words, full causality is freely creating causality, it does not presuppose anything, but establishes everything.

[42]Concerning finality, see R. Garrigou-Lageange, *Le réalisme du principe de finalité*, Paris, 1932; Cl. Schoonbrood, *"Das ontologische Problem der Finalitaet," Alg. Ned. Tijdschrift v. Wijsb. en Psych.*, vol. 47 (1955), pp. 177-184; Andrew G. van Melsen, *The Philosophy of Nature*, Pittsburgh, 4th impr., 1961, pp. 168-171 (the analogy of finality); J. Maréchal, *Le point de départ de la métaphysique*, Vol. 5., pp. 363-372; Thomas Aquinas, *Summa theol*, p. 1, q. 44, a.4; p.I-II, q.1, a.2; *Contra Gentes*, bk.III, ch.2. In his early work *De principiis naturae* he wrote: "Therefore, it is possible for a natural agent to tend to an end without deliberation. This tending is *nothing else* than to have a natural inclination to something."

Finite Beings and Final Cause. One may speak of purpose not only with respect to an efficient cause but also with regard to everything that is active and even simply all that is. In this broadest sense, purpose means that for the sake of which something is. Whatever is has not only a ground but also a meaning or direction: being as being is meaningful, for it is ordered to *being* as its good.[43] However, despite its orientation to *being,* the finite being participates only in a limited fashion in *being* and is dynamically directed to a more intimate participation in *being* through communication with others according to the possibilities contained in its essence.[44] For this reason it may be said that the finite being finds in its activity the purpose to which it is directed according to its nature. Better still, the subsistent being, as fully active, has itself as its purpose.

However, this assertion applies fully only to immanent acts, for only a being which lives, knows and loves attains its self-perfection in itself. Material beings have activity only insofar as they act transiently on others. The question, then, is: where lies the meaning or direction of this action? Evidently, the action cannot be detached from the other being in which it finds its end. For it cannot be conceived as the perfection of the acting being, taken in itself, because it is not a new reality pertaining to the acting being in itself but is the communicated perfection *in* the effect insofar as this perfection comes *from* the causing being—action is in the recipient.[45]

Nevertheless, we must ask whether the effect merely "results" from the efficient cause or whether this cause is "directed" to the effect. Is the cause active for the sake of the effect to be realized, and is the effect the end not only as the terminus but also as the end intended?

Transient Action and Finality. Whatever is, is determined,[46] and every effect is a determined effect. We call something an effect if the determination of its *being* does not find its sufficient ground in the essence itself of the being in question but in something else: the effect is such because there is a cause which produces this effect and no other. How, then, is the cause determined to this effect?

It may happen that a cause determines itself to the effect, but experience seems to exclude this free self-determination in the external

---

[43]Cf. no. 43.
[44]Cf. no 63.
[45]Cf. no. 80.
[46]Cf. no. 41.

action of one extended object on another. Such an action is a natural event in which the cause is predetermined by its nature to definite effects, and these effects follow of necessity as soon as the series of required conditions is present and a prior cause moves the dependent cause to activity.[47] We must, therefore, say that material motions and changes are predetermined in the whole complexus of cause and condition.

Is it possible that at least some effects come about by chance? The answer is affirmative, at least if one means that they originate through a coincidence or a concurrence of several independent series of causes. In such a case the effect is not predetermined in any of the causes taken separately. Nevertheless, chance is not an explanation, but itself needs to be explained. There has to be a further ground why the series of causes concur in this way. This reason is all the more urgent when the effect shows a greater inner unity. Finally, there are no causes which act in absolute independence of one another, for all bodily beings are interconnected in the spatio-temporal order of the universe, no matter how unfathomable this order be for us.

Analogy of Final Cause. Thus it remains true that every effect pre-exists in the whole of its causes. There is a proportion of effect to cause, and the transient action is a change which in every one of its phases runs a determined course. In other words, the cause is directed to its effect, as active potency is directed to its act. Otherwise every effect would be a fortuitous terminus, for, if the cause were indifferent to the effect, anything could follow from anything. If the effect is to terminate the action of the cause, then the effect must be present in the directedness of the cause. This directedness to something definite as an end is called finality.

Finality, however, has to be understood here in an analogous sense. The primary meaning of purpose is that which is intended or pre-exists in a knowing cause, which directs itself to something as an effect to be realized. In a secondary or degraded sense the term indicates that to which a being is ordered through the inclination of its nature, insofar as this thing pre-exists in the directedness of the nature as act pre-exists in potency. Thus there is a correlation of efficient cause and final cause: while one is, the other is also. And the character of the final cause corresponds to the nature of the

---

[47]Cf. no. 95.

efficient cause. A free efficient cause determines itself to its purpose and lets this purpose influence it, while a non-free efficient cause is determined to its purpose by nature and thus is already influenced by this purpose.

Purpose and Nature. In the case of univocal causes, the effect, insofar as its determinate content is concerned, is the same perfection, form, or act through which the cause is in-act, the difference being that in the effect this perfection is realized outside the cause. Accordingly, the effect, which is last in order of execution, is the cause of the cause insofar as it pre-exists in the cause as the determining principle of the cause's operation. It is first in the order of intention. The effect is cause, not because it effects something, but because it orientates the cause to itself as the meaning or direction of causal action.

In beings whose action is a natural event the purpose and the form or act constituting the agent's nature coincide with respect to content. But the purpose is, as it were, the other side of nature— nature *drives* while purpose *attracts*.

Purpose and Perfection of the Agent. In univocal causes the effect, as realized through the power of the efficient cause, depends on this cause, but the efficient cause depends also on the effect, as intended by nature. As we have seen previously, the reciprocal influence of cause and effect characterizes material and finite beings which are together in one order, because they share in the same perfections in such a way that no being is ever the total cause of the other. This reciprocity manifests itself also in the mutual causality of final and efficient causes.

Nevertheless, even in transient actions the purpose does not lie entirely in the perfection of the effect taken in itself. The efficient cause realizes in its action also to some extent the meaning of *its own being,* albeit only by perfecting others whose existence it presupposes. It perfects itself in serving the others according to the order of the cosmos.

However, a higher mode of self-perfection can be the purpose of activity. We are thinking here of a cause that is more truly cause and of an effect that is more truly effect and dependent on the cause. A cause is more truly cause in the measure that it is more free and more independent of the effect; and an effect is more truly effect, the less presupposed it is as a subsistent being with its own nature and purpose, and the more it is raised to the ontological perfection of the cause. The more, then, a cause is cause and an effect is effect, the less the purpose of the activity will lie in the effect's own presupposed ontological perfection, the more this purpose will be the effect's participation in, and relation to the ontological perfection of the cause. The more the cause is cause, the more the purpose is not the subsistence of the effect as opposed to the cause, but the subsistence of the effect as a being which through its participated essence comes *from* the cause, is *in accordance with* the cause, and is *directed to* the cause. This order of effect to cause clearly begins to reveal itself in immanent acts which have a virtually transient influence such as man's influence on things.[48]

---

[48]When the cause is the total and inadequate cause of its effect, and the effect is an analogous participation in the absolute ontological perfection of the cause, the proper purpose is no longer the effect as to be realized by the cause, for this is the case only when the cause needs something else to be itself. The proper purpose here is the efficient cause itself, which attracts everything it has freely caused to itself as the source of all goodness and the proper "why." Accordingly, the perfect final cause and the perfect efficient cause coincide, so that the purpose is not only first in the ideal order but also in the real order. In other words, pure goodness is also pure power (cf. no. 180).

CHAPTER TWENTY-ONE

THE LIVING BEING

109. *The Experience of My Own Being-Alive*

The pre-predicative certainty of my own *being*[1] implicitly contains also the certitude of my being-alive. For I know and love my own *being* and in this knowledge and love I somehow contain all other beings also. The explicitation of this knowing and loving, however, occurs in time,[2] for I can enfold myself only by means of being explicitly directed to other beings with which I am together and which place themselves gradually in my presence, so that by giving and taking we can join one another in the immanence of our acts of life. The multiplicity of my acts finds its unity not only in its origin from me as its source but also in its purpose of being directed to the attainment of my ideal essence.

In my search for insight into essences I depend upon the observation of facts. But perception presupposes that I am sensitively in a spatial and temporal contact with a succession of corporeal beings.[3] This process of experience also, interiorized through memory and expectation, is an unfolding of myself, for I make my surroundings immanent in a certain, albeit degrade way.

The sensitive perceptivity of my organs itself presupposes a vegetative process of exchange between me as a corporeal being and my surroundings. It is precisely this active and passive exchange of matter between me and my surroundings that in organic sensation is raised to the level of touch.[4]

Active Intercourse With My Surroundings. Finally, there is also the undeniable experience I have of my active intercourse with my surroundings. The root of this intercourse lies in the intellective willing and the sensitive tendencies which reveal themselves in transient activities. Sensitive knowledge is even naturally ordered to maintain oneself as a living body through respiration, nutrition, locomotion, etc. In addition, the intellect, on the one hand, uses the

---

[1] Cf. no. 17.
[2] Cf. no. 48.
[3] Cf. no. 77.
[4] Cf. no. 136.

surroundings, whether unchanged or modified, by making them sub-servient to the protection, growth and well-being of corporeal life, but, on the other hand, it is unable to reach its own self-development without constantly using the sensitive, vegetative, and corporeal as symbols and signs in which it expresses and embodies itself.[5]

110. *The Experience of Other Beings as Living*

I do not perceive the beings around me merely as spatially and temporally extended and as constantly changing in a local, qualita-tive, and substantial way through transient activities. Although hith-erto we have viewed perception mainly in this way, its function should be conceived more broadly, for otherwise perception would teach us only about what is common to all corporeal beings. Such a concep-tion would be *abstract,* for it leaves out of consideration the differ-ences existing between the objects of our perception.

The *concrete* course of perception reveals rather the opposite pic-ture. Attention is concentrated primarily on the perception of living and sensitive bodies and even on the perception of those bodily beings which through their *self-expression* in perceptible *symbols and signs* reveal themselves to me and, therefore, just like me, are conscious of themselves.[6] It is only through a more accurate comparison and distinction of perceived beings that I separate these self-conscious beings from other corporeal beings which are merely sensitive or only vegetative because they participate only in a degraded way in my communings with my surroundings. Last of all, I perceive a background consisting of purely corporeal beings which usually act far less as distinct subsistent beings. They are perceived mainly with respect to their usefulness for human activities.

Thus, we find in the beings around us all the grades of life dis-covered in ourselves. However, this view of perception does not ade-quately express the process of our experience, for it is impossible to ascribe precedence to either the subjectively lived experience of my own grades of life or the objective perception of other beings which express themselves in communing with me according to their degree of self-movement. The two condition each other in such a way that in explicit judgmental knowledge perceived beings are in the foreground, and explicit self-knowledge is more characterized by reflection.[7]

[5]Cf. no. 133.
[6]Cf. no. 131.
[7]Cf. no. 48.

For this reason the acceptance of fellow human beings with a vegetative-sensitive-intellectual life should not be conceived as flowing from an analogous reasoning process starting from my self-experience. Rather the opposite must be affirmed. In my dealings with persons, e.g., in conversation, I discover that I also am a person; in dealing with sensitive beings I find that I also am sensitive; in dealing with vegetative beings I see myself also as a vegetative being; just as it is in my contact with corporeal beings that I discover, as we have seen,[8] my own corporeity.

111. *Vital Activity in General*

Although a certain distinction of the living from the non-living lies contained in undeniable experience, this distinction does not suffice to give us an insight into the essence of the living being. Just as, generally speaking, we can arrive at generic and specific concepts only through the observation of activities,[9] so also more detailed knowledge of what life is has to be obtained through a consideration of vital activities which are to some extent open to our understanding by means of external observation of behavior and reflection on our own actions.

Till the present we have considered, alongside our own immanent acts, such as knowing, loving and willing, mainly the transient activities perceived in corporeal beings.[10] However, there are also other activities which do not consist in influences passing from one being to another.

Self-Movement. External observation shows us these activities most clearly in the behavior of the corporeal beings which we call living *par excellence,* viz., man and higher animals. They impress us as self-moving beings.[11] This term is not meant to convey only that in a certain sense they are the source of their activity, for to some extent the same is true of any being endowed with a nature. What is special in the case of living beings is that they actively move not something else but themselves, even though they have to be stimulated to it by their surroundings. In addition, this being-in-motion is a motion to a

---

[8]Cf. no. 78.
[9]Cf. no. 84.
[10]Cf. no. 80.
[11]Concerning life as self-movement see Thomas Aquinas, *Summa theol.,* p. 1, q. 18, a. 1 (where he states also that in non-living beings movement originating in their nature has a likeness to vital action); Th. van der Bom, *Philosophie van het leven,* Antwerpen, 1932; M. Bruna, *Philosophie van de organische natuur,* Antwerpen, 1947.

good to which they tend or a flight from evil from which they flee, for their own sake. When they cease acting in this way, i.e., when their motions are no longer directed to self-preservation, then they are said to be "dead."

This idea of self-movement, however, can be broadened. By movement we mean not only local motion but also any kind of qualitative change. We speak of vital actions with respect to activities whose *principle* and *terminus* are the acting being itself—the principle insofar as these activities originate in the nature of the being, even though others have to influence it, the terminus, insofar as the activities actuate and perfect the acting being itself. To move does not mean here primarily to bring something else to perfection, but to lead oneself to the unfolding of one's own capacities. Thus self-movement in a certain sense is a "reflex", it is a reverting to oneself; for the movement remains within one and the same subsistent being, which is both the origin and the purpose of the vital action.

112. *The Living and the Non-Living*[12]

Self-Perfection and Non-Living Being. To some extent even the non-living being tends to self-perfection, for every finite being can become more perfect through communication. The transient activity of material qualities is a first feeble attempt to self-perfection. But it is only in perfecting others that the material being can attain to self-perfection—namely, insofar as the passive is dependent on the active and thereby testifies to the latter's superiority.[13]

Thus it follows that there is no absolute opposition between the non-living and the living. Some trace of self-movement, of the coincidence of an activity's origin and purpose, is still present even in the non-living.

Subsistence of the Non-Living. Nevertheless, the non-living is active only in the lowest way and therefore also subsistent only in the lowest way. It is always, as it were, "outside itself" both because it is moved by its surroundings as the efficient cause of its activity[14] and because it is attracted by these surroundings as the final cause of its activity.[15] It is precisely because of this mutual dependence and interaction that it is so difficult to indicate the individual subsistent beings in the non-living cosmos. Non-living beings are connected as

[12]Cf. A van Melsen, *Science and Technology*, Pittsburgh, 1961, Ch. VII. Tr.
[13]Cf. no. 91.
[14]Cf. no. 95.
[15]Cf. no. 108.

members of ever larger wholes and ultimately of the cosmos itself, so that with respect to their surroundings they possess only a faint beginning of subsistence.

Nevertheless, there are approximations of subsistence. In certain complex non-living wholes, studied by chemistry, there appears to be a more intimate relationship of the parts to the whole. The more intense this concentration is, the more heterogeneous the collaborating parts are and the more vigorously the whole maintains itself in space and time, the higher the grade of its subsistence is.

However, these higher modes of transient action of parts for the sake of the whole remain essentially distinct from vital activities, insofar as they are unable to assimilate their surroundings for the development of the whole. Because of their stereotyped character, non-living wholes lack the flexibility and adaptability through which the living being is capable of making its surroundings subservient to the constant self-development of the whole.

No Absolute Opposition. The non-living body is not absolutely opposed to the living body for the added reason that the living body exercises the same transient activities as the non-living body. The living body also has the active qualities which interact in an active-passive way with the surroundings. For this reason the experimental sciences of the living body must endeavor to investigate its "physical" and "chemical" activities and passivities and disclose its more complex structures.

Reversely, the non-living body is in potency to the living in many different ways. True, thus far, so it seems, no facts are known which show that the non-living spontaneously, albeit under the influence of higher causes, changes into the living body. But constant experience reveals that under certain conditions and through the influence of living beings, the non-living is integrated into the unity of subsistent living beings. The possibility of such a transition lies in this that the corporeal as such is in a more or less remote way in potency to all forms which can actuate a corporeal being,[16] the corporeal has an "infinite" potentiality, that is filled in a higher way through the transition into the living.[17]

---

[16]Cf. no. 89.

[17]We may mention here also the connection existing in both sensitive and intellectual knowledge between the knower and the known corporeal being, whether the latter is living or not living. The known "as it appears to the senses" or "as it is in itself" is taken into the immanence of the cognitive act, which is the highest form of vital operation. This relation, therefore, also shows the connection between the non-living and the living.

113. *The Corporeal Living Being as Spatial and Temporal*

The relationship of the living corporeal being to extension and temporality becomes intelligible in the light of the general characteristic of vital action described above as self-movement, as directedness to self-development.

The Organism. The living body is at the same time moving and moved. Nothing, however, can be in-act and in-potency in the same respect[18] and, therefore, the self-movement of the living body means that one spatial part moves the other. Consequently, the various parts must have different functions and, therefore, be also qualitatively heterogeneous.

True, heterogenity of parts is found even in many complex non-living beings having a definite configuration of parts. However, in the living whole the structure of the parts with respect to form, quality, and function is such that they collaborate for the well-being and constant development of the whole. They depend on one another to such an extent that a modification of one part entails a modification also of the others and that under certain conditions, despite their heterogeneity, they are capable of taking over one another's functions, and even of regenerating lost parts.

A whole composed of such parts is an organized whole, an *organism*. The juxtaposition of homogeneous parts commonly found in the non-living cosmos is replaced here by a hierarchical order of heterogeneous parts constituting an intimate unit of structure and operation. This hierarchical order manifests itself especially in the distinction between central and peripheral parts. A part is called central or peripheral not merely according to its importance for the whole, but also according to its relationship to the whole's environment.

Organism and Environment. Like all corporeal beings, the living body is connected with the whole of extended beings in communicative interaction. However, contact plays a higher role here. Even for the non-living being it is true that every transient action is received "according to the mode of the recipient." But living recipients will direct the influences they undergo toward their own specific well-being because they have a more distinctive structure and character through which they are directed to their own self-development.

---

[18]Cf. no. 98.

The living body is especially sensitive to influences which are useful or harmful for its development but, on the other hand, remains almost indifferent to other influences. Thus the surroundings lose their homogeneity and receive for each living body a *significance* and *meaning* in accordance with the structure proper to this living body. The surroundings become "environment," *"oikos,"* because some of their factors acquire importance and are placed in the focus of sensitivity.

Because of this significance and meaning of the various parts of the environment, the living body reacts in a specific fashion to certain influences. Taken by itself, the influence no longer explains the nature of the reaction. It becomes a "stimulus" to which the living body replies from within in its original way through self-movement (so-called "irritability"). Accordingly, the living body is active in a higher way than the environment, and the place of causal interaction is taken by a more unilaterally active relationship of the living being to its environment insofar as the living being makes this environment subservient to its self-perservation and self-realization.

The "art of living" consists in a flexible adaptation to conditions which enable the living body to develop itself, even in new, unforeseen, and varied situations, through the utilization of its surroundings.

Relationship of Environment and Living Body. On the one hand, the extension of the living body is a plurality of heterogeneous central and peripheral organs. On the other, the extension of its environment, likewise, is a plurality of heterogeneous more or less important parts, which are valued according to their meaning and importance for the development of the organism. In this way the terms "within" or "inside" and "without" or "outside" assume a higher meaning with respect to vital relationships.

The living body turns from within, i.e., from its central organs, by means of peripheral organs and their surfaces to the outside, where it finds an environment or creates one for itself through a change of place. This environment plays a role in accordance with the *meaning* which the living body discovers in it: from without, the body receives the necessary influences which it intussuscepts through its peripheral organs to make them subservient within itself to its vital development.

When "inside" and "outside" are in harmony, the living body is capable of realizing its own perfection by means of its communication with other beings in a measure of *immanence*.

The Living Body as Temporal. Not only the spatial but also the temporal situation of the living body differs from that of the non-living. As self-movement, vital action is a process of becoming. However, the phases of this change are not parts of a homogeneous time. Like the spatial configuration, so time also is interiorized. The various moments of time acquire a different *meaning and importance* for the living body. They, too, are more or less important according to their function in the development of life. In this process the past exists in the present in a higher fashion than in the case of non-living beings; at least, it leaves clearer traces behind, so that the actual activity cannot be understood without its "prehistory." On the other hand, the actual activity strongly anticipates on the future, because self-movement more clearly carries its purpose in its bosom— viz., the perfection of the individual and the species.

Consequences of This Spatial and Temporal Situation. Because the living being rises to some extent above the dispersion of matter as such in homogeneous space and time, it is also more exposed in its existence and duration. On the one hand, it depends for its continued existence on the assimilation of certain surrounding beings, on a favorable environment, to a greater extent than non-living beings which, because of their lower level, can maintain themselves more easily. On the other hand, the living body has its own characteristic temporal rhythm which regulates the different phases of its development, but at the same time this rhythm is the more fraught with risk the more the future situation is uncertain.

Thus, although the persistence of a living body is of a higher order, it is more precarious also. For this reason the final loss of its subsistence and its transition into "something else" is all the more striking, because it usually means the disintegration of the unstable organization by which different parts were laboriously united into a whole. It is only with respect to the living that we speak of essential change as birth and death.[19] Between these two, there are the intermediary phases of growth, maturity, reproduction, and withering.

114. *The Fundamental Vital Activities of the Living Body*

Nutrition and Growth. All beings having a corporeal life must nourish themselves. This term does not indicate primarily the actions by which animals and men gather and consume food, but rather the

---

[19]Cf. no. 88.

unconscious vegetative process through which the living body, exercising control to some extent over the chemical processes, gradually assimilates a part of the available food to its own chemical structure and admits it into the unity of its own substantial being. This transition of food into the living substance is an expression of the body's need to renew itself materially by borrowing from its surroundings. The opposite of assimilation is the disassimilation or elimination of useless, harmful, deteriorated and consumed parts.

This metabolism of the living body raises the problem of how the identity of the body is preserved in time, even when in the process of assimilation and disassimilation all its component parts are replaced by others.

Growth is closely connected with nutrition and dependent on it. Growth consists in the unconscious vegetative action through which the living body increases in extension and attains to the complete development of its proper structure. It runs its course in continuous cell-division until the full stature, proper to the living being in question, has been reached.

Reproduction. The highest vegetative action is reproduction. It presupposes that the body is fully developed and consists in the action through which the parental organism produces a specially constructed part and prepares it for transformation into a distinct individual, potentially endowed with the same specific perfection as the parent organism. Reproduction may be the action of a single body or the cooperation of two sexually distinct living beings.

Reproduction is an action which is no longer directed to the well-being and development of the individual as such, but aims at the preservation of the species in time by means of the individuals. In a certain sense, therefore, it solves the problem raised by the temporality of the living body which, despite its corruptibility, is dynamically oriented to permanence. The living body remains, not in itself, but in other individuals which derive their origin from the immanence itself of the living body and, therefore, in a sense make it perdure.

Imperfection of Vegetative Operations. The vegetative actions are only in a very imperfect way reflex self-movement. They are still closely related to transient activities and connected with the chemical processes occurring in the living body, to such an extent that, properly speaking, they consist only in the directing of these reactions to the well-being of the individual and the species.

Specifically, the power of nutrition is actuated only through the presence and "co-action" of food that can be intussuscepted. Moreover, the action of the nutritive organs is not primarily for these organs themselves but for the living whole in all its heterogeneous parts and functions.

The power of growth depends on the nutritive actions and is confined within the boundaries imposed by the proper structure required by the nature of the body in question.

The power of reproduction depends on nutrition and growth. It terminates in a fruit which, although of immanent origin, separates from the organism to lead its own independent life and agrees only in the species with the living body from which it springs. Ultimately, therefore, it is true also of the vegetative body that it attains lasting perfection only in *something else* and that it realizes itself only by serving the species and the whole, while perishing as an individual.

If the activities of vegetative life are only very imperfect modes of the becoming and realizing oneself which typify the living being, it follows that the vegetative body is only in a very imperfect way its own origin and purpose and is only very imperfectly subsistent.

115. *Grades of Vital Activity*[20]

The above-described vegetative vital activities themselves are not immediately accessible to us through reflection on our own corporeal being. Only in a mediate way do we discover their existence—namely, when certain feelings, such as hunger and thirst, and actions to which an instinctive urge of nature leads beings endowed with sensitive knowledge and tendencies, are explained in connection with the unconscious processes of nutrition, growth, and reproduction.

Thus it follows that sensitive knowing and tending are higher modes in which corporeal living beings realize their self-development and the preservation of the species. The activities of nourishing and reproducing oneself have much more the character of self-movement in animals than in purely vegetative beings. They become to some extent *deeds* and are no longer wholly anonymous natural events or reactions.[21]

---

[20]Cf. *Mens en Dier*, Antwerpen-Amsterdam, 1954; Th. von Uexküll, *Der Mensch und die Natur*, Bern. 1953, chs. 7-9 (the three grades) ; F. Buytendijk, *Grondproblemen van het dierlijk leven*, Antwerpen, 1938; V. Rüfner, *Die Natur und der Mensch in ihr*, Bonn, 1934, pp. 54-70 (Die Seinsstufen des Lebens).

[21]Cf. no. 91.

Spatial and Temporal Configuration of Animal Beings. In connection with this higher mode of self-movement, we can understand to some extent the difference in spatial and temporal configuration which we observe in the species of plants and animals encountered in our life.

1. A plant has a plurality of ramifications but their organic interconnection is less strict, its roots and leaves act more independently of one another. An animal, on the other hand, is a more closed unit, formed around a center, it has a "body" whose members are more clearly at the disposal of the whole.

2. As a result, it happens more easily in a plant that one part dies, a second is generated, and a third begins to lead a life of its own—the temporal boundaries of coming to be and passing away are less rigidly established. With respect to animals, birth, death, and the cycle of life assume a more profound meaning for the whole.

3. A plant has a favorable or unfavorable environment immediately *around itself,* which its peripheral organs use when they assimilate matter through intussusception. At least the higher animal, however, *faces* a world. The impressions of this world are perceived by sense organs, which in a very special way are oriented to what is important for the way of life proper to the whole, and their meaning and importance is relayed to a central organ. This central organ, to which the peripheral organs report their sensibilities, is absent in plants. Thus, there is a difference between irritability and sensibility.

4. For this reason the plant is less capable of reacting as a whole or of assuming an "attitude." In an animal, on the other hand, the reaction to stimuli is more governed from the center, and expressed by peripheral organs in "deeds."

5. A plant is generally attached to the soil and bound to the actual environment in its immediate proximity. Higher animals, on the other hand, perceive things at a distance, they have a memory and expectations. And if their organs are more in command, this means most of all that they can displace themselves with respect to their environment. Their position regarding the world they face does not merely refer to the immediate present good or evil, but they "see it coming" and therefore, not only seek good and avoid evil, but also assume an attitude with respect to obstacles, by revealing in their

behavior aggressiveness or dispiritedness, hope or fear, despair or courage.[22]

The Self-Movement of Animals is Imperfect. The self-movement of sensitively knowing and tending beings is still very imperfect. First of all, while it is true that to some extent the animal dominates its body as an executive organ, it itself, on the other hand, is dominated much more by the body, insofar as the corporeal well-being of the individual and the species through nutrition, growth, and reproduction is the unconscious driving force of instinctive actions. Although, then, the vegetative serves the sensitive, the sensitive also is subservient to the vegetative, for the sensitive acts and the vegetative processes closely collaborate for the purpose on which they depend— viz., the satisfaction of bodily needs.

Secondly, the animal's self-movement depends also on its surrounding world. True, contrary to plants, which at once react to present stimuli according to their chemico-vegetative nature, the animal is not immediately driven in its self-movement by its bodily nature. The animal supplies its own immediate principle of self-movement through its perceptions and appetencies as immanent acts. It actively addresses itself to the surrounding world as sensitively known and evaluated. Nevertheless, its perceptivity, which includes here memory and expectation, is united with its estimation and tendencies to such an extent that the animal perceives the world facing it only in a very special way—namely, insofar as this world has a meaning and value for the satisfaction of the purposes of the animal's bodily nature. Accordingly, every animal has its own world of perception corresponding to its own nature, and this world consists of the pleasant and the unpleasant, the easy and the difficult. The animal is wholly encompassed by this world, it is bounded by it in its perceptions, appetencies, self-movement and actions, which are still linked

---

[22]Cf. no. 137. In the preceding sections we used the term "body" in the broader sense in which whatever is extended is corporeal (cf. no. 78). The corporeal was said to be material insofar as its essential form is individuated by a principle called "prime matter," but the use of the term "matter" as a collective concept was avoided (cf. no. 89). Here we meet a more restricted sense of the term "body." All beings which we perceive *are* bodies in the broader sense, but only animals, and still more men, have a body in the stricter sense, i.e., an organic whole built of members around a "center," to which the situation is reported and from which the movements are directed. Sensitive beings to some extent *dispose of* their bodies in their perceptive and active dealings with the world facing them. In a certain sense the body is the opposite of the soul when it is conceived in this way (cf. no. 116).

together in an unbroken chain. The animal cannot disengage its knowledge from its instinctive tendencies and actions.

Self-Movement in the Strict Sense is Found in Man. Not before we reach man do we find self-movement which implies true self-determination and autonomy, complete re-flection, and *strictly* immanent acts.

1. As a sensitive being, man is less specialized with respect to perception and less rigid in his reactions. For in man the bond between perception and action is broken through reflection. To a greater degree than animals, even though these have internal senses, man is capable of interiorizing external experiences by means of higher immanent acts in concepts, judgments, and reasoning. From his knowledge of the meaning which the surroundings have for a living body situated in them he is capable of rising to knowledge of the meaning which beings *as* beings have according to their essence and nature.[23]

2. Because of this *objective* knowledge, by which he indicates and assigns names to things, he is no longer simply at the mercy of their influence, but to some extent can dominate and purposively order them. For he knows their activities and sees whether they can serve as means to reach a purpose. His hands are free to "handle" them in the literal sense of the term, i.e., to move them from their place and to change them by utilizing their natural actions. He is capable of making one object serve to change others and thus constructs and uses tools.[24]

3. By removing himself from the influence of surroundings in reflection, he places himself also at a distance from the influence of his own bodily nature. For he realizes its limitations and imperfection in the self-consciousness in which he experiences himself *as* being. This realization that all beings of experience are finite arises from man's universal openness to beings in their *being*.[25] Because of this *spiritual* nature which through knowing and loving is directed to the infinity of *being,* he has a measure of free self-determination[26] with respect to all limited purposes, including the inescapable aims of his *bodily* nature.

[23]Cf. no. 125.
[24]Cf. no. 146.
[25]Cf. no. 16.
[26]Cf. no. 144.

Three Grades of Vital Actions. To summarize the preceding pages, starting from the concept of self-movement, one may try to understand why in all probability experience of life *must* show three grades of vital activity. The more a living being moves itself *of* itself and *to* itself, the higher its grade of life will be. Now motion, in the broad sense of activity, reveals three aspects—

1) the purpose to which it is directed; 2) the form which is the principle according to which there is motion; and 3) the execution itself of the motion. Therefore, there are three grades of vital activities.

1. Some living beings move themselves only in the *execution* of the motion, but its purpose and form are determined by their nature and by the conditions which influence them.

2. Other living beings move themselves not only in the execution of their motion, but also with respect to the *form* according to which the motion takes place, because this form is not determined by their nature but acquired through sensitive knowledge of their surroundings.

3. Finally, other living beings move themselves also with respect to the motion's *purpose,* because through intellectual knowledge they know the relationship of means and purpose and therefore are capable of assigning a purpose to their actions. Nevertheless, even these beings depend on their nature, because this nature gives them the first principles of knowing and the ultimate purpose of acting. They cannot determine themselves in this respect.

In this way the distinction between vegetative, sensitive, and intellectual life becomes intelligible to some extent.[27]

For general metaphysics the important point is not so much to know whether there are boundaries and where they lie, but rather whether there is any *interconnection.* It is not even important that

---

[27]In his *Summa theol.,* p. 1, q. 18, a. 3, St. Thomas presents a philosophical summary of the three grades of life. The foregoing sketch of vital activities, which is mainly based on everyday experience, does not offer more than a probable view. The distinction between the various forms of life can be more accurately determined only by means of specialized research. This task is accomplished, on the basis of chemistry, by means of external observation and experimentation in the biological sciences of nature, and, on the basis of anthropology, by means of internal understanding in biological phenomenology. All kinds of intermediary forms reveal themselves in this research, for the realm of the living manifests a great *richness of forms.* One of the main problems is to classify the species, to show their transition and their origin.

there be three essentially distinct grades of vital activities. What is important is that there are grades and that these grades meet in man, so that man is the being in which the whole world of living bodies is reflected as in a microcosmos.

In the following pages, we will first ask about the essence of the living *as living,* because we suspect that there is a connection between the grades of life and the grades of *being* and even between living and *being.* Thereafter, we will limit ourselves to human life and especially to man's highest activities of life, the immanent acts of knowing and loving, because we suspect that they possess a very special kind of openness, a transcendental openness to beings in their *being.* In this way the consideration of man will lead us back to the problem of the metaphysical starting point.

116. *The Essence of the Living Being*

Life as self-movement or the exercise of vital activity—the so-called "second act"[28] of life—finds its immediate origin in vital powers. These powers, however, emanate from the essence of the living being —the so-called "first act" of life—which is the more remote origin of vital activities. What we want to consider here is the question: In what consists the essence of corporeal living beings?"

Mechanism. The mechanistic theory explains the fundamental operations of life, at least those of the vegetative order but sometimes also the activities of sensitive and intellectual life, through the material composition of the organism, as an interplay of mechanical forces or of chemico-physical processes.

As long as this type of explanation is conceived merely as a particular method guiding man's investigation of vegetative life, there is no need to quarrel with it. If, however, the theory wants to be more than a method and aims at explaining the very essence of life, we can still agree with its claim that vegetative operations take place *by means of* material processes. But these processes alone do not sufficiently explain the unity of the living being, the solidarity of the organic parts, and the orientation of the whole to self-development.

Vitalism. This theory explains the fundamental activities of life by admitting, alongside mechanical and physio-chemical forces, a separate and immaterial force of life, which makes the material parts

---

[28]Cf. no. 93.

with their functions subservient to itself, but allows them to retain their own subsistence.

This type of vitalism should be distinguished from the neo-vitalism which in some philosophers approaches Aristotle's doctrine of entelechy. It is unsatisfactory because it destroys the unity of the living being instead of providing this unity with a foundation. It conceives life too spiritualistically and manages merely to establish an external connection between the living being and its body.

Hylomorphism. The hylomorphic theory,[29] which previously offered a philosophical explanation of the essence of the corporeal as corporeal, assumes a more profound meaning when it is used to explain the essence of the living being.

On the other hand, it must be emphasized that the living being, as we experience it in its self-movement, is essentially a corporeal being and, therefore, extended, mutable, and corruptible. Consequently, it is essentially not an autonomous form, but the *bi-unity of matter and form.* It has no perfect unity, but is a divisible and corruptible being. It can be understood only in the context of other material beings.

On the other hand, however, the living body manifests itself in activities which are more perfect than the purely transient actions of the corporeal as corporeal. Hence, its powers are of a higher nature than the active qualities of the material, even though it is true that the powers in question act only by means of these active qualities. But if the powers are of a higher nature, then the living body must *be* in a higher mode than the non-living body precisely because such activities and powers originate from its essence. Now, the ontological perfection of the corporeal being is derived from its first form. Therefore, the living body can *be* in an essentially more perfect way than the non-living body only insofar as *its first form is more perfect* than the first form of the non-living body.

In every corporeal being the first form is the expression of its proper nature and, therefore, dynamic as the formal principle of activities. Accordingly, in the living body the essential form or first act will likewise be the dynamic principle of the vital activities.

From this viewpoint, as the *animating principle* of the organic corporeal being, the essential form of the living body is indicated by the Aristotelian term "psyche" or soul. The soul, then, is not a subsistent being, something which itself is, but a principle, that by which the corporeal being is animated.

---

[29]Cf. nos. 86-91.

The Soul. Aristotle describes the soul as the first act, i.e., the essential form, of the natural organic body.[30] With respect to this description it is to be noted that the soul, as essential form, should be conceived also as the formal cause of the corporeal and organic modes of *being* pertaining to the living body. For one being has only one essential form[31] and, therefore, it is out of the question to admit a form of corporeity alongside the form which is the principle of life. However, the one soul is virtually many in accordance with the plurality of powers emanating from it.[32] It remains true also that, abstractly considered, the "forming" of prime matter into a body and into an organism may be *viewed* as a first formal causality and that the body thus formed may be considered as a disposition making matter receptive to being further "formed" into a living corporeal being.[33]

------

[30]*De anima*, bk. 2, ch. 1 (412 a 28-b5). Cf. St Thomas' *Comment.*, nos. 212-234. Aristotle sometimes adds to this definition "having life potentially." The term "natural body" is taken in opposition to the mathematical body and the artificially produced body.

[31]Cf. no. 89.

[32]Cf. no. 94.

[33]1. In another definition Aristotle says that the soul is that by which primarily we live, move, perceive, and think (cf. *De anima*, bk. 2, ch. (413 b 10 and 414a 12) and St. Thomas' *Comment.*, nos. 260-261 and 273. See also Stephen Strasser, *The Soul in Metaphysical and Empirical Psychology*, Pittsburgh, 2nd impr., 1961), i.e. the first formal principle by which we, corporeal beings, vegetate, know and tend sensitively, move from place to place, understand (and will).

2. The organic body and the soul are not adequately distinct as prime matter and first form, but inadequately as a being and its form.

3. The besouled body is an organic body, i.e., the corporeal living being is an organized whole consisting of hierarchically ordered parts which constitute a more or less intimate structural and operational unit (cf. no. 113). These organic parts, e.g., in man and higher animals, the vegetative organs, sense organs, and limbs, as well as their component parts, are not homogeneous spatial parts but precisely bearers, in the broad sense, of heterogeneous functions for the welfare of the whole. With respect to the various organs and parts, animation has a constantly different meaning. As metabolism shows, the connection with the whole, i.e., the subsistent living being, may be more or less intimate and permanent. So long as organs and parts are component elements of the living whole, they are not subsistent. On the other hand, they are not accidents. Language refers to them through analogy of attribution by means of nouns and in the fashion of subsistent beings. Actions, vital operations, and even "deeds" are attributed to them. For instance, we say that the lungs breathe, the eye sees, and the hand strikes. However, all these expressions need to be corrected. For the organs and parts are merely quasi-instruments, united with the living being in substantial unity, through which this being unfolds and manifests itself. Especially the sensory and motor organs have a dynamic character as instruments for sensing and working at the service of the sensory and motor powers. But also the parts which act in the vegetative processes lose their autonomy of action and subsistence: they enter into the unity of the living whole through the formative power of the soul as the principle of vegetative life.

Are All Living Bodies Animated? The question may be asked whether it is meaningful to call all living bodies besouled and to speak of vegetative, sensitive, and intellectual souls. As is well-known, Aristotle, for whom biology and psychology coincided, held this view.

Some philosophers conceive the soul only as the origin of conscious activities and, with Descartes, make a sharp distinction between extended or physical being without interior life *(res extensa)* and the unextended or physical being having an interior life *(res cogitans)*. In this view it is a matter of dispute whether animal life should be considered as psychical, i.e., as conscious.

Others more correctly think that a soul and psychical life are present in corporeal beings which through their self-movement and behavior manifest an awareness of their surroundings and a relationship that implies feelings and strivings. No strict consciousness is needed for this, but memory and imagination are required. According to this view, psychical life is to be attributed to the sensitive corporeal being but not to purely vegetative bodies.

The answer to the question raised above is that the relationship of matter and form is not the same in all corporeal beings. There is a *gradation of forms* according as the formal principle "informs" the material principle more, i.e., according as it raises this principle to a higher mode of *being*. This higher mode of *being* manifests itself not only in a more intimate inner structural and functional unity but also in the higher fashion in which the living being incorporates its surroundings through its activity into its own self-development. Even in the realm of non-living beings one could point to a certain gradation. It is quite certain, however, that the vegetative being has a higher essential form than the non-living being, although it itself is surpassed by the sensitive being and this one, in its turn, gives way to the intellectual being as essentially the most perfect.

It is to be noted also that every higher form virtually implies the lower.[35] On the one hand, its activities are based on the lower activities as material dispositions but, on the other, the lower activities are raised to a higher level through their essential connection with the higher.

1. Thus it should be clear that the vegetative form is a higher form. Nevertheless, the *central* meaning of soul and psychical life is used for the form of sensitive being, as revealing a self-movement

---

[35]Cf. no. 97.

which more manifestly originates from a central principle than the manifestations of vegetative life.

2. From the viewpoint of sense life, the form of the vegetative body may be called a soul, but only in a *degraded* sense. Accordingly, it is important not to lose sight of the purely analogous way in which we speak of a vegetative soul and to beware of attributing the properties characterizing the sensitive soul, such as feeling, perceiving, and striving, in the strict sense, to the vegetative soul, which we know only indirectly and very imperfectly through its activities. For this reason it is commendable not to speak of psyche and psychical life before there is question of the level pertaining to the besouled corporeal being of the sensitive world.

3. Finally, again from the viewpoint of sense life, the form of an intellectual being may be called a soul, but now in an *eminent* sense. If, however, this is done, we should not forget the distinction between a purely sensitive soul animating a body and an intellectual soul which, as we will see later, is a spiritual principle. Accordingly, it will be commendable to call the essential form of human life *spiritual* insofar as this form "stands apart" as the principle of self-conscious acts of knowing and willing, and to call it *soul* insofar as it gives sense life[36] to the human body with which it is united in substantial unity.

Interrelation of Vegetative, Sensitive, and Intellectual Beings. The living body manifests in its essence a matter-form structure in which the form "informs" matter in a higher fashion. Life, therefore, is a higher mode of being-oneself, of autonomy, and subsistent *being*,[37] from which consequently a higher mode of activity flows. Life has *grades* which are essentially distinct but, nonetheless, interrelated and realized in the various species of living bodies in higher or lower ways.

The relationship between vegetative, sensitive, and intellectual beings may be conceived in two ways. First of all, living, as such,

---

[36]Cf. no. 153. Apart from the above-mentioned meaning found in systematic philosophy, other meanings are frequently given to the term "soul." Thus we may speak of the soul in a religious sense (the salvation of souls) and in all kinds of metaphorical and analogous senses, whenever there is question of something dynamic or "vivifying." For instance we may say of the members of an organization that they have "one heart and one soul," speak about the "soul of a society," and "the soul of a movement," "soulless resistance," etc.

[37]Cf. no. 65.

may be considered to express only the lowest and poorest grade, so that higher grades are obtained through addition to the lowest. This is the *univocal* view which leads to concepts by means of genus and specific difference, as illustrated by the Tree of Porphyry's *Isagoge*:

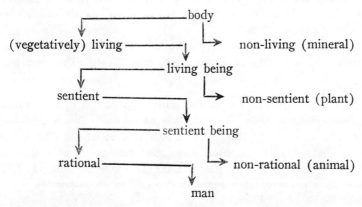

However, this view does not attain the *essence* of the living as living. For vegetative life is in the animal also, and sensitive life is in man also, but *realized in a different and higher way*—by a kind of analogy which may be neglected in the univocal concept of life. Plant, animal, and man are increasingly higher realizations of a rich and all-embracing concept of life. This concept, therefore, is *analogous,* and its content is "present" in lower types of living beings in a degraded and more particularized fashion. This "idea" of life expresses self-possession and subsistence and, at the same time, immanent activity, through which all other beings are admitted into the unity of this being. It is a higher mode of *being,* a more intimate participation in unqualified *being.*

117. *The Relationship of* Being, Knowing, and Living[38]

As we have seen, the exact demarcation of the boundaries between the inorganic, the vegetative, and the sensitive is not the most important problem facing general metaphysics. It pertains to special metaphysics to throw light on this question by means of the rich data supplied by experience concerning living bodies. Nevertheless, even general metaphysics has to consider the question concerning

---

[38]Cf. Thomas Aquinas, *Contra gentes,* bk. IV, ch. 11; *Summa theol.,* p. 1, q. 4, a. 2, *ad* 3; *In De divinis nominibus,* ch. V, lect. 1.

the relations existing between life and *being* as well as between living and knowing.

The Univocal View. To be, to live, and to know are named as the most general modes of *being*. A first, univocal view will conceive "to be" as to be purely corporeal, "to be alive" as an addition and enrichment of being-corporeal, and "to be knowing" as an addition to being-alive. In this view, "to be knowing" is founded, as on a "material" condition, on being alive, and "being alive" on being corporeal.

The Analogous View. In the univocal view no light is thrown on the essence of living and knowing as such. Only the analogous viewpoint can supply this light. From this viewpoint "to be" no longer means to be corporeal, but is all-embracing as unqualified "to be."[39] Life is a particular but higher mode of *being,* and, "to know" is a particular but higher mode of life. Non-knowing life is a degraded mode of life with respect to knowing, and to be non-living is a degraded mode of *being* with respect to life.

Accordingly, there is here not a divergence of concepts, as happens in the univocal view, but a convergence of "ideas."[40] "To be" fully, in the proper sense, is to live, and to live fully, in the proper sense, is to know. Thus to be, to live, and to know, coincide in "to know" as their higher mode of realization. The non-knowing being is a lower realization of the same perfection ("to be") which in the higher grades is called "to know," and the non-living being is a lower realization of the same perfection ("to be"), which in the higher grades is called "to live."

This analogy implies that there is at the same time an essential difference and a continuous transition between beings in their graded perfection. For this reason, it is impossible to posit an absolute oppsition, by affirmation and negation, between the non-living and the living, the non-knowing and the knowing. For all beings participate, though in essentially dissimilar ways, in the same perfection—namely, "to be," which in its fullness coincides with "to live" and "to know."

Moreover, there is a dynamic order in virtue of which the non-living is purposively directed to the living, and the non-knowing to the knowing, so that the "meaning" of the lower lies in the higher.

---

[39] Cf. no. 16.
[40] Cf. no. 84.

In the view explained here, to be *corporeal* does not belong to the essence of the living as living. On the contrary, the living is more living, the more it transcends the spatial dispersion of space and time.

Even self-*movement* no longer functions as the essential determination of life as such in this view. Even if all thought of locomotion is eliminated and movement is conceived only as a temporal transition from being-in-potency to being-in-act, and even if this movement is understood in its broadest sense, i.e., without temporality,[41] self-movement does not pertain to the essence of the living *as* living. Life as life, in its pure "idea," expresses purely immanent activity and does not imply of necessity a transition from *being* to acting, from first to second act. Pure life, as pure immanence and self-identity of "to be" (which coincides with pure "to know"), is pure subsistence, for it means that to-be-of-itself coincides with to-be-to-itself.

---

[41]Cf. no. 79.

CHAPTER TWENTY-TWO

THE EXPERIENCE OF FELLOW HUMAN BEINGS

118. *The Problem: A Plurality of Intellectually Knowing Beings*

The Soul is in a Way All Things. For the central issue of philosophy—the *being* of all that is—the grade of *being* pertaining to knowing beings is more important than that of non-living and non-knowing beings, because knowing beings participate more intimately in the plentitude of *being.* For, cognitive beings are raised above all other finite beings by virtue of the fact that, despite their finiteness, they contain to a certain extent in their immanent activity the modes of *being* pertaining to all these other beings. According to Aristotle's well-known expression, the knowing "soul is in a way all things."[1]

With respect to sensitive beings, Aristotle's statement is true only in a very relative way, for such beings are concerned only with their more or less immediate surroundings, insofar as these surroundings appear externally to a special sense organ and insofar as they have meaning and importance for the corporate life of the individual and the species. The world of sensitive beings is a limited *"Umwelt"* of knowing, tending, and acting.

The situation is different with respect to beings endowed with intellectual knowledge. They transcend corporeal life, and in their immanent activity are concerned with *everything that is,* in any way whatsoever, *as it is.* Of course, it is true that corporeal beings endowed with a finite intellect also are limited in their acts. Nevertheless, the dynamic infinity which drives every being to realize itself through communication with other beings reveals itself for the first time fully in these beings. There is nothing which is *wholly and entirely* outside their range, their horizon is unlimited, i.e., strictly speaking, there is no longer any horizon or limit beyond which their gaze cannot reach at all.

---

[1]*De anima,* bk. 3, ch. 8 (431 b 21) : "Let us now summarize our results about soul, and repeat that the soul is in a way all existing things; for existing things are either sensible or thinkable, and knowledge is in a way what is knowable, and sensation is in a way what is sensible." This and all following texts of Aristotle have been taken from W. D. Ross, *The Works of Aristotle Translated into English,* Oxford University Press, 1950.

The Implication of Fellow-Men. The question to be raised is: Are there any other intellectual cognitive beings apart from myself, from me who has raised the question of *being* and who knows of myself that I am and that I am questioningly directed to all that is? Is the existence of corporeal fellow human beings, of my equals, just as much an undeniable primordial experience as that of my own existence? This question is important for the orderly procedure of our metaphysical investigation. For, if the mode of my *being* enters into my consciousness fully only in my communicative dealings with my equals, than the question of the *being* of all that is, which is that to which my knowing and loving are ultimately directed, can be solved only by means of reflection on the human mode of *being* common to all of us.

What Has Been Established Thus Far. In our previous critical reflection we did not yet explicitly concern ourselves with the existence of fellow human beings. This reflection established the following facts:

1. Something is, no matter what it is.[2]

2. There is at least the one who asks the question whether something is, and this means that "I am."[3]

3. I am not "to be" itself, but a questioning and, therefore, finite being.[4]

4. I experience that I am, and I do not have to have an immediate insight into the question whether my *being* is necessary.[5]

5. I cannot discover who I am by means of an immediate reflection on myself, but only through the fact that I unfold myself *in time* in acts which refer to other beings encountered by me. My self-consciousness explicitates itself in and through *perception,* I experience myself as situated with respect to others.[6]

6. My perception passes from being-in-potency to being-in-act under the influence of beings which present themselves to me in *sense* experience.[7]

---

[2] Cf. no. 16.
[3] Cf. no. 17.
[4] Cf. no. 18.
[5] Cf. no. 20.
[6] Cf. no. 48.
[7] Cf. no. 76.

7. These beings are *corporeal*: they are extended, temporal, mutable.[8]

8. As perceiving these beings, I am also corporeal.

9. Nevertheless, I have some *concept* of these beings by means of their activities, although it is true that this concept is abstract and univocal and therefore falls short with respect to the individuality of these beings.[9]

10. Some corporeal beings manifest vital activities.[10]

11. I also am such a living being.[11]

12. Like me, some living beings are sensitive.[12]

Finally, it was emphasized that the *concrete* process of perception primarily draws attention to those corporeal beings which reveal themselves to me through perceptible signs and symbols and which like me, are *conscious of themselves* and therefore "egos." We mentioned specifically that the admission of vegetative-sensitive-intellectual fellow human beings should not be conceived as flowing from an analogous argument. On the contrary, it is in my social dealings with persons that I explicitly discover that I also am a person.[13]

The last-named point demands our critical attention. For, if it expresses the truth, the question arises whether the "I am," discovered at the beginning of the critique of knowledge, refers exclusively to my individual *being* or contains already a *being-together* with others in a community of beings.

Traditional "realism" usually accepted such a being-together in an unquestioning way and hardly investigated *how* such an experience was possible. Idealism, on the other hand, used to start with an individual ego, but tried in various ways to escape from solipsism and justify the existence of the others as "real" fellow-beings, at least as phenomenal forms of the one "transcendental I."[14]

---

[8]Cf. nos. 78-79.
[9]Cf. nos. 80-85.
[10]Cf. no. 110.
[11]Cf. no. 100.
[12]Cf. no. 115.
[13]Cf. no. 110.
[14]For the problem of idealism and solipsism, see E. Husserl, *Cartesian Meditations*, The Hague, 1900. Fifth meditation.

119. *The Methodic Doubt About the Existence of Fellow Human Beings*[15]

I Have Neither Immediate Experience nor Apodictic Proof of the Other's Immanent Acts. My own immanent acts of perceiving, sensing, thinking, and willing are known to me implicitly in these acts themselves and explicitly through reflection on these acts. They originate in me, and I know myself as their origin. I am conscious of myself.

However, so far as your immanent acts are concerned—so I say in my present skeptical approach—I do not have any immediate experience. Therefore, the only way in which I could know them would be by arguing from your external manifestations to me in my perception. But your speech cannot guarantee your immanent acts, for I do not know whether you tell me what you think; your actions, likewise, offer no proof, for they can be explained in different ways, and I do not have any certainty regarding their motives. Accordingly, it is not possible for me to verify your immanent acts either by means of an immediate intuition or through an apodictic argument.

I Am Not Certain That You have Immanent Acts. Must I admit at least *that* you perform immanent acts? Sometimes I have the impression that I have received thoughts from you by means of communication—but is it impossible that, just like so many other activities, these thoughts originated in an unconscious way from me, for it is *I* who have these thoughts? I can admit that you communicate something to me in conversation and that, consequently, you think, only if I presuppose that you are able to speak and to think. The fact that I have the *impression* of receiving your reply to my questions is not a proof for, as a behaviorist, I can call *all* reactions to a stimulus replies without accepting any immanent life in the replier. A reply is pure behavior, it may be connected with other kinds of behavior, but why should it of necessity be connected with self-consciousness?

The fact that I perceive expressive motions of anger, love, etc., which seem to originate from immanent acts is no proof. For not only do sensitive beings also express their feelings, but it is even possible for me to conceive *everything* I perceive as such a motion—

---

[15] The thoughts presented in this and the following parts of this chapter have been largely borrowed from M. Chastaing, *L'existence d'autrui,* Paris, 1951.

namely, as a motion which is one with what it expresses and, consequently, does not necessarily imply a life of feeling and thinking. I can consider all these so-called expressions to be purely corporeal phenomena.

Likewise, no proof is supplied by arguing from your body movements by way of analogy with my body movements, which I know to originate from immanent acts. First of all, I do not *see* my own movements, such as facial expressions and gestures, in the same way as I see yours, but experience yours through organic sensations, i.e., in a motoric way. Secondly, such a proof can serve only to determine *whether* in a special case another ego is present, but *presupposes* that in general other egos are present.

The fact that in social actions I address myself to you as another ego by speaking to you, showing deference or obedience, etc. is no proof. For in performing these actions I *presuppose* your existence, so that their meaningfulness depends on my belief in you. But just now I am in doubt about the value of this belief. The actions in question originate in me alone, they may have value merely for *my* life, even if you do not exist.

Accordingly, critically I am justified only in accepting the undeniable evidence of *my own* existence and, in addition, the data supplied by the external perception of corporeal beings or even of beings which express themselves. But there is no critical justification for the existence of another ego.

Strictly speaking, solipsism should not even stop here but ask whether the perceived beings exist independently of me as subsistent beings. Is it not possible that the world of objects is merely a projection of the subject, a world constructed by me? Who will distinguish dream from reality if there is no one else to contradict me?

120. *The Impossibility of Solipsism*

It is possible to attempt a methodic doubt concerning the existence of the other egos, but it will remain a mere attempt. However, just as the universal doubt about *being* or consciousness,[16] this doubt cannot be *professed,* for it contradicts itself.

1. The solipsist cannot defend his attitude against others as the correct epistemological position.

---

[16]Cf. nos. 15 and 17.

2. He cannot say: the others are merely my mental images, for then he would first have thought the others as possible real beings and subsequently discarded them. But the rigid solipsist cannot even *think* of the others as real because such a thought would imply that he has already accepted the possibility of other egos.

3. He cannot even speak of his own solitude, his "I alone," for this also presupposes that first a possible society is proposed and then its reality is denied.

4. He is unable to use the term "I" in opposition to "you" or "he." "I" and "mine" are not relative for him, for they do not contrast with any other conscious being. But then "mine" equals "everything," and the result is that the solipsist is no longer a finite knowing and feeling being: his feelings have become all feelings, his thoughts all thoughts.

5. Usually, however, the solipsist arrives at his position from motives of so-called humility, insofar as he agnostically claims not to have access to any other ego. He makes this assertion because he claims to know only what he actually feels and experiences, all other statements being meaningless.

The consequence, first of all, is that he may not admit his own past and future. Secondly, he denies the lived experience through which he *knows* that something is without internally experiencing the *being* of this being; yet such lived experiences are undeniable. Thirdly, he denies the lived experience through which he does not *know* whether something is this way or that way, although he *understands* what it *means* to be this way or that way; yet this lived experience is likewise undeniable.

Thus the solipsist is the victim of a kind of sensualism, which, however, he contradicts as soon as he proposes an imperceptible theory, such as the theory that no fellow-men exist. For he knows very well what the existence of fellow human beings would mean.

6. Accordingly, the solipsist cannot maintain that a statement about the internal life of others or the admission of other egos is meaningless. Likewise, he cannot maintain that he does not know whether other egos exist, for otherwise he would recognize the possibility of the existence of such other egos and, therefore, also the meaningfulness of their existence.

7. The solipsist has never any reason to doubt what he thinks. But his *behavior* shows that he sometimes thinks that others think. Therefore, he cannot accept that he is mistaken in his thought, and experiences evidently the existence of other egos.

121. *The Experiential Evidence for the Existence of Fellow Human Beings*

An Evident Primordial Experience. Before I can deny the existence of fellow men, I have first to ask myself whether there are any other human beings. This question implies that I have considered the possibility of the existence of another ego. But the thought of such a possibility can have arisen only because of my experience of reality.[17] Therefore, I must have thought first that I experienced another ego and then begun to doubt this experience.

How can such a doubt about experience arise in me? Only because I set a contradiction before my mind, i.e., I consider that with respect to one and the same thing the answer could be yes or no. But contradiction implies another ego as the contradictor. Even if I suppose that I myself am my own contradictor, this supposed duplicity has its origin in an experience of really distinct contradictors. Accordingly, it would not be possible for me to posit a doubt regarding what appears to me in experience or to ask a question which can be answered affirmatively or negatively, unless I think that there could be someone else whose experience could be in contradiction with mine.

The objection could be raised that my doubt regarding the supposed actual experience could have its basis in my past experiences. However, in this case I represent myself in the twofoldness of "I-then" and "I-now," and this proposed duplicity also finds its origin in an experience of an actually present twofoldness of experiencers.

My denial, therefore, of the existence of other egos implicitly contains, as a condition of its very possibility, the pre-predicative and undeniable experience of another ego. In other words, my experience of the existence of another ego is an *evident primordial experience,* for in its very denial this experience is affirmed, not through the content of the act of denying but through its exercise.[18]

The Primordial Ego. Despite the evidence of this experience, we have tried to call it into doubt in constructing metaphysics, because

---

[17]Cf. no. 23.
[18]Cf. no. 21.

the starting point of metaphysics is nothing else than the universal question of *being*.[19] Because this question affirms itself as being, and therefore, knows that it is in self-consciousness, the affirmation of *being* implicitly contains the affirmation of the self: "I am."[20] However, as was pointed out, the "I," as first person, in this affirmation could not yet be conceived as explicitly opposed to a possible second or third person. Thus there remained a possibility that this "I" implied either I as the only person (solipsism) or a "We" as a "poly-unity" of persons. We are now in a position to render the initial "I" more precise.

The thinking question whether there is anything, is the starting point. But this questioning thought implies that the questioner can be uncertain. Uncertainty, however, arises from the possibility of two contradictory answers. Now contradiction refers to a plurality of thinkers, one of whom denies what the other affirms. Accordingly, *from the very start the question of* being *is raised in a community* of beings who think together and question one another about the truth of *being*. I know that something is because you reply to the question by *being*, but your *being* is your being-questioning with respect to me, asking me whether anything is. We reply to each other through the *being* of our mutual questioning. The primordial "I am" appears now to have been a "we are," in which the one (I) asks the other (you) whether anything is, and in which the one knows that he also is an "I" through the affirmation in which the self-consciousness of the other (you) reveals itself.

Accordingly, I know that I am because, in listening, I encounter a thinking which I am not and which replies to me. I become explicitly conscious of my *being* by means of you who knows that I am, and vice versa. The *reciprocity of consciousness* is the first concrete form of affirming *being*.

The Perception of You and Your Acts. This "we-experience" is always perceived, with undeniable evidence, only from the viewpoint of one of the many egos. It, therefore, always implies a certain opposition between me and you. For me, I am I and for you I am you, and vice versa. Although my experience of my *being* and my experience of your *being* are both evident, they are very different from each other. The explicit I-awareness has as its intermediary

---

[19] Cf. no. 15.
[20] Cf. no. 17.

the encounter with you within the "we," but I do not experience you immediately in your presence to yourself but only in your making-yourself-present-to-me. On the other hand, I experience myself in my presence to myself, which becomes explicit in reflection. Your acts are not present to me through my internally "living" them but by means of a *perception that is wholly sui generis.* This perception should not be confused with that of the external senses, although it is connected with sense perception and "materially" conditioned by it insofar as I and you are essentially bodily beings. Without falling, on the one hand, into a one-sided sensualism which knows only external perception and, on the other, into a one-sided spiritualism which accepts only an intuition of the other's immanent acts, our analysis of man's cognitive life will have to make room for this *sui generis* perception by which we know our fellow men and their immanent acts of knowing, feeling, and willing through their behavior.

For everyone the experience of the existence of fellow men is an experience that is wholly his own in his individual way, since for each another one is "the other." He who for me is "I" is "you" for you. Moreover, each one is aware of this restricted "we" of "I" and "you" as a particularized and always different experimental certitude projected against the implicit background of a more-embracing "we" containing also various "he's." This background extends without limits over the universal interconnection which unites in their mutual contrast all beings that are like me, you, and him, i.e., all fellow human beings.

Indirect Confirmation of the Experiential Evidence of Fellow Men. The relationship with fellow human beings is subject to all kinds of variations. The following may be considered as the principal and most immediate relationships:

1. The contrast of "I" and "you" as equals, e.g., in conversation, mutual affection, or aversion.

2. The unequal reciprocal order of the one to the other, in which the relationships are essentially different; e.g., in education, caring for, instruction, command, and counsel.

3. The being-directed-together as "we" to a third, e.g., in affection, aversion, care or command, or to the beings of the world, for instance, in research, dealings, or production.

These relationships show that the experiential evidence of fellow human beings—the same applies to the other ways of having experiential evidence—is rendered explicit in communicative intercourse, in and through *activities and passivities*.[21] As will become clear later, language is a privileged form in which personal presence reveals itself. In general one may say that, although the existence of others cannot be proved because it is an experiential evidence, the concrete activities which are directed from you to me or from us to something else are indirect confirmations and further precisions of this evidence. Reasoning from analogy also may play a role here to determine in certain cases whether we have to do with another ego, and especially to interpret the other's behavior, so as to lead us to a more accurate knowledge of his inner life.

---

[21]Cf. no. 71.

CHAPTER TWENTY-THREE

MAN'S COGNITIVE LIFE: SENSES AND INTELLECT

122. *Man's Cognitive Life as Subject-Object Relation*

Man's Ability to Know What to Know Is. Each one of us knows that he lives in a community of sensitive-intellectual knowing and tending beings which both transcends and includes him. By means of reflection on my own "lived" knowledge as well as that received from others, it is possible for me to discover from this experience what the essential structure is of knowing not only as *my* knowing but also as *human* knowing containing me in its universality.

This reflection, through which we not only know that we know but can also learn what it is to know and how knowledge originates, seems to be absent in animals. Although animal behavior shows a cognitive aspect, external perception together with memory and imagination are so closely unified with unconscious tendency and instinctive estimation that attention is paid only to what has meaning and value for the animal's own specific organism in its individual situation. The animal lives to such an extent *in* the world-around-it that it cannot attain to a *known* distinction between the knower and the known and, consequently, not to a *conscious* contrast and connection of subject and object: the animal has neither self-consciousness nor knowledge of beings according to the essence and value which they have *in themselves.*[1]

Man's reflection, however, which is already implicit in every integral cognitive attitude toward objects, can lead him to explicit knowledge of the subject in its acts of knowing.

Meanings of the Terms "Subject" and "Object." Different shades of meaning should be distinguished in speaking about subject and object. Object—literally "what is thrown in front of"—implies a relationship to something or someone opposed to it and actively directed to it, namely, the subject. In this broadest sense of the term every activity and every active power has an object which specifies it. For instance, a transient action will either modify the object on which it acts or produce and realize it.

---

[1]Cf. no. 115.

In a more proper sense there is question of subject and object with respect to immanent acts, because in these acts the relative opposition of subject and object as subsistents as well as their union through identification are more clearly revealed. Starting from itself, the subject directs itself "intentionally" to the object, but at the same time the object, as terminus of the act, is "immanent" in the subject.

Especially with respect to cognitive and intellectual life, in perception, representation, and thought, one may speak of the object as the *immanent terminus* of the intentional directness. (There is here no question yet whether or not the object must be considered to be wholly encompassed by its being-an-object, by being-immanent-in-the-subject.) As such objects we may name that which is perceived, recalled, as well as imagined or dreamed; likewise, what is conceptually thought or represented, judgmentally posited, and argumentally concluded, even if the concept would be incorrect, the judgment false, or the argument illogical. Finally, we may name the idea or plan, engendered in practical knowledge, as a mode of *being* to be realized. The object, in the sense of "immanent terminus" in which it is common to all these different ways of being-an-object, is the pure correlate of a *de facto* actually knowing or thinking subject.[2]

In a stricter sense there is no question of object with respect to everything which is *de facto* and actually "pro-posed" by a subject, but only with respect to that which is *de jure* posited—namely, insofar as by its very nature it is the necessary object of possible human acts of knowing and thinking. Here there is no question of free representations of the imagination or of the practical knowledge contained in activity, but of perception and insight, concept, judgment, and reasoning. The object possesses a *normative* character with respect to the truth of knowing and thinking. When the object is conceived in this way, its correlate is not the fortuitous particular subject in its present activities, but the subject as conscious of its connection with the other subjects in a transcendental directedness to the same object. And, in principle, this subject is accessible also to the knowing and thinking of the others, at least in the sense that they cannot deny this object without falling short of the truth. For epistemological realism[3] the primary object of theoretical *knowing* is not a being which is wholly encompassed

---

[2]Cf. nos. 34, 135.
[3]Cf. no. 34.

by being-the-object-of-a-subject. A distinction has to be made between the object, precisely as object, and the object as that which, because it is in itself, must be the necessary object of possible human acts of knowing. For a thing *is* not because it is the object of human knowledge, but just the opposite: because it *is,* it can be the object of man's knowledge. The object of knowledge is being, as it is in itself, according to all its modes of *being*—and here even its being-an-object can become the object of knowledge. In this sense we call an object of human knowledge anything whatsoever which, in principle, is knowable through genuine human acts of knowledge.

Relative Identity of Subject and Object. To be an object of knowledge it is not necessary that a being be something else than the subject of this knowledge or something else than the act of knowing. If being as being is knowable,[4] then the knower and his cognitive act also are knowable. It is not at all impossible that the subject knows itself in an act of knowledge or that the cognitive act itself is known in the act of knowing.

However, in man's cognitive life there is no possibility of *perfect* identity of the knower, the cognitive act, and the known, of the subject and the object, in such a way that there would be no distinction at all between to-be-knowing and to-be-known, and that "to be" itself would be pure consciousness, active self-illumination. Man's self-consciousness is very imperfect. Although there is an undeniable moment of identity of the knower and the known as pre-predicative being-with-himself,[5] in the explicitation of human self-consciousness it becomes clear how imperfect and relative this identity is and how much it is accompanied by the opposition between the subject-ego and the object-ego. Here are the reasons:

1. Man's consciousness is experiential knowledge, for I find myself to be; there is a priority of my *being* with respect to my consciousness.[6]

2. Although human self-consciousness is implicitly present in the acts of knowing and willing, these acts are primarily directed to the other beings, and especially to my fellow men, as their objects. It is

---

[4]Cf. no. 42.
[5]Cf. no. 16.
[6]Cf. no. 20.

only through reflection on these acts of knowing and willing that self-consciousness becomes explicit.

3. What man knows of himself in reflection is first of all his own activities as originating from him, i.e., his actual perceptions, feelings, thoughts, deeds, etc. These he experiences directly. Only through continued reflection does he discover the connection between his present and past acts and experience himself as a stream of consciousness. At the same time, however, he discovers also that there is a certain bond between this stream of consciousness and the sensitive-vegetative bodily life, of which he does not have any immediate awareness. For this reason he is never able to penetrate into the innermost depth of the connection between, on the one hand, his cognitive and tendential life in the realm of the sensitive and, on the other, this same life in the intellectual realm. In many respects he remains a secret to himself. His habitual dispositions, such as temperament and character, and his own individual nature are even less accessible to him.

4. In the process of this continued reflection on himself man leaves behind his immediate experience. His self-knowledge becomes a reconstructive type of representation, understanding and thinking, in which he uses the representations, concepts and thoughts, known to him from his social dealings with fellow men and from their way of expressing their inner life in language. In this fashion his explicit interpretation of his acts and attitudes has as its intermediary his knowledge of the others in a society. He has become, as it were, "someone else" for himself, he sees, understands, and judges this "other" from the perspective of his fellow men. Evidently, the possibility of error, which is absent in pre-predicative self-consciousness,[7] is always great in this explicit and categorical self-knowledge; hence he obviously needs self-criticism and the aid of others to arrive at the truth.

The Object in Integral Human Knowledge. Thus for man the first explicit object of his act of knowing is not he himself, whether as actually knowing or as subsistent being, but "something other" than himself, another active and subsistent being, which either exists with respect to external sense perception or in a personal encounter posits itself as another ego facing his knowing and tending ego. If this assertion is true, then, from the viewpoint of integral human

---

[7]Cf. no. 21.

knowledge, the term "object" assumes a still more specialized sense than that of being, as it is in itself, with all its modes of *being*. Object here is something which not only as the *known* faces the *knower* as knower—this sense belongs also to human self-consciousness—but also places itself as "another" subsistent being before the knower as a subsistent being.

Accordingly, man is a knowing being in such a way that, as it were, bypassing himself, he is directly oriented toward the other beings around him as facing him, and explicitly discovers himself as a knowing being only by reverting to the starting point of this intentional direction.[8]

For a human being knowledge of the others as objects and knowledge of himself as subject are two poles between which his knowing oscillates and which refer to each other. All knowledge of the others comes back to him to enlarge his self-knowledge, and every conscious experience of his own inner life goes toward a better understanding of the others.

Man's transcendental openness, through which he somehow includes in himself everything *that is,* as it is,[9] goes hand in hand with his initial orientation to the beings presenting themselves as *others* facing him in encounters that occur in the course of space and time. The union of these two reveals itself most clearly in the dependence of intellectual understanding on sense experience.[10]

Especially in the sensitive moment of cognition man is "outside himself" and with the external, while in the intellectual moment of cognition there is a return from exteriority to interiority. We speak of "moments" here with respect to these two structural elements of integral human knowledge to emphasize their mutual interconnection. On the following pages we must investigate their general structure in order to see how it is possible to arrive at an understanding of "what beings are in themselves" by starting from the experience of "how the beings around me appear to me in their exteriority."

123. *The External Senses*

The Receptive Character of Sense Experience. Sense experience is the cognitional contact of a living corporeal being with its bodily

---

[8]Cf. no. 48.
[9]Cf. no. 16.
[10]Cf. no. 76.

surroundings before it becomes conscious of the opposition and connection of subject and object.[11] What is given by the external senses
possesses the mark of indubitability, but only insofar as it is recep-
tively accepted in a kind of intuition and insofar as its meaning and
importance are not yet interpreted by the internal senses and the
intellect.

The receptive character of sense experience finds its philosophical
explanation in the transient action exercised by the surroundings.
By means of physical changes this action produces a physiological
change in the organic sense organ, and at once a modification is
caused in the sense "animating" this organ, the cognitive power.
Because whatever is received, is received according to the mode of
the recipient, this modification is of a physical nature. It is an
"interiorization" with respect to the physiological changes and therefore is called an impressed cognitive image. As such it prepares
the sense, as a "fully ready first act,"[12] for cognitive activity, but
this cognitive activity itself is a spontaneous reaction which, as an
immanent act, finds its origin and terminus in the sense power
itself.

"Active Qualities." The "active qualities" perceived by the senses
are real characteristics of corporeal beings, but only insofar as their
action is received in the sense organ and in the sense power. They
are, therefore, dependent on the conditions of both the object and
the subject, and in this sense they may be said to be relative. They
are the meeting ground, as it were, of our living body and the outer
world.[13]

For this reason the active qualities of the various external
senses have an original meaning and importance:[14] they *refer* to both
the object and the subject.[15] The subject is a corporeal living being
which for its life *needs* other beings (objects). However, contrary
to what happens in purely vegetative living beings, these objects
are not immediately present and therefore have to be *sought;* hence
the subject directs itself centrally by means of self-movement to the
objects and in this way experience distance and time.[16] For in its

---

[11]Cf. no. 77.
[12]Cf. no. 94
[13]Cf. no. 84.
[14]Cf. no. 113.
[15]Concerning the original meaning and importance which perceived active
qualities have, see J. Nogué, *La signification du sensible,* Paris, 1936.
[16]Cf. no. 115.

turning from within to without, it encounters the active qualities as manifestations of the objects it seeks. These manifestations reveal the objects in their external character. In this way the subject has a possibility to recognize some objects as good and useful, others as evil and harmful, and to regulate its behavior accordingly.

The sense of touch reveals to us in this way the limits of the sphere of our actions. Taste distinguishes the tasteful from the distasteful in connection with actively nourishing oneself. The sense of heat and cold makes us live in a "sphere" which is favorable or unfavorable to the vegetative processes. Hearing and sight, as higher senses, are directed to the perception of what is still *distant*. Hearing perceives through sound the announcement of an event approaching us. It is mainly temporal. Sight, on the other hand, perceives through color and light the simultaneous configuration of objects at a certain distance as well as the relationship of their mutual motion. It is mainly spatial. Sight and touch, as, e.g., putting one's hand around something, collaborate to make us distinguish object as permanent "things."[17]

In addition to these external senses, there is sometimes question of others which perceive the conditions and motivity of the body. The latter is called the kinesthetic sense. However, one may question whether these senses should be sharply distinguished from those that are directed to an object. It is always in connection with movement from within to without and, therefore, with external perception that one's own body is experienced as the central starting point of a perspective in which the objects in a certain structural whole are discovered.

The above-mentioned meanings of active qualities are the most fundamental. However, through the integration and combination of external data in the *internal* senses new meanings are synthetized, so that the external world is experienced as a field of references to richer characteristics of the objects.

124. *The Internal Senses*

The Central Sense. The common or central sense is the first of the internal senses which synthetizes the manifoldness of the specialized external senses. It is the common origin and the common purpose of the *cognitive* life proper to the sense organs and possesses a higher form of immanent activity than the external senses.

---

[17]Cf. no. 78.

First of all, the central sense harmonizes the distinct fields of perception, especially the extension discovered through active touch, and the field of vision, and thus gives greater clarity to depth, the third dimension. Moreover, to some extent, the central sense initiates the process of identification, although not without the aid of memory and imagination, for instance, of this-round-here with red, warm, fragrant, and tasty, and thus prepares the discovery of the thing-like object, e.g., apple. This integration of the sense data is a first step toward the discovery of objects as subsistent beings.

Secondly, the central sense to some extent unifies the sense organs and the senses themselves: it is the same animated body which at the same time touches, sees, smells, and tastes by means of organic activities that, though distinct, originate from the same center and revert to it. This integration of the senses is a first step toward the discovery of the subject as a subsistent being.

For this reason the central sense is sometimes called "sense consciousness," as if through it I would know already somehow that it is *I* who touches, sees, tastes, smells, etc. However, the incipient reflection performed in the central sense does not go that far. True, this sense distinguishes and connects not only the *data* of the external senses but also their *acts* and, we may add, even the acts of the internal senses, affections, emotions, and tendencies. Nevertheless, this synthetizing knowledge of one's own sense life has more the nature of a spontaneous *"living"* of experiences which is still fully encompassed by them than that of a reflex *consciousness,* i.e., one which implies that the distinction between knower and known, tending and being tended-to, and consequently, the opposition of subject and object as beings, are *known* as such. Accordingly, not only sensibility, taken by itself, is not conscious, but also the knowing and tending of the internal senses, taken by themselves are not fully conscious.[18]

The Estimative Sense. As a kind of sensitive value judgment, this sense connects the central sense with affective and appetitive life.[19]

---

[18]Accordingly, a distinction should be made between, on the one hand, sense experiences as "material" conditions for the emergence of consciousness and, on the other, the pre-predicative and wholly implicit consciousness which is present in man because his knowledge of being pervades his sense experience (cf. nos. 16 and 82).

[19]Concerning the cogitative and estimative sense, which Alfarabi and Avicenna considered a distinct power, see G. Klubertanz, *The Discursive Power,* St. Louis, 1952; Thomas Aquinas, *De veritate,* q. 10, a. 5 and especially his division of the internal senses in *Summa theol.* p. I, q. 78. a. 4 and *De anima,* a. 13.

Perception is primarily directed to the discovery of the value which the surroundings have for the vital needs of the subject. True, even in the central sense itself, the objects are experienced as agreeable or disagreeable, but this experience is limited to what immediately affects the life of the senses, e.g., seeing, hearing, etc.

However, there are also other tendencies toward or away from the perceived objects,[20] which cannot be explained by means of the immediate experience of the agreeable or disagreeable—namely, the instinctive actions directed to the seeking of a good, the fleeing from an evil that is still in the future and unknown from past experience, a good and evil with respect to the well-being of the individual and the species. Such tendencies presuppose that the sensitively knowing being *interprets* the objects as good or evil, harmful or useful with respect to its natural good: the wolf is to be avoided, mother is to be sought, a nest is to be built, a web is to be spun. This discovery through presentiment of a hidden meaning is the animal's estimative power, which changes perception into "practical" knowledge.

Man also instinctively connects perceived objects with his sensible good. Nevertheless, his estimative power is less obscure and less determined, because of its connection with intellectual knowledge. Man's estimative sense is more adaptable because his past experiences play a greater role in the interpretation of his perceptions. Because of this influence of memory and imagination, the human estimative sense stands on the *boundary* between sensitivity and intellect. For this reason it is called "particular reason" or "cogitative power," because it proceeds from particular experiences to new particular judgments and appreciations. This power is indispensable for the "practical" knowledge of the individual and reveals itself especially in prudence.[21]

Memory and Imagination. As was previously pointed out, the perception of spatial distance and temporal succession, which is performed especially by the higher external senses, is not possible without memory and expectation, i.e., without the sensitive retention of what is no longer present and the sensitive projection toward what is not yet here.[22] For this reason the internal senses, in the most proper sense of the term, are those which *represent* to themselves, imagine absent sense-perceptibles.

---

[20]Cf. no. 137.
[21]Cf. no. 158.
[22]Cf. no. 75.

The power of imagining which interiorizes the temporal dispersion of the perceived, is conditioned by an extremely refined organic structure in which sense perception leaves behind its impressions. However, the continued action of the past should be conceived neither as an organic event nor solely as the influence of habit on actual behavior. The past *itself* is still intentionally present in a way in the immanent acts which contain a re-presentation (making present again) of the perceptions and their objects.

This re-actuation of past perceptions and their objects reveals itself in manifold ways. It may be a pure reproduction without any awareness of the fact that its content has been perceived before. But it may also be a re-collection of the perceived, with a certain awareness of its having been perceived before. In this last case we speak of *memory*.

Memory in its vaguest form is present when we "recognize" the actually perceived objects implicitly or more explicitly. We know that we are familiar with them and, therefore, capable of supplementing what we here and now actually perceive. Concretely, as it *de facto* occurs, perception is even always a recognition of objects by means of a few actually "given" signs and an anticipation, based on memory, of the experiences which would fill the gaps in our actual perception.

In recognition there is not yet any explicit presence of the past *as* past. This presence pertains to reminiscence: we have again before us the perceived objects themselves or the past events and experiences themselves. Reminiscence may leave the time of these past experiences vague or estimate this time more accurately in its connection with the whole stream of our experiences. This reminiscence of time may arise spontaneously, be provoked by our present situation, or be consciously and deliberately caused.

Alongside the retention and re-actualization of past impressions and events, with or without awareness of their pastness, we have the capacity of combining images and synthetizing new ones from elements derived from experience. This capacity is called "creative" imagination. It plays an important role in the development of our cognitive life and is difficult to distinguish from reproductive imagination and memory. Creative imagination refers especially to the future, which it anticipates. It makes purposive activity possible.

In addition, there is the wholly unrestricted power of fantasy, by which we form all kinds of fancy worlds with fancy events in a fantasy space and a fantasy time. The awareness of the distinction between fancy and actual reality is subject to great variations. It may even disappear in whole or part, as in dreams. The free play of fantasy is the sensitive foundation of all higher cognitive and mental life, of discovery and invention, arts and letters, history and science.[23]

From the epistemological viewpoint, a distinction must be made between perceptive *knowing* and free *imagination*. Perceptive knowing is directed to the objects as they *really* are, have been, or will be; hence not only perception, but also memory and expectation are limited by reality. The free representing by the imagination, on the other hand, taken in itself, is not knowledge, but is the sensitive aspect of *thinking* and, consequently, is governed only by the forms of *possibility*.

Cognitive Species. Although perception, *insofar as* it has an intuitive character, needs an impressed species or cognitive image, it does not produce an expressed species in the central sense. It also gives rise to an impressed species in the imaginative powers. Memory, expectation, and imagination, on the other hand, essentially produce their object in an expressed species. This phantasm or representative image,[24] in the broad sense of the term, is meant as a reference to the real object insofar as memory and expectation are concerned. In free imagination, however, the phantasm refers in a peculiar way to a fancy world which exists "objectively" only at the discretion of the imagining subject. To determine what the mode of *being*, the spatiality and temporality of the fancy image are, is one of the most difficult problems of epistemology.[25]

---

[23] Cf. no. 148.

[24] Cf. no. 81.

[25] Cf. nos. 34, 122 and 165. The original meaning of the term "species" is shine, form, appearance, shape, or image. In its technical sense it means the representation or likeness of the known in the knower. Because this representation is the terminus of the knower's activity, it is called "expressed species." Apart from the phantasm (the representative image of the internal senses) the thought image, i.e., concept, judgment, or reasoning, also should be conceived as an expressed species.

The expressed species is immanent in the knower, but at the same time refers to the object itself insofar as this object transcends the cognitive act.

The expressed species is knowable through reflection on the act of cognition and may even be *experienced* in this reflection. However, only by means of *reasoning* are we forced to admit that the expression of the known by the knower must have been *preceded* by an impression of the thing to be known in the receptive knower. This impression is called "impressed species." In the external senses this species arises from the surroundings, but in the intellect it originates from the collaboration of the intellect's spontaneity with the phantasm.

125. *The Origin of the Intellectual Phase of Cognition*[26]

Transcendence of the Individual and Concrete. Fully developed, the sensitive phase of cognition is the merger of the central sense and the cognitive power or particular reason with the riches of memory and expectation into what we may call in a special way "sense maturity": there is an intimate familiarity with the changing concrete world insofar as it has meaning and value for the sensitive living subject. However, the experience implied in this maturity remains knowledge of the objects in their *relative meaning* for *this* individual subject, at least as long as we methodically abstract from the intellectual phase of knowledge. This relativity is not known as such. Likewise the relativity of the perspective in which this subject spatially and temporally arranges the active qualities appearing to it is not known as such. In other words, the level of the individual and factual is not transcended.

Nevertheless, man knows that his knowledge contains more than the individual and factual. He expresses his experience in a judgment,[27] and this judgment implies a concept of what he has experienced, which to a certain extent expresses the mode of *being* proper to that which he has experienced.[28] Because what is experienced is understood as being in a determined way, it is placed in an absolute, all-embracing order—the order of participation in *being*.[29] Finally, he expresses what pertains to beings as beings in absolutely general judgments, first principles, which are implicitly contained in the particular judgments of experience.[30]

No matter how imperfectly the judgment expresses the essence of the experienced being and how much the intellectual knowledge remains subject to being rendered more perfect, the judgment implies an *absolute* position, which posits the sensitively experienced as a being in itself. The judgment is directed to the truth as the agreement of the knowing subject with the known object as it is in itself. Consequently, this truth is not merely related to this individual subject but pertains to all knowing subjects: what reveals itself to

---

[26]For nos. 125-128 see D. M. de Petter, "Impliciete intuitie," *Tijdschrift v. Philosophie,* vol. 1 (1939), pp. 84-105; "intentionaliteit en identiteit," *ibid.,* vol. 2 (1940), pp. 515-550; "Zin en grond van het oordeel," *ibid.,* vol. 11 (1949), pp. 3-26; "De oorsprong van de zijnskennis," *ibid.,* vol. 17 (1955), pp. 199-254.
[27]Cf. no. 85.
[28]Cf. nos. 83-84.
[29]Cf. no. 35.
[30]Cf. nos. 36-44.

me as true may still be concealed from you, but it can never reveal itself to you as not true.

Interpenetration of Intellect and Senses. How can the origin of such an intellectual knowledge of the sensitive be explained? First of all, its adequate origin cannot lie in the sensitively known precisely *insofar as* sensitively known. The schematic image or phantasm remains an individual representation;[31] it has all the relativity proper to sense cognition, so that of itself it can never reveal the object as it is in itself, i.e., *as* object and, consequently, neither the subject *as* subject.

Secondly, this intellectual knowledge cannot find its origin in a perfect intuition of the subject in itself. True, we always have an implicit self-consciousness, and *in* this consciousness of ourselves as intellectual beings there is always an implicit presence of all other fellow-beings to which we are open insofar as "in a way we are all things." Nevertheless, this implicit self-consciousness is explicitated only by means of intellectual acts of cognition that are explicitly directed to the other subsistent beings *as objects*. But these objects are known to us from sense experience, which does not produce what it experiences but receives it.[32]

Thirdly, still less is it possible for this intellectual knowledge to derive its origin from a perfect intellectual intuition of unqualified *being,* for we do not have any such intuition.[33] True, in the absolute affirmation of *being,* which has something of an intuition, we know that "to be" is all-embracing. However, from *being* we do not know which beings are possible, real, or necessary.[34] If we did possess this knowledge, we would not need experience to arrive at an intellectual insight. But it is only through experiential knowledge of what *de facto* is that the essence of the necessary can be known to us:[35] to arrive at intellectual knowledge, we have to discover that the "data" of experience *are* in this way or that way.

Accordingly, intellectual knowledge must find its origin in a mutual interpenetration of the senses and intellect, and in this interpenetration the phantasm is needed to arrive at a kind of knowledge that transcends the sensitive although it cannot dispense with it. We

---

[31]Cf. no. 81.
[32]Cf. no. 24.
[33]Cf. no. 19.
[34]Cf. nos. 29-35.
[35]Cf. no. 26.

will have to determine more accurately how the intellect discovers the objects as objects and, consequently, also itself as subject in the light of an intuition of *being* which raises the sensitive to the level of intelligibility and which cannot attain the knowledge of beings in their modes of *being* without this elevation of the sensitive.

Receptive and Active Intellect. Two opposed aspects must be admitted in the human intellect which in their "bi-unity" make intellectual knowledge of the sensitive possible.[36]

On the one hand, the human intellect is a receptive power, a so-called potential intellect. It proceeds from no knowledge, from question and doubt to knowledge, reply, and certainty and, therefore, passes from being-in-potency to being-in-act in a process running its course in time.[37] Although this transition is an active self-unfolding, it does not take place without the influence of the objects presenting themselves to the intellect.

However, the intellect's receptive openness is not of the same nature as the receptivity of the senses. The openness of the senses finds its explanation in the transient action of bodily surroundings on the sense organs, through which the sense powers themselves are brought to their first act and react to the impressed species in a cognitive activity that is one with the organic event. Intellectual knowledge, however, transcends the here-and-now that characterizes the sensitively present insofar as it is individuated by prime matter. For the intellect understands every being as being, i.e., as connected with the all-embracing synthesis of *being*. The intellect is concerned with the universal, which is not yet actually made present in the particular as known by the senses. The actual sensible is only potentially intelligible and, therefore, cannot be the adequate explanation of the receptive character of the intellect.[38]

On the other hand, the human intellect is a spontaneous and active power, a so-called "agent intellect." Man is characterized by a certain measure of active interiority or self-presence. And this

---

36 Concerning the distinction of agent and potential intellect, see Aristotle, *De anima*, bk. III, chs. 4-5 and St. Thomas' *Comment*, nos. 671-745. Also *Summa theol.*, p. 1, q. 79, *De anima*, aa. 4-5. Further, K. Rahner, *Geist in Welt*, pp. 97-101; A. Dondeyne, "L 'abstraction", *Revue néo-scolastique de philosophie*, vol. 41 (1938), pp. 348-371; A. Marc, *Psychologie réflexive*, vol. 1, pp. 165-290.

37 Cf. no. 72.

38 Cf. no. 83.

self-consciousness, as the transparency of *being* to itself, includes actively also all other beings as beings.[39]

Nevertheless, this active immanence by which the intellect posits itself and all else should not be conceived as a perfect identity with everything that is. On the contrary, the intellect is "everything" only *to a certain extent*. For man's active intellect is essentially related to the passive intellect without, however, entirely coinciding with it. This *distance* of spontaneity and receptivity has as its *intermediary* the other as other. Only through this intermediary does implicit or habitual self-consciousness become actual self-consciousness.

To express it differently, the light of actual intelligibility, which is present *in* us as ever-shining, is not immediately shining *for* us, it is not what is known explicitly first, but makes the receptive intellect pass from being-in-potency to being-in-act by illuminating the sensitive phantasm which arises from the action of the object. Through this illumination the potentially present intelligible meaning and value of the sensible is made actual. It is only by means of this elevation of the sensitive datum to the level of actual intelligibility that the intellect can determine itself to the cognitive act and, then, by reflecting on the origin of this act that is directed to the object, can become conscious of its own actual intelligibility and active interiority.

Accordingly, the receptive understanding of the other as other, which is based on the sense experience, is the deficient and participated mode of being-self-conscious proper to man.

126. *The Intellectual Species*

The Impressed Species. The necessary union of spontaneity and receptivity in man's knowledge is expressed especially in the theory about the origin of the intellect's impressed species. The human intellect does not have any "innate" ideas. Ideas or concepts arise in dependence on the senses and, therefore, on bodily dispositions.[40]

This dependence on the senses does not mean that the sense image is merely a condition of intellectual knowledge—as it is for those who admit innate ideas—but the phantasm is a cause of this knowledge.

---

[39]Cf. nos. 17 and 35.

[40]This dependence is not intrinsic but extrinsic. For, precisely *insofar* as the concept transcends the phantasm of the inner senses, it does not arise from experience but from thinking (cf. no. 85).

However, as the expressed species of the senses, the phantasm cannot be the proper and principal cause of the impressed species which determines the receptive intellect to the act of knowing. For the lower is unable to exercise influence on the higher by virtue of its own power. The principal cause of the impression made on the receptive or potential intellect is the intellect itself, as spontaneous or active intellect.

Accordingly, the intellect determines itself from within to the knowing of objects, but it does so by means of the phantasm as an instrumental cause. This determination takes place insofar as the agent intellect strips the schematic phantasm of its spatial and temporal conditions, i.e., of materiality, and especially insofar as it causes an intelligible characteristic to appear in which the similarity and dissimilarity of the phantasmally represented object to other objects reveal themselves.[41] This universal characteristic that lies hidden in the individual and is revealed by the light of the agent intellect, as impressed species, determines the receptive intellect to the act of knowing.

It would be wrong to interpret too literally this theory which speaks of instrument and principal cause, abstraction and illumination. The theory is an attempt to express in a systematic way that in the unity of human cognition the synthesis established on the sense level is natively oriented to the higher synthesis pertaining to the intellectual level and that, reversely also, thinking is interpenetrated with perception. Accordingly, there is not first a schematic sense image, from which then the general concept is formed next through abstraction. There is no question of a relationship of cause and effect in the proper sense of the term, for everything takes place within one and the same knowing being. Properly speaking, there is likewise no matter-form relation as if the sense content were the matter, and the intelligibility the form of our cognitive objects, for matter and form refer to temporally and spatially extended beings and may not simply be transferred to the plane of intellectual cognition. All such expressions are "analogies" which help us in making to some extent a conceptual analysis of the ineffable, inexpressible unity of senses and intellect which, despite everything, we experience in ourselves.

The Immanent Act of Understanding. The reception of the manifold sense data in the unity of an intelligible species is merely a prepa-

---

[41]Technically the stripping is called to *abstract from,* and the manifestation of the intelligible characteristic is spoken of as *to abstract* (cf. no. 51.).

ration for the cognitive act itself. The subject has to let itself be
modeled by the object in an attitude of sympathetic intimacy before
the *immanent act of cognition* ("cognition in the second act") can
emanate from the power thus prepared ("cognition in the first act").
Accordingly, the act of cognition itself is an activity of the subject
which through the action of the agent intellect has fused with the
object, and by means of this act the subject both becomes *conscious*
of the presence of the object and, as actually knowing, cognitionally
is the actually known object.

It is only in the act of cognition that the *act* of the knower and the
act of the known become one in such a way that there is no longer
question of the knower being related to the known as potency is to
act or as matter is to form—relationships in which the two compo-
nents give rise to a third. Retaining his *own* actual mode of *being,*
the knower includes in his immanent act the known according to the
mode of *being proper* to the known, i.e., the otherness of the object as
a being in and for itself is safeguarded.[42]

The Expressed Species or Inner Word. The cognitive act must
necessarily have an immanent terminus, for, unlike transient action,
it does not produce a change in the other. As regards man's act of
cognition, which expresses a subject-object relationship, this immanent terminus is an immanent "opposite," i.e., the act terminates in
an immanent object. The *being* of the object as immanent terminus
is restricted to being-the-object-of-a-subject.[43]

At the same time, however, in receptive knowledge the object
known transcends the knower, for this object is another possible or
real being whose *being* is not restricted to being-known by the sub-

----

[42]The "in-being" of the known in the cognitive act has nothing to do with
"in-being" in a spatial sense or with having-before-oneself in place. Likewise, it
does not bear comparison with the "in-being" of food in nutrition, for in the
process of assimilation the otherness or independent *being* of food is lost. In
cognition there is question of an "in-being" in which the object remains "itself,"
yet is also immanent in the subject. We may even say that through this immanence it becomes more "itself," at least in the case of a plurality of material individuals, which in the cognitive synthesis is reduced to the unity pertaining to
them in their origin from the universal.

The higher mode of "in-being" pertaining to the material in intellectual
knowledge arises from the power of the active intellect to dematerialize its
objects, a power which flows from the intellect's own immateriality as transcending the here-and-now of matter. Immaterial reception is the opposite of the
material reception in which potency limits act or matter limits form, since in
immaterial reception the act of knowing does not limit but enlarge and elevate
the act of the known.

[43]Cf. no. 122.

ject. As transcendent, the object is that which, because of its own mode of *being* in itself, becomes the object of human knowledge.

That the object as "in itself" and as object of human knowledge are not fully identical is a result of the fact that man's knowing, as theoretical knowledge, is not only merely a receptive and not a creative knowing, but also fails to know the known being fully. Much of the being-to-be-known remains concealed from our imperfect knowledge, which is not a perfect intuition. For this reason there is a *distance* between what is known of the object and the object as it is in itself.

This distance means that in our act of knowing the immanence of the object is deficient. The immanence consists in an *intentional* directedness to the object to be known. This intentional directedness to a being, as it is in itself, implies that this being is only in a certain respect the immanent terminus of the cognitive act: its presence is limited. For this reason we construct thought contents, whose *being* is restricted to being-the-object-of-a-subject, and *in* these contents we have the object present to us in certain respects as a being in itself. Such a thought content is called the *expressed species* of thinking or also the "inner word."

Accordingly, this word is an inner reconstruction of the being known in the knower. Our knowing has not only a receptive but also a constructive character. However, this constructive character or *thinking,* as the forming of thoughts, is directed to, and a means of knowing the object as it is in itself, and is ruled by the truth of being.[44]

The dynamic character of man's imperfect way of knowing reveals itself most clearly in thought. We constantly form new concepts in order to arrive slowly at more adequate knowledge of the object which in its full richness transcends us. As a temporal process, the progress of our knowledge advances not only through the broadening of experience in new observations, but also through making our insight more profound in new concepts.

127. *Concept, Judgment, and Reasoning*

The Concept. The concept is a representation of the intellect, a thought in which an intelligible content is expressed. This content is a possible mode of *being* or "essence," in the broadest sense

---

[44]Cf. no. 85.

of this term. In the formal-concrete concept this mode of *being* is
viewed as pertaining to a bearer that is not further determined. For
this reason the first and all-embracing concept, the transcendental
idea "being," is something which *is* in a way that remains to be determined more accurately. The original more determined categorical
concepts owe their origin to the collaboration of sensitive passivity
with intellectual activity. Thus a distinction is sometimes made between so-called direct and reflex concepts. Direct concepts, also known
as empirical concepts, are the expression of the intelligible meaning
and value which the intellect discovers in the transient active qualities
of the objects presented to it in the phantasm.[45] Reflex concepts, on
the other hand, are an expression of the immanent activities of the
subject itself, which in the formation of concepts is intelligibly present
to itself.

On the basis of these original concepts and in the light of the
idea "being," our thought forms new concepts through synthesis and
analysis. In doing so, the intellect enjoys even more freedom than
the imagination, for it can think anything whatsoever, as long as it
does not include a contradiction.[46]

The Judgment. The concept, separately considered, does not yet
have any cognitive value, for it does not say anything about the *being*
of beings. To arrive at cognitive value, a reflection is needed which
views the concepts as means for obtaining knowledge of the being
apprehended in experience. The abstraction of the concept through
the phantasm from the object experienced must be understood *as* an
abstraction, i.e., it has to reach its term in the fusion of the concept
through the phantasm with the object. This fusion takes place in the
judgment, in which a statement is made about the state of beings in
themselves and in which the object known, *as* object, is posited against
the knowing subject, *as* subject, i.e., the object is posited as transcendent and opposite to this subject, but at the same time as immanent to,
and understood by it.[47]

Accordingly, in the direct judgment the *being* of the object known
reveals itself thematically, but at the same time the *being* of the knowing subject manifests itself in a non-thematic way. For this reason
the subject can become known thematically according to its immanent
activity in a reflex judgment. The fact that for the thematic knowl-

---

[45] Cf. no. 84.
[46] Cf. no. 85.
[47] Cf. *ibid.*

edge of the subject a judgment is needed and, consequently, a subject-object opposition in which the subject places itself facing itself, shows clearly how imperfect our judgmental knowledge is. The opposition and connection of subject and predicate of the judgment is a reflexion of the opposition which, despite the cognitive immanence, remains between the object as it is in itself (the subject of the judgment) and the object as it is inadequately understood in a concept (the predicate of the judgment). Accordingly, no matter how much man possesses an implicit self-consciousness which somehow embraces everything that is, nevertheless his explicit self-consciousness is a knowing of himself by means of a concept which can express the knower only in his object-directed activity but not in his individual essence. As a result, the distance, on which the subject-object relationship is built, is not wholly eliminated.

The singular direct or reflex judgments of experience imply universal judgments. These judgments express the necessary essential relationships which reveal themselves in the way the beings of experience *de facto* are.

The most immediate and all-embracing universal judgments are the first principles. Just as every concept falls within the synthesis of the idea "being," so every judgment falls within the synthesis of the principles of *being*. These principles are not separate judgments alongside other, just as the idea "being" does not stand alongside other concepts, but in the deficient form of a judgment they express the transcendental openness of human knowing to "everything that is, as it is." Thus they find their explanation in the spontaneity of the active intellect, which in a way contains all knowledge as its source and which by means of transcendental ideas determines the receptive intellect to the formation of the transcendental judgments. According to these judgments we judge whatever comes to our knowledge, for the less general and the singular judgments are nothing but the unfolding of what is already present, though only in a confused way, in the principles.

Nevertheless, we are unable immediately to derive the particular beings from the principles of *being*. We need sense experience, abstraction (concepts), and concretion (experiential judgments) to discover what is possible, real, and necessary through *being*.[48]

Reasoning. Thus we see why the human intellect is called "reason." It constructs reasonings in order to arrive, through thinking,

---

[48]Cf. no. 125.

from imperfect knowledge at more perfect knowledge by means of explicitation. Reasoning is an attempt to supplement what we lack in intuition. However, reasoning cannot transcend judgmental knowledge, for it terminates in a new, though more explicit, judgment.

We speak of deductive reasoning, or the syllogism in the stricter sense, if at least one of two connected judgments is more universal than the conclusion. Reasoning is inductive if the premises are more particular and the conclusion more universal. Deduction makes us grasp the particular in its hypothetical necessity, while induction makes us observe the universal, which in itself is necessary, as *de facto* true.

By means of reasoning it is possible to learn more about the relations between beings. We may even be induced to admit beings which themselves are not perceived but to some extent present in what is perceived as, for instance, the cause is present in the effect.

128. *Human Knowing as Participation*

We can approach the essence of knowing by reflecting on the pre-knowledge of what it is to know that is contained in the exercise of the cognitive act. For, strictly speaking, we do not know something until we know that we know it and thus in a way know what it is to know.

For this reason sense experiences, in which consciousness in the strict sense is lacking, may be called cognitive acts only in a degraded, analogous sense, as a kind of participation in understanding. Likewise, the perceptive observing of the fact that something is or is this way or that way is a diminished way of knowing as compared with the insight into, and understanding of the reason or ground why it has to be or has to be this way.[49] To know in the strict and proper sense is to understand a being in its truth, i.e., in its interconnection with everything else in *being*.

The Antinomy of Immanence and Transcendence. Man's mode of knowing manifests itself as a special subject-object relationship. It is immediately directed to the other beings facing the subject and only reflexively to the being who knows. Idealism[50] and phenomenalism[51] attempt to explain the origin of the object either wholly or partially

---

[49]Cf. no. 21.
[50]Cf. no. 24.
[51]Cf. no. 25.

by means of the subject's spontaneity. Empiricism[52] and realism,[53] on the other hand, have to explain how the cognitive act of finite man can extend also to the other beings in such a way that these beings are noetically in him. For, man is not these other beings because they are ontically outside him and opposed to him. Isn't it an antinomy if we have to accept that the object is, on the one hand, transcendent to the knower and, on the other immanent in him?

"Physical" and "Intentional" Modes of Being. Intellectual knowledge is directed to being as it is in itself; therefore, this being has to become immanent in the knower and, consequently, to know the other being means to become the other *as* other.

To explain how the knower can become the other as other, a distinction is made between the mode in which the being is in itself and its mode of *being* in the knower. The object, so it is said, is in itself in a material way, but in the intellect it is immaterially, i.e., when it is in itself, matter limits the form to the concrete and individual,[54] but in the intellect the form is stripped of the limitations of matter and thus becomes abstract and universal. Accordingly, the knower becomes the other in an immaterial way.

This becoming-the-other of the knower is explained through the production of the *concept*. Although this concept is a thought produced by the action of the intellect and, therefore, strictly an immanent object, nevertheless, it is also essentially a re-presentation of the being as it is in itself because it is similar to it and as a *cognitive* image refers to it.

Thus a twofold way of *being* is distinguished:

1. The "physical" mode of *being,* which the object has as it is in itself, i.e., as being in the real world around us and also in the realm of the possible, to which our cognitive acts are directed.

2. The "intentional" mode of *being,* which the object has precisely insofar as it is represented by the concept in the intellect. The cognitive presence of the object to the subject is a presence by means of an "intention"—i.e., the concept, which as immanent terminus originates in the intellect but nevertheless is essentially directed to the object as it is in itself and therefore transcendent to the subject.[55]

---

[52]Cf. no. 23.
[53]Cf. no. 34.
[54]Cf. no. 90.
[55]Generally speaking, intention means the dynamic directedness of one being to another being in view of its perfection (Cf. no. 63). In this sense every

Insufficiency of this View. As long as the concept and the being to which this concept refers are placed in *opposition* to each other, it is impossible to explain why we do not know first our concepts but the being as it is in itself. This being itself has to be immanent in us, for what is not immanent in the knower is not known.

A certain identity of concept and being, therefore, is required. This identity is found in considering the concept not according to the mode of *being* it has as something belonging to the intellect, but according to its intelligible content, for according to this content it is a *likeness* of the subject in itself.

However, likeness is not a sufficient explanation. For similarity says both agreement and difference. By means of likeness it is possible to explain how I know the being precisely insofar as the concept is similar to this being. But it cannot explain how I can know this being precisely insofar as it differs from the concept, i.e., according to the mode of *being* it has in itself as a physical being, and how, as happens in judgment, I see my concept *as* (or *as not*) more or less adequately resembling or agreeing with "that which is as it is in itself." Therefore, the difference also must be immanent in me. But how? By means of another concept? And so on to infinity?

To escape from this difficulty, the concept is said not to be an ordinary sign, i.e., something which has to be known first before it can give us knowledge of something else. The concept is not an instrumental sign but a formal sign, something which, without having to be known first, immediately makes something else known. It is not first in itself and then in addition refers to something else, but its whole being consists in being-a-sign-of, in referring to.[56]

Nevertheless, even this reply does not settle the problem of how we know objects. For the sign remains distinct from the signified; it has a mode of *being* (to be a sign) which the signified does not have; consequently, it does not explain how we could know the signi-

---

finite activity is intentionally directed to its object (Cf. nos. 93 and 122). Especially of knowing and loving is it said that they contain their object in themselves in an intentional way. Accordingly, intentional is whatever is connected with immanent acts as the expression of their directedness; for example, concept, representation, word, gesture, symbol, sign, and even all behavior and cultural products. In a special sense intention means the tendential directedness to a purpose to be attained by the use of certain means. In this sense it is usually opposed to "execution" (Cf. nos. 108 and 141).

[56]Cf. John of St. Thomas, *Cursus Philosophicus, Logica,* tr. II, q. 22, a. 1-2; *De anima,* q. 4, a. 1; q. 6, a. 2-3; q. 10, a. 2; q. 11, a. 1-2. J. Maritain, *Les degrés du savoir,* pp. 769-819. For a critique, see D. M. de Petter, "Intentionaliteit en identiteit," *Tijdschrift v. Philosophie,* vol. 2 (1940), pp. 515-550.

fied according to its own mode of *being,* distinct from that of the sign, as long as only the sign is immanent in the knower.

The Essence of Knowing. Thus, we have to maintain that the being, as it is in itself, according to its *own* mode of *being,* is immanent in the knower. The knower in the act of knowing *is* the known in the act of being known. Knowing can never be understood by means of an intentionality "taken by itself," but has to be conceived as the *identity of an act with an act.*

The identity of an act with an act, however, is not in the first place that of one act with another act, for such an identity can only be relative, but is the identity of an act with itself. Let us see what this identity means.

A material being is to some extent identified with the form through which it is "such," but it is only here-and-now "such." The form by itself does not constitute the essence of this being, but is united with a limiting principle of mutability and multiplication. It is given to matter, estranged from itself, it is "with matter" and not in perfect self-identity "with itself," And, although the form in itself is a principle of intelligibility, *as* a materialized form, it is not actually intelligible but only potentially.[57]

If, on the other hand, a form by its very nature is not a form-of-matter but by itself constitutes the essence, the form is "with itself." The immaterial being is essentially not a bi-unity of matter and form, but the non-composed unity of a form with itself.

This immanence of the immaterial form as essential act in and with and for itself, in active identity with itself, this being-interior-to-itself, is the essence of knowing—it is the coincidence of the knower and the known in a single act without any opposition.

Although we are unable to express knowing in any other way than by means of the opposition of the knower and the known and then declaring that the two are identical, the subject-object relationship does not pertain to the essence of knowing *as* knowing. The same is *a fortiori* true of the subject-object relationship in which the object is a different and opposite being. To know is not to stumble on something, to touch something or to catch something opposite us. Such expressions are imperfect representations arising from the sensitive experiences of touching, hearing, and seeing.

---

[57]Cf. no. 125.

To know is to be oneself in pure inner activity, in immanence of *being,* which is the highest and most proper mode of being-oneself or identity. Accordingly, "to know" and "to be" should not be conceived as two spheres which are first distinguished and then brought together in a kind of intentional connection by means of a representation or cognitive image. They are an original unity, and where this unity is present in all its purity, there knowing is perfectly present.

Both one-sided idealism and one-sided realism tend to concentrate on the problem of the subject-object relationship and forget that "to be" expresses identity, and therefore in its perfection includes to-be-known and to-be-knowing in unity.

Participation and Knowing. If to know is to be self-illuminating for oneself, the transparence of the self for the self, self-consciousness (expressed by the term "I"), and if, on the other hand, to know is also an active identity with *all* that is, as it is—for whatever is, is intelligible—, then pure knowing will be an infinite openness of knowing to *being* and of *being* to knowing, a reciprocal openness which is all-embracing self-consciousness.

The question arises, however, how a *finite* knower would be possible and especially a knower who is primarily directed to the *other* as an object? The reply is that *participation* is possible, i.e., a knower who in a finite way participates in the intimacy of knowing and being-known which of itself is infinite. The analogous grades of cognitive participation are the grades of participation in the actuality of *being* according to a greater or lesser immateriality. Wherever, therefore, "to know" is realized in a particularized way, the reason for the particularization will be that the identity of the knowing being and the being-to-be-known is not perfect, so that there remains a duality or opposition of these two within the immanence of the cognitive act. This limtied immanence or *merely relative identity,* in which the knower and the known as subsistent beings do not wholly coincide with actual knowing and actual being-known, finds expression in intentionality as immanent directedness of a subject to a transcendent object by means of a cognitive image.

The Imperfection of Man's Knowledge. Against the background of an absolute ideal of knowing that coincides with the fullness of life and the fullness of *being,*[58] the imperfection of man's cognitive act reveals itself in its intentionality.

---

[58]Cf. no. 117.

First of all, on the one hand, the all-embracing horizon of *being* has already manifested itself to some extent to man, who in his pre-predicative awareness of *being* is "in a way all things." Otherwise, how could he know that he does not know everything knowable and even that he does not totally know anything at all?

On the other hand, this infinite openness is a dynamic infinity. With the growth of his knowledge, man becomes also increasingly aware of it that he does not yet know everything; hence man's process of knowing in time remains always both extensively and intensively perfectible and is never finished. Every immanence of the already-known is essentially an intentional directedness to the not-yet-known.

Secondly, man *is* not his act of cognition, for his cognitive transition from being-in-potency to being-in-act implies the distinction of essence, power, and activity."[59] Consequently, his *being* is prior to his actually-being-known-by-himself, his consciousness: he experiences that he himself is and does not know his *being* down to its deepest ground.[60] Even in finite self-knowledge, therefore, there is a distinction between the known as it is in itself and the known precisely as it is known. Because of this inadequacy, self-knowledge has to be expressed in a word, concept, or cognitional image which does not wholly coincide with the ego and contains an intentional directedness to the ego as a not-yet-revealed mystery.

Thirdly, man becomes actually conscious of his self-presence only by means of reflection on the cognitive act in which he perceives the *other* beings with which he is interconnected in the course of his life. But this perception itself of objects is likewise deficient, for it can take place only by means of the sense experience of their external appearance at a certain moment of time and from a certain spatial perspective. What is already known about the object is provisionally synthetized in a representation or cognitional image, in whose structure memory, imagination, and the formation of concepts play a role, and this inner reconstruction is referred to the object through the judgment. However, since the object *as a being* in itself is immanent to the cognitive act in pre-predicative experience, prior to any analysis, the judgment is able to realize that the abstractly-general predicates fall short. Thus it can become the start-

---

[59] Cf. no. 94.
[60] Cf. no. 19.

ing point and basis of new experiences and concepts, of inductive and deductive reasoning processes.

Finally, even our apodictic insights into the universal and into essential relationships are inadequate, for they presuppose abstraction.[61] We know, however, there must be concretely-general "specific ideas" which give rise to individual possibilities of realization. For this reason our universal concepts and judgments reveal an intentional directedness to the overcoming of abstract univocity in analogous knowledge, which synthetically unites both the similarity and the difference of beings.

However, it is precisely this absolute synthesis of beings in unqualified *being* which we approach in the most inadequate way, for we approach it in the form of judgments about being as being and, therefore, by means of analogous concepts, from which we cannot derive the particular modes of *being*. We are unable to place ourselves on the viewpointless "standpoint" of the absolute. Nevertheless, the absolute origin of all beings is present in a way in our perspective as soon as we affirm of any being whatsoever that it *is*. Accordingly, despite everything, there is in us a certain immanence of "everything that is," as it comes forth from its source. This immanence, however, is potential and becomes actual only through the intentional movement of our knowledge from the factual, the many, the finite, and the mutable to their source.

129. *The Possibility of Error*

The imperfectness of human knowledge shows itself not only in its incompleteness and intentionality but even more in the possibility of error. When we recognize that a proposed situation does not agree with the way that beings are related and therefore reject it, we form a true judgment. But one who assents to an incorrect proposed situation makes a false judgment and errs.

A judgment is false if it "affirms of what is not that it is or of what is that is not." The false judgment does not agree with that which is as it is. This lack of agreement must not be conceived as merely a deficient agreement, but as a positive deviation. If it is merely a question of being incomplete or deficient, we have to do with imperfect truth but not with falsity. He who errs posits the false judgment with the claim of truth. Accordingly, such a judgment presents itself as the expression of knowledge.

---

[61]Cf. no. 84.

Its Possibility. Experience shows us that we err frequently. Our former views contradict new experiences and insights or the views voiced by knowledgeable persons. In this way we are led to reject our former views as errors.

Still, it is difficult to understand how error is possible. For the judgment presents itself as an act of thinking based on knowledge. But knowledge can be understood only as "to have within oneself beings as they are." How, then, can knowledge induce us to an act of thought which thinks these beings other than they are? In other words, how is merely "putative" knowledge possible?

Knowledge agrees with beings as they are when it is governed by the evidence of experience or insight[62] or by the trustworthiness of a person who testifies about these beings.[63] For human knowledge is a receptive knowing—to such an extent that even our apodictic insights have this receptive character and are governed by being as being.

Erroneous or merely putative "knowledge," therefore, is possible only insofar as the one who judges does not allow himself to be determined in his judgment by evidence or truthworthiness, but by a representation of beings which does not agree with these beings as they are, and gives his assent to this incorrect representation.

Its Origin. Accordingly, the immediate cause of error lies in lack of evidence, in ignorance. But how does it happen that despite his ignorance, a person falsely assents to something which he does not see, into which he does not have an insight, or which he has not heard from a reliable witness? The cause lies in a lack of attention to the beings as they are in themselves. This lack of attention itself may arise from carelessness, i.e., the failure to apply oneself to perception and thinking, or from undue haste and impatience in making a judgment.

The lack of reverence for truth which reveals itself here can originate in this case—in contrast with the case of faith[64]—only in an unjustifiable influence of the will, which therefore is the remote cause of the error. The will, which natively is rational, lets itself be guided by sensitive moods, emotions, and passions, instead of controlling them.

---

[62]Cf. no. 21.

[63]Cf. nos. 8 and 132.

[64]Cf. no. 132.

All kinds of motives may play a role here. For instance, the desire to have an opinion or to impose this opinion on others, the desire to dominate others, to contradict what others say or, as usually happens, to go along with them, the desire not to be troubled or, reversely, to remain forever a restless seeker. Heredity, education, and milieu play an important role in the origin and permanence of purely putative knowledge and erroneous prejudices.

The occasion for forming incorrect representations and making errors lies in the inexhaustible wealth of aspects possessed by beings. For in sense experience they reveal merely their external appearance, and in understanding and thinking they reveal their essence only gradually, to a limited extent, and usually also only mediately.

The ultimate root of the possibility to err lies in the finiteness of our intellect. It does not coincide with truth, but is only intentionally directed to it as to a goal to be attained. In the process of the development of knowledge the will exercises a determining influence and, as finite, the will can deviate from its norm because it does not coincide with its goal in full identity.

Error as Known Disagreement. Just as the truth is the known agreement of the proposed version of a situation with the beings in question, so falsity must be the *known* disagreement of such a version. But if this is true, the error, which is the assent to an incorrect proposed version of a situation, must contain also to some extent knowledge that the judgment is false.

This knowledge, however, seems to be impossible, for one who errs considers precisely the false judgment to be true and explicitly affirms it as true. Therefore, the knowledge that the judgment is false cannot be explicit as long as the erring person errs, for as soon as he knows explicitly that he is mistaken, he no longer is fully in error.

It follows, then, that the contradiction which in a way is known to exist between the false judgment that is considered to be true and the true state of affairs must lie on the level of implicit knowledge. As a matter of fact, the false judgment is an incorrectly performed reflection on the origins of the judgment. Not everything implicitly contained in the false judgment is false, for it is based also on experiences and insights which are evident. By reverting to the origin of the false judgment and by renewed reflection on the evident starting points, it is possible to "take back" the assent, and by means of more attentive formation of concepts referring to the being to be judged the falsity can be removed from the judgment.

CHAPTER TWENTY-FOUR

THE ROLE OF THE SUBJECT AND THE OBJECT IN THE GROWTH OF OUR KNOWLEDGE

130. *The Formation of Concepts*

Taken in itself, the concept does not yet have any cognitive value. It expresses a possible mode of *being,* but does not yet assert anything about the *being* of beings.[1] It is only when it plays a role as the concept-of-something and thus is either explicitly or implicitly connected with a judgment that it becomes a true or false concept, an adequate or inadequate concept, because in this way it is governed by the truth with respect to the being in question.

The Difficulty of Essential Knowledge. Sometimes our first approach to a being is by means of a negative or undetermined concept, e.g., not-green, not-sympathetic. But even a positive concept may still be a very obscure and vague indication of what is meant, as when we call a thing "a kind of machine." Even when we possess a well-defined concept of a thing, a concept which distinguishes it from whatever this thing is not, this concept is usually derived from the thing's external activities and forms of appearance,[2] which indicate how to recognize the thing rather than its proper essence. For instance, we may say that man is a sentient being having two hands and two feet. A more distinct concept is obtained when it is possible to describe the properties of a being, as when man is described as a sentient being which can speak, work, and live in a society.

The strictly constituent essence of the subsistent and even of the accidental is attained only exceptionally, and even when it is reached, we often have to rely on partially negative indications as, for instance, when we say that man's soul is immaterial. True, the idea is sometimes put forward that we have a strictly essential concept of at least certain beings or aspects of being, e.g., mathematical entities or certain intentional attitudes studied in phenomenology, such as perception, judgment, love, fear, hope, patience, courage, happiness. However, even with respect to these objects we may ask whether we understand them adequately and wholly intuitively. It may be true

[1]Cf. no. 127.
[2]Cf. no. 84.

that we have an insight into the relationships between numbers, nevertheless it remains a fact that the essence of a number is the object of laborious study in the investigation of the foundations of mathematics. And as far as phenomenology is concerned, it proved necessary to devise a careful method for the purification of concepts in order to arrive at an approximation of essences.[3]

Purification of Concepts. There is another reason why concepts have to be purified. Because the intellect and the senses are intimately connected, especially in the estimative sense or particular reason,[4] in our prescientific dealings we evaluate beings primarily from the viewpoint of practicality, of having to deal with them.

Our concepts seize beings insofar as they are useful or agreeable for the development of our life. However, it is not in these utilitarian relationships that the essence and proper meaning of the objects consists, and especially not when these objects are living beings and fellow-men who, as subsistent beings, have a value of their own and are themselves the purpose of their development in immanent acts. Accordingly, purified intellectual concepts have to present the objects with respect to what they are in themselves and for themselves according to the proper and original mode in which they participate in *being*.

Univocal and Analogous Concepts. Our concepts are universal, i.e., they can be predicated of a plurality of beings which, in principle, is limitless. Two clearly distinct modes of being-universal must be contrasted:

Univocally-universal concepts, which are ordered according to genus and species, and whose content is in inverse ratio to their extension. These concepts arise from the abstraction that is made of specific and individual differences. The abstraction in question is ontologically based on the matter-form composition of corporeal beings.[5]

Analogously-universal concepts, or ideas, which are transcendental. They are all-embracing not only with respect to extension but also regarding content. They contain the various particular modes in an actual, though confused, way. The origin of these concepts lies in

---

[3] This approximation is sometimes called "eidetic vision."
[4] Cf. no. 124.
[5] Cf. nos. 51, 54, 84, 86, 116.

the imperfect intuition of *being* whose ontological foundation is the participation of every being in *"to be"* according to its essence.[6]

Intermediary Concepts. The question may be raised whether there are not all kinds of intermediary forms between all-embracing ideas and univocal concepts which abstract from all differences. For there are *grades* in the matter-form relationship, in such a way that the higher forms rise more and more above individuation through matter and approach individuation through their essential form.[7] The individuality of living and knowing beings is not a mere repetition here-and-now of the same thought content, but has a greater originality because of the higher mode of immanence, intimacy and active directedness to a purpose proper to these beings. Especially the individual human being displays a measure of free self-determination[8] in the activities which are based on intellectual knowledge, such as loving, willing, and social and cultural activities. Accordingly, concepts which express these higher modes of *being* and acting will include, despite their universality, the richness of the various possibilities in which they can be individually realized as gradual approximations of an "ideal." Unlike univocal concepts, they do not express only the lowest mode of being-realized as pertaining to all in a homogeneous way.

Univocity reveals itself most clearly in mathematical concepts,[9] in concepts expressing the "materials" of which tools and utilitarian "things" are made, such as water, iron, wood, and air, and in physical and chemical concepts. But concepts of living species begin to fall short of pure univocity, for there is a certain latitude between the minimal and the maximal realization of the species-idea.

With respect to concepts of physical activities and the powers that give rise to them, analogy shows itself still more clearly: the outer and inner senses are realized in different ways in animal species and man.[10]

---

[6]Cf. nos. 49, 52, 56, 117. Not only the ideas of being, the one, the true, the good, and the beautiful are transcendental (cf. nos. 36-44), but also the idea of the active and all concepts expressing an activity which does not include any imperfection in itself, even though it is true that these concepts are not predicated unqualifiedly of all beings but only of those which more perfectly participate in *being,* such as the living, the knowing, and the loving (cf. nos. 117, 128, 144).

[7]Cf. nos. 90, 113, 116.

[8]Cf. no. 143.

[9]Cf. no. 168.

[10]Cf. no. 124.

A fortiori this analogy applies to the concepts expressing the activities, powers, abilities, and functions proper to man as man. They are *ideal concepts* implying a certain infinity, which is realized by each individual in an essentially different particular way. This assertion applies especially to the concepts of intellectual, technical, artistic and moral abilities, for they do not exclude but imply the rich variety of their concretizations.

For this reason all concepts of the cultural sciences are raised above pure univocity. We mean not only the historical-descriptive cultural sciences, but also those which are critical-normative and axiological. Examples of the concepts in question are the following: law, authority, king, democracy, state, family; lyrics, drama, classicism, romanticism, impressionism; parental love, gratitude, politeness, civilization, welfare.

By way of conclusion we may say that every realm of *being* and activity and every science of nature or culture has its own way of forming concepts and its own way of predicating these concepts in judgments. The two opposite poles between which the concepts of experience move are, on the one hand, the univocal repetition of exactly the same abstract content, which is most clearly exemplified by mathematical concepts, and on the other hand, the analogous inclusion of all distinctions in concrete identity, which reveals itself in its purest form in metaphysical notions.

Individual Concepts. Do we have individual concepts? The ideal of knowledge is to understand the individual in itself, for, whether real or possible, the individual is a being in the original sense.[11] The experiential judgment shows that we have somehow a concept of the individual, although this concept shows general characteristics and is always subject to being perfected through more accurate experiences and reflections.

The question, however, is whether we have individual concepts in the sense of concepts which apply *only* to this individual. It is true that we refer to individuals which are most important to us by means of proper names, such as John, France, etc., and not only by adding a demonstrative pronoun to a universal concept (*this* house). Likewise, individual and original products of science, art, or culture, whether produced by one man or by a society, can become a "concept" for us; for instance, the Ninth Symphony, the Divina Comedia, the Cathedrals, the tales of chivalry.

---

[11]Cf. no. 90.

Thus we cannot say that such an intellectual knowledge of the individual is in its individuality is wholly denied to us. But it obviously presupposes and implies a sensitive contact. It is based on becoming familiar with the other persons, their mentality, and activity, and this intimacy produces in us an "impressed species" with a richly variegated content. Alongside the self-communication of the object, the moods of the subject play an important role in the formation of this "impression," which is the resonance of the object in the subject. For this reason there is presupposed a measure of affinity and of corresponding intuitivity, i.e., one must have a "feeling" for, and openness to the object in question. In the personal individual and his work the subject discovers a certain affinity, a reflection of all-embracing *being,* hence *the transcendental idea of "being" is made more explicit through such knowledge.*

Nevertheless, this individual grasping of the individual, which is not simply communicable to others, is not an individual concept in the strict sense of the term. The opposite assertion, it seems to us, is even a contradiction. If our knowledge of the individual were fully intuitive—which is impossible for us—there would be no need of a concept as an intermediary cognitive image. Therefore, if there is a concept, the reason is that this knowledge also is imperfect and inadequate. We say "inadequate," because it has to make use of univocally or analogously universal concepts as converging toward knowledge of the concrete individual. Accordingly, our concept of the individual, even in its richest form, implies universal concepts as its constituent elements and thus remains intentional.[12]

We must now investigate what conditions must be fulfilled by both the subject and the object if man is to approach the individual in its innermost core.

131. *From Knowledge of Exteriority to Knowledge of Interiority*[13]

Knowledge of Exteriority. The external senses perceive spatially and temporally dispersed beings insofar as these beings are purely corporeal. Such beings have no other actions than the transient activities which flow of necessity from their nature. If we enter into

---

[12]Cf. A. Brunner, *La connaissance humaine,* pp. 103-219 (degrees of knowledge) ; pp. 231-248 (the problem of individual concepts).

[13]Cf. Hans Urs von Balthasar, *Wahrheit,* vol. 1, Einsiedeln, 1947, especially pp. 80-141 (*Wahrheit als Freiheit*). See also Edith Stein, *Zum Problem der Einfühlung,* Halle, 1917.

contact with them, they influence also our sense organs through their transient actions. The qualities experienced, therefore, depend on our organism.[14] In an attempt to arrive at "objectivity," science endeavors to separate the roles played by the subject and the object in perception. It is successful in this respect insofar as quantitative relationships are concerned, although even here the general laws remain approximations. But we have no direct insight into the qualitative and specific differences, the essence itself, of non-living beings.

Nevertheless, the essence in question should not be conceived as an interiority which lies hidden beyond the appearances and manifests itself only in external qualities. There is no interiority in the proper sense here, but there are only extended interacting parts. What "to be" means for the purely extended is something which we can understand only in an approximate way because this grade of *being* is too distant from our own grade, the grade of being-alive and knowing.

Accordingly, corporeal beings are open to some extent to our perception because of their activities, they reveal themselves of necessity and have "nothing to say" about their knowability. Their being-known takes place, so to speak, without their consent.

Knowledge of the laws governing spatially and temporally dispersed objects does not demand of the subject more than businesslike attention to facts, memory, imagination, and intellect. To anyone who is willing to be open in this "objective" way, the phenomena will reveal themselves in the same way. It is possible to verify one another's statements in these matters by means of facts that are, in principle, equally accessible to all, because the "facts" in question are not the events in their individuality but events insofar as, under an abstract aspect, they repeat themselves in the same way in the same circumstances.

A First Approach to Interiority. The external senses do not exclusively or even principally serve for the perception of pure exteriority. Although exteriority is the "material" condition of further knowledge, the external senses are organs of a living being and, therefore, are primarily sensitive to those configurations of the external environment that are experienced as manifestations of life.[15]

This level is reached as soon as a spatial part does not present itself merely as a more or less autonomous shape, as can happen also in the case of mere "things," but also as a center which moves itself

---

[14]Cf. no. 84.
[15]Cf. no. 110.

from its mysterious interiority to what is outside itself in order to make the environment subservient to its self-development.[16]

Thus, the spatial and temporal expansion of the living begins to manifest to some extent the character of a kind of self-revelation; an *internal* dynamic principle (form or soul), full of potentialities, *exteriorizes itself* in growth, bloom, and bearing fruit.

For this reason the workings of such a principle cannot be known by merely observing and measuring the spatial changes. They demand a higher approach, i.e., they must be understood as expressions of an immanent purposiveness. In their analogous similarity with human behavior they bear a remote resemblance to "language."[17]

To understand this "language," the subject has to assimilate the data of the external senses in the internal senses. By means of his imagination, he has to place himself inside the interiority in question, so as to take part from within in its orientation to the exterior. With his estimative sense, he must endeavor to "feel" the meaning of the environment, and with his memory and expectation, he must direct himself from the living object's "now" to its past and future.

It is very difficult for us to arrive at such an emphatic understanding of self-exteriorizing interiority insofar as purely vegetable being is concerned. Plants do not have any interiority or immanent acts in this strict sense, but only in an analogous sense. Even in my own life, the vegetative process is not immediately open to me. Nevertheless, the growth and bloom of plants which we perceive speak to us and demand to be recognized as a higher mode of being-subsistent and a higher mode of being-one's-own-purpose. Although it is true that, just as in the realm of the non-living, we cannot adequately understand what kind of a mode of *being* this self-development is that is devoid of self-sensing, nevertheless to recognize the secret of life, manifesting itself in the splendor and wealth of shapes and forms, opens the way to further knowledge.

Knowledge of Sensitive Interiority. It is only in sensitive life that there is question of immanent acts and of interiority in the strict sense of the term. However, the tactile, perceptive, and appetitive association or contact with objects, which makes animals to some extent subjects in an analogous sense, is a domain that is strictly proper to each sensitive being. Its "intimacy" is wholly individual, for its "lived experiences" are something which only the subject itself can

---

[16]Cf. no. 113.
[17]Cf. no. 133.

have immediately; in themselves, they can never become the immediately present cognitive object of another finite being.

Nevertheless, all sensitive immanent acts tend to *express themselves*. They are spontaneously embodied in movements and actions.
It is by perceiving this behavior *as* behavior, i.e., by placing ourselves
in our imagination in the unknown interiority of the animal to experience, as it were, from within the expressive movements, that it
is possible for us to acquire an indirect knowledge of the interiority
of sensitive beings.

However, the "language" of animals, which is not yet the strictly
objectifying symbolic language of man, remains for us largely a secret
that we will never learn to understand fully. For the animals live in
a world that is extremely specialized for each species.[18] We can only
guess how, in the absence of conscious opposition of subject and object, they are perceptively and appetitively related to this world, that
is not directly known to us. On the other hand, even more than in
the case of knowing vegetative beings, the recognition that we have
to do with an interiority is a condition for the understanding of the
animal's external behavior in its meaning and value as an expression
of its interiority.

Knowledge of the Sensitive Life of Fellow Men. Our knowledge
also of our fellow men in their animated bodily *being,* i.e., insofar as
they are sensitively receptive, imaginative, emotional and appetitive,
depends on the perception of their expressive movements. It is only
here that perception begins to reach the objects to which it is most
sensitive—fellow subjects—but provisionally only insofar as their sensitive emotional life is concerned. True, the perceived object is present also as an extended, moving, and colored whole, but as such it
does not become an object in itself. Perceptive intentionality goes
directly to the interiority expressing itself, it is usually hardly aware
of the external particularities and at most conscious of them in a summary fashion, but it is all the more aware of the psychical element
which it encounters in these particularities.

The reason why we thus immediately grasp the human body in its
form and movement as animated lies in this that sensitively cognitive,
emotional and appetitive life is constitutively connected with its motor
expression. Just as perception implies a bodily orientation to the
object presenting itself, so also feelings and tendencies spontaneously
fuse into seeking-for or fleeing-from, shrinking or expanding, strain-

---

[18]Cf. no. 115.

ing or relaxing; we may even say that they constitute an unbreakable unity with them in such a way that the exterior *"is"* to some extent the interior, just as soul and body are in a sense identified.[19]

The unity in question, however, is not absolute because the feelings transcend their expression. Perceiving experiences remains different from "living" them. Their perception is a spontaneous interpretation based on the general and indubitable recognition that fellow subjects exist, but does not exclude the possibility of error and generally does not attain to more than probability. This probability, however, may become increasingly more certain through our memory of past experiences.

Nevertheless, expression should not be conceived as a sign made for the purpose of referring to something else which is absent. It is a natural "symbol" which makes the animated psychical being itself perceptible.

Accordingly, while it is true that we cannot "live" the sensitive life of someone else, we can perceive it in his bodily behavior. Moreover, we may, as it were, place ourselves emphatically in his interiority, which we recognize without "living" it, and in an analogous way share the expressiveness of his perceptive, emotional, and appetetive life. In this emphatic perception we may become at the same time more clearly aware of the expressiveness of our own interior life. The other's perceived body is a center-there of perceptive perspectives, expressions of feelings, and appetitive actions with respect to objects, just as my internally "lived" body is a center-here.

The other's internally "lived" experiences, therefore, are for us both absent insofar as they are individual and internal, and present insofar as they are embodied in behavior. The recognition of the perceptible as the self-expression of a subject is a "material" condition for the intersubjective social dealings of human persons without, however, being this social contact itself. It is only in communication with the others that this contact is reached.

132. *Communication*[20]

Human Interiority. Man's interiority in its *self-consciousness* transcends the interconnection of sensory impression and motor expression. Although the active self-presence of the subject is very imperfect because it is reached by means of the perception of objects,

---

[19]Cf. no. 116.
[20]Cf. Edith Stein, *Zum Problem der Einfühlung,* Halle, 1917.

nevertheless man experiences that the horizon of his consciousness is not the limited horizon of perceptible objects but the all-embracing horizon of *being,* which no longer is a horizon.[21]

This infinite openness, through which man can see the truth and goodness of his objects in their finiteness and relativity, is the foundation of his freedom to take a stand in his own way with respect to every object.[22]

Insofar as every man in his self-consciousness and self-responsibility encompasses the whole of all beings to some extent, i.e., insofar as he is a spiritual person,[23] he is no longer only a besouled body which through interaction with its surroundings exteriorizes its inner feelings in movements. The distinction as well as the necessary interconnection between interior and exterior, between within and without, disappear on the higher level of spiritual interiority, which is all-embracing.

Nevertheless, human beings remain distinct even as spiritual persons, not because one is here and the other there, but because each one is related in his own original way to "everything," each one is his own microcosmos with his own vision and evaluation of all beings in their *being.*

Of course, this "mentality," which is grounded in the individual essence of each man, is still in an incipient stage, it has not yet reached full clarity, is usually still estranged from itself and not yet free from contradiction. Nevertheless, it is for each one his own intimacy of thinking, loving, and deciding. The others do not have in any way immediate access to this personal domain through perception, even though it is true that the different perspectives of all are directed to the same all-embracing horizon.

Self-Communication. Despite this lack of immediate perceptibility, there is in every person, precisely because being-a-person means universal openness, orientation to knowledge of the personal interiority of others. But this orientation to the other object-as-a-*subject* can be filled only from the other subject itself insofar as this subject makes itself known, reveals itself, in free *communication.*

Accordingly, with respect to the other's interiority, being-known undergoes a radical change. This change, however, has been gradually prepared on the level of the vegetative and the psychical through

[21]Cf. no. 118.
[22]Cf. no. 142.
[23]Cf. no. 153.

their expressive movement. While purely corporeal beings do not in any way control their knowability, the spiritual being freely disposes of its knowability. Its being-known is based on a free act of imparting knowledge, and the act of taking knowledge depends on this free act.

Thus, spiritual interiority is a domain which does not lie passively open to the observer or exteriorizes itself of necessity. Intimate personal life reveals itself only if the person actively shows it in freedom, if he lets himself be known through self-communication by bearing witness to the other about that of which he is the sole immediate witness and to which no one else has immediate access—namely, his subjectivity.

Its Conditions. Every being is knowable as a being.[24] However, the higher the mode of its *being,* i.e., the more it is immanent to itself, the more conditions have to be fulfilled on the part of both the object known and the knowing subject if the truth is to be reached. Truth is no longer equally accessible to all.

For knowledge of spiritual beings it is required, on the part of the being known, that this being *reveals* itself, and this revelation is a free act. On the part of the knower, it is necessary that he *believe* in this revelation, and this believing likewise is a free act.

To believe, in the strict sense of the term, is a mode of knowing which does not rely on the experience and insight of the knowing subject himself, but on the testimony of another subject who communicates his experiences and insights. Faith, therefore, is an indirect way of acquiring certainty regarding a truth.

If intersubjective faith is to possess a critically justified cognitive value, two conditions must be met:

1. The other should know through experience or insight that of which he bears witness. He must be or have been present to the cognitive object.

2. There must be agreement between the content of his cognitive act and the content of his communication, between his thinking and speaking.

Intellectual and moral trustworthiness, therefore, are decisive for the truth value of the communication. To be able to believe

---

[24]Cf. no. 42.

in what someone says, we have to believe first in him who speaks as a witness of the truth.

Thus faith is an intellectual act having a moral aspect. It is an attitude of surrender to the freedom of another, an appeal to his freedom, asking him to speak as he thinks. It is an act of trust in him, based on the conviction that he deserves this trust.

Trusting Surrender. From what we have seen it follows that it is impossible to arrive at knowledge of the other's spiritual interiority unless the knower:

1) recognizes the other as an autonomous person;

2) respects the other's freedom to reveal himself or to conceal himself; for, if against the other's will he wants to force access, the other will close himself; therefore, knowledge of the other has to be accepted as a gift coming from the initiative of the subject to be known;

3) assents to the communication even before he has even heard it; for faith aims at the communication's content only by means of trust in the communicator.

If these conditions are fulfilled, it will become possible for a subject to acquire knowledge of what is directly accessible only to another subject, to enter into the other's spiritual interiority and from there to see, as it were through the eyes of the other subject, the beings as they can be seen only from the viewpoint of the other subject. To believe is the road to enlargement of knowledge by means of communicating with another knower.[25]

The Justification of Faith. The trusting surrender on which the knowledge of faith is ultimately based must be justified. For a person has, in addition to the possibility of revealing or concealing himself, also the possibility of truthfully or untruthfully revealing himself. Moreover, there are limits to the reliability of the communication because of the finiteness and bodily character of the communicator. Not being pure self-consciousness, the communicator cannot know himself adequately; he, too, has only a limited insight, obtained by means of acts and attitudes directed to objects, into

---

[25]Cf. A. Brunner, *Glaube und Erkenntnis,* München, 1951; J. Mouroux, *Je croix en toi,* Paris, 1949.

the deeper motives of his life and the origin of his acts from his individual essence.

The justification of the trust one has in another differs according to the grades of intimacy of the communication. Because self-knowledge is obtained by means of the subject's orientation to objects, self-communication likewise will take its course through communication of the subject's vision on objects.

If the communication of a person refers to objects which the other could reach also without the testimony of the other, or if the truth of his testimony can be verified through convergence of witnesses, then it will be sufficient that the probable trustworthiness of the witness be confirmed by our general knowledge of men. Life in society is based on such probabilities.

If, however, there is a question of a person's genuine internal self-communication concerning objects having a central significance precisely for this person, so that indirect verification is not easy or even impossible, then the past actions of this person may be able to offer some reason to trust him. Ultimately, however, this criterion falls short, and the full understanding of the self-communication depends on a *personal affective inclination* which is no longer justifiable through general considerations. Nevertheless, this inclination does not mean that one blindly accepts whatever the other says. Precisely because this inclination is directed to the true welfare and the development of the other's essential potentialities, it accepts also the deficiency of his self-knowledge, his self-communication, and even of his trustworthiness, and attempts to know him, through and in spite of his defective communication, even better perhaps than he explicitly knows himself. In this way faith in the other can contribute to bringing him, as it were, to himself.

133. *Speech and Thought*[26]

Communication and Expression. Although communication, as the free revelation of the thinking and willing of persons, transcends the level of sensitive impressions, it cannot take place without the intermediary of expression, just as thinking is not possible without the

---

[26]Cf. L. Van Haecht, *Taalphilosophische beschouwingen,* Louvain, 1947; J. Peters, "Over de oorsprong van het woord," *Tijdschrift v. Philosophie,* vol. 13, (1951), pp. 163-248; M. Merleau-Ponty, *Phénoménologie de la perception,* Paris, 1945; L. Lavelle, *La parole et l'écriture,* Paris, 1942.

imagination[27] or willing without feelings.[28] Accordingly, it will be necessary to reconsider what has been said about spiritual interiority because of the interconnection between communication and expression.

Insofar as man's intellectual life is one with his sensitive and vegetative life, his being-a-person is already to some extent exterior-ized. He cannot prevent his bodily structures from being perceptible or his organic and psychical activities from expressing themselves in his behavior. Thus his "mentality," his intimate spiritual attitude, is to a certain extent unconcealed and accessible to others even without any communication on his part.

However, man is not encompassed by the forms of necessary ex-pression which he shares with all living beings. To some extent these forms are at his disposal, so that the relationship between the interior and the exterior, between consciousness and behavior, is more flexible and more governable. For the same reason, however, it is also less univocal and more subject to different interpretations.

Although in themselves the sensory-motor movements of expres-sion are dynamic developments of imaginative, affective and appetitive life, they do not direct themselves intentionally *to* other persons. Nevertheless, man can make *use* of them to address himself to a fellow man and to speak to him in communication. In this way the expression becomes an instrument which is intrinsically raised from being a natural "symbol" to a freely-made sign that communicates something to someone else and finds the goal of its meaning in the being-known of the signified. It is here that we must seek the origin of human language, in the proper sense of the term. It communicates the internal word[29] to others by means of the external word with which it consti-tutes a unity.

Language and Spontaneous Expression. For *empiricism,* language is only a set of complex reaction to complex stimuli. Words do not transcend the level of expression, they have meaning only in concrete situations, they are not universally-valid signs of universal concepts about objects.

For *rationalism,* on the other hand, thought is complete in itself without expression. If, however, thought wants to communicate itself, it needs perceptible signs. For this reason thought constructs a system of signs from different variations of sounds. This system is wholly

---

[27]Cf. no. 125.
[28]Cf. no. 144.
[29]Cf. no. 126.

detached from what it signifies and can be arbitrarily replaced by another system, another language, or even by a language of written signs. Speaking and thinking are supposed to have only an extrinsic connection, and every thought is perfectly translatable.

In contrast with these views we must maintain that, on the one hand, language remains intrinsically connected with spontaneous expression but, on the other, it transcends this expression in freedom.

Although movements of expression do not yet direct themselves intentionally *to* the other, they can be understood by the other in perception because, as natural "symbols," they make what they signify itself present. Especially sensitive emotional life becomes visible in mimicry and gestures, it attains audibility as a cry or sound in the differentiation of breathing which is closely connected with the vegetative process. It is especially through the correspondence of vocal sounds and hearing that there can arise finely shaded expressions which the utterer himself can perceive and psychically dominate.

Mimicry, gesture, and vocal sound express in the first place a certain life rhythm of the subject. Even as such, they can be directed intentionally *to* the fellow human being to pour out to him the subject's emotional and affective life and to communicate to him the manner in which the subject "lives" his world of objects.

However, as a kind of initial, sketchily expressed attitudes and activities directed to objects, these symbols may draw the attention of fellow human beings to these objects themselves with respect to their meaning and value for the subject. In this case, they become subtle deictic gestures, whose sense is immediately given through the concrete situation.

If later these gestures or vocal sounds are made when the object is absent, they can by virtue of their deictic character recall this absent object to the fellow man and communicate to him the speaker's attitude with respect to the object that is present to the speaker only as projected by his imagination. If subsequently these sounds or gestures occur again in similar situations, they can indicate present objects according to the similarity which these objects have for the speaker with respect to the first object for which they were used. In this way gestures and especially vocal sounds may be gradually lifted out of concrete and individual situations, repeated freely, and recognized as the same means of expression to indicate "one and the same aspect that is found in different objects." In this way words receive a general meaning—they have become instruments to communicate to others how the subject sees similarity and dissimilarity in a plurality of objects, how he conceives the objects *as* being "this way or that way," in other words how he judges and thinks.

Once a mutual understanding of their thoughts about present or absent objects has been established between speaking beings by means of the expressivity of their bodies, the words, carrying a first layer of meaning with which they still coincide as the expression of emotions, may be charged with new meanings and references in the above-described way. They are capable of being extended to even-widening circles of objects, which they connect with what was first signified. Thus, meanings are added to meanings, and in the course of the use of a language there are constant shifts in significations. The first meanings may retire to the background, and the later senses come to the foreground. The sound themselves of the words may also gradually alter, even though the meaning remains the same.

Language, however, does not aim primarily at isolated words, but at their synthesis in a sentence or proposition. The proposition connects events, as activities and passivities, with their subsistent subjects; it indicates whether they refer to the past, present, or future; it determines the spatial relationships, causal connections, etc. These categorical determinations of an indicated event may be expressed, for instance, by the composition of a sentence from separate words, such as verbs, nouns, adjectives, adverbs, prepositions, and conjunctions, by conjugation and declension, and in many other ways through all kinds of constructive elements. In this way an historic process of evolution through man's free disposal of sound-expressions gives rise to the different languages. They are complex systems of signs, which have been gradually formed in a society of speaking beings and are more or less understood by all.

Language as a Community of Thought. A society of many human beings who understand one another's communications is at the same time a community of *thought*. For the individual man always is "already speaking" with others and, by speaking, he awakens to thinking. From his fellow men he not only learns to understand the current sentences and words, but he also acquires a certain interpretation of events and beings.[30] Let us see why.

A word indicates a plurality of subsistent beings, qualities, activities and relations insofar as, considered under the same aspect, they

---

[30]Cf. no. 121.

constitute a unity. Through its similarity or opposition to other words it contains a reference to the similarity or dissimilarity with other beings, qualities, activities, and relations. However, the wealth of interconnections between beings, as they are in themselves, is so great that all of them cannot be taken into consideration. In the unity of meaning attributed to a word a choice has already been made among the many possible interconnections. Every language has its own way of uniting beings in words, so that every language shows them in a certain order and according to certain perspectives. Other interconnections are pushed into the background in such a way that it is only with difficulty that they can be expressed in that language. Each language is a definite interpretation, a certain vision and evaluation of the beings in their *being,* an expression of the "mentality" proper to the particular community of language.

To grow up in a community of language, therefore, means to become acquainted with the corporeal, living and spiritual "world" as preceding generations have interpreted and understood it in the names they have given to it. Nevertheless, everyone receives this traditional interpretation in his own way and according to his own degree of originality.

For, if in speaking and thinking a man passively holds fast to the current meanings, language does not become for him an approach to the beings in their *being,* but rather substitutes itself for them. "Wordism" alienates thought and speech from their proper purpose, viz., to say how beings are.

Language reaches its own potentialities only when its user actively re-thinks what was pre-thought in the words and thus personally enters into contact with beings in his own way. In the context of his speaking, the words will receive from him new meanings, which either imply a return to more original "visions" obscured by later usages, or refer to ontological connections which were hitherto unexpressed and still concealed. By "recoining"" in this way the traditional linguistic tools, he will make the current meanings serve to express individual and original, hitherto unexpressed, aspects of both his inner life of thinking and feeling and the beings about which he makes a communication.

All those who live in a community of language live in a certain mutual understanding. However, this understanding is never perfect, but is accompanied by misunderstandings. Avoidance of such misunderstanding will be easier when the objects spoken about are equally present or accessible to all, but more difficult when they can become known only through someone's communication. This is especially the case with the self-communication, in the strict sense, of one's personal life. More than anywhere else it is here that the deficiency of words is felt as a barrier to communication. Sometimes unarticulated silence, as a wordless word, is more eloquent than a plurality and concatenation of verbiage.

Transcendence of Thought. The connection between thinking and speaking reveals itself as so essential that there is no thinking without a beginning of speech. Even when a thinker does not address himself explicitly to a fellow human being in a dialogue to be contradicted, corrected, supplemented, or affirmed by him, his thinking has a dialogical character, for he asks himself how beings are, poses problems to himself, and endeavors to supply himself with an answer. Thus he is constantly engaged in the task of putting his experiences and insights into words. The phantasm, without which he is unable to form any concepts, judgments, and reasonings,[31] is usually not merely a phantasm of perceptible beings but also a phantasm of the speakable words which name these beings.

Even in this solitary dialogue, the deficiency of the word and the transcendence of thought reveal themselves. The thinker has in himself all kinds of unspoken thoughts, feelings, and attitudes. They are richer than words but also more confused. They demand to be clarified by means of language. But whatever term he assigns them, he is dissatisfied—his thinking remains a never-finished attempt to explicitate the all-embracing wealth of what is implicitly present to him.

---

[31]Cf. no. 125.

CHAPTER TWENTY-FIVE

THE AFFECTIVE LIFE OF MAN:
SENTIMENT AND WILL

134. *Introduction*

The intentional knowledge resulting from perception, conception, judgment, and reasoning is only one side of man's integral communication with beings. Alongside intellectual immanence, there is also affective immanence and the striving, willing and acting flowing from it.

Relationship of the Two Kinds of Immanence. From our own experience we know that these two kinds of immanence do never wholly coincide in us, but constitute distinct aspects of one and the same integral relationship. The foundation of this duality lies in the deficiency of our knowledge which, because of its intentional character, is unable to effect the perfect immanence of the object in the subject. The known may to some extent be present in the knower as it is in itself, but it always is so in a defective way—namely, by means of representations and inadequate concepts. For this reason knowledge is dynamically oriented to the completion and perfection of immanence on another level, the level of the basic interconnection of beings in *being*. Knowledge may *reveal* to the subject that in *being* it is fundamentally connected with the object, but the inclination itself to the object and the resulting *actuation* of the interconnection belong to affective life, which is distinct from cognitive life, although not separate from it.

On the other hand, cognitive life develops in the direction of the coincidence of intellectivity and affectivity, of understanding and loving. For knowledge of another person's intimacy, which is the highest possibility of knowing that is immediately given to us in experience, is believing in the other and, as such, it is not only conditioned by the affection binding the knower to the person known as his "other ego", but is also an essential aspect of this affection itself: in their personal love the communicating persons become to some extent transparent to each other.

Thus there is an interaction and a tendency to mutual compensation between the intellectual and the affective aspects. This ten-

301

dency is closely connected with the mutual compenetration of the true and the good as properties of being as being.[1] Just as every being in an analogous way and according to its own level is true and good, so also every grade of *being* implies and presages to some extent the intellectual and affective aspects.

In the preceding pages we have seen how the intellectual aspect is rooted in the sensitive, the vegetative and the corporeal.[2] In a similar way we will find affectivity in the sensitive life of feelings and appetency, in vegetative processes, and even in the transient actions of the corporeal, albeit only in a degraded sense and in potency.

135. *The Natural Tendency*

In every finite being the essence as *nature* is the origin of its capacity for self-realization.[3] The foundation of this dynamic character proper to the essence lies in its participation in unqualified *being*. Because of this participation, the particular being is not isolated from the others, which are in different ways, as their absolute negation, but is connected and related with them. Self-realization, then, consists precisely in the actuation of this radical being-together through communication in imparting and partaking, in activity and passivity.

Connaturality of Beings. If we call the perfection to which a being is dynamically directed in this way its *natural good,* then two aspects should be distinguished. By participating in the perfections of related beings, a being becomes more itself, but by making the others share in its own perfection, it perfects them in its turn. For the good of a "part" is not only its own perfection in itself, but also the perfection of the other "parts" for the welfare of the whole.

Thus, we see that the ultimate explanation of dynamism as a tendency to the good lies in a fundamental relationship of being-together and kinship, a *connaturality.* This relationship is the order of beings to intercommunication as to their good.

The name which is given to this fundamental order of connaturality on the level of the conscious and free communication of persons is *love.* In a degraded way, however, this order may be found on other levels as the root of the animal's behavior toward its own kind and its world, as the root of the "sensitivity" plants show

---

[1] Cf. nos. 42-44.
[2] Cf. no. 125.
[3] Cf. no. 64.

for their environment, and even that of the interactions through affinity between the bodily beings. Hence this term "love" may be transferred by analogy of proportionality to every connaturality which unites beings radically with one another.

Accordingly, we will speak of *natural love* as the foundation of all tendency and activity, even though we know very well that this "affection" for the good is essentially different in each being according to its own grade of *being*.[4] Allowing for all kinds of different nuances, it may be described as a certain harmony, consonance, agreement, coadaptation, proportion, similarity, complacency, etc. Everywhere, however, this love is the ontological foundation for the, likewise analogous, "tendency" to the good as a purpose.[5]

Aversion to Evil. In finite beings this natural orientation to the good has its counterpart in their natural aversion to evil. Especially in material beings, which because of their spatio-temporal character are corruptible, these two aspects constitute an unbreakable unit.

For, the finite, and especially the temporal being still "tends" to its good—its self-perfection—through union with the others. What is the reason why it has not yet reached the goal to which it tends? The answer is that the others, precisely insofar as they are the *others,* keep it separated from its goal. Therefore, for a tending being, which by virtue of its natural love is directed to the others as its good, the others do not immediately mean good, for otherwise there would be no tendency but an immediate presence and possession of the good. However, precisely insofar as one is not the other and different beings with their own "mine" and "thine" are opposed to one another as competitors, they prevent one another from reaching their full development through communication. Insofar as each of them tends to its own particular good, it prevents the other from possessing this same good. The enrichment of the one means the impoverishment of the other.

The mutual interaction of bodily beings illustrates this point very clearly. The change caused by it implies the loss of the preceding state and, if this change is essential, even the loss of the body's being-itself,[6] for the coming-to-be of the one takes place at the expense of the other's passing away. Thus all bodily beings are exposed to the

---

[4] Concerning natural love, see Thomas Aquinas, *Scriptum super sententiis,* p. III, d. 27, q. 1, a. 2; *Summa theol.,* p. I-II, q. 26, a. 1.

[5] Cf. no. 108.

[6] Cf. no. 88.

impending and corrupting influences of the others, so that in this respect these others are an evil for them, making it impossible for them to reach their own good in a definitive way—they are subject to corruption.   For this reason their search for the good must always be accompanied by the flight from evil.

The Conquest of Obstacles to the Good.   Nevertheless, this two-fold relationship of search and flight does not solve the problem, as appears from the analysis of any continuous "movement" to the good. If there were no obstacles impeding a moving being, it would already have reached its goal.   Movement, as a successive event occurring in time, presupposes of necessity that beginning and end are separate by an intermediary.   Hence the good cannot be reached immediately. But flight from the obstacle, which because of its resistance is a rela-tive evil, means that the goal can be reached even less.   The only way to attain the goal is to *conquer the difficulties.*

Thus there remain only two ways in which the arduous good can be reached:

1.   The obstacle gives up its otherness and actuates its being-to-gether with the tending being.   It ceases to be an obstacle and enters into communication with the tending being, either as a "means" that becomes "useful" for making the tending being reach its own goal, or as a striving-together-with this being to a common goal.

2.   The obstacle retains its otherness and its orientation to its own good as contrary to the good proper to the tending being.   In this case it becomes a "danger" which threatens to "damage" the striving being, so that this being has not only to defend itself, but must also attack the obstacle, chase it away or destroy it, if it wants to attain its own goal by conquering the resistance.

Wherever, therefore, there is space and time and, consequently, "the other" as an obstacle between a being and its good, there is no possibility of immediate enjoyment of the good.   Trouble and efforts are needed to reach it.   The good can be attained only in a mediate way, i.e., by means of activities which are not good or pleasant in themselves but only intentionally directed to the good and the pleasant, insofar as they attempt a reconciliation or union with the opposing obstacle and, if it continues to be an obstacle, try to chase it away or destroy it.

In this way, the nature of corruptible beings is not only a principle of *tendency* to the good and *flight* from evil, but also a principle of *utilizing* the surroundings for self-development and of *defense* against whatever threatens its continued existence.[7]

"Sensitivity." The various aspects of orientation to the good which to some extent are discernible in every "movement" of a being to its good reveal themselves more clearly in the self-movement of the living. Life is precarious, for the living being can maintain its superiority over its environment, on which it depends for its self-realization, only under a complex of favorable conditions.[8] For this reason the urge to assimilate and to utilize other beings, as well as the urge to defense and aggression, are more strongly developed. The living being is less passively dependent on the "favor" of the other beings around it and more actively organized to assimilate or repel them.

However, in vegetative life the process of mediation between the living being and its goal takes place only through a "natural" reaction to a present stimulus. Vegetative "sensitivity"[9] is conditioned by the *immediate* presence of the agreeable or disagreeable; the vegetative being does not have any contact with the good or evil that is still at a distance and merely approaching; it cannot have a presentiment of what will be useful or harmful in the future. Although, alongside its assimilative apparatus, it possesses a defense apparatus—e.g., closing itself, pilosity, thorns—both apparatus begin to operate only when they are in immediate contact with the favorable or the dangerous.

The sensitive living being, on the other hand, is characterized by sensitivity at a distance. Through the estimative sense, in conjunction with memory and expectation, it feels that something favorable or unfavorable is "coming."[10] Thus it is enabled to take precautions: it can change its positions, come closer or move away. The estimative sense appears to refer not only to what is felt as a real present good or evil, but also to what may possibly be useful or harmful.

---

[7]Thomas Aquinas explicitly asserts that resistance and tendency go together in all corruptible beings: "In corruptible natural bodies there is of necessity not only a tendency to attain the suitable and to flee from the harmful, but also to resist corrupting and opposing influences which impede the suitable and cause harm." *Summa theol.*, p. I. q. 81, a. 2.

[8]Cf. no. 113.

[9]Concerning the differences between vegetative "sensitivity" and sensitive feeling, see S. Strasser, *Das Gemüt*, Utrecht, 1956, pp. 128-141; "Zur Gefühlssteuerung des menschlichen Aktes," *Zeitschrift für philos. Forschung*, vol. 7 (1953) pp. 171-190.

[10]Cf. no. 124.

This complexity of affective attitudes, which presupposes a certain knowledge of the concrete situation in relation to past and future, becomes even more complex in man's effective life, because man's sensitivity is permeated with his intellectual life, and the estimative sense is raised to being a "particular reason." Nevertheless, it is important to distinguish sensitive feeling and intellectual willing in the structure of effective life, without, however, separating them.

136. *Sensitive Feeling, Desiring and Loving*[11]

Meanings of "to Feel." In its broad sense, "to feel" includes also sensitive knowing insofar as in this knowing there is an immediate non-distanced, "lived" presence of the felt in the feeler. "To feel," therefore, is used especially for the following senses:

1. The sense of touch, insofar as in this sense subject and object are together in the least separate way.[12]

2. The central sense, insofar as in this sense the subject "feels itself" in its "lived events," as well as its global organic and psychical states.[13]

3. The estimative sense, insofar as in this sense the subject has the most immediate "feeling" and "presentiment" of the meaning and value of the object with respect to its inner vital development.[14]

The most essential aspect, however, of feeling is not its cognitive moment but the "lived" state itself in which the subject is through the presence of the object: the subject is touched, moved, affected by the object.

Like sensitive estimation and intellectual judgment, feeling is characterized by the opposition between the negative and the affirmative. This opposition assumes here the form of the agreeable and disagreeable as the fundamental modes of feeling.

Feeling and Consciousness. The subject is in the affective state of *delight* (pleasure, joy) when the present object is experienced as a good which satisfies the subject in its self-unfolding; it is in the state

---

[11]The analyses of nos. 136-138 have been taken from Thomas Aquinas' treatise *De passionibus animae* in the *Summa theol.*, p. I-II, q. 22-48. See also *De veritate*, q. 25-26.

[12]Cf. no. 77.

[13]Cf. no. 124.

[14]*Ibid.*

of *sadness* (grief, sorrow) when the present object is experienced as an evil which hurts the subject.

Although the states of feeling, therefore, are intentionally connected with present objects, felt to be good or evil, this orientation may be more or less explicitly present in our consciousness. Sometimes we do not know why we are depressed or joyful, although there is a vague realization that there must be something which motivates our feeling. On other occasions, however, the object giving rise to our state of feeling stands more in the foreground.

Feelings and Desires. In the strict sense, states of feeling are not temporal processes. Of themselves, they are permanent because they refer to the *present* as such. On the other hand, sensitive life is a dynamic process of development in a changing world. Neither good nor evil are definitively present to the subject. As long as life runs its course, the good attained does not fully satisfy nor does the evil that befalls mean utter destruction. Moreover, the situation constantly changes: good as well as evil come and go, approach and depart.

The sensitive living being knows about this coming and going through its memory and expectation. For this reason it is already in relation with the good and evil even before they are present. It moves toward and seeks the good to be attained, it turns away and flees from the evil to be avoided. These movements of affection toward the agreeable and away from the disagreeable are *desires* and appetencies flowing from the desires. In contrast with the states of feeling in the strict sense, they imply a standpoint with respect to the *future*.

Basis of the Desires. Just as in every movement-toward the terminus is to some extent present and in every movement-away-from the starting point somehow is included, so likewise and *a fortiori* the "intentional" presence of a good or evil that is not "actually" present must be contained in the psychical movement toward or away from this good or evil.

Accordingly, desire and appetency presupposes a more profound fundamental *orientation* of man's affective life to certain objects as good and to their opposites as evil.

This orientation, which is a "lived" proportion or disproportion, consonance or dissonance, of subject and object, is the supporting substructure and the motivating explanation both of the appetitive movement with respect to the absent object and of the affective reaction with respect to the present object. The orientation reveals itself only *in* the phases of movement and rest, but this does not make it less important. It is best indicated by the terms *love* and *hatred* in the analogously enlarged meaning of these words. In this way sensitive love and hatred are the modes in which perceptive beings "live" this "natural" inclination and aversion through the intermediary of knowing.

The fact that an object is felt in love or hatred as, respectively, good or evil may be based on the experience of delight or sadness in a previous experience of the same or of a similar object. However, it may also happen that even prior to such experiences a proportion or disproportion to the object is felt. In this case it is the estimative sense which acts as intermediary in the rise of an instinctive like or dislike.

Such instinctive inclinations reveals themselves especially when the object means the satisfaction of the needs pertaining to vegetative life, i.e., self-preservation, nutrition, growth, and reproduction. However, there are also objects which are agreeable or disagreeable for sensitive knowing itself and which, therefore, because of this proportion or disproportion, are sought or avoided. Finally, because of the interconnection of sensitive and intellectual life, there are sensitively experienced objects which are felt to be convenient or inconvenient with respect to the more complex needs and ideals of the whole man in his relationships to the things of the world and his fellow men. In this case the cogitative sense or particular reason serves more especially as the intermediary.[15]

"Concupiscible Appetite." Love and hatred, as a mysterious kind of memory, desire and flight, as movements to or away from the future, delight and sadness, as rest or acquiescence in the present good or evil, are actuations of one and the same power. Because the desire for, and the tendency toward the agreeable good is the central phase of these actuations and draws more attention, this power is called the *concupiscible appetite* or the power of desiring.

With respect to this appetite, the good that is sought and the evil that is avoided present themselves in an uncomplicated way in their immediate harmony or disharmony with the bodily, vegetative, or sensitive nature of the subject.

---

[15]Cf. no. 124.

137. *The Sensitive Tendencies to Utilize and to Resist*

The relationships of good and evil to the sensitive subject are not as simple as sketched above with respect to the concupiscible appetite. In its concrete situation the subject is spatially and temporally together with other living beings in a perishable way that is always full of danger. Because our inner senses, i.e., the estimative sense in conjunction with memory and expectation, give us advance knowledge of the future good or evil that is still absent but coming closer, a certain *ambiguity* affects the object which is sought-for or fled-from on the basis of our fundamental orientation of love and hatred. For our feeling, the object is no longer simply a good or simply an evil.

The Absent Good and Evil. Every good that is still absent is seen as separated from us through "the other." It cannot be immediately reached as a purpose and thus in this respect is to a greater or lesser extent a hard-to-reach or "arduous" good. To attain it requires steps and activities which are not agreeable and wanted for their own sake, sometimes they are even disagreeable or prevent us from remaining with the immediately agreeable. We may be weary of making an effort, and even the slightest trouble may be too much for us. Viewed from the aspect of difficulty, the good which is to be reached through the use of means or the overcoming of difficulties is something disagreeable. For our feeling, it is only a relative good. If despite the difficulty, the goodness of the object prevails and we see its attainment as possible, we turn toward the good. If, on the other hand, the difficulty impresses us more than the goodness of the object, so that we see its attainment as impossible, then we turn away from the good.

In a similar way the evil which is not yet present is not an unqualified evil that is simply to be avoided. An object which comes closer in a threatening way is a "danger." It does not yet hurt us, but will hurt if it acquires power over us. For our feeling, it is a relative evil. If the conviction prevails that the evil cannot be avoided or overcome, we will view it as an evil. We are powerless with respect to it and succumb. If, on the other hand, the view prevails that we can avoid the danger or even conquer it by chasing it away or destroying it, then we appreciate it as a way to the good. We turn toward the threatening object in defense or attack, we resist it in the hope of being able to turn the situation to our advantage through victory.

Even if the evil is already present, if we have been overcome by it and the good has not been attained, we may realize that the situation is not definitely settled. In an intense affective straining of energy we rise in revolt against the evil and do not want to acquiesce in it.

Need for Another Appetitive Power. Thus we see that the good that is difficult to attain or the evil that is hard to overcome may arouse in us *contradictory* attitudes of striving. According to the position we take, either a turning-toward or a turning-away-from is possible with respect to the same object. The simple sensitive orientation of feeling proper to the concupiscible appetite is a being-affected by the object in its immediate agreement or disagreement with the development of our life. It has therefore, a more passive character. But in the more complex relationships to good and evil, the aspect of arduousness presages something of the free choice of position which arises from intellect and will.[16]

Since the arduousness experienced is an addition to the experience of the goodness or evil of an object, we must admit, alongside the concupiscible appetite, another more complex and different power. Moreover, the tendency to the immediately agreeable can come into conflict with the tendency to the attainment of the useful or the destruction of the harmful.

This new power is directed to the good as accessible not immediately but only through changing obstacles into means of attainment. Thus, it does not directly aim at what is good and agreeable in itself, but at the realization of means which in themselves are not good (whence they cannot be in themselves objects of delight, pleasure or joy), but are good only insofar as they prepare the way for that which is good in itself. We may, therefore, call this new power the *tendency to utilize.*

In the second place, this power is directed to evil as something to be destroyed by avoidance or conquest. Thus it is directly oriented to resist danger and difficulties. We may call it the *power of resistance* against the non-definitive evil. Since resistance reveals itself most acutely when the threatening evil has already become a reality, in anger, fury and revolt, the Ancients used to call it the "irascible power."[17]

---

[16]Cf. no. 141.

[17]The division into concupiscible and irascible appetites stems from Plato, who alongside the rational part of the soul posited the non-rational part and divided the latter according to *thumos* (courage), and *epithumia* (desire). See

"Irascible" and "Concupiscible" Appetites. If the concupiscible power is compared with the power to utilize and to resist, it is of the greatest importance to emphasize the dependence of the latter on the former. The power to resist has only a subservient function as a frontline fighter and defender, although it makes higher forms of behavior possible. The process of affective movement finds its permanent substructure in the proportion of affection and good, called "love," which is the tendency toward the corresponding object that satisfies it. Its final orientation is directed to repletion by this object, terminating in the state of feeling called delight, pleasure, and joy. Whatever lies in between this object and this state, the phases of tendencies and resistances, of means and obstacles, must always be seen in function of the rise and development of the fundamental attitudes which transcend movement and therefore are definitive—namely, love and satisfaction. These alone have value in themselves. The relationship to the means and obstacles is not autonomous and derives all its value from its connection with the fundamental attitudes. The useful and the harmful are good and evil only through analogy of attribution or relation, i.e., through their reference to that which in pure affection is experienced as immediately good or evil.

138. *The Various Affective Movements*

From the fundamental orientation of the sensitive living being to the completion of its essence as its natural good the whole scale of affective movements can be understood in its *formal structure* according to the tri-partite distinction of 1) the affirmative and negative (good and evil); 2) the turning-to and the turning-away-from; 3) the temporal phases of presence and absence.

The starting point lies in the concupiscible appetite (love and hatred); the intermediary phase (desire and flight) begins there also but develops in the tendency to utilize and resist (hope and fear, despair and courage); a provisional terminus lies in anger, but the

---

Republic, 435-441 (even in the State there is a tripartite division); *Phaedrus*, 246; *Timaeus*, 70. This classical division of the affective movements shows a resemblance with the contrast modern authors make between the propensity to tenderness and to aggressiveness (H. Kunz, *Die Agressivität und die Zärtlichkeit*, Bern, 1946), to sympathy and to defensiveness (E. de Greeff, *Les instincts de défense et de sympathie*, Paris, 1947), to appropriation and resistance, based on a need from within or a pain from without (M. Pradiness, *Traité de psychologie générale*, vol. I, Paris, 1943).

definitive resonance of love and hatred occurs again in the concupiscible appetite (delight and sadness).

Analytic Classification. With St. Thomas, who calls the affective movements "passions," we may distinguish the following types:

1. *Love* and the inclina-
   tion-to
   =proportion, harmony of affectivity
   and good; the pleasing of the good.

2. *Hatred* and aversion
   =disproportion, opposition between
   affectivity and evil; the displeasing
   of the evil.

3. *Desire* and longing
   =the movement toward the attainment of the loved good when it is
   still absent.

4. *Flight* and abhorrence
   =the turning away to avoid the hated
   evil when it is still absent.

If the desired good is difficult to attain, the detested evil difficult to
avoid or conquer, the tendency to utilize and to resist plays a role:

5. *Hope* and confidence
   =the movement toward a future and
   difficult good whose attainment is
   considered possible.

6. *Despair* and discour-
   agement
   =the turning away from a future and
   difficult good whose attainment is
   considered impossible.

7. *Fear* and anxiety
   =the depressive state of one who
   thinks that a future and threatening, difficult to avoid, evil cannot
   be resisted.

8. *Courage* and daring
   =the aggressive state of one who
   thinks that a future and threatening, difficult to avoid, evil can be
   conquered.

9. *Anger* and fury
   =the attitude of him upon whom evil
   has fallen, but who resists it and
   seeks to avenge himself; the revolt
   against present evil.

Finally, the affective movement finds its terminus in:

10. *Delight*, pleasure, joy=the rest in the good, the employment
    of the present good.

11. *Sorrow*, sadness, dis-=the acquiescence in present evil: the
    pleasure   bearing of it.

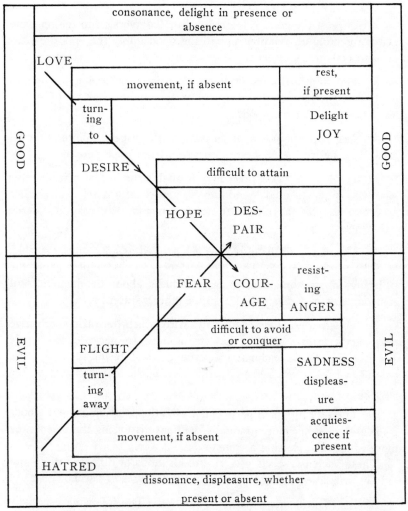

Synthesis of the Movements. This analysis of the effective movements must be supplemented by a synthesis. In making it, we should keep in mind that the various aspects distinguished above are present in one another.

1. Love contains already a certain joy because of the "intentional" presence of what is loved in the immanence of the lover. In a similar way hatred and aversion contain a certain sadness. Reversely, just as striving, so also joy and sadness are manifestations of the fundamental attitudes of love and aversion.

2. Love of the good is the reason for the aversion to the opposite evil. In general all relationships to the good imply the opposite relations to evil, and vice versa.

3. The four attitudes of hope, despair, fear, and courage also imply one another. Hope of victory gives courage, fear of difficulties leads to despair of the good.

4. Anger presupposes displeasure with respect to present evil, as well as desire for vengeance; it flows from hope and courage.

Other Aspects. The preceding formal structure of affective life has to be supplemented by additional considerations regarding other aspects that play a role in these movements. We may name the following:

1. The nature of the objects which are felt as good and agreeable, as evil and disagreeable. Thus, for instance, pity is sadness about the suffering of someone else, envy is sadness about the happiness of someone else, evil glee is delight in the other's sufferings.

2. The greater or lesser intensity with which the various affective movements toward definite objects attempt to pervade the whole affective life. Some inclinations, strivings, and feelings will become central, while others remain peripheral in the development of the subject.

3. The way in which particular inclinations, strivings, and moods come and go either more gradually, without disturbing the balance, or more eruptively, causing a commotion.

These various aspects give rise to all kinds of differentiations not only in ordinary language but also in the analyses of psychologists.

Moods, Sentiments, Emotions, Passions. The following especially should be distinguished. They are sometimes indicated by the same names, but occasionally also known by different terms.

1. General *fundamental moods*.[18] The subject is always "tuned" by the experiential world as a whole in which he "finds" himself and which in a more or less permanent way has a particular resonance in him. These moods have no distinct objects, but they may exercise influence on definite feelings toward determined objects or be caused

---

[18]Concerning moods, Cf. O. F. Bollnow, *Vom Wesen der Stimmungen*, Frankfurt, 1943.

by these feelings. Of themselves, however, the moods precede the explicit distinction of subject and object, of the organic and the psychical. They are closely connected with the "natural" love and aversion of the subject. Although they are not directly controllable, they are of fundamental importance for the higher life of intellect and will, for certain ontological aspects allow a more adequate access only by means of these differentiated moods. For instance, the elating moods of cheerfulness, happiness, and bliss make us feel time as a participation of eternity, while the depressing moods of melancholy, sadness, dejectedness, and especially dread[19] make us feel time in its passing character and fatality.

2. Normative *feelings,* in the strict sense of the term.[20] They are intentionally directed to particular objects and are adapted to the changing situations, so as to secure in a sense an undisturbed development of affective life on the basis of the fundamental moods.

3. Violent *emotions* or affections. At critical moments they interrupt the regular course of feelings and throw us out of our equilibrium by their suddenness. They are accompanied by much more violent expressions than are feelings, and they begin and end also more abruptly. Compare, for instance, fright with fear or fury with anger.

4. Lasting *passions.* They tend with a kind of impetuosity to dominate other feelings toward other objects and even man's higher life of intellect and will; they endeavor to become so dominating that man's whole conduct falls under their control. Thus, for example, we speak of a passion for pleasure, money, and power, but also for sports and games, science and justice.

139. *Intellectual Affectivity*

Love in the Strict Sense. Every being has a relationship to the natural good appropriate to it. In an analogously enlarged sense we have called this relationship "love."[21] Man also has a nature, and therefore, there is in him, too, such an unconscious order to self-realization through the development of his corporeally-living, sensitive, and intellectual nature.

---

[19]Since Kierkegaard dread is usually considered a fundamental mood. It should be distinguished from fear, which is directed to a particular object.

[20]Concerning feelings, emotions, and passions, see Stefan Strasser, *Das Gemüt,* pp. 179-213; Pradines, *op. cit.,* vol. I, pp. 659-733, vol. II, p. 2, pp. 304-338.

[21]Cf. no. 135.

However, because man has also an intellectual nature, the character of his inclination undergoes a change. Purely sensitive beings are aware of their inclinations in their acts of appetency and resistance but, because they do not know themselves *as* beings, their inclination is not consciously directed to their *being* as such. Man, on the other hand, knows about his *being* and consciously loves it as his good.[22] Thus, unconscious "natural" love culminates in him as love in its first and proper sense, as a conscious inclination and a consciously taken attitude.

Man loves himself in the first place. He cannot do otherwise than seek his self-perfection. He will seek whatever perfects him, whatever is good for him. But his conscious love of the good is guided by his knowledge: he will seek what he recognizes and values as good. While sensitive estimation is limited to the here-and-now in the concrete situation, intellectual estimation discovers being-good as such. Thus the circle of attractive objects is enlarged "to infinity." For whatever is, under certain conditions is capable of being esteemed as good or evil for man. At least, whatever is, has a possible cognitive relationship to man because in a way he is "everything." Consequently, he can at least love all beings as good for his knowledge.

Love of Others. Because in his intellectual knowledge man is open to the other beings as beings, his affective attitude to the others is not solely determined by their aspects of being-good or being-evil for his own self-development.

While sensitive knowledge as such is encompassed by the meaning which objects have for one's own vital development, i.e., their usefulness or harmfulness, their agreeable or disagreeable character, intellectual knowledge estimates objects also according to the value they have for themselves. Through analogy with his own directedness to his *being* as his good, man is capable of experiencing the others as directed to their *being* as their good. He can recognize their autonomous purposiveness and *let* them be. Through reverence man, knowing about the *being* of the others, respects them in their own nature and does not merely consider them as good-for-him, i.e., as useful. This reverence can be exercised best toward those beings whom he views as fellow men because, like him, they also know that they *are* and consciously love their *being*.[23]

---

[22]Cf. no. 17.
[23]Cf. no. 121.

The affection for others may go beyond this. Man is capable not only of considering them as others, as independent beings facing him, but also of viewing them as united with himself, as beings with which he is-together in a society. As soon as he truthfully loves himself "as he is," he discovers that his *being,* as a particular mode of participating in unqualified *being,* implies of necessity relationships to those which in other ways participate in the same all-embracing *being.* If he loves himself according to these connecting relationships, he also loves those who are united by this connection, his fellow beings.

This broadening of self-love, through affectively "living" man's ontic being-together that is discovered in intellectual knowledge, is in principle without limits because of the universal interconnection of all beings. Thus, human communication breaks through the closedness which characterizes the surrounding world of subhuman beings. Nevertheless, this fundamental all-embracingness of intellectual affectivity may not be cut loose from self-love, because man is not connected with all beings in the same way. As a person, he is more related to personal beings than to the sub-personal. As this individual person, he is closer to one person than to another because of descendence, milieu, and mentality. Accordingly, the love of other beings is rooted in an awareness of unity, relation or resemblance, but this awareness may be at the same time a realization that different persons are supplementary poles and complement one another.

Self-Love and Love of Others. Accordingly, conscious self-love is the root and foundation of affective life and especially of man's love for the other. Because and to the extent that man loves himself, he adheres to his own good for his own sake. Thus he will love also with an analogous love those whom he knows to be united with him and in whom he discovers himself as "another ego"; he will adhere to their good because of them. He will love their good to the extent to which he knows himself to be united with them, and of himself affirms and accepts this unity in a free decision. For this reason there is in principle no contradiction between true self-love and the love of the other. There is, of course, opposition between egoism and altruism, but egoism is the attitude of one who wrongs the other for his own benefit, although in doing so he really wrongs himself because his being is essentially a being-together with the others.

To love, then, means to adhere to the good of a subject in order that this subject may *be* good through something which perfects him. Unlike, e.g., joy, love is not a reaction to a present good, but

an active and somewhat creative taking-of-a-position in favor of a
being and an entering into the proportional orientation of this being
to its "ideal essence" as its good that is to be realized.[24]

What is loved in the proper sense is the subsistent subject with
whom the lover feels himself united and wants to be united always
more closely. This loved subject is in the first place the loving subject
himself for his own sake: self-love is the most natural and most
necessary love. Self-love is necessarily connected with *being* itself.
In the second place, in an analogous way and through participation
in self-love, the loved subject may be another being which is experienced as being-together with the loving subject: in the love of
the fellow-being self-love unfolds itself in a wealth of manifestations.[25]

Self-love and the love of others for their own sake may be indicated by the general terms "love of benevolence" and "love of
friendship."[26]

On the basis of this love of subjects in the strict sense of the term
"love" the love of concupiscence directs itself to objects implying
a perfection for the loved subject, especially in reciprocal love, which
the loved and the beloved want to give to each other to make each
other happy.

Accordingly, love of friendship and concupiscence are nothing
but two aspects of one and the same integral loving affectivity. Both
are present, therefore, as integral constituents in self-love as well as
in the love of the other. Therefore, it is false to oppose love of
friendship and of concupiscence as "disinterested" and "interested"
love. One may say that every love adhering to a subject for his own
sake is "disinterested," whether this love be self-love or love of
another; likewise, we may speak of "interested" love with respect

---

[24]Cf. no. 63.

[25]Some forms of love refer only to certain limited realms of life, while
others are broader in scope. In some forms the persons assume more the
attitude of standing side by side in orientation to the same objects, but in
others they are more or less face to face, directed to mutual encounter, union and
encompassment. In some the immediate present feeling perdominates, in others
more the permanent state of affectivity. In some it pertains to the very
essence of love that the other knows about his being-loved and reciprocates
this love, in others these elements lie in the background because dedication
prevails. Sometimes the other individual is aimed at because of a motive
that is more or less general, but in others the individual is loved precisely
because of his original individuality. In some forms the contrast of man and
woman plays a more central role, but in others this contrast is of peripheral
value.

[26]Concerning love of benevolence and love of friendship as aspects of
integral loving affectivity, see Thomas Aquinas, *Summa theol.*, p. I-II, q. 26,
a. 4. See also, J. Peters, *Liefde, (Wijsgerige grondbegrippen)*, Roermond, n. d.

to any true love, because it is not possible for me in "disinterested" love of the other to detach the other from the connection he has with me and I with him. I, therefore, love him "because" I love myself.

140. *Intellectual Striving, Desiring, Willing*

Striving. In the intellectual sphere also love is the dynamic substructure of the tendency to what is good for loved subjects. Like loving, striving attains here a certain all-embracing character because of the unlimited horizon of intellectual knowledge.

Even in the sensitive tendency to utilize objects the individual subject is capable of turning-toward or away-from one and the same object, because the future arduous good may be viewed under the aspect of evil. Nevertheless, the norm of tendency remains here the instinctive estimation of the individual object as useful or harmful with respect to the individual subject here-and-now in the concrete situation.

The intellectual *value judgment,* however, refers every object to the all-embracing norm of being-good or being-evil as such. Just as every individual being participates in a particular and consequently deficient way in unqualified *being,* so also every individual good participates only in a deficient way in unqualified goodness. For this reason the intellectual knower can see every desired object as being only relatively good and every abhorred concrete object as being only relatively evil.

Because of this relativity every particular object to be reached or realized in the future can be judged either worthy of our striving, insofar as it is capable of satisfying to some extent the limitless tendency to the good, or unworthy or being strived-for, insofar as it is incapable of fully satisfying this tendency because its way of giving satisfaction excludes the other ways. Thus man can assume a standpoint with respect to the attractiveness exercised by the objects. If he allows himself to be influenced by their attraction, he makes this concerete good a *purpose* which he wants to tend to.

Desiring. The first expressions of this tendency to a purpose are desiring and wishing. Love directly aims at a subject, a subsistent being, one whose good we want, but desire and wish are not immediately directed to an autonomous subject, but to a certain situation that is not yet real but whose future realization we propose to ourselves; e.g., that this or that may happen, that I may pass my examination, that Peter's health may be restored.

Willing. The first question that arises is whether the desire can be fulfilled, the aim reached or realized. Such a realization may be brought about in two ways: 1) the use of our own forces if, in our opinion, the realization lies within our powers; 2) the influence of someone else, who will use his power because he loves us and wants our good.

In the second case we speak of *hope* in the most proper sense of this term, which is more restricted than the vaguer meaning the same term has when one leaves out of consideration whether the difficult good becomes possible through myself or through someone else.[27] In the first case we have to do with *willing* in the most proper sense of the term, which is more restricted than the vague sense in which the entire intellectual life of sentiments and strivings is referred to as will.[28]

A situation which is beyond our control may have our affective approval or disapproval, we may hope for it or fear it, it may sadden or gladden us when it occurs, but we cannot will it in the strict sense. Object of our willing is only the situation whose realization we cannot only hope for, but also bring about in the future through our *causal* influence, our action. When we will something, we take the initiative to make it be and, insofar as our will remains constant, we do not rest until we have executed what we have planned. Accordingly, the active will, based on the foundation of love and desire, is a dynamic process of realization.

141. *Categorical Analysis of the Process of Willing*[29]

Although it is sometimes meaningful to say that "we do not know what we really want," the process of willing reveals a high degree of consciousness because it is supported by progressive acts of judgment regarding the end intended and the means to be used. It is

---

[27]Concerning hope, see G. Marcel, *Home Viator,* London, 1951, pp. 29-67 (Sketch of a Phenomenology and a Metaphysic of Hope).

[28]Language expresses experience, knowing, and believing in the indicative mood, desiring and hoping in the optative, and willing in the imperative mood.

Hoping and believing are related insofar as to believe is to communicate in the knowledge of someone else and hoping is to communicate in the willingness and ability of the other.

[29]This analysis has been taken over from Thomas Aquinas, *De actibus humanis, Summa theol.,* p. I-II, q. 8-17.

permeated through and through with the deliberation and organizing activity of reason. Keeping this interconnection of intellect and will in mind, we may analyze the formal structure of the whole process of willing in the following way:

1. An event or situation is conceived as a possible attainable good which can be posited as a purpose. This is an affective judgment or evaluation of the object in question.

2. This good is posited as a purpose to be realized. This is the pure act of *willing* the purpose as wanted for its own sake. This act of positing a purpose permeates the entire subsequent process and is the transcendent motivation of all following phases.

3. The judgment is made that this purpose, as a still-absent good, can be realized only through the use of means.

4. The good is *intended,* aimed-at, by the turning of the attention to the means. This intention connects the pure willing of the good with the subordinate phase of occupying oneself with the question of means.

5. The subject *deliberates* with himself or with others concerning the kinds of means that can lead to the purpose.

6. He *agrees* that various proposed means are suitable for the purpose intended.

7. The deliberation is brought to an end through an *ultimate practical judgment*: all things considered, this particular means here-and-now appears to be most suitable for reaching the purpose.

8. He then *chooses* this means, i.e., he *decides* to use it. This choice or election is the central act of the process of willing—the preceding deliberation aimed at it, and the subsequent execution flows from it. Especially in the choice, reason and will constitute such an intimate bi-unity of "phases" that they presuppose each other. For, the concrete judgment implies the orientation of the will, and this orientation is not blind but guided by the concrete vision of the individual situation.

9. By virtue of the choice, the order is established in which the executive powers must be put to work. This *command* is an act of the organizing intellect under the influence of the choosing will.

10. The moving *influence of the will* puts the executive powers to work.

11. The *executive powers* themselves begin to operate and proceed to execute what has been commanded. The command which intervenes in the future and regulates the execution may refer to various activities:

a) The actuation of the subject's own inner potentialities, i.e., the powers of thinking, perceiving, imagining, and sensitive striving, which to some extent are governed and directed by the will insofar as their exercise is concerned, albeit not with respect to their content.

b) The motion of the subject's own limbs, which through the sense appetite are under the control of the will, to exercise a transient influence on the surrounding world, to take action.

c) Especially, the turning of the subject through speech to fellow human beings on whom he can exercise a "moral" influence, based on friendship, authority, or power, by means of request, proposal, counsel, insistence or command, in order to secure their collaboration in the project which he has decided to realize.

12. Finally, when the purpose is reached through the use of the means and is known to have been attained, the process of willing finds its completion in *fruition* of the good, in *enjoyment* as rest in the presence of the good.

This analysis shows how intellectual affectivity leads from willing and intending through deliberation to choice or decision, and how command and execution, as causal influences on the future, flow from the immanent act of taking a position, i.e., of choosing or deciding.

Synthesis of the Process of Willing. Like the analysis of affective sense movements, the analysis of willing has to be completed by a synthesis. Not every means is purely a means. It usually has also something of a purpose with respect to subordinated means; consequently, it is appreciated, willed, and intended. Often also it is only in our deliberation about what should be done in concrete situations that we become fully aware of our purposes and intentions. It may even happen that in the execution the purpose intended undergoes a gradual change, as also an artist or author brings the idea of his opus to maturity while working on it. Because of the mutual implications of the various acts, concrete willing cannot be neatly schematized. Life is infinitely richer than our categorical analysis of it.

142. *The Decision of the Will as a Free Act*[30]

The will's decision is accompanied by a feeling of freedom. Man has the impression that he determines himself to his future acts, that, as an ego in the full sense of the term, he is the origin of his deeds and consequently responsible for them. The question is whether we are justified in considering freedom as a property of willing.[31]

A necessary, though insufficient, condition for the freedom of an act is its spontaneity. An activity is spontaneous if it is not wholly determined from without in its concrete situation through the causal influence of other beings, but in spite of the influence exercised by its surroundings finds its ultimate explanation in the nature of the being itself from which it flows, because it tends to realize something to which this being is inclined by its very nature.[32]

---

[30]Concerning freedom, see A. D. Sertillanges, *S. Thomas d'Aquin*, vol. 2, pp. 191-229; C. Barendse, "De metaphysische grondslagen der vrijheid," A. van Leeuwen, "Over wilsvrijheid en zedelijkheid," and J. C. Y. de Jong, "Ziekelijke stoornissen van de wilsvrijheid," *Verslag 11e Alg. Verg. der Ver. v. Thomist. Wijsbegeerte*, Nijmegen, 1946.

[31]Freedom is an analogous concept. Negatively, as being free-from something, it may be described as not-being-fettered and necessitated; positively, as being free to do something, it should be viewed rather as a higher mode of being-able-to, of being the origin of something.

1. With respect to external self-movement a being which is capable of executing what it is innerly urged to do has freedom of movement. It is not forced by its surroundings to do something or not to do it, insofar as it is not locked up, imprisoned, fettered, or restrained.

2. With respect to man as living in a society, we speak of social freedom in all kinds of grades and shades, insofar as the individual or the society is capable of acting according to his or its own insight and decision in a given realm without being hindered by law or custom, threat or pressure, power or force. In this sense we speak of free men in opposition to slaves and serfs, of national freedom as independence from foreign domination, of political or civil liberty, of economic freedom as in free-trade, of freedom of conscience, religion, etc.

3. In moral life the freedom to do or not to do something means that there is no moral obligation: it is permissible.

4. At present, however, we are concerned with freedom in its most fundamental sense, i.e., the capacity of a rational being to determine itself with respect to its inner attitude, freedom of will, which is called also freedom in the psychological sense.

[32]Cf. no. 64.

Voluntariness and Free Will. This spontaneity may be called voluntariness in a very broad sense. It exists to some extent in every subsistent being according to its grade of *being.* The lowest grade of voluntariness is typical of non-living beings, for in an interaction of passivity and activity these beings are more driven by the others than driving themselves.[33]

Living beings reveal a higher degree of spontaneity, for they make their environment subservient to a more immanent self-movement.[34]

Sensitive beings possess a certain knowledge, which is the immanent principle and guiding norm of their action. In the estimative sense they even reveal a kind of "judgment" regarding the object as either useful or harmful for the well-being of the subject. Nevertheless, this instinctive judgment is determined by the subject's natural tendencies. Sensitive beings have "free movement," but no "free judgment."[35]

An action is not merely voluntary but freely-willed in the proper sense only when the given nature of the being does not predetermine the attitude that will be taken. The being has control over its judgment and consequently also over the attitude of the will which coincides with the ultimate practical judgment or decision.[36]

Human Freedom. To what extent concrete individual decisions and actions are free or not is something that can be determined only in a probable way. Man can easily be mistaken in this matter and mistakenly consider free what is predetermined in many ways. Thus the introspective feeling of freedom is not an apodictic proof for the genuine freedom of a decision—man is not pure self-consciousness, not even in his highest activities.[37]

What has to be maintained as beyond doubt is not the factual freedom of individual decisions, but freedom as a human possibility, as the general orientation of the human being. Just as man is essentially directed to knowing being as it is in itself, although he

---

[33]Cf. no. 91.

[34]Cf. no. 111.

[35]Cf. no. 124.

[36]Freedom of will implies: 1) the power to take a standpoint with respect to an object or to abstain from taking one, to will or not to will, to act or not to act. This is called "freedom of exercise"; 2) while taking a standpoint, the power to accept an object as a good or to reject it as an evil and to turn to another object, the power to will this or that, to do this action or that action. This is called "freedom of specification."

[37]Cf. no. 128.

may err in particular judgments, so also is he essentially directed to internal self-determination, although it may happen that in particular decisions he is not free but merely thinks that he is free. His orientation to freedom is implied in the undeniable experiential evidence of his *being,* knowing, and loving.[38]

The Foundation of Human Freedom. The very nature of man's intellectual knowledge implies that it is in general possible for him to make opposite judgments regarding every particular object which possesses some attractiveness for him. The intellect's knowledge of value is an all-embracing orientation to the good *as* good and thus transcends the concrete situation.

The good as good can be realized in infinitely many ways, but none of these ways is the complete and integral realization of unqualifiedly being-good. Precisely because the particular good falls short and is not able fully to satisfy the universal orientation, it can be evaluated as a relative evil. Therefore, the intellectual judgment concerning concrete and individual objects is not of necessity determined to affirmation or to negation. It retains a certain indetermination because different considerations and viewpoints are possible and may lead to contradictory evaluations.

Thus every concrete striving for a determined good presents itself as a limited application of a tending power—the will—which in itself is unlimited and transcends this limited application.

Self-Determination. From the preceding considerations it follows that the intellect which judges the good, i.e., the practical intellect, is determined by the will's orientation to the good, but in such a way that every particular judgment can always be revised in the light of this universal orientation. In other words, the intellect can reflect upon its own judgment, it can direct its attention to the attractiveness of another object and turn away from the first.

If man were to continue his deliberations in this way, he would never arrive at a decision. The question, then, is how a determined attitude of will arises from an undetermined cognitive power. We may not appeal to theoretico-practical knowledge, for this knowledge always sees the relativity of the particular object and is not necessitated to pronounce this object definitively good or evil. The practical intellect arrives at the decision because *in union with the will* it brings the concrete affective *inclination* of the subject to bear

---

[38]Cf. no. 17.

on the judgment. This inclination, however, which reveals itself in the ultimate practical judgment or decision, is not necessitated by the particular attractive good, but allows itself to be influenced from within by this attractiveness and thus puts an end to the deliberation.

Accordingly, the deliberate and decisive selection of a position finds its explanation in the unity of knowing and willing. These two are not separated but together in reciprocal "reflection." They constitute a circle, in which the intellect illuminates the will, and the will moves the intellect. In different respects they are prior to each other, i.e., they constitute each other as principles of a single integral act. The choice, therefore, is not blind, and the judgment is not without motive. The choice *is* the judgment.

Outside the free act of will, however, there is nowhere a sufficient ground for making the choice. The man who chooses, insofar as he is free, is not determined by any motive lying in any particular being outside himself. He actively determines himself—not without any reason or ground, but he himself is the reason insofar as he *makes himself be.*

Because action is that through which the finite being actuates its relationships to the other beings and thus realizes its essential possibilities, a free act is the power of a being to dispose to some extent of its own mode of *being* and thus actively to determine its concrete individual "essence" at least to a certain extent.

143. *Determinism and Indeterminism*

These considerations show the solution of the objection which determinism raises against free acts: since whatever is, insofar as it is, is necessarily determined,[39] how is it possible that a determined act of will originates from the indetermination of practical knowledge?

The reply is as follows. Whatever is, insofar as it is, is determined, for it is *what* it is. However, this statement does not mean that the determinate is therefore limited also to this or that, i.e., that its being-determined makes it also particular and limited. On the contrary, *being* itself, as all-embracing, is the ground of determination, for it is not determinable by anything outside itself. Accordingly, the more something *is,* the more determinate it is.

---

[39]Cf. no. 41.

Likewise, the determinateness of all that is does not mean that the determinate must be determined by something other than itself, i.e., its being-determined does not mean that it is also dependent and necessitated.

On the contrary, since *being* itself is the ground of its determinateness, the more a being *is,* the more it is self-determining and the less it is determinable by something outside itself.

Degrees of Determinateness. Thus we may distinguish various degrees of determinateness. First of all, not every determination is a being-determined through the passively received influence of an *external cause.* Such a determination is the most imperfect form of determinateness. It is accepted as the explanatory ground of the activity proper to a being which in its action depends on its surroundings, i.e., the reaction of material beings. Nevertheless, even in non-living beings this determination from without is not total, because these beings possess a nature and therefore a measure of originality and spontaneity of reaction.

Secondly, not every determination is a being-determined by a passively received *inner essence or nature.* Such a passive reception also is an imperfect kind of determination. It is accepted as the explanatory ground of the spontaneous activity proper to a being which participates in a particular way in *being* without having any influence on this mode of *being.* However, in finite beings endowed with life and knowledge this determination is no longer present in the form just described, because these beings reveal a certain self-movement which foreshadows freedom. They utilize the changing conditions of their surroundings for their self-development in a way that defies our prediction because the more perfect their life is, the more they are individually differentiated.

Thirdly, the highest and most original meaning of determination is active *self-determination,* i.e., in and of itself a being constitutes its own ground for its way of *being* and acting. To the extent that a being is self-determining, it is unconditioned, i.e., independent and not-necessitated.

To some extent man participates in this active determinateness devoid of passive determination—namely, insofar as he is the master and author of his ultimate practical judgment regarding future acts and thus actively constitutes from within the sufficient ground of his will and acting. To the extent that he deliberately and freely performs his acts, he is in the proper sense the "origin" of his mode of being-active and consequently also of his mode of *being*.

144. *Human Freedom as Participation*[40]

In a free-will decision man is determined neither by the particular attracting objects nor by his own particular subjective inclinations. He transcends their limitations. This transcendence is possible because he actively determines himself from his universal orientations to all-embracing unqualified being-good. Accordingly, his freedom testifies to his infinite openness.

Limitations of Freedom. On the other hand, his freedom is very limited. For it is the freedom of a being which is limited, because it is at some time somewhere in the material, living, and social world. Man's self-determination can mean only that he assumes a position with respect to this unavoidable situation and freely gives it orientation and meaning in reference to his infinite elan. Thus, his freedom is essentially related to the non-free and determined realm that is *in* him and *around* him. Torn loose from its roots in the given world of experience, freedom would be pure arbitrariness, an absurd kind of jump motivated by "nothing."

Just as man comes to understanding only by starting with sense perception, so also he comes to willing only by starting with sensitive feeling and desiring. Sensitive affective life is the substratum of freedom. And this life, in turn, is conditioned by the physiological organism and physico-chemical processes. The individual material, vegetative, and sensitive determination of man is the "matter" which of necessity functions as a determining, albeit further-determinable, factor in the formative activity of the will. Without these more or less controllable dispositions, without this "matter" of freedom, human self-determination would be empty. As far as man is concerned, self-determination means gradually and through trials and errors to regulate the life of the passions in a way which has his own personal consent.

Thus man's freedom is at the same time a coming-to-be-free, a developing and temporalized freedom. The whole past of the individual and of his ancestry continues to act in a determining way. A

---

[40]Cf. A. van Leeuwen, "Over wilsvrijheid en zedelijkheid," *Verslag der 11e Alg. Verg. v. Thomist, Wijsb.,* 1946; J. Hollak, "Vrijheid als zedelikheid," *Studia Catholica,* vol. 20 (1944), pp. 151-162.

person's destiny is to give, in an historical process of development through the phases of youth, maturity, and old age, a meaning and direction to this imperfect past with respect to the future, to perfect it in the direction of what he himself chooses as his "ideal *being*." His freedom therefore is busy unfolding itself in a process of growth. It is not so much the individual decisions that are free but it is more the course of life itself which reveals a greater or smaller measure of freedom, without ever definitely attaining to perfect freedom as long as life lasts.

In his history man is essentially together with fellow human beings. He belongs to societies in which free subjects encounter one another intersubjectively. Man is free to choose the position he will take with respect to the freedom of others, but he has to take a position. Even if we disregard or neglect one another, even if we hate or destroy one another, we take into account the other's inner freedom of will as something which escapes our freedom and is not subject to it.

The ground of this social restriction of freedom lies in this that, despite the fact of everyone's orientation to all-embracing goodness, each can determine himself only from a particular situation and therefore participate only in a limited and one-sided way in the possibilities open to man. By means of loving communication with the freedom of others, the individual can widen his self-determination and become in a more universal way the man he chooses to be.

Accordingly, just as he arrives at full self-consciousness only by means of the affirmation of others,[41] so he attains full freedom only by recognizing the others' freedom and even placing his freedom at the disposal of theirs, i.e., by loving them.

Freedom of Self-Realization. These bonds of freedom are special modes of human finiteness. A finite being, which has a limited essence distinct from "to be," is never capable of giving itself its own essence in self-determination. If it were the origin of its own essence, it would not limit itself, for a being does not want to particpate in unqualified *being* in a limited way but as unlimitedly as possible.[42] A self-determination of the very essence itself would be an infinite and absolute freedom and would make the essence coincide with the plenitude of *being.*

---

[41]Cf. no. 121.
[42]Cf. no. 43.

Accordingly, a finite being is determined to its particular essence by an origin transcending it. Its self-determination can refer only to the further unfoldng of its pre-given essence, which as nature is dynamically directed to unqualified *being*.

This unfolding of the essence takes place by means of accidental free acts which are distinct from the being's nature and originate in it. These acts revert also to this nature as to their purpose because, as non-subsistent realizations of the essential possibilities, they perfect the subsistent being.

If finite freedom has both its origin and purpose in necessary nature, it is connected with the natural good, which is tended-to because of a natural inclination.[43]

How is it possible that a free movement to the natural good originates from a determining nature? The only reply is that human nature is a complex nature, i.e., as the *particular* nature of a particular being, it is a principle of necessity, and at the same time as a *spiritual* nature which "in a way is all things," it is a principle of freedom.

Accordingly, the natural good may be considered from two viewpoints. On the one hand, if man is considered as this individual being with these tendencies to vegetative life, to sensitive-intellectual knowing, feeling, enjoying, to companionship with his fellow men, every object filling these tendencies is by necessity of nature attractive and good.

On the other hand, with respect to his intellectual nature man is open to being as being and consequently to the good as good in its universality. Although he experiences the attractiveness of the above-mentioned objects and is aware of the tendencies that flow of necessity from his nature, he is capable of referring these objects and tendencies to unqualified being-good as the universal norm. In the light of this norm he can judge every particular good as merely relatively good. It is within his power to consent or not to consent to a tendency directed to a good which is judged to be only a relative good.

Motive and Self-Determination. Man does not create the attractiveness of the object to which he freely tends as a good. His willing is not without a motive but has its ground in the goodness reason dis-

---

[43]Cf. no. 135.

covers and proposes to him in the object at which he freely aims because it satisfies his tendencies.

Nevertheless, considered in itself, the motive is not compelling and determining as long as the practical intellect continues to consider the goodness of the object as merely relative. The motive becomes the sufficient and determining ground of the free act only when man in his decision unites his infinite elan with the finite attractiveness of this motive, makes it *his* motive and thus makes "himself" the motive. For through his assent he raises a natural good, which in itself is merely relative, to an unqualified good for "himself," because he wants to consider and realize "himself" as naturally directed to *this* good.

Thus it may be admitted that there is an aspect of motivelessness in freely willing—namely, if this term is used to express that the decisive motive does not lie outside the self-determination but coincides with it. In a sense also the attractiveness of the good is caused by the free choice—namely, insofar as man "makes" himself be *such* that *this* good ultimately becomes for him *the* good. To this extent there is a core of truth in philosophical systems which claim that an object is good because it is appreciated and loved.[44]

Motivelessness, or rather having "oneself" as the motive, reveals itself still more clearly when we no longer consider the free willing of what is good for a subject but the root of willing, i.e., the love for the subject for whom one wills the good.

Whether the beloved be the lover himself or someone else, ultimately the beloved is loved not *because* he is already good, but *in order that* he may be good. The sufficient motive of the love, therefore, is not the state of perfection or goodness proper to the beloved, but can be only the beloved subject himself *for his own sake*. Accordingly, it is meaningless to ask "why" one loves somebody. It is not possible to put forward certain characteristics of the beloved as the *ultimate* motive, but only he himself in his unicity, i.e., in his being himself, is the sufficient ground of the love. Thus this love is not merely a kind of reaction, but it is the active choosing of a position in favor of a subject, in consequence of which the tendency of the lover is directed to the realization of what is good in itself with respect to this subject which is united with him.

---

[44]Cf. no. 43.

Finiteness of Human Love.   Nevertheless, human love is only a finite and particular mode of love, for "to be," to-be-loving, and to-be-loved do not coincide in full identity.[45]   Man's self-love is not identical with the *being* itself of the self-loving subject, but flows of necessity from "finding" oneself as already being.   And to love others does not make them be subsistent, but presupposes that they are already connected with the lover; it merely affirms emphatically that their essence is a turning toward their good and, therefore, presupposes their nature as already determined.

---

[45]*Ibid.*

CHAPTER TWENTY-SIX

HUMAN ACTIVITIES

145. *Introduction: Knowing, Tending, and Acting*

Knowing. Sense perception, tendency, and motion constitute an unbroken chain. Man has the capacity to break the immediate connection between knowing and acting through the reflection of the intellect, which not only evaluates the perceived objects according to their agreeable or disagreeable, useful or harmful character for the subject in its concrete situation, but also is open to *being* and the value which these objects possess in and for themselves.[1]

Man's highest activity is not his active influence on the surrounding world but the immanent act with its mutually compenetrating aspects of *understanding and loving.* In this act the communication with "that which is" is realized in the highest way, especially when there is question of the reciprocal self-revelation of personal beings.[2] Unlike sense perception and sense strivings, such an act is not directed to external activity but, as a terminal act, it is a supratemporal permanent attitude,[3] an actual state of presence which brings rest and joy rather than a progressively developing event which ends when the goal is reached.

Tending. Nevertheless, as long as man lives in time, his possession of beings in knowing and loving togetherness is essentially incomplete. Our knowing is intentional and therefore only an imperfect way of having the beings in ourselves,[4] our loving is only a beginning of affective union.[5]

For this reason knowing and loving are not only the ideal terminus or purpose but also the real starting point: they dynamically unfold themselves in *striving and willing.* Although striving and willing are immanent acts, they transcend immanence in the direction of external activities through which as-yet-not-present situations come to be realized in the future. They are, therefore, virtually transient actions and consequently the cause of the changes.[6]

---

[1]Cf. no. 115.
[2]Cf. no. 132.
[3]Cf. no. 93.
[4]Cf. no. 128.
[5]Cf. no. 93.
[6]Cf. no. 93.

Acting. The influence of the act of will extends first of all to the intellectual and sensitive powers, and through the sensitive tendencies also to bodily movements. However, the mutual influencing of the hierarchically ordered powers remains within the unity of the subsistent subject. It is a self-influencing, a self-movement. It is, therefore, not efficient causality in the strict sense, but an "emanative" causality of the subject with respect to its acts.[7]

Secondly, by means of his motor organs man can knowingly and willingly exercise efficient causality on other corporeal beings. This exercise of influence on the surroundings is called activity *par excellence*.[8]

Human Causality. In his actions man is an efficient cause in a higher way than sub-human beings are. Physico-chemical and vegetative processes are still more or less anonymous events of nature, which occur of necessity as soon as the conditions of spatio-temporal contact are fulfilled.[9] The univocal cause has no control over its causality, and it is connected with its effect on one and the same level of perfection.[10]

As soon, however, as knowledge begins to direct the exercise of influence, one may speak of initiative in the strict sense. To some extent such initiative exists in the spontaneous behavior of animals, but it reveals itself more clearly in man's free activities. It depends on man's decision whether or not the effect will come to be, and it depends on his concept or plan whether the effect will be of this or that kind. He is responsible for both the existence and the nature of what he produces.

Practical reason conceives an idea containing the projected essential features of a structure of beings which does not yet exist but is possible, e.g., the idea of a house to be built, an operation to be performed. This idea is a kind of general source of individual realizations which in principle can be multiplied "to infinity." In this way, by means of his universal practical idea, man transcends the univocal causal influence of the individual on the individual and becomes the eminent cause of a mode of *being* which things would not possess without his intervention.

---

[7] Cf. no. 103.
[8] Cf. no. 115.
[9] Cf. no. 91.
[10] Cf. no. 107.

On the other hand, however, the actual execution of the idea proposed by his practical intellect is wholly dependent on man's bodily movement, for only by means of this movement is man capable of controlling the surrounding material world. We do not want to consider here the "moral" influence which man may have on his fellow human beings through his movements of expression, but only the "physical" influence which he exercises on bodily beings. This influence consists primarily in a spatial arrangement of pre-existing beings, a mechanical change of place. But by means of this change of place man manages to produce the most far-reaching alterations in the world through his technique and art and to permeate the given material world with the organizing power of his intellect.

146. *Technical Activity*

Man is naturally less protected and more helpless than animals. His estimative sense is less determined and less certain. However, as a biped, man has his hands free to intervene in the situation of his surroundings. He is not only capable of moving around and "behaving," but can literally "handle" things, i.e., guided by his reason, as in forming things, his hand is the subordinate principle in the execution of forms he conceives.[11] He seizes food and carries it to his mouth. Inquisitive as he is, he lays his hands also on what is not immediately agreeable and by trial and error he learns to know what is useful to obtain his food or prepare it, to protect himself against the climate by clothes and dwelling, to defend himself against animals or to hunt them. Taking a stone in his hand, he makes fire or shapes wood and other materials into objects that can serve as missiles, bows, vehicles, plows, cooking utensils, or furniture.

Inventions. Man invents useful objects because by means of his intellect he is able to discover the general nature of the objects and the laws governing their actions. His knowledge does not remain limited to the perception of successive conditions of individual objects. He is capable of seeing the same qualities in many objects and of classifying them under an abstractly general concept as examples of a species. These qualities, however, are at first the modes in which objects act transiently on one another, the modes in which

---

[11]Aristotle calls the intellect "the form of forms" and the hand "the instrument of instruments." For his comparison of intellect and hand, see *De anima*, bk. III, ch. 8, 432 a 1.

they causally influence one another especially through mechanical locomotion. By means of comparative observation and experimentation man can discover which elements of the causes are essential or accidental with respect to the effect. Thus he arrives through induction at abstract-general judgments expressing the connection of cause and effect.

Because these general laws refer to repeatable situations, they are valid also for the future. Thus man can calculate and foresee what will happen under certain conditions. Insofar as he controls these conditions through his mastery of the bodily movements by which he relocates objects and thus makes them act upon one another, he controls also the future actions of objects and invents general uses for them.

Homo Faber. By means of his hands or of the tools he manipulates man has the possibility of acting in such a way on the beings around him that they become the "matter" from which he can make something new. The "matter" in question is amorphous, homogeneous, specific material, such as clay and stone, or later in history, copper, bronze, and iron. He has power over these materials because of his knowledge of their natural activities and passivities with respect to other objects. He uses, for instance, the hardness and sharpness of stone to give softer mtaerials the desired stature, shape or form.[12]

The matter thus shaped, which as a product of his labor stands out against the surroundings, he indicates by the name of "thing." The thing appears in the world of the *homo faber* as a separate individual something, a concrete incarnation of a general guiding idea. This idea which presided over the fabrication of the thing is its "form," insofar as the thing through this form is suitable for the "purpose" its maker had in mind while making the thing, such as to use it for throwing, cutting, hitting, hammering, or for dressing in it, or dwelling in it.[13]

---

[12] Cf. no. 89.

[13] The theory of the four causes—matter, form, purpose, and agent (cf. no. 103)—arose from the cultural activity of *homo faber*. Matter contains a capacity for form; form corresponds to purpose and is present as an idea in the intention of the artificer before it is realized in matter through executive labor. This theory is transferred to the level of the natural mutual influences of beings, because all modes of causality are analogous and especially because man's productive activities presuppose the workings of nature and share their characteristics. However, when these concepts are thus broadened and rendered more profound by giving them a general metaphysical meaning, one must keep in mind the remark which we previously made with respect to act and potency—namely, the similarity must not make us lose sight of the difference

Work. The laborious and explicit exertion of oneself to the causing of a useful or agreeable effect in the surrounding world is called "work" or "labor." Work is spoken of in opposition to:

1. Games and recreation. Although these may require exertion, they are not undertaken for the sake of useful or agreeable results which lie outside the activities themselves, but for the sake of the agreeable aspect which is contained in the use itself of the player's capacities.

2. Immanent acts as such. These acts, as final state of joy, exclude all exertion, e.g., the contemplation of the true, the love of the good, and the pleasure of the beautiful.

True, there is an aspect of work in the *exertion* necessary to attaining to the evidence of truth (study and investigation in opposition to contemplation), in the acquiring of good morals (asceticism in contrast with virtue), in the formation of esthetical good taste, the maintaining of the health and skills of body (hygiene, sports, gymnastics), and in general in everything which we may call the cultivation of our own powers. Nevertheless, all these exertions are not work in the proper sense of the term.

On the other hand, in the strict sense, work does not consist only in "making," i.e., producing useful, agreeable, or beautiful things. Every exertion to realize a useful or agreeable condition in the world of objects and every service to fellow humans is work. As such we may name alongside industry the operations of agriculture, mining, cattle-breeding, commerce, transportation, and ordinary housekeeping. The planning and organizing of productive labor is the work of guidance which sometimes, as intellectual work, is less correctly opposed to manual labor.

Work is not its own purpose, but reaches out to something else— the result achieved through labor. Nevertheless, work as work is not merely a means to a goal. As the exercise of ingenuity, as the

---

(cf. no. 98). Any attempt to interpret nature by means of analogy with culture has to be on guard against anthropomorphism.

A fortiori great prudence is necessary when the transcendent cause of beings in their totality is conceived as their efficient, final, and exemplary cause. It is not correct, for instance, to conceive God as the "Architect of the universe." To be capable of being a cause is an absolutely general or transcendental property of *being*, but to "make" things is a human and therefore particular and finite mode of causality.

control of the activities of the world in which we find ourselves, of "nature" in the collective sense,[14] it is a good for man as man. Through work, this "nature" is humanized, i.e., it is raised to an order which of itself it possesses only potentially and in this order man's intellect sees a reflection of itself. For this reason labor is not only a source of useful things, but can also be a source of joy.[15]

Technique.[16] Expertness, skill, or technique is the ready well-ordered capacity to arrange a thing in such a way that it serves the purpose assigned to it. In its broadest sense technique is the rational and methodic mastery of the rules governing the use of means in all realms of human activities. In this sense we speak of the technique of weaving, but also of the technique of playing the violin, singing, speaking, studying, and governing.

In the proper sense, however, technique refers to expertness in the realm in which the center point lies in the relationship of means and purpose, i.e., pure usefulness predominates. Control of the material to be handled is not just an aspect but the whole meaning of the activity: subhuman and especially non-living beings are considered merely in their relationship to man, i.e., insofar as the actions of these beings can serve as instruments to satisfy man's needs, his desire for self-development, and his welfare. Thus technique in the proper sense is the art of producing useful things.

Instruments. Techniques becomes more perfect in direct ratio to the extent to which the causality proper to "nature," which of itself is independent of man, is given a calculated role to play. Technical ability develops through constantly more accurate knowledge of the quantitative proportions between cause and effect, expressed in the laws of the mathematico-physical sciences.

Causes controlled by man and made subservient by him as means to a purpose are called *instrumental* causes. The simplest of these are manual tools which merely transmit the motion imparted to them by the craftsman. Man, however, invents also tools which transform

---

[14]Cf. no. 64.

[15]Concerning work, see Remy C. Kwant, *Philosophy of Labor*, Pittsburgh, 1960. Tr.

[16]Cf. P. de Bruin, "Philosophie der techniek," *Studia Catholica*, vol. 13 (1937), pp. 437-464; F. Tellegen, *Aard en zin der technische bedrijvigheid*, Delft, 1953; H. van Riessen, *Philosophie en techniek*, Kampen, 1949; M. Pradines, *Traité de psychologie générale*, Paris, 1948, vol. 2, pp. 21-117; N. Devolder, *Arbeid en economische orde*, Antwerpen, 1946; Andrew G. van Melsen, *Science and Technology*, Pittsburgh, 1961.

a motion in an autonomous way. Above all, the wheel is an ingenious means for obtaining localized, regular, calculable, and arbitrarily transformable motions, especially when drive and brake are combined in a well-regulated way.

Tools may utilize for driving purposes either forces of nature which are readily present, such as water and wind, or forces that are artificially produced, as steam, gas, electricity, and atomic energy. In this way there arises an automotive machine, a structure composed of mobile and immobile parts, adapted to one another in such a way that they take in motor power, transform it, and apply it to materials to produce in them the desired pre-calculated changes.

The introduction of machines means a revolution in the process of labor. The intellect concentrates on invention, and the executive work becomes mechanical, for everything is pre-arranged in the smallest details and insofar as man's regulating intervention is still needed, it is determined by the tempo of the machine which he "serves." Even this intervention is more and more eliminated by so-called "cybernetic" machines which regulate themselves, find the necessary information, and adapt themselves to new situations.

The progressive autonomy of the machine, which is a development arising from the very character of technique, represents a higher form of man's dominion over material "nature," provided he retains control of the machine. The more he is technically capable of doing, the more important the question becomes of what he freely wants to. This point is no longer a question of technique, for technique is essentially subservient to him. However, technique remains itself only when it becomes constantly more subservient, i.e., when it is not guided in its production by what it is capable of doing, but by the product's purpose which transcends the production.

Purpose. The purpose is, indeed, the decisive factor with respect to all work and all production. The object produced derives its unity from its purpose. So far as this unity is concerned, it is of no importance whether the material, considered in itself, as a being of "nature," is a single subsistent being or more than one. For the making of things produces a unity of order, which unites a plurality of parts through accidental relationships of orientation to a single purpose.

This purpose can be expressed only in terms of human activities. The thing's purpose is that we use it or consume it. A knife, a machine, a house are *one* because we can do something with them in a unified way: they serve to cut, to produce, to live in, etc.

The purposes, however, of things are hierarchically ordered: one thing serves another thing, and this in its turn serves a third. Ultimately all these service relations are not directed to the things themselves, but to man as the "why" of all technique. They aim at providing for the satisfaction of his needs and the fulfillment of his desires for self-unfolding.

147. *Economic Activity*

Technique as practical knowledge, teaches us *how* we are *able* to produce things through the actions of "nature." However, this transient action on the material world is not the ultimate activity man has in view. For this reason work is not sought for its own sake but because of its product, and this product in its turn because of its usefulness for the purpose of man's life.

Economy reduces work as a means to its purpose. It determines *what* we *will* produce. It organizes the work.

Its Nature.[17] Economy regulates the application of the means to the attainment of a pre-established purpose. Economy is necessary only where the means are not readily and abundantly available, but have to be managed with foresight and sparingly in order to produce the maximum output.

As far as spiritual goods, truth, goodness, and beauty, as such, are concerned, the acquisition of one does not mean the loss of the other, nor does the fact that one has them imply that the others cannot possess them also. Spiritual goods do not exclude but include one another and can be multiplied in many subjects. For instance, one who communicates the truth to others, does not lose it, but possesses it fully precisely through this communication.

Economy, then, arises where everything cannot be present to everyone at the same time because of *spatial and temporal dispersion.* In such a situation what is present has to be used sparingly and becomes costly. Because it is not possible to satisfy immediately all the desires of everyone, preference has to be given to what is most necessary, and this necessary good has to be equally divided among all.

Its Proper Sphere. The most proper sphere, therefore, of economic management is the domain of material utilities. Nevertheless, spiritual

---

[17]Cf. P. de Bruin, *Economie, een geesteswetenschap,* Roermond, 1946.

goods are likewise subject to costs insofar as it takes time and energy to acquire them and insofar as their communication requires material means and demands that other possible works of economic value be sacrificed.

Thus economy does not only organize the supply of material goods but of all goods or means of satisfying desires, insofar as these goods are not unlimitedly available but have to be produced and distributed in space and time according to a certain choice. It is not its thing-like character which makes something an economic good, but economic value is possessed by everything which has value in itself for human self-development insofar as it has to be managed systematically and judiciously.

Economy does not consist merely in the individual's care of his own needs. It is only through the division of labor and exchange of commodities that it becomes possible for man to satisfy his reasonable wants. The more work is specialized and integrated in a well-ordered social organization, the more also it becomes possible to offer to many less basic but more valuable goods. Accordingly, the economy is essentially of a social nature. It organizes a system of exchange of services according to fixed rules. In this system the specific "economic" value of the services is not determined by the needs of the individual but by their evaluation by the society.

Economic Value. The immanent purpose of economy is the realization of what is economically valuable. "Economic" value or costliness, *as* such, depends on the rarity of the object or service. The less readily available it is and the more difficult it is to produce it, the higher its economic value will be. Thus the economic evaluation of an object or service in the social system of exchange will be determined by the relationship of supply and demand.

Nevertheless, the economic evaluation presupposes a pre-economic value judgment of the offered services that is independent of their rarity. They have first to be considered by society as valuable *in themselves* for the attainment of the purposes of human life. Thus economy is dependent on a transcendental purpose—viz., the self-development of man as he himself freely conceives it. Economic activity is an organization of the means, but it is not the ultimate activity which brings rest and joy to man's tendencies.

On the other hand, there is an intimate connection between the fundamental tendencies of man as man and economic possibilities.

Man's orientation to self-development through spiritual-corporeal communication with beings in truth, beauty, justice, and love is *essentially* unchangeable, but the mode in which man freely makes this tendency concrete by directing it to certain objects and activities is co-conditioned by the means that are technically and economically attainable. In this sense technique and economy exercise influence on the free self-determination of man.[18]

148. *Artistic Activities*

Man does not give form and shape to the beings around him merely for reasons of utility and usefulness. The motive of self-expression also drives him to "make" things. He wants to express in a visible or audible work his "intuitive" feeling of the *being,* meaning, and value of the world in which he lives.

In former times, *art* extended to both servile and free or fine arts. It was defined as "right reason in regard to the making of things."[19] Nowadays the term "art" is preferably reserved for the ability that is not directed to the production of the useful as such, but of things whose contemplation or audition moves aesthetically.

Techniques and Art. This modern usage of the term should not make us forget the bond between technique and art. Man does not merely make his artifacts manipulatable, adaptable, and efficient, but also gives them pleasant forms, so that their very appearance shows forth his control of matter and his ingenuity in finding elegant solutions. Clothing not only protects against the weather but shares in the expressiveness of gesture, movement and pose.[20] Especially man's dwelling, and even more the representative structures dedicated to worship, government, and recreation, create through their interplay with light and space a certain sphere which acts as a symbol of the spirit reigning in them.

Man's expressiveness does not limit itself to arranging spatial forms in orderly fashion, but extends also to things which simply are

---

[18]Cf. no. 155.

[19]Cf. no. 94. For this definition see Aristotle, *Ethica,* bk. VI, ch. 4 (1140 a 16) and St. Thomas' *Comment.* nos. 1053-1060. See also J. Maritain, *Art and Scholasticism,* London, 1930; M. de Corte, "Ontologie de la poésie," *Revue Thomiste,* vol. 43 (1937), pp. 361-392 and vol. 44 (1938), pp. 99-125; A. van Groenewoud, "De schoonheidsleer van de H. Thomas," *Bijdragen,* vol. I (1938), pp. 271-311; L. van der Kerken, *Religieus gevoel en aesthetisch ervaren,* Antwerpen, 1945; E. de Bruyne, *Het aesthetisch beleven,* 1942; *Philosophie van de kunst,* Antwerpen, 1948.

[20]Cf. no. 131.

representations of, or references to others. Thus he sculptures flowers on the friezes and animals on the bases of columns and paints tableaux of human life on the walls. The way is opened for works of art which serve no other purpose than to be contemplated. They are free expressions of man's affective life.

Some arts are spatial, such as decorative arts, landscaping, architecture, sculpture and painting; others are spatio-temporal, such as the dance, theatre, and film; but there are also purely temporal arts of hearing—namely, music and the art of language. Music with its rhythm, melody, and harmony is the most direct expression of feelings, and the reference to things plays a more peripheral role. In the art of language, on the other hand, words may retain their musical and emotional origin, as they do in lyrics, but the signifying power, which they have by virtue of the fact that in daily life they communicate our views about things, events, and relationships, becomes an instrument of free expression. The poet will even charge his words with new suggestions, references, and meanings.[21]

Arts and Symbols. In all the arts the sign plays a central role. Shapes, bodily movements, and sequence of sounds are not produced for their own sake but as incarnations of the unseen and the unheard. In art, however, the sign is not merely a purely conventional substitute for something absent which we have already learned in other ways. It is a *symbol* understood in this sense that it is a sense-perceptible shape which is essentially expressive, so that the signified itself appears to some extent as present in the sign, just as body and soul to some extent coincide.[22] That which is signified in art is not separable from the sign. In science, on the other hand, the sign is usually a pure means which in principle could be replaced by another sign without any loss of meaning. Art is verbal expression, in a broad sense, but its word cannot be separated from imagination and emotion.

In a way it may even be said that in artistic work everything is figurative language provided the term "figurative" is understood as referring not only to visual images but to all the senses.[23] Art is the symbolization not in one but in two ways: a world of the imagination is exteriorized by its expression in symbols, but this world of

---

[21]Cf. no. 133.
[22]Cf. no. 131.
[23]Cf. no. 124.

imagination itself is the artist's reproduction of what he in his poetic knowing experiences as the deeper meaning of the real world.

Poetic Knowledge. Poetic knowledge, which literally means "making" knowledge, is a mode of practical knowledge, as are also, e.g., technical and moral knowledge. What is proper to poetic knowledge is the bi-unity of making and experiencing, of expression and emotion, of "ex-spiration" and inspiration. Its truth consists in the agreement of these two elements; poetic truth is the pure expression of pure emotion.

The element of aesthetic emotion is a being-struck-with-admiration in the presence of the universal interconnection which makes all beings intelligible. However, unlike what happens in philosophy, this all-embracing ontological interconnection is not reflectively understood in the most general or transcendental ideas and first principles, but is spontaneously sensed as present in a particular concrete sense-perceptible something. Thus even if the object is contemplated only by accident in perception or imagination, it attains a luminosity and clarity, a charming or enrapturing beauty[24] which fills the whole subject. This moment in which there is coincidence of senses and intellect, of subject and object, makes the moved subject feel himself, as it were, at the source of all beings and urged freely to call forth from himself, in imitative creativeness, contingent concrete reality in an expressive fashion.

On the other hand, however, it is only in this creative or "poetic" moment, in imaginative fancy and production, that the universal "idea" concealed in every thing, event, or situation reveals itself to him. The poetic idea grows with the needs of the opus, with the resistance and the possibilities of the material. Outside his creative work he is unable to tell either himself or anyone else what he feelingly contemplates.

Art Appreciation. Delight in a work of art is not passive contemplation but an active participation in the creative emotion which gave rise to the work, an imaginative placing of oneself at the origin of the inspiration and a sharing in its move toward exteriorization in the visible and audible. It is only when one feels the same urge which the artist freely obeyed in making his work in this way and not in any other, that one understands what the work of art wants to say. It is even possible that one can then give a truthful explicita-

---

[24]Cf. no. 44.

tion which goes beyond what was explicitly in the mind of the artist himself. For the artist also is not always fully conscious of everything that is implied in his poetic knowledge.

Every work of art contains all kinds of non-aesthetic aspects, though not always in the same degree. The more immediately moving arts, such as music and lyrics, are more purely aesthetic, while the descriptive, narrative, and dramatic arts, such as epics, novel, theatre, and film, and also the plastic arts, objectify the emotion in human persons, situations, and actions. Especially in these objectifying arts, opinions and views of a philosophical, scientific, social and religious nature play an important role. In them there is a closer connection of the artistic with the other human realms of thought, desires and actions.

These non-aesthetic aspects must be evaluated by non-aesthetic norms. However, the properly artistic aspect does not consist in these other aspects, taken in themselves, but in the integration of their contents and forms in the free expression of emotion. What the artist as artist has to express and what, consequently, has to be considered in the evaluation of his work of art, is not the non-aesthetic truth or falsity of his work, but the emotion which he experiences in his wonder over the connection of the concrete and the universal. If he expresses this emotion in a pure way, his work of art is aesthetically valuable—even though it is true that the perfect work is attained only when no wrong is done to the human truth of the realms of life that enter into his product.

Aestheticism. Aesthetic delight and artistic creation are not sought for the sake of something else for which they are useful. Their non-utilitarian character raises them above all technical works and economic concern. They are the pause in which man experiences the relativity of work and becomes free for the proper life of the spirit. In a certain sense it may even be said that they are a prelude of man's immanent final activity, insofar as feeling and imagination, senses and intellect, contemplation and creation, subject and object, coincide in a moment of harmony.

Nevertheless, aesthetic delight and artistic creation are not the highest possibility of human communication with all that is. For they are volatile and frail, bound as they are to the instability of sensitive feeling and imagining. Although in man's aesthetic emotion, truth and goodness are to some extent united,[25] neither one nor the other

—————
[25] Cf. no. 44.

is reached fully. For, although the contemplation of the beautiful may lead from the concrete sense object to the interconnection of all beings, it does not understand them explicitly in their own mode of *being*. Even aesthetic delight refers to the beings in their appearance to the subject rather than in their own mode of *being,* their own essence and value. The disinterested surrender to beings, as they are in themselves, is not perfect in the aesthetic moment.

For this reason man has to transcend the aesthetic in scientific knowing and moral willing. There is danger that he will cling to effortless delight in his course of life, that the subjective state of delight will become his purpose, and the real world of nature and society will be merely an occasion for delight. In contrast with this aestheticism, the genuine aesthetic and artistic attitude, as a partial fecundating and animating aspect of man's whole life, remains connected with his works and cares as well as with the immanent activities of knowing and willing, of wisdom and love.

149. *Scientific Activities*

Various Forms of Knowing. Man is dynamically directed to communication with all that is. Knowing, however, is not merely a condition of this communication but also one of its forms.[26] There are many forms of human knowledge; for instance, experience of life, general knowledge of man, knowledge of the individual through personal contact, technical knowledge, poetic and aesthetic knowledge.

In contrast to these pre-scientific modes of knowing, scientific knowledge is knowledge for the sake of knowledge. Its purpose lies in itself as the perfection of man's capacity for knowledge, even though it may be important for man's activity and even though it may be precisely this importance which as a rule gives rise to the study of science.

The statement that scientific knowledge is knowledge for its own sake applies not only to theoretical sciences but also to the so-called practical sciences. True, these sciences have praxis as their object, they seek the norms for doing and acting correctly, and they may move from the more general norms to the less general. Nevertheless, as long as they remain science, they retain a speculative character and are distinct from the so-called practico-practical abilities, such as skill and prudence, which preside over the execution of the individual action.[27]

---

[26]Cf. no. 128.
[27]Cf. no. 155.

Scientific research and aesthetic emotion have this in common, that both of them are interested in the cognitive object in a non-utilitarian way. The aesthetic object, however, is the concrete and sense-perceptible presence in its concrete form or shape, as a symbol of suggested more profound interconnections. The scientific object, on the other hand, is not the being as it speaks to us and moves us immediately in contemplation, but as it can be seized in judgments expressing its own nature and laws. While the rest of contemplation which follows laborious research may offer aesthetic delights, research does not have this delight as its purpose, but is oriented to expressing the ontological interrelationship by logical means.

Meanings of "Science." Science is a more special and more eminent way of knowing than the other ways described above. It is certainty about beings that has been acquired methodically and justified critically. This certainty does not extend only to the fact *that* things are, but if possible also includes *what* they are and the reason *why* they have to be as they are. Science aims at insight, i.e., at knowledge of grounds or causes, knowledge of connection and relationship.

The term "science" can have several meanings. It may refer first of all, to the actual exercise of such an eminent way of knowing. Secondly, it may express the habitual ability to know in this way. Thirdly, by way of analogy, it may indicate the whole of the cognitive objects, precisely insofar as they constitute the content of scientifically systematized knowledge at a given time or in a given society. In this last sense science is a whole of propositional contents, a system.

The concept of science develops together with science itself in an historical process of evolution. According to the Aristotelian view, there is question of science in the strictest sense only when we know why something is in this way and cannot be other than it is.[28] Thus science refers to the necessary and the general, as foundation and cause of the actual and the individual. Such a deductive kind of knowledge starts with principles which are open to insight and do not themselves have to be proved, but from which all other statements are proved.

Mathematics. In this view of science, however, two questions arise. First, do these principles of insight supply us with the real grounds

---

[28]Cf. Aristotle, *Analytica priora,* Bk. I, c. 2 (71 b 9) and St. Thomas' *Comment.,* lect. 4, Cf. St. Thomas views about the relationship of physics, mathematics, and metaphysics, *In Boethium de Trinitate,* qq. 5 and 6. See also J. Hoogveld-Sassen, *Inleiding tot de wijsbegeerte,* vol. I, Nijmegen, 1947; A. Brunner, *La connaissance humaine,* Paris, 1943, pp. 301-409.

or causes of the beings? And, secondly, is it possible for us to deduce the real and possible beings from these principles? Critical reflection makes us doubt that we have the capacity to perform such a deductive demonstration in a general way. Only within very narrow confines do we have an insight into the necessity of beings as flowing from their immediate and adequate grounds.

The deductive character is found most strikingly in the mathematical sciences, which proceed in a more constructive way than the others. Mathematics, however, doesn't study empirically perceived beings in their dependence on final and efficient causes, i.e., in their process of qualitative development. Through a very special kind of abstraction mathematics isolates the quantitative relationships, it measures and counts the repetition of "equal" or the "same" by means of purely univocal concepts.[29] Going beyond this, in free thought representations it posits all kinds of imaginary magnitudes, assigning to them by definition an "essence" and deducing from this "essence," by means of "operations," the implied properties and relationships to other magnitudes. Mathematics reasons only from the formal cause, which is usually posited in an imaginative way, and is distinguished from the formal logic of univocal concepts insofar as it still retains a somewhat determined content—namely, magnitudes that can be constructed in thought.[30]

Positive Sciences of Experience. The beings that come to be in our experience are not known to us either through their substantial essence or through their final and efficient causes. Critical reflection on our inability to intellectually intuit and rationally deduce these beings, in modern times led quickly to the autonomy of so-called "positive" sciences of experience. They broke away from philosophy and sought their method mainly in accurate observation and repeated experiment. Only by means of induction is it possible for us to proceed from the observed "phenomena," i.e., accidents and effects, to more general concepts and propositions concerning the nature and causes of observed beings.[31]

These propositions, however, unlike the first principles of thought, are not self-evident. They are hypotheses which, if admitted, are capable of putting the known facts together in an orderly fashion and of making them to some extent intelligible. But then hypotheses are not admitted as objectively true unless we can first show that they

---

[29]Cf. no. 78.
[30]Cf. no. 168.
[31]Cf. nos. 84, 102, 127.

are the only possible hypotheses. It is for this reason that, in contrast to the conclusions of mathematics, they have to be verified not only as free from internal contradictions but also as in agreement with our growing experience and as able to lead us to the discovery of new facts.

Accordingly, the concept of science implied by the autonomous "positive" sciences of "nature" as well as of the "mind" is more modest than the ideal pursued by mathematics and metaphysics. But it has proved itself more fruitful for the expansion of our knowledge. The emphasis lies no longer on the necessity and universality of the object known, but the contingent and the individual also can be the object of science, provided all subjective prejudices are excluded through critique and method. An object of science is anything which is in principle accessible to all subjects in unprejudiced observation and which has to be affirmed by all of necessity, even if it is known only in its interconnection with the other "phenomena" and not in its general essence and its necessary causes.

That "positive" science can only approach the ontic conditions from afar reveals itself very clearly in the laborious process required for the formation of concepts in any of its realms, the deficiency of judgments, and the fact that the reasoning process usually provides only a proof *that* something is but only rarely a proof *why* it is so, based on its immediate and adequate ground of *being*.

Philosophy. This self-limitation of the sciences, accompanied by an unheard-of expansion of its interest to all realms of *being* and activity, and an ever-increasing in specialization and co-ordination, throw a new light on the relationship of positive science and philosophy. Philosophy is no longer possible without a reflex critique of knowledge, i.e., a critique whose function it is to show that certain insights and experiences of pre-scientific knowledge are still presupposed in scientific knowledge and are undeniable conditions of all knowledge as knowledge. Only that which can resist radical doubt is acceptable as the starting point of metaphysics. Thus philosophy has been freed from its admixture with the scientific hypotheses and theories pertaining to any particular period of history, which usually are only of a probable nature and may be replaced in subsequent developments by others.

Like experimental science, however, philosophy does not proceed in a purely deductive way, but endeavors to penetrate to the ultimate ground of beings by means of an analysis of that which is always present and all-embracing. Whether and to what extent we possess the power to attain the ontological first principle is something which can become clear only in the development of metaphysical thought itself. However, the finiteness of the starting point and man's imperfect mode of *being* and knowing militate against an adequate knowledge of being as being in its ultimate grounds. Accordingly, metaphysical knowledge also and even especially is essentially finite and incomplete. It is usually expressed in negative judgments, even though we know that the infinite in itself is the absolutely positive. It has to admit that what is fully intelligible "in itself" can be a mystery "for us."[32]

Science and Purpose of Life. A result of this development of the idea of science is a profound realization that knowledge for knowledge's sake is insufficient. On the one hand, the sciences are sought for their own sake and, unlike other activities which are oriented to further purposes, they pertain to the final purpose of human nature. On the other hand, however, they cannot possibly satisfy man's tendency to communication and self-perfection; they remain dynamic and offer only a relative and provisional rest.

Insofar as they perfect our cognitive capacity, the sciences cannot be evil, for rest in truth is always a good. But because they cannot fully realize happiness, they are only a shadow of, and a participation in an absolute happiness which transcends scientific contemplation. For this contemplation remains always obscure, it does not give any direct contact with the concrete and individual beings but only a contact mediated by arguments of probability and analogy, general judgments, abstract concepts, and all kinds of systematizing representations, symbols, and models. For this reason, without being in itself a means to the goal, science is not the absolutely ultimate goal for which man will sacrifice everything.

Accordingly, like poetic and aesthetic knowledge, scientific knowledge is always a moral good in regard to its specific essence, but its study by concrete man has to be governed by the norms of morality. Knowledge as knowledge knows no measure, but the pursuit of knowledge is good only when it is in harmony with the development of man's other bodily and mental capacities. Thus it finds its norm in its integration in the whole of life. Science, as we pursue it laboriously in time, is not the final purpose itself of human existence.[33]

---

[32]Cf. no. 42.

[33]Cf. Rousselot, *L'intellectualisme de S. Thomas d'Aquin,* Paris, 1936, pp. 172-229.

CHAPTER TWENTY-SEVEN

MAN AS A MORAL BEING

150. *Introduction: Norms of Conduct*

Value Judgments. While instinctive behavior is guided by the estimative sense, the specifically human activity arising from the will is directed by practical reason.[1] Practical reason sets goals and assigns means to reach these goals. It judges also actions which have been done, or are to be done, according as they agree or disagree with the purposes to be reached.

Practical reason proposes something as a purpose to be reached because it is evaluated as a good, as possessing a value for the self-unfolding of man. It does not aim at what we perceive as actually existing, or understand as possible, but at what we posit as an ideal to be realized.[2]

Value judgments have a normative character. They judge objects or activities as true or false, good or evil, beautiful or ugly, agreeable or disagreeable, suitable or unsuitable, just or unjust. They formulate rules which action "must" follow to be "right," i.e., to reach the goal which gives meaning to the action. Accordingly, the necessity implied by the norms is a necessity referring to a purpose, a kind of hypothetical necessity.

Norms and Purpose. The ultimate norm governing every realm of human activity is the purpose of this realm itself. And the question to be asked is: On what basis is this purpose posited as necessarily to be attained? Is the purpose of a definite realm of activity judged to be valuable of itself or does it derive its value from a higher and more absolute value with which it is connected?

Technical production is governed by the norms of skill. But the exercise of technical skill is motivated by the utilitarian value of the products, for these products are evaluated according to their useful-

---

[1]Cf. no. 142.

[2]Value is the basis on which we esteem something as a good: it actuates and perfects a capacity. We attribute value, first of all, to the objects to which our activity is directed as the perfection of our essence and our capacities. By analogy of attribution we ascribe value also to the activities and skills directed to these valuable objects.

Value is a formal-abstract concept, indicating a property *of* objects and activities. A less fortunate modern use in so-called axiology applies the term also to the being or act which "has" value.

ness to do this or that. Economic judgments govern the priority rules for the realization and distribution of the products in view of the widest possible satisfaction of needs. This means that the economic judgment of value presupposes a pre-economic evaluation of utility. Hence the technical and economic norms are dependent on a transcendent purpose.

Likewise, the norms governing bodily well-being and the development of strength and agility, e.g., in the care of health, hygiene, sports and games, find their meaning in a transcendent purpose, for biological values are subordinated to psychical and spiritual values.

Accordingly, it appears that the purpose of human self-unfolding must be sought in cultural activity—the term "culture" being understood here not in its broadest sense as extending to all human activities, but somewhat more restrictedly, as the pursuit of a certain unselfish communication with beings in their truth, goodness and beauty, or also as the exercise of immanent activities and their exteriorization in historical society.[3]

Absolute Norms.   Must we say that the norms governing the knowledge of the true, the love of the good, and the delight in the beautiful, which are studied in logic, ethics, and aesthetics, are ultimate norms and therefore independent of higher norms? In a certain sense the answer has to be affirmative. Truth, goodness, and beauty pertain to all beings as beings; hence the activities which refer to these values cannot be ordered to higher, broader, and more profound activities, but are ultimate activities having their meaning and value in themselves. Accordingly, insofar as their *specific essence* is concerned, they are always good for man.

Nevertheless, there is a difference in absoluteness between the norms governing the knowing of the true, the enjoying of the beautiful, and the loving of the good. With respect to their specific essence, intellectual and aesthetic activities are governed by truth and beauty, but in their pursuit they, as well as *all* other human activities, are ruled by the ethical norms. The ethical norms, therefore, have an absoluteness that transcends all other norms.

The reason is as follows. No matter in what realm of values the specifically human activity occurs, whether it be a question of technical, economical, social, medical, pedagogical, artistic, or intellectual endeavors, insofar as it is a free human act, it ultimately origi-

---

[3]In a still narrower sense culture is often understood as the study of science and liberal arts or even as poetic creation and aesthetic enjoyment.

nates in a decision through which man is self-determining.[4] In this decision he takes a stand with respect to his *essence as a whole,* his nature as the common dynamic root of *all* his abilities in their interconnection, and he gives an all-embracing and ultimate purpose to his whole life. Although this self-determination to an ultimate purpose is not so much to be conceived as an explicit momentary event but as a more or less implicit attitude or orientation, nevertheless, it explicitates itself dynamically in all the particularized and momentary decisions referring to particular situations.

The norms which govern human acts, precisely insofar as they are *free* deeds or self-determination, are called moral norms. They are not concerned with any branch of human activities in particular, but with every deed insofar as it is specifically human. Man does not always act as a technical, economical, political or scientific being, but insofar as he acts *freely* he always acts as man. Accordingly, although every deed, such as technical labor, hygiene, education, artistic creation, or scientific endeavor, is ruled by its own norms corresponding to its object, nevertheless, as a specifically human deed, it falls under the norms of ethics which connect man's integral nature with the integral purpose of his life.

151. *Man's Integral Nature as the Fundamental Norm of Ethics*

Human Freedom and Absolute Norms. Ethical norms have an absoluteness that is wholly proper to them. All other norms are concerned with a hypothetical necessity, i.e., a necessity flowing from a hypothetical purpose. Ethical value judgments, however, aim primarily at the absolutely necessary purpose itself of integral human nature. They posit this purpose as something that *has to be of absolute necessity.*

On the other hand, as we have seen, ethical or moral norms are concerned with human activity precisely insofar as this activity is a *free* act, a self-determination of man to a purpose that is freely made. For it is only for free deeds that man is morally responsible.

Thus the question arises of how it is possible that a free act, precisely in its freedom, is governed by an absolute norm having a necessitating character.

The ground for this normalized character of human freedom must be sought in the *finiteness* of this freedom.[5] Freedom, as freedom, is self-actuation, i.e., actuation through which a being is the autonomous

---

[4]Cf. no. 143.
[5]Cf. no. 144.

ground of its *being*. As such, freedom cannot in any way be necessitated by anything outside itself, but has its intelligibility and goodness in and of itself. Just as freedom has itself as its motive, so also is it its own law or norm. Freedom cannot obey, because it is not subject to any rule by which it should be evaluated.

Finite freedom, however, is freedom through participation. It is not pure activity but presupposes a passivity, a finding-oneself-to-be. The free act is not the essence itself of the finite being, but an accidental perfection which is distinct from the previously given substantial essence. The unchangeable individual essence, therefore, as nature, is the *source* from which free acts emanate. Moreover, these acts are not their own purpose but, as non-subsistent determinations, are directed to the *purpose* which of necessity is prefigured in the nature of their subject.[6] Thus they share in the necessity, in the having-to-be which characterizes the "natural good" of every being.[7]

Necessary Purpose and Free Nature. The tendency of non-free beings to the natural good is characterized by necessity, but intellectual finite beings are capable of freely taking a stand with respect to the necessary good of their nature and thus are able to determine "themselves," even though this natural good normalizes their free acts. The question, therefore, remains how such a free self-determination with respect to the necessary good is possible. How can nature be a norm, freely to be accepted by finite intellectual beings?

The explanation lies in the above-mentioned complexity of human nature. As a particular nature, it is of necessity orientated to definite objects, but as a spiritual nature, which is open to the good as good, it can evaluate every definite object as merely relative good.[8] As a spiritual nature, man's nature is a *free nature*. This means that it is the dynamic source of a *free* orientation to a *necessary* purpose. This purpose "has to be," though not in the sense that man cannot do anything but realize it, but in the sense that the natural good appeals to his freedom freely to accept his nature with its dynamic orientation to the good and thus personally to realize himself.

Accordingly, freedom, which as freedom is not subject to any norms, as finite freedom, is normalized by a nature which does not determine the acts originating in it by a necessity of nature, but *appeals* to the judgment of practical reason. In the light of this

---

[6]Cf. no. 100.

[7]Cf. no. 64.

[8]Cf. no. 144.

universal norm of good as good this practical judgment is capable of understanding in a particular way the particular goods to which human nature is ordered and of directing human activities in accordance with this understanding.

However, not every way in which man freely interprets his natural good is of equal value. True, although man has to make a choice, he is free in his practical judgment regarding the way in which he must realize his natural good. Nevertheless, his nature, as it is "in truth" demands of him that he recognize his "true" natural good as it is and that he allow his acts to be normalized by this recognition. Man is capable of determining "himself" *freely,* but he is *obliged* to accomplish this self-determination in accordance with the *ideal* as it is prefigured in his "true essence."

The meaning, therefore, of integral human nature as ethical norm is as follows. This nature does not impose itself with a natural necessity, but, as the true and higher ego of man, appeals to reason and freedom to conform with nature, so that man freely "becomes what he is" by nature. Human nature is a gift that is at the same time a task, a call to authenticity as faithfulness to truth in man's deeds.[9]

---

[9]1. Every finite activity is directed to the natural good and thus itself is called good by analogy of attribution (cf. no. 64). In this sense every free act of man is naturally good.

2. As a *free* act, however, a human act has a special relation to the natural good. The bond between nature and good is effected by means of the practical judgment in which man raises a good that in itself is merely relative, to "his" good.

3. As judgment, the ultimate practical judgment is governed by the norm of truth, but it may either agree or disagree with this norm. An error in the practical judgment is an error in self-determination. Man is responsible for this error insofar as he is conscious of the conflict between his self-interpretation in the ultimate practical judgment and the judgment of "conscience" (cf. no. 155).

4. We call an act ethically good when through it man directs himself freely to self-realization as it is "in truth" the good of his "true" integral nature. Such an act, then, is done knowingly and willingly according to the ethical norm. On the other hand, an act is morally or *ethically evil* when it is done knowingly and willingly despite its deviation from the ethical norm.

5. A morally evil action is a deed of a free nature which, as a *deed,* implies of necessity a kind of self-realization and orientation to the good and which, as a *free* deed, is a certain attainment of freedom. However, it is deficient in a characteristic that ought to pertain to it precisely insofar as it is a deed of a free *nature*—namely, the willing of self-realization as it *ought* to be willed, as it lies "in truth" implied in the orientation of the nature to the natural good.

6. The morally good action is a "truthful" realization of man's *being* as a deed, as a free deed, and as the deed of a free nature. For this reason such an action has a meaningfulness that is lacking in the morally evil act—namely, to make man more integrally "man." Thus it contributes to man's happiness, for happiness is the affective reaction of nature to the possession of its true good.

152. *Right Practical Reason as the Formal Moral Norm*

In calling man's integral nature as orientated to the integral human good the norm of morality, we indicate the *foundation* of the norm. For, *formally* as norm, the norm is a rule or dictate of "right" practical reason, i.e., reason insofar as it "in truth" reveals what "must be done" freely.

First Principle of Practical Reason. The first principle of the practical reason is an immediate, absolutely apodictic evidence:[10] the good must be done and evil must be avoided. This most general ethical norm is a concrete expression of the universal principle of *being* which states that for a being as being the fullest possible "to be" is lovable, good, and perfective.[11] When this principle of *being* is brought to bear on the *being* of man himself who enuntiates it, then it reveals itself as the general norm of morality.

The point may be clarified as follows. I who am and know that I am—the same applies to everyone else who like me is conscious of his *being*—find myself naturally inclined to the fullness of *being* as my good. I "have to" be in fullness according to the mode of the possibilities implied by my essence. This "having-to" which is proper to *being* as good and lovable is not for me, whose essence as a spiritual nature is a free nature, a necessity imposed on my activity in a coercive way, but a necessity proposed to it as to be freely accepted. "Having-to" has for me the character of a *moral* necessity.

This necessity, then, is precisely the first moral norm. Strictly speaking, it should be expressed in this way: I, and all who are like me, must tend to the good in freedom.

As the expression of our tendency to the good, this first value judgment has the *optative* mood—it expresses an *ideal* of human dignity. As an appeal to our freedom to remain faithful to this tendency, it has an *imperative* mood—it expresses a *duty*.

The apodictic evidence of this judgment is immediately open to every human being who obtains an intellectual insight into his own essence. It is anchored in the very nature of the intellect as a spontaneous or active power.[12] Thus man's intellect itself implies the ability

---

[10]Cf. no. 21.

[11]Cf. no. 43.

[12]Cf. no. 125.

to have an insight into the first principles of practical reason. This insight is called *synderesis.*[13]

The Universal Norm and Man's Essence. The first ethical norm is so general that it cannot immediately serve to direct man's actions. True, the idea of the integral human good in its analogy embraces all more particular purposes of life, both with respect to its extension and with regard to its comprehension or, to say it differently, not only potentially but also actually.[14] However, it embraces them only in a confused and implicit way. Just as it is not possible for us to derive the particular beings from the universal idea of being,[15] so we are likewise unable to deduce the more particular norms from the first universal norm.

In order to explicitate the all-embracing fullness of the universal norm of the good in more particular value judgments and to be able to guide man in the various realms of life, practical reason has to reflect further on the "essence" of being-man. All that is necessary for this purpose is to become conscious of the natural inclinations in which this essence reveals itself. These natural inclinations manifest themselves in the capacities and activities flowing from man's nature.

Thus there is an intimate connection between theoretical and practical reason with respect to knowledge of man's essence itself. Both constitute a single reason which proceeds from experience to insight and from insights to norms. The ontic order of the relationships of man's nature to other beings is the foundation for the deontological order.

The question of what man is in his most profound essence, in what his self-realization consists, and what the goal and meaning of his life and activity are, always receive an answer implying an ethical aspect. Man's ontology cannot be separated from axiology, nor vice versa. For man has a spiritual and, therefore, a free and moral nature. The replies to the question of how by thinking he finds himself to be and how by willing he makes himself be, are mutually related. True, his essence is given to him as a nature, but the unfolding of this essence lies in his own hands, to be executed according to the interpretation which his theoretical and practical reason gives to this essence.

In this ethical perspective we must raise the question regarding the truth of human nature and ask what constitutes the true essence or mode of *being* of man.

---

[13]Cf. no. 94.
[14]Cf. no. 52.
[15]Cf. no. 53.

153. *By Nature Man is a Spiritual-Material Person*

Man is a Subsistent Being. In his perceptive and active dealings with the beings around him man is conscious of his own *being*: he is "I" for himself, the conscious bearer, origin, and purpose of perceptions and action.

In his perceptions and actions he knows also that he is an organic living being, for he knows that his vegetative processes are his. And he knows about his being spatially and temporally in a definite place and at a definite moment, for the material events occurring in, and affecting his body concern him and pertain to him, albeit in a different way than his conscious acts.

Next, through memory and expectation he knows that he is the same "I" who unfolds himself in a plurality of successive acts.

Finally, he ascribes to himself a life of imagination and representation, of understanding and thinking, of desiring, wanting, and willing.

All these different activities and passivities originate from the same "I" in diverse ways—as wholly unconscious, sensitively experienced or intellectually conscious—and are supported by this "I." They are interconnected, influence and condition one another.

Accordingly, man is aware of himself as one being, in the primary sense of being—namely, a *subsistent* being or supposit, which underlies the plurality of powers and the changing accidental activities and passivities.[16]

Material-Spiritual Character of Man. This one human being is certainly corporeal, vegetatively and sensitively living. His essence, therefore, must be composed of determinable prime matter and a determining essential form. This essential form is the formal principle of both man's organic corporeal being and his vegetative and sensitive life. Viewed in this last respect, as the dynamic principle of life animating a body, the essential form is called "soul".[17]

This one human being, however, is also intellectually knowing and willing. The intellectual activities of life are of a wholly proper nature and rise above all vital activities based on being-corporeal. For in their orientation to objects they are not limited to the material being appearing here and now, but possess a transcendental openness to everything that is, as it is—to the true, the good, and the beautiful, as such. Because human knowing and loving aim at the *being* of

---

[16]Cf. no. 67.
[17]Cf. no. 116.

beings, albeit in a very imperfect way, and because outside being nothing is, man has in his intellectual powers an infinity of horizon, transcending the material—he is "in a way everything."[18]

Activity and object, however, are proportioned to each other.[19] Therefore, the activities also which are directed to the supra-material must be supra-material in their subjective mode of *being*. They cannot be intrinsically organic activities, as sense experience and sense appetite are, no matter how much the exercise of these activities is conditioned by sense experience and sense appetite.

We give the name "spiritual activities" to activities which, because of their all-embracing openness for the *being* of beings, are supra-material. These activities must originate from spiritual powers. And these spiritual powers, in their turn, must emanate from a spiritual principle of essence which is intrinsically independent of corporeal being.

Insofar, however, as a form transcends the limitation of being-here-and-now in space and time, it may not be conceived as merely the form of individuating matter. For a material form constitutes the individual essence only in conjunction with matter and limits the "to be" of the being to this or that specific mode of being-material.[20] The "to be" of man, on the other hand, insofar as it is the root of the spiritual activities of understanding and willing, is a spiritual "to be." It is the "to be" of a being which can know about *being,* which in an infinite openness is knowingly and lovingly related to unqualified *being.* Accordingly, insofar as the form is an essential principle of such a being-spiritual, it is not a form limited by matter but a subsistent, supra-spatial and supra-temporal form.

Must we assume, then, that there are two formal principles in man: one through which he is spiritual, and the other through which he is here and now corporeal, vegetative, and sensitive? Such an assumption would militate against the unity of man, for one and the same being which thinks and wills also senses and experiences, moves and nourishes itself. But a single being has only one essential form.[21] Therefore, the many human powers must flow from a single formal principle. The spiritual principle is also the first formal principle of vegetative life and sense life: by virtue of an essential necessity, man's "spirit" fulfills the role of "soul" with respect to the organic living body.

---

[18]Cf. no. 118.
[19]Cf. no. 93.
[20]Cf. no. 90.
[21]Cf. no. 89.

Accordingly, man is a being whose essence is a unity composed of spirit, which as soul is first form, and prime matter. The implication of this assertion is that man is a spiritual being of such a nature that he is corporeally living because of his being-spiritual, and that he is actuated to his being corporeally living through a spiritual principle. Although considered in itself the human spirit has "to be" as its "own to be," nevertheless, in order to attain self-realization through its actions, this spirit has to be an animating principle.[22]

Man as a Person. The individual man is a single subsistent being, i.e., neither a non-autonomous part nor a property or attribute of a whole, but a being which "itself is in itself" and makes "to be" its own according to the essential mode in which it participates in *being*. This appropriation of *being* consists in the modification which the essence exercises with respect to *being*.[23]

Subsistence, however, is an analogous concept, which can be realized in higher and lower modes. Man is subsistent is a much higher way than all other living and sensing beings. For he is the supposit of a rational nature, i.e., a self-conscious and free-willing, and therefore self-determining nature. His subsistence, then, does not mean only that he appropriates "to be" according to a mode which is wholly determined by his essence and according to activities which in given conditions flow of necessity from the essence as nature. His subsistence means that he appropriates "to be" according to a mode which, albeit determined by his essence, leaves him the liberty to interpret this essence in his activities by the judgment of his reason and to realize his essence according to this interpretation. He himself is responsible for the explicitation of his essence; he is the master of his acts insofar as they arise from reason and will. Thus in his free actions he appropriates "to be" in a higher way than beings which do not have a free nature.

We speak of *person* with respect to a being which is subsistent in such an eminent way that it is capable of making itself be, of being the free origin of its own *being*. To be a person is the highest mode of being-subsistent. The person, therefore, is the highest and most

---

[22]Concerning the difficult problem of the relation between *psyche* and *nous* in Aristotle (*de Anima*, bk. III cc. 4-5), see F. Nuyens, *L'évolution de la psychologie d'Aristote,* Louvain, 1948. For St. Thomas Aquinas' view of the soul, see *Summa theol.,* p. 1, qq. 75-76 and especially the extensive and masterly explanations of *De spiritualibus creaturis* and *De anima.* See also Stephan Strasser, *The Soul in Metaphysical and Empirical Psychology,* Pittsburgh, 2nd impr., 1961.

[23]Cf. no. 65.

eminent of all subsistent beings and may even be said to be properly and really a being in the full sense of the term. All sub-personal beings are imperfectly themselves and imperfectly subsistent, they do not dispose of their *being* because they are neither conscious nor free. The person, on the other hand, has a very special relation to *being* for to the extent that he is a person his *being* is essentially to-be-active, self-determination or "auto-position."[24]

If we call a man a person,[25] we indicate that he has a spiritual nature which makes him not merely be a subsistent part of the material universe, individuated through "here-and-now," but also causes him to transcend and comprehend this universe through his powers of intellectual knowledge and love; consequently, he is capable of consciously and freely taking a position with respect to particular beings, including himself insofar as he is material, vegetative, and sensitive, or insofar as his own natural inclinations are concerned.

Insofar as man is a person, he is a whole that exists of itself, *in* itself, and for itself, a being that can *make itself be* in an original, unrepeatable way, determined by itself through acts for which it itself is responsible.[26]

---

[24]Cf. no. 143.

[25]Concerning the concept of person, see P. Ellerbeck, "Functie en inhoud van de term persoon in de psychologie"; J. Peters, "De plaats van de persoon in de hedendaagse philosophie"; D. M. de Petter, "Het persoon-zijn onder thomistisch-metaphysische belichting"; all in *Verslag der 13e Alg. Verg. v. d. Ver. v. Thomist. Wijsb.*, Nijmegen, 1948.

[26]The term "person" originally meant "mask," and consequently also role, character, function, dignity. It soon received the concrete meaning of indicating the rational and free, individual subsistent being. The formal-abstract term "personality" is used in several senses.

1. In its purest form it means that through which a being is a person, that through which a being can freely appropriate "to be" to itself (cf. the term "subsistence" in no. 65).

2. Thus it came to mean also the characteristic of being a person.

3. Concretely, personality, means someone who through free self-determination has become "himself" in a striking way. Sometimes it is used in a neutral and more psychological sense in reference to someone who in his essence and actions reveals himself steadfast despite the change of his own moods, the opinion of others, and the variable situation. More appropriately and in an ethical sense, it indicates one who does the good and approximates his ideal essence in full freedom, from an interior affective inclination, without tension between his various powers.

4. In a less correct usage, "personality" means the power to recognize oneself as the same perduring being. In this sense there is sometimes question of a "split personality" (Th. Ribot).

5. Still less appropriate is the use of the term for the concretely given whole of capacities and inclinations which characterizes an individual or class with respect to affective life and will and distinguishes it from others (K. Schneider's psychopathic personality). The aspect of self-determination, which is clearly present in the concept of person, has disappeared almost completely in this usage of the term.

Man, however, is only a finite person. He is not absolute freedom, but merely possesses the power for actions which are distinct from his essence and flow from it as from a free nature that nevertheless is a nature. He is determined in many ways; his freedom consists in giving meaning to these determinations.[27] Man is an embodied person, a spiritual being which is essentially material, a transcendental directedness to the *being* of beings *from* a definite situation in the spatio-temporal world.

The Embodied Person as Subject of Morality. Only the person is a subject of morality, but not the person as person—for freedom as freedom is its own norm—but the finite and embodied person. For the acts of such a person are not wholly autonomous, but normalized by the necessary purpose of his nature. Although this nature is essentially one, it is complex in its aspects, as appears when we consider the many powers emanating from it. This nature is spiritual and as such directed to the all-embracing *being* of beings, but it is also sensitive, vegetative, and material and therefore limited and determined. Accordingly, the norms will refer to the *hierarchy* of the various powers and their acts, they will prescribe that the "natural" order of values be maintained in the free acts. In other words, they will order the person to behave in accord with his personal dignity, i.e., as a rational being, in every situation in which he finds himself through his complex nature.

For the material, vegetative, and sensitive powers and inclinations emanate from nature as material dispositions for the spiritual, but the spiritual powers are the formal and final causes of the material. Therefore, man's natural inclinations, as a subsistent being to self-preservation, as a living being to nutrition, growth, and reproduction, as a sensitive being to sense pleasure and the avoidance or conquest of whatever is an obstacle, must be kept in order by reason and raised to being instruments and concrete expressions of the universal good of man as a spiritual person. They are the "matter" of moral virtues,[28] as they are also the "matter" of freedom.[29]

The moral process of becoming man, of becoming "what one is," is a process of order, of mutual compenetration and integration of the various aspects of being-man. It is a spiritualization of the corporeal or also an embodiment of the spiritual.

---

[27]Cf. no. 144.
[28]Cf. no. 157.
[29]Cf. no. 144.

154. *Man as a Person is Naturally Social*

The Meaning of "Social." Every finite subsistent being by virtue of its essence, properties, activities and passivities, refers to all other beings by relations of agreement and difference, of exercising influence and being influenced.[30] This being-together of beings expresses itself more particularly in the dealings which living beings, and especially sensitive beings, have with their surroundings.[31]

However, just as man because of his spiritual nature is subsistent in an eminent way, so also has he an eminent relationship to the other beings through his intellectual powers of understanding and loving—in a kind of immanence he "is in a way everything."

Above all other relationships which man as a person has naturally, we must place his relations to fellow men who, like him, through their spiritual nature are free persons. Before the level of man is reached, relations are not relations in the full sense. Insofar as man by his very nature is directed to such interhuman relations, we speak of his social nature—the term "social" being derived from the Latin *socius,* companion.

In a degraded sense of "social" one could attribute a certain social instinct to animals insofar as some animals for their self-realization need to live together with others of their species, to which they owe their lives or with which they band together for a shorter or longer time to secure food, security, or reproduction.

Man, who is less self-sufficient than animals,[32] depends more and longer on others of his species. The utilization of the world through technique, labor, and economy is at once collaboration with fellow human beings, and in this collaboration the useful result is increased through specialization and commerce. Although higher cultural life, as it manifests itself in beauty, art, and science, is a matter of eminently personal activity, it too is no less essentially a social affair which runs its course in the interchange of spiritual goods. Language, which alongside the hand and tools is the instrument *par excellence* of human activity, and which because of its signifying function is indispensable for the development of the person even in his most personal thought,[33] is accepted from the forebears, modified, and transmitted to the descendants. Thus from his very birth man lives

---

[30]Cf. no. 163.
[31]Cf. no. 115.
[32]Cf. no. 146.
[33]Cf. no. 133.

in a world that is already shaped and named by human beings, he lives in a cultural milieu that is essentially social.

Personal Social Relationships. Man, however, does not only *need* fellow human beings in order to search his own natural good. The proper and primary sense of the social nature of man *as a person* is that man is related to the others *as persons,* as subsistent beings whose self-realization is a purpose in itself and who may not be used by others as *pure* means. Man is naturally orientated to *personal* relationships.

Persons possess a closed subsistence but, precisely because of this, also universal openness: through knowledge they are related to the other in his individual originality without losing themselves. "True" knowledge of fellow men begins by acknowledging that they are persons. It is only when they have been recognized as such that affirmative or negative affective attitudes follow, such as to esteem or despise, to love or to hate, to seek or to flee, to hope or to fear, to bear with or to be angry, to envy or not to envy.[34]

These intellectual and affective attitudes are the foundation of *social acts* in which human beings reciprocally meet and speak to one another about other beings or about themselves in the indicative, optative, or imperative moods, questioning and replying, warning and exhorting, requesting and counseling, begging and commanding, obeying and resisting.

In this social intercourse persons can manifest the sentiments which they have for one another. They are capable of responding to these sentiments in reciprocal affective acts, all of which imply either something of hatred or something of love.[35] When there is mutually expressed affectionateness, a personal bond arises, which can vary from an initial rather general benevolence through all levels of friendship to strictly personal love.

On the basis of social acts and actual affective expressions there may arise more permanent relationships of one human being *to* another, and if they are reciprocated, also permanent relationships

---

[34]Cf. no. 138.

[35]Cf. J. van Boxtel, *Herstel der liefde in de sociale wijsbegeerte,* Nijmegen, 1948. Concerning the distinction between affective attitudes, social acts, personal bonds, permanent relations, societies, etc., see D. von Hildebrand, *Metaphysik der Gemeinschaft,* Augsburg, 1955. See also A. Oldendorff, *De psychologie van het sociale leven,* Utrecht, 1953; Chr. Barendse, "Intersubjectief verkeer en lichamelijkheid," *Lichamelijkheid,* Utrecht, 1951, pp. 85-119.

between human beings. In some cases the subjects of these relationships have been given special names; for instance, we speak of man
and wife, relatives, friends, colleagues, parents, and children, teacher
and pupil.[36]

Moral Social Obligation. The first moral duty flowing from man's
social nature as a person is the recognition that every other human
being, no matter who he is, is a fellow man, an "other ego," an
intellectual and moral person, at least in capacity and vocation.

This recognition, which implies a certain initial benevolence, has
to be maintained and developed in our dealings with our fellow men.
It is the foundation of all social virtues, and first of all of justice.[37]
The explicitation of this initial benevolence in friendship and love
for some human beings with whom we find ourselves connected by
special bonds or with whom we freely bind ourselves is the crown
and the purpose of the social virtues.

Seen in this light, the self-realization of a being whose mode of
being is a being-together implies a certain loving dedication to others.
For this reason the concrete norms of morality do not explicitly speak
of self-love, but of our relationship to fellow human beings. It is only
through the practice of faith,[38] hope and charity[39] toward the others,
as determined by the bond flowing from the spatio-temporal situation
which we have accepted or freely chosen, that man becomes what he
should be—more himself by means of a more intimate participation
in the mode of *being* of the others.

What has been *ontically* stated regarding the tendency of every
being to *self-realization* through activity[40] is, therefore, ethically understood in a more profound sense for man as a person when we say:
"A finite personal being becomes more himself according as he enters
more in true *communication* with others, by including the true well-
being of fellow persons in his own well-being and taking care of it
in the same way." Thus we understand better that subsistence and
relativety do not exclude but rather include each other.[41]

---

[36]In their social acts men influence one another *as persons*. There is question here of a special and eminent form of efficient causality (cf. no. 102),
which is closely connected with final exemplary causality: it proposes to the
other's freedom a purpose to be attained, and moves him by means of motives
freely accepted by him (cf. no. 144). This kind of causality is exemplified
by human authority, for such authority is not an external compulsion.
[37]Cf. no. 159.
[38]Cf. no. 132.
[39]Cf. no. 139.
[40]Cf. no. 63.
[41]Cf. no. 164.

Person and Society. The fact that man as a person is by nature social has still another meaning—namely, that he is essentially connected with societies, which transcend the individual. The habitual relationships between human beings under certain conditions give rise to objective wholes, each of which presents itself as if it were one being. Relations exist *between* persons, and a society *contains* persons, as its members. By means of analogy with individual persons, the society is the subject of activities, attitudes, and relations. It presents itself, therefore, as an ordered unity of persons,[42] having a quasi-substantial essence and existence, quasi-proper powers, acts and activities.

The question must be raised whether man's being-a-person does not exclude that he can be a means for something else, so that he cannot be a non-subsistent part of a greater subsistent whole. Is his being-a-person not in contradiction with his membership in a society?

The reply is in the negative if one does not conceive the unity of a society as the absolute unity of a single subsistent being, but as the relative unity of many subsistent beings. Although in language and concept we attribute a quasi-subsistence to a society of persons, when we investigate the conditions under which such a quasi-subsistence is possible, we find that the many individual persons are considered precisely insofar as they are together and collaborate in orderly fashion to one and the same purpose. Thus not the society itself is the ultimate subject of powers and acts, but the persons composing it in their mutual relations. If, then, we substantialize society in speech, we merely use a concise form of expression to indicate the many ultimate subjects insofar as their thinking, willing, and acting run their course in connection with the thinking, willing, and acting of the others. The personal pronoun "we" indicates each "I" in its polar reference to the other "I's". The society, therefore, is nowhere else really present than in each of the persons and as a network of relations. However, it is present in each of the members in a different way, according to the place which this member occupies as one of the many poles or terms of the network.

Natural and Free Societies. Two fundamental kinds of society may be distinguished, although concrete societies will usually have something of both types.

---

[42]Concerning society as a "moral" unity of order, see Angelinus, *Wijsgerige gemeenschapsleer,* Nijmegen, 1949, pp. 55-87; F. Tellegen, *De Gemeenschap,* I-II, Roermond, n. d.

First of all, the social relations themselves may be essential for the self-realization of the person. In such a case living-together is sought for its own sake, precisely as living-together, as social communication and mutual enrichment. The purpose of such a society of *life* coincides with the very purpose of each person taken separately. The society aims at making each person attain his natural good in active and passive communication with his fellow men.

Secondly, social relationships may be directed to the attainment of a purpose which for each of the members is a "means" to his personal self-realization. In the production and distribution of these useful means a norm is imposed by the harmony of mutual interests and by the requirements of the *utilitarian* society itself as a quasi-subsistent being, directed to self-preservation and self-development. The production of the useful goods has to be regulated by mutual consent, which is arrived at either in consultation with the interested parties or by following the directives of a few bearers of authority. The possession also of these goods must be divided according to the merits and needs of the members. This coordination limits the individual in his freedom both to produce such goods and to appropriate what is produced or discovered.

By nature man is a member of the all-embracing society of human beings. This society, however, is too vast to act as a unit; the rights which it confers and the duties which it imposes are no others than the above-mentioned moral relations of man to man. The membership of this all-embracing society, therefore, has its intermediary in the membership of societies with smaller numbers, which as particular centers of relations can present themselves to other persons and other societies.

By nature man holds membership in the limited society of the family in which he is born and raised and the nation to which he belongs through descent, language and customs. To reach its welfare, the family needs to live in a broader organization, so that in this sense the family is not a "perfect" society. Hence we may say that man is by his very nature directed also to "civic" societies, such as the village, city, region, state, federation, and commonwealth, which contain more members and therefore make it possible to arrive at greater specialization and a broader satisfaction of needs. However, such societies are less naturally given with human nature itself than are family and nation in this sense that their limits and organizations depend more on the free will of the members, as this will manifests itself in human history. The first, but not the only, task of a civic society is to create a positive order of law.

Finally, marriage is also a natural society in a very fundamental sense. For its essence and purpose lie anchored in the very nature of human beings as man and woman. On the other hand, contrary to the society of the family at least insofar as the children are concerned, every individual marriage bond depends for its origin on the free self-determination of the partners.

Alongside the natural societies, there are also free societies, such as union, associations, groups, parties, fraternities, etc. While the purpose of the natural societies is determined by human nature itself, that of free organizations is established by positive human decisions. Although it is true that the rise of free societies is in line with man's social nature, nevertheless, the concrete individual free organizations arise only through being freely established by man. The entrance also in an existing free organization is an act of self-determination.

155. *Man as a Person is Naturally Historical*

Conscience and Man's Temporal Dispersion. As a spiritual nature, human nature is the same in all men, insofar as all human natures by virtue of their reason are directed to truth, goodness and beauty. But human nature is different in each one, insofar as each views the same absolute from a different perspective. The particular standpoint in question is determined by each one's individual essence as the original mode in which he is man.

Because man, as a spirit-in-matter, is the transition between individuation through form and individuation through matter,[43] each one's spiritual nature cannot be understood without its relation to the corporeal and individual. It is only from his "situation," conditioned by place and time in the material world, from sense experience, sense feelings and sensitive desires, that man comes to intellectual acts.

Thus each man's individual nature is a limited participation in unqualified being-man. Nevertheless, each one is called to realize the ideal of being-man in his own original way.

Man cannot obtain knowledge of his individual destiny by a simple deduction from the general moral norms contained in synderesis.[44] Likewise, this destiny is not known to him through a clear and perma-

---

[43]Cf. no. 90.
[44]Cf. no. 152.

nent intuition of his individual nature and its capacities. For he is a
temporal being which developes in a process of becoming. His life
is dispersed through the ages of youth, adulthood and decline. Even
his freedom is temporalized, it is not always capable of everything,
but only of one thing after another. Man arrives at self-knowledge
through reflection on his particular acts, but his individual nature
reveals itself only in changing conditions. Thus the demands of this
nature are not always equally strong or concerned with the same
object.

The *judgment of conscience* which expresses what is demanded of
man here and now and which is the norm of the individual action
has to take into consideration man's present situation.

All this, however, does not mean that the judgment of conscience
is not guided by the general and absolute norms of synderesis. On
the contrary, for, temporal as he is, by means of memory and expectation and especially through his intellectual knowledge, man knows
about his temporality. In this way it is possible for him to reduce the
dispersion of his life to a certain unity. He is capable of accepting
the past deliberately and of giving it a meaning freely by means of
his decisions about the future. This unification of past and future
takes place when man, reflecting on the past, discovers his supra-
temporal spiritual nature as transcending the changing acts and in
the light of this discovery judges the present situation.

Man's Historical Character. We do not use the term "historical"
with respect to every being that is in time or for every event. A
being is correctly spoken of as "historical" if to some extent it is
capable of comprehending its temporal becoming as a unity and, consequently, able to orientate this becoming from the standpoint of supra-
temporal and absolute purposes and norms. An event is spoken of as
historical if it is a free act pertaining to such a being which realizes
itself in time and nevertheless transcends time.

Man, therefore, is naturally historical, for his individual spiritual
nature, on the one hand, is normalized by what is true, good, and
beautiful in itself,[45] but on the other, it has to unfold this orientation
to the absolute in a plurality of successive, individual acts which occur
in changing situations.[46]

---

[45]What is true, good, and beautiful in itself, as such has neither past nor
future but is simply actual and present (cf. no. 75).

[46]Cf. no. 72.

Especially man's life as a social being is historical. Even societies and communities which are quasi-subsistent, pass through a period of evolution, and in this process their quasi-self-knowledge, their judgments about their own essence, purpose, and means, is not always equally perfect. It is within such societies having a common mentality or "spirit" that the life-story of the individual person unrolls. The judgment of his conscience regarding what his own individual nature demands of him here and now will have to take into account also the place he occupies in the historical development of the different societies of which he is a member.

Man, then, cannot simply derive the norm of conscience from the norms of general human nature. He needs the experience of his historical course of life, both as individual and as member of society, to discover what his supra-temporal individual nature demands of him at every moment. The passage from the general to the particular is made by means of prudence,[47] which implies an evaluation of the situation in the light and under the impulse of the first moral principles.

However, it would be erroneous to think that the judgments of conscience can come into conflict with the absolute general norms. On the contrary, the conclusions of prudence are implicitly contained in the general norms. It is only because of our imperfect knowledge of human nature and its orientation to its purpose that we are not simply capable of intuitively surveying the consequences which the principles contain under certain conditions and have to make use of a process of prudent reasoning. This reasoning process, however, is led by the general norms, and only in the estimations of prudence does the fullness contained in the absolute norms reveal itself. We may even say that the more the general norms assume a concrete shape in virtues, in the life of sentiments and will itself, the more man will more or less intuitively discover the particular in the general and, "connaturally" in tune with the norm, "feel" what his individual nature demands of him as man here and now. The virtuous man finds in his ordered inclination itself the rational norm of the individual acts to be done in changing time.

156. *Man as a Person Has an Eternal Destiny*

Man Transcends the Temporal. Man is an historical being because, despite his temporal character, he transcends this temporality to some extent through his spiritual nature, which is directed to the

---

[47]Cf. no. 158.

atemporal, the ever-actual and ever-present, the "to be" of beings. Although every temporal dispersion in past and future must be conceived as a kind of participation in absolute presence or eternity,[48] man participates in eternity in a much higher way than subhuman material beings. What is meant by this higher mode of participating in eternity?[49]

Man is born and dies. His course of life is encompassed by a time in which he did not yet live and in which he will no longer live as this material person among the material beings of this world. As this spiritual person, however, he transcends all moments of time to some extent, for *all* temporal beings, no matter when they were or will be, somehow fall within the perspective of his all-embracing openness as a spirit. But if this is so, his "to be" also, insofar as it is spiritual, must escape the corruptibility of everything temporal.

Man's Nature and Immortality. It is possible for philosophical reflection to render the statement acceptable that man's general desire for immortality is based on, and arises from human nature itself. In such a reflection we must keep in mind that man's essence is constituted by a spiritual principle, which as "soul" is the first form of the body, and by prime matter.[50] The spiritual soul, however, *as* spiritual, is a subsistent form and, as such, is raised above the limitation to the here-and-now of place and time. This subsistent form is not intrinsically dependent on the body in its "to be," although it communicates its "to be" to this body in substantial unity. Therefore, although man's death means the cessation of the formal actuating influence which the spiritual soul exercises as soul of the organic body, it does not mean that the spiritual soul ceases to be precisely insofar as it is a subsistent form. Moreover, it is unthinkable that the spiritual soul itself would "die." As a subsistent form, it does not have any capacity for essential change, for becoming something else, because such a possibility arises only from a being's composition of matter and form.[51]

Different Forms of Duration. As soon as one admits that man has a spiritual soul, he has to admit also that this spiritual soul has a higher mode of duration than the temporality implied by corruptibility.

---

[48]Cf. no. 75.

[49]Concerning immortality, see A. Marc, *Psychologie réflexive,* vol. 2, pp. 311-342.

[50]Cf. no. 153.

[51]Cf. no. 88.

However, it is not possible for us to seize and express in adequate concepts the soul's supra-temporality as a higher participation in absolute presence or eternity. We say that with respect to his spiritual soul man has a supra-temporal destination and that, as far as this spiritual soul is concerned, "after" death man "continues to exist" in an "eternal life." But we should beware of conceiving this immortality as an "existence without end" in the *same* temporal process which characterizes material beings and man himself in his bodily *being*. The "after-existence" and "persistence" should not be conceived as a *longer* but as a *higher* form of "duration," as a self-presence which is not divided by temporal dispersion.

As far as the positive content of this eternal life is concerned and the question of how man in his spiritual soul can live a life of knowing and loving without actually turning to sense experience, imagination, and sensitive tendencies, we are faced with a philosophical "mystery" which our thought simply has to accept but cannot of itself fathom.[52]

On the other hand, we are able to assert that the way in which man on his temporal road to self-realization makes his free moral acts harmonize or disharmonize with the integral purpose of his integral nature is decisive for the question whether or not he will attain his supra-temporal destiny and his ultimate happiness.[53]

157. *Corollary: the Moral Virtues*

In the preceding pages we have laid the metaphysical foundation of ethics. Ethics is the science of moral ideals and norms. It should not be confused with the practical reason of every man, who for himself explicitates the all-embracing norm of the good by reflecting on his natural inclinations in connection with his concrete situation. Ethics is the science of moral praxis, but not this praxis itself.[54] Its task is to investigate in a general way the progressive process of

---

[52]Cf. no. 42.

[53]Some philosophers have thought that the spiritual soul, as a subsistent form, pre-exists prior to its formal influence on the human body and that for some reason or other, e.g., to expiate a fault, it is united with the body. Such a pre-existence, however, is not acceptable, once it is admitted that soul and body constitute a substantial unity and that the spiritual soul is *essentially* the soul of a body and therefore related to prime matter. For the individuation of such a soul would not be intelligible without the relationship to the corporeal.

When the unity of the spiritual soul and the body is thus strongly emphasized, it has to be admitted that the spiritual soul, even when "after" the death of the body it "continues to exist,'" retains a certain bond with the bodily temporal life to which it owes its individuation.

[54]Cf. no. 149.

concretization of ideals and norms. Thus ethics will discover how each of man's natural inclinations demands to be rationally ordered, and how this order gives rise to a hierarchical whole of interrelated and mutually compenetrating moral attitudes which perfect the person in his self-determination through the free act of communication. This critically justified general knowledge which ethics supplies with respect to ideal moral attitudes and their mutual connection will be of importance for prudence in directing praxis itself.

We will add here a very concise survey of the ideal moral attitudes derived from the natural inclinations of man, as they have been synthesized by Thomas Aquinas.[55]

The morally good man does not merely do actual deeds that are morally good because they are directed to the true purpose of man's self-perfection. His permanent or habitual mode of *being*, his attitude, is permeated with moral good. This permanent disposition, which becomes, as it were, a second nature and implies an ever-increasing ability and ease to act spontaneously in a morally good way, is called a "virtue."[56] Virtue may be a gift which a person has received together with his individual nature for his course of life, but it can also have been acquired through previous moral decisions, especially at the cross-roads of life.

Four main or cardinal virtues are distinguished—prudence, justice, fortitude, and temperance. These virtues may be considered in three ways:

1. As four fundamental aspects of every morally good disposition.

2. As the four great realms of moral life in connection with the four fundamental inclinations and powers of rational knowing and willing, of the tendencies to utilize and to enjoy.

3. As special virtues occupying a central position in each of the four realms. Moral life "hinges" on them—whence they are called *cardinal* virtues, (the Latin *cardo* means hinge).

158. *Prudence*

Prudence, which may be called also caution or circumspection, is defined as the right norm of moral action (*recta ratio agibilium*)[57]

---

[55]St. Thomas' treatise of the virtues fills almost the whole II-II of his *Summa theol.* The moral virtues are spoken of in qq. 47-170.
[56]Cf. no. 94.
[57]Cf. no. 94.

or as the perfection of practical reason by virtue of which this reason arranges the realization of the means fittingly with respect to the purposes of life. These descriptions show the importance of prudence: not a single morally good act is accomplished without prudence.[58] Prudence induces us, prior to the doing of an act, to consider means and purpose in the light of the general moral norm, next to evaluate the means to be used here and now, and finally to command the appetitive powers to direct themselves to this means.[59]

Prudence may be divided into personal prudence, which aims at the individual's personal life, and prudence of government, which is concerned with the ruling of a society and subdivided according to the nature of this society.

Prudence, which occupies the right "mean" of reason, is infringed upon by excess or defect. Too little counsel is present in haste, thoughtlessness, nonchalance; too much in slyness, cunning, craftiness and over-concern.

159. *Justice*

Justice is defined as the permanent and stable will to give each one his due. The first object of justice is what rightfully belongs to the other, the "right" of the other.[60]

General or legal justice induces the rulers and subjects of a society to give this society its due. Particular justice leads to giving individuals and groups what is due to them. It is divided into distributive and commutative justice.

Distributive justice induces the rulers of a society to divide the available goods according to the merits and needs of the subjects. Its opposite is the rulers' undue respect of persons. Commutative justice leads individual persons or groups to give to others their strict dues. It is against commutative justice to steal, not to return what has been borrowed, to harm another's good name, and to judge them rashly.

In certain relationships it is not possible to render fully and in equal values to the other what is owed to him. Thus we speak of

---

[58]Cf. no. 155.

[59]Cf. no. 141.

[60]If something belongs to a man on the basis of the general and immutable nature of man, we speak of a natural right. If, however, man's relationship to certain objects varies according to the particular situation, society will determine through agreement, custom, or law what pertains to a particular person. In such a case we have to do with purely positive right.

the virtue of religion, through which we render to God what we owe Him in the form of external and internal worship: adoration, sacrifice, prayer, and dedication. Through filial piety we give to parents and country what we owe to them. Reverence induces us to bestow due honor on persons who are to be respected. With respect to persons holding authority over us, reverence becomes obedience to their commands.

The above-mentioned virtues are due to the other in the strict sense. If justice is taken more broadly, it extends also to virtues aiming at that which it behooves man to perform. Thus, for instance, gratefulness is generally considered an attitude owed to a benefactor; cruelty and over-indulgence are blameworthy, although in certain cases it may be fitting to aim at the authoritative punishment of an evil-doer—the so-called virtue of vindicativeness (not to be confused with vindictiveness). Veracity, which is based on simplicity, i.e., not wanting to appear to others differently from what one is internally, manifests itself, for instance, in the fulfillment of promises. Veracity is due to the others because, just as we ourselves, the other does not have an explicit intuitive knowledge of persons with whom he associates and, therefore, has to depend on the exteriorization of their interiority, on their word.[61] Defects against the virtue of veracity are, on the one hand, lying and hypocrisy and, on the other, indiscretion and the violation of secrets. Liberality is the equable mean between wastefulness and avarice. Benevolence is due to fellow men because, as affective beings, men are related to one another.[62]

160. *Fortitude*

Fortitude is defined as the virtue through which man tend to what reason sees as good, despite all sentiments that would make him turn away from the good. Fortitude manifests itself in the twofold form of attack and forebearance: one has to be strong in patiently enduring difficulties while shutting out fear, and in courageously attacking difficulties while moderating audacity. Fortitude lies mainly midway between fear or cowardice and rashness. Because fear and courage

---

[61] Cf. no. 132.

[62] Friendship in the strict sense is not "due" to the other and, therefore, is not called a moral virtue. Yet friendship is the more praiseworthy, the more it is based on communication in the moral life. Relations which are based mainly on reciprocal usefulness or enjoyment are only in an improper sense friendship.

are the proper subject matter of fortitude, this virtue is the proper perfection of the tendencies to utilize and to resist.[63]

Through the first-named aspect (to attack), fortitude is related to magnanimity. This virtue stands midway between conceit, ambition, and vain glory on the one hand, and pusillanimity on the other.

In reference to the second aspect (forbearance), we may name patience, steadfastness or perseverance. The opposite poles of these virtues are, on the one hand, impatience, softness, and flightiness and, on the other, impassiveness, obstinacy, and stubbornness.

161. *Temperance*

Temperance is defined as the virtue which moderates the tendency to pleasure according to the rules of right reason. Because this tendency is directed to the well-being of both the individual and the species, temperance has a distinct aspect with respect to both.

Temperance with respect to the well-being of the individual is directed to the right use of food and drink. It is more specifically called sobriety. It is violated through gluttony and dipsomania.

Temperance, viewed as the order of actions aiming at the well-being of the species, is called chastity insofar as the sexual act itself is concerned, and modesty insofar as it aims at what is more remotely connected with this act. The excesses against it are called unchastity and immodesty.

Just as justice contains a group of virtues which are due only in a broader sense, so also temperance contains a number of virtues which are only in a wider sense perfections of the tendency to pleasure. Thus, for instance, studiousness is the equable mean between curiosity and indifference to knowledge, humility the mean between pride, haughtiness and vanity on the one hand, and abjectness on the other; gentleness the mean between irascibleness and phlegmatic indifference; urbanity the means between affection and unmannerliness.

---

[63] Cf. no. 137.

CHAPTER TWENTY-EIGHT

THE INTERCONNECTION OF BEINGS

162. *Introduction*[1]

Modes of Being. The first meaning of real being is subsistent being.[2] There are many finite subsistent beings, but they are not all subsistent in one and the same sense. Hence there is analogy of subsistence. The person as person is subsistent in the most perfect sense, but sensitive, vegetative, and material beings are subsistent only in a degraded sense.[3]

Although the finite subsistent being is subsistent, its further perfection depends on the bearing of accidental determinations—it is a substance.[4] These determinations are either logically necessary or logically accidental.[5] The former are properties which flow of necessity from the essence, the latter are variable characteristics which further perfect the being. The attribution of these characteristics to the subsistent being is made according to accidental categories or predicaments.

The accidental categories are all connected with activity and passivity.[6] Those mentioned specifically thus far are the following:

1. Transient action and the undergoing of this action, so-called action and "passion." They coincide with the change of place, quality,

---

[1]The explanations of relationships presented in this chapter depend largely on the excellent study of A. Krempel, *La doctrine de la relation chez. S. Thomas,* Paris, 1952. This book surveys nearly all of St. Thomas' statements regarding relations and offers a very original synthesis. Its main purpose is to show that the so-called "transcendental relation," which Cajetan definitely introduced into Thomism, was not a real relation for St. Thomas himself but only a logical relation with a foundation in reality, a "necessary logical relation," as Krempel expresses it. In this point the author goes counter to the general tendency of neo-Thomism, which wants to explain the potency-act structures through the theory of transcendental relationship. In this central issue the study of the author seems to lack sufficient clarity and distinction, for he would have to deny the "real" distinction of essence and "to be," of matter and form, and of power and activity. Nevertheless, it seems possible to us to make use of his penetrating critique, not to reject the transcendental relation, but to acquire a more profound understanding of its ontological value.

[2]Cf. no. 65.
[3]Cf. nos. 91, 112, 116, 153.
[4]Cf. no. 67.
[5]Cf. no. 69.
[6]Cf. no. 71.

or essence, considered in its twofold relationship to the changer or agent and the changed or "patient."[7]

2. Immanent action. Although vegetative operations of life foreshadow them, immanent actions appear in the proper sense only in knowing, loving, striving, and willing. Immanent operation pertains to the category of quality.[8]

3. Active potency. It, too, is a quality, as are also the abilities and skills which perfect it.[9]

4. Quantity, which is proper to corporeal beings. It gives rise to the categories of "where" and "when" as denominations of place and time.[10]

Relation. We still have to treat relation. The fact that it has not yet been explicitly spoken of, does not mean that there was not constantly question of all kinds of relations. On the contrary, the *leitmotiv* running through the whole treatise and connecting all its parts has been that the finite and material subsistent being is essentially relative, as may appear from this brief enumeration:

1. A finite being is perfectible because its mode of *being* is not the absolute negation of the *being* of others, but is together with them, and this being-together has to be explicitated through communication, active and passive participation.[11]

2. Individual man especially, as a person, is essentially related to his fellow-men as persons in all kinds of societies.[12]

3. It is for the sake of self-realization in communication with the others that powers emanate from the essence, and these powers also are dynamically related to activities which, in their turn, are so related to their objects.[13]

4. Being as being is true as the terminus of the cognitive relation, and good as the terminus of love and striving.[14]

[7]Cf. nos. 80, 91.
[8]Cf. nos. 93, 111, 122, 145.
[9]Cf. no. 94.
[10]Cf. no. 78 f.
[11]Cf. no. 63.
[12]Cf. no. 154.
[13]Cf. nos. 93-95.
[14]Cf. nos. 42-44.

5. The mutable is temporal, but the relations between past, present, and future states, as well as the complete *being* of the temporal and mutable are fully actual only in a perceiver who remembers and expects.[15]

6. Finally, within the finite being itself, the essence is related to "to be", matter to form, accidents to the substance, and in general potency to act.[16]

In the following pages, however, the question of relation, reference, or proportion must be explicitly considered. Relation is the last, and in a sense the weakest, addition received as a perfection by a being. It does not even change the being in itself. Nevertheless, it pertains to this being, and we may even say that our knowledge of the being is brought to perfection only through the consideration of its relationships. For it is only in its interconnection with all others that a being is what it is and attains to its meaning and purpose.

The interrelations of beings call forth two fundamental questions that are decisive for metaphysics. The first is: If every subsistent being is itself, does not this identity or absoluteness exclude relationship to other beings? And reversely, if all beings are essentially related to one another in a static order and especially in a dynamic order, are they still subsistent? The second question is: With respect to the whole of finite beings which are mutually related in an order of interconnection, must we say that this whole, taken as a whole, *is* absolutely in the full sense of the term? Or is this whole likewise only a relative whole, related to an absolutely transcendent ground of *being*?[17]

163. *The Structure of Relation*

Nature of the Relation. Relation is an original category and cannot be properly defined. However, it can be clarified by means of the opposition of the relative, as the not self-sufficient and conditional, to the non-relative, as self-sufficient, unconditional or absolute. Absolute in the strictest sense is that which is not only *in itself* but also *of itself* and does not need an extrinsic ground of *being*—it is independent in its subsistence. Absolute in a diminished sense is that which is *in itself* but not ultimately *of* itself—the dependent subsistent

---

[15]Cf. nos. 75, 79.
[16]Cf. nos. 97-101.
[17]Cf. no. 172.

being.[18] Absolute in a still more degraded sense are accidental determinations which, although they are related to the subsistent as something "of" and "in" this being, further enrich the content of the subsistent being *in itself;* for instance, powers and activities.

On the other hand, the relative, as such, is a being not insofar as it is in any definite way *in itself,* but insofar as it precisely refers to something else. Relation, taken in the formal-abstract sense, is nothing else than *esse ad,* to be in reference to something else. Relation as relation, therefore, does not add any further determination of content to a being in itself. For this reason language usually expresses relations through grammatical cases (except the nominative), prepositions, and conjunctions. If, however, relations are to become subject of judgments in science or philosophy, they have to be expressed as being in themselves, through abstract or concrete nouns, such as resemblance, difference, simultaneity, friendship, double, half, father, son, teacher and pupil.

A relation cannot be *in* itself. It essentially includes the beings that are related and is always a relationship of something to something. The relatives are the two terms between which the relation is and on whose nature it is wholly dependent. Ultimately the principle and terminus of a relation are distinct subsistent beings or at least beings conceived as distinct and subsistent. In addition, the principle or subject of the relation must have a foundation or reason why it is related to the other being. In the term of the relation there must be a characteristic corresponding to the foundation present in the principle.

The Two Foundations of Relationship.[18a] According to the difference in foundation and term all kinds of distinct relations are possible. However, all relations can be reduced to two groups because the foundation of the relation, considered formally as foundation, can be twofold.

The first formal foundation is sometimes called *quantity.* But this term should not be understood as referring merely to the category of bodily extension (size and number), but in a much broader and transcendental sense as the *measure* of absolute perfection of a being in the order of *being.* Thus all absolute categories fall under this term,

---

[18]Cf. no. 65.
[18a]Cf. Aristotle, *Metaphysica,* bk. V, ch. 15 and St. Thomas *Commentary,* nos. 1001-1032. See also the clear discussion of Krempel, *op. cit.* pp. 195-243.

whether they be the substantial essence, quantity in the strict sense, or qualities.

On the basis of their quantity of *being* beings are related to one another according to the agreement or difference of their content. These static relations arrange related beings either in the same rank or in higher or lower ranks. Static relations resulting in the same rank are given the same name, regardless of the term from which they are viewed. They are reducible to relations of identity and equality. Identity is the agreement of a being, or of a determination of *being* conceived as a being, with itself. Equality is the agreement of two beings in genus or species, in sizes or number, or in qualities. Static relations giving a lower or a higher rank do not express unity or agreement but plurality or difference. They are relationships of inequality; for instance, half or double, tall or short, broad or narrow, high or low, quick or slow, early or late. Similarity belongs to these kinds of relations insofar as it expresses not perfect qualitative agreement but only a more or less intense approximation. Accordingly, the "analogy" of beings essentially implies dissimilarity as well as subordination and superiority.[19]

The second formal foundation is sometimes called *activity and passivity*. However, these terms should be understood in the broadest sense, so that all mutual conditioning of beings is comprised in them, i.e., all modes of giving rise to, influencing, moving, changing, and causing. This foundation is present whenever a being "makes" another being "be" in any way whatsoever. Contrary to the relationships based on quantity of *being,* the present relations are dynamic. Among them we must enumerate also the relationships of powers to activities and of activities to their objects.

All relations of dependence are essentially of a hierarchical order. Their terms have opposite names; for instance, foundation and superstructure, premises and conclusion, mover and moved, cause and effect, father and son, master and servant, teacher and pupil.

All dynamic relations imply also static relationships of agreement and difference between cause and effect if they are considered precisely with respect to their content or determination of *being*. In univocal causality the terms have a univocal agreement or at least an approximation with respect to a univocal determination of being.[20] In analogous or higher causes, on the other hand, the perfection is

[19]Cf. no. 56.
[20]Cf. no. 107.

realized in a superior way, but possessed by the effect only in an inferior, more particular and imperfect way—the cause *is* by its essence what the effect *has* through participation.

Reciprocity. It is a property of relation that the reference of the principle to the terminus always implies also a reference of this terminus to the principle. We cannot conceive relation in a non-reciprocal way, but the question whether or not this reciprocity is always really present will be examined later.

Reciprocity implies, first of all, that the related beings, as related, are always together and are known and understood together in their reciprocity—relation is a mode of being-one. Secondly, reciprocity implies that the related beings are always to some extent opposed to each other. However, relative opposition is the weakest of the four types of opposition and comes closest to identity.[21]

A Problem. A relation cannot be caused directly, but flows from the modifications occurring in the principle and terminus. It is the mode of *being* which is farthest removed from being-subsistent, from being really *in*-itself. For with respect to its *content,* it implies nothing but a "to be to something else," and, with respect to its *being,* it raises the question whether a relation is a real mode of *being* because it does not add anything to the content of a being. Must we say perhaps that relation is only something pertaining to intellectual comparison?

164. *Real Relations*

Epistemological Positions. To understand means to see interconnection, to connect the many in a unity by means of an all-embracing glance. Thus relation belongs *par excellence* to the domain of the mind. Man's spirit does not rest until he has made everything be-together in a single whole devoid of any contradiction.

For this reason absolute idealism says: to be related or relation is the "to be" itself of beings; but relation is something of the mind; therefore, "to be" is nothing but to be thought.[22]

The absolute realism of ideas, on the other hand, argues exactly in the opposite way: being, as it is thought by man, agrees fully with being, as it is in itself; therefore, whenever we conceive

---

[21]Cf. no. 38.
[22]Cf. no. 24.

necessary relations between beings, these relations are an immediate and adequate representation of real relations.[23]

The epistemological problem reveals itself in an urgent form in the problem of relation, precisely because the concept of relation does not necessarily include that it is a possible or real ontological determination of beings. For of itself the relation does not add any new determination of content to being taken in itself; hence it seems to be not something intrinsic but something extrinsic to the being. For this reason the empirical conceptualism of Occam,[24] which accepts the reality of beings, does not attribute to relation any reality outside the absolute characteristics of beings and recognizes only relative names or concepts. For the same reason the idealistic conceptualism of Kant[25] attributes to the relation a central position in our knowledge, but conceives relation as an *a priori* concept of our thinking, through which we arrange the data of experience in an orderly fashion.

In this matter especially, moderate or critical realism of concepts which implies a certain amount of conceptualism,[26] shows its strength by carefully distinguishing between, on the one hand, the mode according to which a being is in itself, which is only imperfectly understood in our concepts, and, on the other, the mode according to which we understand and signify this being—the *modus essendi* (the mode of *being*) does not wholly coincide with the *modus intelligendi* and the *modus significandi* (the mode of understanding and the mode of signifying). Through the mode of our understanding there arise respects which are established by thought itself and which do not simply represent real relations, even though these purely-thought relationships have a foundation in beings and in their possible or real connections. Nevertheless, not all relations are purely-thought relationships. There are undoubtedly also relations which do not arise from our intellectual comparisons.

The Reality of Relations. As soon as on the basis of experience we admit the reality of a finite being, we cannot conceive its particular mode of *being* otherwise than as opposed to other possible particular modes of *being* and as connected with them in a common universal origin. As soon, however, as it is certain that many

---

[23]Cf. no. 83.
[24]Cf. no. 83.
[25]Cf. *ibid.*
[26]Cf. *ibid.*

distinct beings are real, their being-together is not merely thought by us but real. Against absolute pluralism,[27] we must admit that these beings constitute necessarily a unit because plurality itself is a participated unity.[28] But the distinction of beings which are together is opposition through relation, for in relation the opposites include one another.

Accordingly, the most profound foundation of all more particular relationships between beings is their participation in *being*—each being resembles the others analogously, i.e., proportionally, in that precisely in which it differs from them, viz., "to be."[29] If, then, we want to understand what each being is, we must investigate also the place occupied by it in the real gradation of *being,* its quantity of *being* in relation to other beings.[30]

The participation in *being,* however, is not only the foundation of static relations but also of dynamic respects. For every being is naturally—according to the mode of its essence—directed to active-passive communication with the others in order to receive and to give a share in the fullness of *being.*[31]

This real interconnection of everything with everything reveals itself specifically in the knowing and loving of finite persons. By virtue of their spiritual nature, these persons are orientated to open themselves to all beings as true, good, and beautiful. True, their particular approximations of the universal makes each one of them be other than the others, but even in this opposition they are interconnected and dynamically orientated to reciprocal self-evaluation.[32]

Finally, spatial and temporal beings are interconnected in simultaneous or successive dispersion according to time and place. Temporal dispersion gives rise to relations which are present only virtually and potentially in beings, but spatial being-together presents itself as a whole of actual relations.[33]

Thus we see that the beings which are open to our experience are interconnected in many kinds of orders. By *order,* taken concretely for that which is ordered, we mean a whole of many subsistent beings which are united in some respect according to dynamic relationships

---

[27]Cf. no. 45.
[28]Cf. no. 39.
[29]Cf. no. 56.
[30]Cf. no. 57.
[31]Cf. no. 64.
[32]Cf. no. 132.
[33]Cf. no. 168.

of collaboration.[34] According to the different realms of being we may distinguish the orders of the material, the living, the psychical, the spiritual; in the realm of human activities we may speak of the economic order, the legal order, the moral order, etc. However, all these realms of "nature" and "culture" together constitute a hierarchically structured unity of many in which all particular beings and events are interconnected—namely, the unity of order called the "world."

Conditions of Real Relations. The following conditions must be fulfilled if a relation within the whole of relationships of an order is to be a real relation in the strictest and most proper sense of the term:

1. The substratum must be a real subsistent being.

2. The foundation must be a real form or perfection of this being, i.e., its essence, an essential property, or an accidental quantitative or qualitative determination.

3. The terminus must be a distinct real subsistent being.

If these conditions are fulfilled, the relation is really distinct from its foundation.[35] It is an accidental determination. *As* a relation it has a "to be *to*" the terminus, but as an accident, it has a "to be *in*" the principle: it inheres *in* the subsistent subject as a relative determination *of* this subject.

Nevertheless, the relation is inseparably connected with the subsistent subject as soon as the foundation and terminus are present. Its reality is derived from the subject which according to the foundation is the emanative origin of the relation,[36] but its specification comes from the terminus—taken formally with respect to its content—, which is the condition for the presence of the relation.

Reciprocal Real Relations. A real relation of one being to another has a corresponding real relation of the other to the first only if both the principle and the terminus are related in a real order of interdependence, so that they pertain to a single "whole" as subsistent parts which refer to each other.

[34]Concerning order, see Angelinus, *Wijsgerige gemeenschapsleer*, Nijmegen, 5th ed., 1949, pp. 63-87, 151-165; A. Silva-Tarouca, *Thomas heute*, Vienna, 1947, pp. 55 ff.
[35]Concerning the problem of distinction between relation and foundation, see Krempel, *op. cit.*, pp. 245-271.
[36]Cf. no. 100.

If, however, the terminus is not dependent on the principle, but transcends the "order" to which the principle belongs, then this terminus is merely *conceived* as reciprocally related to the principle, so that there is no question of a real relation of the terminus to the principle.

Such a non-reciprocity of real relationship occurs, strictly speaking, always in the dynamic relationship of cause and effect when the cause is considered *as* cause. For the cause, as cause, is not dependent on the effect. However, in the case of finite efficient causes, the cause, and especially the univocal cause, depends in many ways on that which it influences, so that the dynamic relation is reciprocal.[37] However, insofar as beings exercise a formal-intrinsic causality as objects of theoretical knowledge, and insofar as they exercise final causality as objects of love, they are not modified through their influence on the knower and lover. Accordingly, the real relation of the subject to the transcendent objects of its immanent acts is a non-reciprocal relation.[38]

165. *Pure Beings of Thought*[39]

Concept, Judgment, and Real Being. To understand why, alongside the real relations discovered in the objects of our experience, we necessarily conceive relations of which we know that they are not formally present in real beings as their determinations, we must keep in mind that our knowledge is perfected in the judgment. True, our original concepts, as far as their content is concerned, express possible or real modes of *being*. But these concepts are general, and though the modes of *being* expressed by them are thought of in reference to concrete subjects, the concepts do not yet determine which subjects *are* according to these modes. The question of *being* comes up only in the judgment which asserts: this or that is in this way or that way.[40]

The proportionate object, of which the structure of the judgment is the proper expression, is a be-ing which acts as the bearer of *being* without coinciding with it—it participates in *being*.[41] Moreover, although is is a being which is here and now in this way, in principle

---

[37]Cf. nos. 105-107.
[38]Cf. no. 122.
[39]Concerning beings of thought, see Thomas Aquinas' *Scriptum s. Sentent.*, p. 1, d. 2, q. 1, a. 3; d. 19, q. 5, a. 1; d. 30, q. 1, a. 3.
[40]Cf. no. 85.
[41]Cf. no. 18.

other beings can be determined according to this mode of *being* and, in addition, this being is not once and for all determined according to this mode of *being*. It is material and changeable.[42]

If in an affirmative judgment on the basis of experience it is asserted that such an individual material being in this or that, the verbal copula "is" not only expresses the truth of the proposition, but also states immediately the real "*to be*" of the being—it states that this being is something which itself is really as indicated by the predicate, although this predicate does not express the individual mode of *being* of the subject in an adequate way but only according to an aspect in which it agrees with others.[43] Accordingly, at least insofar as the attribution of *being* is concerned, there is here an immediate agreement between the being as it really is and as it is understood.

Beings of Thought. However, not all our judgments are concerned with positive modes of *being* pertaining to really present, individual, subsistent bearers of *being*. As we will see, we form also other kinds of judgments, such as judgments about concepts, judgments, and reasoning processes, judgments with a negative predicate, judgments in which the subject is predicated of itself, judgments about past and future beings, and judgments which are not concerned with subsistent beings but with constituent principles of beings considered in themselves.

In all these cases the judgment may be true, so that the verbal copula "to be" expresses the truth of the proposition. But here this copula is not the immediate expression of the possible of real *being* pertaining to an ultimate subject that is. We conceive as a being something which in itself is not a possible or real being in the primary sense of the term. We construct purely-thought-beings, whose "to be" is wholly encompassed by being the object of a thought representation, but we know that their "to be" is purely a being-thought and not an immediate expression of the *being* pertaining to the beings in themselves.

Such pure beings of thought are necessary for our sense-bound thinking as subjective means to arrive at knowledge which transcends momentaneous particular experience. It is only through these indirect means of negation and reflection that we are able to explicitate

---

[42]Cf. no. 86.

[43]Concerning the verbal copula "to be," cf. Aristotle, *Metaphysica*, bk. V, ch. 7 and St. Thomas' *Comment.*, nos. 895-896. See also *Quodlibet.* 9, a. 3.

what remains implicit in the imperfect intuition of *being* contained in the direct affirmative experiential judgment.[44]

Only Relations are Pure Beings of Thought. Only relationships can be pure beings of thought. For every positive determination of thought content, every absolute characteristic, is either in itself or at least in its constituent elements a direct expression of a perceived possible or real mode of *being* or, at least of "appearing to be" of beings. The representations also of free imagination are combinations whose elements are perceived aspects of reality which we project as existing in a world of fancy.[45] Only relations, as such, do not express in their concept any positive determination of content, so that they are capable of having a "to be" purely through the acts of the comparing, connecting, and dividing intellect.[46]

166. *Logical Relations*[47]

Truth and Relations of Reason. When we conceive purely thought relations after the manner of beings it may still be possible sometimes to predicate these relations of real beings in true judgments or to form true judgments about these relations themselves. For a judgment is true when the proposed situation agrees with "that which is" in what it *intends* to express, even if the mode of understanding and

---

[44]Cf. no. 16.

[45]Cf. no. 124.

[46]Cf. no. 34.

[47]We use the expression "logical relation" in a narrower sense. Many authors identify logical relations simply with relation of reason or being of thought, which is not quite correct, it seems. Thomas Aquinas clearly indicates the difference between what we will call "first degree relations of reason having a foundation" and "second degree relations of reason having a foundation": "The relation of reason consists in an order of the understood things. This can happen in two ways. In one way, according as this order is invented by the intellect and attributed to that which is spoken of relatively; for example, the relations which the intellect attributes to the things understood precisely insofar as they are understood, such as the relations of genus and species. For these relations are invented by the intellect when it considers the order of what is in the intellect to what is outside [the intellect] or also the order of understood things to one another. In another way, according as such relations follow from the mode of understanding, i. e., the intellect understands something in reference to something else, although it does not invent this reference, but rather this reference is necessarily consequent on the mode of understanding. This kind of relation the intellect does not attribute to what is in the intellect but to what is in reality. It occurs when certain things which in themselves do not have an order are understood as if they had an order. However, the intellect does not judge them to have this order, for otherwise it would be false." *De potentia,* q. 7, a. 11. Cf. Krempel, *op. cit.,* p. 359.

expressing does not fully equate the mode in which the expressed being is in itself.

However, the truth of such a judgment requires that the relations constituted by thought are *founded* on real beings and on their real relationships. There can be no question of a justified use of the verbal copula "to be" unless what we think in this way about a being ultimately refers to what in itself is a being in the primary and most proper sense—namely, an individual subsistent being.

Such pure beings of thought which are founded on real beings are called *necessary relationships of reason*. The necessity of our thinking to constitute such relations arises, on the one hand, from the proper nature of the being, which is the foundation of true knowledge and, on the other, from the proper nature of our knowledge, which is founded on being.

All founded relations of reason agree in this that they are concepts which do not immediately correspond to something real in beings. In this way they are opposed to original concepts which, though they are general, have a content that directly, albeit imperfectly, expresses a real mode of *being* of a subsistent being, e.g., an absolute characteristic, such as essence, quantity, or quality, or also a relative characteristic.[48] Accordingly, relations of reason have only an indirect foundation in reality. They do not immediately express being, but express being mediately, by means of the mode of understanding proper to the structure of our intellect.

Logical Relations. Two degrees of mediateness may be distinguished. Relations of reason of the first degree are concepts which originate from our proper mode of conceiving beings as they are in themselves, but are predicated in true judgments of the beings themselves. This kind of relation of reason will be discussed presently. First, however, we will say something about the relationships of the second degree. They arise when we *reflect* on the mode in which we know beings only by means of concepts. We predicate them in true judgments of beings not as they are in themselves, but precisely insofar as these beings have been given a being-thought in our representative and conceptual thinking.

Relations of reason of the second degree are arrangements which reason puts into its own thoughts precisely as self-produced intentional means of knowledge of beings. If our knowledge were perfectly

---

[48]Cf. nos. 84, 127, 130.

intuitive, it would not need the intermediary service of general concepts and the consequent judgments and reasoning processes. But because we have to make use of the process of abstraction, we know a being by characteristics that can be present also in other beings.[49] When the intellect reflects on the possible presence of the conceptual content in many, it forms the relationship-of-reason of formal universality and consequently of formal predicability: a conceptual content may be predicated of individual beings as expressing their genus, species, property, etc.[50] In the judgment a synthesis is made between the universal concept and the individual datum of experience according to the predicable relationships between subject and predicate. Reasoning processes posit relationships of implication between propositions.[51]

All these relations of reason between thoughts are reflections upon contents of concepts or "second intentions."[52] They are constantly formed by man's thoughts about beings, without themselves becoming explicitly objects of his judgment. It is only in formal logic that the products of our thinking or founded relations of reason are singled out and made the object of consideration. Their interconnection constitutes the logical order, and for this reason we best call them *logical relations.*

The judgments of logic, in which these logical relations of predicability, predication and illation of consequence assume the position of predicates, have as their subjects our concepts, judgments, and reasoning processess as such, and not real or possible beings.

167. *Negative and Privative Concepts*

Relations of Reason of the First Degree. Founded relations of reason pertaining to the first degree are purely thought beings in a less strict sense. They are closer to the foundation in real beings and are predicated of these beings themselves. They arise as a necessary consequence from our mode of understanding when we attempt to express our knowledge of beings in judgments.

A clear example of such a relation of reason is the predicate "to be known" or "to be loved." Through it, we express a relation of beings to our understanding and loving, although we know very well

---

[49]Cf. no. 82.
[50]The so-called "predicables" (cf. no. 83).
[51]Cf. no. 130.
[52]Cf. no. 83.

that our acts depend on the objects called "understandable" and "lovable," while the objects of theoretical knowledge and motivated love, as such, do not depend on our acts. Hence to-be-known is not a real mode of making a being be in an added way. Of necessity we conceive the relation as reciprocal, but we know that there is a real relation[53] only from the knower and the lover to the object known or loved.[54]

Negative and Privative Concepts. There are still other purely thought beings pertaining to the first degree, which flow of necessity from our way of understanding and signifying. First of all, we have so-called negative and privative concepts.

The "to be" of beings is not yet taken into consideration in the concept but only in the judgment. The judgment, as reply to a question, is a verdict concerning two proposals: Is this so or is this not so? From its inception our knowledge is marked by the relation between affirmation and negation. It progresses through demarcation and definition, i.e., it aims primarily at the many particular beings, approaching them in their positive particular mode of *being* by means of questions which have perhaps to be answered in the negative, for we usually know what a being is *not,* before we have a clearly defined concept of what it really is.[55]

Negations, however, can be illuminating or even necessary only for a mode of knowing which is based on progressive experience, does not proceed in a fully intuitive way but abstractively, and consequently forms thoughts which do not fully coincide with the being to be known. Such a mode of knowing is a thinking knowing.[56]

The negation may pertain either to the copula or to the predicate. If it belongs to the copula, not-to-be is posited as a quasi-to-be; for instance, this wall is-not white, i.e., it is not true that this wall is a white wall. If the negation belongs to the predicate, non-being is posited as a quasi-being; for instance, this wall is not-white, i.e., it

---

[53]Cf. no. 164.
[54]Practical knowledge also gives rise to all kinds of relations between real or possible beings in its planning; the architect, for example, plans the arrangement of building materials in the construction of a house. These relations are neither actual real relations nor pure relations of reason whose "to be" is encompassed by being-thought. They are, therefore, relations which are proposed as "to be realized": they are not yet actually real but will possibly become "real"—namely, when our activity will have exercised its causal influence on that which is. (cf. nos. 141 and 145).
[55]Cf. no. 130.
[56]Cf. nos. 45, 128.

is true that this wall is a non-white wall. Not-to-be and non-being
are thus brought into relation with to-be and being, although we know
that "in themselves" not-to-be and non-being are not capable of having a relation to to-be and being, for to be related a thing must first
be. To-be *as* to-be and being *as* being are related precisely "to
nothing" outside themselves, they do not have any "other than themselves" to which they could be related.[57] Accordingly, our ways of
thinking and expressing diverge from what we intend to seize cognitively. Nevertheless, the negative concepts are founded on beings and
can be used as predicates in true judgments.

Absolute and Particular Negations. There is, first of all, the idea
of the absolute nothing, the negation of all reality and even of all possibility. This idea is attempted by absolute nihilism and absolute
skepticism.[58] In the principle of non-contradiction absolute being
assumes the form of a predicate, but what we want to state is precisely that it can never be a predicate. For our way of thinking the
principle of identity and all-embracingness is clarified through the
negation of the absolute negation.

Next, there are concepts of relative or particular non-beings, i.e.,
not being this or that, as proposed predicates. These concepts are
either privative or purely negative. They are privative when the
very absence of a positive characteristic in a subject which can or
should have this characteristic is conceived as a characteristic—the
so-called defect. For instance, to be blind, intended as a characteristic
of a sensitive or living being. They are purely negative when the
absence of a characteristic is conceived as a characteristic without saying anything of the subject. For instance, to be sightless, which can
be predicated also of non-sensitive and non-living beings, e.g., of a
stone.

These concepts can be predicated in true judgments because they
have a foundation in the positive characteristic pertaining to the being
of which there is question in the negative or privative judgment:
every particular mode of *being,* as such, is opposed to other particular
modes of *being* and sometimes excludes them positively, but at least
it does not of necessity include them actually.

Foundation of the Particular Negation. Thus, the particular negation implies a particular affirmation as its foundation. When we say,

[57]Cf. nos. 36-41.
[58]Cf. nos. 13-16.

for instance, of this subsistent real being, this man, that he is blind, we represent matters as if to-be-blind were a real mode of *being,* a form, a determination pertaining to the subject. But to-be-blind is not such a mode of *being.* Nevertheless, "to be" is correctly used as the verbal copula when this man with respect to his eyes is positively in such an organic condition that the presence of the positive characteristic of sight is excluded.

Thus *evil* in general is something in real beings, it *is* in a derivative sense of the term "to be." But it is not itself something unqualifiedly real, it is not a "being" in either the subsistent or the non-subsistent sense, for being as being is good.[59] Evil is a real being insofar as we conceive it, by means of a founded reference of reason as a relation of disagreement with "what should be," i.e., the normative good. On the basis of the positive elements which are present in the evil being, although only in a defective way, we ascribe to this being a relation of reason to being-evil in a true judgment.

168. *Local and Temporal Relations Between Beings*

Are the relations which we ascribe to beings on the basis of their extension in time and space real relations or relations of reason? The question is not easily answered. We will speak here first about the relations between distinct beings, for we view the relationships of a being to its own parts and moments to be so-called transcendental relations. They will be considered later.[60]

Local Relations. Through indications of place, such as here or there, above or below, in front or behind, close-by or far away, we denominate a being extrinsically[61] but on the basis of its immediate or mediate contact with a surrounding being, conceived as immobile.[62] The category "where," then does not add a new intrinsic mode of *being* to the subject. But what about the foundation of this denomination, the spatial relationships?

True, we always determine these relationships from the viewpoint of a reference system conceived as immobile which is chosen as the starting point, and if we place ourselves imaginatively at a different starting point, we discover different relations of distance. Moreover, concretely speaking, our "lived" experience of closeness, distance, etc.,

---

[59]Cf. no. 43.
[60]Cf. no. 170.
[61]Cf. no. 70.
[62]Cf. no. 78.

is conditioned by the fact that we "ex-sist"[63] as sensitively striving and acting beings in a "human" world. Nevertheless, this twofold "relativity" of our spatial judgment does not prevent us from considering the discovered relations of distance as real relations as long as we do not take into account the progress of time and, consequently, local motion, but speak only about the relations between simultaneous extended beings, i.e., beings which are present at one and the same moment. For we assume that they are really together; hence the real relations in question are the modes of really being-together of distinct beings.

Accordingly, though it is absolutely impossible for us to perceive the real order of the dispersed parts of the material universe in its totality—for our perception always takes place from a place within this whole—, nevertheless, it is possible for us to know *something* about this real order—namely, the meaning which it has with respect to certain bodily beings that are to be chosen as the center of our perspective within the whole which we cannot encompass.[64]

---

[63]Cf. no. 66.

[64]Mathematics has quantitative relations as its object. If we do not accept that geometric and arithmetical magnitudes exist in themselves either really or ideally, we face the difficult question of replying to the question as to what mode of *being* pertains to mathematical beings. Are they accidental determinations which through formal abstraction are separated but actually exist in subsistent beings? Or are they relations which exist at most potentially in beings and become actual only through the abstractive act of mathematical representation? Whatever the answer may be, it must be admitted that mathematics forms also purely-thought beings by way of analogy with perceived quantitative relations. Such are, first of all, imaginary homogenous space extending "to infinity," *a fortiori* the non-Euclidean space representations, and also negative and imaginary numbers. The specific nature of these founded relations of reason would have to be determined accurately.

However, we should go beyond this and say that mathematics as such abstracts from the question whether or not its objects are real or possible. Mathematical objects *as* such are pure beings of thought, founded relations of reason. This objectivity suffices for its purpose, for the truth norm of mathematical propositions is not experience but "imagination."

Perhaps we may express the bond which, despite everything, mathematics seems to retain with the experience of bodily beings in the following way. Mathematics is the science of all possible formal relations that can be conceived as existing between beings which present themselves as individuals of a species precisely insofar as they present themselves in this way—in other words, insofar as these beings can be conceived as pure repetitions of "the same" by thought process which forms univocal concepts. The formal logic of the univocal finds its purest application in the mathematical object (cf. no. 149).

Concerning mathematics see Aristotle, *Metaphysica*, bk. XIII, chs. 2-3; E. W. Beth, *Wijsbegeerte der wiskunde*, Antwerpen, 1948; A. Kockelmans, "De betekenis van de term 'materia intelligibilis' in de werken van S. Thomas," *Tijdschrift v. Philosophie*, vol. 15 (1953), pp. 71-114, and "S. Thomas' opvatting over de zijnswijze der wiskundige entiteiten in het licht der aristotelische traditie," *op. cit.*, vol. 16 (1954), pp. 419-464; P. Hoenen, *De noetica geometriae origine theoriae cognitionis*, Rome, 1954.

Temporal Relations. Let us revert to the simultaneity which is implied in the very concept of spatial relations. This simultaneity is a real property belonging to the beings and events that are at a distance from one another. The fact that this property is real, however, does not determine under what conditions simultaneity of one thing with respect to another has to be affirmed or denied. Perhaps simultaneity is something which pertains to a being in reference to another being only in dependence on the question of whether or not it is in locomotion with respect to the standpoint, conceived as immovable, of this other being, so that a change of standpoint would imply also a change of simultaneity. We prefer to leave unanswered here the question about the interconnection of time, place, and motion, which is closely connected with the theory of relativity, and make only the remark that the point is not whether simultaneity can be a real property—in our opinion, the answer should be certainly affirmative—but which presuppositions are implied by the very concept of simultaneity with respect to distant beings.

Temporal indications, such as then and now, denominate a being extrinsically,[65] on the basis of its simultaneity or non-simultaneity with a phase of another being's motion, taken as the measure of time. Accordingly, the category "when" does not add a new intrinsic mode of *being* to a subject. But what about the foundation of this denomination, the temporal relationships?

The difficulty which arises against the reality of the temporal relations between distinct beings is this: excepting simultaneity, these relations are put between events that are not actually together but precisely exclude one another in their actual reality. But to give rise to real relations, beings have really to be-together.

Because temporal relations bring together events which are not actually together, they presuppose the activity of thought. Through memory and expectation, thinking makes actually present in a single thought that which is no longer actually present or not yet actually present and that which is actually present at the moment when the

---

From *In I. Sentent.*, d. 2, q. 1, a. 3, we are inclined to derive the conclusion that according to Thomas Aquinas abstract mathematical "intentions" follow from our mode of thinking and, therefore, are founded relations of reason.

Concerning "imagination" as the truth norm of mathematical propositions, see Thomas Aquinas, *In Boethium de Trinitate*, q. 6, a. 2.

Concerning the bond of mathematics and experience, see Andrew G. van Melsen, *The Philosophy of Nature*, Pittsburgh, 4th impr., 1961, pp. 155-159.

[65]Cf. no. 70.

act of thinking occurs or the moment at which this act places itself.[66]
The relations, therefore, of "before" and "after" are founded relations
of reason pertaining to the first degree.[67] They can be predicated
of events and beings in true judgments, but do not intend to assert
that the "priority" or "posteriority" in question are formally as such
a real ontic determination of a being, for the actual being cannot
be actually related to the non-actual as such, i.e., that which is no
longer or not yet.

Real Foundation. Nevertheless, we should keep in mind that the
foundation of these relations itself is real, because past and future
beings are together with actually present beings in a broader and
analogous sense—namely, insofar as all are interconnected in the
spatio-temporal universe by means of the causal bond of becoming.
Even being-temporally-at-a-distance from one another is a deficient
way of being-together. This assertion becomes clear especially when
one considers that every event was always already present in its
causes and will always still be present in its effect, so that in a
degraded sense everything is in someway contemporaneous with
everything else. However, this potential simultaneity of the material
is rendered actual only through the synthetizing acting of the intellect.

In all our judgments the verb implies temporal relations. The
present expresses the simultaneity of the judged object with the
perceptive act of the perceiver. The past and the future tenses do
not express events from the standpoint of the "now" proper to these
events themselves—with respect to this "now" all events are present
with themselves—but from the perspective proper to the moment
of time, the "now" of the observer. Yesterday we said: "John will
leave"; today: "John is leaving"; tomorrow: "John has left." The
judgment, then, concerning one and the same fact differs in its
temporal expression according to the temporal positions of the same
observer in the course of his life or of different observers situated
at different times. Of course, we can also make ourselves present
in our imagination at a different moment of time and make our
statement from this imagined temporal location.

---

[66]Cf. no. 75.
[67]Cf. St. Thomas, *In I Sentent.*, d. 26, q. 2, a. 1: a relation of reason may
be "a relation of a being to a non-being, as when we are said to be before those
who are still to come. For such a priority is not a relation according to reality
but only according to reason, because a real relation requires that both extremes
be in-act." See also *De veritate*, q. 1, a. 5, *ad* 16; *De potentia*, q. 7, a. 11.

Accordingly, these temporal relations of past and future with respect to the chosen moment of "now," implied in every experiental judgment, are founded relations of reason.

169. *The Relation of Identity*

Identity is a Relation of Reason. To be real, relations must be concerned wtih distinct subsistent beings. However, even insofar as a being is not related to another being, i.e., precisely insofar as it is absolute, we conceive it as related—namely to itself. We express the identity through which a being is what it is by saying that it is itself. Thus we place it first in our thought in opposition to itself and then deny the distinction: a being is not opposed to itself as to something other than itself, but coincides with itself.[68] The relation of identity, therefore, is not a real relation but a founded relation of reason pertaining to the first degree.

Even and especially self-consciousness and self-love, which are the highest modes of being-identical are thought of as intentional relationships of the subject to himself as object: the known is the knower himself, and the loved is the lover himself.[69]

The reason why we conceive identity and self-consciousness as "reconciled" opposites lies in this that identity is not absolute in any finite being and that self-consciousness is not perfect in any finite knower. Thus there remains a certain opposition within the finite—the being is only imperfectly itself, and the knower knows himself only in an imperfect way. There is a certain otherness, a certain distance, between the realized and the ideal essence of every being that is finite and therefore dynamic.[70] In every self-consciousness that is finite and consequently dynamic,[71] there is a certain otherness between me insofar as I am and me insofar as I know myself.

Why a Plurality of Principles is Needed to Express the Absoluteness of Being. For this reason our assertions about being as being, which intend to express the absoluteness of *being,* are inadequate with respect to that which they intend to express. The way in which we think the primary principles of *being* means making use of founded

---

[68]Cf. Thomas Aquinas, *ibid.*; see also *Summa Theol.,* p. 1, q. 13, a. 7: "Insofar as reason apprehends the same thing twice, it posits them as two, and thus it apprehends a kind of relationship between a thing and this thing itself."
[69]Cf. nos. 122 and 139.
[70]Cf. no. 63.
[71]Cf. no. 18.

relations of reason.   Thus it is necessary for us to explicitate the absoluteness of *being* in more than a single first principle.   Each of the primary principles we use to explicitate this absoluteness attributes to being as being a distinct transcendental property.

The principle of *identity* is meant to express the absoluteness of a being on the basis of its *being,* but it does so by conceiving the absolute as in reference to itself.   The principles of *non-contradiction* and of *excluded middle* intend to express the all-embracing character of *being,* but do so by first conceiving "not-to-be" and "neither-to-be nor not-to-be" after the fashion of a quasi-*being* and then denying this quasi-*being.*   In this denial they deny at the same time the possibility of the initially proposed all-embracing negation and the initially proposed all-embracing abstention or indifference and thus posit the primacy of affirmation.[72]

Unity, likewise, intends to convey the absoluteness of *being,* but it does so by denying division or opposition, i.e., by denying that "to be" and "not-to-be" are together within the identity of *being.   Infinity* intends to express the all-embracing content of *being,* but in its mode of expression it is the denial of finiteness.   *Determinateness* is conceived as the denial of the possibility of being further determined.[73]

Alongside these transcendentals, which express the absoluteness of a being as being either by way of reference to itself or by means of a reference of negation, there are *truth, goodness,* and *beauty* as ideas that refer the absolute to the powers of understanding and willing, which are oriented to the absolute.   The relations expressed by intelligibility and lovability are not real, but a purely-thought mirroring of the relationships of knowing and will to *being.*   Truth, goodness, and beauty express the absolute "to be" of being as the foundation of these relations of reason.[74]

Thus all transcendental concepts or ideas coincide with respect to that which they intend to express, "the thing signified," but are distinct with respect to the way in which they conceptually express this selfsame thing.   We cannot conceive the absolute otherwise than in an plurality of transcendental ideas which are distinct by relations of reason, but we know at the same time that these ideas, insofar as their intended content is concerned, are identical in the absolute

---

[72]Cf. nos. 36-38.

[73]Cf. nos. 39-41.

[74]Cf. nos. 42-44.

itself. Absolute truth, for instance, even *as* truth, *"is"* absolute goodness.[75]

170. *Transcendental Relations*

Principles of Being and Relations. The subjects of our judgments are not always subsistent beings, whether as individuals or in general. We form judgments also about what itself is not an ultimate subject of *being,* but only a determination of *being,* a form, or perfection through which a being is. We separate these constituent principles in formal-abstract concepts[76] and attribute to them a "to be" and a mode of *being* as if they were beings. But what we conceive in this way after the manner of a being in the primary sense, an *ens quod,* is only a being in a derivative sense, an *ens quo,* a being by analogy of proportion.

All sciences proceed in this way. They form judgments about colors, sounds, sizes, distances, numbers, motions, processes, functions, powers, abilities, virtues, activities, events, situations, etc. Especially metaphysics is full of this kind of judgments, in which within the unity of the concrete being its constituent principles are distinguished, contrasted, and related to one another.

We reserve the name "transcendental relations"[77] for all those relations which are not between subsistent beings but within a single concrete being between this being and its constituent principles or between different constituent principles themselves; for instance, the relations between being, essence and "to be," between matter and form, substance and accident, active potency and activity, passive potency and act.[78]

We call these relations "transcendental" because they can be comprehended under the relation of potency and act, taken in their broadest analogous sense, and consequently occur in all categories of finite being.

---

[75]Cf. no. 189.

[76]Cf. no. 51.

[77]Concerning transcendental relations, see especially Louis de Raeymaeker, *The Philosophy of Being,* St. Louis, 1954, pp. 105-107 (see also the text of Cajetan quoted on page 106) 255-256, 307, 334. Our description of this relation does not fully coincide with that of de Raeymaeker on p. 105. See also A. Pattin, "De verhouding tussen zijn en wezenheid en de transcendentale relatie in de twede helft der 13e eeuw," *Verhandelingen v. d. Kon. Vlaamse Academie van Wetenschappen,* Brussels, 1955, who claims that the transcendental relation is implicitly present in the works of Thomas Aquinas and the first Thomists.

[78]Cf. nos. 92-101.

The question about the nature of such transcendental relations is one of the most difficult metaphysical problems. If constituent principles are "really" distinct, then, so it seems, their relations can be ascribed only to a real being, i.e., a subsistent being, as a mode of *being* in reference to other subsistent beings. In what sense, then, do we ascribe such relations in true judgments to principles of *being* within the unity or identity of a single concrete being?

The Nature of Transcendental Relation. Every being, as being, is what it is. We conceive this identity as a reference of the being to itself. However, no finite being perfectly realizes this identity and, therefore, neither the other transcendental properties of *being,* viz., non-contradiction, unity, infinity, determinateness, truth, goodness, and beauty. Within the finite being there is only deficient identity and consequently also opposition, plurality, division, indeterminateness, and determinability. Thus there are of necessity *opposite aspects* in such a being, and these aspects do not arise merely from our imperfect way of knowing but find their foundation in the imperfect mode of *being* proper to the being in question.

For, when we judge the finite material being as "something that is such or such," explicitation of what is implicitly contained in this judgment reveals the following:

1. The finite being is not "to be" itself, but participates in *being* in a particular way. Because of this distinction between the particular essence and "to be," the finite being is really related to the many other particular beings with which it is together in the static and dynamic order of *being.*[79]

2. The material being is not in its own essential form, but participates in an individual way in this essential form. Because of this distinction between individuating matter and specifying form, the material being is really related to others of the same species and to all material beings with which it is together in the static and dynamic spatio-temporal order.[80]

The foundation, therefore, of the real relations between subsistent beings lies in the immanent composite structure of each being according to transcendental relations, and these transcendental relations are expressions of the fundamental fact that each being *is* not the perfec-

[79]Cf. nos. 57-64.
[80]Cf. nos. 86-91.

tion of *being* and of the essential form of identity, but merely possesses them through participation, so that it is dynamically orientated to accidental increase of perfection through active and passive communication with the other beings.[81]

With respect to what they intend to convey, our judgments are true when we assert that in the single concrete being essence and "to be," matter and form, active potency and activity, passive potency and act, though they are identified to some extent, do not fully coincide but are opposed to each other. However, our mode of conceiving and expressing them is inadequate, because the form of the judgment implies that we conceive the constituent principles as subjects to which predicates are attributed, i.e., as subsistent beings. But what is not something that itself is, in the primary sense of being, is not a bearer of real *being*. If then, "to be" pertains to constitutent principles only in a derivative and analogous sense, to-be-distinct and to-be-related likewise belong to them only in an analogous way.

Accordingly, the metaphysical judgments in which we set constituent principles apart in formal-abstract concepts and predicate of them that they are "really" distinct and "really" transcendentally related will be false if we forget that there is no question here of subsistent beings. We have constantly to keep in mind that our expressions fall short and that the intention of these judgments is to explicitate in the form of judgments—our only way of expressing our thought—the evident insights which lie contained in the experiential judgments— namely, the transcendence of unqualified *being* with respect to every particular finite being and the transcendence of the essential form with respect to every individual material being. It is only in this defective way that we can approach the universal source in which the finite and the material participate.

The Meaning of Real Distinction and Real Relation in Metaphysics. Thus "real" distinction and "real" relation receive a new and analagous meaning in metaphysical judgments. There is question of distinction and relation not between beings but between aspects which, without wholly coinciding, are nonetheless essentially connected and related within one and the same concrete being. Such aspects are, for instance, this being as being *and* as only a limited being, this being as being this way *and* as being only here and now this way.

---

[81]Cf. nos. 67-71.

In the concrete being these aspects essentially imply a reference to each other. For this reason we do not conceive the transcendental relations as accidental determinations of the constituent principles but as constituting these principles: the "to be" of the principles, we say is a "to be related to each other."

On the other hand, it is impossible to conceive these principles as *pure* relations, for in that case nothing would be conceived as *that which* is related. That which we have to conceive as the substratum of the transcendental relations cannot be anything else than the being itself which, considered in one respect, is related to itself as considered under a different aspect. Insofar as this respect in the being itself does not fully coincide with another respect and nonetheless necessarily evokes this respect, we speak of a "real" transcendental relationship. This relation, therefore, has its foundation in the imperfect identity of the being with itself, an identity which we conceive as a two-in-oneness and consequently in the fashion of a "real" relative opposition.

Provided "real" is understood in a secondary and analogous sense, we may say that the principles are "real"—namely, in the sense that they are principles of reality through which the real is really as it is. In the same sense we may speak of "real" distinction and "real" relations: they are non-coinciding aspects which call forth each other, they "make" the real be or be this or that way, but they themselves are not, or are not this or that way.

Real Transcendental Relations. The last sentence once more shows the inadequateness of our expression, for how can something make something else be unless it itself be first? All we can do is conceive the principles of a being in the fashion of beings which are constitutively related to each other and to the being which they constitute and then recognize that this way of expression is inadequate and deficient by adding that there is no question of considering them as beings in the primary and proper sense. While correcting our expression, however, we maintain the truth of what we wanted to say through it.

Accordingly, the transcendental relations occupy a peculiar position between the real relations in the first and proper sense and the founded relations of reason. They have the character of founded relations of reason when we consider our way of understanding and expressing ourselves—namely, insofar as we conceive the transcendental relations in the fashion of real relations between subsistent beings. On the other hand, they have the character of "real" relations in the derivative and analogous sense when we pay attention to what we want to express by them. For what we have in mind is the imperfection and the consequent opposition existing within the self-identity of finite and material beings. This relativity aspect is "real"; it is the way in which the relation of dependence on a transcendent source of *being* and of essential form reveals itself in beings;[82] and at the same time it is in these beings the foundation of their relationship to all those which participate in *being* and essential form.[83]

The Importance of the Transcendental Relation. The above-explained theory of transcendental relations is important for all sciences but especially for the sciences of man. In our thinking we have to analyze man's integral activity into "really" distinct acts flowing from "really" distinct powers. Vegetative processes are to be distinguished from psychical acts, sensory aspects from motor aspects, external perception from memory, expectation, and imagination, sense knowledge from sense striving, emotions from one another, observing and thinking from loving and willing. We may, and even must, say that the sensitive "influences" the intellectual, that the intellect "moves" the will, and vice versa. However, we should not forget how inadequately we express in this way these transcendental relationships between powers and acts and between different kinds of acts. It is not the intellect which understands but man, it is not the intellect which illuminates the will, but it is the knowing man who illuminates the striving and the acting man.

The analytic substantification of powers and acts must constantly be corrected through a synthesis which interconnects all powers and acts as constituent principles of a single complex and varied human activity.[84] The causal relationships within man are not relations of efficient cause and effect in the proper sense but only in an analogously broadened sense,[85] which we attempt to express by speaking about quasi-efficient or emanative causality, quasi-exemplary and quasi-final causality. The same precaution should be exercised when there is question of the interrelations between different cultural realms.[86]

---

[82]Cf. no. 104.
[83]Cf. nos. 62 and 90.
[84]Cf. nos. 125, 138, 141.
[85]Cf. no. 100.
[86]Cf. nos. 145-150.

Alongside the above-mentioned relation of activities and active potencies as accidental determinations, which essentially imply a relation of in-being or inherence to the subsistent subject as their bearer, origin and purpose, attention has to be paid to 1) the relation of passive potency and act in temporal and changing beings, 2) the relation of essence and "to be" in finite beings as finite beings. This last consideration brings us back again to the starting point of metaphysics.

171. *The Transcendental Relationship of Potency to Act in the "Becoming" Being*

Becoming. Becoming is the transition from being-in-potency to being-in-act which occurs in time. Considered as transition from one state to another, becoming is change or motion, in the broadest sense of these terms.[87] But only one indivisible state of this process is actually real—namely, the state in which that which is becoming is at this moment of time. Transition in this actual state itself, considered precisely in relation to states which are no longer or are not yet.

Accordingly, changing being has its complete "to be," the totality of its interrelated determinations, never *actually* together, for in actuality these determinations exclude one another. Nevertheless, despite this dispersion of its *being,* changing being remains somewhat itself, the same which was and will be. The past and future states, therefore, must be present somehow in the being which actually is in this determined state. However, they cannot be present actually, but are present either virtually, insofar as they continue to exercise influence, or potentially, insofar as they already announce their coming.[88]

Temporality and Identity of the Mutable Being. This virtual and potential presence admits degrees, for living beings and even more sensitive beings bring their past and future closer together in their activity.[89] Nevertheless, of a temporal being, precisely insofar as it is temporal, it is never true that its temporal parts are together in full actuality at this moment, this "now"—the participation of the temporal in eternity is very imperfect.[90]

It is only in the perceptional perspective of an intellectual knower, who through memory and expectation is capable of having the past as

---

[87]Cf. no. 73.
[88]Cf. no. 87.
[89]Cf. no. 115.
[90]Cf. no. 75.

past and the future as future intentionally present, that the dispersed states of the temporal being are actually brought together.

Because a relation can be actual only when the related beings are actually together, the relations of one and the same temporal being to its "before" and "after" can be present only virtually and potentially in this being itself. These relations are actuated in the act of the intellect which encompasses and compares the dispersed states of the temporal being. For the intellect essentially transcends time, although its dependence on sense perception makes it unfold itself in time.

If, then, we conceive the changing being as necessarily related to its past and future states, we place this being in its present state in opposition to this being in its past and future states, so that we oppose one being to another. Next, we bring it into relation with itself, conceiving this "itself" as if it were "something else."

It is evident that we have to do here with transcendental relations, remaining within the unity of a single being. According to our mode of thinking and expressing ourselves, these relations are founded relations of reason which from the indicated moment of perception, the "now," synthetize the temporally dispersed states of complete *being*, the duration of the changing being, into a unity of order.

On the other hand, considered from the viewpoint of what we intend to express through them, these relations of reason correspond with a fundamental and analogously "real" relation in the being itself— namely, the imperfect self-identity of the changing and corruptible being. It presents itself in this actual state, but it is only here and now this or that way, for it can be also different without losing its identity.[91] Considered in itself, it does not exclude the ontic determination according to which it is actuated now but, on the other hand, neither does it necessarily include this determination.[92] Of itself, it is only in potency to this act or form as one of its possibilities; it is in potency also to many other acts or forms, even though they be opposite and mutually exclusive states which can be actuated only in an order of succession.

"Real" Distinction of Potency and Act. Accordingly, by speaking about the "real" distinction of potency and act and their transcendental relation, we express the imperfect identity of the "becoming" being with its actual mode of *being*. These formal-abstract concepts

[91]Cf. no. 73.
[92]Cf. no. 74.

are substantifications of the opposite characteristics of "becoming" being which is separated from the totality of its mode of *being* and merely on the road to self-realization insofar as it tends to reach self-realization through a plurality of successive determinations. Although it is always "in-act," it *is* not this act. For at the same time that it is in-act with respect to *this* form or ontic determination, it is also in-potency with respect to other forms according to which it will be actuated in the future. Even now it carries within itself potentially its future being-different, so that it never identifies itself fully with any actual state whatsoever. It is mobile.

Potency and "To Be." In the changing being we conceive potency as a constituent principle that is distinct from the successive acts, although it is essentially ordered to them. Of itself, potency is un-determined because it refers to many acts, but it is determined by the particular act which actuates its capacity.

However, whatever is, insofar as it is, is determined and there-fore actual. The determinable *as* determinable cannot be.[93] How, then, can we say that potency *is*? Certainly it is not a subsistent being having its own "to be." But how, then, can we attribute to potency a being-distinct and being-related? Moreover, the acts to which the potency is conceived to be related are not actually present as termini of the relation, except the actually present state. In addition, these acts are not distinct beings but possible constituent principles of the same being which of itself is in-potency.

It will not do to reply that the potency is nothing but relation to acts, for in that case nothing would be related to these acts. Every relation presupposes a related subject, and this subject itself must be actually something if it is to be related actually, even though the relation in question flows of necessity from its essence.

The difficulty disappears if attention is paid to the fact that potency is never without an act. For either potency itself is an act, considered under the aspect of further perfectibility, or of itself it is pure potency (primary matter) but always already actuated according to an act (a primary form). Accordingly, to potency *as* potency it does not pertain to be, but when we say that potency "is" in a derivative and analogous sense, we refer to the potency either insofar as it itself is an act or insofar as in union with the act it constitutes a being. Considered in this way, actuated potency is nothing else than

---

[93]Cf. no. **41.**

the concrete being itself, albeit not precisely insofar as actuated according to this act, but insofar as *of itself* it is not necessarily actuated in this way but can be actuated also according to other acts.

Thus it is from the act that the potency derives its "to be." When we conceive potency precisely *as* potency, as opposed to all acts and related to them, we posit a relationship of reason, which is founded in the intrinsic "relativity" or imperfect self-identity of "becoming" being.

This situation reveals itself most clearly in primary matter, which we conceive as pure potency.[94] Prime matter does not have any predicates: it is not some thing, not of any size, not of any quality, and therefore, neither related. When we conceive prime matter as related to all possible substantial forms, we mean to express the radical mobility of every spatio-temporal being, which is not actuated by any definite substantial form in such a way that it cannot lose this form to become "something else."

Relation of Act to Potency. Acts also are conceived by us as essentially related to potency. Nevertheless, there is no perfect correlativity of potency and act. If the potency were "nothing else than" relation to act, and act "nothing else than" relation to potency, potency and act would not be distinguished in any way, so that they would of necessity coincide fully. But in every individual changeable being there is a certain infinity of the individual potency: no specific act perfectly fills the capacity of the being in question, but it remains related to other specifying acts as its possible perfections. On the other hand, there is also a certain infinity of act: specifically the same act is capable of actuating not only the individual potency of this being here and now, but also the potency of other beings at different times and different places.[95] Potency and act transcend each other in opposite respects.

Every specific accidental act or accidental determination implies a relation to a subject as its substratum whose determination it is and which individuates it.[96] Every specific substantial act which is the essential form of a body implies a relation to a primary matter as its principle of individuation.[97]

---

[94]Cf. no. 89.
[95]Cf. no. 86.
[96]Cf. no. 68.
[97]Cf. no. 90.

If, however, act is understood in its broadest analogous sense, so that even "to be" is still conceived as an act with respect to essence, then the question must be raised whether act, considered purely as act, must necessarily be conceived as *related* to a potency which is distinct from it, limits it and renders its multiplication possible. Can act be by itself? Especially, is "to be" of necessity the "to be" *of* this or that being according to a particular mode of *being* or essence? This is the critical question in which the metaphysics of *being* culminates.

CHAPTER TWENTY-NINE

THE ULTIMATE GROUND OF BEINGS

172. *Introduction: the "To Be" of Beings*

The relativity of all beings brings us back to the starting point of metaphysics. If the many, because of their being-real, are not only identical with themselves but also related to all others with whom they participate in the unqualified *being* common to all (*esse commune*),[1] this universal interconnection in *being* may be able to throw some light on the problem concerning the "why" of beings —what is the ultimate ground explaining the proper "to be" immanent in every being?

Can We Speak of "To Be"? It does not seem possible to speak about "to be." Structurally, the perfect cognitive act or judgment is immediately directed only to here-and-now experienced finite, nay material, beings to express in what way they are subject of real *being*: this or that is such or such.[2] Directly, as subjects of the judgment, the individual bearers of *being* are considered, and indirectly, as predicates, the modes of *being;* the "to be" itself, however, of beings does not become thematic but remains implicit in the synthetizing function of the judgment. This function does not even always have to be expressed in a separate verbal copula, but is already present in the act by which the content of thought is connected with a bearer, insofar as this act is not only a predicative synthesis but claims also to be a truth-positing synthesis.[3] If, however, the verbal copula "to be" is explicitly used and in an affirmative judgment predicated of individual here-and-now experienced real beings, then it does not only mean that the proposition is true but also expresses immediately the *actus essendi,* the being-real of the being in question.[4]

---

[1]Concerning unqualified being or *esse commune* in St. Thomas, see L. Oeing-Hanhoff, "Ens et unum convertuntur," *Beiträge Baeumker*, vol. XXXVII, no. 3, Munster, 1953, pp. 77-91. See also the articles of Louis de Raeymaeker and J. van Boxtel quoted in Section 101, and St. Thomas, *De divinis nominibus*, V, lect. 2.

[2]Cf. no. 165.

[3]Cf. no. 15.

[4]Cf. no. 165.

Not all our judgments, however, are concerned with really present positive modes of *being* pertaining to really present subsistent subjects of *being*. For instance, we may attribute also negative predicates; especially, we can make the subject of a judgment something which itself is not in the primary sense an actual subject of *being,* i.e., a be-ing, as, for example, the past or future, the merely possible, the purely imagined or purely thought, the constituent principles, properties, activities, and relations *of* beings. Even then the first thing said of such subjects of judgments is that they are. However, in such cases the verb "to be," which continues to express the truth synthesis, the being-true of the proposition, is not an immediate and adequate expression of an ontic situation. It no longer means the being-real, the *actus essendi,* of a real subject which appropriates this "to be" to itself, the being-real of a be-ing in the primary sense of the term. Depending on the context, "to be" receives all kinds of analogous meanings, such as pertaining to the essence, existing in the imagination, founded being of thought, etc. However, all these meanings are connected with and have to be reduced to the unmodified and central sense of unqualified *being,* the to-be-real pertaining to real subsistent beings.[5]

The Concept "To Be." Accordingly, it seems that in the judgment "to be" itself, no matter in what sense it be taken, does not become thematic, for the judgment aims at a subject of *being* that is at least proposed by our thought or imagination. "To be" itself remains implicit in the synthetizing function of the judgment.

Nevertheless, from the verb "to be" we form not only the predicate be-ing (as a participle) and the subject being (as a noun), but we may even substantify the infinitive of the verb "to be" to express a concept—namely, "to be." This concept can function as the subject of a judgment. To evaluate this concept, we will have to examine its origin and nature in a critical way.

The concept "to be" is a formal-abstract concept, formed through reflection upon the act of *being* which is co-signified in the formal concrete concept "being." Formal-abstract concepts express not something which itself is, in the primary sense of being-real, but the constituent principle through which something is as it is.[6] What in the act of judgment is posited as a mode of *being pertaining to* a being,

---

[5] Cf. no. 29.
[6] Cf. no. 51.

for instance, to-be-healthy, predicated of a living being, we conceive "after the fashion" of something subsistent, for instance, to-be-healthy or health, in order to use it as the subject of new judgments.

The first thing, however, which we predicate of all possible subjects of a judgment is that they are in one way or another. The verbal copula, therefore, makes all concepts predicates, and all predicates are modifications of *being*. From this it follows that when the copula "to be" is substantified to "to be" or beingness, it encompasses all formal-abstract concepts as its modes in an actual, albeit confused, way.

"To Be" is Not an Adequate Object of Knowledge. Metaphysical thought has to reflect upon the ultimate reference to the act of being-real which is implicit in every act of judgment and thus has to detach "to be" itself, as a constituent principle, from the being it judges. Hence it cannot do otherwise than substantify the act of *being* in a formal-abstract concept and make it the subject of a judgment. This procedure, however, is not without danger. For to make something the subject of a judgment means to predicate "to be" of it and to give a further determination of its mode of *being*. The subject, then, of a judgment is conceived "in the fashion" of a being composed of a bearer and a form, of essence and "to be." But as a simple act, "to be" itself transcends this composition; it itself is not again the bearer or subject of *being*. Accordingly, we are not capable of conceiving "to be" adequately in a concept, because every concept formally contains the complex "something that is in this or that way." Therefore, it is likewise impossible to judge it adequately.

When, in spite of all, metaphysical judgments express "what 'to be' is" and apply "to be" as a verbal copula to "to be" as the subject of a judgment, such a judgment is not an adequate expression of an ontological structure: it is not possible to say of "to be" that it *is* in the primary sense of the term. We have to do the best we can with the synthetizing *form* of judgment, which is designed primarily for formal-concrete be-ing in the first sense of the term, to explicitate to some extent what we cannot express in an adequate way. However, the very fact that we have to speak in judgments about "to be" shows that we do not fully understand "what 'to be' is," even though "to be" is the light in which we understand whatever we understand.

It should be evident, therefore, that the formal-abstract concept "to be" does not indicate anything which we encounter as "something which itself is" in the primary sense of the term, i.e., as a subsistent subject of *being*. Nevertheless, it is just as erroneous to think that our judgments regarding "to be" intend to speak about our formal-abstract concept "to be" as such, that is, that these judgments belong to logic.[7] On the contrary, the concept "to be," functioning as the subject of judgments, refers to the affirmative judgment, and the copulative function which it exercises in such judgments, i.e., the self-identity which in the truth synthesis of subject and predicate, is attributed to every subject that we can experience, conceive, or imagine.

Moreover, because all our judgments concerning any subject of judgment ultimately go back to the affirmative experiential judgment about an individual subsistent being in the primary sense of the term, the concept "to be" refers to the act of *being* which in this existential judgment is attributed to the being in question. And because the individual judgment of experience does not have the source of its evidence within itself,[8] but is based on a pre-predicative knowledge, we encounter "to be" most originally in the all-embracing pre-predicative knowing of *being*.[9] In this knowing "to be" is not yet *signified* either by a verb (as in the existential judgment) or as a noun (as in the formal-abstract concept "to be"), but it is *exercised,* or rather it exercises itself as the actuality of the knowing subject as well as of the known or knowable objects, as the act of acts.

Accordingly, it is not possible for us to pursue metaphysics without reflectively substantifying the act of *being* and conceiving "to be" in a formal-abstract concept "in the fashion" of a being. However, what we *intend* by this concept is to refer to the "to be" itself which cannot be adequately seized in a concept and in this sense is trans-conceptual, viz., "to be" as the constituent act through which every real subsistent being is real and to which even the accidental, the possible, the purely thought, the purely imagined, etc., still imply a certain reference.

"To Be" as the First Concept. Apart from the general reason, which is applicable also to the modes of *being,* that the constituent principles of being cannot be considered as subjects or bearers of *being* in the primary and proper sense, there is still a special reason why precisely "to be," in the primary sense of to-be-real, escapes our judgments. It is not possible for us to attribute to "to be" predicates referring to its constituent parts. For otherwise we would have to

---

[7]Cf. no. 166.
[8]Cf. no. 20.
[9]Cf. no. 16.

have at our disposal concepts which are more elementary than the idea "being" and by means of which we should be able to construct the idea of "being." But all other concepts, whether formal-concrete or formal-abstract, presuppose the idea "being" and its implied reference to unmodified "to be" as to-be-real. Hence we cannot explicitate what "to be" *is* by means of something which is prior to it and a necessary condition of it, but only by means of something that is posterior to it and its necessary consequence, a property in which it reveals itself, such as identity, infinity, perfection, determinateness, unity, truth, goodness, activity, etc. "To be" as the immanent ground of all that is can be explicitated only by showing how everything in beings is explained through their measure of participation in *being*.

"To Be" and Beings. This does not mean that the metaphysical explanation of beings is finished when the wealth of modes in which beings can participate in *being* has been analyzed and synthetized. Far from it. Although "to be" as "to be," does not need an explanation and although "to be" is the immanent explanatory ground of finite beings, this does not explain *why this* and *that* and the *many de facto* existing beings are, are as they are, and exercise the activity which they exercise. For "to be" is multiplied in many beings; it is limited to to-be-this or to-be-that; it is together with particular modes of *being* a constituent principle of many bearers of *being* which are distinct from "to be" itself. The fundamental question is: This multiplication of "to be" in many beings, this particularization to this or that being, this composition with different modes of *being* in the *de facto* existing concrete beings as they are and operate, in one word, this given world, as be-ing through "to be," does it belong of necessity to unqualified *being?* Or reversely, does to-be-real belong of necessity to these, and only to these, many, particular, composite beings which we experience or are able to experience?

If the answer were in the affirmative, i.e., if all finite and real beings were absolutely necessary, then unqualified "to be" would of necessity include its participation into precisely these finite real beings. In that case not only would everything real, exactly as it is, be absolutely necessary, but there would also be no room for any possible but *de facto* not really existing being. The modes of possibility, reality, and necessity would wholly coincide.

The question remains, however, how *we* could know that everything real is absolutely necessary and that everything possible is necessarily realized. On the contrary, we have reasons to doubt that it is so. For we *experience* finite beings only in their *de facto being;* hence there *seems* to be room for the strictly contingent, i.e., the real which is real neither because of an intrinsic necessity of essence nor because of a necessitating cause which by its very essence is of necessity; and consequently, there seems to be room also for the purely possible, i.e., what can be but is not real.[10]

In this second case the question arises of what the ground is for the reality of the strictly contingent: How can it be real without having the necessary and sufficient ground of its being-real either in itself or in a necessitating cause which itself is of necessity? At the same time a question must be asked about the possibility of the purely possible: How can it be related to being-real without itself being real?[11]

173. *The Transcendental Relationship of Essence and "To Be" in the Finite Being*

In the real finite being we have admitted a distinction between its to-be-real and its individual essence as its constituent principles. Let us reflect on this distinction.[12]

If "to be" as that through which the being is, and essence, as that through which the being is in this or that particular way, themselves are not beings in the primary sense but are only conceived and expressed by us in the manner of beings,[13] we cannot say that they are distinct in the primary sense. For only that which itself is something that is can have the property of being distinct from something else that is. In concrete being, therefore, essence and "to be" must be conceived as to some extent identified with each other.

The Foundation of the Distinction Between Essence and "To Be." Nevertheless, when we conceive essence and "to be" as necessarily distinct from each other and from the finite being itself, our

---

[10]Cf. no. 31.

[11]The problem raised by the relationship of the modes of *being* is ultimately the problem of *immanence* or *transcendence.* Is the world of *de facto* existing finite beings fully self-explanatory because the ultimate ground must be found in unqualified *being* which has of necessity to particularize itself in these particular modes of *being,* and especially in intellectual beings which are open to *being,* so that ultimately unqualified "to be" coincides in one way or another with the totality of finite real beings? Or must we maintain that there is a distinction between the possible and the real, that not everything possible is of necessity also realized, even that everything finite and real is strictly contingent, so that "to be" finds its ultimate ground in a ground that wholly transcends finite beings, a cause which does not of necessity have to cause whatever it causes?

[12]Cf. no. 60.

[13]Cf. no. 172.

distinction has an ontic foundation. For this reason our judgments concerning this distinction are true judgments with respect to
what they intend to convey, the thing signified: they offer an explanation, inadequately expressed as it is, for the imperfect identity of the
finite being with itself in *being*. Although the finite being, as being,
is identical, one, infinite, perfect, determinate, and connected with
all others, as a *finite* being, it is divided, finite, imperfect, determinable, and exclusive of the others through its particularity. It is this
"finite infiniteness," which means a dynamic orientation to, and consequently also a certain distance from unqualified *being* that we
explain by means of the distinction between essence and "to be."

We conceive this distinction in the manner of the distinction
between beings, but we know that it is a "real" distinction in an
analogous sense, a distinction *within* the one, albeit only imperfectly
one, real being.[14]

However, if the distinction between essence and "to be" in the
real being is a distinction between constituent principles, then the
relation which we necessarily conceive between the two is not an
immediate and adequate expression of a real relation between one
being and another being. First of all, essence and "to be" are not
purely relations, for otherwise they would presuppose a foundation
from which they flow, and a distinct starting point and terminus which
through essence and "to be" are related. We must say, therefore,
that essence and "to be" *have* relations, that they are "essentially"
related to each other and to the being which they constitute.[15]

Nevertheless, we cannot say that essence and "to be" are related
in the primary sense. For to be proper bearers of relations, they
would first have to be subsistent and really distinct beings in the
proper sense.

A Necessary Relation. Yet it remains true that essence and "to
be" have to be conceived as essentially and of necessity related.
Specifically the essence has to be conceived as wholly and entirely
related to, and dependent upon "to be." For the essence expresses
a content which is conceivable only as a possible limiting modification
of *being* and therefore is inconceivable without a relation to it. A
limitation is not thinkable save in connection with something positive
whose limitations and circumscription it is. The "to be" of a being,
likewise, must be conceived as *de facto* limited through the essence

---

[14]Cf. no. **170.**
[15]Cf. *ibid.*

and therefore as related to the essence, although as "to be" it transcends every limitation. For in the experiential judgment in which
we enunciate the "to be" of finite beings, "to be" always presents itself
as the "to be" *of* this or *of* that, i.e., as an immanent constitutent principle that is limited through the individual essence. Accordingly, we
always conceive "to be" as related to the essence and connected
with the essence in the imperfect unity of the finite being.

The relations which we conceive of necessity between essence
and "to be" should be conceived as "transcendental" relations, which
are "real" in a derivative and analogous sense—namely, insofar as
they express the merely imperfect identity and consequently the
duality-in-unity of the one real finite being.

Contingency and the Distinction of Essence and "To Be." The
distinction and relation between essence and "to be" offer an explanation for the finiteness of the being, the limited and particular
mode in which it is. At the same time they make us realize fully the
above-mentioned problem: Is not every finite being contingently real?

For, if the individual essence and the real "to be," despite the
fact that in the finite being they are *de facto* somewhat identified
with each other through their transcendental relation, do not *of
themselves* coincide but are distinct, it seems to our thinking not
absolutely impossible that this finite being would not really be.

Let us examine this point a little more closely. When we consider
this finite being only with respect to its essence, with respect to
what it is, we find that on the basis of the confluence of its essential characteristics into a single essence it is ordered to being-
real by necessity of nature, but there is nothing which warrants that
this order has to be brought to realization. *Of itself,* the finite
being, considered in its essence, presents itself to us merely as a
possible being. Whether it really exists or not we cannot deduce
from the individual essence itself, precisely because this essence
does not coincide with unqualified *being,* but merely contains a possible particular mode of *being.* Only through the *experience* of its
de facto reality do we know that the possiblity of being-real has been
fulfilled and that the finite being participates in being-real without
fully coinciding with being-real.

If this consideration, which we offer here only in a provisional
way, is correct, it follows that the finite being, insofar as it *de
facto* is realized, has real "to be" as an immanent constituent princi-

ple; for this reason, insofar and as long as it is real, it cannot be non-real. Its being-real is hypothetically necessary. But *of itself* it is not of necessity real because, in our view, it does not include being-real by virtue of its essence. To be real, at least in our view, is not an essential predicate of the finite real being.

Of course, it could still happen that it would be absolutely necessary because of a dependence on a cause which of itself is necessary as well as *necessitating*. But the question regarding this cause is precisely the fundamental problem: Must all finite reality be conceived as ultimately dependent upon a non-finite cause or does the whole of finite beings explain itself? And if we must accept a nonfinite or infinite cause in whatever sense such a cause should be understood, does this cause cause its effects of necessity or freely?

Before the problem of distinction and relation between essence and "to be" in the finite being and the implied participation in unqualified *being* make us raise the problem of causal dependence, it will be necessary to raise first in a more explicit way the question of the modes of contingency, possibility, and necessity. For, despite the finiteness of the beings which we experience, perhaps it is possible to deny their dependence upon a cause distinct from them and to see them as absolutely necessary constituent elements, parts, or aspects of the All-One.

174. *The Merely-Real or Contingent*

Contingency. Contingency is a mode of reality—namely, not-necessary reality or mere-reality. Contingent is that which is real, but, while being real, could also not have been.[16]

However, with F. Grégoire[17] and others, we must make a distinction:

1. In the strict sense contingent is that which neither is of necessity by virtue of its own essence nor *proceeds of necessity* from a cause which is necessary by virtue of its own essence. The strictly contingent is the opposite of the absolutely necessary in the broad sense, which extends not only to what is of itself necessary but also to what of necessity proceeds from a cause that of itself is necessary.

---

[16]Cf. no. 30.

[17]"Condition, conditionné, inconditionné," *Revue philosophique de Louvain*, vol. 46 (1948), p. 33. See also A. Grégoire, *Immanence et transcendence*, Brussels, 1939, pp. 40-42; L. de Raeymaeker, *The Philosophy of Being*, St. Louis, 1954, pp. 93, 286 ff. (especially footnote 14), 124 f. (Avicenna), and 297 ff.; "Le principe de causalité à la lumière des controverses récentes," *Acta III Congr. Thomist. Internationalis*, Turin, 1951, pp. 153-156.

2. In the broad sense contingent is that which is not of itself necessary although *it is not excluded that it proceeds of necessity* from a cause which is of itself necessary. The contingent in the broad sense is the opposite of the absolutely necessary in the strict sense, i.e., that which is necessary by virtue of its own essence.

Contingency and Chance Occurrences. We know the real primarily only from experience and therefore in its *de facto being*.[18] It does not immediately reveal itself as necessary. Thus we readily speak of contingency and think that beings and events could have been also different from what they *de facto* are. True, we have a kind of insight into necessity, but this insight is primarily concerned with hypothetical necessity. We understand, for instance, that if, and as long as a being is, it cannot not-be.[19] We sometimes understand that some definite being, once its essence is given, of necessity gives rise to certain properties or powers,[20] and that under given conditions it will necessarily perform certain activities or operations. We understand also that finite and spatio-temporal beings have of necessity certain static and dynamic relations with other presupposed beings, so that to some extent everything is connected with everything in the order of *being*.[21]

All this, however, does not prevent us from continuing to speak about contingency with respect to the existence of certain determined beings here-and-now: the individual, so we think, is contingent, and the concrete order of individual beings could have been different from what it *de facto* is, even though aspects of necessity are present in all beings, events, and situations.

For this reason we use the term "contingent" or "chance" as eminently applicable to events which are brought about through an unexpected, unforeseen or unintentional concurrence of circumstances.[22] This contingency is considered to be a property of an effect which we cannot explain through a single cause or series of causes or through a single tendency of nature but only through a complex of causes which, so far as our knowledge is concerned, are not evidently interconnected. Contingency may not be ascribed without any

[18]Cf. no. 21.

[19]Cf. no. 23.

[20]Cf. no. 100.

[21]Cf. no. 164.

[22]Concerning chance, see Jacques Maritain, "Reflections on Necessity and Contingency," *Essays in Thomism,* New York, 1942, pp. 25-37.

further ado to the ontic conditions themselves, for series of causes acting in complete independence cannot exist because everything is connected with everything, no matter how remote this connection may be.[23]   Accordingly, the problem has to be raised again in the form of the question to what extent it is possible for us to discover the more profound co-ordination hidden behind the actual collaboration of causal series, and whether this co-ordination is absolutely necessary or strictly contingent.

It is clear that our *ignorance* regarding the whole of observable finite beings, does not give us the right simply to consider an individual finite being or a group of individuals to be contingent in the strict sense of the term.

Contingency and Corruption.   Even the datum of experience that certain beings begin or cease to be, and the insight that they are essentially orientated to coming-to-be and passing away are not signs of contingency in the strict sense.   For, strictly speaking, contingency does not mean that a being, although it is really now, can not-be at a different moment, but that a being *at the very moment* at which it is real, i.e., while it is hypothetically necessary, could also have not-been.   In other words, it is not only not of itself, not absolutely necessary, but also not through a *necessitating* cause which of itself is necessary.   This contingency, then, does not immediately follow from the fact that something is now and is not then.   For one could offer provisionally an explanation by saying that what is necessary by its very essence, whatever it may be, implies of necessity also that certain beings exist at certain times and not at other times.   In that case it would be impossible that this being here and now, perishable as it is, could have not-been.   True, we must admit that this absolute necessity of this actual perishable being can be deduced neither from its essence nor from this necessitating cause.   However, we cannot yet exclude the hypothesis that the only way of explaining the real world without any contradiction would consist in admitting that all *de facto* existing beings flow of necessity from the absolute, just as consequences follow from the premises.[24]

---

[23]Cf. no. 108.

[24]The strict contingency of perishable beings cannot be demonstrated by this argument: since every being maintains the identity of its essence, coming to be and passing away show that to-be-real does not pertain to this being through an essential necessity. For we do not know the individual essence of this being adequately, and, therefore, we cannot determine whether it pertains perhaps to the essence of this individual, e.g., the human person, who is essentially historical, that it *can* be realized only at certain moments and not at others.

Contingency and Free Will. Contingency in the strict sense reveals itself clearly to us only with respect to the effects originating in the free will of man. Even the free-will decision is not brought about until the complex of its sufficient conditions is fully present, but among these conditions there is at least one which is a non-necessitating condition. Like everything that is real, the free act of will is fully determined, but its determination is not a *necessary* effect of the presence of its conditions. Ultimately, man determines himself to his act: the ultimate practical judgment and the choice of will determine each other under different aspects.[25] Moreover, whatever flows from the decision, whatever man causes freely, has a sufficient ground of *being,* but is only hypothetically necessary in the strict sense, because the hypothesis, i.e., the decision, is contingent in the strict sense. Thus man, as a free being has the capacity for real possibilities which are contradictorily opposed. For both contradictory opposites a sufficient ground of *being* is really present, but only one of the two is realized, and this without necessity. Accordingly, with respect to a freely realized effect it may be asserted that it is not necessary either of itself or because of a *necessitating* cause—it *could* also not-be at the very moment when it *de facto* is. And with respect to the contradictory opposite of the *de facto* realized effect it is fully true that it is really possible, without *de facto* being realized.

In a diminishing and analogous sense one may speak of a certain contingency and therefore, of active determination with respect to the prefigurations of freedom in animal and vital activity.[26] Here, too, causality presents itself as a kind of superiority over the environment and, consequently, as a kind of determination which, though not free, is spontaneous and active.[27]

The strict contingency of finite beings in their totality can be proved only in one of the following two ways:

1. By proving that everything finite, even if taken in its total interconnection, is ultimately dependent on a *free* First Cause;[28]

Even in this case such a being would be real only through participation, so that its essence and "to be" remain distinct, but the contingency implied by this distinction could be merely a contingency in the broad sense.

The only thing which we can say provisionally is this: the individual perishable being has a sufficient ground for its *being* at the moment when it is, while at the moment when it is not, a necessary condition for its being is lacking.

[25]Cf. no. 142.
[26]Cf. no. 143.
[27]Cf. no. 115.
[28]Cf. no. 180.

2. By showing, as Nicolai Hartmann wants, that necessity can never be more than hypothetical, so that the concept of absolute necessity implies a contradiction. For in that case the absolute, i.e., the unconditional whole of finite beings, is contingent precisely because it is unconditioned.[29]

175. *The Purely Possible*

We know that something is possible first of all from its reality. But, because the real presents itself to us primarily as *de facto* being, we think that the events could have been different from what they are and thus conceive the purely-possible. As we conceive it, the purely-possible is a being, but has no actual reality, so that what remains is only a *de facto* non-fulfilled order to being-real.

Intrinsic Possibility and Real Possibility. We know that in order to be capable of being-real, a thing must be individual and fully determined.[30] If, nevertheless, we sometimes assert of the general that it is possible, we cannot mean the general *as* general, but we refer to an individual being which, however, we consider only according to the characteristics indicated in the general concept. We say, for instance, that a mountain of gold is possible, but what we mean is this: it is not at all excluded that somewhere sometime there would exist a definite individual something in which the characteristics "mountain" and "gold" go together. If there is question of characteristics which in our experience we have at some time or another seen together in an individual being, then there is no objection against such an assertion. It refers to the so-called objective intrinsic possibility in principle, which is sometimes called "logical possibility." However, if we ourselves bring the characteristics in question together in an "essence," in the broadest sense of the term, then the fact that we do not see anything in this essence which implies a contradiction is not a sufficient reason for concluding to an objective intrinsic possibility, although we may provisionally and subjectively consider such a being as possible. For we do not know any "essence" adequately with all its properties and relations hence we cannot exclude that there would be contradiction in the proposed combination of the characteristics. Accordingly, objective intrinsic

[29]Cf. no. 176.
[30]Cf. no. 90.

possibility requires that we positively see the impossibility of there being any contradiction in the combination of characteristics.[31]

However, even the objective intrinsic possibility, taken in itself, is not yet a *real* possibility or *"realizability,"* at least when there is question of a being which is dependent on conditions or causes. If such a being is to be realizable, it must, first of all, be also *extrinsically* possible in principle, i.e., there must not be any contradiction in the necessary and sufficient condition of this being, and these conditions themselves must be intrinsically possible. Secondly, all the *sufficient conditions* must already be *really present* or at least it is to be expected that they will be present. Moreover, with respect to the realizable, the question is whether these sufficient conditions are or are not necessitating conditions. For, if they are necessitating, they will entrain their effect of necessity; when they are present, the really possible is of necessity realized, so that it is not purely possible.

Real Possibility and Free Will. The really purely-possible reveals itself to us clearly only where we have the power to determine ourselves in free acts. Man is a being of possibilities, i.e., in him "to be able" or active potency[32] assumes an analogously higher sense because of his freedom: to the extent that he is free, he can "make" himself be in this or that, albeit only accidental, way, without being necessitated by previous conditions. True, his abilities are very limited, especially because of the material-spiritual nature given to him; nevertheless, he must be called to some extent the master of his acts because of his self-determination. The effects also of these acts, insofar as he in his free actions intervenes in the course of events, are not fully determined by the presence of vital and physical forces, but through control over his bodily motions he is capable of organizing these forces and making them subservient to his freely chosen purposes. Thus his dependence on other beings is not total, but through his "yes" or "no" he himself is in someway a source. This means that he discovers possibilities which are real possibilities because the sufficient conditions of their realizations are present, yet these possibilities will not become real of necessity because their realization depends upon his free initiative.

---

[31]Concerning the different types of possibility and the distinction between "not seeing a contradiction" and "seeing no contradiction" cf. the careful article of F. Grégoire, "L'acte de mésurer et la notion général d' infini," *Mélanges J. Maréchal*, vol. II, Brussels, 1950, pp. 94-97. See also F. Grégoire, "La preuve réelle de Dieu, étude critique," *Revue philos. de Louvain*, vol. 54 (1956), pp. 112-119.

[32]Cf. no. 72.

In a degraded and analogous sense we may speak of the purely-possible, as well as of the contingent, in animal and living activities. Here also several ways of realization seem to be left open, and they are "judged" by a spontaneous but not strictly free judgment of the estimative sense.[33]

It depends on the question concerning the ultimate ground of the world, whether or not, even under conditions different from the actual ones, in principle everything is *realizable* of which we think that it is in principle possible because we see, so we think, that no contradiction is included either in its essence or in its necessary conditions. Let us assume that the wholly unconditional or absolute,[34] would be such that it would of necessity bring forth everything possible as real. In that case we would have to conclude that whatever is *de facto* non-real—even though we consider it in principle possible in the sense of not-absolutely-impossible—is, strictly speaking, absolutely impossible, despite the fact that we do not see the reason for this impossibility. On the other hand, if the absolute is of such a nature that it is an infinite but free cause, then whatever does not include a contradiction can in principle be realized by this infinite cause, even though *de facto* this has not been done.

---

[33]1. If on the level of necessitating causes we oppose the really possible to what is already real, we usually refer to the really possible in a somewhat broader sense—namely, that which according to our limited prescience will *probably* follow, i.e., that whose sufficient conditions are partly realized, while in view of the known situation it is to be expected that the missing conditions also will be realized. (cf. J. Hessen, *Lehrbuch der Philosophie,* vol. III, München, 1950, pp. 60-65).

2. It is a restriction of the concept "really possible" to follow Nicholai Hartman (*Möglichkeit und Wirklichkeit,* Berlin, 1938) when he applies it only that for which the totality of its conditions is already realized and adds that such a possible will always take place of necessity. First of all, there is the above-mentioned broader concept, in which the really possible is still distinct from the real by this that it will become real only through the actual occurrence of the expected condition which ultimately completes the totality and renders it sufficient. Secondly, if one calls really possible only that of which all conditions are present, it is still possible that among these conditions there is a non-necessitating condition (as in the case of a free act). Thus the effect would be contingent in the strict sense, and its opposite really possible, but not real.

3. Real potency in the proper sense (cf. nos. 92-96), whether active or passive, skills and habitus (cf. no. 94) are something real which can be the dispositive or emanative (cf. no. 100) source of certain activities, perfections, forms, or acts. In a finite being this potency is usually a necessary but never the sufficient ground for the acts or operations to be done or the perfections to be acquired. Accordingly, they do not make the activities or acts really possible in the strict sense, but may do so in the broader sense.

[34]Cf. no. 176.

176. *The Absolutely Necessary*

Hypothetical Necessity.   Necessity[35] is known to us primarily on the basis of observed facts as a hypothetical necessity implied by these facts.   But hypothetical necessity has a twofold meaning.   In the *strict* sense, it implies that the hypothesis could also not have been, so that it is strictly contingent.   In the *broad* sense, it does not say anything about the necessity or contingency, and even about the possibility or impossibility, of the supposition. Hypothetical necessity, as we know it, usually has this broad sense.   We consider only the necessary connection between the supposition and its consequence, but leave the mode of *being* itself of the supposition out of consideration: it does not matter whether the supposition agrees with the (necessary or non-necessary) facts or only with all kinds of merely proposed combinations which we do not even always consider possible.

This necessity presents itself first as the mode of general judgments which are concerned with beings considered according to a more or less general *essence* and indicate what relations exist between the intrinsic constituent principles of the essence or what properties and relations flow from the essence.   Only a hypothetical necessity is possessed by such general judgments whose truth is either directly seen or indirectly known through reasoning.   For we do not know whether or not the beings which we presuppose to be according to certain modes of *being* are absolutely necessary.   In some sciences man constructs even "essences" of which he does not yet know for certain whether they imply a contradiction and can state only that we do not see that they are unintelligible.

However, with respect to the very first evident judgments or axioms about being *as* being, we must admit that we are not dealing with hypothetical judgments in the proper sense.[36]   The hypothesis "something is, no matter what and no matter how" is not merely fulfilled but fulfilled with absolute necessity. As we have seen before,[37] the supposition that nothing would be is absolutely impossible not only for me but also *in itself,* even though I *know* this absolute impossibility only because it is implied in my factual reality.

---

[35]Cf. F. Grégoire, "Condition, conditionné, et inconditionné," *Revue philosophique de Louvain,* vol. 46 (1948), pp. 16-21.

[36]Cf. no. 35

[37]Cf. no. 23.

The Absolutely Necessary and the Unconditional. Is it possible to show that not only of necessity something is, no matter what it may be, but also that there is something which is in every hypothesis, something which *of itself is absolutely necessary?* The answer is in the affirmative if we take this "something" in the broadest analogous sense, i.e., if we understand by it not only a determined being which participates in *being* but also, if need be, unqualified "to be" itself, or even "something" in which essence, "to be," and being would wholly coincide. In this broadest possible sense, we must certainly admit that there is "something" which is of itself absolutely necessary.

The reason is as follows. Whatever is, is either conditioned or unconditioned. The conditioned implies that its fully sufficient condition exists. In its turn, this condition could also be conditioned by the first conditioned in such a way that the two are together in a symmetric relationship and condition *each other*. Then the question arises whether or not this *whole* is conditioned. Since every condition which itself is conditioned is an insufficient condition, every such condition presupposes its condition. Hence, ultimately everything conditioned must refer to the unconditioned totality of its conditions. At present we are not concerned with causality and, therefore, it does not yet matter whether or not this unconditioned totality of conditions coincides with the "whole" constituted by individual members which, each taken separately, are conditioned. In any case we must admit that the "whole" is absolutely unconditioned, i.e., it does not have any condition outside itself, provided the "whole" is taken as the whole of everything that is possible and real, of everything that *is* in any way whatsoever, even that which no longer merely participates in *being* but is identical with it—in other words, the whole in the broadest sense, so that only absolute not-to-be falls outside it.

However, the absolutely unconditioned is not simply to be identified with the absolutely necessary. For why should it be impossible that the unconditioned "whole" or the unconditioned First in the whole, would be only *de facto* but not of necessity? As a matter of fact, this view is taken by Hartmann. Every necessity, he says, is a relation of the necessitated to the necessitating and, therefore, is always relative or hypothetical. Finally there has to be a non-necessitated necessitating condition. But this last condition, as being unconditioned, is precisely no longer necessary because there is nothing *else* on the basis of which it would be necessitated. Accordingly, the absolutely necessary cannot be thought. What we mean by it, the absolutely first both in the order of knowledge (the first insight) and in the order of *being* (the first cause), strictly speaking, is precisely the absolutely contingent. Hartmann considers it a contradiction that something would be "of itself" absolutely necessary. Thus for him the principle of ground and consequently also the intelligibility of being as being is not absolutely general but restricted, not only in the sense that *we* are not capable of grasping everything in our knowledge, but also in the sense that *in itself* and for the most perfect intellect not everything is intelligible, and certainly not the *being* of the absolute and unconditioned.[38]

It must be admitted that what of itself is absolutely necessary can be called necessary only in an analogous sense, for it differs essentially from the only necessity that is immediately known to us—namely, the hypothetically necessary, in the broader or stricter sense, which is necessitated to be by *something else*. However, we should not forget that, apart from the conditioning of one being by another being, there is also within a single being the conditioning of its constituent principles, properties, and relations. We find here a necessity based on something that is *immanent* in a being, albeit not in perfect identity. But what is of itself absolutely necessary is something which is not in any way necessitated by anything other than itself— not by another being, not by a superior logical principle or law, and not by any other constituent principle which does not wholly coincide with its essence. Yet we have to conceive it as related to itself in perfect identity in such a way that it founds *itself*, is itself the ground of its *being*. If this analogy is kept in mind, it is possible to show that the absolutely unconditioned or absolutely independent is of itself absolutely necessary. The proof is as follows.

Self-Identity and the Absolutely Unconditional. Hypothetically necessary is that which only in a certain hypothesis is real. But the absolutely unconditioned, which is the condition of all conditions, is real in *every* hypothesis, no matter of what kind. Its "to be" is not conditioned by anything, so that it cannot be abolished by the absence of anything. Because the absolutely unconditioned is prior to every hypothesis, it cannot not-be in any hypothesis.

However, the fact that it is not necessitated to be by anything else does not yet mean that of itself it can just as well not-be as be,

---

[38]Cf. no. 42.

that it is indifferent with respect to *being* and not-being, that it is contingent in the broad or the strict sense of the term. Contingency, i.e., being capable of not-being, is not at all a perfection but rather points to an imperfection—namely, not having in oneself the ground of one's *being*. But the fact that the unconditioned is not necessitated to be either by something else or by a constitutent principle which does not perfectly coincide with its essence means precisely that it is in no way passive but *is of itself active through the perfect coincidence of itself with its* being. The unconditional is not prior to its *being,* nor posterior to its *being,* but is active "to-be-itself," which perfectly grounds, explains, and renders itself intelligible. Its essence cannot be anything else than active identity or rather, according to our mode of thinking, self-identification that always "has already been made."

Accordingly, like the conditioned, the unconditioned also has a ground for its *being.* However, the sufficient reason for the *being* of the conditioned does not lie entirely in the immanent *being* of the conditioned itself, but is found in its dependence on the condition, whereas the reason or the "why" of the unconditioned lies solely in its *being,* considered as its essence which the unconditioned is *of itself.* It is itself its groundless ground.[39]

---

[39]Cf. F. Grégoire, "Condition, conditionné, et inconditionné," *Revue philosophique de Louvain,* pp. 25-31. See also the extensive and profound considerations of the same author in *Questions concernant l'existentialisme,* vol. II, *Essai d'une phénoménologie des preuves métaphysiques de Dieu,* Louvain, 1953.

It must be admitted that in speaking of perfect identity, active identification, and self-constitution, we make use of relations of reason (cf. no. 169) to express conceptually, to some extent and in an analogous way, the perfect *simplicity* of that which we intend to express. Our concepts are not an adequate expression of what we conceive to be, negatively, absolutely unconditioned and independent (not *from* something else) and, positively, as grounding itself (*of* itself). The analogon which most closely but still imperfectly approximates this coincidence of independence and necessity is the act in which we are supremely ourselves—the free self-determination originating in ourselves. This act is what it is, determinately and undeniably but, on the other hand, insofar as it is free, it is not determined through determination from without but through self-determination (cf. no. 143).

The germ of truth contained in Nicholai Hartmann's view is that the unconditioned transcends *our* finite concepts of necessity and contingency in the unity of an immanent necessity and a transcendental independence. Immanent necessity makes us understand that to-be-able-not-to-be cannot be conceived as a positive perfection; transcendental independence makes us see that "to be" in its highest form may not be conceived as a "made-to-be," received under certain conditions, but should be seen as the *act of being,* the *actus essendi.*

177. *The Absolute*[40]

Let us summarize the preceding considerations. *There is some-thing which is wholly unconditioned*—at least, the "whole" in its broadest sense, i.e., everything which is in any way whatsoever with all its conditions and consequences. The unconditioned must not be conceived as contingent but as of itself absolutely necessary in the sense that it *perfectly founds and explains itself*.

This conclusion still proceeds somewhat the distinction between theism and certain forms of atheism, between emanationist or dialectic monism and the doctrine of creation. It affirms only that the uncon-ditioned is intelligible in itself and does not have to be wholly unintel-ligible for us. Thus it has become a question which philosophy cannot simply leave alone. Especially the relation of the finite beings of our experience to the unconditioned has become a problem. We have to attempt to clarify this relation at least to some extent by determining it more accurately.

The Unconditioned is Wholly Uncaused. It is not difficult to see that the unconditioned must be absolutely uncaused. To be caused, according to any form of causality, is a way of being conditioned. Therefore, there must of necessity be "something" that is not caused. Although we must conceive the unconditioned as founded on itself through identity, we may not say that it is the cause of itself. For the caused has a real relation of dependence to the cause and, con-sequently, is "really" distinct from it—whatever sense we may attach to the term "really"—even if the cause in question is a so-called internal cause. The question, however, whether or not the uncaused itself is the cause of something distinct from itself still remains here out of consideration.[41]

The Unconditioned is Supremely Subsistent. The unconditioned must also be said to be supremely subsistent in an analogous sense. First of all, it should be clear that it is not an accident, an immanent further determination flowing from a presupposed subsistent subject, for it is absolutely independent and, therefore, not dependent on any supporting subject.[42] Secondly, the unconditioned is of itself, i.e., it is its own sufficient ground of *being*. But in that case it has "appro-

---

[40]The considerations of nos. 177-181 are inspired by the reflections of **F.** Grégoire in the second work quoted in footnote 39.

[41]Cf. no. 180.

[42]Cf. no. 68.

priated" its "to be" in the highest possible way,[43] for through self-realization in identity it is the active source of its own *being*. The dependent subsistent being of our experience is *in* itself, but its *"in* itself" does not imply "of itself," so that its "to be" cannot be explained of itself. The unconditioned, however, as being of itself, is *a fortiori* absolutely *in* itself or subsistent.[44] For this reason it cannot properly and strictly be said to be "ex-sisting" insofar as to "ex-sist" expresses having its source in something else and, therefore, being conditioned by it.[45] Provisionally we leave out of consideration whether or not there are "really" distinct immanent and modifying determinations which flow from it either of necessity or without necessity.[46]

The Unconditioned is Absolute. The unconditioned must also be called absolute or non-relative, by which we mean provisionally that it is not *of necessity* related to something *other* than itself through a real relation. For whatever is really related is related to something else.[47] But a relation arranges beings either as equals or according to inferiority and superiority, it is reciprocal or non-reciprocal. With respect to the reciprocal relation one can ask whether or not the *whole* of correlates, as such, again is related to something else, and with respect to the non-reciprocal relation the question may be asked whether or not the *terminus* of the relation, as such, again is related to something else. Ultimately one has to arrive at something which is no longer necessarily related to something outside itself. At least, the "whole," in the broadest sense of the term, of all correlates and termini of relations is no longer so related. Accordingly, the absolute is indubitable. However, the relation of the relative to the absolute and their mutual distinction remain out of consideration here.

178. *Is the Absolute Finite or Infinite?*

Finite and Infinite. The ways of philosophers part when the question is raised whether the absolute should be called finite or infinite.[48]

---

[43]Cf. no. 65.
[44]Cf. no. 163.
[45]Cf. no. 66.
[46]Cf. no. 179.
[47]Cf. no. 163.
[48]Concerning finite and infinite see F. Grégoire, L'acte de mesurer et la notion générale de l'infini, *Mélanges Maréchal, vol. II,* Brussels, 1950, pp. 97-109: "The idea of the infinite is the idea of such a magnitude that the mind cannot even ask itself if a greater magnitude is possible."

The term "finite" is used first with respect to extension and number and next also with respect to time. From the concept "finite" arises the concepts "endless" (endlessly continuing) and "infinite." On the level also of the transcendental plurality of analogous beings[49] one may speak of the finite, endless, and infinite. We will use the term *"extensive* infinity" for ontically infinite plurality, because the term "extension" is customarily used in connection with the denotation of concepts.[50]

In addition, we may speak of comprehensive finiteness or infinity, i.e., the presence or absence of limits with respect to content. First of all, the term may be used in relation to the greater or lesser intensity or degree of perfection according to which certain characteristics or modes of *being,* such as heat or cold, colors, feelings, are realized. At present, however, we are concerned with the greater or lesser intensity of the absolutely general perfection called, "to be," with the quantity[51] or degrees of *being.*[52] By comprehensive or *intensive* infinity we mean unlimited intensity of *being.*

"Finite" or "limited" is a negative concept. As applied to the intensity of *being,* it presupposes that in the progressive movement of our thought we conceive a more perfect "to be" and then deny this "to be" of the being in question by saying that it is only this and not also that or that it is this only to this extent and not to that extent also.

We experience only finite beings and we judge them *as* finite, i.e., we attribute to them a limiting essence. If such is the case with respect to all possible beings which we can experience, this means that we have the power to conceive *endlessly* beings which would be in a more intensive way. For every limitation presupposes that in our thinking the limit is somehow transcended, and it is this transcendence which the limitation denies.

This power to conceive endlessly more perfect beings implies, as we will show now, not only the conceived transcendence of the limit through more intense *being,* but also a certain idea of an infinite intensity of *being.* By "intensively infinite" we mean here with F. Grégoire: that which is denied by every limitation of *being,*

---

[49]Cf. no. 78.
[50]Cf. no. 51.
[51]Cf. no. 163.
[52]Cf. no. 57.

i.e., that which we have to conceive in such a way that the question of a possible greater intensity of *being* cannot even be raised.

The fact that we can endlessly conceive more perfect beings means that no limit is necessarily the last one, beyond which nothing more intense can be conceived. But in that case the hypothesis that at a given moment we would have to say: "This is the most perfect being which *we* can think of," although we thought of it as *limited,* is an impossible hypothesis. For on what ground would we conceive it as limited? The only possible ground would be a transcendence of the limit at least in thought. Accordingly, we cannot conceive anything as the most perfect being that can be thought, unless in principle it does not permit any further transcendence of the limit. But that which in principle does no allow such a transcendence is that which is conceived as excluding *every* limit.

Therefore, the concepts themselves of finite intensity of *being* and of an endlessly progressing thought imply the previous concept of an infinite intensity of *being* that is at least proposed problematically. To call a proposed being "finite" is to assert that it does not realize every perfection of *being,* to deny that it is all-perfect. Hence not only is infinity the denial of finiteness, but also finiteness is the denial of infinity: finiteness presents itself against the background of an absolute infinity which, albeit denied with respect to the being in question, is first proposed at least problematically. But in that case, for our thinking, that which is of itself absolutely infinite does not imply an immediately perceived contradiction. Nevertheless, at present we may not yet conclude that we positively see that contradiction is excluded and that therefore, the "of itself absolutely infinite" is in principle intrinsically possible.[53]

The Infinity of Unqualified "To Be." How does it happen that we have the power endlessly to conceive beings which are in a more intensive way, so that we conceive every definite being as excluding all other possible modes of *being,* as finite? This manner of thinking is based on the mode of *being* proper to the beings known to us. Every being of our experience *is* in a particular way, and the possibilities of particularization are inexhaustible. But in that case "to be," when it is no longer considered as the "to be" *of* this or *of* that, but as unqualified "to be," is in principle not subject to any limit.

---

[53]Cf. no. 175.

"Absolutely considered, 'to be' is infinite, for it can be participated in by infinitely many beings and in infinitely many ways."[54]

However, we must critically investigate in *exactly* which sense unqualified "to be" can be called infinite, for it is always the "to be" *of* this or *of* that being and cannot be placed outside the beings whose constituent principle it is.[55]

Some say that unqualified "to be" is a general concept, obtained through abstracting the proper determined "to be" present in every individual being. When we leave aside all determinations, there arises a concept of "to-be-in-general," predicable of all beings. It may be called infinite in this sense that it allows all possible determinations but does not exclude any of them. This infinity, however, is merely that of the absolutely-undetermined determinable. It applies only to the concept as it exists in its generality in our mind, but there is nothing in reality which corresponds to this infinity. For every "to be" of an individual being is perfectly distinct from the "to-be's" of the other beings and it is determinately only a to-be-this or to-be-that.

This view, which attributes to "to be" an empty infinity, cannot be accepted for two reasons. First of all, because this view does not harmonize with the way in which we have explained the concept "being";[56] secondly, because "to be" does not reveal itself to us primarily in a concept but in a judgment.

"To Be" as of Itself Infinite. First of all, the concept "being" does not arise through proper abstraction from the determinations of beings. On the contrary, as a transcendental and analogous idea, it contains precisely all particular beings in an actual but confused way. It is all-embracing not only with respect to extension but also in regard of comprehension. It is not a concept alongside other concepts but the concept of all concepts. The endless movement of our experiential thinking is precisely the progressive immanent explicitation of the wealth implicitly contained in the idea "being."[57]

To what does this idea owe its possibility of endless explicitation? Not to this that it indicates in beings a certain *opposition* between the subject which is and the "to be" through which the subject is, but to this that it indicates also a certain measure of *identity* of beings

---

[54]Thomas Aquinas, *Contra gentes,* bk. I, ch. 43.

[55]Cf. no. 40.

[56]Cf. no. 51.

[57]Cf. nos. 50-56.

with "to be." In other words, it owes this possibility to the fact that it refers to "to be" as that which reveals itself to some extent in every conceivable being, no matter how deficient this revelation may be.

Accordingly, the "to be" which is co-signified in the idea "being" is the source of the endless movement of thought that is consequent **on this idea.** Therefore, "to be," considered in itself, has to negate every limit and must be a constituent principle of the many and finite beings which *of itself* is one and infinite.

Secondly, it is not correct to think that the infinity and unity attributed to unqualified "to be" are meant to be applicable to our concept of "to be," precisely and solely as a universal concept derived through our thinking from the many and finite beings.[58] In our view it is to the very "to be" itself, as *actus essendi,* as act of *being,* that this unity and infinity pertain. However, this unity and infinity should not be misunderstood.

Let us begin by admitting that unqualified "to be," as the constituent principle through which the many finite beings are, is always multiplied and particularized. It is not something which exists in itself, outside beings, as *absolutely* one and *absolutely* infinite. Nevertheless, it is a principle which *of itself* implies unity and infinity, and it is not merely conceived as one and infinite by virtue of our abstracting way of thinking.

1. That "to be" is finitized in beings does not mean that it would be finite of itself and would have merely a privative infinity as a concept in our thought because we would leave behind the determinations present in each of the individual beings. For these "determinations," insofar as they are opposed "to be," do not have the nature of enrichments but that of limitations.[59] "To be" is finitized, not because of itself it would imply finiteness, but because its infinity does not come to fullness in any of the individual beings. However, to the extent to which each being participates in "to be," it is orientated to infinity, i.e., it is endlessly perfectible.[60]

2. That "to be" is multiplied in beings does not mean that there is only a pure plurality of separate immanent principles of *being* which we would *a posteriori* synthetize in a single universal concept. For the very plurality of beings *is* a mode of unity, albeit only imperfectly.[61]

[58]Cf. no. 172.
[59]Cf. nos. 41 and 63.
[60]Cf. no. 63.
[61]Cf. no. 39.

"To be" is multiplied, not because *of itself* it would imply plurality, but because its unity does not come to fullness in any one of the many beings. However, to the extent to which each being participates in "to be," it is one with all the others. For it is not only itself— although imperfectly because it "becomes"—, but according as it becomes more and more identical with its ideal essence through self-realization,[62] it includes also more and more the others as others. That which in each being is most intimate and proper, and through which it distinguishes itself from what it is not, its immanent "to be," is also the ground of its connection with all, without making them lose their subsistence. Every being not only has ever more intimate relations with the others that are actually together with it according as it grows more in intensity of *being,* but it has also potential relations to the infinite multiplicity of all beings that are ever really possible.[63] No matter how much beings are opposed to one another and mutually exclusive, there is a certain, albeit very imperfect, mutual dependence and relational immanence with respect to all others, not only on the level of knowing but even in the lower regions of *being.*

Infinity of Possible Beings. We are unable to deduce the possible particular modes of *being* from a perfect intuition of *being,* but know the possible only from what we *de facto* experience as real. This experience never extends to the "totality" of all reality. For this reason we do not fully know the degrees of intensity according to which "to be" can finitize itself. As we have seen, however, the endless progress of our cognitive movement has its ground in the pre-predicative awareness, present in every judgment, that unqualified "to be" *of itself* implies not opposition but unity, not finiteness but infinity. Thus it follows that endlessly other beings than those encountered in our limited experience must be possible. This limitless possibility means not merely that *we* do not see any contradiction in the existence of other beings, but also that these beings *de facto* do not imply a contradiction either in their essence or in their conditions. In other words, in principle they must be intrinsically and extrinsically possible.[64]

However, even this is not sufficient. The inexhaustibleness of *being* demands that the being-real of other beings must be *concretely* possible, even though we do not know which other beings can be real.

---

[62]Cf. no. 64.

[63]Cf. no. 168.

[64]Cf. no. 175.

Their being-real must not be in contradiction with the "totality" of all reality. But the being-real of other beings would be in such a contradiction if the sufficient conditions for the possibility of these beings were never really present. Hence we must conclude that endlessly other beings than those experienced by us must be *really* possible, i.e., capable of realization.[65]

Is Relative Infinity Grounded in Absolute Infinity? As long as we remain on the level of unqualified *being,* we cannot speak of absolute infinity, but only of the *relative* infinity implied in the limitless possibility of finite beings. For we should not forget that unqualified "to be" is the to-be-of-all-beings in their universal interconnection. Although *of itself* it does not imply any modification and limitation through an essence, nevertheless, it is always in *relation* to finite and material modes of *being.* True, absolutely speaking, as the actuality of all acts and form of all forms, "to be" has the primacy—even the essence ultimately derives its determining power from "to be," which actuates *everything* in all beings.[66] Yet there is a relative priority of the receptive bearer and its content determinations, because "to be," as the perfecting and crowning actuality, needs that whose actuation it is—"to be" follows form. It cannot actuate without letting itself be modified.

The question, however, is whether this reciprocal causality of essence and "to be," which is the highest truth in experience that is immediately accessible to our understanding, is capable of fully satisfying our search for the ground of beings. For there is a kind of opposition here: on the one hand, unqualified "to be" is of itself and in principle not subject to any limit but, on the other, it is encountered only as limited, as the actuation of particular and contrary modes of *being.* Does this contrast not urge our thought to continue its search for identity? Do we not have to transcend this purely relative infinity, immanent in the finite, to discover as the ultimate explanatory ground, not the unqualified "to be" inherent in be-ings, but a subsistent Ground,

---

[65]Cf. no. 62. This conclusion does not give us positive knowledge of *what* is really possible; nevertheless, we do know that no limit is ultimate either with respect to ontic multiplication (extensification) or with respect to ontic interiorization (intensification). No matter how intense but limited the mode of *being* is, no matter how far-reaching but still surveyable the whole of beings is, it is not the greatest that is really possible. To deny the limitlessness of the really possible is to deny the dynamism itself of our cognitive movement, and, consequently, the infinity of unqualified *being.*

[66]Cf. no. 60.

transcending all opposition, multiplicity, and composition, which is absolutely one and absolutely infinite?[67]

The problem raised at the beginning was: Is the absolute—whatever it may be, even the "whole" of all finite beings in the broadest sense—absolutely infinite, i.e., does it have an infinite intensity of *being?* Does it contain in perfect unity all perfection of *being* without any limit, measure, or degree?

Let us try to answer in the negative. And assuming that the unconditioned is "nothing else" than the "whole" of all real and really possible finite beings, let us call these beings in their interconnection "the world."

We want to abstract here from the question whether the world is finite or infinite (transfinite) with respect to extension, predicamental plurality or number,[68] and temporality. We will not even raise the the problem whether or not such questions are meaningful, nor whether or not the world has also supra-temporal and supra-spatial aspects. We do not even want to raise any questions about the ontic, transcendental, or analogous plurality of beings i.e., we do not ask whether the "whole" of all beings is finite or infinite with respect to the extension of *being*. We accept, however, that in any case the world consists only of beings which are finite with respect to the intensity of *being* and, therefore, not *absolutely* infinite but only relationally and dynamically infinite. And we suppose that the world is unconditioned and self-grounding.[69]

---

[67]Some philosophers see in the limitlessness of the really possible an *a posteriori* proof for the real possibility of the absolutely Infinite. Because this absolutely Infinite must be the previously accepted self-grounding ground, they go on to conclude from the real possibility of the absolutely Infinite to its reality. This procedure avoids the difficulties of the so-called ontological proof of God's existence. However, we will not follow this line of thought, but proceed more cautiously by eliminating all other solutions.

[68]Cf. no. 78.

[69]The hypothesis of a self-sufficient world needs to be examined, for without necessity one should not accept anything as real. Moreover, the admission of the absolutely Infinite implies difficulties. First of all, what possible meaning could still be attached to the dynamic movement of beings, and especially knowing beings, to absolute intensity of *being*, i.e., what could be the meaning of the development of "nature," of man and humanity, of history, if the absolutely Infinite would always be already fully "realized"? Secondly, does not the absolutely Infinite contain a contradiction for our way of thinking? It would be "something" which we can seize neither in the formal-concrete concept "being" because it does not participate in *being* according to a distinct determining essence, nor in the formal-abstract concept "to be" because it is not the "to be" *of* something but stands apart as absolutely subsistent. Thus, what would be the use of speaking about something which can neither be thought or expressed?

Every Particular Being Refers to an External Ground. Let us make then the hypothesis that *the finite world fully grounds itself.* As should be clear, not a single *part* of this "whole," considered separately, *fully* grounds itself. For every particular being, as an analogate, has relations of proportional similarity and dissimilarity to the other beings whose existence is a condition of these relations.[70] In addition, it has relations of dependence, at least with respect to some of its accidental determinations.[71] Such a being, even if it were the ground of its own substantial *being,* does not perfectly ground itself, because it is not the sufficient ground of its relations. Moreover, we must add that it is not the perfect foundation of its activities. Every particular being is dependent in its activity: transient activities presuppose a properly disposed subject matter;[72] the immanent activity of theoretical knowledge presupposes the object;[73] and the immanent activity of striving and willing, even in free acts, presupposes purpose and motives.[74]

However, is it possible to maintain the hypothesis that the particular being, perfectly grounds itself at least with respect to its substantial *being?* The reply is in the negative. First, temporal and corruptible beings are dependent upon conditions and series of causes even where their substantial "to be" is concerned.[75] Secondly, even incorruptible particular beings, if such exist, cannot perfectly ground themselves as regards their substantial "to be." For, as *this* being, the particular implies a connection of contrary opposition to all other possible modes of *being*: every being possesses something proper and original, which the others may encompass to some extent in immanence but can never *be* through *perfect* identity, for the other, *as the* other, is co-original with it. Accordingly, from the *essence* itself of the particular as particular it follows of necessity that the particular is connected through opposition to all other possible particular beings. Once this is granted, it should be clear that no particular being can ever perfectly ground itself with respect to its substantial *being.* Its very *essence* implies the connection of opposition to all other beings; hence, to ground itself perfectly, it would at the same time have to ground *all* others and the "whole"; consequently, it would no longer be particular because particulars as such are co-original. But if the

[70]Cf. no. 164.
[71]Cf. no. 80.
[72]Cf. no. 93.
[73]Cf. no. 122.
[74]Cf. no. 144.
[75]Cf. no. 106.

particular does not perfectly ground itself, it cannot be the perfect ground of *all* others or even of a single one of the other beings: it is always a conditioned condition and, therefore, causes the *being* of the other only in a limited respect but never with respect to its *being* as such.

However, the fact that a being does not perfectly ground itself does not mean that this being grounds itself perfectly in one part but not in another. The expression means that the immanent grounds— "to be" and essence (form and matter, substance and accidents)—are not of themselves identified in this particular being, but *as* grounding this being they refer to a further grounding of the immanent ground, which, as the ground of the immanent ground, must be called transcendent. The particular finite being is dependent upon a non-reciprocal condition distinct from this being, upon an external cause.

In a previous chapter we left unsolved the question regarding the validity of the principle of causality with respect to the finite *as* finite.[76] Now we may say that *whatever is in a particular way, whatever participates in unqualified being is the effect of an external cause.*[77]

---

[76]Concerning the metaphysical principle of causality, see, e.g., J. van der Kooy, *Het oorzakelijkheidsbeginsel,* Antwerp, 1950 (extensive bibliography); J. van der Kooy, O. van Costerhout en F. Tellegen, *Het causaliteitsprobleem* (*Verslag v. d. 9e Alg. Verg. der Ver. v. Thom. Wijsb.*), Nijmegen, 1942; A. Grégoire, *Immanence et transcendance,* Brussels, 1939; J. Defever, *La preuve réelle de Dieu,* Brussels, 1953; H. Geurtsen, "De innerlijke structuur van het Godsbewijs," *Tijdschrift v. Philosophie,* vol. 6 (1944), pp. 3-54, 207-282; "Les preuves de l' existence de Dieu," *Bijdragen,* vol. 9 (1948), pp. 285-291; C. Nink, "Modalanalyse und Kausalprinzip," *Scholastik,* vol. 24 (1949), pp. 161-181; C. Scheltens, "Het probleem van de metaphysische causaliteit in de neo-scholastische philosophie," *Tijdschrift v. Philosophie,* vol. 14 (1952), pp. 455-502.

[77]Cf. no. 107. When there is question here of external cause, this term provisionally retains a certain indefiniteness. Undoubtedly, it indicates that every part of the "whole" does not fully ground itself, therefore, must have a cause which somehow *transcends* this part. Precisely as transcendent, this cause is called "external." However, the nature of this transcendence has to be clarified through further analyses. For instance, we are not yet able to exclude that the "external" cause in question has the character of the quasi-emanative causality, similar to that which is proper to powers with respect to their activities (cf. no. 103) and, in general, to the subsistent relative to its accidental determination (cf. no. 100). In a broader sense, this emanative causality may be called *external* causality. For the subsistent is not only the support of its determinations but also their quasi-efficient source, so that these determinations are a quasi-effect and a quasi-purpose. On the other hand, the determinations are not distinct from their source as subsistent beings but only as immanent perfections. In this respect emanation must be called an internal causality, although it should not be put on a par with the constituent inner causality exercised by matter and form with respect to being. For, emanation presupposes that the being in question is already constituted as subsistent.

The Whole of Particular Beings as Grounding Itself. The admission of an external cause does not say anything explicitly about the nature of this cause. Perhaps it could be identified with the "whole" itself which transcends each of the particular finite beings. Let us, therefore, continue our hypothesis and express it more precisely in this way: it may be granted that *every particular being refers to an external ground,* but the "whole" as their synthesis, *"the world" grounds itself.* The world in question is a *finite* world, insofar as the intensity of *being* is concerned, and consists of "nothing else" than the "whole" of all beings which "ever" are real.

However, why do we call this world limited with respect to the intensity of *being?* The only reason can be that we accept that other and higher grades of *being* than those which are realized in this world are really possible, even though we do not positively know which ones. These grades of *being* must be really possible in the strict sense, i.e., the sufficient conditions must be present both for the limitless perfecting of every real being and for the realization of always different and higher beings. Moreover, these possible grades may not be fully realized in the world as a "whole." Only if these conditions are fulfilled, may we call this world really *finite.*

For, if the world as a "whole" would *fully* realize *all* really possible grades of *being,* so that all perfections of *being* would be attained in the "whole," then there would be no reason why the world should not be called intensively infinite. (Though it may be admitted that this "whole" would escape our complete grasp and, consequently, could be considered as endlessly incomplete insofar as *our* limited viewpoint is concerned.) For outside the reality of this world, absolutely *nothing* else could be; because this world would fill the total possibility of *being,* it would be without a limit; even the very question of limit could not meaningfully be raised with respect to this world. Accordingly, it would be *absolutely* infinite.

Let us consider, therefore, the world as fully grounding itself, as *self-sufficient,* yet *finite* in the sense that there are non-realized real possibilities. Where in this world lies the sufficient ground for these non-realized but really possible intensifications of *being?* It can be only in the real world itself which, according to the hypothesis, is identified with the absolute. Though finite, this world therefore, has within itself the sufficient ground for being more intensively than as a "whole" it is. It can realize higher grades of *being* than it does realize. It has of itself, without being conditioned by anything outside itself, the absolute and infinite power to be, to be without any limitation, yet it is limited.

There are two ways in which we can show that such a world, in the hypothesis of its being the absolute, *has to be absolutely unlimited despite its being limited.*

The World as Absolutely Infinite Because of Its Self-Limitation. What is the ground by reason of which this world is limited to the restricted grade of *being* which it really possesses? On the one hand, as of itself necessary, the world cannot be contingent, indifferent with respect to *being* or not-being. It, too, has a reason why it is, and is as it is. This reason is the world itself in the active identity in which it gives itself "to be" as its essence.[78] Consequently, the world is not necessitated by anything else to have "to be" in any limited grade, for in its *being* it does not depend on anything else or anything prior. On the other hand, in the hypothesis of its being-infinite, the world, even as a "whole," possesses "to be" only in a limited grade and, therefore, is essentially related to other possible grades of *being* with which, as other, it has a connection of opposition. In other words, it is at the same time infinite power and finite actuality with respect to *being.* This means that the world *limits itself.* But *self-limitation,* in the strict sense, i.e. purely active self-limiting without being *passively* limited by something else, pertains only to the *absolutely infinite* which is not already limited by virtue of the particularization of its essence. Only that which in its essence "is" nothing else than subsistent and intensive infinity of *being* would be strictly capable of limiting itself. Accordingly, in the hypothesis under consideration, the finite world would be not only of itself absolutely necessary but also absolutely infinite.[79]

The World as Absolutely Infinite Because of Its Self-Perfection. Can a finite world have within itself the sufficient ground of everything really-possible which it does not realize in itself? One could think that, since finite being implies infinite perfectibility,[80] it must also have within itself the sufficient ground for the actuation of its perfectibility. However, is this line of thought correct? If perfectibility is viewed only from the standpoint of the finite *as* finite, it does indeed include capacity and tendency or passive and active potency, but this inclusion is not sufficient to make the actuation of the per-

---

[78] Cf. no. 176.
[79] We do not want to determine here as yet whether or not self-limitation in the absolute sense implies perhaps a contradiction. (cf. no. 179.)
[80] Cf. no. 63.

fectibility in question really possible in the strict sense.[81] The fully sufficient ground of being-actual in a higher and more intensive way cannot lie in being-actual in a lower and less intensive way, precisely *as* lower and less intensive. For otherwise the ground of perfection and "to be" would lie in imperfection and "not to be," taken aѕ such— a thing would be ın a more unlimited way according as it would be in a more limited way.

Accordingly, the fully sufficient ground for further perfection or intensification has to be found in one of these two—either, while being-actual in a less intensive way, something is "really" already actual in a more intensive way, or the less intensive being is influenced in its intensification by something "else" which is already actual in a more intensive way.[83] To express it differently, every transition from being-in-potency to being-in-act, even in the case of active potency, finds its ultimate sufficient ground in being-already-in-act. We abstract here from the question whether being-already-in-act pertains to the changing being itself or to something "else," to an external cause.[84] However, since in the hypothesis of a self-grounding world the sufficient ground of a really-possible perfection cannot lie in a cause transcending this world, we have to admit that the world can *perfect itself.* But *to perfect itself,* taken in the strict sense, as purely active self-perfection without being perfected by something else, could pertain only to the *absolutely perfect,* which would not be, by virtue of its essence, merely in a potency, distinct from its actuality, to the actual perfection, but would already actually possess the perfection that it is supposed to give to itself in the perfecting process. Accordingly, in the hypothesis of a self-grounding world, the imperfect but endlessly perfectible world is not only fully its own ground, but also absolutely perfect or absolutely infinite.[85]

---

[81]Cf. no. 175.

[83]Cf. St. Thomas, *In librum De causis,* prop. 6: "The First Cause, insofar as it is infinite 'to be' itself, is above being, and being is said of that which participates in 'to be' in a finite way. This being is proportionate to our intellect, whose object is essence." Cf. also *Summa theol.,* p. 1, q. 3, a. 4; *De potentia,* q. 7, a. 2.

[84]Cf. no. 95.

[85]We abstract here from the question whether or not self-perfection in the strict sense of the term implies perhaps a contradiction (cf. no. 179).

It is likewise impossible to defend the hypothesis that the self-sufficient world, identified with the absolute, as a "whole" is not infinite but only an *endlessly* self-perfecting "whole." As was pointed out, the question is not that the world could not be viewed as such from *our* limited standpoint. However, considered as a "whole," the world would have to include the multiplicity of its perfection *in itself* as a unity and, therefore, would have to be intensively infinite.

The Absolute as Absolutely Infinite. We may draw this conclusion: *presupposing* that the absolute coincides with the world as a
"whole," either everything possible is realized in this world, and this
world is *absolutely infinite* in the intensity of *being,* or not everything
possible is realized in this world, and this world is *finite.* But even
if it were finite, it still would have to be *absolutely infinite* in our
hypothesis, for its finiteness could be explained only either as self-
limitation or as self-perfection, and only the absolutely infinite would
be able to limit or perfect *itself* in the full sense of the term.

Accordingly, *the absolute is absolutely infinite in any case,* even
in the supposition that it is not transcendent to the world as a "whole."
The absolute is the subsistent and full intensity of *being,* no matter
how this intensity may be related to the many finite beings or to the
world as the "whole" of the finite beings.[86]

The Absolutely Infinite and Man's Judgment. It is not possible
for our finite knowledge to seize the subsistent absolute intensity of
being in a *proper* concept, at least when by this term we mean a concept which is an *immediate,* though inadequate expression of what is
proper to that which is signified in the concept. For our highest and
widest concepts, which actually but confusedly contain what they intend to express, the formal-concrete concept "being" and the formal-
abstract concept "to be," insofar as their *logical structure* is concerned, do not unqualifiedly apply to the absolutely infinite. This
infinite is not "something which is," i.e., something which participates
in *being,* nor is it "to be" as the to-be-*of*-something, as an immanent
principle which is always finitized and multiplied. The absolutely infinite is neither concrete or abstract. It is not possible for us, therefore to attribute in affirmative judgments to the absolutely infinite
predicates expressing real modes of *being* of which the infinite would
be the really distinct "subject."

Nevertheless, our knowing is not without connection with the absolutely infinite, because the infinite is the terminus of a metaphysical
inference, of mediate knowledge. When we realize that whatever we

---

[86]The same conclusion follows in the hypothesis that the absolute is constituted by one or more finite beings within the "whole" of the world, which,
at least in their substantial *being,* are not dependent upon any other beings
and, therefore, unconditioned. Moreover, from the absolutely intensive infinity
it follows that, if there were several of such absolutely unconditioned conditions or uncaused causes, they could be the absolute only together in unity
and not each one taken separately, because each of them would be particularized by the others.

know directly or indirectly in itself is known to us as conditioned or caused, as relative and finite, we become aware of the fact that what we can know contains a reference to the unconditioned and uncaused, the absolute and infinite. If this is true, however, then this reference must be present also in the source of our knowing—in its deepest ground, intuititive pre-predicative knowing of *being* must contain an *implicit* reference to the absolutely infinite.

It is possible to some extent to explicitate this implicit reference of what is prior for us to what is prior in itself by means of the *act of judgment*. True, this act refers primarily to the mode of being-real of concrete beings. Nevertheless, in reflection it can be used also to speak, e.g., about non-concrete, non-complex principles of *being,* about generalizations thought out by our mind, about relations of reason, etc., which we conceive "in the manner" of beings. In such cases "to be" receives analogous meanings in which the general fundamental meaning, the truth of the proposed situation is retained.[87] In this way we may also form judgments about the absolutely infinite as termini of inferences or reasoning processes. As such we may name:

1) Affirmative judgments of relation, in which we conceive the absolute as that to which the relative, the conditioned, the composite, etc. refer.

2) Negative judgments of attribution, in which we deny of the absolute the predicates—including "to be" and the transcendental properties of *being*—which we attribute to finite beings, because of the relativity and finiteness implied by the mode of signification proper to our concepts.

3) Affirmative judgments of attribution, in which we assert that "to be" and the transcendental properties of *being* must be realized in the absolute, though in an eminent and infinite way which is unknown to us.

The most positive affirmations which in this way we are able to make regarding the absolutely infinite are the following two:

a. The absolutely infinite *is* "Being," but not as participating in "to be," but as by his very essence absolutely identical with its fullness.

---

[87]Cf. no. 172.

b. The absolutely infinite *is* also "To Be," but not as concretized in a distinct subject, but as the subsistent "To Be" itself.

Because the absolutely infinite wholly transcends the opposition of being, essence, and "to be," even in these judgments the verbal copula "is" cannot indicate real-to-be as pertaining to a subject, but conveys the truth of the proposition by which we *intend* to say that "to be," as *actus essendi,* and being, as that whose act it is, must be conceived here as *absolutely* identified. The analogy of the idea "being" reaches its highest possibility when we bring whatever participates analogously in *being* in relation with the absolute, conceived as Subsistent "To Be" which wholly transcends even unqualified "to be."

Thus we have left the level of unqualified "to be," for this "to be" cannot subsist in itself but is essentially characterized by its merely *relative* infinity. It is always multiplied and finitized as only the "to be" *of* beings. Nevertheless, the question about the relation of the finite to the absolutely infinite remains, including the hypothesis that perhaps Subsistent "To Be" would have to finitize itself as the "to be" *of finite* beings. In this hypothesis unqualified "to be" would be the aspect under which the absolute manifests itself *to us.*

When in subsequent pages we speak of the Infinite, without further qualification, we mean the subsistent absolutely infinite, and to indicate that it transcends the opposition of the concrete and the abstract, we will spell it with a capital letter—the Infinite.

179. *The Relation of the Finite to the Absolutely Infinite*

Philosophers travel even more divergent roads when they attempt to answer the question about the relation of the finite to the Infinite. Is the particular being a part of the Infinite, and more especially, is man perhaps a part without which the "whole" is not itself, a part in which the "whole" becomes conscious of itself? Or is the finite a subsistent being which in its subsistence, and even in its self-responsibility, is wholly dependent upon the Infinite as its transcendent, and even free and freely-giving cause? The reply to these questions is not only decisive for our attitude, but also itself is an attitude in which we personally more or less approach the Infinite. Though philosophy does not pronounce the last word in this matter, it has to endeavor as much as possible to explicitate by means of reflection what is implicitly present in pre-predicative knowledge of *being.*

Hegel's Formulation of the Problem. Each one of the many finite beings "is" in one of the many analogous senses of *being*. Even the Infinite "is" in a limitlessly distant sense of *being* which, however, reveals itself to be the sense on which all others are founded. How are these truths interconnected? How is it possible that both the finite and the Infinite "are"? Hegel[88] formulates this problem with all desirable clarity as follows.

If the particular finite being is said *not* to be the Infinite, it seems to follow that reversely the Infinite is *not* the finite. This leads to a further consequence: if the Infinite is *not* the finite, and the finite is something positive, then the Infinite is limited—namely, by the finite which it is *not*. But such an Infinite would be particular and co-original with the finite; the two would be together. The true Infinite, therefore, would be the being-together or the unity of the finite and the Infinite. If, however, this Infinite again is conceived as transcendent to its parts that are together and as distinct from them, then this Infinite likewise would *not* be the parts; therefore, it, too, would be particular and not yet the true Infinite. And so on to infinity.

From this line of thought Hegel concluded that it is impossible for the finite and the Infinite to be *in truth distinguished from each other* and *opposed* as lower and higher or highest, as inferior and superior, at an endless distance from each other. It is even impossible to conceive the finite as subsistent, as being *in* itself outside the Infinite. Moreover, it is impossible to conceive the Infinite as transcendent if transcendency means that it leaves the finite as something other than itself outside and below itself. This transcendence itself, insofar as it places the negation of the positively conceived finite in the Infinite, must be transcended to see in the Infinite the only true positive, which negates the finite as truly negative and thereby preserves it in itself in a higher way.

Moderate Monism. Thus we arrive at the position taken by monism. Although absolute monism is not contradictory,[89] it goes against experience, which leads us to recognize finite modes of *being* as real.[90] However, the question must be raised whether perhaps moderate monism, which explains the plurality of the real particular

---

[88]*Wissenschaft der Logik*, vol. 1, ed. Lasson, pp. 103-146; *Enzyklopädie*, par. 93-95; *Phänomenologie des Geistes*, ed. Lasson, pp. 123-129.

[89]Cf. no. 35.

[90]Cf. no. 45.

modes of *being* as necessary realizations within the unity of the Infinite, cannot provide a solution of the problem.[91]

Let us make the hypothesis that there is nothing else than the world of actual or possible experience which constantly changes in time and space. "Beings" are localized and temporalized aspects of this unique reality. The processes of coming-to-be and development in this world are explained through the origin of all that is from a self-founding *material* substratum, which gradually through self-determination raises itself from a state of indeterminacy, from non-living to living, from non-psychical to psychical or conscious, and from non-spiritual to spiritual—insofar as man's cultural life must be called spiritual.

If we bring this hypothesis in connection with the previously established principle that the absolute is absolutely infinite, we must make the following assertions about the hypothesis:

1. In no case can this self-founding "whole" be merely an endless progress, save from the viewpoint of *our* limited knowledge—*in itself* this spatio-temporal "whole" which is supposedly self-sufficient must be infinite, at least extensively.

2. Especially, the "material" substratum cannot be conceived as being only in passive potency to its perfections or acts, in the way "prime matter" is in potency according to the theory of hylomorphism.[92] Moreover, even active potency is not sufficient, but the substratum, taken as a "whole" and not in its separate phases, must be the fully sufficient condition of its perfecting and, consequently, actually include the perfections which it gives to itself. It has to be in itself actually living, psychical, and spiritual, in order to be able to move itself from a self-accepted lower condition to these higher levels of *being*. But if this is so, why should we continue to call it the substratum, as distinct from its perfections, and why should we still call it material? The only suitable name should be subsistent "To Be" itself which, however, in this hypothesis has to develop itself in the way we experience it.

3. The difficulty remains whether or not the absolutely Infinite can degrade itself to the status of a material substratum and subsequently raise itself in a gradual way. This is the question whether or not self-limitation and self-perfection imply a contradiction. We will consider this point later.

---

[91]Cf. no. 46.
[92]Cf. no. 89.

We may make the hypothesis that the Infinite is the *formal* constituent principle of the finite beings, the whole of the subsistent *Essences* of which finite beings are particularizations.[93]

However, if we want to maintain intrinsic causality, these Essences must be conceived as concrete generalities in the sense that they necessarily include in themselves the realization of their particularizations. Secondly, these Essences can be put forward as the unconditioned Infinite only if they are taken together as united. But this unity is "To Be," for the essences are modes of *being*.

Let us suppose, therefore, that the Infinite is subsistent "To Be" which, however, as the formal constituent principle, as unqualified "to be," must of necessity realize itself in many finite beings.

In this supposition the first question to arise is: Does subsistent "To Be" have to realize all possible finite beings? In that case the world as a "whole" is intensively infinite. But one may legitimately question whether the world is infinite in this way. The second question is: Are the beings admitted in this view still subsistent beings, appropriating "to be" as their own and as distinct from that of the others? Or must finite beings not rather be considered in this view as necessary particular aspects or modes which flow of necessity from the subsistent "To Be" as conclusions flowing from premises?

Spinoza. With Spinoza one could make this hypothesis: the Infinite is the one and only Substance.[94] For only that is absolutely substantial which does not need anything outside itself to be and to be understood, i.e., that which is not related to anything else but is its own ground. Outside the one Substance nothing can be. Finite beings, therefore, are not substances, but non-subsistent particular modes or inherent determinations,[95] which through emanative but immanent causality[96] originate of necessity from the Infinite in an infinite plurality and diversity.

The questions arising in this hypothesis are:

1. Is the non-substantial character of finite beings not against our experience of their substantiality, especially with respect to the many human *persons,* who to a certain extent are free and self-

---

[93]Cf. Thomas Aquinas, *I Scriptum s. Sentent,* d. 8, q. 1, a. 2; "Whether God is the 'to be' of all things" and *Contra Gentes,* bk. 1, ch. 26: "That God is not the formal 'to be' of all things." Cf. also *Summa theol.* p. 1, q. 3, a. 8.

[94]*Ethica,* I, *De Deo.* In order not to change Spinoza's terminology, we use here "substance" rather than "subsistent being" or "subsistence." (Tr.)

[95]Cf. no. 68.

[96]Cf. no. 100.

responsible for the deeds originating in them? Should we not accept, therefore, that substance, despite its absoluteness, can be a merely relative absoluteness, a to-be-*in*-itself, without implying necessarily to a to-be-*of*-itself?[97] Is it not possible that substantiality be realized in a degraded and analogous way[98] in many, which, not so much despite, but rather because of what they are in themselves, are related to other substances, since all finite beings participate in finite ways in the absolute Substance of the Infinite?

2. According to this hypothesis, in this world as a "whole" whatever is really possible is also of necessity realized. The world is not finite, and there is no room for contingency in the proper sense. But is not this position contrary to the world as we experience it, for at least man's freedom contains unrealized real possibilities?[99]

3. If the Infinite does not only realize all possibilities of *being* in an eminent way through absolute identity in its very *Essence,* but also makes all limited modes of *being* arise of necessity *as realized* from itself, must we not say that the Infinite is somehow *dependent* upon the finite modes? True, the modes are said to be wholly dependent, because they originate from the substantial through immanent emanative causality. However, as soon as one accepts, on the one hand, that there is a certain *distinction* between the modes and the substantial, and, on the other, that the realization of the modes pertains to the very Essence of the Infinite, it necessarily follows that the Infinite is not wholly itself if it does not realize the modes. But in that case the Infinite is further determined by the modes, and, therefore, as substantial, is further determinable or potential. It *needs* the modes, with which it is not fully identical in its Essence, to be identical with itself. Accordingly, the Infinite "is" on condition that it realize the distinct finite modes and thus it is not absolutely unconditioned and independent.[100]

Dialectic Idealism. With dialectic idealism one could make this hypothesis: the Infinite is not the Subsistent vaguely conceived as a "thing" with determinations, but it is transcendental *Ego,* self-conscious *Subject,* it is Idea, it is Spirit. However, to be self-conscious and therefore identical with itself in the most proper sense of the term,[101] bespeaks a relationship of the self to the self. Thus the

---

[97]Cf. no. 65.
[98]Cf. no. 162.
[99]Cf. no. 175.
[100]Cf. no. 46.
[101]Cf. no. 128.

Absolute would have to place itself opposite to itself in order to become identical with itself through overcoming opposition. But to make itself into the other-than-itself is to limit, determine, and negate itself, while to find itself in this other and negate the other as other is to perfect itself. Now the other than the *Logos* is *Physis*. Thus the Absolute becomes estranged from itself and places itself outside itself as Nature, but reverts to itself as Spirit by reconciling Nature as its object with itself as subject. For Perfect Knowing means overcoming the opposition of subject and object, and therefore must first posit this opposition. Consequently, the Absolute as subsistent "To Be" is dialectic Thought which attains full concreteness through the elimination of its abstract moments, beginning with the elimination of contradiction between the initially undetermined to-be and the just as undetermined not-to-be in the synthesis of coming-to-be, and so on.

Identity and Contradiction. Dialectic idealism raises the problem of identity and contradiction with all possible clarity. In this problem we must keep in mind that *our way of thinking is imperfect* lest we uncritically transfer this way to the mode of *being* pertaining to that which we intend to convey with our judgments.

First of all, it is only according to *our* way of thinking that identity includes the distinction and opposition of the self as subject and the self as object. We are not capable of expressing identity otherwise than through a founded relation of reason,[102] because only the finite is known to us in itself and implies a "real" distinction of constituent principles which, albeit proportioned to each other according to transcendental relations,[103] do not coincide in perfect identity. Precisely, however, because identity is realized only imperfectly in the finite, the principle of identity[104] forces us to look further and to accept subsistent "To Be" which transcends all composition as the self-grounding foundation of *being* of the finite. What this to-be-perfectly-itself, this absoluteness "is" in itself transcends our understanding. We can approach it only imperfectly through analogous knowledge starting from composite being, which is always to some extent divided against itself and therefore in many ways relative to the "other." Negatively, however, it is certain that in the Infinite there can be no question of a tension between unlimited and limiting counterparts, between act and potency, between one par-

[102]Cf. no. 169.
[103]Cf. no. 170.
[104]Cf. no. 36.

ticular and another, or between subject and object as limiting each
other.

Secondly, the absolute contradiction between being and non-being
is conceived by *us* "in the manner" of a contrary opposition between
two positives.[105] The reason is that our groping way of knowing
needs negation alongside affirmation[106] and in negation we must posit
non-being as a quasi-being, so that being and non-being, as opposed
to each other in our thinking, have something in common—namely,
to-be-thought. We even bring them into relative opposition as if
they posit and include each other, as if they were together.

Nevertheless, in our negative judgments the mode of expression is
clearly distinct from what we intend to convey by means of it. When
we say "being is not non-being,"[107] we conceive, it is true, "to be"
as the negation of the negation, but we do not intend to say that
"to be" itself is a negating act. By saying that being as being does
not negate anything, we want to express as strongly as possible that
"to be" is purely positive and that, therefore, being, to the extent
that it is, cannot have in positive opposition to itself something "else"
which limits it and with which it would be reconciled in a common
"mean."[108] Accordingly, absolute not-to-be cannot be predicated
of anything, for everything, even purely-thought "non-being," participates to some extent, no matter how degradedly, in *being.*[109]
Absolute negation is impossible.[110]

---

[105]Concerning the various modes of opposition see *De quattuor oppositis.*
(Grabmann considers this little work, attributed to St. Thomas, authentic on
the basis of the manuscripts, while Mandonnet views it as non-authentic.)
The value of this work, especially in reference to the problem raised by
Hegel, was discovered by B. Lakebrink, *Hegels dialektische Ontologie und die
thomistische Analektik,* Cologne, 1955. See, e.g., pp. 129-152 (*Dialektischer
und analektischer Widerspruch*); pp. 175-201 (*Die Modalität*); pp. 252, 260-
266. Cf. F. Grégoire, *Aux sources de la pensée de Marx: Hegel et Feuerbach,*
Louvain, 1947, pp. 55-67.

[106]Cf. no. 167.

[107]Cf. no. 37.

[108]Cf. no. 38.

[109]Cf. Thomas Aquinas, *De veritate,* q. 2, a. 11, *ad* 5: "Being and non-being
have something in common in an analogous way, for non-being itself is called
a being in an analogous sense, as is clear from *IV Metaphys.*" *Summa theol.,*
p. 1, q. 16, a. 3, *ad* 2: "Non-being does not have anything in itself through
which it can be known. It is known however, insofar as the intellect makes
it knowable. Hence truth is founded in non-being insofar as non-being is a
kind of being-of-reason." *Scriptum s. Sentent.,* I, d. 24, q. 1, a. 3, *ad* 1:
"Every respect of being to negation or non-being is merely a relation of
reason. Hence the relation by which being is referred to non-being exists
only in the mind; likewise, the privation through which non-being is denied
of being exists only in the mind as a privation of privation or a negation
of negation."

[110]Cf. no. 37.

On the other hand, relative not-to-be, i.e., not-to-be-this or not-to-be-such, may sometimes be predicated in true judgments. Such a judgment, however, does not intend to say that a kind of not-to-be really *belongs* to a being, for a negative judgment is not the immediate expression of "that which is." Nevertheless, our negation may be founded. Thus, for example, the negations of particular modes of *being* in a particular being are founded in this that the Infinite positivity of *being* does not fully manifest itself in this being but is limited by the essence; hence this being, as being merely such or such, stands in privative, contrary, or relative opposition to other positive modes of *being* which it excludes or at least does not include.[111] These privative, contrary, or relative oppositions participate to a greater or lesser extent in the absolute contradiction between to-be and not-to-be; for instance, white and black is also white and not-white, superior and inferior is also superior and non-superior. But the opposition is less, the exclusion is not absolute; for instance, what is actually white can become black and thus is potentially black; grey is white in one respect but in another black; superior and inferior constitute a society. Accordingly, in these diminished forms of opposition which merely participate in contradiction there may be all kinds of intermediaries, harmonies and transitions. Especially coming-to-be, changing, and developing may sometimes have the character of a dialectic process.[112]

The fact that in finite beings we always find oppositions, intermediaries, and transitions, both in their internal structure and their interconnection with others, means that we have to do with beings which in their *being* reveal a relative contradiction and an intermediary state conceived by us as in between to-be and not-to-be. For this reason the principles of excluded contradiction and excluded middle force us to look further and to accept as ground of the finite-in-opposition pure subsistent "To Be" itself, which is without any participation in contradiction and perfectly free from it.

What this all-embracing oppositeless Infinite in itself "is," we are unable to understand. In a negative way we will conceive it as that which absolutely and in all respects excludes not-to-be from itself, the absolute counterpole of the impossible, that which absolutely cannot not-be.[113] Consequently, it is conceived as that which has

---

[111]Cf. no. 38.

[112]Cf. no. 73.

[113]Cf. no. 32.

neither any privative or contrary opposition in itself nor any relative opposition, *insofar* as such an opposition would mean the mutual exclusion of absolute contents. However, when in this way we deny of the Infinite both absolute not-to-be and the relative not-to-be implied in the contrary finite modes of *being,* we do not intend to assert that the Infinite is the negating act "elevating and overcoming" (*aufheben*) the finite, which, therefore, it first had to posit. All this is merely *our* mode of thinking. What we intend to say is this: subsistent "To Be" in its pure positivity does not contain the particular modes of *being* according to their own *deficient* degrees of participation, in which precisely they are opposed to one another, but according to an infinite, *eminent* mode in absolute identity. Thus the Infinite is not the negation of the finite, but that which makes possible the being-real of limitlessly many, mutually opposite beings, precisely because in contradictionless identity it transcends all oppositions in *being.* The Infinite is absolute Omnipotence, the abundantly sufficient ground on which whatever is intrinsically possible is really possible. To express it differently, whatever is not wholly impossible in itself, because it eliminates itself through absolute internal contradiction, is possible in dependence upon the absolute identity of subsistent "To Be."[114]

Self-Limitation, Self-Perfection, and the Infinite. If we have to interpret the characteristics which the Infinite has for us in this way, we will have to *revise* the previously proposed *hypothesis* that the Infinite coincides with the finite "whole" of beings, the world, because it limits *itself* and perfects *itself.* Is there not a contradiction involved in such a dialectic process through which the Infinite posits *itself as this* in opposition to *itself as that* and then reconciles these two aspects with each other?

---

[114]The critical distinction which, as has been said, should be made between our mode of thinking and the absolute identity and contradictionlessness of the Absolute in itself applies also to the other transcendental ideas. Subsistent "To Be" is *one,* not because it does not contain the positive "other" in itself, but because it alone does not imply in any way absolute not-to-be in itself and undividedly embraces all perfection of *being* (cf. no. 39). Through this infinity it is also *distinct,* not as distinct from some positive perfections of *being,* considered *as* perfections, but as wholly distinct from absolute not-to-be, from impossibility (cf. no. 37). Subsistent "To Be" is *perfect,* not as the result of a process of perfecting, but through the active identity of its essence with the fullness of *being* (cf. no. 40). It is *determinate,* not as limited or circumscribed by the positive "other," nor as completed actuation of determinability, but through actual all-perfectness (cf. no. 41). It is *individual,* not as one among many participating in unqualified "to be," but as Subsistent "To Be" itself (cf. no. 90).

First of all, self-limitation does not imply a contradiction when there is a question of a being which is already limited by its essence and contrarily opposed to others with which in its endless perfectibility it wants to enter into ever more intimate relations through its activity. Because it is unable to communicate with all at the same time, the finite being has to make a choice and direct itself intentionally to one or a few particular objects in order to obtain access to their inner essence through more intense knowledge, love, and action. Through this contact with the few it is then better able to understand the many, for what is most intimate in each is also the meeting point with all. For the finite being, specialization is the road to universalization.

As was pointed out above,[115] of *self-limitation in the absolute sense,* i.e., without being limited by something else, there could be question only with respect to the absolutely infinite. However, the possibility of this hypothesis is *excluded,* for otherwise the Infinite would be at the same time limited and not-limited. We cannot escape from this conclusion by saying that it would be non-limited in its power but limited in its act—in other words, in different respects. For as we have just seen, these aspects can arise only from *our* imperfect mode of thinking, but in the Infinite itself, active potency and act coincide in absolute identity.[116] True, we may call the Infinite the "coincidence of all opposites," provided we understand this of contrary opposites which are not realized in the Infinite according to their own degree of *being,* but in an eminent way that implies no opposition. But there can be no question of absolute contradiction in the Infinite. Hence it is not in identity finite and not-finite, although whatever is positive and perfect in the finite is implied in an infinite way in the identity of the Infinite with itself.

Secondly, self-perfection, self-movement,[117] does not imply a contradiction when there is question of a being which by its very essence is imperfect but endlessly perfectible. By means of its active potency it is capable of making activities emanate from itself, some of which merely perfect others,[118] and others, as immanent acts, such as living and knowing, are an unfolding of the self.[119] Nevertheless, the finite being does not have within itself the fully sufficient ground

[115]Cf. no. 178.
[116]Cf. no. 95.
[117]Cf. no. 111.
[118]Cf. no. 93.
[119]Cf. nos. 117 and 128.

for its transition from being-in-potency to being-in-act, but needs to be influenced by another being which is already in act.[120] The self-movement of the living finite being is ultimately a moved moving.

As was pointed out above,[121] *self-movement or self-perfection in the absolute sense* could be spoken of only in reference to the absolutely perfect. But even in the case of the absolutely perfect this hypothesis is *excluded* because otherwise the absolutely perfect would have to be at the same time both perfect and imperfect-but-perfectible. We cannot have recourse to the distinction "perfect in power" and "imperfect in act." For, as pure self-identity, it is also pure act without any distinct potency.[122]

The Infinite and the World. From the preceding considerations we may draw this conclusion: the absolutely Infinite does not co-incide with the world as a "whole," nor is the world as a "whole" the constitutively necessary immanent unfolding of the Infinite. The reason is that self-founding subsistent "To Be" is pure Identity with Itself, Unity without component parts, and does not have in itself

---

[120]Cf. no. 95.

[121]Cf. no. 178.

[122]Cf. no. 95. Subsistent "To Be" therefore, likewise cannot be identified with pure *becoming*. Becoming (coming-to-be) neither is in contradiction with *being* nor is it the reconciliation of absolute to-be with absolute not-to-be. It is an imperfect mode of *being*, proper to that which is not yet through its essence whatever it *can* be, and now "begins" to be actually what it was not yet actually. It is only with respect to the finite being—strictly speaking, even only with respect to the temporal being—that there can be question of becoming as the successive synthesis of the privative opposition between, on the one hand, not-to-be-real according to a particular mode of *being* and, on the other, to-be-real according to this same mode of *being*. When, in addition, it is taken into consideration that what is not yet real according to the substantial or accidental mode of *being* in question was already real according to another mode of *being*, we speak of movement or change and of the synthesis of contrary modes of *being* (cf. no. 79).

In a similar way one cannot conceive as a kind of supra-temporal immanent process of the Infinite itself the causal origin of finite being, whether temporal or supra-temporal, *as* being, from infinite subsistent "To Be" (cf. no. 79). This causal origin, which will be discussed later, is no longer a transition from being-in-potency to being-in-act occurring in time, but is merely conceived as such a transition. For this reason this origin is still called "being-in-motion" by the metaphysician, though only in the broadest analogous sense, insofar as to-be-real is the "fulfillment" of a possibility.

Although dialectic idealism does not deny the principle of non-contradiction, it does not pay sufficient attention to the merely analogous and degraded sense which contradiction has in privative, contrary, and relative opposition. It too easily calls these oppositions unqualifiedly "contradictions" and thinks, therefore, that the Absolute, which *we* have to conceive as the negation of opposite aspects in a higher synthesis, itself likewise "originates" through the process of a reconciliation which elevates and eliminates (*aufheben*) these oppositions.

any contrary opposition between particular aspects. The world as a "whole," on the other hand, is the unity of realized opposite modes of *being* which, it is true, are to some extent immanent in one another, but only according to the imperfect or participated identity which is otherness. Therefore, (1) the absolutely Infinite is not constituted in itself by the possible particular modes of *being* according to their contrary finite realizations, but contains these modes in an eminent infinite way in absolute identity; (2) the particular modes of *being,* when they are realized in the world according to their own degraded, mutually exclusive ways, are distinct from the absolutely Infinite.[123]

Thus finite beings cannot belong to the Essence itself of the Infinite. First, because this would be against the perfect unity and identity of the Infinite. Secondly, because otherwise the Infinite would need the finite, *as* realized in a finite way, to be itself. This point is immediately clear when the Infinite is conceived as the result of overcoming the plurality and otherness of the finite beings. But even if we emphasize that the Infinite is the origin of its immanent determinations, these determinations would have a certain immanently final priority over their origin because they would perfect the Infinite and "bring it to itself." But in such a case the Infinite would no longer be the unconditioned and self-sufficient absolute.

The Problem of External Causality. If *immanent emanative causality,* i.e., the self-unfolding of the "whole" into its parts, moments, phases, aspects, phenomenal forms, modes, etc., does not bring any solution, then the priority of the unconditioned Infinite over conditioned real finite beings must be understood as *external causality in the stricter sense,* i.e., as efficient, exemplary, or final causality.[124] This reply becomes all the more urgent according as, on the basis of experience and especially human self-experience, one gives more emphasis to the subsistence of the finite.[125]

Hence the question arises of what analogous sense the concept "external cause" has in this problem. For we *conceive* the cause and the caused as "the one" and "the other." But thus the problem of the relation of the finite to the Infinite comes back with an almost insoluble urgency. With Hegel, it was pointed out—and it appears impossible to argue against it—that we cannot say of the Infinite that it

[123]Concerning the individuality of Subsistent "To Be," cf. Thomas Aquinas *In librum De causis,* prop. 9 (*in fine*).
[124]Cf. no. 103.
[125]Cf. nos. 47-48.

is not the finite if the finite is considered in its positivity and perfection. But if the finite depends upon the Infinite according to external causality, then the finite in its own immanence is not the Infinite.

The problem, therefore, is: if dependence according to external causality, causal dependence, is admitted, is it still possible to reconcile the otherness or positive "ownness" of subsistent finite beings with the necessary all-embracing character of the absolutely Infinite?

180. *The Finite as Causally Dependent on the Infinite*

The Exemplary Cause. When we arrange the beings of experience in orderly fashion according to their analogous degrees of *being,* we determine the measure of their participation in unqualified *being.*[126] After the preceding analyses we must add that at the same time we place them in relationships of proximity to, or distance from the absolute intensity of *being,* i.e., of subsistent "To Be." We conceive this intensity as the universal primordial model, the archetype, which beings imitate in manifold expressions in particular ways.

A difficulty which can be raised is the following. How do we know that the Infinite, conceived as the all-surpassing mode which finite beings approximate only in a deficient way, is not merely an auxiliary representation created by thought, an "idea," to which nothing has to correspond in reality?

In reply, let us begin by pointing out that in our analyses we did, indeed, begin with this problematic representation of the infinite intensity of *being.* However, previously we had already established that the self-grounding unconditioned, whatever it may be, is real. Next, we attempted to see whether or not it is possible to consider the absolute as finite. The failure of this attempt showed that everything finite *as* finite refers to the absolute as an explanatory ground which must be absolutely infinite. Once the reality of the Infinite is shown, it follows that the Infinite is, not only for our way of thinking but also in itself, the eminent measure by which the limited "to be" proper to particular beings is measured. However, the concept of measure needs to be analogously refined and rendered more precise in the following way before it can be used in this connection:

1. The Infinite is not a measure in the same way as the univocal unit of number as a minimum is the measure of the numerable

---

[126]Cf. no. 57.

many,[127] but in the way the maximum perfection as ideal is the measure of the more or less perfect.

2. The Infinite is not the empirical maximum, which is merely greater than the others, but transcends all comparison, and the finite reveals only a deficient and one-sided resemblance with this Infinite. If we may use a comparison here, we may say that the finite resembles the Infinite as a portrait more or less resembles a person, and not that the person resembles the portrait.[128]

3. Especially, the Infinite is not the first which *we* know explicitly and through which we approach the others. Rather the reverse is true: we begin by discovering that what is first known to us *is* only according to a limited grade of *being* and therefore implies a relationship of both distance and approximation to what transcends every grade absolutely; and only then do we come to the question whether or not there must be "something" which, though it is hidden from us in its essence, is nonetheless the ultimate ground of intelligibility of everything that appears to us.

Provided these precisions are admitted, we may call the Infinite the exemplary cause of everything that is or can be. However, the exemplarity in question should not be understood as if *another* being, a demiurge, views this primordial exemplar and by imitating it makes the world be. For otherwise the Infinite would not be the only absolute. Accordingly, the efficient cause may not be sought outside the exemplary cause, but the fact that for our way of thinking all particular possibilities of *being* pre-exist in the Infinite in an eminently exemplary way is the ground of the Infinite's omnipotence.

Final Cause. In a previous chapter we have understood the orientation of beings to endlessly continued further perfections as the natural tendency to the most intensive possible participation in unqualified *being*.[129] We may now add that this endless tendency to self-unfolding receives its full explanation only through the orientation of the finite to the absolutely Infinite, to subsistent "To Be."

A difficulty that arises here is the following. Is not the Infinite as purpose to be considered an absolutely unattainable "ideal"? The reply is that an affirmative answer will not be acceptable if it is admitted that the orientation to the Infinite flows from the very

[127]Cf. no. 78.
[128]Cf. no. 163.
[129]Cf. no. 63.

essence or nature of the finite. For there must be a certain proportion between what by its nature is ordered to something and the something to which it is ordered. If there were no such proportion, hope[130] would be destroyed and the tendency would be meaningless.[131] However, the concept of purpose needs to be analogously refined and rendered more precise in the following way before it is used in this context:

1. The Infinite cannot be a purpose which is realized through the tendency to self-unfolding, not even that of the world as a "whole." For the purpose of tending to self-unfolding is the state of perfectness. If the realization of the Infinite consisted in this self-unfolding, then the finite, becoming perfectly itself, would "raise" itself to the Infinite. But the Infinite is not the result of a tendency, for it is unconditioned and self-grounding.[132]

2. The purpose to be attained does not pre-exist except in the intention of the tending subject and in its being-real depends upon this subject insofar as it is last in the order of execution.[133] The Infinite, however, cannot be anything else than a purpose which does not depend upon the tending subject in its being-real. It is not a resulting but a pre-existing purpose. It does not come to be in the future, but *is* in perfect self-presence, above time and motion. It is purpose, not as an inherent perfection of the tending subject, but as subsistent perfectness in itself.

3. More and more to attain this purpose does not mean to realize it, but to adhere to it and approximate it, to participate more intimately in its perfectness, to be more assimilated to it, not through the loss of subsistence, but on the contrary through becoming more fully "mature" in itself and a greater source of wealth for others.

If these precisions of the concept of "purpose" are accepted, we may call the Infinite the final cause or purpose of all that is. However, the attraction of this subsistent Purpose cannot consist only in this that it comes to be present in the "intention" of the tending subject but consists mainly in this that the Purpose first makes the tending subject itself *be* according to a *nature* directed to this Purpose. As a final cause, the Infinite is at the same time efficient

[130]Cf. no. 138.
[131]Cf. no. 43.
[132]Cf. no. 179.
[133]Cf. no. 108.

cause. Thus it is not an efficient cause which directs itself to the effect to be caused, but an efficient cause which directs the effect to be caused to itself. Hence the caused is not the purpose of the cause, but the cause is the purpose of the caused. And this efficient cause makes itself purpose of the effect to be caused not because it needs something of the effect in question, but reversely, because, as the Good, it wants to communicate itself as a free gift.[134]

Efficient Cause. The infinite is not efficient cause because it directs itself to a presupposed being to perfect it through transient action, either by bringing a new form to actuality from the potency of primary matter[135] or by making new accidental determinations emanate from the substance.[136] For otherwise the efficient cause would not itself be absolute but the absolute would be, by inner necessity, a duality of opposites, e.g., a pure act and a pure potency or "world stuff"—which would be against the absolute identity and unity of the absolute. The activity of the Infinite as efficient cause, then, is not change and motion in the proper sense, for these motions presuppose a passive object which is changed or moved.[137] Likewise there are no conditions, circumstances or impediments which influence the activity.[138] The Infinite does not find any idea, model, plan, or law outside itself. Likewise, there is no purpose outside the Infinite which induces it to exercise its activity.

Thus the Infinite is an absolutely *uncaused cause* according to all three aspects of external causality—viz., idea, motive, and power. In the activity of finite beings exemplary, final, and efficient causality never coincide perfectly; they influence one another in different respects; for instance, the effect as realized depends upon the efficient cause, but the efficient cause depends upon the effect as intended.[139] The Infinite, however, is by identity primordial exemplar, purpose, and agent; hence the effect is not prior to the cause in any respect, whether as material, as idea, or as motive.

The actual causing also of an effect cannot be an activity emanating from the Essence of the first Cause and distinct from it. First of all, it is not a transient activity, for there is no presupposed re-

---

[134]Cf. no. 108.
[135]Cf. no. 89.
[136]Cf. no. 68.
[137]Cf. no. 79.
[138]Cf. no. 80.
[139]Cf. no. 108.

cipient of action;[140] secondly, it is not an activity which would be an immanent self-perfecting of the cause, for through the absolute identity of Essence and "To Be" the Cause is already pure Activity.

The Cause of Being. The uncaused Cause, as subsistent or essential "To Be," is the cause of real beings precisely *as* beings, as participating in *being.* And as the cause of *being,* it presupposes nothing but posits everything. Our way of thinking, which is derived from the influence which one finite being exercises on a presupposed other finite being, inevitably falls short with respect to the uncaused Cause.[141]

If beings are caused in their *being,* then *everything* in them is caused. "To be" is most intimate in all, the constituent principle from which is derived the actuality and, consequently, also the meaning and value not only of subsistent beings as bearers of "to be," but also of the other constituent principles which modify "to be," viz., essence, properties, abilities, activities, relations, etc. Accordingly, everything in every respect depends upon the cause of *being* as such.

According to our mode of thinking, the cause of *being* includes the three causal aspects in perfect identity. As exemplary cause, it is the measure of all beings, for every being imitates the uncaused Cause's infinite intensity of *being* to some extent on its own scale according as it more or less approaches this intensity. As efficient cause, it is the inexhaustible source which distributes and divides its fullness over many. As final cause, it attracts all to itself in order that each one may approach it and resemble it as closely as

---

140Cf. no. 80.

1411. We present matters as if "nothing" is the material out of which beings are made. But to presuppose nothing does not mean to presuppose nothingness, i.e., nothing as a kind of subject-matter. The intention is precisely to exclude all material causality. Accordingly, such concepts as making, forming, effecting, etc. have to be purified and used only in an analogous sense.

2. We speak about the coming-to-be of beings as if they pass from not-to-be to to-be. But absolute not-to-be is not a real previous state of beings. It is only with the being-real of beings that the measure of their duration, time, is present (regardless of whether their duration is finite or endless). What is intended when we say that beings pass from not-to-be to to-be is precisely that their dependence in *being* is not a transition occurring in time.

3. We present the situation as if beings pass from being-possible to being-real. But possibility, likewise, is not a real previous condition which beings have in themselves. The ground of their intrinsic possibility lies in their exemplary cause and that of their real possibility in their efficient cause. Thus what is intended when we say that beings pass from being-possible to being-real is precisely that their being-real comes from the same cause which is the foundation of their possibility.

possible in accordance with the possibilities implied in each one's essence. Thus all beings *are* in the measure of their causal relation of approximation *to* their primordial exemplar, origin, and purpose; they are relative in the most profound sense—namely, by a dynamic relationship.[142]

Participation. If we call also this tri-unity of causal relationships participation,[143] this term acquires a more profound and intimate sense than it has enjoyed hitherto. From a first provisional concept of participation we have now arrived at a more definitive idea.[144]

By participation in the metaphysical sense we meant to realize "to be" and the transcendental properties of *being,* such as unity, truth, and goodness, in a particular way. A being through participation was a being which participates in unqualified "to be" according to a distinct limiting essence and through an immanent "to be" of its own.

The analysis of beings, especially in their mutual relationship, induced us to raise the question whether unqualified "to be," which is always finitized and multiplied, as a constituent principle could really be called the ultimate ground of finite beings. We discovered that the unconditioned and in itself absolutely necessary had to be not only relatively infinite but absolutely infinite. In other words, unqualified "to be" referred to an absolute ground transcending all relative *beings.* Thus we could say that *whatever is by participation is caused by an external cause.*[145] The causality of *being* revealed itself as an *a priori* condition for the possibility of participation in *being.* This external cause, as we have seen, could not be anything else than that which is no longer through participation but through the perfect identity of Essence and "To Be." But, continuing our analysis, we saw that this *subsistent "To Be"* which is the cause of the particular beings cannot be conceived as a cause which produces the many, distinct, particular, real beings within the unity of its Essence as constituent parts of itself, whether through material,

---

[142]Cf. no. 194.
[143]Cf. Thomas Aquinas, *Summa theol.,* p. 1, q. 44, a. 1, *ad* 1: "Although the relation to the cause does not enter into the definition of the being that is caused, nevertheless, this relation is consequent upon what pertains to this being's nature, for from the very fact that something is a being through participation it follows that it is caused by something else." See also aa. 3 and 4 of the same question.
[144]Cf. no. 57.
[145]Cf. no. 178.

formal, or emanative causality. Such a conception would be against the subsistence of the finite beings as well as against the absolute simplicity of subsistent "To Be" and against its identity which transcends all contrary oppositions. For this reason the ultimate ground of beings through participation is the *absolutely* transcendent Infinite, which in unity is their exemplary, final and efficient cause.

In this way the idea of participation has changed from being formally static to being causally dynamic. To participate, as *having* partially, refers to par*taking,* as receiving in dependence on an external cause. And to par*take* refers to the *imparting* through which the subsistent universal intensity of "To Be" *makes* the particular being be.

To summarize these considerations, when a being is only in an *imperfect* way, it is internally structured or *composed* of essence and "to be" and essentially connected with other particular beings with which it is together as *one.* Imperfection, composition and multiplication are three signs indicating that "to be" does not belong to this being by virtue of its essence. But if "to be" does not belong to a being by virtue of the essence, then this being is caused in its "to be" by that to which "to be" belongs essentially—namely, subsistent "To Be."

181. *The Infinite as a Free Cause*[146]

A Difficulty. Does the causal relationship solve the proposed difficulty as to how both the finite and the Infinite can "be"? On the contrary, the problem seems to become even greater. If subsistent "To Be" because of its simplicity does not cause through the emanation of a distinct activity but through its very *Essence,* then it is a necessary cause. Consequently, the caused, the world also is absolutely necessary, though not of itself but because it proceeds of necessity from a cause that is of itself necessary.[147] In this way the difficulties raised against moderate monism revert with a vengeance against the theory of causality. For, if the Infinite is the cause of this world through its Essence, it cannot be without the world, but the world is its necessary completion and climax. And precisely because the world is proposed as a whole of subsistent

---

[146]Cf. Thomas Aquinas, *Summa theol.,* p. 1, q. 19, a. 4; *De potentia,* q. 3, a. 15, A. D. Sertillanges, *S. Thomas d'Aquin,* vol. 1, pp. 221-226; A. Grégoire, *Immanence et transcendance,* pp. 178-188.

[147]Cf. no. 174.

beings, it is even more evident that the absolute is not solely the first cause taken separately, but the togetherness or unity of two correlates—the cause and what is caused of necessity. But in that case, why should we speak of external causality in the strict sense, since the true Infinite embraces in unity both cause and effect?

The Real Reciprocity of Cause and Effect in the World. The objection conceives the concept of cause according to the meanings it has with respect to relations between beings within the world. But this concept has to be analogously purified from every imperfection which is implied by our way of thinking and thus, through negation and eminence, brought somewhat closer to the uncaused cause about which the objection speaks. It is true of course, that we always *conceive* cause and effect as reciprocally related and, consequently, as together in mutual opposition. However, reflection on the pure essence of causality will show that, as has been noted repeatedly,[148] cause as cause *is* not really related to effect.

In the world of our experience one thing is dependent upon another, but always only to a limited extent, only in the acquisition or retention of certain substantial or accidental characteristics.[149] The reason is mainly that what in one respect is influenced by a cause in other respects always influences its cause. This influence often is a condition of actual causality.[150]

---

[148]Cf. nos 103, 107, and 164.

[149]Cf. nos. 79 and 88.

[150]Reciprocal influence of cause and effect is present, for instance, in the following cases:

1. If the object to be influenced is presupposed as something passive, e.g., as raw material and can be to a greater or lesser extent in the necessary disposition for the undergoing of influence.

2. If the other is not only passive but also reacts efficiently; for example, in the interaction occurring in the material world (cf. no. 91), between the living and its environment (cf. no. 113), in the social intercourse of human beings (cf. no. 154), not only as equals but also as superior and inferior (teacher-pupil, ruler-subject).

3. If the effect to be realized is the purpose of the action and, therefore, cause of the cause (cf. no. 108). This happens, for instance, in every tendency of nature, for nature is ordered to its purpose even with respect to self-perfection, in such a way that, the cause itself is unable to assign a purpose to its activity (cf. no. 108). The same situation exists when a cause in causing is dependent upon a prior cause, for in such a case the higher cause directs the lower cause to the purposes of the higher.

4. More generally, wherever the causing of an effect means an enrichment of the cause. This is the case of human activities with respect to objects when the result obtained serves for cultural development (cf. no. 146). The same is true of the unselfish enrichment of other persons, because the communicator attains also his own perfection in his communication (cf. no. 132).

From this influence exercised by the effect it becomes clear once more that no particular being is the total foundation of any other particular being, i.e., it is not the cause of *being* with respect to the other.[151] As particular beings they are co-original, and each one has something proper which it does not derive or receive from another particular being. For this reason they constitute together an *order* or interconnection of reciprocally related beings.[152] It is only within this order that there can be question of relative superiority and inferiority, relative dependence and independence in different respects.

Cause as Cause is Not Reciprocal to Effect as Effect. Accordingly, in the world of our experience the cause and the caused are really mutually related, for instance, as the active and the passive, which demand and need one another, which are together as unequal equals in all kinds of proportions. The question, however, is whether the relation of cause, purely *as* cause, to effect, purely *as* effect, is likewise a real relation. Is the relation to the effect essential for that which is cause, just as the actual relation to the cause is essential for that which is effect? We must reply in the negative to this question.[153]

It is true, of course, that we *call* a being a cause in reference to its effect. But if a being which is called a cause, of necessity causes actually, as soon as it is has fully its own nature or character and the conditions are fulfilled, then such a being cannot *be* without the effect. It is itself only when it is together with the effect, it needs the effect to be itself. Accordingly, with respect to a cause that causes of necessity, the effect is to a certain extent of equal dignity as the cause and even relatively prior to it, it is not absolutely dependent upon the cause. The *necessitating* cause is a *necessitated* cause. It is necessitated by something other than itself—namely, an order which transcends the bi-unity of cause and effect and connects them. Such a cause is imperfectly a cause, and its effect is not purely its effect.

On the other hand, if a being is nothing but an effect, it is totally dependent in its *being* and unable to exercise any influence on the cause, whether as a material or presupposed recipient subject, as an efficient cause, as an idea or motive, as a purpose to which the cause is directed, or as a necessary means for the self-perfecting of the cause.

---

[151] Cf. no. 178.
[152] Cf. no. 164.
[153] Cf. no. 103.

If this is so, then that which is nothing but pure cause is so absolutely self-grounding and self-sufficient that it does not undergo any modification, receive any enrichment *when* it has effects dependent upon itself. It cannot be said to be a "moved mover"[154] in any respect, whether in the order of exemplary causality, in that of final or that of efficient causality.

Thus the relation of causality as such is *unilateral,* i.e., only of the effect to the cause, but not vice versa. For what is purely effect presupposes what is purely cause as the absolutely prior, independent, and subsistent, as that which it itself is not but to which it is so essentially related that it cannot be without being related to it. On the other hand, that which is pure cause does not presuppose what is pure effect as something which, as idea, as purpose, as subject of influence, or in any other way, stands opposite the cause as co-original. Thus the pure cause cannot possibly be related to the pure effect by a real relation, for a real relation originates from its principle and terminus as presupposed beings.[155]

The Uncaused Cause as a Free Cause. Subsistent "To Be" as the pure cause of *being* which does not presuppose anything but posits everything, cannot be a cause that is moved to its causing. It is, on the one hand, in its infinity the perfectly sufficient ground for the realization of everything possible and, on the other, in its self-sufficiency not necessitated to bring about this realization since it does not depend on anything else as its purpose or as its indispensable means of self-perfection. Its causality is fully at its *disposal,* it has power over its power because it does not need the exercise of its powers to be itself. Of itself it is pure Act in such a way that its active potency or being-able is already completed by the identity of this potency with the act,[156] so that it does not need to manifest itself "externally." As absolutely independent, the pure Act is pure freedom to produce effects or not to produce them, to produce them in this way or in that way. Not the cause which necessitates because it is necessitated is the pure uncaused cause, but the cause which does not necessitate because it is free is the pure uncaused cause.[157]

---

[154]Taking this term in the broadest sense. Cf. no. 79.
[155]Cf. no. 164.
[156]Cf. no. 95.
[157]We are unable to form an adequate concept of the absolutely free cause, whose actual causing is at the same time free and yet not distinct from its Essence. For we conceive the act of causing as a transition from being-in-

Consequences of the Uncaused Cause's Freedom. If the uncaused cause is a free cause, all kinds of consequences follow of necessity. First of all, the cause will have to be conceived as *Will*. Not being blindly directed to the finite as its purpose or means, the uncaused cause is not a passively-being ordered, but an active ordering. It does not order itself to beings, but orders the beings to itself. In causes in them a being-ordered which does not lie outside their *being,* it makes them be according to an essence that is "nature" or dynamic orientation to their infinite cause as their Purpose.

Only practical reason, however, is capable of ordering and correlating. Therefore, the free Will, which orders beings in a constituent hierarchy to itself and to one another, which interconnects them in the

---

potency to being-in-act, as a perfecting, although we know that change, properly speaking, takes place only in that which is influenced, but in the cause merely insofar as it is an influenced or moved cause.

We have a kind of imperfect experience of free causality in our own freedom: because of its superiority to any particular good, the will determines the ultimate practical judgment without being absolutely determined to this judgment (cf. no. 143.). However, this analogy is very defective. For in many ways we are determined through our material-spiritual nature, we are dependent upon motives which have a certain goodness and attractiveness in themselves, although it remains in our power to make these motives our own (cf. no. 144). Moreover, every act of our freedom is an accidental self-perfecting, distinct from our essence, and at the same time a self-limitation with respect to the many possibilities according to which we could actuate ourselves.

The free Act, on the other hand, which is identical with its Essence is, as we have seen, neither an act of self-perfecting nor of self-limitation (cf. no. 179), but freely makes subsistent beings real. While our free act itself, as distinct from our essence, can be and not-be and, therefore, is strictly contingent (cf. no. 174), with respect to the infinite free act contingency pertains only to the finite beings which are not realized of necessity. True, *we* cannot conceive this cause otherwise than as related to particular beings in self-identity, while these relations of causality could also not have been. However, as we have seen, these relations are not real, but merely relations of reason, founded on the real relations of dependence which merely hypothetically necessary beings have to their free cause.

If we say that the Infinite causes the finite by a necessity of nature, this assertion, just as moderate monism, contains a contradiction. If, on the other hand, we say that the Infinite causes freely, that it can cause and not-cause, our way of thinking makes it appear as if the contingency lies in the Cause itself, as if this Cause proceeds or does not proceed to a decision. However, this way of thinking is deficient; hence we deny its suitability and add that there is no transition whatsoever either in the infinite subsistent "To Be," whose free act is identical with its Essence, or in the finite beings which by being caused do not pass from one state to another (cf. no. 180), but are wholly dependent upon the Cause in their *being* and in *all* that they are, even in their duration, permanence, and change. This Cause transcends them infinitely and, therefore, is not ordered to anyone of them, but orders them all to itself by making them be without necessity. By accepting the freedom of the First Cause, we make the *contradiction* disappear, but in its stead we find an ineffable and inscrutable *mystery.* Yet, despite its obscurity, this mystery is the light in which the whole of all finite beings, the world, becomes to some extent intelligible.

participation of *being,* is at the same time Reason creating order. We have to conceive it as infinite *Intellect,* which coincides with Essence and Will.[158]

As the infinite Intellect, which is perfectly identical with itself as the Intelligible, the Infinite is absolute Self-consciousness. And in its comprehensive knowledge of its All-perfectness it knows at the same time all particular modes of *being* as possible participations of its universal intensity of *being.* The ultimate ground, therefore, of the *intrinsic* possibility of finite beings is the absolute Essence knowing itself as the eminent archetype. And through the infinite Power everything that is intrinsically possible is also *really* possible, although not always in the world as it is now, because the more than sufficient ground for its realization is never missing.

From the freedom of the infinite Power it follows that every *de facto* existing finite being must be called *contingent* in the strict sense if it is viewed in relation to its first cause. However, this contingency does not mean that in the world as it *de facto* is there are not many kinds of *necessities* if we view the beings of this world in their own nature and their interconnection. Nothing can be so contingent that it does not participate to some extent in the absolute necessity of *being* which as internal self-ground is the Essence of subsistent "To Be." For instance, whatever is, insofar as it is, cannot not-be. Whatever is has of necessity sufficient internal and external grounds on which it is, viz., its constituent principles, its essence, and its external causes. Of necessity it has its emanating essential properties. Of necessity, as a nature, it is directed to the good as its purpose. Of necessity it has static and dynamic relations of connection with other beings. Of necessity, as soon as the conditions are fulfilled, its activities emanate from it. Even if it is a free being, it is necessitated to take a position with respect to its inner nature and its external milieu.[159]

Accordingly, the necessities existing in the world, which the sciences endeavor to express in general judgments as laws, are not at all against the contingency of beings with respect to their first

---

[158]Cf. no. 188. The same conclusion, moreover, follows from the absolute intensity of *being* pertaining to the first cause. "To be" attains full reality only in living, knowing, and understanding (cf. no. 117). Subsistent "To Be," therefore, as the cause of everything that through participation is, lives, knows, and understands, must not only *have* life and knowledge but has to *be* subsistent Life and Knowledge.

[159]Cf. no. 144.

cause. They are, on the contrary, marks indicating their dependence upon an intelligent and free creator of order.[160]

The Freedom of the Uncaused Cause and the Identity and Distinction of the Finite and the Infinite. We must now investigate how the unilateral character of the causal relation and the consequent freedom of the uncaused cause make it possible for us to think without contradiction, though only in a very inadequate way, about the unity and distinction of the finite and the Infinite.

Both the finite and the Infinite are positive. For this reason the contradictory opposition between non-being and being and the privative opposition between lacking and possessing a perfection are excluded here. Likewise, they are not opposed as contraries or as correlates.[161] For otherwise they would be distinct by virtue of the particular mode of *being* proper to each: the one would be this and the other that, one would have something the other does not have, *and* vice versa. Ontically they would stand "outside" each other. No matter how intimately they would be united through agreement in something common or through activity and passivity, no matter how much they would require each other and not be able to exist without each other, they would be co-original and, therefore, in this sense isolated from each other, each one being both subsistent and related on a ground of its own.

---

[160]From the contingency of the world it becomes easier to understand why it must of necessity be finite. A hypothetical world that is absolutely infinite in the intensity of *being* would fully coincide with the Infinite itself; hence it would no longer be a "whole" of particular beings in contrary opposition, it would no longer be a world. Every "whole" of finite real beings is a finite whole so far as the intensity of its *being* is concerned. With respect to the first Cause, it is a contingent whole. Another world is possible, a world with differently ordered and differently perfected beings or even beings of other kinds than those pertaining to the world of our experience. No world is possible which would be the best that can be, for all goodness in a world is relative. The caused never equates the uncaused cause, but merely approximates it analogously without ever being able to bridge the abyss. Thus the world, as a finite world, is always a world of contrary oppositions which have not yet been reconciled. Despite the fact that they relatively include one another, particular beings always also exclude one another to a certain extent. There always remains undetermined determinability, progressive unfolding in time, and a tendency to the solution of conflicts without ever reaching final harmony and lasting peace. We may even say that finite freedom implies not only imperfectness and deficiency, but even the possibility of deliberately turning away from the true good. But we may ask: Would the infinite Power, which communicates to beings "to be," subsistence, causality and freedom-in-causing, not be able to draw good even from moral evil—albeit in a way that transcends *our* understanding—and make it enter into the order of the world to its first Cause as its ultimate End?

[161]Cf. no. 38.

However, there is another way in which positives can be distinct—namely, precisely on the ground of the purely unilateral dynamic relation. Cause and effect are not distinct by virtue of their own particularity, but only because the cause *is* fully and in a universal way through identity with the essence the perfection which the effect *has* in a deficient and particular way through participation. Cause and effect are not two relatives but are the absolute and the related-to-the-absolute.

It is in this way that the identity and the distinction of the finite and the Infinite should be conceived. For here, and only here, causal dependence is participation in absolute perfectness, in transcendental perfection of *being*. Thus there is no longer question of a relation between two beings in the sense of two participants in *being,* which is the first sense of the term for us. Our thought has to transcend the familiar oppositions between beings *within* the order of *being.* There is no longer question here of two which participate in *being* in their own way, analogously and more or less intensely, according to agreement and differences, and which can be joined by us because together they contain a greater fullness of *being* than each taken separately. The particle "and" has to be given a new meaning here, for the perfectness of the participating being does not lie as something co-original in any way "outside" the absolute intensity of *being* pertaining to the first cause.

How the Infinite and the Finite Include Each Other. The finite and the Infinite must be called "one" provided we accurately determine the meaning of this unity. They include each other, but in a way that is radically different on the part of both.

The participating beings include the cause imparting "to be" in themselves, but not as their constituent principle, as the "to be" which they appropriate as their own. Subsistent "To Be" again is the ground of this immanent ground, it "makes" unqualified "to be" the formally constituted ground on which beings are. It is, therefore, as it were, the soil in which unqualified "to be" is rooted and still more intimate to beings than the "to be" which they appropriate. It is present in beings as in its effects, through causal in-being, as pure Activity—more intimate to me than my own intimacy.

The imparting cause of *being,* on the other hand, also includes the participating beings, but not as properties or modifying determinations emanating from it. Subsistent "To Be" includes the real beings because, and insofar as in spontaneous freedom it acts as the groundless ground which "makes" unqualified "to be" be the ground on which these and the other particular beings are. Finite beings are present in subsistent "To Be" as in their cause, through dynamic in-being—it is all as the cause of all.[162]

How the Infinite and the Finite Exclude Each Other. The finite and the Infinite must likewise be called distinct provided, of course, we accurately determine the meaning of this distinction. They exclude each other, according to our way of thinking, but in a way that radically differs on the part of both.

What do we mean by the negative judgment that the finite is *not* the Infinite? It does not mean that the positively proper entity through which the finite is itself, cannot at all be found in the Infinite, so that the Infinite would be "totally other" with respect to the finite. It means that the finite possesses only in a deficient and contracted way that which is proper to it—namely, the "to be" which it has received from the Infinite. The distinction of essence and "to be" in the finite, which makes the finite being dynamically perfectible and never absolutely perfect, is the foundation of our negative judgments: the finite is only in this or that way and, therefore, it is not the other particular beings and *a fortiori* not the Infinite, despite the fact that its own "to be" must be understood as a "to be" according to, from, and toward, the Infinite. It is distinct and at an "infinite" distance from the Infinite because it *is* in a purely relative way, which we conceive as a relative not-to-be. It is not distinct through its *being* as such, for in the measure that it is, it most intimately includes in itself the Infinite as its present cause.

Secondly, what do we mean by the negative judgment that the Infinite is *not* the finite? For our way of thinking this judgment is the reverse of the negative judgment that the finite is not the Infinite. However, here it is even more evident that the negation is a way of thinking and does not apply to what we intend to express by it. The Infinite is not a negative act; taken in itself, it is not even the immediate foundation of negative judgments because it is not a particular

---

[162]Cf. St. Augustine, *Confessions*, bk. III, ch. 6: the Infinite "is all as the cause of all." Thomas Aquinas borrowed the text from Pseudo-Dionysius, *De divinis nominibus*. See his *Comment.* Ch. V, lect. 1. The text in question reads: "magis autem neque est, sed est ipse esse existentibus," i.e., (we may say) even (that) He is not, but that He is the "to be" of existent things. St. Thomas understood the text in a causal sense and not formally (see no. 264 of the text and no. 630 of the Commentary in the Pera edition, Rome, 1950). Cf. also *Summa theol.*, p. 1, q. 4, a. 2 and q. 6, a. 4.

being.[163] The foundation of the negation lies in *our* starting point—namely, the experience of the finite and material. We cannot conceive the Infinite without saying that it is not finite, not temporal, not "becoming" and perishable, not spatial and material, and consequently we say also that it is not the finite and material beings.

The fact that in this way we conceive the Infinite as not only contradictorily opposed to absolute-not-to-be but also as contrarily and relatively opposed to positive beings does not mean that we attribute to particular beings something proper which the Infinite would not contain eminently in the identity of its Essence. On the contrary, the foundation of our negative judgment is the relative positivity of the finite compared with the absolute positivity of the Infinite. We deny that the Infinite possesses the perfectness of *being* in the degraded way of the finite and assert that it includes all perfections in an eminent way. The Infinite is distinct from the finite through the pure intensity of its *being*.

Thus the opposition which the negation intends to place in the Infinite with respect to finite beings as its contraries and correlates is merely thought and *not real* as if the Infinite and the finite were together as equals. Just as the real relation, the real opposition here is unilateral: it comes from the finite, which is not the Infinite, but particular. Accordingly, although we say correctly that the Infinite is *not* the finite, the expression is inadequate. It is not intended to make the Infinite something particular, but only to emphasize its universality and eminence with respect to everything particular. The negation is our way of expressing the transcendence of the absolutely affirmative.[164]

---

[163]Cf. no. 37.

[164]The term "transcendence" likewise should not be misunderstood. According to our *way of expression,* it includes a relation to that which the transcendent transcends. However, according to our *intention,* the Infinite transcends also this relative transcendence and is not the higher or highest in a relative sense. The Infinite is the incomparable, which, precisely because of the absolute intensity of its *being,* can make itself freely present through causal immanence in the inner depth of every dependent finite being. For every particular being the other particulars are in a sense strangers, because what is most intimately proper to the one is not most intimately proper to the other, and vice versa. But every being is akin with the Infinite in the sense that the most personal particularity of each is a weak reflection of what the Infinite is in all fullness through its essence. Everything finite points to the Infinite as its more profound and true "self," but a "self" that is transcendent and, therefore, not included in the finite as a constituent principle but as its archetype, source and purpose. Through reflection on itself the finite finds its all-transcending cause and naturally adheres to it in love. Immanence and transcendence are two inadequate modes of thinking by means of which we attempt to approach along different roads the mystery of the free first cause that remains inscrutable for us.

The Spiritual Nature of Subsistent "To Be." If we understand that subsistent "To Be" as free cause has to be also subsistent Life, Knowledge and Will, we conceive it as spiritual. This insight is implicitly contained in the insight that the unconditioned is absolutely its own ground,[165] for as active self-identification it must be a knowing—being-known and a loving—being-loved,[166] without distinction of subject and object.[167] Thus as subsistent "To Be" it is also the absolute "Ego."[168] And if we conceive being-a-person as the highest mode of being-subsistent,[169] we have to conceive subsistent "To Be" also as a personal Being.

However, difficulties arise when we think of the infinity and all-embracing character of subsistent "To Be." For we think of a person as a determined individual, distinct from others, who delineates himself through free acts, behaves in a characteristic way arising from his originality in a milieu of things and other persons, associating with them in mutual exchanges, and revealing himself to them to a greater or lesser extent. A person is for us a dynamic being, which is essentially social and historical, having a situation and a destiny.[170]

The Infinite, however, cannot be a person in this way, for it does not limit and perfect itself,[171] it does not express itself in contingent free acts distinct from its essence. Nevertheless, it should not be conceived as infra-personal, as unconscious and non-free. Viewed from *our* concept of person, it is rather supra-personal. More correctly expressed, as the cause of the personal and especially of man's free acts, it must be personal in an *eminent* way unknown to us, and should be called the primordial person rather than the primordial thing. To be a person in our social and historical way is an effect of our particularity and perfectibility, but does not belong to the pure perfectness of personal *being*. To be of itself, *in* itself, and to itself must pertain to the Infinite in all their purity, and consequently interior life and self-communication belong to Him. The same must be asserted regarding the possibility of freely revealing His hidden intimacy, not to presupposed other persons, but to personal

---

[165]Cf. no. 178.
[166]Cf. no. 17.
[167]Cf. no. 122.
[168]Cf. no. 18.
[169]Cf. no. 153.
[170]Cf. nos. 154 and 155.
[171]Cf. no. 179.

beings having in Him their first source and ultimate goal, who through knowing and willing are connected with Him.[172]

182. *The Ultimate "Why"*

Why is there something and not rather nothing? In these words we may express the fundamental philosophical wonder. The question presupposes that there must be a reason or ground why the beings of our experience *de facto* are and that on this ground they can be understood in their necessity.

As we have seen in the beginning of our study, our knowledge does indeed transcend the experience of facts. What is *de facto,* is possible; however, *de facto*-being is not a condition of possibility but, on the contrary, possibility is its condition. Therefore, in every case, even if the facts would not be, there is the absolute possibility of what *de facto* is. Consequently, the real ground of the possibility of what is *de facto,* is absolutely necessary. It is impossible that there be nothing.[173]

Irrationalism and Rationalism. Irrationalism seeks to doubt this possibility. It admits that we have an insight into necessary connections, but considers all necessity to be hypothetical.[174] Therefore, the ultimate "why" of all, the ground on which everything else rests,

---

[172]In our explanations we have constantly spoken of the unconditioned, the absolute, the infinite, as "it." The use of the neutral appears now to have been a methodic *epoche,* i.e., we left out of consideration the personal character of the Infinite. Just as in the beginning of philosophy we said that "something is," without implying that this "something" meant an opposition to "somebody" or a preference for the impersonal (cf. nos. 15 and 17), so also must the hitherto used neutral be understood as an abstention from making any assertion about the thing-like or personal, the unconscious or conscious, nature of the Absolute. Now that a decision has been reached in favor of the personal—in an immanent sense—the train of thought would have to be retaken in this new light.

It is possible to follow the path of thought over which we have traveled starting from unqualified *being,* in a similar but analogous manner by starting with any of the transcendental ideas, such as unity, truth, goodness, beauty, etc. Likewise, and *post factum* even with greater justification, one could start with the active, absolutely perfect modes of *being,* viz., life, feeling, knowing, understanding, willing, loving, freedom, communication, etc. Such a rethinking would be a revision and deepening of the whole of metaphysics in a personalistic sense. It would be a mode of thinking which would appeal to us more immediately in our concrete and integral way of being-man, and thus would be more fruitful. Accordingly, now that we have arrived at the end of the road which we have chosen for methodic reasons of prudence, we see that we still stand at the beginning. Everything has to be done over. And at every new end of a travelled road new perspectives will open up, inviting us to another round. *Docta ignorantia,* learned ignorance, remains characteristic of man's endless movement of thought (cf. no. 16).

[173]Cf. no. 23.

[174]Cf. no. 176.

as a groundless ground does not have any ground on which it is. The unconditioned first could just as well be as not-be, it is purely *de facto* real. The absolute is *contingent*. Every rational explanation ultimately terminates in a reference to what is no longer explainable by reason—the pure "facticity" of "that's the way things are."

Rationalism, on the other hand, admits, first of all, that the groundless ground in itself is its own ground and that, consequently, it is of itself absolutely necessary. Next, however, it admits also that whatever is grounded on this ground flows *of necessity* from it, as conclusions flow from premises. The ground grounds not only everything possible, but cannot do otherwise than thinkingly realize everything possible in a logical process of development. Everything, therefore, in every being is absolutely necessary, so that there can be no question of contingency in the strict sense.[175]

The One-Sideness of These Views. If, however, the groundless ground of being is an intelligent, free, and personal Being which wholly transcends us, then both purely contingent facticity and purely deductive necessity one-sidedly and untruthfully explain the "why" of the *de facto* existing world as a whole.

First of all, it is not meaningless to inquire into the "why" of this world. For whatever is must be intelligible in its *being*[176]—in this point rationalism is right. Since, however, this world is finite and not identical with the absolute intensity of *being,* it refers to something above itself as its "why." Only the Being which is identical with the fullness of *being,* as fully grounding itself, does not have a "why" outside itself but is of itself real by absolute necessity. Therefore, the ultimate "why" of the existing world lies nowhere else than in the subsistent "To Be."

Secondly, it does not at all follow, as rationalism claims, that the existing world is of necessity deducible from its transcending ground. On the contrary, this deduction is not only impossible for our limited and deficient knowledge, but is also in itself absolutely impossible

---

[175]If, in addition, one admits that we possess, at least to a certain extent, this all-grounding ground in our most fundamental concept and in our first principles of thought, he will attempt to construct a deductive metaphysics which, in its logical progress, independently of experience, is a reflection of the necessary process by which the beings flow from their ground. Through thinking, this metaphysics claims, we are capable of discovering the "why" of everything.

[176]Cf. no. 42.

because the Being which of itself is absolutely necessary is an intelligent and free cause.[177]

The "Motive" of the Free Uncaused Cause. Why did the free cause decide to cause finite beings, to cause *these* finite beings and no others? The initial question regarding the "why" of the world of experience terminates in this final question regarding the "motive" which the first cause in its freedom has to cause these beings. Is is possible for us from our finite and caused viewpoint to ask the cause this question?

The Infinite cannot have any motive outside Himself which induces Him to cause. The effect to be caused derives its goodness and attractiveness from the cause and thus cannot be its motive.[178] The question, then, is in what senses He Himself may be called the motive of His causing.

It certainly cannot be in the sense that the world to be caused would be for Him a necessary means to attain Himself as Purpose. For He possesses Himself in perfect identity and gains nothing from His causality. He does not cause from a tendency or desire to possess.

On the other hand, He cannot assign any other purpose to the world to be caused than Himself.[179] His Goodness, which is identical with His Essence, is the attracting power which leads whatever proceeds from Him back to Himself. For the good of the effect as effect lies in its return to the cause through approaching and becoming similar to Him. As Aristotle expressed it with respect to the first Mover, He "produces motion as being loved."[180]

If, however, the return of the caused which is ordered to its cause as to its purpose does not perfect the cause, but is a perfecting only of the caused, then the *free* cause is a liberal, i.e., *freely-giving* cause.[181] That the Infinite as subsistent Goodness makes Himself

[177]True, subsistent "To Be," as it is known by itself as Intellect, can be participated in endlessly many particular ways and is the ground on which finite beings are possible. For this reason everything which will ever be real, as originating from the infinite Intellect, will be rationally ordered. However, the realization of the possible comes from the Freedom of the intelligent cause without any necessity. Consequently, although the actually existing world is of necessity intelligible and meaningfully organized, it is strictly contingent. Cf. Thomas Aquinas, *Contra gentes,* bk. III, ch. 97: "Providence dispenses things according to some rational order (*ratio*); yet this order is selected on the basis of God's will." See also the end of this chapter concerning the "reason why."

[178]Cf. no. 181.

[179]Cf. no. 180.

[180]*Metaphysica,* bk. XII, ch. 7, 1072b 3.

[181]Concerning the liberality of the first cause, see Thomas Aquinas, *Contra gentes,* bk. I, ch. 81 and 93; *Summa theol.,* p. 1, q. 44, a. 4, *ad* 1; *De potentia,* q. 5, a. 4.

the purpose of the finite, i.e., that He orders all finite beings to Himself, means the same as that He orders all beings to their own perfection, to be attained through a more intimate participation in Himself as subsistent Goodness.

The Infinite is not moved to causing by any motive outside Himself. The reason "why" He imparts of His own Goodness cannot be found anywhere else than in Himself. This "why" is His pure Goodness, understood as superabundant liberality. But this Goodness should not be conceived as overflowing by necessity of nature, but as freely-flowing, as a personal decision which in this sense is without a motive, above reason, and not deducible from anything else. The adage "the good is diffusive of itself," i.e., communicates itself, may not be understood as a law extending to subsistent Goodness, but should be conceived as an expression of the bottomless freedom pertaining to the ultimate Ground of *being,* who gratuitously calls everything finite to *being* and goodness. The motivelessness or the being-a-motive-for-oneself, which is valid to some extent even with respect to human free acts and human love,[182] applies here in a perfect way: it is not because beings are good that they are loved by Him, but because they are loved by Him, they participate in *being* and in goodness.[183]

The Infinite orders everything to His good. But His good is not only His Goodness in Himself, which is the motive why He loves us and makes us worthy of being loved. It is also our own good, as a received proportional likeness of His subsistent Goodness. He wants us to have all good, because He wills that we are and thereby resemble Him. Thus, from His viewpoint, there can never be opposition between His interests and ours. For He makes us be, be causes, and even be free causes. He wants the greatness of man and the world. Whoever thinks that he has to belittle the finite to glorify the Infinite is mistaken and fails to understand Omnipotence, Wisdom, and Goodness. He forgets that the "to be" of the finite being is a "grace," i.e., a free gift. He forgets that the ultimate "why" for the glory of this world and its endless dynamic perfectibility is called Creating Benevolence—Benevolence which for us is the inscrutable mystery of subsistent "To Be," Knowledge, and Love.

---

[182]Cf. no. 144.

[183]Cf. no. 43. One could perhaps ask: Why call *these* beings into being and call them *as* they are? Why create this world order and not another? But such questions pervert the acquired insights. For they mean once more that the motive is sought outside the Infinite Himself in a goodness which these beings would have independently of the free act of causality through which they were called into existence.

CHAPTER THIRTY

CAN WE KNOW THAT GOD IS?

183. *Belief in God and the Proof of God*[1]

God and the Philosopher. "This being we call God." With these words St. Thomas concludes each of the various ways in which he arrives at an unmoved mover, an uncaused cause, etc. We may ask to what extent the terminus of the metaphysical search for the ultimate ground of beings coincides with the God whom the believer adores.

The so-called proofs of God cannot start with an adequate definition of God's essence borrowed from Faith, for to the believer God is the Inscrutable and Ineffable. The philosopher likewise usually, at least in the beginning, does not claim to have an adequate essential knowledge of the absolute which he seeks. Thus his only starting point can be a nominal description, a provisional concept.

It is not very difficult for the philosopher to show in his investigation that there is something absolute. No one escapes from admitting something in which he "believes" absolutely, whether this "something" be the unknowability of the absolute, absolute relativity, mutability and temporality, a permanent and fixed law, fate, the world or humanity as a whole, the value of beauty, work, pleasure, freedom. What is important for the philosopher is to *render more precise* the relation between the relative and the absolute, the contingent and the necessary, the temporal and the eternal. The task of the investigation, which after its result is called the proof of God's existence, lies primarily in safeguarding the purity of the concept of the absolute and in protecting it against deformation.

Thus the questions *whether* God is and *who* God is are inseparably connected. The very denial of God shows the truth of this assertion, for the denial is not the negation of something absolute, but usually the rejection of God as he is conceived and adored by some human beings in this or that particular way.

---

[1] Cf. H. Geurtsen, "De innerlijke structuur van het Godsbewijs," *Tijdschrift v. Philosophie,* vol. 6 (1944), pp. 3-54 and 207-282; "Les preuves de l'existence de Dieu," *Bijdragen,* vol. 9 (1948), pp. 285-291.

God and the Believer. For the believer God is the One who freely
has revealed Himself to us. In the supposition that God is a personal being, the knowability of human persons[2] can throw some light
on the manner in which God can be known to the believer. If His
Essence is pure interiority, He fully disposes over his being-known.
In that case our knowledge is passive, totally-dependent upon His
free manifestation to us. His unverifiable word of revelation will give
us knowledge only if we accept it exactly as it comes to us, only if we
believingly accept His testimony about Himself. The motive why the
believer believes, therefore, lies *within* the act of faith itself: it is
God Himself in His word, which is understood by the listener.

The believer, however, admits also that God speaks not to him
alone but to all, and that each one who is well-disposed and receptive
to the word hears what he himself hears. He believes, moreover, not
only that God has made Himself known in His intimate essence
through supernatural revelation, but also that He has manifested
Himself *to some extent* through creation. He believes that in the very
structure of human nature, in the infinite openness of our knowing
and loving, there is an implicit desire for, and an implicit recognition
of God as the infinite ground of finite beings.

The believer, therefore, admits also that there is a possibility of
a purely philosophical reflection on the structure of the finite and
that this reflection, unlike the incommunicable personal act of
trust which is faith, proceeds in the manner of a *science*, open to
verification by, and *critique* of a community of fellow-thinkers.
While such a reflection may be inspired by supernatural faith, it
will have to proceed along the roads of pure reason.

The Character of the Proof of God. The fact that the reflection
on the grounds of finite beings has to proceed along the roads of
reason alone does not mean that the so-called proof of God's existence
is a pure deduction of a particular conclusion through the application
of a previously accepted general principle, e.g., the principle of causality, to a particular case. If the causality of the first cause is conceived
as a particular case of causality, then the caused discovered will certainly not correspond to the God who is adored by the believer. In
the so-called proof of God's existence the *a posteriori* fact and the
a priori principle are not foreign to each other, but in the *a posteriori*
the *a priori* appears to us, and whoever has discovered the principle

---

[2]Cf. no. 132.

as the explicitation of what is implied in the fact has discovered also the first universal cause.

It is, likewise, not possible to conceive the so-called proof of God as an inductive process of reasoning and of collecting facts. For, its conclusion is not an abstract-universal truth, but an individual reality that is not particular but causally universal.

Nevertheless, the proof of God is a rational reflection, a process of thought, for we do not have an explicit intuition of God which would fully satisfy our knowing and willing. So far as our explicit knowledge is concerned, God is not first but last, even though in Himself God is ontologically first.[3]

---

[3] Alongside the *a priori* proof, which proceeds from what is ontically prior to what is ontically posterior, and the *a posteriori* proof, which argues from the ontically posterior to the ontically prior, there is sometimes also question of an *a simultaneo* proof. In this proof the middle term is not a char· acteristic which is really district from the predicate of the conclusion, but is conceived in our thought as prior in order to deduce the predicate from it. The so-called ontological proof of God's existence is such a proof. According to St. Anselm of Canterbury (*Proslogion*, chs. 2 and 3. For a critique of it see, e.g., Louis de Raeymaeker, *The Philosophy of Being,* St. Louis, 1954, pp. 289 ff.; Thomas Aquinas, *Summa theol.,* p. 1, q. 2, a. 1 and *Contra gentes*, bk. 1, chs. 10-11), God is the being than which none greater can be thought. But such a being is of necessity real. For a being which can not only be thought but also is real is greater than a being that can only be thought.

In reply to this argument we may say that we cannot doubt that something is of necessity real, as soon as we experience that something is *de facto* real (cf. nos. 29 and 176). However, that this being is infinite or "than which nothing greater can be thought" does not immediately follow nor that it is distinct from the finite beings of our experience (cf. no. 179). Moreover, the argument does not want to start from experience but merely from being-thought. Now, that we "think" the greatest conceivable being as being-real may have two meanings. First of all, it may refer to the judgment or assertion. In this sense it is certain that the being than which nothing greater can be thought and of which we assert—on what grounds?—that it is real, if it really is, is of necessity real. Secondly, it may refer to the concept or representation. In this sense it is not immediately evident that what we think of as "the greatest conceivable" and which we therefore represent of necessity as being-real exists also in reality.

Leibniz (*Monadologia*, no. 45; concerning Scotus' "coloratio," see A. Epping, "Scotus en het anselmiaans Godsbewijs," *Doctor Subtilis,* 's Hertogenbosch, 1946, pp. 29-60. See also the bibliography quoted by P. Descoqs, *Praelectiones theologiae naturalis,* vol. 1, Paris, 1932, pp. 617-618.), is right when he says that first one has to show that the "thinking" of which there is question here cannot have the sense of "not seeing that there is contradiction," but must have the sense of "seeing that there is no contradiction" (cf. no. 175). As a matter of fact, once it has been shown that the absolutely infinite in intensity of *being* is intrinsically possible, it can be shown also that this infinite is real. For the infinite cannot have the ground of its possibility in a reality outside itself, but only in its own reality. Leibniz himself wants to prove the possibility of the infinite from the concept itself which we have of the infinite. However, we do not have an adequate positive concept of the infinite and can demonstrate the possibility of the infinite only *a posteriori* from finite beings which we experience as real—and therefore as really possible—insofar as these beings imply the infinite as a condition of their possibility (cf. no. 178).

The proof of God's existence is an original and unique train of thought, which cannot be compared with other cognitive processes. It is not a demonstration in the strict sense, such as those of mathematics and the experimental sciences. Nevertheless, it makes sense to speak here of a demonstration or proof in the broader sense, because there is question here of mediate knowledge, knowledge of the infinite in and through a reflective analysis of the finite.

The "proof" of God is not an explicit intuition in the strict sense. Yet it is meaningful to speak of an intuitive moment in this proof. For God, who is explicitly last known to us, is ontologically first and most knowable, and a shadow of this primacy may be found even in our thinking—namely, insofar as our striving for absolute happiness, our search for absolute truth are ultimately nothing else than an implicit desire for Him and an initial bond with Him. Our most fundamental undeniable apodictic evidences are reflexions of His presence in all that we know.[4] The proof of God is the explicitation of this presence that lies contained in our pre-predicative knowing of *being*.

Accordingly, the proof of God is the "explanation" of finite being in syllogistic form with "scientific" means. In this proof the first principles—of identity, of ground, of meaning—which lie contained in every act of judgment concerning beings are systematically developed; the realization of the properties of *being* in the beings of experience is seen as imperfect; and in this way our thinking pushed forward to the discovery of absolute identity, of the groundless ground, the meaning which makes everything meaningful—"To Be," Truth, and Goodness.[5]

The proof of God's existence is essentially unfinished in the conceptual form given to it, no matter how relatively perfect and elabo-

---

[4]Cf. no. 128.

[5]It should be evident that this "explanation" can be made more or less skillfully, dependent as it is, on the one hand, upon the wealth of human experience which supports philosophical thought and, on the other, upon the rigorous logical sequence and the absence of contradiction in human thinking. If one objects against this or that particular explanation, he does not immediately throw doubt on the affirmation of God's existence, for in its implicit form this affirmation precedes the explanation. Moreover, in life itself, the affirmation may have developed in many concrete ways, such as affective intuitions in the broad sense of the term, i.e., through synthetically seeing one another in an unanalyzed and more immediate way, and also through an act of faith in God. The object of the quest is merely to arrive at a conceptual justification of God's existence that is increasingly less incorrect. As a rational being, man cannot escape from constantly again attempting to perform this rational explanation. More than anywhere else it is here that one may apply Plato's word: "The unexamined life is no life for a human being." (*Apology*, 38 a).

rate the form may be. For it is the thought movement itself of a metaphysics that is essentially unfinished and endlessly perfectionable. Every metaphysical system will offer a different brand of proof for the existence of God. However, the main reason why the proof remains unfinished is that it always discovers the Infinite as the Unknowable, so that the question who God is remains without an answer. Yet the question whether God is and who He is are inseparably connected.[6]

In the history of philosophy we find the "Itinerary of the Mind to God" (St. Bonaventure) more or less systematically conceptualized in a variety of shades. One has only to think here of Plato, Aristotle, Plotinus, St. Augustine, Alfarabi, Moses Maimonides, St. Thomas Aquinas, Scotus, Descartes, Spinoza, Leibniz, Kant, Hegel, Bergson, Blondel, and Lavelle. Among the medieval scholastics Scotus has left a very systematic explanation.[7] In the following pages we will survey the five ways followed by Thomas Aquinas in his *Summa Theologica* which, provided they are understood in their broader context, are the crown of the Thomastic metaphysics of *being*.[8]

---

[6]One could raise this objection. To discover whether God exists, we must know first who He is (if He exists) and then investigate whether or not there exists such a being. But we do not know God's essence; hence we cannot know whether He exists.

In reply, we must distinguish two types of proofs—namely, the proof *"propter quid"* or *"why"* and the proof *"quia"* or *"that."* The proof "why" shows not only that something is or is as it is but also indicates why it is or is as it is on the proper, immediate and adequate ontic ground of the being in question. Such a proof has to start from an essential definition and is always *a priori*. But there is also an imperfect kind of proof, the proof "that," which merely shows that something is or is as it is without giving any complete insight. Such a proof may be able to deduce an effect from more remote and common causes or ascend from the effect to the cause. In such a proof one cannot start from an essential definition of the cause as it is in itself, but only from its nominal description in connection with the effect whose essence we do know to a certain extent. It should be clear that the question concerning the "why" of God's reality can find its answer only in God Himself and that our "itinerary" to God is merely an unfinished ascent from known finite reality toward Him.

[7]*De primo principio*. See about Scotus' proof of God, e.g., A. Epping, "De structuur van Scotus' Godsbewijs," *Studia Catholica*, vol. 18 (1942), pp. 86-98; E. Gilson, *Jean Duns Scot*, Paris, 1952.

[8]*Summa theol.*, p. 1, q. 2, a. 3; Cf. *Contra Gentes*, bk. 1, ch. 13. Concerning his proofs see, e.g., F. van Steenberghen, "Le problème de l'existence de Dieu," *Revue Philosophique de Louvain*, vol 45 (1947), pp. 8-20, 141-168, 301-313; "Réflexions sur les quinque viae," *Acta Tertii Congressus Thom. Intern.*, Turin, 1951, pp. 237-241; *Ontologie*, pp. 159-164; A. Grégoire, *Immanence et transcendance*, Brussels, 1939; H. Robbers, 'De geestesgang van het bestaan der wereld naar het bestaan van God," *Verslag der 16e Alg. Verg. der Ver. v. Thomist. Wijsb.*, Utrecht, 1951, pp. 17-33.

184. *The First Way: the Unmoved Mover*[9]

There exists beings which are in motion.

The most striking characteristic of corporeal beings present in our observation is their being-in-motion.[10] Motion in the narrowest sense is locomotion,[11] but in a broader sense the term applies also to increase or decrease, and to change according to sense-perceptible qualities and even to instantaneous essential change.[12] Moreover, we conceive here as motion also every transition from being-in-potency to being-in-act, including the transition from active potency to activity.[13] Accordingly, all forms of vegetative development, sensitive and intellectual perception, remembering, thinking, reasoning, all affective movements, desires, strivings, decisions, and action fall under being-in-motion or being-dynamic in the broad sense intended here.

But what is in motion ultimately is moved by something else as its mover.

For nothing is *in motion* or transition save insofar as it is still only *in potency* to that to which it is in motion.[14] Therefore, it must have a ground on which it becomes actual, i.e., it is moved by a mover. But precisely *insofar as* it is in motion and consequently moved, it itself cannot be this mover. For nothing is *moving* save insofar as it is *in-act* with respect to that to which it actively moves.[15] Now the same cannot be both still-in-potency and already-in-act in the same respect, for these two states exclude each other.[16] Accordingly, what is in motion is moved by "something else."[17]

---

[9] Cf. E. Winance, "Le premier moteur," *Doctor communis*, vol. 7 (1954), pp. 4-26.

[10] Cf. no. 79.

[11] Cf. no. 73.

[12] Cf. no. 79.

[13] Cf. no. 95.

[14] Cf. no. 74.

[15] Cf. no. 106.

[16] Cf. no. 74.

[17] One could object that a living being moves itself (cf. no. 110). In reply, we may say that the living is moved in one respect, but moves in another. In organic living bodies one part moves another part. In sensitive and intellectual life one power actuates another, or also, actual knowledge of the premises moves to actual knowledge of the conclusions, and the actual willing of the purpose moves to the choice of means. Moreover, the appetitive powers move both the cognitive and the bodily powers to the execution of activities. Ultimately, however, the finite living being is moved to its activity by another being, not only by its objects but also and especially, by a higher being which is already in activity, and under the influence of this being the ready potency goes into activity (cf. no. 95). The transition of the finite being which is ready to act to the exercised activity cannot be fully explained through the spontaneity of this being, because the complete self-actuation and self-perfecting of the finite is a contradiction (cf. nos. 95 and 179).

The mover is either a mover moved to its moving—and this cannot be continued to infinity—or a mover which is not moved to its moving.

If the mover itself is in motion to its moving, then it is moved by something else to this being-in-motion. The series of moved movers may be continued endlessly, but nowhere will one find the sufficient ground of the being-in-motion. For even in an endless series of moved movers each mover remains just as unexplained in its moving as the being-in-motion which it is supposed to explain. Moved movers as such do not bring us closer to an explanation.

The explanation, therefore, of the moved movers lies in this, that each of them ultimately is a mover only by virtue of another mover which is *not* moved to move and does not take its place in the ranks of moved movers, but is a mover that transcends being-in-motion and is unmoved.

Therefore, there exists ultimately an unmoved mover.[18]

The reality of a mover which absolutely transcends all beings as *finite* beings and is unmoved in every order of motion is demonstrated only when motion is understood not merely as a transition from being-in-potency to being-in-act but as a being-moved to-*being*.[19]

For, if we understand motion as the transition from being-in-potency to being-in-act, we have to understand the unmoved mover as the being which does not pass from being-in-potency to being-in-act. Although such a being would be supra-temporal, it could nonetheless still be a finite being, a being which *would not pass* from being-in-potency to being-in-act but would still be *composed* of potency and act in the broadest analogous sense—namely, of essence and "to be."[20]

Accordingly, motion should be understood in the broadest metaphysical sense. Thus considered, being-in-motion does not necessarily imply a transition from being-in-potency to being-in-act, but only that the being in question, though it possesses its act, "is" not this act through its very essence.[21] In this sense *every* finite being is moved with respect to its "to be," without there being question of a transition from the state of non-being to that of being or of

---

[18]If we start from local motion, we arrive at an unmoved mover transcending the order of local motion. A similar transcendence holds for each of the above-mentioned special kinds of motion.

[19]Cf. no. 79.

[20]Cf. no. 101.

[21]Cf. no. 79.

coming-to-be in the proper sense.[22] To explain this metaphysical motion, there is needed an unmoved mover which is unmoved with respect to the act of being. It is only in this way that the investigation of the finite being-in-motion leads us to admit as the ground of this finite being-in-motion a mover to which "to be" pertains through its essence itself, a pure Act.

This pure Act is Subsistent "To Be."

185. *Second Way: the Uncaused Cause*

There are beings which are efficient causes.

This assertion may be clarified as follows. Corporeal beings **are** mutually active and passive. Their own activity is a transient action exercised upon something else. This action occurs as an anonymous event of nature as soon as there is contact with the other. This contact, however, is reciprocal; hence the object which in contact has to become open to influence, itself in its turn also exercises influence.[23] The living body likewise is interconnected with the whole of extended beings in communicative interaction. However, the surroundings have a special meaning and value for each corporeal living being—they constitute its "milieu." Thus the living body reacts to definite influences in a specific way.[24] Sensitive and intellectual beings are influenced by their objects,[25] and they themselves influence their surroundings, modifying them through the execution of their plans.[26] Man produces cultural objects, whose purposive form points to a meaning given to them from the standpoint of a goal and an idea.[27] Man's "moral" influence on his fellow-men as persons is the most proper form of human causality.[28]

Now, a cause is either caused by something else in its causing—and this cannot be continued endlessly—or is uncaused in its causing.

The reason is as follows. First of all, the cause which is caused in its causing is caused *by something else* in its being-a-cause. For nothing is its own cause *because* nothing is prior to itself.[29] Secondly,

---

[22]Cf. no. 181.
[23]Cf. no. 91.
[24]Cf. no. 113.
[25]Cf. no. 122.
[26]Cf. nos. 146-148.
[27]Cf. no. 105.
[28]Cf. no. 154.
[29]Cf. no. 103.

an endless series of causes that are caused in their causing—so-called directly subordinated causes—does not offer a satisfactory explanation, for each of them itself needs to be explained just as much as the cause with which we started. If there were no first cause, there would be no caused causes. By "first cause" we mean here a cause which is not merely first relatively to others, but an absolutely first cause which wholly transcends the series of caused causes.

Therefore, there exists ultimately the uncaused cause.

Every cause causes a perfection.[30] The caused cause, however, does not cause the total perfection of the object influenced by it, but only the acquisition or preservation of certain substantial or accidental determinations,[31] i.e., it causes the being in question only with respect to its modes, its particularizations of the perfection of *being*. The uncaused cause, on the other hand, as a pure cause, has the effect totally dependent upon itself, not only with respect to particular modes of *being* but with respect to *being* as such. The uncaused cause, as causing "to be," must possess the perfection of *being* in such a way that it is absolutely independent of prior causes in its *being*.

Accordingly, the uncaused cause has "to be" through its essence. *It is subsistent "To Be."*

186. *Third Way: the Being Which is of Itself Absolutely Necessary*[32]

There are beings which by their very nature are corruptible, as is clear from the fact that they come to be and pass away. These beings are material beings, which are subject to change not only with respect to their accidental determinations but also in their essence.[33]

But is impossible that everything *that is, is by its very nature in all respects corruptible.* For what is corruptible by its very nature, will ultimately cease to be. If, however, everything is corruptible in *all* respects, everything would already have passed away in its entirety and nothing would ever have been. In that case there would

---

[30] Cf. *ibid.*

[31] Cf. no. 181.

[32] There have been many discussions of this third way. For its historical origin, see, H. Holstein, "L'origine aristotélicienne de la tertia via de S. Thomas," *Revue philosophique de Louvain,* vol. 48 (1950), pp. 354-370. Yet both Avicenna and Moses Maimonides have influenced this proof. For a good explanation of the third way, see Sertillanges, *S. Thomas d'Aquin,* vol. 1, pp. 138-141; U. degl'Innocenti, "La validità della terza via," *Doctor communis.* vol. 7 (1954), pp. 41-70.

[33] Cf. no. 88.

be nothing now, for what is not, begins to be only as caused by something that is. However, something is now. Therefore, not everything is corruptible in all respects.[34]

If the corruptible is not in *all* respects corruptible, there is something which by its very nature is incorruptible—for instance, prime matter, which in essential change is the *permanent* substratum and the reason why the passing away of one thing is precisely the coming-to-be of the other.[35]

The incorruptible, that which by its very nature must always be, is necessary, at least in the broad sense.[36] For, if it is not of itself absolutely necessary, it derives its necessity from an actual causing cause. (We abstract from the question whether this cause causes the incorruptible of necessity or without necessity.) If this cause in its turn is not of itself absolutely necessary, then it is caused with respect to its necessity. Ultimately, the explanation of everything necessary that is not of itself absolutely necessary has to lie in a transcendent cause which does not have a cause of its necessity but is of itself absolutely necessary.

Therefore, *there is a being which of itself is absolutely necessary.*[37]

---

[34]If the objection is made that something which by its nature is corruptible could de facto not be corrupted, we reply that this incorruption would be due to a cause that is incorruptible; hence the supposition admits that not everything is corruptible in every respect.

[35]Cf. no. 89.

[36]Cf. no. 176.

[37]One could proceed also in this way. Whatever is by its very nature in such a way that it is not always but can be and then not-be or vice versa, i.e., what comes to be and passes away, has a cause of its *de facto* coming-to-be. For it is not real by virtue of its essence, because otherwise it would have to be always and could never not-be. Ultimately, it has to find its cause in something which transcends coming-to-be and passing away, something which by its nature has to be always and in this sense is necessary. And so on (Cf. Thomas Aquinas, *Contra Gentes*, bk. 1, ch. 15).

Another way of proposing the same argument is as follows. The contingent in the broad sense, i.e., what is not of itself absolutely necessary, insofar and as long as it is, cannot not-be (cf. no. 37); it is at least hypothetically necessary in the broad sense (cf. no. 176). But every hypothetical necessity refers to a ground of its necessity and ultimately to that which is of itself absolutely necessary.

This proof remains incomplete as long as it is not shown that what of itself is absolutely necessary is not the "whole" of beings that come to be and pass away, or their permanent substratum (prime matter), or their immanent law, or coming-to-be (change) itself, or unqualified "to be" as an immanent constituent principle. Only when this point has been proved, may one conclude that what is of itself absolutely necessary, that whose Essence is "To Be," transcends everything which is not of itself absolutely necessary and consequently is the free cause of both the incorruptible and the corruptible.

187. *Fourth Way: Infinite Unity, Truth, Goodness, and Beauty*[38]

There exist finite beings to which we attribute the properties of unity, truth, goodness and beauty, but always only in a limited way according to "more or less." Yet these properties *of themselves* do not include any limitation or measure, any imperfection. Therefore, finite beings merely participate in these perfections.

In other words, we discover in beings ontic aspects which *of themselves* do not include any limitation—namely, the transcendental properties of *being*[39] which pertain to every being as being. These properties are not realized in a univocal way in the many but only analogously—in each of them differently, according to a wealth of original variations.[40] Everyone of these variations with respect to the fullness of the property in question means a particularization implying a deficiency. We conceive these variations as the unequal presence of the same property and, therefore, a presence according to a gradation.[41] This gradation is most evident when we compare the grades of the material, the vegetative, the sensitive, and the intellectual—everywhere we see at the same time distance as well as transition. However, even with respect to each individual being and especially each person, we admit that this being realizes the transcendental ideas in an original and unrepeatable way, not wholly known to us, according to the measure of its essence and activities.

Now, what possesses only "more or less," in a particularized manner, the properties of being which of themselves are infinite, is one, true, good, and beautiful only through participation or receptive *approximation to* Unity, Truth, Goodness and Beauty, not merely as relatively greatest but as absolute and subsistent. For, a being which possesses only in a diminished way and in a limited degree a perfection that of itself is infinite, *is* not this perfection through its *essence,* since what a being *is* through its essence it is simply, by identity, and without measure or grade. If, however, it *is* not this perfection through its essence, the ground on which the perfection is present

---

[38]This way also has been subject to much criticism. Nevertheless, it seems to be the most fundamental. Cf. C. Fabro, "Sviluppo, significato e valore della quarta via," *Doctor communis,* vol. 7 (1954), pp. 71-109. See also St. Thomas, *Contra gentes,* bk. 1, ch. 13; *De potentia,* q. 3, a. 5; *Prologus in Ev. Joannis; De substantiis separatis,* a. 3. The fourth way applies also to finality; see *Contra gentes,* bk. 1. ch. 38, 3rd argument.

[39]Cf. no. 52.

[40]Cf. no. 56.

[41]Cf. no. 57.

can lie only in its dependence—in all three ways of the metaphysical relationship of causality—upon the pure cause which *is* this infinite perfection essentially.

Therefore, what is one, true, good and beautiful through participation presupposes what is one, true, good and beautiful through its Essence in three ways: 1) as that to which it is similar as its exemplary cause; 2) as that from which it derives as its efficient cause; 3) as that to which it is directed as its final cause. And that which is one, true, good and beautiful through its Essence is no longer a mere concrete subject of the properties of *being*, but is subsistent Unity, Truth, Goodness and Beauty.

But the properties of *being* refer to "to be" as their common origin. Therefore, all graded beings, i.e., *all finite beings, point beyond themselves to subsistent "To Be."*[42]

188. *Fifth Way: The Intellectual Regulator of Natures*

Every finite being has a proper nature. This nature is an orientation of its essence to its activity and, consequently, to a predetermined purpose, and this orientation has not been estatblished by the finite being itself.

This assertion may be clarified as follows. Man consciously and freely sets himself goals. These purposes pre-exist intentionally in his knowledge and exercise attraction even before they are realized through execution.[43] This is the primary sense of purpose: that which in practical knowledge is posited as the intended terminus of activity.[44] However, man does not posit consciously and freely all purposes of life. The ultimate purposes lie prefigured in his nature itself. He tends to them naturally, although through reflection on his natural tendency he is able to know his natural good to some

---

[42]This way is valid for all characteristics which do not imply any imperfection in their essence and which it is always better to have than not to have. All of them refer to God as transcending them. Let us name a few examples after first making the remark that not all concepts listed here have equally passed the stage of analogy of improper proportionality or metaphor to be predicated in the proper proportional way of the higher and the highest (cf. no 55). With unity, truth, goodness and beauty are connected identity, selfhood, individuality, determinateness, constancy, harmony, plentitude, wealth, nobility, light, splendor, etc. Alongside these, we must name deeds, powers and abilities (virtues) which, and insofar as they are directed to the infinity of *being:* power, strength, life, fertility, communication, knowing, intellect, willing, freedom, joy, peace, wisdom, justice, faithfulness, etc.

[43]Cf. no. 108.

[44]Cf. no. 144.

extent, interpret it, and determine more specifically the ways in which he wants to realize this good concretely.[45] These specific ways constitute his freely-posited purposes.

Accordingly, even man *finds himself pre-ordered* to his purpose—namely, self-realization as an ever-increasing participation in *being*.[46] In an analogous way he is similar in this respect to non-knowing beings and even all finite beings—all have a natural tendency to their predetermined good. It does not matter whether this good, self-realization through communication with others, is reached through transient action and efficient causality or through immanent acts of life. In any case beings are ordered to one another and to the good of each one as well as that of the whole, as is evident from their non-conscious activities. This attractive good, which is the reverse side of nature as urging, must to some extent pre-exist in the natural tendency, even as act lies prefigured in the dynamic orientation of potency. This good must be called purpose in an analogous way.[47]

This "connaturality"[48] or natural tendency which unites finite beings into an orderly world does not find its adequately sufficient ground in these beings themselves. For this tendency flows of necessity from their essence, and these beings themselves do not constitute their essence through self-determination because their essence is not their "to be" and, consequently, they *are* determined to their essence

Now, the orientation of a being according to its nature to its activity and consequently to a pre-established purpose, presupposes active direction by a directing intellect whose practical reason assigns a purpose as the purpose of the nature in question.

The reason is as follows. Every order, as the being-directed of one being to another, presupposes an active direction. This active orientation of the one to the other consists in the constituting of accidental or substantial determinations and characteristics of the one in such a way that these characteristics are the foundation from which relations to the other can flow. However, only practical reason, which combines the many in a structural unity of order, is capable of activity founding the relationships of one being to another. This applies especially to the active ordering of a being to a purpose that has not yet been attained. Such a purpose has to exercise its attrac-

---

[45]Cf. no. 151.
[46]Cf. no. 64.
[47]Cf. no. 108.
[48]Cf. no. 135.

tion on the being ordered to it and, therefore, must be prefigured as a direction or intention in the characteristic which is the foundation of the relation. The characteristic has to be dynamically proportioned to the purpose assigned to the being in question.

Accordingly, if finite beings according to their very essence as nature are ordered to activity and, consequently, to a pre-assigned purpose, and if they do not through practical reason direct themselves actively to this purpose, then they presuppose their active orientation by the practical reason of a directing intellectual being who is not identical with them.

Therefore, *there exists an intellectual being who directs the natures of finite beings as such.*

And because nature is the essence itself of the finite, the "director" of natures is the cause of the essence in its orientation to participation in *being* as the natural good. But the cause which actively directs the essence of the finite to *being* is the cause which makes the finite participate in *being,* for the fact that the finite is actually directed to *being* means that it actually is.

This directing intellectual being, who is the exemplary cause of the essential order through his knowledge, is therefore, at the same time the efficient cause of the finite beings through his power, and the final cause of the order of activity through his goodness.

He Himself, however, cannot have a "nature" in this sense described above, i.e., in the sense of an orientation of His essence to a predetermined purpose which He Himself has not constituted. In Him orientation to purpose and the purpose itself coincide by identity; His good is not distinct from His essence itself. Therefore, *His essence is "to be," He is subsistent "To Be."*[49]

---

[49] In his *Summa Theologica,* St. Thomas starts from beings of nature which, lacking knowledge, act for a purpose because they always or at least most of the time attain the best result. In *Contra gentes,* bk. 1, ch. 13, he starts from the order of various beings to an harmonious whole. We have broadened his argument somewhat in order to be able to arrive at the conclusion that there is a directing intellectual being who does not presuppose the beings to be directed but causes all finite beings to be.

CHAPTER THIRTY-ONE

CAN WE KNOW WHO GOD IS?

189. *Our Way of Thinking About God's Essence*

No Proper Concept of God's Essence. As systematic reflections upon our implicit knowledge of God, the proofs of God's existence can contribute to a certain rational justification of our belief in God. These proofs, however, were not merely concerned with the conviction the God exists, but offered at the same time a certain explicitation of the concept "who God is," which, despite its very implicit character, served as the provisional starting point.

If the question is asked whether we do know now who God is, the answer has to be in the negative. The Essence of God is not conceptually accessible to our finite-infinite purely human knowledge. The only thing we grasp conceptually is what God is not and how everything finite is related to Him. Even our highest concepts, the transcendental ideas, have a certain imperfectness, if not with respect to their intended content, at least insofar as the human mode is concerned in which *we* conceive and understand this concept. For example, we conceive "being" primarily as the bearer of "to be," i.e., as something which participates in "to be." Though we *aim* at the act of *being,* we are unable to seize this act adequately in a concept even if we were to use the formal-abstract concept "beingness."[1] Again, we conceive identity in the fashion of a relation, and unity in the manner of a negation.[2]

Nevertheless, the relative and negative judgments about God must contain a certain affirmative moment as the condition making these judgments possible, for negation and relation are never first. But this affirmative moment transcends our explicit concepts. Although it lies in the line of concepts, it is beyond them. This affirmative moment is the implicit pre-predicative and not directly conceptualizable knowledge that the transcendental ideas are realized primarily in God in an eminent and infinite way with respect to their intended content, although their primary meaning for us lies in the finite way in which they are found in the beings of our experience.

---

[1]Cf. no. 172.
[2]Cf. no. 169.

Accordingly, we must distinguish between, on the one hand, our way of thinking and expression and, on the other, that which we *intend* to convey in our thinking and expression. Let us first investigate how, without having a concept of God expressing what is proper to Him, we, nonetheless, have some understanding of Him,[3] i.e., how in rational thought we can formulate judgments which are not direct judgments about God Himself—for the Ineffable is above our judgment—but express *how* the beings of our experience contain a reference to God by means of a deficient and analogous similarity. Next, we will devote critical attention to the purely relative value of these judgments in which we attribute predicates or names to God.

Our Analogous Knowledge of God. Every philosophical system will use a different central idea as an instrument in its attempt to acquire a more profound view of God. In Thomism, as the philosophy of "to be,"[4] the *Leitmotiv* which brings our way of thinking somewhat closer to God's Essence is the idea "being" and its implied reference to unqualified "to be." Through analogous refinement we arrive at the concept of God's essence as "To Be" itself in pure infinite intensity and plenitude.

The fundamental difference between the finite and the Infinite thus lies in this that the finite is only through participation, it is a be-ing whose essence and "to be" are distinct, transcendentally related constituent principles. God, on the other hand, is neither a formal-concrete subject of *being* nor formal-abstract "to be," but is subsistent "To Be."

Consequently, formal-abstract unqualified "to be" is that which *in* finite beings is the reflexion of their transcendent origin, and which as a formally constituent immanent principle *in* them bears witness to their dependence upon subsistent absolutely infinite "To Be."

When, according to our mode of thinking, we conceive subsistent "To Be" as God's Essence, this means that we are able to see whatever we can predicate of God in our judgments as flowing from "To Be" as its roots. We do not mean that we are capable of deducing God's properties from His Essence, but that we are able to reduce His properties to this first source, beyond which nothing can be thought by us. For all other concepts, even the transcendental ideas,

---

[3] Cf. no. 130.
[4] Cf. no. 101.

are rooted in the idea of "being," as referring to "to be." This idea is presupposed by all others and not reducible to anything more original.

Accordingly, we have to investigate how subsistent "To Be" can be conceived by us as the foundation of God's properties or attributes, even though we know that in God there is no distinction at all between essence and emanating properties and that God's identity does not even offer us a foundation for this distinction of reason between, e.g., His goodness, wisdom, and justice. The ground of the distinction we make here lies wholly on the side of the finite beings that are first known to us. In God His goodness is, even formally speaking, His Wisdom, and His Justice.[5]

190. *The Ultimate Ground of the Properties of Being*

Identity. Being as being, i.e., considered precisely to the extent that, and according to the mode in which it *is,* is itself. Despite all distinctions, it is always to some extent identified with its "to be." For this reason unconditionality, necessity and absoluteness also pertain to being as being.[6] On the other hand, God, as subsistent "To Be" does not merely participate in identity but, according to our way of thinking, *is* absolute contradictionless identity, which imparts identity to everything that is.[7]

Unity. Being as being is itself and not not-itself. It absolutely excludes non-being from itself. Therefore, in being as being there is no opposition, it is undividedly itself, not divided from anything, it is one.[8] Distinction, composition, and multiplicity are the degraded modes of unity proper to the finite. God, on the other hand, as subsistent "To Be," does not participate in unity but *is* the absolutely indivisible Unity, which makes whatever is in a particular way, i.e., through composition of parts, be one.

Infinity. Outside being as being there is nothing, so that being does not have any opposite which is excluded from it as "something else." But what is not cannot limit as "something else." Therefore, being, insofar as it is, is unlimited.[9] An absolutely finite being, consequently, is impossible.[10] However, the infinity of the finite, which as

---

[5]Cf. no. 169.
[6]Cf. no. 36.
[7]Cf. no. 169.
[8]Cf. no. 39.
[9]Cf. no. 40.
[10]Cf. no. 61.

this being is opposed to others as *that* being, is only a) a dynamic infinity, i.e., it is endlessly perfectible,[11] and b) a rational infinity, i.e., there is an endless plurality of possible finite beings,[12] and to all of them it has potential relations of being-together.[13] God, on the other hand, as subsistent "To Be," does not in any way have anything positive as His opposite to which He would be related. He is intensive or comprehensive Infinity.[14] God may be called dynamic only insofar as through His all-perfectness and Goodness He exercises attraction on the finite.[15] He may be called related only insofar as He makes everything that is or can be relative to Himself.[16] As the first cause and the last end, He is the transcendental ground of the dynamic and relational infinity of the finite.

Determinateness and Individuality. Being as being is what it is, it is "already" itself, it has the perfectness which it should have. Insofar as it is, it is not still undetermined and determinable, but already determined and individual.[17] Subsistent "To be," on the other hand, is perfect and complete, absolutely distinct through its pure plenitude and not subject in any way to an additional determination. God is perfect Determinateness and Individuality, the transcendent ground of the imperfect determinateness and individuality of the beings.

Truth, Goodness and Beauty. Being as being, to the extent of its *being,* is intelligible[18] and lovable.[19] God, as subsistent "To Be," must be conceived as absolute openness or unconcealedness, as Truth. He is not true by participation in *being,* but because in Himself He is through identity the groundless ground of all intelligibility. Consequently, He is also of necessity the concealed or the mysterious for all finite understanding. Likewise, He is subsistent Goodness— not made-good through participation in *being,* but imparting goodness to everything by making it participate in His plenitude. He is Beauty in Himself, manifesting Himself to Himself to His own delight and

---

[11]Cf. no. 63.
[12]Cf. no. 178.
[13]Cf. no. 35.
[14]Cf. no. 178.
[15]Cf. no. 181.
[16]Cf. no. 182.
[17]Cf. nos. 41 and 90.
[18]Cf. no. 42.
[19]Cf. no. 43.

freely revealing His glory in the integrity, harmony, and splendor of His works.[20]

191. *The Ultimate Ground of the Properties of the Finite*

Subsistence. The principle of identity applies in the most proper sense to that which appropriates "to be" to itself and identifies it with itself—namely, the real individual subsistent being.[21] The finite subsistent being appropriates "to be" only imperfectly, it merely participates in subsistence. God, on the other hand, appropriates "to be" to Himself in a perfect way, He is "To Be" without any modification and, therefore, He is perfect Subsistence, not only as a being *"in* itself" but at the same time as self-grounding, as "of itself."

Act. The finite subsistent being is dynamically infinite and, therefore, tends to appropriate "to be" more and more by means of activities. As unfolding itself, it is the substratum of accidental inherent determinations.[22] God, on the other hand, as perfect Subsistence, cannot be a substratum of additional perfections, forms or acts. He does not "possess" anything, but through His very Essence *is* the perfect or pure Act.

Simplicity. God does not possess any attributes that are really distinct from His essence. What the finite has through composition He *is* through simplicity, without any distinction of constituent principles.[23]

Activity and Power. The finite being perfects itself through actuation of its being-together with the others that is radically "already present."[24] This gradual actuation, insofar as it emanates from the finite itself, is its activity.[25] The root of this emanation is the permanent power, capacity or active potency, which through skill and abilities may be more or less readily disposed to activity.[26] Essence, power and activity are distinct in the finite being. God, on the other hand, as pure Act, does not have any accidents distinct from His Essence. He, therefore, is absolutely Immutable. His activity does not emanate from His Essence, but He Himself *is* the perfectly imma-

---

20Cf. no. 44.
21Cf. no. 65.
22Cf. no. 67.
23Cf. no. 98.
24Cf. no. 63.
25Cf. no. 71.
26Cf. no. 94.

nent Act, which does not need to manifest itself externally.[27] However, His power to manifest Himself and to be an actual cause is unlimited, for His power is His Essence—He is the all-powerful or Omnipotence.

192. *The Ultimate Ground of the Properties of the Corporeal*

Space. The corporeal is extended in parts alongside parts.[28] We conceive it as placed in space, it is here or there. God, however, is neither here nor there, because He does not have any parts outside parts and, therefore, He is not extended or spatial. He is not encompassed by any place. On the other hand, He is the cause of beings even in their extension, which is a deficient way of being-together and presence. The here-or-there of extended beings, therefore, is grounded in God who as their cause makes them be dispersed and distinct. In this sense God extends to all places and is omnipresent—not as a body is present to another body through proximity, nor as the spiritual soul is present in all parts of its body, but as the cause is present in its effect, through causal presence.

Time. All beings known to us from experience are temporal. Their "to be" is dispersed in successive states of then, now, later. To being as being no mode of non-being pertains and, consequently, neither being-not-yet nor being-no-longer. Being as being is present. Temporal beings, however, merely participate in an analogous way in this presence, according as their successive moments compenetrate one another to a greater or lesser extent.[29] God, on the other hand, as subsistent "To Be," is without any development of moments, but "at the same time" wholly present to Himself. He is pure self-presence or Eternity. As such, He is undividedly present to each of the temporal moments, He is contemporaneous with everything because, through participation in His eternity, He interconnects the beings whose "to be" He disperses in moments.

Form. God is not corporeal, not composed of prime matter and primary form.[30] However, as subsistent "To Be," He is the absolute Form, and all material and finite forms are limited reflexions of His Essence.

---

[27]Cf. no. 182.
[28]Cf. no. 78.
[29]Cf. no. 75.
[30]Cf. no. 89.

193. *The Ultimate Ground of the Properties of the Living*

Life. Although self-realization in an analogously enlarged sense pertains also to the non-living, self-movement and self-perfection in the primary sense are found only in the living.[31] However, just as beings merely participate in unqualified "to be," so also living beings merely share in unqualified life. In these living beings life is particularized to the life *of* this or *of* that living being, it is finitized and multiplied, and dynamic orientation to life rather than fully life. For unqualified life in itself does not imply any imperfection, it may not be understood as self-perfection but should be conceived as perfectly being oneself.[32]

God, as subsistent "To Be," is perfectly Himself and, therefore, subsistent Life. His life is not self-movement, not transition from being-in-potency to being-in-act, but purely immanent act, not distinct from essence and power. For this reason all vegetative-organic processes, all internal and external sensitivity, all passive feeling and active tending must be excluded from God's life. However, vital acts which of themselves do not imply any being-in-motion, such as knowing, loving, and willing, may be ascribed to Him.

Knowledge. Although man's intellectual act of knowing contains the aspect of taking an absolute position,[33] nevertheless, it is merely a participation in unqualified knowing. It is a subject-object relationship, characterized by intentionality, in which the knowing subject is known only through reflection on the other.[34] Unqualified knowing, however, of itself is active interiority, being-with-oneself, even though we can find it only as particularized, as the knowing act *of* finite knowers.

God, on the other hand, as subsistent "To Be" and subsistent Life is also subsistent knowing, active self-illumination, pure self-consciousness without any intentionality, in identity of the knower, act of knowing, and the known: in God "thinking is a thinking on thinking."[35]

Willing and Loving. Because of its connection with intellectual knowledge, man's intellectual affectivity implies a broadening of self-love to a love which in principle is not subject to any limit.

---

[31]Cf. no. 111.
[32]Cf. no. 117.
[33]Cf. no. 125.
[34]Cf. no. 128.
[35]Aristotle, *Metaphysica,* bk. XII, ch. 9, 1074b 34.

Yet it retains the character of being-affected-by and reacting-to, it remains an emotive movement.[36]   God, however, as subsistent "To Be," is also pure Willing and pure Love—self-love which is at the same time a liberal self-giving love for all whom His goodness calls into being.[37]

Freedom. God's Willing is also freedom.   His necessity is not a being-necessitated by something prior to Him, but means that God *is* in every hypothesis and, therefore, independently of any hypothesis.   This necessity, then, is identical with His absolute independence.   As perfectly self-grounding, it may be called freedom in the highest analogous sense.   However, it does not have the contingency pertaining to the free acts of finite beings, for this contingency is an imperfection.   In a more restricted sense God is free with respect to the actual causing of finite beings.   But here also, the contingency does not lie in the free causing, which is identical with God's Essence, but only in the effects which are not caused of necessity.[38]

Personality. The individual human being is more perfectly subsistent than infra-human beings.   He possesses a nature which through reason and freedom gives the subsistent being to some extent the power to dispose of its own *being* through self-determination.[39]   God, on the other hand, as self-grounding Subsistence, must be conceived as eminently personal, for His Knowing and Loving are pure *active* "To Be" itself.[40]

194. *The Ultimate Ground of the Reality of Beings*

The names we attribute to God are based not only on the properties which according to our mode of thinking He possesses in Himself, but also on the relations which He has to that which He causes.

---

[36]Cf. no. 139.

[37]Cf. no. 182. Of the other emotive movements only joy, which presupposes the presence of the good, can be attributed to God in a proper sense.

[38]Cf. no. 181. Even finite freedom is to some extent, albeit only imperfectly, without a motive (cf. no. 144), but infinite freedom is perfectly its own motive (cf. no. 182). Finite freedom is normalized by nature (cf. no. 144), but infinite freedom is its own norm. Normalized freedom is the freedom of a moral being. Morality implies being-in-motion, tension between reality and ideality, between what is *de facto* and what ought to be. For this reason God is not a moral being, even though as Goodness itself and as the absolute Ideal He is the highest norm of morality.

[39]Cf. no. 143.

[40]Cf. no. 176.

True, these relations are merely relations of reason, modes of our thinking which do not adequately express what we intend to convey through them. However, they are founded in the real relations of dependence which caused beings have to their cause. For this reason we may and we have to call and recognize God truthfully *according to what He is for us.*

God is the uncaused cause. The effect, therefore, has no kind of priority over Him. Neither as idea nor as motive or purpose has it any influence on the cause; hence the cause in question is a *free* cause.[41] The effect, likewise, does not pre-exist in capacity in a matter that is independent of the cause; the cause, therefore, is the cause of the *being* of the effect and, consequently, the cause of everything in the effect, its *total* cause. The effect is in no way a perfecting of the cause; therefore, it is not an immanent determination of the cause, but a *subsistent* being, distinct from the cause, although it implies the cause according to causal immanence.

Freely to cause a real subsistent being, distinct from the cause in its entire *being* and in everything it is, can do, and does, we call "to create."[42] God is called the *Creator.* Creation, taken actively, is identical with God's Essence and, therefore, eternal. This eternal act, however, makes the temporal *be* and be temporal. The effects only of the act are successive, changeable, and following one another according to a freely established rational order. They are, moreover, strictly contingent, but this does not exclude that they participate in necessity in varying degrees.[43]

Taken passively as coming-to-be-created or rather to-be-created, creation is not a change undergone by a creature, but is this creature itself considered according to the real relation of its total *being* and of all that it is, can do, or does to its Creator.

The Nature of this Relation. Although the finite being is related to God in its whole *being* and in all its aspects, it *is* not a relation but *has* a relation. The reason is that—abstracting from the question regarding subsistent real Relations, which would have to be the Infinite Itself—a real relation demands as its substratum a subsistent being and as its foundation a perfection of this being.[44] The

[41] Cf. no. 181.
[42] Cf. A. D. Sertillanges, *L'idée de création,* Paris, 1945.
[43] Cf. no. 181.
[44] Cf. no. 164.

real relation is something *pertaining* to something, an inherent determination or accident in the metaphysical sense.[45]

On the other hand, creation in the passive sense is a unique kind of relation of dependence. First of all, it flows of necessity from the substantial *being* itself of its subject and from all further determinations of this subject in its essence, power and action—whatever there is in the subject as actuality or potentiality is related to, and dependent upon the first cause. Secondly, although this relation with respect to its *being* flows from the subject whose relation it is, nevertheless, one cannot say that the subject is the emanative cause of this property which it has of necessity. On the contrary, in its own *structure* this relation in a sense is prior to the subject because it connects the subject with what we conceive as the relation's correlate—namely, the free act of creation, which is not really related.

Accordingly, to our mode of thinking, this relation stands between the Creator and the creature, and in this sense, as that through which the creature is creature, it is prior to the creature. Thus it is an *essential* relation proper to every finite being as finite; hence it is not surprising if it is sometimes spoken of as a "transcendental" relation, especially when one considers that the relation of creation is one pertaining to *all* categorical determinations. In this connection, however, the term, "transcendental" should be understood as "connected with all categories";[46] in other words, it no longer has the precise meaning previously attached to it when we spoke about the relation between constituent principles.[47]

Relativity and Subsistence. Despite all distinction between subsistence and relativity in the finite, one should not forget that these two aspects do not exclude but include each other. This assertion applies not only to the relation of one being to another with which it is together, especially insofar as the self-realization of human persons is concerned,[48] but also and even more to the relation of the

---

[45]Cf. no. 68.

[46]Cf. no. 52.

[47]Cf. no. 170. According to St. Thomas Aquinas, creation in the passive sense is an accident. Cf. *Summa theol.*, p. 1, q. 45, a. 3, *De potentia*, q. 3, a. 3. However, as Sertillanges, *L'idée de la création*, p. 58, remarks correctly: "It does not follow that it deserves to be placed in the category of relation in any other way than by analogy. It is a relation which is unique in its kind. Because it is concerned with the whole being, including the relation itself, it presents itself as a general form of the categories insofar as they refer to the First Principle." Cf. Thomas Aquinas, *Summa theol.*, p. 1, q. 60, a. 5: "Every creature naturally, according to what it is, pertains to God."

[48]Cf. no. 154.

finite to the Infinite. Precisely where the finite subsistent being is most itself, and, consequently, *is* in the highest degree—namely, in the free personal decision—the causal influence of God is strongest and therefore also the relationship of dependence. Reversely, the finite being becomes more *itself* according as it directs itself more to God. For man, to direct himself more to God means to bring himself in harmony with God in knowledge and love. By becoming more deiform, the finite becomes more itself, for in a sense God is the eminent "self" of the creature.[49] Love of God and self-love do not exclude but include each other. Creator and creature are not opposed to each other as this being is to that other being. The opposition arises only from the eminent universality of the Infinite and the deficient particularity of the finite. But in its whole essence, power and action, the finite is dynamically related *to* the Infinite, which it has present in itself through causal in-being and through whose presence the finite is, is itself, is subsistent, capable, active and free.

By virtue of His single act of creation, God may be given different names: 1) Creator, in the stricter sense, when created being is considered insofar as it comes to be; 2) Conserver, when created being is viewed as perduring in time; 3) Ruler or Providence, when the creature is regarded insofar as it is directed to God as its highest Good; 4) Consummator, when created being is considered insofar as it is united with God as its highest Good.[50]

195. *The Inadequacy of Our Knowledge of God*

Negative Knowledge of God and Pre-Predicative Positive Knowledge. We must now critically reflect upon the road we have travelled thus far in order to emphasize that only a relative value may be assigned to the judgments in which we affirm positive predicates or names of God.[51] For the judgments in which we merely say that the finite is related to Him or in which we merely deny the content of our concepts of Him, because of their unpretentiousness more closely

---

[49]Cf. no. 181.

[50]It is proper to human nature, as a nature which is conscious of its first Cause, to recognize the first Truth and to love the first Goodness. But what is proper to a nature "ought" to be in the moral sense: it is a duty freely to be done. While previously we understood the *metaphysical* dynamism of self-realization (cf. no. 64) *ethically* in its deeper sense as dedicated social intercourse with our fellow men (cf. no. 154), we may now conceive it in its most profound sense from the *religious* viewpoint as the dedication of man to God.

[51]Cf. no. 189.

approach and more adequately express what they intend to convey than the judgments in which we affirm the contents of our concepts of Him.[52]

This does not at all mean that we have to take refuge in pure agnosticism. For it would be impossible for us to know only *that* God is insofar as everything is related to Him without knowing something in any non-negative way about what He is. The negative judgment, which is always merely our way of thinking the positive,[53] has as its function to render more precise, clarify and enrich the affirmative knowledge which it necessarily presupposes. This affirmative knowledge, as implicit knowledge, is the source from which the negation springs and, as explicit knowledge, is the purpose intended by the negation.

To discover how the negative knowledge of God is subservient to a primordial positive pre-predicative knowledge which is the source of inspiration for our hesitating and groping attempts to form concepts, judgment and reasonings, we have to reflect on the threefold way followed by our train of thought about God—namely, the way of causality, the way of negation, and the way of eminence.[54]

The Way of Causality. The beings of our experience cause one another, but only in certain definite respects. How did we arrive at the conclusion that they are caused in their very *being* and in all

---

[52]Let us illustrate the point with a two-edged difficulty: If God is, He is through His essence. On the one hand, we may say: we do not know God's essence; therefore, we cannot know His "to be" either. On the other hand, however, one could also say: we know the "to be" of God; therefore, we also know God's essence. How, then can you maintain that, on the one hand, we do not know God's essence and, on the other, that we do know God's "to be?"

The reply is as follows: If by God's "to be" we mean the act itself of *being*—which in God is not that through which He is, but is perfectly identical with God Himself and with His essence—then we do not know God's "to be" any more than His essence. If, then, the judgment in which we attribute "to be" to God nonetheless is true, it cannot be an immediate and adequate expression of what we mean to convey by it. It is a judgment that does not have its immediate foundation in God Himself but in the world of our experience. Our quasi-existential judgment, "God is," is founded in this: all beings which we experience existentially, presuppose as the ground of their possibility and as the cause of their reality something which we do not immediately know in itself, the Unknown, called "God." Although as the transcendent ground of experienced reality, He must be more "real" than all experienced reality, the way of His being-real infinitely transcends *our* concept of reality. We may, therefore, admit that in the judgment, "God is," we do not know what God's "to be" is and, therefore, neither know God's essence, even though we correctly say that God's essence is "to be."

[53]Cf. no. 167.

[54]Cf. no. 178.

respects and that this conclusion applies also to the world as a "whole"? In other words, how did we arrive at the metaphysical principle of causality that every being, taken separately, as well as all beings, taken together, are caused by an uncaused cause which transcends all beings? The answer is because every being taken separately and all being together participate in unqualified "to be," they are particular and therefore, finite. But unqualified "to be" and the transcendental properties of *being,* such as unity, truth, goodness, as well as the highest grades of *being,* such as unqualified to live, unqualified to know, and unqualified to love, of *themselves* do not express any imperfectness and imply infinity. In they are multiplied and finitized, they do not pertain to the finite being by virtue of this being's essence. Accordingly, the beings of our experience fully explain neither themselves nor one another. Precisely insofar as they *are,* are one, are living, are knowing, etc., they refer to a transcendent cause.

Thus we are forced to attribute also to the cause, by analogy of relation, being, unity, life, and knowledge in the causal sense, just as medicine is called healthy because it is the cause of health.[55] "To be," to be good, etc., then, are predicated primarily and intrinsically of finite beings and only causally of God who is the cause of goodness, life, et.

All this, however, does not say anything about God, considered in Himself, so that we are still agnostics. Let us, therefore, raise the crucial question: "Is" God only insofar as He causes "to be," i.e., by denomination according to the effects, without being in Himself? The affirmative reply is impossible. What is not, cannot be a cause. "To be" is a condition of "being-cause," but "to be cause" is not a condition of *being.* "To be" is unconditioned, but "to be cause" is a mode of all-embracing *being* and therefore of necessity implies that the cause *is.*

The same line of thought applies to God's goodness as the cause of goodness and to all other transcendental properties of *being.* They are intrinsic to every being and can never be attributed to anything *only* from without through analogy of an added relationship.

However, all this does not tell us anything about the mode in which the first cause *is,* is good, is true, etc. Nevertheless, the critique of the analogy of extrinsic attribution contains a reply to this difficulty. For nothing can be the cause of an effect unless it possesses the per-

---

[55]Cf. no. 55.

fection which it imparts to the effect at least in the same degree as the effect. The dynamic relationship of effect to cause implies of necessity also a certain static relation of similarity.[56] The effect resembles the cause because it shares in the perfection of the cause. The question, now, is how this similarity should be understood.

Way of Negation. God is the ultimate cause of everything in all beings—their extension and temporality, colors and forms, all their qualities and relations, their powers, tendencies and actions. Must we say, then, that in exactly the same sense as these beings He is extended and temporal, colored and formed, vegetative and sensitive, tending and acting? Such a reply would be correct if we were dealing with a univocal cause, i.e., a cause which belongs to the same order as the effect and is determined in its causing to a single kind of effect.[57] God, however, is the all-embracing universal cause. He is not cause of the colored merely as colored, of the vegetative merely as vegetative, etc. He is the cause of *all* modes of *being,* precisely because He causes the "to be" of beings and their transcendental properties. Therefore, limited qualities can be attributed to Him at most in a metaphorical sense, according to analogy of improper proportionality, as when we say that He is the "Sun of Justice." In their proper sense, however, such qualities must be denied of Him. He is not material, not temporal, not sensitive, He does not ask and seek, He neither desires nor tends, He does not have within Himself a single one of the perfections which imply any *essential imperfection.*

What about the transcendental perfections, which are *essentially perfect* or of themselves infinite, such as "to be," goodness, truth, beauty, as well as life, knowledge and love? May we intrinsically attribute them to God as cause in the same sense in which they are found in the world as effect? The answer is in the negative, when these perfections are understood in the sense in which we conceive them in our concepts. Our concepts of these perfections are analogous by analogy of proper proportionality, for the perfections in question are realized in finite beings according to "more or less," i.e., according to degrees.[58] For this reason the *concepts* which we have of these perfections always imply imperfection, for conceptually we cannot separate the perfection and its finite grade.

---

[56]Cf. no. 163.
[57]Cf. no. 107.
[58]Cf. no. 56.

The situation reveals itself most clearly with respect to the perfection "to be" itself, which we conceive in the idea "being"—the unqualified "to be" which we find in beings is always merely relatively infinite: the being is a subject of "to be," and the "to be" is only the "to be" of a subject. We know "to be" immediately only as participated by beings whose infinity is merely dynamic and relational.[59] The situation is manifest also from the distinction which we make between the perfection "to be" and the other pure perfections—our knowledge unfolds itself in a plurality of primary judgments concerning being as being which do not coincide, because our acts about beings, such as to affirm, to deny, to love, to enjoy, etc., which are the foundation of these judgments, are really distinct from one another.[60]

God, however, does not belong to the series of "more" or "less," but stands above all finiteness and all gradation and outside the order of participants in *being*. With respect to Him there can be no question of an analogous perfection in the same sense as when we compare and grade analogous beings. He is not the "most being" and the "most good" in the relative sense of the term. First of all, as the transcendent cause, He is not a participating be-ing, in which bearer and perfection are distinct; therefore, He cannot adequately be seized in judgments expressing that He is one, good, knowing, etc. Secondly, in Him there can be no "really" distinct aspects of *being*—there is no distinction of essence, power, and act, of truth and goodness, of mercy and justice, of necessity and freedom, of knowledge and love. His knowing *is* His loving itself, His justice *is* His mercy, His necessity *is* His freedom.[61]

Thus it happens that we have to deny of God all our concepts, taken according to the structure which they have as *our* concepts and according to their original human mode of signification. He is not a being, for He is not concrete; He is not *beingness* for He is not abstract; He is not good, for the good is contrasted with the true; He is not knowing, for knowing is contrasted with loving; He is not necessary for, according to our way of thinking, necessity is contrasted with freedom. He is nothing of whatever we can immediately seize and express through our concepts, be they our highest ideas.

---

[59] Cf. no. 178.
[60] Cf. no. 169.
[61] Cf. no. 189.

Way of Eminence.   Must we say, then, that agnosticism is the only refuge? No, for the transcendental perfections are not denied of God because of His deficiency but on the ground of His eminence. Precisely because we know that these perfections of *themselves* do not imply any finiteness, we know that we conceive them in imperfect concepts. We do not know what is meant by "to be" in the absolutely-eminent way, at least we do not know it conceptually. We know that in their most profound essence unity, truth, life, knowledge, and love escape us. However, in this knowledge we have of not-knowing them, they do not escape us fully—in our inadequate concepts we *aim* at a pre-predicative implicit knowing which we have about *being* and the perfections in question. Thus we are not without a perspective on the Absolute, even though the Absolute transcends the transcendental ideas themselves insofar as the manner is concerned in which *we* conceive and signify them.

This perspective on the Absolute is the innermost essence of our intellect and our will as spiritual powers—a participation in the knowing and loving of God by God. We will never be able to express this implicit aspect fully in concepts and judgments, although it nourishes and inspires all our thinking about the *being* of finite beings. Because of this perspective, our thinking is endless movement. For this reason we have to affirm the transcendental ideas of God, not according to the way they are in our thought and expression, nor according to their explicit content, but according to an all-transcending eminent "way" which is conceptually unkown to us although it is what we ultimately intend and signify with our concepts. We can approach the Unapproachable to some extent in our thought because we carry Him within ourselves or, rather, because through causal immanence.   He bears us in our *being,* knowing, and loving.[62]

Thus our affirmative judgment of God is true, not with respect to the manner of signification, but with respect to what is distantly signified by it. God is eminently Being, Essence, and "To Be" in absolute identity of the concrete and the abstract. He is the Good and Goodness. He is knowing, the act of knowing, and the known, without distinction. He is knowing which is loving, Essence which is pure Act.[63]

---

[62]Cf. no. 181.

[63]Nevertheless, we cannot say that we have a proper concept of God. We merely project our concepts toward identitv, we know that in Him they coincide, but also that in Him they no longer are human concepts. Explicitly we know only their convergence, but not their identity. The "mode" of absolute infinity

God in Himself cannot be understood in any human concept, yet we have to some extent an understanding of God. This assertion does not mean that, by abstracting from the differences between Creator and creature, we are capable of forming a univocal minimal concept of "being" which in its indeterminateness would indicate precisely what they have in common. Such a univocal concept has already been rejected previously in connection with the idea of "being" as predicated of finite beings.[64] We certainly cannot admit it here, for Creator and creature may not be put alongside each other according to similarity and difference.[65] On the other hand, the assertion does not mean either that we form an analogous concept which in its confusedness would somehow "comprehend" actually, though only implicitly, both what is proper to God as what is proper to beings. Nothing is prior to God—not even the content of an objective concept —which we could conceive, prior to the distinction of Creator and creature, as analogously or to a greater or lesser extent applicable to both. Yet it remains true that through our analogous transcendental ideas we have a measure of understanding of God. How, then, should these analogous ideas be conceived?[66]

The analogy of proper proportionality is valid for individual finite beings. But their distinction according to a greater or lesser presence of the same attribute is founded on the fundamental contrary modes of *being,* based on not-having and having, which are related to one another as the perfect and the imperfect.[67] Let us name a few examples: necessary and contingent, one and many, infinite and finite, substantial and accidental, in-act and in-potency, present and past. In these contrary modes of *being* the remarkable point is that the second of each pair always is related to the first and participates in it and that the first transcends the second. Nevertheless, we are not able to conceive these transcendental modes in their purity, because we find them only as related to, and connected with their contrary inferior

---

escapes our ideas, which retain the creatural mode derived from their origin in the sensitive and the finite. They aim to some extent at God, but do not seize Him. To some extent they signify Him, but the mode of signification is finite, they do not comprehend Him. The distance separating the sign and the signified is not wholly overcome.

[64]Cf. no. 54.

[65]Cf. no. 181.

[66]Cf. P. Kreling, "De betekenis van de analogie in de kennis van God," *Verslag der 8ste Alg. Verg. der Ver. v. Thomistische Wijsb.,* Nijmegen, 1942, pp. 31-54; A. van der Putte, "Over de waarde van onze Godsnamen," *Verslag der 16e Alg. Verg. der Ver. v. Thomistische Wijsb.,* Utrecht, 1951, pp. 34-51.

[67]Cf. no. 56.

counterpart. What we know immediately is only the unity of the
many, the infinity of the finite, subsistence revealing itself in accidents,
act as the fulfillment of potency, the present which was prepared in the
past and itself is already becoming past. The same applies to the
opposition of good and evil, true and false, free and not-free, etc.

For this reason, according to our defective mode of thinking, in
the transcendental ideas there always is a tension through which the
superior sense of the idea is only relatively perfect because we cannot
think of this sense without a reference to the inferior sense, as the
contrast with which it is together. Though we say that being *as*
being is infinite, every being we know is finite. Being *as* being is
perfectly determinate, but every being we know is determinable; being
as being is good, but every being we know falls short of the good.

How, then, can we escape from the relativity which is proper even
to the analogous ideas as they apply to beings, in order to obtain
through these analogous ideas a certain understanding of God? There
is no other way than causality. To see that beings are only hypothetically necessary, only finitely infinite, only through supporting accidents subsistent, only through fulfillment of potency actual, means for
us that we cannot find the ground of their necessity, infinity, subsistence, actuality, presence, etc., in their essence, but have to seek it in
a *cause*. In this way we transcend the deficient way in which we
think of the ontological perfections by groping for the ungrasped-but-
aimed-at pure necessity, infinity, subsistence, actuality, presence, for
subsistent "To Be."

This subsistent "To Be" is for our way of thinking a derivative
sense and primarily a causal sense—namely, to be the cause of necessity, actuality, etc. Peculiar as it may seem, however, reflection
teaches us that this sense is not merely a causal sense, but also a
sense which intrinsically belongs to the cause and even the sense which
is most intrinsic and *in itself* the first and absolute sense of *being*.

Thus the relative analogy proper to the meanings of the ontic
perfections in their reciprocal relations as superior and inferior *within*
the realm of beings terminates, so to speak, in an analogy of the second degree. All the immediately known relative meanings of *being*
and of the pure perfections of living, knowing, and loving constitute
together the meanings that are primary for us, and in the proof of
God's existence we discover that these meanings are related to another meaning which for us is secondary and derivative but in itself
absolute. We are unable to grasp this meaning that is secondary for

us explicitly in a concept, but we know it through the causal approach and the "analogous" or proportional similarity of the meanings that are primary for us with this absolute meaning.

If this is so, we must abstain from considering this absolute meaning, which is not reciprocally related to the meanings that are primary for us and, therefore, not relatively the first among many meanings, as one of the cases of the analogous idea—be it the highest of all. God is not one of the analogates of the transcendental idea of being, but should be called rather the *analogans*.[68] As subsistent "To Be," He makes come forth from Himself, through free imparting, all the other deficient and relative meanings of the perfections of *being* according to a greater or lesser similarity with Himself.

We know that He is the One who is, properly speaking, signified in all our transcendental ideas of *being,* life, knowledge, and love. He is the One to whom the whole metaphysics of *being* refers. Nevertheless, we know His "To Be," which transcends all measurable proportions and is identical with His Essence, only through the proportional relations which finite beings have with Him. And the similarity of proportion is one-sided and always includes a dissimilarity which is still infinitely greater.

Thus we remain in a learned ignorance, for with our natural reason we are never capable of travelling the distance separating us from the essence of the first Cause.

196. *Conclusion*

Initially metaphysics is the question regarding the ground and meaning of the beings encountered in our experience. It begins as a general ontology and discovers that every being participates in "to be" in an original way. This participation is the foundation of an endless movement, which metaphysics endeavors to understand by investigating the structures of essence and "to be," matter and form, power and activity, as they are analogously found in material, living, and knowing beings. It discovers the highest degree of dynamism in man, who in his understanding and loving is "to some extent everything." Precisely, however, in the highest human activities, which, beyond the material, the temporal, and the finite, grope toward the spiritual, the eternal, and the infinite, finiteness reveals itself most strikingly.

---

[68]This term is used by H. Schillebeeckx, "Het niet-begrippelijk kenmoment in onze Godskennis," *Tijdschrift v. Philosophie*, vol. 14 (1952), pp. 411-454.

Ultimately metaphysics is the acceptance of infinite subsistent "To Be" as the free cause accounting for the reality of the possible beings. This reply, however, is at the same time a question—What is the essence of the first Cause?

All beings revert to their source as to their purpose. Man alone is able to become conscious of this desire for God and to accept it freely. But the One whom he desires is not accessible to man in His inner essence by way of human reason. Nevertheless, the recognition of God, when it becomes a deed of the whole man, directs itself with the power of love to the Reality Itself which is present to reason only in a veiled way.

Is not all human dissatisfaction and insufficiency understandable in the light of this unfilled deepest desire of man—to come close to Him who is the ground of everything as He is in Himself? And would the hypothesis be absurd that this desire, which from the viewpoint of our finiteness cannot be filled, could still be filled by Him to whom it is directed?[69]

---

[69]Cf. H. Robbers, *Wijsbegeerte en Openbaring*, Utrecht, 1948.

BIBLIOGRAPHY

Introduction to Philosophy

Josef Pieper, *Wass heisst Philosophieren?*, München, 1949.

Louis de Raeymaeker, *Introduction to Philosophy*, New York, 1948.
A survey of the problems and history of philosophy and extensive information about the organization of philosophical life, periodicals, congresses, universities, standard works and text books.

Jacques Maritain, *An Introduction to Philosophy*, New York, 1937.
Greek philosophy till Aristotle; definition and division of philosophy; a clear introduction into the problems from a Thomistic viewpoint.

E. Baudin, *Introduction à la philosophie*, I, *Qu'est-ce que la philosophie?* Paris, 3rd ed., 1939.

R. Le Senne, *Introduction à la philosophie*, Paris, 1949.

Introductions to Thomism

Etienne Gilson, *Le Thomisme, introduction à la philosophie de S. Thomas d'Aquin*, Paris, 6th ed., 1948.
An historical masterpiece.

A. D. Sertillanges, *La philosophie de S. Thomas d'Aquin*, Paris, 2nd 1940.
Very profound.

Les grandes thèses de la philosophie thomiste, Paris, 1928.
A concise summary.

H. D. Gardeil, *Introduction to the Philosophy of St. Thomas Aquinas*, St. Louis, 1957 ff.
Four small volumes. Largely based on Aristotle and St. Thomas' commentaries on Aristotle.

P. Grenet, *Le Thomisme*, Paris, 1953.
A systematic survey.

M.-D. Chenu, *Introduction à l'étude de S. Thomas d'Aquin*, Paris, 1950.

Josef Pieper, *Über Thomas von Aquin*, Leipzig, 1940.
A biography.

Thomas von Aquin, Frankfurt-Hamburg, 1956.
Short aphoristic philosophical and theological texts.

Th. Gilby, *St. Thomas Aquinas, Philosophical Texts*, London, 1951.

Frederick C. Copleston, *Aquinas*, Harmondsworth, 1955.

P. Wyser, *Der Thomismus* and *Thomas von Aquin,* Bern, 1951 and 1950. Volumes 15/16 and 13/14 of *Bibliographische Einführungen in das Studium der Philosophie.*

Philosophical Dictionaries

R. Jolivet, *Vocabulaire de la philosophie,* Lyon, 3rd ed., 1951.
Rather concise.

W. Brugger, *Philosophisches Worterbuch, Frieburg,* 1953.
Brief and pertinent articles.

A. Lalande, *Vocabulaire technique et critique de la philosophie,* Paris, 7th ed., 1956.
A standard work.

Bernard Wuellner, *Dictionary of Scholastic Philosophy,* Milwaukee, 1956.
Vocabulary and brief definitions and divisions.

Dagobert D. Runes, *Dictionary of Philosophy,* New York, 1941.
Dictionary of Names and Topics. Brief signed articles.

Text Books

Charles Boyer, *Cursus philosophiae,* Paris, 2nd ed., 1950.
Brief and clear, but lacking in inner connection.

Joseph Gredt, *Elementa philosophiae aristotelico-thomisticae,* Freiburg, 9th ed., 1948.
Solid and thorough; difficult for beginners; usually follows John of St. Thomas.

F. X. Maquart, *Elementa philosophiae,* Paris, 1937-38.
Orderly and well-arranged; polemic with Suarez and modern philosophers; conceived in the spirit of Maritain.

Vincent Remer, *Summa philosophiae scholasticae,* Rome, 7th ed. (revised by P. Geny), 1947 ff.
Extensive and complete; closely adheres to the text of St. Thomas, which is often quoted literally.

R. Jolivet, *Cours de philosophie,* Lyon, 1947 ff.
In close contact with the sciences and modern thought.

F. J. Thonnard, *Précis de philosophie en harmonie avec les sciences modernes,* Paris, 1950.

General Epistemological Studies

Fernand Van Steenberghen, *Epistemology,* New York, 1949.
Clear and concise; analytic or descriptive epistemology; critical epistemology; conclusions; the affirmation of being is seen as the absolute norm of knowledge.

P. Geny, *Critica de cognitionis humanae valore disquisitio,* Rome, 1927.
Certitude, scepticism; defense of the objective value of knowledge against idealism; value of deduction, induction, acceptance on faith; methodology of the sciences.

A. Brunner, *La connaissance humaine,* Paris, 1943.
A very independent study, starting from dialogue as an undeniable phenomenon; critique of the sciences.

G. Van Riet, *L'épistémologie thomiste,* Louvain, 1946. A very complete and critical explanation of the opinions held by neo-scholastic philosophers from Balmès to Brunner.

P. Rousselot, *L'intellectualisme de S. Thomas,* Paris, 3rd ed., 1936.
A penetrating study of intellectual life as highest and final activity and of the insufficiency of man's intellectual life in time; the natural desire for the vision of God.

J. Maréchal, *Le point de départ de la métaphisique,* Cahier V: *Le Thomisme devant la philosophie critique,* Paris, 2nd ed., 1949.
A famous attempt to understand Thomas in the light of Kant; justification of realism from the dynamic orientation of knowledge.

J. Noel, *Le réalisme immédiat,* Louvain, 1938.

Jacques Maritain, *The Degrees of Knowledge,* New York, 2nd ed., 1959. Extensive explanations based mainly on John of St. Thomas; somewhat antiquated in its critique of the sciences.

M.-D. Roland-Gosselin, *Essai d'une étude critique de la connaissance.*
I: *Introduction et première partie,* Paris, 1932.
Only first volume was ever published. It studies the judgment as directed to being, by way of discussions with French idealism.

Karl Rahner, *Geist und Welt. Zur Metaphysik der endlichen Erkentnis bei Thomas von Aquin,* Innsbrück, 1939.
A profound interpretation of the relation between intellect and senses and of the mediating role played by the phantasm.

Nicolai Hartmann, *Grundzüge einer Metaphysik der Erkenntnis,* Berlin, 4th ed., 1949.
Realism as dependence of knowledge on the known, but conceived too empirically.

General Studies of Metaphysics

Louis de Raeymaeker, *The Philosophy of Being,* St. Louis, 1954.
Considers the fundamental question of Thomistic metaphysics in an extensive, very synthetic, and personal way; historical digressions about the development of the problems.

Fernand Van Steenberghen, *Ontology,* New York, 1952.
Progressive development into four part: being and its properties; the order of finite beings; infinite Being; return to the order of finite beings.

Henry J. Koren, *Introduction to the Science of Metaphysics,* St. Louis, 1955.
Brief but clear.

J. Webert, *Essai de métaphysique thomiste,* Paris, 1927.

Jacques Maritain, *A Preface to Metaphysics,* New York, 1948.

Reginald Garrigou-Lagrange, *Dieu, son existence et sa nature,* Paris, 6th ed., 1933.
Defense of the first principles against agnosticism and modernism; systematic explanation.

D. Feuling, *Hauptfragen der Metaphysik, Einführung in das philosophische Leben,* Heidelberg, 1949.
A leisurely introduction to personal thinking, though one would hardly agree with the author in all points.

N. Balthasar, *L'abstraction métaphysique et l'analogie des êtres,* Louvain 1935.
A very profound monograph.

A. Forest, *La structure métaphysique du concret selon S. Thomas d'Aquin,* Paris, 1931.
An important historical study of the problems concerning essence and "to be," matter and form, etc.

André Marc, *L' idée de l'être chez S. Thomas,* Paris, 1933.

C. Fabro, *La nozione metafisica di participazione secondo S. Tommaso d'Aquino,* Torino, 1950.
Together with the work of Geiger, this book caused a revolution in the view taken of Thomism.

L. Geiger, *La participation dans la philosophie de S. Thomas d'Aquin,* Paris, 1942.
Two opposite forms of participation; how St. Thomas connects them.

J. de Finance, *Etre et Agir,* Paris, 1945.
The first major study of action in Thomism.

A. Marc, *Psychologie réflexive,* Paris, 1949.
Dialectique de l'affirmation, Paris, 1952.
Dialectique de l'agir, Lyon, n.d.
A trilogy about thinking and willing, being, moral action, as viewed from St. Thomas in confrontation with French idealism and spiritualism.

L. Lavelle, *Introduction à l'ontologie,* Paris, 1947.
A valuable little study about being, existence, reality; good, value, ideal.

B. Lakebrink, *Hagels dialektische Ontologie und die thomistische Analektik,* Cologne, 1955.
Martin Heidegger, *Einführung in die Metaphysik,* Tübingen, 1953.

INDEX OF NAMES

The numbers refer to the sections and not to the pages.

515

INDEX OF SUBJECT MATTER

The numbers refer to the margin.

48, 65; in the highest sense it is the person, 153; so that the transcendental idea of being is explicitated especially through knowledge of personal beings, 130, see also *Subsistent;* beings are not properly numerable, 62, see also *Number;* all beings in secondary sense are related to being in the primary sense, and are modified senses of the primary sense, see *Modes of Being.* We may name:

(4) *accidental,* 47, 68; see also *Accident.*

(5) *merely possible,* 175; see also *Possible.*

(6) *pure beings of reason (thought),* in the broadest sense, as opposed to the real and the possible, 28, 34; pertains to a) proposed state of affairs which is merely thought to agree with the real or the possible, 34, 129, see also *Error;* b) quasi-real beings in a world of fancy, 34, 124, see *Imagination, Representation;* c) in the strict sense, relations conceived by reason which can be stated in true judgments (founded relations of reason), 165, 166; first degree founded relations of reason arise from the mode in which we understand real or possible beings as they are in themselves, 166, 167, see also *Negation, Privation, to Think,* mode of; founded relations of reason, second degree, are respects created by reason between its own thoughts as intentional means to arrive at knowledge of beings, 166, see *Predicables,* logical.

Body, (1) the *extended* in general, 78, see *Extension;* the corporeal as in motion, 78; as composed of matter and form, 86-90; the merely-corporeal and the living, 112, 117; individuality and corporeity, see *Individuality;* ultimate ground of the properties of the, 192.

(2) the *mathematical,* 78, see *Mathematics.*

(3) the *organic,* of animal and man, 115; soul and, 116; spiritual soul and, 153; does not belong to living as living, 117.

Categories, 52, 69, 70; activity as guide to the, 71; as division of the

direct universal, 83, see *Universal;* transcendental and categorical concepts, 52, 169, 187. See also *Subsistence, Accident, Extrinsic Denomination.*

Cause, (1) *in broad sense,* as applicable to internal and external, 102, 103; origin of the theory of four, 146, see also *Matter, Form, Emanation;* deficiency of the internal, 104.

(2) in narrower sense, as *external cause,* exemplary, final, efficient, 103, see also *Purpose, Exemplary Cause;* whatever, being capable of change, changes or does not change in time is caused, 107, 178; the causal relations within man are only analogously efficient, exemplary, and final causes, 170, see also *Emanation.*

(3) in the narrowest sense, *efficient cause,* 105, 106, 107; instrumental, 146; moral influence as quasi-efficient, 102, 145, 154; emanation as quasi-efficient, see *Emanation;* there are no fully independent series of efficient, 108, 174.

(4) *cause as cause,* 102, 103, 107, 108, 181, see also *Effect;* relation of effect to cause is unilateral, 103, 164; this relation conceived as mutual, 181; the effect influences the finite cause as material, idea, purpose, motive, 181, 108; the necessarily causing, is not a pure, 181; human freedom and, 143; must cause and caused always be conceived as this and that?, 179, 181.

(5) *the absolutely uncaused cause,* 180, 185; is free, 181; is free-giving, 182; way of causality, 195, see also *God,* proof of existence.

Certitude, as cognitive condition, 8, see also *Evidence, Doubt;* spontaneous or reflex, supposed or motivated, 8; of faith, see *Faith;* spontaneous, of human life, 10; pre-predicative, of "to be," 16; of one's own "to be," 17; of all that is, 35; of fellow-men, 121; of the Absolute, 183.

Chance, 108, 174; see also *Contingent.*

Change, is formally abstract concept, 73; perception of, see *Perception;* in the first sense, as modification of observable qualities, 79; essential, 79, 88, 85; birth and death, 113; spiritual soul cannot essentially,